International Conference on Interfaces and Human Computer Interaction 2018, International Conference on Game and Entertainment Technologies 2018 and International Conference on Computer Graphics, Visualization, Computer Vision and Image Processing 2018

Held at the Multi-Conference on Computer Science and Information Systems (MCCSIS 2018)

Madrid, Spain
17 – 20 July 2018

AA005297

Editors:

Katherine Blashki
Yingcai Xiao

ISBN: 978-1-5108-7015-4

Printed from e-media with permission by:

Curran Associates, Inc.
57 Morehouse Lane
Red Hook, NY 12571

Some format issues inherent in the e-media version may also appear in this print version.

Copyright© (2018) by International Association for Development of the Information Society (IADIS)
All rights reserved.

Printed by Curran Associates, Inc. (2018)

For permission requests, please contact International Association for Development of the Information Society (IADIS) at the address below.

International Association for Development of the Information Society (IADIS)
Rua Sao Sebastiao Da Pedreira
No. 100, 30, 1050-209
Lisbon, Portugal

Phone: 351 21 3151373
Fax: 351 21 3151244

secretariat@iadis.org

Additional copies of this publication are available from:

Curran Associates, Inc.
57 Morehouse Lane
Red Hook, NY 12571 USA
Phone: 845-758-0400
Fax: 845-758-2633
Email: curran@proceedings.com
Web: www.proceedings.com

INTERNATIONAL CONFERENCES ON

INTERFACES AND HUMAN COMPUTER INTERACTION 2018

GAME AND ENTERTAINMENT TECHNOLOGIES 2018

and

COMPUTER GRAPHICS, VISUALIZATION, COMPUTER VISION AND IMAGE PROCESSING 2018

part of the

MULTI CONFERENCE ON COMPUTER SCIENCE AND

INFORMATION SYSTEMS 2018

PROCEEDINGS OF THE INTERNATIONAL CONFERENCES

INTERFACES AND HUMAN COMPUTER INTERACTION 2018

GAME AND ENTERTAINMENT TECHNOLOGIES 2018

and

COMPUTER GRAPHICS, VISUALIZATION, COMPUTER VISION AND IMAGE PROCESSING 2018

Madrid, Spain
JULY 18 - 20, 2018

Organised by
IADIS
International Association for Development of the Information Society

Copyright 2018

IADIS Press

All rights reserved

This work is subject to copyright. All rights are reserved, whether the whole or part of the material is concerned, specifically the rights of translation, reprinting, re-use of illustrations, recitation, broadcasting, reproduction on microfilms or in any other way, and storage in data banks. Permission for use must always be obtained from IADIS Press. Please contact secretariat@iadis.org

Volume Editors:
Katherine Blashki and Yingcai Xiao

Computer Science and Information Systems Series Editors:
Piet Kommers and Pedro Isaías

Associate Editor: Luís Rodrigues

TABLE OF CONTENTS

SHORT PAPERS

INTERFACES AND HUMAN COMPUTER INTERACTION

REFLECTION PAPERS

POSTERS

COMPUTER GRAPHICS, VISUALIZATION, COMPUTER VISION AND IMAGE PROCESSING

FOREWORD

These proceedings contain the papers and posters of the: 12th International Conference on Interfaces and Human Computer Interaction 2018, 11th International Conference on Game and Entertainment Technologies 2018 and 12th International Conference on Computer Graphics, Visualization, Computer Vision and Image Processing 2018, which was organised by the International Association for Development of the Information Society, from 18 - 20 July, 2018. These conferences are part of the Multi Conference on Computer Science and Information Systems 2018, 17 - 20 July, which had a total of 617 submissions.

The Interfaces and Human Computer Interaction (IHCI) 2018 conference aims to address the main issues of concern within Interface Culture and Design with a particular emphasis on the affective aspects of design, development and implementation of interfaces and the generational implications for design of human and technology interaction. This conference aims to explore and discuss innovative studies of technology and its application in interfaces and welcomes research in progress, case studies, practical demonstrations and workshops in addition to the traditional submission categories.

This conference seeks to cover both technological as well as non-technological issues related to these developments.

Submissions were accepted under the following topics:

- Affective User-Centred Analysis, Design and Evaluation
- The Value of Affective Interfaces / Systems / Application / Interaction
- Generational differences and technology design
- Measurement of success of emotional technology / interfaces
- Supporting user populations from specific Generations
- Supporting user populations with Physical Disabilities
- Supporting user populations with Intellectual Disabilities
- Creativity Support Systems
- Emotional Design issues / methods / experiences for novel interfaces including tangible, Mobile and Ubiquitous computing, mixed reality interfaces and multi-modal interfaces
- Usability
- User studies and fieldwork
- Methodological implications of Emotional User Studies
- Participatory design and Cooperative design techniques
- Ethical issues in emotional design
- HCI and Design education
- Eliciting User Requirements

The Game and Entertainment Technologies (GET) 2018 conference aims to bring together research and practice from creative, social and business practitioners and researchers in this challenging field. The focus of this conference is on design, development and evaluation of games, entertainment technologies and the nature of play.

Known to have been enjoyed since at least 30 BC, games and entertainment are a universal part of human experience and present in all cultures. Games and entertainment activities contribute to the social, emotional, psychological and physical well-being of human society. As game and entertainment technologies become increasingly more pervasive we are continually challenged in our work, learning and personal life by increased access to virtual spaces and communities that offer opportunities for everyday needs and aesthetic experiences. The 'Creative Industries' require design and development structures, techniques and methodologies that enrich, enhance and encourage new interaction modes, metaphors and in-depth co-creation.

Topics of interest include, but are not limited to the following areas:

- Development methodologies
- Design issues
- Controversial issues – we welcome debate and dissension, for example; games as art, entertainment as purely for monetary returns etc
- Special Effects
- Animation
- Mobile and ubiquitous games and entertainment
- Serious Games –applications, critiques
- Philosophical issues
- Prototypes
- Social and cultural uses of/for Play
- Tools and technologies
- Skills, strategy, rules and chance
- Genre
- Immersiveness and engagement
- Research methodologies in creative practice
- Usability and playability
- User/player centered design
- Psychological, social, and cultural differences in perception and participation
- Communities, networks, social interaction and social capital
- Cross-cultural and intercultural approaches
- Assessment of exploratory learning approaches
- Emerging practices

The Computer Graphics, Visualization, Computer Vision and Image Processing (CGVCVIP) 2018 conference intends to address the research issues in the closely related areas of Computer Graphics, Visualization, Computer Vision and Image Processing. The conference encourages the interdisciplinary research and applications of these areas.

Submissions were accepted under the following 5 main topics:

- Computer Graphics
- Visualization
- Computer Vision
- Image Processing
- Other Related Topics

These events received 238 submissions from more than 33 countries. Each submission has been anonymously reviewed by an average of five independent reviewers, to ensure that accepted submissions were of a high standard. Consequently only 37 full papers were published. The overall acceptance rate corresponds to about 16 %. A few more papers were accepted as short papers, reflection papers and posters. An extended version of the best papers will be published in the IADIS International Journal on WWW/Internet (ISSN: 1645-7641) and also in other selected journals, including journals from Inderscience.

Besides the presentation of full papers, short papers, reflection papers and posters, the conferences also included a keynote presentation from an internationally distinguished researcher. We would therefore like to express our gratitude to Professor Dr. Paloma Diaz, Director of the Digital Living Academic Unit and Director of the Interactive Systems Research Group (DEI-LAB), Universidad Carlos III de Madrid, Spain, for accepting our invitation to be the keynote speaker.

This volume has taken shape as a result of the contributions from a number of individuals. We are grateful to all authors who have submitted their papers to enrich these conferences proceedings. We wish to thank all members of the organizing committee, delegates, invitees and guests whose contribution and involvement are crucial for the success of the conference.

Last but not the least, we hope that everybody had a good time in Madrid, and we invite all participants for the next edition of these conferences, that will be held in Porto, Portugal.

Katherine Blashki, Noroff University College, Norway
Interfaces and Human Computer Interaction 2018
& Game and Entertainment Technologies 2018 Program Chair

Yingcai Xiao, The University of Akron, USA
Computer Graphics, Visualization, Computer Vision and Image Processing 2018
Program Chair

Piet Kommers, University of Twente, The Netherlands
Pedro Isaías, The University of Queensland, Australia
MCCSIS 2018 General Conference Co-Chairs

Madrid, Spain
July 2018

PROGRAM COMMITTEE

INTERFACES AND HUMAN COMPUTER INTERACTION CONFERENCE & GAME AND ENTERTAINMENT TECHNOLOGIES CONFERENCE

PROGRAM CHAIR

Katherine Blashki, Noroff University College, Norway

COMPUTER GRAPHICS, VISUALIZATION, COMPUTER VISION AND IMAGE PROCESSING

PROGRAM CHAIR

Yingcai Xiao, The University of Akron, USA

MCCSIS GENERAL CONFERENCE CO-CHAIRS

Piet Kommers, University of Twente, The Netherlands
Pedro Isaías, The University of Queensland, Australia

INTERFACES AND HUMAN COMPUTER INTERACTION CONFERENCE

COMMITTEE MEMBERS

Alessandro Casavola, University of Calabria, Italy
Alexander Gelbukh, Instituto Politécnico Nacional, Mexico
Alexander Kröner, Technische Hochschule Nürnberg Georg Simon Ohm, Germany
Andre Constantino da Silva, Instituto Federal de Educacao, Ciencia e Tecnologi, Brazil
Antonio Maria Rinaldi, University Napoli Federico II, Italy
Arianna D Ulizia, IRPPS-CNR, Italy
Caterina Senette, Istituto di Informatica e Telematica, CNR (Pisa), Italy
Celia Martinie, Universite Paul Sabatier, France
Connie Veugen, Vrije Universiteit Amsterdam, Netherlands
Corina Sas, Lancaster University, United Kingdom
Eduardo Tanaka, Eldorado Research Institute, Brazil
Elaine Hayashi, University of Campinas, Brazil
Francisco Madera Ramirez, Universidad Autónoma de Yucatan, Mexico
Hanan Salam, University of Pierre and Marie Curie-Paris 6 (UPMC), France
Hiram Calvo, National Polytechnic Institute, Mexico
Isabela Gasparini, Universidade do Estado de Santa Catarina (UDESC), Brazil
Jesuk Ko, Gwangju University, Republic of Korea
Jorg Muller-Lietzkow, University of Paderborn, Germany
José Antonio Macías Iglesias, Universidad Autónoma de Madrid, Spain
Kamila Rios, Universidade Federal de São Carlos, Brazil
Keith Nesbitt, University of Newcastle, Australia
Khaled Khankan, Taibah University, Saudi Arabia
Leonelo Almeida, Federal University of Technology, Paraná, Brazil
Lira Nikolovska, Self Employed, USA
Lucía Vera, University of Valencia, Spain

Luciana Alvim Santos Romani, Embrapa Agricultural Informatics, Brazil
Marcelo Romero Huertas, Universidad Autonoma del Estado de Mexico, Mexico
Maria Claudia Buzzi , IIT - CNR, Italy
Mark Apperley, University of Waikato, New Zealand
Mathieu Raynal, University of Toulouse, France
Maxim Bakaev, Novosibirsk State Technical University, Russia
Michael Hobbs, Deakin University, Australia
Miguel Sicart, IT University of Copenhagen, Denmark
Monica Bordegoni, Politecnico di Milano, Italy
Nadine Vigouroux, IRIT, CNRS, Paul Sabtier University, France
Nayat Sanchez-Pi, Universidade do Estado do Rio de Janeiro, Brazil
Niklas Ravaja, University of Helsinki, Finland
Otniel Portillo Rodriguez, Universidad Autonóma del Estado de México, Mexico
Philip Breedon, Nottingham Trent University, United Kingdom
Rodica Mocan, Babes-Bolyai University, Romania
Rodrigo Bonacin, Dssd - CTI Renato Archer, Brazil
Rommert Casimir, Tilburg University, Netherlands
Sandro José Rigo, UNISINOS, Brazil
Silvio Cazella, UFCSPA, Brazil
Sylvia Tzvetanova Yung, University of Bedfordshire, United Kingdom
Toni Granollers, University of Lleida, Spain
Victor M. R. Penichet, Escuela Superior de Ingeniería Informática (ESII), Spain
Xiaokun Zhang, Athabasca University, Canada

GAME AND ENTERTAINMENT TECHNOLOGIES

COMMITTEE MEMBERS

Alessio Ceccherelli, Tor Vergata University, Italy
Alf Inge Wang, Norwegian University of Science and Technology, Norway
Ali Arya, Carleton University, Canada
Carla Hoekendijk, Independant Consultant/Developer, Netherlands
Castulus Kolo, Macromedia University of Applied Sciences, Germany
Christos Bouras, University of Patras and Computer Technology, Greece
Connie Veugen, Vrije Universiteit Amsterdam, Netherlands
Daniel Cermak-Sassenrath, IT University of Copenhagen, Denmark
Ellen Brox, Norut - Northen Research Institute, Norway
Emanuele Carlini, ISTI, CNR, Italy
Eric Gressier, CNAM - Cedric, France
Evi Sampanikou, University of the Aegean, Greece
Gabriele D`Angelo, University of Bologna, Italy
Hanna Wirman, Hong Kong Polytechnic University, Hong Kong
Harry Agius, Brunel University London, United Kingdom
Isabelle Astic, CNAM, France
Jerome Dupire, CNAM - Cedric, France
Jouni Smed, University of Turku, Finland
Kai Kimppa, Turku School of Economics, Finland
Marcia Medeiros, UniFANOR (Devry Brasil), Brazil
Michael Katchabaw, University of Western Ontario, Canada
Michel Simatic, Telecom Sudparis, France
Miguel Sicart, IT University of Copenhagen, Denmark

Niklas Ravaja, University of Helsinki, Finland
Pilar Lacasa, University of Alcala, Spain
Rommert Casimir, Tilburg University, Netherlands
Ruck Thawonmas, Ritsumeikan University, Japan
Thrasyvoulos Tsiatsos, Aristotle Univerisity of Thessaloniki, Greece
Vagelis Kapoulas, Computer Technology Institute & Press "Diophantus", Greece
Windson Viana, UFC, Brazil
Yoshihiro Okada, Kyushu University, Japan

COMPUTER GRAPHICS, VISUALIZATION, COMPUTER VISION AND IMAGE PROCESSING

COMMITTEE MEMBERS

Aiert Amundarain, CEIT, Spain
Alessandro Artusi, University of Cyprus, Cyprus
Ana Serrano, Universidad de Zaragoza, Spain
Angelica De Antonio, Universidad Politecnica de Madrid, Spain
Anna Tomaszewska, Technical University of Szczecin, Poland
Bruce Campbell, Rhode Island School of Design, USA
Carlo Nati, Working Group for the Development of Tecnoscientific Knowledge, Italy
Celmar Guimarães da Silva, University of Campinas, Brazil
Chang Ha Lee, Chung-Ang University, Republic of Korea
Charalambos Poullis, Concordia University, Canada
Charalampos Georgiadis, The Aristotle University, Greece
Chien-hsing Chou, Tamkang University, Taiwan
Christos Gatzidis, Bournemouth University, United Kingdom
Creto Vidal, Federal University of Ceará, Brazil
Daniel Thalmann, EPFL, Switzerland
Elefelious Getachew Belay, Università Degli Studi di Milano, Italy
Fatima Nunes, University of São Paulo, Brazil
Giuseppe Patanè, CNR-IMATI, Italy
Gleb Nosovskiy, Moscow State University, Russia
Hongchuan Yu, Bournemouth University, United Kingdom
Ingemar Ragnemalm, Linköping University, Sweden
Isaac Rudomin, Barcelona Supercomputing Center, Barcelona
Jairo Sanchez, Vicomtech-IK4, Spain
Jian Chang, Bournemouth University, United Kingdom
Jose Remo Ferreira Brega, Sao Paulo State University, Brazil
Josip Almasi, Open Computing Ltd, Ireland
Juan Manuel Gonzalez Calleros, Meritorious Autonomous University of Puebla, Mexico
Julio Marco, Universidad de Zaragoza, Spain
Krzysztof Okarma, West Pomeranian University of Technology, Poland
Krzysztof Walczak, Poznan University of Economics, Poland
Leandro Fernandes, Federal Fluminense University, Brazil
Lihua You, Bournemouth University, United Kingdom
Linda Giannini, Smart Educational Ambassador, Italy
Luca Grilli, Department of Engineering, University of Perugia, Italy
Luciano Soares, Insper Instituto de Ensino e Pesquisa, Brazil
Marc Daniel, Ecole Superieure D ingenieurs de Luminy, France

Marcelo de Paiva Guimaraes, UNIFESP / FACCAMP, Brazil
Matteo Paolo Lanaro, The University of Milan, Italy
Mu-Chun Su, National Central University, Taiwan
Patrick Gioia, Orange Labs, France
Pawel Forczmanski, West Pomeranian University of Technology, Poland
Pedro Cano, Universidad de Granada, Spain
Peter Dannenmann, RheinMain University of Applied Sciences, Germany
Pierre-Frederic Villard, University of Lorraine, France
Piotr Lech, West Pomeranian University of Technlogy, Poland
Quan Wen, University of Electronic Science and Technology of China, China
Raffaella Fontana, INO-CNR Istituto Nazionale di Ottica, Italy
Rene Rosenbaum, meeCoda, Germany
Richard Kulpa, M2S - University of Rennes 2, France
Roman Durikovic, Comenius University in Bratislava, Slovakia
Shaun Bangay, Deakin University, Australia
Simon Richir, Arts et Metiers ParisTech, France
Stefano Valtolina, University of Milan, Italy
Sung-Hee Lee, KAIST, South Korea
Theresa-Marie Rhyne, Computer Graphics Consultant, USA
Wojciech Maleika, West Pomeranian University of Technology, Poland
Xenophon Zabulis, FORTH, Greece
Xiaogang Jin, Zhejiang University, China
Xiaosong Yang, Bournemouth University, United Kingdom
Xuejun Hao, Columbia University, USA
Zhong-Hui Duan, University of Akron, USA

KEYNOTE LECTURE

VIRTUAL AND AUGMENTED REALITY: AFFORDABLE AND USEFUL EXPERIENCES IN EDUCATION

Professor Dr. Paloma Diaz,
Director of the Digital Living Academic Unit and Director of the Interactive Systems Research Group (DEI-LAB), Universidad Carlos III de Madrid, Spain

ABSTRACT

Virtual, augmented and mixed reality provide many learning affordances that could be exploited in formal and informal education not only to promote student's engagment but also to improve the learning or teaching process. Even though there is extensive evidence of their learning affordances, immersive technolgies are not yet as propular as expected. In this talk I will review different approaches to support immersive experiences and the learning affordances they provide. Two key issues that might justify the lack of acceptance of these technologies to highlight the need to look for platforms and approaches that guarantee that immersive experiences are affordable, sustainable and useful.

Full Papers

REDESIGN OF THE BANK RECONCILIATION INTERFACE OF THE CONTAAZUL SOFTWARE

João Antonio de Menezes Neto and Victor Rafael Laurenciano Aguiar
Master's Degree in Design (PPGDesign), University of the Region of Joinville, Joinville, Santa Catarina, Brazil

ABSTRACT

This paper details the redesign process of the bank reconciliation interface of ContaAzul, an online cloud-based financial management software for small businesses in Brazil. The reconciliation is a feature that allows the users to import bank account statements and easily register them into the software, generating automated reports that help the financial control of the small companies. The research problem was motivated by use cases that are not covered in the current version of this feature, as well as by recent technological advances, such as application programming interfaces (APIs) and similar software available in the market, justifying the redesign. Interaction design was chosen as the project approach and Garrett's five planes as the methodology. As the final deliverable, a prototype was composed of static, bitmap screens, elaborated from a participatory design perspective, which was presented to the software engineering team for further implementation. This research was developed as a course conclusion project in the Master's Degree in Design of University of the Region of Joinville, which is focused on industry-based, applied research and development. The first author of this paper is one of the design coordinators of ContaAzul company and co-responsible for the aforementioned feature.

KEYWORDS

Interaction Design, Small Business, Bank Reconciliation

1. INTRODUCTION

This paper details a Master's Degree in Design course conclusion project that had as a general objective to redesign the ContaAzul software's bank reconciliation interface. The company, eponymous to the software, has its headquarters in Joinville, Santa Catarina, Brazil, and the first author of this essay is one of its design coordinators.

Bank reconciliation is a feature that is a part of the financial module of the ContaAzul software. Its purpose is to facilitate the registration of the money received, paid or transferred by the user, as presented in his or her bank account statement. By registering this information, it becomes possible to generate automated financial reports, helping the user to control his or her finances (ContaAzul, 2017).

The need for a redesign was primarily motivated by use cases not covered in the actual version of the feature, pondering the hypothesis that the redesign can contribute to the satisfaction of the company's customers. As a central research question, the following framing was delimited: how to redesign the ContaAzul software's bank reconciliation interface, considering use cases not covered and the deadline of April 2018, as demanded by the company, taking into account current users' difficulties and the utmost importance of this interface to the whole platform?

Regarding the structure of this text, it is divided into three sections. The first one is a contextualization about small businesses and the technological advances of banks in Brazil, along with a brief review about the ContaAzul company and its software, focusing on the current reconciliation interface. The second one introduces the theoretical and methodological basis of the project, listing interaction design as the approach and Garrett's five planes (Garrett, 2010) as the methodology, with adaptations due to the context. The last section details the practical phases of the project, correlating each of Garrett's five planes to a specific objective: strategy, scope, structure, skeleton and surface.

The final deliverable of the project was a static prototype of the redesigned interface, presented with bitmap screens. This prototype was elaborated from a participatory design perspective, that is here considered as an approach in which users co-design solutions and have an active role in the system (Rosa et al., 2012). The prototype was then handed over to the software engineering team of ContaAzul for a technical analysis for further implementation.

2. RESEARCH CONTEXT

This section contextualizes the field of activity of the ContaAzul company, discussing a brief profile regarding small businesses and banks in Brazil, which are, respectively, its clients and partners. Other topics covered here are the firm's timeline, the features present in its software and the disposition of its design team.

2.1 Small Businesses and Banks in Brazil

According to the Brazilian Small Businesses Support Service (Sebrae, 2017), there are 6.4 million small businesses in Brazil. These companies are responsible for 52% of formal labor contracts in the private sector, equivalent to 16 million workers. The fields of activity of this kind of company are varied, permeating industry, commerce, services and civil construction. In addition to the formal labor context, there are also 10 million informal workers in Brazil (Papp, Gerbelli, 2016). As no requirement for formal qualification in the administrative area to open a business is needed, there are different initiatives in the country, such as Sebrae itself, that provide support and advice to entrepreneurs.

Besides, it is important to recognize banks as stakeholders of influence in relation to financial management. In the Brazilian scenario, the first institution officially established was *Banco do Brasil*, in 1808 (Banco do Brasil, 2017b). As platforms evolved, another bank, *Bradesco*, was the first one in the country to allow online transactions through personal computers, in 1996 (Bradesco, 2017).

More recently, in 2017, *Banco do Brasil* was the first national institution to use APIs of open banking, making possible transactions through third-party platforms in a secure and stable manner (Banco do Brasil, 2017a). In the future, these APIs will admit software similar to ContaAzul to serve as white label platforms for financial services (Computerworld, 2017). The API is open to the community and can be used by technology companies that plan to develop integrated solutions.

2.2 The ContaAzul Company

Initially called Ágil ERP, the ContaAzul company began its operation in 2007, in the city of Joinville, Santa Catarina, Brazil. In 2011, already using the new nomenclature of ContaAzul, the first round of foreign investments was obtained, and its founders participated of intensive capacitation courses in California, United States (ContaAzul, 2017). As for 2018, ContaAzul has had more than 800,000 users testing its platform, issuing more than one million invoices (ContaAzul, 2017).

The software operates through web browsers, in a cloud-based microservice, and has a single-page application structure. The menu is comprised of five main modules–Sales, Purchases, Financial, Reports and Accounting–, and each of them has a specific set of features.

The ContaAzul design team is under its Research & Development core, whose responsibilities are to assist in the identification of opportunities and strategies, validate hypotheses with users, prototype interfaces and monitor the development of features, among other activities (Zanini, 2018). Each designer pairs with product managers, business analysts and software engineers, and has independence to delimit his or her design methods, as long as they favor the interoperation of teams in an agile development environment. This modality aims to reduce the bureaucracy present in traditional software development environments, decreasing the documentation required, since the software source code is seen as a document in itself (Fowler, 2017).

The author of this paper is the design coordinator of the Financial module team and co-responsible for the user experience of the bank reconciliation interface. This fact highlights the relevance of this research, as it might positively affect the contributions of design to the strategies of the company.

2.3 Bank Reconciliation Interface

The current ContaAzul software's bank reconciliation interface consists of two columns: on the left, the imported information from the bank statement is displayed; and on the right, there are input fields to register the information as a new transaction into the referred software. The central button, *Reconcile*, is only enabled after typing all of the mandatory information (description, category, date and value). If desired, the user can add supplementary information, such as department, and attach digital receipts. The software also suggests automatic reconciliation when identifies a description, value or date similar to transactions previously registered as provisions.

From a technical perspective, the ContaAzul software's bank reconciliation is managed by a complex set of business rules based on use cases and their accounting counterparts. Although the interface is simple, with a few graphical elements (Figure 1), its ideal logic must comprise a wide range of financial events, adapting itself to fit the user's necessity.

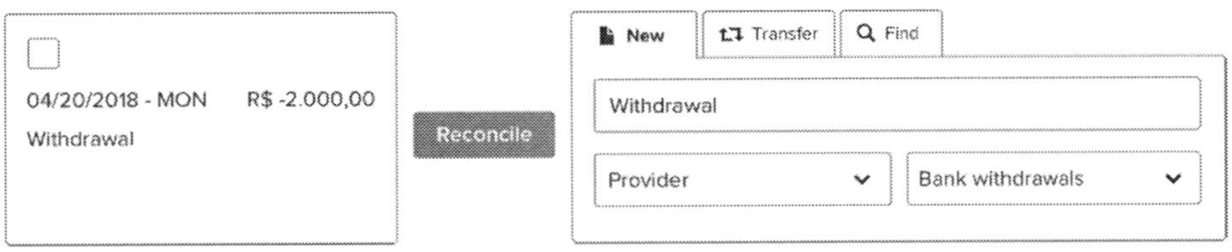

Figure 1. Current reconciliation interface, adapted to fit the formatting guidelines of this paper and translated from Portuguese to English with demo information

By the comparison between the examined software and five competing ones, it was possible to observe that there were use cases not covered by the current version of ContaAzul's reconciliation feature. These cases were: 1) allow the user to search for transactions and create ones at the same time; 2) permit the user to search for and reconcile mixed-type transactions, such as money received (inbound) and its incurring taxes (outbound); 3) make it possible for the user to create transactions and reconcile mixed-type ones simultaneously. From that standpoint, it has been hypothesized that amplifying the use cases covered may enable users to interact with the ContaAzul software in a more precise way, having the information registered in it as a truthful reflection of the financial events of his or her company, inducing a higher level of satisfaction.

Taking into account these aspects, the central research question was framed: how to redesign the ContaAzul software's bank reconciliation interface, considering use cases not covered and the deadline of April 2018, as demanded by the company, taking into account current users' difficulties and the utmost importance of this interface to the whole platform?

3. THEORETICAL AND METHODOLOGICAL BASIS

This section reviews references and concepts that contributed to the practical development of the project. It is important to emphasize that this section has the function of providing the theoretical and methodological basis for the project, but adaptations were necessary due to different variables, especially considering the deadline stipulated by the company.

3.1 Interaction Design as a Project Approach

Interaction design is a contemporary design approach that has gained momentum with the popularization and development of personal computers. According to Preece et al. (2013), in order to plan interactions, identifying human needs and consequently conceptualizing solutions are essential activities, and these solutions may be radical or incremental products and services.

In the interaction design field, it is important to take into account some usability and user experience best practices. Usability, for instance, is closely related to ergonomics. When applied to the context of interfaces, usability aims to adapt and recognize elements in order to guarantee the correct fulfillment of the user's tasks (Preece et al., 2013). User experience, on the other hand, is fundamentally subjective, being a complimentary perspective to usability, as it goes beyond the graphical layers of an interface. Strategies that adhere to the target audience of a solution, for example, can also provide satisfaction, since user experience is associated with the behavior of products and services in the real world (Garrett, 2010). For Kalbach (2017), one of the ways of mapping the user experience is to consider it as something holistic, personal and situational, i.e., directly dependent on a context.

In addition, for Preece et al. (2013), the evaluation of interfaces is important to balance the different stipulated user needs. Some methods of evaluation rely only on the researcher, and other ones have participation and collaboration of more people. The approaches suggested by Preece et al. (2013) are "quick-and-dirty" (based on informal feedback from users), usability testing (using camcorders, eye tracking software, among others), field study (performed in real use environment), predictive assessment (experts in user groups) and heuristic evaluation (recommendations suggested and validated by specialists).

With those concepts in mind, interaction design was chosen as the project approach for this research, as it is directly compatible with the general objective, especially due to its deep correlation to interfaces, usability and user experience.

3.2 Garrett's Five Planes Methodology

Garrett's five planes methodology, or "the elements of user experience" (Garrett, 2010), uses a layered metaphor, separating the stages of the project into sequential phases. The level of abstraction or concreteness of each step is defined from the hierarchy of these layers. The author considers a vertical division in the planes, dividing them in software interface and hypertext system.

According to Garrett (2010), in an ideal scenario, the next phase must only start when the previous one is complete. The five planes are, from the most abstract to the most objective one: strategy (concentrating commercial and communication goals), scope (defining the elements of the strategy that will be used), structure (mapping user flow of interaction), skeleton (focused on blueprints or wireframes), and surface (elaborating the visible, graphic layer of the interface). This methodology was chosen because of its direct correlation to digital interfaces, favoring a more productive and clear development phase.

The next section details the methods applied in each plane, describing the adaptations conducted in order to reflect the context of the project and, mainly, the ContaAzul company's *modus operandi*, that prioritizes the participatory design perspective in its initiatives.

4. PROJECT DEVELOPMENT

The development of the practical part of the project began after the approval in the qualifying examination in the Master's Degree in Design Program, in December 2017, having as a mandatory deadline April 2018. Some of the data considered during the project was collected in previous opportunities, arising from the first author's daily experiences as a ContaAzul company employee. In addition, this whole research was reviewed and approved by the Local Ethics Committee of the University of the Region of Joinville.

As commented in the previous section, different methods were connected to each of Garrett's planes, that served as specific objectives of the research. The methods are presented in the following sections, detailing their application, as well as the results obtained in each phase.

4.1 Strategy Plane

The strategy plane, in short, delimits the reach of action of the project (Garrett, 2010). In order to achieve it, it is necessary to parallelize the requirements of the company, the tendencies of the market and the general profile of the target audience of the solution. After obtaining data sources that represent the verbalization of users, either directly or indirectly, it is possible to mitigate research and design biases.

Based on this, it was decided to apply three methods in this phase: a review of ideas submitted by ContaAzul customers, a review of support tickets, and a questionnaire.

From the first analysis, 98 clients' suggestions connected to the bank reconciliation thematic were curated, from 2,479 ideas registered in the ContaAzul company's database, all of them read in full. Then, as a complementary method, 250 support tickets from customers were also read–the tickets were related to usability issues in the current reconciliation interface. Lastly, an anonymous online questionnaire was sent to customers, partners and customer service employees of the company.

Regarding the questionnaire, its main objective was to identify the frequency of use of the bank reconciliation feature, the incidence of usage difficulties and the recurrence of these difficulties. The responses occurred between March 16, 2018 and March 23, 2018. Thirty-seven answers were received, and all respondents indicated that they had had difficulties in ContaAzul's bank reconciliation.

From these insights, the team responsible for the bank reconciliation feature wrote a list of strategic objectives, in a session moderated by the first author of this paper.

As company requirements, the team suggested three aspects: 1) to assist its customers and partners to input financial information with reliability; 2) to highlight the market positioning of the ContaAzul company as a complete platform; 3) to enhance user experience in order to retain current customers and possibly expand to new customer niches.

In reference to market tendencies, the team summarized as follow-up actions: 1) to consider the changes and fluctuation of the Brazilians' perception in relation to the money they earn and spend; 2) to take advantage of the technological advances, such as APIs, that remove friction in the user experience; 3) to keep the team up-to-date with improvements and innovations released by similar software companies.

At last, in a user's perspective, the strategies of consensus were: 1) to be aware that opening a small business is sometimes a latent life necessity, and that it does not require technical training; 2) to equalize language, voice and tone of the interface, communicating the use cases in a clear and simple interface; 3) to offer flexibility to the user to input information as a reflection of the real events occurred in his or her business, avoiding forced adaptations or imprecisions.

4.2 Scope Plane

For Garrett (2010), the strategy plane can be interpreted as a "vision", while the scope plane, detailed in this section, is an "agreement". The main purpose of the scope plane is to change the question from "why are we designing this software?" to "what are we actually going to develop?". Based on this approach, the first author of this paper and his team wrote "user stories", that represent the translation of use cases into practical situations experienced by the person using a platform (Ventura, 2017). Along with this, a technical evaluation of complexity was done by the software engineering team.

The user stories were divided into three parts–user need, qualifying factor, and expected result–, written considering the information obtained in the previous phase, as well as prior projects conducted by the same team.

After the exercise of user stories was complete, the engineers evaluated the complexity of implementation of each of them. The participation of engineers early on was important, because, as advocated by Preece et al. (2013), bringing together people with different backgrounds and contexts can boost the amount of ideas and the originality of the solutions. This step was also relevant as the reconciliation feature already exists, so there were limitations in relation to database, programming (Java) and other similar aspects.

4.3 Structure Plane

In order to map an interaction flow that takes into account the requirements defined in the strategy and scope planes, a spatial user journey map was chosen to be used. For Kalbach (2017), the referred instrument considers the tasks to be performed by a person using direction and navigation metaphors, reminiscent of a "compass", having a correlation to the navigability present in graphic interfaces.

With this in mind, the authors of this paper created and divided the map into three chronological layers, thinking about the user's perspective: 1) generator fact (e.g., the act of selling or buying a product or service at a small business); 2) accounting evidence (e.g., the act of receiving or paying money for that previous product or service); 3) reporting (e.g., the act of analyzing the result, as of profit or loss).

The map was developed in a collaborative session, pondering the multiple views of the team responsible for the reconciliation interface.

4.4 Skeleton plane

The skeleton plane, by definition, is characterized by the development of blueprints or wireframes (Garrett, 2010). Considering the relevance given by the ContaAzul company to participatory design, this phase had a diverse set of methods and stakeholders involved. The activities developed involved a co-creation session, sketches, interface layout in editorial software, generation of alternatives, participatory interface evaluation, and usability testing.

In relation to the co-creation session, the original plan was to recruit ContaAzul's customers and accountants. However, due to timing and personal scheduling, the invited participants could not be present in the originally booked date. As it was impossible to call the session off due to the project's deadline, an adaptation was necessary. With that in mind, five ContaAzul company employees, from different departments, that had not had contact with the research until that moment, were invited to join the session. The participants were:

1. an accountant;
2. a financial analyst, that uses the ContaAzul software's reconciliation interface on a daily basis;
3. an implementation analyst, in charge of the software's customer consulting and onboarding;
4. a support analyst, responsible for telephone, e-mail and chat support to customers;
5. a front-end software engineer from a different team.

It is important to notice that, even though the participants were employees of the company, an aspect that was not originally planned, all of them have had wide experience with customers and were aware of pain points in the use experience of the ContaAzul software.

The first author of this paper acted as a moderator of the session, projecting on a monitor the user stories and difficulties found in the research until that moment. The group discussed each topic, and, as soon as the debate was over, the second phase of the session started. It focused on ideation, giving opportunity for the participants to suggest solutions to the difficulties, relating them to graphic interfaces or not. The participants were invited to speak out loud all the ideas they had for each topic. The author served as a graphic facilitator, drawing sketches on sheets of paper as the ideas were exposed. As a result, these drafts ranged from "buttons" and "boxes", in a reference to graphic interfaces, to intangible, generic ideas, such as "teach the users".

As the session finished and the participants were dismissed, the author started wireframing, in paper, interface layouts based on the suggestions of the group. These suggestions were later refined and transposed to an editorial software. The alternatives, in the total of six, were then shared with the team of the ContaAzul reconciliation feature and with the participants of the co-creation session. All were invited to evaluate the potential of each alternative to reduce the difficulties previously pointed out.

After the evaluation was over, the group agreed as a consensus to choose one of the alternatives. The screen flow was then prototyped, as well as the alternative for an initial round of usability testing was prepared. The tests were conducted remotely, via videoconference and screen sharing, with nine ContaAzul software's users, recruited considering a diverse set–service, commerce, industry; and entrepreneurs and accountants–, following the standard protocols of the company, that has a structured list of processes for usability testing. The results of the tests allowed iterative improvements to the screen flow, until, as a consensus, the team decided to move forward with the one of the alternatives.

4.5 Surface Plane

The surface plane, according to Garrett (2010), comprises the creation and application of a graphic layer over the wireframes. However, considering that ContaAzul has a preestablished interface elements library, called "design system", this phase was quick to produce, giving efficiency to the process.

As commented before, as soon as the alternative was refined and chosen, there was a new round of refinements and usability testing, especially because by this phase of the project all of the screen variations, that respond to the new use cases, were complete. This time, four users participated in the tests. The results were satisfactory, as the users were able to complete the tasks required during the test, with the sensibility to connect it to their own reality and market characteristics. The new and final interface is presented in Figure 2.

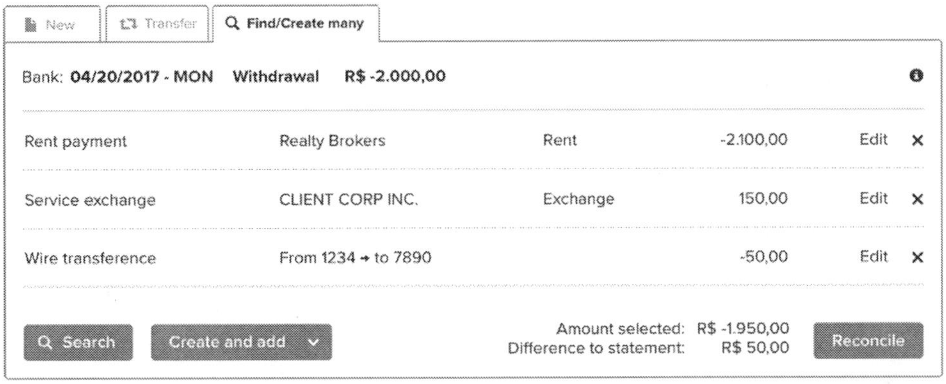

Figure 2. New reconciliation interface, adapted to fit to the formatting guidelines of this paper and translated from Portuguese to English with demo information

With the concept validated, the final prototype, in static, bitmap screens, with all the variations, was produced and handed over to the software engineering team, accompanied by business rules and design direction documentation. The prototype is available online, at the link http://bit.ly/ca-con. This deliverable concludes the scope of this research, which had the prototype as a final milestone.

As of the next steps, considering the agile development approach, which is used by ContaAzul, the engineering team is now in charge of delimiting a roadmap and release plan, dividing the deliveries into different stages. This exercise is collaborative and will have alpha and beta phases with customers. The expected implementation of the project in a production environment is July 2018.

5. CONCLUSION

Revisiting the original objective, which was to redesign the ContaAzul software's reconciliation interface considering the use cases not covered, it is possible to affirm that a valid result was achieved, but its real efficiency can only be evaluated, after its implementation. The new interface, that was a collective work of people from different disciplines, from inside and outside the company on focus here, will allow, as far as the evidences raised to the present moment go, more precise financial events in the software.

In relation to the specific objectives, which were directly connected to Garrett's five planes, the partial results obtained were also satisfactory. Although the co-creation session had to be adapted at a very short notice, due to scheduling conflicts of the invited participants, it contributed to the studies of the usage difficulties and the alternatives to mitigate them. Direct sources of user information, such as suggestions and support tickets, were also important, even though they might generate biased interpretation if not analyzed correctly. The fact that some adaptations were necessary to Garrett's five planes, a methodology that dates back to 2010, also shows changes in the design practice in the contemporary context, as, for instance, the existence of a preestablished library of interface components.

In addition, ContaAzul utilizes agile development concepts, which is a positive catalyst for user experience, since the incremental deliveries will make it possible to correct any necessary routes with the new reconciliation interface, as soon as it starts being coded, reducing risks and cost.

Considering the ContaAzul company's mission and vision–help small businesses and accounting firms in Brazil to reach success–, it is possible to affirm that the results of this research tend to help in relation to financial information maturity, as the software will be more robust and complete. As commented earlier, small businesses are very representative in the Brazilian society, making the results of this research even more relevant to its local context.

On a personal level, the experience of working in the technology industry and being able to report that as a central Master's Degree in Design project was flattering. It was an opportunity to connect academia and industry, with an immediate impact to the community–both by the process detailed and the results achieved.

ACKNOWLEDGEMENTS

The authors would like to thank ContaAzul, with special acknowledgements to Vinicius Roveda Gonçalves, Joaquim Torres, Anderson Borges, José Carlos Sardagna, Thiago Godoy, Laudifer Sfreddo de Castro, Victor Zanini, João Paulo Villa Mello, the Financial Module Engineering Team "Spartans", the Design Team "Lumos", the Customer Experience Team "CX", the Administrative Team "Wall Street", and all the participants of the project, as well as the faculty and students of the Master's Degree in Design (PPGDesign) of the University of the Region of Joinville (Univille), along with our families and friends.

REFERENCES

Banco do Brasil, 2017a. *Banco do Brasil lança plataforma de Open Banking* [online]. Available at: http://www.bb.com.br/pbb/pagina-inicial/imprensa/n/55574/Banco%20do%20Brasil%20lança%20plataforma%20de%20Open%20Banking#/ [accessed 1 Apr 2018].

Banco do Brasil, 2017b. *Nossa história* [online]. Available at: http://www.bb.com.br/pbb/pagina-inicial/sobre-nos/nossa-historia#/ [accessed 1 Apr 2018].

Bradesco, 2017. *Nossa história* [online]. Available at: https://banco.bradesco/html/exclusive/sobre/nossa-historia.shtm [accessed 1 Apr 2018].

Computerworld, 2017. *ContaAzul conclui integração de sua plataforma com o Banco do Brasil* [online]. Available at: http://computerworld.com.br/contaazul-conclui-integracao-de-sua-plataforma-com-o-banco-do-brasil [accessed 1 Apr 2018].

ContaAzul, 2017. *Sobre a empresa* [online]. Available at: https://contaazul.com/sobre/ [accessed 1 Apr 2018].

Fowler, M., 2017. *A nova metodologia* [online]. Available at: https://medium.com/desenvolvimento-agil/a-nova-metodologia-69b8f8a379c7 [Accessed 1 Apr 2018].

Garrett, J. J., 2010. *The elements of user experience*. 2. ed. New Riders, New York, USA.

Kalbach, J., 2017. *Mapeamento de experiências: um guia para criar valor por meio de jornadas, blueprints e diagramas*. Alta Books, Rio de Janeiro, Brazil.

Papp, A. C., Gerbelli, L. G., 2016. *Trabalhadores informais chegam a 10 milhões no país* [online]. Available at: http://economia.estadao.com.br/noticias/geral,trabalhadores-informais-chegam-a-10-milhoes-no-pais,10000071200 [accessed 1 Apr. 2018].

Preece, J., et al., 2013. *Design de interação: além da interação homem-computador.* Bookman, Porto Alegre, Brazil.

Rosa, J. G. S, et al., 2012. *Design participativo.* Riobooks, Rio de Janeiro, Brazil.

Sebrae, 2017. *Pequenos negócios em números* [online]. Available at: https://www.sebrae.com.br/sites/PortalSebrae/ufs/sp/sebraeaz/pequenos-negocios-em-numeros,12e8794363447510VgnVCM1000004c00210aRCRD [accessed 1 Apr. 2018].

Ventura, P., 2017. *Entendendo definitivamente o que é um caso de uso* [online]. Available at: http://www.ateomomento.com.br/o-que-e-caso-de-uso/ [accessed 1 Apr. 2018].

Zanini, V., 2018. *How we built our user experience team (UX) at ContaAzul, Brazil* [online]. Available at: https://medium.com/design-contaazul/how-we-built-our-user-experience-team-ux-at-contaazul-brazil-93ef648472f7 [accessed 1 Jun. 2018].

INSTANT CHURCH: A DATA-DRIVEN EUCHARIST REALIZED AS A CHRISTIAN PERFORMANCE SLOT MACHINE

Danny Schott, Carsten Greif, Sinah Herrklotsch, Michael A. Herzog and Dominik Schumacher
Faculty of Engineering Science und Industrial Design, Magdeburg-Stendal University of Applied Sciences
Breitscheidstr. 2, 39114 Magdeburg, Germany

ABSTRACT

Falling attention and acceptance of the church in society, resignations and falling memberships, lack of use of digital technology and interactive media in this context needs to be investigated and new approaches should be tested. In this Paper our contribution transfers the eucharist celebration into a data-driven slot machine using a Design Based Research methodology. The sensor and microcontroller-based artifact uses real time social media data analytics to start actuators and a laser engraving process, triggered by a coin slot of the user. With that interactive machine the religious service is translated into a design fiction and tested for its acceptance in a public exhibition with around 700 visitors. In doing so, we examined the question of whether religious processes can be automated and whether social media can be used in conjunction with a digital artifact in order to generate an intensive dispute about religion. The qualitative evaluation shows that almost all younger users reflected positively about the interactive exhibit while some of the 40+ religious people showed strong negative emotions. The possibility of generating new views on the faith and questions to the ecclesial community could be shown with such a controversial digital artefact.

KEYWORDS

Religion, Automation, Digitization, Interaction Design, Design Fiction, Social Media Data Analytics

1. MOTIVATION AND RELATED RESEARCH

1.1 Project Context

Christian churches are registering a steady decline in membership. According to current figures from the German Bishops Conference, 162,000 Catholics and 190,000 evangelists left German churches in one year 2016, mainly due to the evolution of demographic change. The alienation from faith or lack of commitment to the church as an institution were mentioned as main reasons for a conscious withdrawal (Riegel et al., 2018). In a study of the diocese of Essen has been investigating further motivations since March 2017 in cooperation with the University of Siegen for church exits. Exemplary statements from this study of active and former church members show a mood:

> *The church will become more modern and open. God wants us all to love and just as we like. (Catholic, 41-60 years, Duisburg) – I do not need a parish festival with sausages, I want to know something about faith, but there's no time for it (Catholic, 41-60 years, Bochum)*

There are generalized exit motivations that show church tax is not the main reason why people leave the church. Rather, an emotional bond and a practical benefit is missing [http://zukunftsbild.bistum-essen.de/die-bistums-projekte/die-bistumsprojekte/initiative-fuer-den-verbleib-in-der-kirche/kirchenstudie/ergebnisse-stimmungsbild-und-interviews/, 2018- 05-21]. The represented morality also no longer fits into a modern world view, especially for young people. Digital technology driven approaches could encourage the gain of new and young members of the churches in an internet society. This should create many new opportunities for support, as well as the co-creation and fundamental reorganization of many social services (Hagemann 2017). »Engaging in social communication through the most innovative platform is a great start, but without awareness of the particular form, mode, and content intelligible in the digital age, this could lead to a frustrating experience.« (Zsupan-Jerome 2014)

In order to promote this trend, attempts are made to bring religious traditions into modern forms and to stimulate discourses among different cultural strata. In this context, the question arises as to whether religious traditions can be digitized and thus endure in our fast-moving, consumer-oriented and Western-influenced society.

1.2 Related Work

YouVersion with its famous »Bible« App is an excellent example of a religiously-shaped technology, designed to use digital media in the service of classic evangelical ambitions. (Hutchings 2014, p. 14). The Smartphone App, running on over 300 million devices [https://www.youversion.com/products/, 2018-05-18], contacts its users once in a day to encourage them remembering faith, doing a good deed, contributing and connecting to the religious community. YouVersion »is a case study in how technology can change behavior when it couples the principles of consumer psychology with the latest in analytics.« (Eyal 2013). Considering the concerns from our own exploration, the success of the YouVersion platform contradicts the often-mentioned mismatch of Christian values and Social Media. Although other work reported how »the idea that pastors might become dependent on a mobile app has caused some resistance from Christian observers« (Hutchings 2014, p. 22). Church as an institution seems to be confronted by several challenges on its way to digitization.

In various papers Twitter as a Social Media channel is discussed as a very appropriate way to spread the teachings of the Bible through limited use of characters in one tweet (Cheong 2010), (Hutchings 2014, p. 23). In the past technological innovations always supports the Christian understanding and interpretation of the bible, (Hutchings 2014, p. 26).

Faith-Based Design is an approach to develop and design products that help maintain traditional faith and religious practices. Christians are using modern technologies to communicate with friends and family or to measure their workdays. The same technologies now are used by them to receive the words of god daily for example bible verses (Gorman 2009, p.18). »Whatever one's religion, using a ringing, beeping electronic device that one carries on one's body – as opposed to an inert book or calendar that sits ignored on the shelf – is a new means of remembering, affirming and reflecting on belief.« Because these products now exist in the physical world, they are more amenable to the practice of Christian rituals (Gorman 2009, p.19).

In a design research case study, the use of Christian symbols was investigated under assistance of sketching relied on digital technology to support their faith practices. In an approach participants sent photographs to digital screen at the front of a churches' sanctuary to bless them which is a common strategy for diffusing the negative influence that may be embedded in the picture (Wyche et al. 2012 p.5). »Given that a goal of our project was to imagine how future technology could be used to support these practices, imagining ways new technology could support users' religious practices seemed logical« After presenting the concept drawings the desire to appropriate new technology was more nuanced to the participants. For the users it was okay to use technology to practice their faith (Wyche et al. 2012, p.7).

Digital Church Conference gives interested church communities access to social media. In order to get in touch with their church members and acquire new members in this medium. The conference seeks to free open priests and church leaders from the fear of using social media and helps entire communities to take advantage of this technology to practice their faith. In addition, the presence in these media promotes a higher visibility in the otherwise difficult to reach for the young target group (https://digitalchurchconference.com [May 18, 2018]).

2. RESEARCH CONCEPT

The presented prototype Instant Church stands for a critical perspective on the described transition process in churches and religion. Therefore, an interactive artefact for public space was designed on the basis of the design science methodology (Hevner 2004). Therefore, we used the Design Science Research Methodology Model (DSRM) of Peffers et al. 2007 and adopted it to structure our own research process (Figure 1). The project started in the context of several workshops bringing together public relation professionals working at a German evangelist cathedral with scientists and students from Human Computer Interaction, Interaction Design and Electrical Engineering. About 10 projects added interactive extensions to religious objects or art in the cathedral. For instance, in the »Nachthimmel« project a light show using projection mapping and real-time music processing was created to augment an organ concert in the Magdeburg Cathedral.

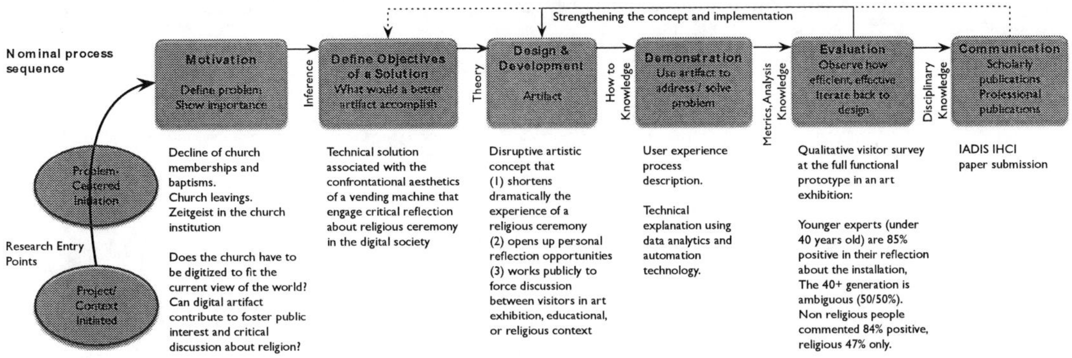

Figure 1. Design Science Research Methodology Model applied to the Instant Church Project

The Instant Church approach was reflected and discussed regularly in the professional design and engineering community (10 projects in the same context). First weekly concept meetings, then monthly reflection meetings over a period of 16 weeks helped to iterate the DSRM cycles based on several creativity techniques. The consultation with the professional design and engineering community of the above-mentioned projects, and interim presentations with the customer helped to iterate the design process and improve the concepts as the designed and programmed artifact.

Figure 2. Design Process: Discussion in a Concept Meeting

Figure 3. Intermediate concept of the Instant Church Slot Machine in a vertical version

The approximation to a final prototype – used and evaluated in a 4-day public exhibition – resulted in a total workload of approximately 1,000 working hours. Two research questions »Does the church have to be digitized to fit the current view of the world?«. and »Can digital artifacts contribute to foster public interest and critical discussion about religion?«, but also the enormous challenges described in the motivational chapter above leads to several variants and approaches.

3. USER EXPERIENCE AND FINAL DESIGN

The Instant Church design installation is a critical digital artefact that stages essential elements of the Catholic liturgy (opening, liturgy of the Word, celebration of the Eucharist, dismissal) for the user in the aesthetics of a machine. Figure 4 visualizes the automaton's actions (1...6) in relation with the Catholic worship service.

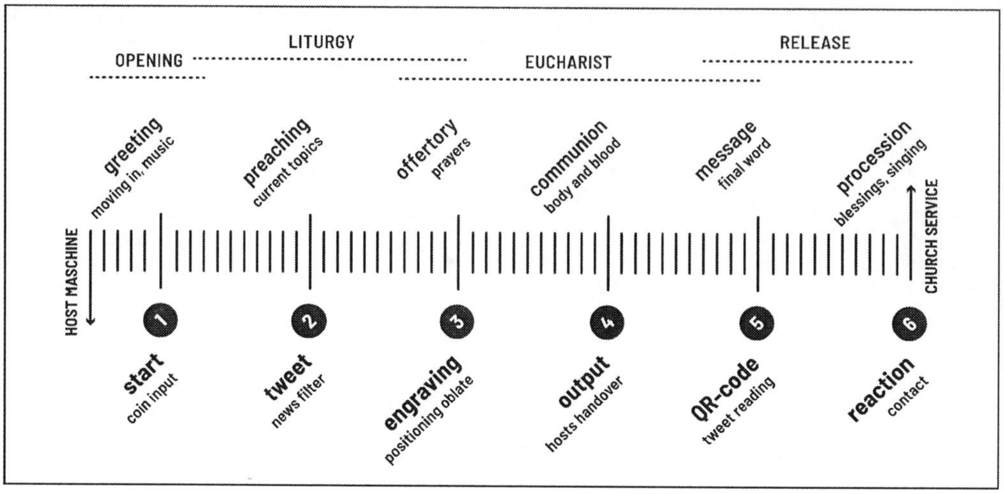

Figure 4. Process overview shows the analogies of catholic worship (duration about 60 minutes) with the vending machine in use (duration about 12 minutes)

1 **Greeting** The shortened and digitized Eucharistic celebration starts at Instant Church with the insertion of a coin (Figure 5). As a greeting a bell sounds, the playing of organ music marks the beginning of worship. The so-called opening (Entry, Confession, Kyrie, Gloria and Daily Prayer) stands as an accompanied entry into the church with the church choir.

Figure 5. User inserts a coin and starts the process of Eucharistic celebration

Figure 6. The wafer is transported from the tabernacle to the conveyor belt

2 **Preaching** After the opening, the next part of a Catholic service is the Liturgy of the Word (Old Testament readings, response psalms, Gospel readings, preaching, creeds and intercessions). The automaton translates the part of the sermon with the start of an animation on the whole semitransparent base plate on which the conveyor belt and all other elements stand. The animation visualizes how a software uses special algorithms to analyze the social network Twitter for current political issues and to filter out hate tweets. The realization of this is explained in more detail in Section 4 TECHNICAL IMPLEMENTATION.

3 **Offertory** Now follows the most important part of a catholic church service, the actual eucharistic celebration (giving of gifts, high prayer, Lord's Prayer, peace greeting, Agnus Dei, communion). The gift preparation is translated by Instant Church as positioning of the wafer from the lavishly lit tabernacle (acrylic glass tube) on the conveyor belt (Figure 6). Then, the conveyor belt transports the wafer into the black box by holding a laser engraving machine. The QR code generated in the step is now lasered onto the wafer and visualized by a complementary light animation.

4 **Communion** The conveyor belt begins to move again after the laser process and conveys the engraved wafer to a funnel through which the wafer rolls in an inclined rail to the ejector. The user could now take in the holy bread for him that represents the body of Christ (Figure 7). The experience of the Catholic worship by the automaton does not end at this point, but, like the actual service, has been extended by the announcement of the so-called dismissal.

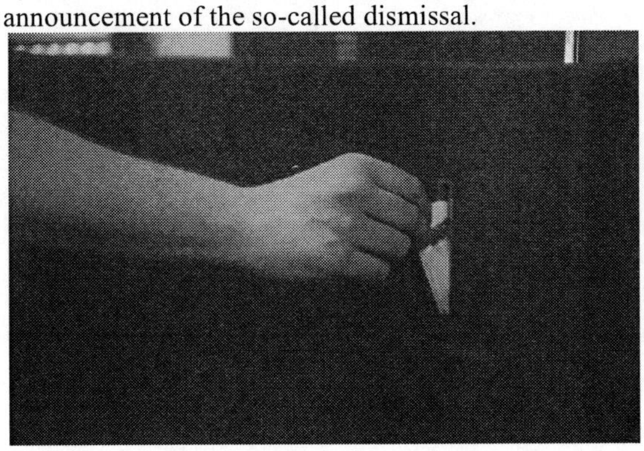

Figure 7. User is getting the holy bread out of the box

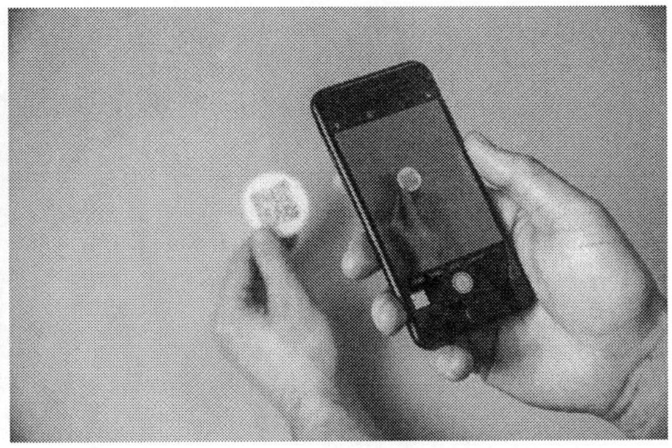

Figure 8. Scanning the engraved QR code, which referenced the posting on Twitter

Figure 9. General view of the data-driven slot machine Instant Church

Figure 10. The engraving process of the wafer realized with microcontrollers and laser technologies

5 **Message** The dismissal (announcement, blessing, dismissal, excerpt with singing) starts at Instant Church with the scanning of the QR code on the wafer (Figure 8). With the smartphone, the user is now linked directly to the hate tweet on the Twitter platform and could read the message. Since it is not just a tweet, but a special hate tweet, it is the user's job to form an opinion.

6 **Procession** The dismissal or excerpt, in the figurative sense, is now to contact the author of the tweet or to respond in a different way to the hate tweet. This act is thought-provoking, calling for action and promoting greater communication and freedom of expression in the global community. Finally, the user can absorb the body of Christ and complete the communion. The user of an indulgence performed an action to receive the purification. The process ends with the eating of the sacramental bread and this closes the holy communion.

An appropriate design has been applied, in order to motivate the user to approach the interactive object (Figure 9). The aesthetics of a mobile automaton serves as an allegory for the drastic reduction, compression and digitization of the service and is intended to visually underpin the critical theoretical provocation. The designers have created an appealing aesthetic for attention with various design elements and style elements and created a visual bridge to the topic of religion and digitization. In concrete terms, this is evident in the black lower part of the entire body in which the technology is installed; this does not by chance remind of the cult stone on the Kaaba in Mecca, but creates a visual reference to Islam and represents openness and tolerance for the world religions. Other important design elements to attract the attention of users are, for example, the small golden cross on the cover of the engine directly in front of the tabernacle (represents the donation in church), the conspicuously illuminated cross hole on the box in which the laser engraving (represents the consecration) on the wafer is created. The greatest attention is drawn to the fact that the upper cover (represents the church window), which protects the precious and sacred elements, is fully illuminated by an animated lighting installation. And thus, the edges of the acrylic glass, both before and during the ceremony, are effective »be enlightened«.

4. TECHNICAL IMPLEMENTATION

By using modern microcontroller and rapid prototyping methods, Instant Church is be transformed into a functional prototype. The technological structure is divided into two parts: the software which is created using the programming language Java and a hardware part. The software uses a real-time algorithm to analyze the social media network Twitter by using their API. Once the algorithm has detected a tweet, the URL is loaded into a temporary memory and, using a specially developed routine, transferred to a machine-readable QR code and subsequently transferred to a G-code readable by laser-cutter. This G-code consists of simple numerical instructions for a microcontroller. The most common problems appeared in software development at the interplay of interfaces and algorithms. In doing so, the error-free transformation of a URL into a vector-based QR code and subsequent G-Code poses a great challenge. This was solved by consistently using a variety of proven open source frameworks. The program checks each pixel and transfers it to a pixel array which released into a G-Code file. Another challenge was the control of the feeder to arrange the wafer to be engraved at correct points. The correct positioning under the laser was a critical step which was solved by an optical sensor network fail-safe. The isolation of the laser and its dangerous emission was a particular difficulty in the exhibition context. The laser process not visible to the viewer is shown in Figure 10. However, the functionality of the laser was essential for the evaluation.

The process of technical lasering, as focused divine energy, is an excellent metaphor. (Professor, 42)

The mechanical part mainly included classical design tasks, which were supported by a CAD program and implemented mainly in the 3D printing process. Oblate ejection with its complicated mechanics posed a challenge as it had to be reliable as well as produced in the 3D printing process.

5. USER EVALUATION

As part of a 4-day art and design exhibition in February 2018, the installation was presented in public. In the context of a cathedral exhibition with several exhibits related to religion were a range of visitors specifically invited. Included mostly academics, as well as middle-school and college students, including active church members. Approximately 700 visitors from Germany, Great Britain, Romania and Italy have interacted with the exhibit. Semi-structured interviews and numerous open discussions about Instant Church were conducted, 31 interview records were qualitatively evaluated and criteria for socio-demographic and religious affiliation were categorized. The statements were rated positive, negative or neutral in terms of subjective opinion and presented by age group or religiosity (Figure 11).

Younger participants of the interviews, under 40 years old, showed a 85% positive reflection about the experience and mindset of the installation, fully positive in K-12 school classes where students from different schools showed a lot of enthusiasm and emotions.

Perhaps not quite serious but interesting approach to get young people excited about the church. (Chorus singer, female, 19 years old, religious) – If this would happen anywhere, then I would often participate in the church. (Student, 16, non-religious) – The installation emphasizes the zeitgeist of the constant availability of information. (Student, 19, unknown religious orientation)

The 40+ generation discussed rather ambiguous about it (50/50%) but also showing rarely some strong negative emotion.

> *The machine opens up a novel approach to the church, especially for non-religious people. (Catholic School Teacher, 62, religious) – That's pure blasphemy! (Church member, 68, religious) – The church committees would never tolerate such a thing! (Theist, High church official, 66, religious)*

Non-religious people commented the concept 86% positive, but religious people only by 47%. Also, there was no one from the non-religious group who commented negative. In the religious group, negative response reached almost 30%.

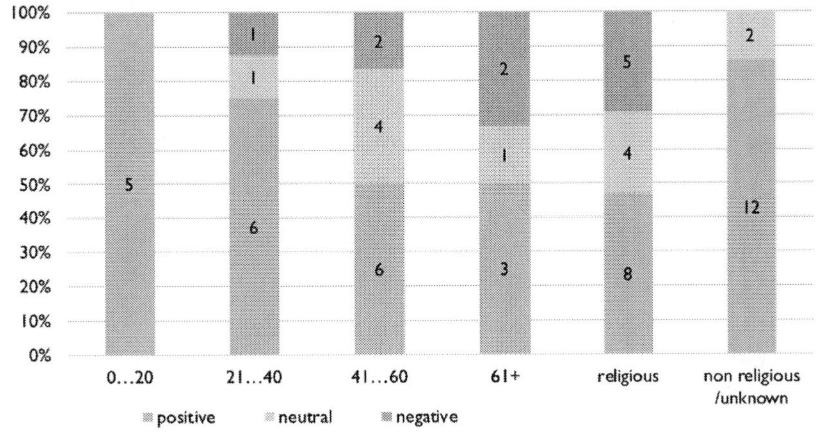

Figure 11. Comparison of categorized qualitative statements from the memorandum. (n=31)

6. IMPLICATIONS AND CONCLUSION

Our artifact caused controversy and discussion in terms of religion in the target group, especially with young and non-religious participants. As shown in the study »Now the Bible is an App« participants show affection for use of digital technologies in context of religion, which can be used as an entry point and intermediary to the younger generation, as demonstrated in our study. The related project »Nachthimmel«, what was created in the same context, had a similar effect and reaches an untapped target group for the church. During a regular organ concert, usually a maximum of 100 visitors are attracted to a rather older target group. However, on two evenings, the performances were sold out, attracting 1,200 visitors – mostly a younger audience - with classical music from the 20th century.

The Instant Church exhibit gained attention from at least 700 visitors within the 4 days exhibition and forced controversial discussions a lot as shown in the evaluation. Furthermore, the prototype as a mediating learning technology in the sense of Bloom's taxonomy (Anderson et al. 2001) evidently addresses not only remembering and understanding, but also transfer-aspects like analysis and evaluate in the education process, triggered by our machine.

> *Even an active member of the church could not explain the process of the Eucharist celebration so exactly. (Journalist, 26, non-religious)*

Despite an initially negative impression of the often-religious participants, it was possible to build up an emotional access to this critical topic after further explanations, which increased the acceptance of the artifact. Real physical products, such as Instant Church, can also support the practice of faith as outlined in »religion on demand: faith-based design« and »using sketching to support design research in new ways«. In the high level of acceptance of the participants in our study and other research show that the church as an institution should use new technologies to connect with different target groups.

So far, a few documented projects describe interactive objects in the context of religion. Our study shows the potential of using interactive technologies to attract a greater audience – especially younger people that don't have a religious affiliation yet. Based on that there is an opportunity for churches to use such objects as a polarizing door opener and to keep up with the prevailing trend of digitization. The accomplished evaluation illustrates this opportunity, although Instant Church takes up only a small part of the Religious tradition, the Eucharist. But this chance also carries risks, which has been shown when visitors explored it by themselves with no additional explanation: Instant Church was sometimes interpreted as blasphemy. The illustrated automated process of the Eucharist may not work as a simple solution for current problems of the Church, like the devastating loss of members.

But it serves as an attempt through a vision of the future to encourage people to go new ways. Even if the audience understood the whole process of the automated Eucharist, the last and meaningful step of engraving a hate tweet on the oblate turned out to be a hardly understandable metaphor.

Why do you tattoo the Body of Christ? (Professor, 42, unknown religious orientation)

In a reworked version of Instant Church, the provoking part could be left out and the focus could step back to the original religious ceremony of just giving the oblate to the user, but in an automated and digitized form of blessing.

There are some ideas so wrong that only a very intelligent person could believe in them. (George Orwell, 1903 - 1950, complicated relationship with his catholic church, Kershaw 2012)

REFERENCES

Anderson, L.W., et al., 2001. *A taxonomy for learning, teaching, and assessing: A revision of Bloom's taxonomy of educational objectives, abridged edition*. Longman, White Plains, NY.

Cheong, P. H., 2010. Faith Tweets: Ambient Religious Communication and Microblogging Rituals. *M/C Journal*, 13(2). Media/culture, Queensland, Australia

Eyal, N., 2013. The App of God. *The Atlantic, July 24, 2013*, Washington DC, USA, http://www.theatlantic.com/technology/archive/2013/07/the-app-of-god/278006/ [May 18, 2018]

Gorman, C. R., 2009. Religion on demand: Faith-based design. *Design and Culture*, 1(1), NY State University, New York City, NY, USA, pp. 9-22.

Hagemann, T., 2017. Digitalisierung und technische Assistenz im Sozial- und Gesundheitswesen. *Gestaltung des Sozial- und Gesundheitswesens im Zeitalter von Digitalisierung und technischer Assistenz*. Nomos Verlag, Baden-Baden, Germany, pp. 9-18.

Hevner, A. R., March, S. T., Park, J., & Ram, S., 2004. Design science in information systems research. *MIS quarterly*, 28(1), Carlson School of Management, Minneapolis, MN, USA, pp. 75-105.

Hutchings, T., 2014. Now the Bible is an app: digital media and changing patterns of religious authority. *Religion, Media, and Social Change*. Routledge, Oxford, UK, pp. 151-169

Kershaw, T., 2012. The religion and political views of George Orwell, Brennan, M.G., *George Orwell and Religion*, Bloomsbury Publishing, London, UK

Peffers, K., Tuunanen, T., Rothenberger, M. A., & Chatterjee, S., 2007. A design science research methodology for information systems research. *Journal of Management Information Systems (JMIS)*, 24(3), pp. 45-77.

Riegel, U., Kröck, T., Faix, T., 2018. Warum Menschen die katholische Kirche verlassen. Eine explorative Untersuchung zu Austrittsmotiven im Mixed-Methods Design, *Etscheid-Stams M., Laudage-Kleeberg R. & Rünker T. (ed.), Kirchenaustritt oder nicht - wie Kirche sich verändern muss*. Herder, Freiburg, Germany, pp. 125-207.

Wyche, S. P., & Grinter, R. E., 2012. Using sketching to support design research in new ways: a case study investigating design and charismatic pentecostalism in São Paulo, Brazil. *Proceedings of the 2012 iConference*, ACM, New York City, NY, USA, pp. 63-71.

Zsupan-Jerome, D., 2014. *Connected Toward Communion: The Church and Social Communication in the Digital Age*. Liturgical Press, Collegeville, MN, USA, p. 112.

COMPARATIVE USABILITY EVALUATION OF MOVERIO AND SMARTPHONE

Valeria Orso[1,2], Patrik Pluchino[1,2], Andrea Beretta[2], Giulio Jacucci[3,4] and Luciano Gamberini[1,2]
[1]*Human Inspired Technology Research Centre (HIT), University of Padova*
[2]*Department of General Psychology, University of Padova*
[3]*Helsinki Institute for Information Technology HIIT, Dept. Computer Science, Univ. Helsinki, Finland*
[4]*Helsinki Institute for Information Technology HIIT,*
Department of Computer Science, Aalto University, Finland

ABSTRACT

Mobile apps embedded with Augmented Reality (AR) have recently spread among the general public thanks to technological advances, e.g., smartphone with faster processing speed, and the reduction of costs. AR technology has been exploited to enhance the experience of tourists and numerous apps have been experimented. However, it is not free from shortcomings. In the present study we assessed and compared the usability and user experience of two types of devices, namely a head-mounted display (HMD) and a smartphone, enabling environmental exploration with an AR app. We found that participants were equally accurate and fast at accomplishing the three tasks required, i.e., reading a text, reaching a landmark and finding the nearest places. Prior to the test, users had high expectations toward both devices and they were concerned of appearing weird to bystanders while using the HMD. Overall, the differences between the devices leveled out after the actual usage. Furthermore, users surprisingly assigned lower scores of the ease of use to the smartphone at post-test. Together, our findings suggest that the urban exploration is effectively supported by both technologies.

KEYWORDS

Mobile Augmented Reality, Usability, User Experience

1. INTRODUCTION

Augmented Reality (AR) technology enables the user to visualize digitally created elements superimposed onto the real environment and to interact with them in real time (Azuma, 1997; Olsson et al., 2012). The benefits brought about by AR have soon been exploited in the touristic context. Mobile AR apps allow the user to visualize historic ruins at their original location and magnificence (Vlahakis et al. 2002), to supplement actual landmarks with descriptive information (Hsieh et al. 2018), to inform visitors of the upcoming events in the city (Cabral et al. 2014) and to provide navigational guidance (Ruta et al. 2015). Smartphones are a powerful platform for supporting mobile AR applications (Haugstvedt & Krogstie 2012). Wearable computers, that are fully functional self-contained computers that the user attaches on the body and enable the continual access to information (Spagnolli et al. 2014), have also been experimented with mobile AR apps, especially as head-mounted displays (HMD). Head-worn viewers, also referred to as smartglasses, have the big potential to provide the user with a larger amount of always-available information in an unobtrusive manner, thus preventing distractions, which is extremely desirable in a mobile context (McAtamney & Parker 2006, Costanza et al., 2006). Nevertheless, a number of shortcomings, e.g., screen reflections, the need to hold up the device, can potentially hamper the interaction with the device (Schmalstieg & Höllerer 2015). In the present work we aimed thus to compare the usability and the user experience with a mobile AR app using a HMD and a smartphone in an experiment run in the field.

The remainder of the paper is organized as follows: first we outline related research that have investigated usability of devices supporting mobile AR apps. Then we report on the methodological details of the experiment and research and the results. Finally, we draw conclusive remarks, acknowledge the limitations of the present study and propose future developments.

2. RELATED WORK

Despite the proliferation of AR apps in the touristic domain, the main focus of the evaluations seems not to be on usability and experience of use, concentrating on the assessing of technical challenges and constraints (Düsner et al. 2007). Concerning smartglasses, only few studies have investigated the usability and the user experience so far, and to the best of our knowledge the interest toward touristic AR apps is still limited. Brusie at al. (2015) compared the ease of use of Google Glass and Vuzix M100 in a surgical application domain. Unfortunately, they report the devices to be not robust enough to undergo to a proper evaluation. Brancati et al. (2015) presented a wearable AR system to support the exploration of different point of interests (POIs) in the city of Naples (Italy). They based their evaluation on questionnaires assessing the usability and the user experience and they reported positive evaluations on both aspects. The evaluation of mobile AR apps running on hand-held devices have attracted only limited interest so far as well (Ko, Chang, & Ji 2013), nevertheless in general users seem to receive positively such apps. Lee et al. (2012) asked participants to try CityViewAR, a mobile AR app superimposing original buildings over a city devastated after an earthquake, and then to fill in a short usability questionnaire. They found the experience of use in the AR condition slightly better than the non-AR condition. No analysis was conducted on participants' performance. Morimon et al. (2010) presented MobiAR, a smartphone-based AR app to explore the city of San Sebastian (Spain), but they provided no evaluation of it. Williams, Yao and Nurse (2017) proposed ToARist, which was meant for the touristic exploration of the city of Oxford (UK). They had a group of overseas participants evaluating the app and they report it to be generally usable and easy to use.

3. MATERIALS AND METHODS

In the present section we first report the experimental design, then we describe the equipment and the materials employed. Next a description of the experimental sample and f the procedure is provided.

3.1 Experimental Design

We designed a within-subject experiment with a two-level factor, being the device in use, i.e., HMD or the smartphone. Among all of the possible activities involving a tourist, we selected three tasks: a first task required the participant to locate a target POI that was out of his/her view and to walk to it following the indications provided by the device; in a second task the participant was asked to identify the three nearest POIs belonging to a given category and to report their names to the experimenter; a third task required the participant to access the textual description of a specific POI and read it out loud. Two sets of analogous tasks were devised to prevent familiarity effects. The presentation of the different devices was counterbalanced across participants. The experiment took place in the center of a mid-sized city.

3.2 Equipment

We deployed an Epson Moverio BT-200 (developer version) as an AR-HMD. This device is a see-through AR viewer allowing 3D vision of the objects overlaid onto the surroundings. The input of commands is enabled by a touch-based hand-held pad. The device run Android™ 4.0. In addition, we used a Samsung S4 (4.3''), which run Android™ 4.2. In both conditions, participants used Junaio AR Browser, a commercial AR app. The app shows the POIs in the surroundings of the user as digital labels overlapping onto the real environment through the camera of the device (Figure 1).

Figure 1. A view of Junaio

3.3 Materials

A total of three questionnaires were employed. A pre-experience questionnaire collected respondents' expectations regarding the devices and was filled in before the experience. More specifically we investigated the expected ease use (3 items), that is the extent to which the user foresees that the use of the device will be simple and effortless (adapted from Davis, 1989); the expected usefulness (1 item), which refers to the device being an effective support for achieving the users' goals (adapted from Davis, 1989); the expected self-impression (2 items), amounting to users' possible concerns regarding the way bystanders see them while using the device (adapted from Buenaflor and Kim, 2013); and the expected comfort (2 items devised *ad hoc*), which refers to the extent to which users expected that the device is comfortable to use. The post-experience questionnaire included the same dimensions as the pre-experience one, plus visual comfort (2 items), that is the extent to which the user perceives that the information displayed is clearly organized; and satisfaction (3 items), which is the extent to which users consider the experience of using the device pleasing. The phrasing of the items was adjusted to make them consistent with the condition. A third questionnaire by Spagnolli et al. (2014) investigated participants' intention to use the HMD in the future.

3.4 Participants

A total of 18 people took part in the study. However, data from seven participants were excluded due to technical issues (6) or inability to perform one of the proposed tasks (1). The final sample included 11 users (7 of them were women). The mean age of the sample was 25 (*SD*= 4.38). All of them but three owned a smartphone and used it on a regular basis.

3.5 Experimental Procedure

Participants were first debriefed on the overall procedure and purpose of the experiment, then they gave their informed consent to take part in the study. The experimenter trained them to use the app with both devices. When participants felt confident in using the devices the actual experimental session started with the request of filling in the pre-experience questionnaire. Then participants were given the device, either the HMD or the smartphone, according to the randomization order of the device, and then they were asked to perform the three tasks. After participants had completed the three tasks in a given condition they were asked to complete the post-experience questionnaire(s). The second experimental phase followed with the same procedure. The entire experimental session was video-recorded to allow off-line computer supported video-analysis.

3.6 Measures

Different metrics were considered:

- *Performance accuracy.* The extent to which participants were able to effectively complete the assigned tasks.
- *Time on task.* The temporal interval needed to accomplish the various tasks.
- *Pre-test questionnaire.* The expectations with respect to the overall experience of use (i.e., ease of use, usefulness, self-impression, and comfort).
- *Post-test questionnaire.* The actual evaluations in regard to the above-mentioned dimensions of usability and user experience after having used the devices. In addition, visual comfort and satisfaction were assessed.

4. RESULTS

The following analyses were performed by means of generalized mixed-models (in accordance with not normal distribution of the data) or non-parametric tests.

4.1 Performance Accuracy

Three generalized mixed-models were carried out to evaluate differences in the performance accuracy on the three tasks respectively: reaching the POI, finding the nearest POIs, and reading textual information. The independent variable was the device type (HMD vs. smartphone). In consideration of the three tasks a main effect of device type did not emerge (all p's $> .05$). No differences emerged in the accuracy of performing the various tasks when utilizing any of the two AR devices.

4.2 Time on Task

Three Wilcoxon tests were performed regarding the time needed to accomplish the above-mentioned tasks. Here again, no difference due to the device utilized for carrying out the three tasks was shown (all p's $> .05$).

4.3 Pre-test Questionnaire

Five Wilcoxon tests have been performed considering as dependent variables the users' evaluations of perceived usefulness, ease of use, comfort, as well as the user expected self-impression and the visual comfort, as recorded in the questionnaires. Two differences emerged, firstly concerning the self-impression ($V = 66$, $p < .05$) participants assigned higher scores when using HMD ($M = 3.68$, $SD = 0.75$, $Mdn = 4$) in comparison to the smartphone ($M = 2.05$, $SD = 0.85$, $Mdn = 2$). Secondly, in regard of the experienced comfort ($V = 61$, $p < .05$), users evaluated more positively the HMD ($M = 3.09$, $SD = 0.49$, $Mdn = 3$) compared to the smartphone ($M = 2.32$, $SD = 0.60$, $Mdn = 2$; all p values were adjusted with BH corrections, Benjamini & Hochberg, 1995).

4.4 Post-test Questionnaire

Five Wilcoxon tests have been conducted considering as dependent variables the scores regarding the perceived usefulness, ease of use, comfort, user expected self-impression, visual comfort, and satisfaction. No differences emerged concerning all the user experience and usability dimensions (all p values $> .05$ and they were adjusted with BH corrections, Benjamini & Hochberg, 1995).

4.5 Pre- vs. Post-Questionnaire

Two series of Wilcoxon tests were carried out to compare participants' expectations related to the perceived usefulness, ease of use, comfort and self-impression and their scores after the actual usage of the devices. The Moverio BT-200 and the smartphone were considered independently. In regard of the HMD device, no differences emerged as a function of time (pre- vs. post-test). In consideration of the smartphone, the only difference that emerged was related to a reduction in the perception of ease of use ($V = 66$, $p < .05$; at pre-test, $M = 3.39$, $SD = 0.25$, $Mdn = 3.33$, while at post-test, $M = 2.61$, $SD = 0.40$, $Mdn = 2.67$).

5. CONCLUSIONS

In the present experiment, we comparatively investigated the same touristic mobile AR app, namely Junaio, running either on a HMD and a smartphone. We assessed participants' expectations of using the devices before the experience and then we measured their opinions after the actual usage. Participants foresaw that using both devices would be generally effortless and simple. In particular, they predicted that using the HMD would be more comfortable than the smartphone. At the same time, they showed higher concern regarding being stared at by casual observers nearby while wearing the HMD. Interestingly, such differences leveled out after the actual use. Participants considered equally easy, useful and comfortable both devices. It is worth noticing that the perceived fear of attracting undesired attention was similar for both the HMD and smartphone after the experience. As a matter of fact, users' performance in terms of accuracy and completion time did not differ between the devices. Unexpectedly, the perception of simplicity of use decreased from pre- to post-test only when participants were using the smartphone. This may be due to the frequent need to shade the smartphone to contrast light reflections on its screen, as noted during the video-analysis.

Taken together these findings support the feasibility of exploiting hands-free devices for the exploration of the urban environment. Mobile AR apps based on hand-held devices (i.e., tablet, smartphone) for visiting cultural sites were found to disconnect the tourist from the surroundings, as the need to hold such tools built a physical and experiential barrier with the real world. Indeed, in this situation tourists' attention is focused on the technology rather than on the environment (Jylhä et al. 2015). In order to design cutting-edge AR systems for enhanced urban exploration different sensorial channels should be included. The integration of auditory and tactile messages may relieve the visual channel, yet presenting the users with the same amount of information (Hsieh et al. 2018).

In the future, additional comparisons should be run between more advanced AR head-mounted displays (e.g., Microsoft Hololens) to determine the features that best support the user in an urban exploration context. Additionally, it should be considered that touristic visiting is oftentimes a group experience (Brown and Chalmers 2003), therefore such technologies should be evaluated as operated by several users simultaneously.

Finally, it should be interesting to assess the extent to which recent AR head-mounted displays can be deployed for a full touristic visiting experience, tailoring the route to the needs and priorities of the users (e.g., time availability, preferences) and the POIs in the area.

ACKNOWLEDGEMENT

The present research was partially funded by the European Union Seventh Framework Programme (FP7/2007-2013) under grant agreement n°601139 CultAR (Culturally Enhanced Augmented Realities).

REFERENCES

Azuma, R. T. (1997). A survey of augmented reality. Presence, 6(4), 355-385.

Benjamini, Y., and Yekutieli, D. (2001). The control of the false discovery rate in multiple testing under dependency. Annals of Statistics 29, 1165–1188.

Brancati, N., Caggianese, G., De Pietro, G., Frucci, M., Gallo, L., & Neroni, P. (2015, November). Usability evaluation of a wearable augmented reality system for the enjoyment of the cultural heritage. In Signal-Image Technology & Internet-Based Systems (SITIS), 2015 11th International Conference on (pp. 768-774). IEEE.

Brown, B. and Chalmers, M., Tourism and Mobile Technology. In Proc. ECSCW 2003, Springer (2003) , 14–18.

Brusie, T., Fijal, T., Keller, A., Lauff, C., Barker, K., Schwinck, J., ... & Guerlain, S. (2015, April). Usability evaluation of two smart glass systems. In *Systems and Information Engineering Design Symposium (SIEDS), 2015* (pp. 336-341). IEEE.

Cabral, D., Orso, V., El-khouri, Y., Belio, M., Gamberini, L., & Jacucci, G. (2014, October). The role of location-based event browsers in collaborative behaviors: an explorative study. In *Proceedings of the 8th Nordic Conference on Human-Computer Interaction: Fun, Fast, Foundational* (pp. 951-954). ACM.

Costanza, E., Inverso, S. A., Pavlov, E., Allen, R., & Maes, P. (2006, September). Eye-q: Eyeglass peripheral display for subtle intimate notifications. In Proceedings of the 8th conference on Human-computer interaction with mobile devices and services (pp. 211-218). ACM.

Dieter Schmalstieg and Tobias Höllerer. 2015. Augmented Reality: Principles and Practice. Addison Wesley Professional.

Haugstvedt, A. C., & Krogstie, J. (2012, November). Mobile augmented reality for cultural heritage: A technology acceptance study. In Mixed and Augmented Reality (ISMAR), 2012 IEEE International Symposium on (pp. 247-255). IEEE.

Jylhä, A., Hsieh, Y. T., Orso, V., Andolina, S., Gamberini, L., & Jacucci, G. (2015, November). A Wearable Multimodal Interface for Exploring Urban Points of Interest. In *Proceedings of the 2015 ACM on International Conference on Multimodal Interaction* (pp. 175-182). ACM.

Kaufmann, H., & Dünser, A. (2007, July). Summary of usability evaluations of an educational augmented reality application. In International Conference on Virtual Reality (pp. 660-669). Springer, Berlin, Heidelberg.

Ko, S. M., Chang, W. S., & Ji, Y. G. (2013). Usability principles for augmented reality applications in a smartphone environment. International Journal of Human-Computer Interaction, 29(8), 501-515.

Lee, G. A., Dünser, A., Kim, S., & Billinghurst, M. (2012, November). CityViewAR: A mobile outdoor AR application for city visualization. In *Mixed and Augmented Reality (ISMAR-AMH), 2012 IEEE International Symposium on* (pp. 57-64). IEEE.

Leue, M. C., Jung, T., & tom Dieck, D. (2015). Google glass augmented reality: Generic learning outcomes for art galleries. In Information and Communication Technologies in Tourism 2015 (pp. 463-476). Springer, Cham.

Marimon, D., Sarasua, C., Carrasco, P., Álvarez, R., Montesa, J., Adamek, T., ... & Gascó, P. (2010). MobiAR: tourist experiences through mobile augmented reality. *Telefonica Research and Development, Barcelona, Spain.*

McAtamney, G., & Parker, C. (2006, April). An examination of the effects of a wearable display on informal face-to-face communication. In Proceedings of the SIGCHI conference on Human Factors in computing systems (pp. 45-54). ACM.

Olsson, T., Kärkkäinen, T., Lagerstam, E., & Ventä-Olkkonen, L. (2012). User evaluation of mobile augmented reality scenarios. Journal of Ambient Intelligence and Smart Environments, 4(1), 29-47.

Ruta, M., Scioscia, F., Ieva, S., De Filippis, D., & Di Sciascio, E. (2015, December). Indoor/outdoor mobile navigation via knowledge-based POI discovery in augmented reality. In *Web Intelligence and Intelligent Agent Technology (WI-IAT), 2015 IEEE/WIC/ACM International Conference on* (Vol. 3, pp. 26-30). IEEE.

Spagnolli, A., Guardigli, E., Orso, V., Varotto, A., and Gamberini, L. (2014). Measuring user acceptance of wearable symbiotic devices: validation study across application scenarios. *Proceedings of the International Workshop on Symbiotic Interaction.* Springer, Cham, pp. 87-98.

Vlahakis, V., Ioannidis, M., Karigiannis, J., Tsotros, M., Gounaris, M., Stricker, D., ... & Almeida, L. (2002). Archeoguide: an augmented reality guide for archaeological sites. *IEEE Computer Graphics and Applications*, *22*(5), 52-60.

MODELLING USER EXPERIENCE: INTEGRATING USER EXPERIENCE RESEARCH INTO DESIGN EDUCATION

Gülşen Töre Yargın[1], Sedef Süner[1,2] and Aslı Günay[1]
[1]*Middle East Technical University, BILTIR-UTEST Product Usability Unit*
Department of Industrial Design, Dumlupinar Bulv. Universiteler Mah. No: 1, 06800, Ankara, Turkey
[2] *TED University, Department of Industrial Design*
Ziya Gökalp Caddesi No.48 06420, Kolej Çankaya, Ankara, Turkey

ABSTRACT

The last two decades have given a new lease of life to the interpretation of users' interactions with products in human-computer interaction (HCI) and design domains. As a fast growing field, user experience (UX) brought along multifarious endeavors to frame this new field's definition and components. In the midst of this burgeoning field, many design related domains started to embrace the terms experience, services, and systems rather than a mere product focus. Academia's efforts to define what UX really is, influenced the practice by trying to investigate how UX can be put in action. Hence, growing demand from industry created a need for fully trained and specialized UX designers, turning the attention back again to academia. Although one of the most critical components of UX is research to understand users, their interactions, environments, and even the invisible factors; selecting and applying appropriate methods and tools are of high challenge due to concomitant dependence of experiences on subjective perceptions, contextual ties, and timewise conditions. In this light, we have devised a course to be integrated into design education at graduate level with the aim of teaching how to comprehend, interpret, and communicate UX to present input for the design process with a special approach. The particular approach is "modelling UX" because designing for experience and evaluating the success of design output, as well as bethinking scientific improvements and improving the practice, entail investigating experiences with opportune research methods. After delineating background for devising a UX course, this paper dwells on the objectives, content, structure, and outputs of our course; which would be a scaffolding resource for efforts to integrate UX research into design education.

KEYWORDS

User Experience, Design Education, User Research, Modelling Experience

1. INTRODUCTION

For design and HCI disciplines, twenty-first century started with a construction of a new UX paradigm and continued to be replete with studies about the term's meaning, its constructs, and jointly accepted models. UX rooted in, but diverged from traditional usability concept with the positioning of many novel interactive technologies in everyday life. This has not only widened the scope of emotional concerns of users, but also exposed designers to novel interaction issues (Cockton, 2013; Djajadiningrat et al., 2004). As Jordan (2000) asserted, the traditional focus on mere physical and cognitive aspects of users and instrumental characteristics of interaction started to fall short; and hence, a holistic view towards users' interaction with products has been adopted, placing a premium on hedonic aspects and encompassing users' emotions, objectives, expectations, and dreams. In a nutshell, accumulative discussions and frameworks about UX demonstrates that UX involves three main components: users, products/systems, and context in which the interaction occurs; and embraces a broader and more complex social, cultural, economic, and temporal spectrum (e.g. Desmet and Hekkert, 2007; Forlizzi and Battarbee, 2004; Hekkert and Schifferstein, 2008; Karapanos et al., 2009).

Apart from extensive discussions about this new field's definition and components, escalating numbers of UX related conferences, seminars, workshops, and journals; as well as ascending numbers of members in communities, such as User Experience Professionals Association and The Interaction Design Association (see UXPA, 2018; IxDA, 2004-18) can depict the rapid growth of the interdisciplinary UX field.

The aforementioned disciplinal growth and UX awareness has been accompanied by demand from industry for fully trained and specialized UX designers, which is evident in increased number of UX relevant job postings, hence turned the attention to academia (Getto and Beecher, 2016; Vorvoreanu et al., 2017; White and Kapakos, 2017). UX focused online courses, internship programs, workshops, and camps also address the immediate necessity for practice-ready UX designers; yet a sustained education agenda for UX has not been commonly achieved. Gonzalez et al. (2014) reported that students in design related domains do not feel ready for a career in UX; as education programs aiming to raise UX practitioners are almost unavailable and even most practitioners are self-taught by having been involved in a related job (Getto et al., 2013).

Considering the aforementioned need above, this paper presents a UX course we devised and offered for graduate level industrial design students. Acknowledging the centrality of user experience research (UXR) in UX paradigm, the course has given weight to user research methods and a specific tool we have developed to model UX - User Experience Research Method Matrix (UXMx). To orient readers to the particulars of the course, we first present spearheading examples of curricular adjustments for implementing UX, as well as emerged paradigms for implementing UX in design education. Subsequently, we discuss how an integrated model of UX education would be. After capturing the broad picture about current situation and discussing the integrated model of UX education, we account for centering UXR. Then, exhaustive content is allocated for the explanation of the introduced course - Modelling UX - with its objectives, scope, and outputs.

2. CURRENT PARADIGMS IN UX EDUCATION

Although UX education mostly takes place in extracurricular events, the increasing demand in tech-industry for job-ready UX professionals has impact on curricular adjustments in both undergraduate and graduate level. Academy-industry collaboration is one way to ensure that students gain the skills necessary for UX practice. One of the first undergraduate degrees in UX design was recently offered by Savannah College of Art and Design in the US in collaboration with Google (SCAD, 2018), as others emphasize the importance of introducing students to real-world design problems through apprenticeship models (Getto and Beecher, 2016; Getto et al., 2013), and partnering with external clients in studio projects (MacDonald and Rozaklis; 2017).

It is widely accepted that we should train future UX experts in academy and perhaps establish fully fledged UX programs, yet there are challenges to developing curriculum standards, teaching strategies or models. Firstly, UX theory and practice intersects with a set of knowledge and skills shared by different disciplines. Literature shows recent effort on helping students with varying backgrounds acquire skills associated with designing for UX, like human factors (Gonzalez et al., 2017), HCI (Faiola and Matei, 2010), industrial design (Budd and Wang, 2017), interaction design (Bødker and Klokmose, 2012), and technical communication (Getto and Beecher, 2016). Different disciplines require diverse methods, skills and processes, which are shared by contemporary UX practice. Naturally, the disciplinary approach to aligning curriculum and course content with UX-relevant skills is to introduce methods and tools traditionally attributed to other disciplines. This not only leads to redefinition of the scopes of the disciplines, but also gradual convergence of boundaries. For example, HCI and human factors programs traditionally show affinity towards testing and quantitative measurement, and are advised to acquire a human-centered perspective beyond usability, especially early qualitative user research (Faiola, 2007; Gonzalez et al., 2017; Hanington, 2010). Industrial design and interaction design have traditionally adopted human-centered design principles (Hanington, 2010), but might benefit from integration of digital prototyping skills such as coding and making (Budd and Wang, 2017).

The reverberation of this multidisciplinary landscape makes it difficult to frame standardized skills and methods. Another challenge is the diverse nature of the industry-based UX practice. The UX job market has started to become diversified, as companies are now opening different positions such as UX Design, UX Engineering, UX Research, and UX Writing (Gonzalez et al., 2017). Moreover, in an analysis of the required skills in UX-related job postings, Gonzalez et al. (2014) found inconsistencies between the job titles and required skills. Finally, being a technology-driven field, UX is in a state of flux, and teaching all the tools and skills that would be relevant in the near future is simply not possible (Getto and Beecher, 2016).

Despite challenges, there is evident effort to build strategies for developing theoretically informed curriculum and course content in UX related fields. Existing educational strategies point out to an integrated model with a balanced intersection of theory and application through real-life or simulated project processes (Bødker and Klokmose, 2012; Faiola, 2007; Faiola and Matei, 2010; Getto and Beecher, 2016). The recommended curricular content can be matched with this model as: UX as awareness, skills, and process.

UX as awareness refers to the efforts to equip students with UX-related theories and models. Theories dedicated to explain the interaction between the user and the artefact or system, such as Activity Theory (Bødker and Klokmose, 2012) and Norman's notion of affordances (Faiola and Matei, 2010), are made available in the curriculum in order to familiarize students with the conceptual understanding about the extent of the effect products have on the subjective experience of the user. At graduate level, where UX education mostly takes place, the focus is dominantly on theoretical aspects of the UX rather than practical, although a balance between and integration of the two is recommended (Getto et al., 2013).

UX as skills encompasses the breadth of the required tools and techniques to be utilized at different stages of the UX design process. Various skills harbored by the UX practice are proposed to be made explicit in the curriculums, such as interviewing and ethnographic research, prototyping and testing, computing, visual design, oral and written communication, and so on (Budd and Wang, 2017; Gonzalez et al., 2017; Hanington, 2010; Vorvoreanu et al., 2017). While it holds true that industrial practice may demand vast number of skills with no universal standards in job definitions and requirements, specialization started to take place as different UX positions are being made available by the companies (Gonzalez et al., 2017).

UX as process points out to the project lifespan, beginning from early user research to empathize with the users, to design ideation, iterative prototyping and usability testing. As Getto et al. (2013) suggest, "A balance between [theory and practice] is necessary, and teaching tools is an opportunity for students to put theory into practice" (p. 67). Hence, going through the steps of a real or simulated UX project is considered to be an opportunity for students to put theory into action in an integrated curriculum (Bødker and Klokmose, 2012; Faiola and Matei, 2010; MacDonald and Rozaklis, 2017; Vorvoreanu et al., 2017).

Given the historical connection of UX to user-centered design, UXR is naturally a central skill embedded in the UX process. UXR has been emerging as a separate expertise as a result of further specialization within professional UX practice, and a recent survey shows that knowledge and experience on research methods are among the most valuable skills according to UX professionals (Gonzalez et al. 2017). Similarly, Churchill et al. (2016) reported that two surveys conducted with students, academics, and industry practitioners show a consistent consensus about the importance of design and empirical research methodologies. User research is usually recommended as a core module of the curriculum, with particular emphasis on qualitative methods to inform the early design phase with user-driven directions, such as ethnography (Faiola, 2007), requirements gathering (Getto et al., 2013), and generative/ participatory methods (Hanington, 2010).

In the ever-changing context of the technological landscape and the professional practice within, the importance of the ability to independently plan, conduct, analyze and communicate user research is evident. Thus, within the broader scope of UX education, we focus on UXR and put effort in devising a course to raise awareness and enable students to acquire skills in UXR and experience UXR as a process in accordance with the integrated model of UX education. In the following sections, we present objectives, content, structure and outputs of the course which aims to integrate UXR into design education at graduate level.

3. A COURSE ON INTEGRATING UXR INTO DESIGN EDUCATION

3.1 Objectives and Scope

To integrate UXR into graduate design education, we adopted the approach of "modelling UX" as a bridge between the phases where user insights are generated and used to design products. Hence, the course focuses on understanding specific experiences and studying them to communicate to the design process through modelling. In scientific terms, modelling is one of the most crucial means for understanding a phenomenon or a theory (Deutsch, 1952). Models are used for abstracting scientific data or concepts in order to analyze, organize, teach, and present (Frigg and Hartmann, 2009); meanwhile allowing to focus on major blocks of the reach topic rather than less significant parts. Correlatively, UX is multidimensional, dynamic, and complex by its nature and making sense out of an experience is essential for developing products and services relevant to that experience. Hence, investigation of UX through modelling is valuable to discover, comprehend, and convey such a complex paradigm. Our approach to modelling is more qualitative; rather than generating UX measurement models (Law and van Schaik, 2010) our focus is on understanding the holistic experience and underlying paradigms. Such holism requires utilizing qualitative methods, such as interviews and ethnography, and data visualization skills to represent results beyond statistical modelling (Gonzalez et al., 2017).

Effective modelling requires mastery in selecting and applying appropriate research methods. Therefore, within the scope of the course, objectives involved enabling students to raise their *awareness* towards current concepts in UX, UXR methods, tools and techniques; obtaining *skills* for researching and modelling UX and conducting UXR in different settings; and acquiring hands on experience in conducting UXR as a *process*.

3.2 Structure and Content

The fourteen-week course involves several stages, which have been planned for raising awareness and delivering theoretical knowledge about UXR, planning a UXR case, applying the research, analyzing the results and modelling and communicating them by generating user insights. These stages are introduced in this section.

3.2.1 Course Introduction

At the beginning, an introductory meeting is scheduled to present course objectives, scope and content. Students are encouraged to indicate interest areas and choose an experience that can be the topic of their research project in the course. By asking their interest areas, we aim to (1) elevate motivation as the project requires intense work and (2) maintain diversity in subjects dealt with during the course. Such diversity enables variety in the UXR methods applied and allows students to observe how different methods are employed in practice other then they personally experience throughout the course. In this phase, to sensitize students to the topic, they are also lectured on definitions of UX, current approaches in UXR, models and modelling in UX.

3.2.2 State-of-the-art UXR Methods and Introduction of the UXMx

After the introductory phase, an extensive database of UXR methods[1] are briefly presented to demonstrate an exhaustive overview of possibilities in conducting research in this area. To guide students in selecting a method for a specific case, we developed the UXMx tool. It aims to guide method selection process with five major questions to be answered by the researcher (Table 1). These questions refer to the criteria for categorizing UXR methods[2] and such categorizations help the researcher to understand the considerations to choose a method.

Table 1. Method selection questions, method categorization criteria and categories of UXR methods used in UXMx

METHOD SELECTION QUESTIONS	CATEGORIZATION CRITERIA	CATEGORIES
WHY? What is the purpose of the research?	Categorization according to the phases of the design process	GENERATIVE / EVALUATIVE
HOW? Which approaches will be adopted by the researcher?	Categorization according to the way of application	DIRECT / INDIRECT
WHAT? What kinds of data will be gathered through research?	Categorization according to characteristics of the user information	ATTIT. / BEHAV. / IMAG.
WHY? What will be the time frame for the research?	Categorization according to time / duration of the study	CROSS-SECTIONAL / LONGITUDINAL
HOW? Which contexts are appropriate for conducting the research?	Categorization according to the research setting	CONTRIVED / NATURALISTIC

[1] Around 60 methods, techniques and tools are available in the database. In the paper, these ‘methods, techniques and tools’ are referred to as ‘methods’ for the sake of brevity.

[2] The categorization criteria used in UXMx is an adapted version of the criteria for user research methods presented in Töre Yargın (2013). For an extensive overview of these categorizations see Töre Yargın (2013) and Süner (2018).

After lecturing on method selection criteria and questions, and overviewing database of methods, the UXMx is presented to the students. We plan two different use cases for UXMx to train the students in using it for real practice. The first one involves an assignment for which the students review published work on UXR and locate the utilized methods in the UXMx. To do that, the latest issue of a journal publishing UX studies is assigned to each student[3]. Students are asked to review each individual paper which involves an empirical study with users, and analyze the utilized methods by considering why it is chosen, how it is justified by the researchers, and benefits and drawbacks. After, a workshop is conducted to locate the methods in the UXMx. In this workshop, students are asked to consider their analyses of the published work when locating them on the UXMx and mark the relevant method selection criteria. The objective of this phase is to familiarize the students with methods and the selection criteria, while reviewing recent academic studies in the field.

For the second use, the UXMx is employed as a guide to select the methods for students' research cases. For each case, together with each student we decide on two methods by considering the selection criteria in the UXMx. As the tutors of the course, we assist the student in the selection process by indicating which criteria should be primarily taken into account considering the practicalities of the research setting and the type of experience that the student would like to explore.

3.2.3 Research Planning

After acquiring knowledge about UXR methods and how they can be selected, students start to plan their own UXR projects. At first, they are asked to conduct a literature review on the assigned methods and discuss their advantages and disadvantages; and then they plan their own studies by considering how the two methods should be devised to complement each other and allow them to understand and model the experience they focus on.

3.2.4 Research Application and Analysis

Followed by the planning stage, students revise their methodology plans based on our feedback and organize pilot studies to test their applicability. At this stage, a lecture is given on practicalities of laboratory and contextual observation and usage of observation equipment in these settings. Afterwards, pilot studies are conducted with representatives from their sample. Following the pilot studies, students are lectured on early stages of qualitative data analysis and data coding; and a coding workshop is scheduled to initiate the analysis process of students' research projects. In this workshop, students work on transcriptions of pilot studies and develop their preliminary code books which are used in data analysis, as well as when developing their models. For the consecutive few weeks, scheduled critique sessions are organized to supervise and guide the data collection and analysis processes of students.

3.2.5 Research Communication

Towards the end of data collection and analysis phases, a lecture on data displays and visualization is given. The lecture conveys several examples of modelling approaches towards UX as follows: representing activities and works of users, representing the user, representing the concepts and their relations, representing experience over time, and representing design recommendations based on user insights (Table 2). After the lecture, a workshop on data display and visualization is conducted to direct students to choose a modelling approach for their projects and plan their final models. As the outcome of the course, a poster is prepared for each project to communicate the aim, methodology, scope, and the experience model that is developed as the result. First, the draft posters are evaluated by the students in a peer evaluation session. In this session, each student gets familiarized with others' work and has a chance to scrutinize how different methods are applied by their peers. The lecture is finalized with an exhibition and a poster presentation event. This public event is open to the participation of all students and the staff at the faculty, which is another chance for the students to receive feedback on their UXR projects and final models.

---

[3] Journals such as Human–Computer Interaction, International Journal of Human-Computer Studies, Computers in Human Behavior, Ergonomics, Behaviour & Information Technology, ACM Transactions on Computer-Human Interaction (TOCHI), International Journal of Child-Computer Interaction and Journal of Usability Studies are involved. While assigning them to the students, interest areas which are indicated at the beginning of the course are considered.

Table 2. UX Modelling approaches presented in the course

MODELLING APPROACH	TYPES OF MODELS	SOURCES
Representing activities and works of users	Work models in contextual design involving the flow model, the cultural model, the sequence model, the physical model and the artefact model	Holtzblatt, Wendell, & Wood, 2004
Representing the user	Personas (both data-driven and inspirational)	Pruitt & Adlin, 2006
	Task-based user segments based on mental models	Young, 2008; Authors' unpublished project work
Representing the concepts and their relations	Hierarchical Value Maps (HVM) based on laddering interviews	Wansink, 2003; Reynolds & Olson, 2001; Miles & Rowe, 2004; Abeele & Zaman, 2009; Töre Yargın, 2013
	Conceptual Maps / Cognitive Maps	Farsides, 2004; Miles, Huberman, & Saldana, 2013; Töre Yargın, 2013; Authors' unpublished project work
	Cross Impact Analysis (CIA) based on laddering interviews or Repertory Grid interviews	Töre Yargın, 2013; Kuru, 2015; Süner & Erbuğ, 2016
Representing experience over time	Experience maps representing user experience over time	Karapanos, Zimmerman, Forlizzi & Martens, 2009; Richardson, 2010; Karahanoğlu, 2013
Representing design recommendations	Mental models	Young, 2008
	Design recommendation infographics	Authors' unpublished project work

3.3 Outputs: Student Projects

The course has been offered in Spring 2016-17 and Fall 2017-18 semesters and taken by twenty-one graduate students from Middle East Technical University, Department of Industrial Design. During the course, depending on the type of the project and academic level of the students, some projects are carried out individually, whereas others are encouraged to be conducted as couples. Nine couple projects and three individual projects were carried out throughout these two semesters. In some of the projects, students were able to find collaboration opportunities, including science parks, application developer companies and maker communities, as well as academic institutions. Table 3 presents an overview of these twelve projects indicating their titles, methods used, the UXMx criteria considered when choosing the methods and types of the models presented as outcomes of the projects.

Table 3. Summary of all projects carried out in the course

TITLE	METHOD	WHY	WHAT	HOW	WHERE*	WHEN	MODEL REPRESENTING
Exploring Sensory Modalities: The Case of Listening Music with Headsets	UX Curve						• Concepts and their relations • Experience over time
	Mental Imagery						
	RGT						
Budget Management Experience of College Students	Laddering						• Concepts and their relations • Experience over time
	Diary						
	Interview						
Ride Sharing Experience of Students with the 'TAG' Application: Commuting between METU and Eryaman	Interview						• Experience over time
	Device Logs						
	Diary						
	Interview						
Redesign of Syrian Refugees' Registration Process in Ankara	Observation						• The user • The activities / works • Recommendations
	Interview						
	Workshop						
3D Modelling and Printing Experience	UX Curve						• Experience over time
	Diary						
	Interview						
The Use of Online Tools in Industrial Design Education	Survey						• Concepts and their relations
	Experience Sampling						
	Interview						
Lunch (Break) Experiences of METU Technopark Employees	Diary						• The user • The activities / works • Recommendations
	Interview						
Makers' Experience of Self-Learning Arduino via Online Platforms	Interview						• Concepts and their relations • Experience over time
	UX Curve						
	Task Completion (with TA)						
Exploring Employees' Experience of Physical Space in Teknokent Incubation Center	Cultural Probes						• Concepts and their relations
	Interview						
Role and Importance of Idea Generation Techniques in Industrial Design Education	Interview						• Concepts and their relations
	Focus Group						
Enhancing Children's Healthy Eating Experience: A Contexmapping Study	Interview						• Concepts and their relations
	Diary						
	Workshop						
Consumers' Shopping Experiences in Super-markets and Online Markets Mobile Application	Shadowing (with TA)						• Concepts and their relations • The activities / works • Recommendations
	Laddering						

* Empty cells indicate settings, where decision was made based on availability. TA: Think Aloud

As it can be seen in the table, there were an array of methods applied by the students including interview methods, such as traditional interviews, laddering, repertory grid, mental imagery and UX Curve interviews and focus groups; observational methods, such as naturalistic observation, shadowing and collecting device logs to observe behavior; diary methods, such as traditional diaries, experience sampling and cultural probes, and workshop methods conducted with users and designers. Consequently, for each of the project, different UX models were generated representing concepts and their relations, experience over time, activities or works, the user and design recommendations. Such variety enables students to observe different types of UXR processes and thereby support learning from their peers, which is an important goal of this course.

4. DISCUSSIONS AND CONCLUSIONS

The course schedule described so far involves lectures, assignments and workshops. Figure 1 illustrates how targeted learning outcomes, course content, tools, and activities align with dimensions of the integrated UX education model. For raising *awareness towards UX* and UXR throughout the course, students are lectured on several topics including concepts and models on UX; UXR methods; usage of the UXMx to choose a method; operation of observation equipment and considerations in contrived and naturalistic settings; and data analysis and visualization. Theoretical knowledge is supported with assignments and in class activities, which enable students to apply knowledge and acquire the required skills for conducting UXR and modelling UX. All these lectures, assignments, and workshops guide the student to experience *UXR as a process*. Through acquiring hands on experience with such a process, our aim is to equip students with necessary *skills* and knowledge to function as UX researchers. This serves the industry's need for training job-ready UX practitioners, as well as facilitating academic development of students in conducting empirical research.

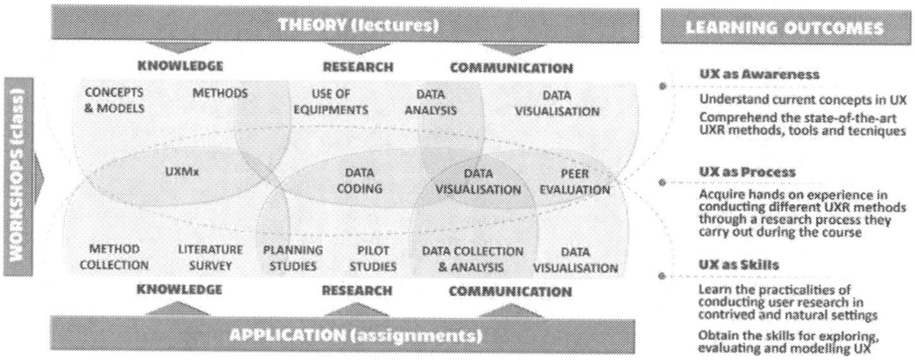

Figure 1. Theoretical structure of the course

Although there is a plethora of methods that should be learned and applied to have mastery in UXR, students have chance to experience merely three methods at most. So, we aspire to maintain variety in research cases and encourage peer learning by facilitating in-class presentations and activities. This enables students to discuss on different UXR cases, thereby learn from peers. To train students in UXR, another critical issue is educators' competence in conducting UXR in real life (Gonzalez et al., 2017). In this course, guiding students in deciding on their topics and selecting methods for their research projects required educator's mastery in UXR. We have varying experience (from nine to fifteen years) including industrial collaborations with different firms. This is helpful in leading the course and guiding students when choosing topics, using UXMx, and building models.

Given our integrated UX education model, it is also crucial to reflect upon the role of the UXMx. We intended to devise UXMx as a decision making aid that can be utilized in multifarious cases both in education and industry. Hence, major portion of the implications of the course revolves around UXMx. We believe that UXMx leads to valuable and rich educational, professional, and academic implications. Bethinking educational ones, as UXMx is used to benefit from appropriate method selection criteria and able to locate students' project among constellation of research methods, students have gained knowledge on how to select methods and present research findings. For professional implications, UXMx has potential to be directly utilized in practice. While being a guidance for industry, for which knowledgeable UX researchers is of current necessity, it can also be used both for choosing the right methods and communicating the research outcomes within a firm or to other stakeholders. Beyond these core implications, UXMx can be a guide as an academic implication, by structuring method reviews and by being a classification tool for manifold UXR methods.

This paper describes the objectives, scope, content, and outputs of a course, which aimed to provide training on UXR. By describing these, the goal is to discuss the theoretical structure of the course (Figure 1). For this reason, the paper only focuses on presenting the course's content and structure; and overviews the current outputs. To understand how well objectives have been met and how well the course corresponds to students' and industry's needs, evaluations should be conducted both during the course and at the end of each semester. The effect of knowledge and skills acquired during the course on real life circumstances and how students who took the course benefit from it should be explored to understand the course effectiveness and value. Future studies will focus on these issues to improve the course and draw lessons for developing educational strategies for UX. Furthermore, although this course has been facilitative in training UX researchers, it is important to note that it is limited with time restrictions and capacity of a semester-long course, since it is offered as an elective in the Department of Industrial Design. We believe that lessons learned from the execution of the course as well as its theoretical structure can be informative for educational curriculum development in UX.

ACKNOWLEDGEMENTS

The course presented in this paper was designed as part of a research project funded by Middle East Technical University (Project number BAP-08-11-2017-008). We would like to thank all of the students who participated in our course.

REFERENCES

Abeele, V.V. and Zaman, B., 2009. Laddering the User Experience! *User Experience Methods, Interact 2009.* Sweden.

Bødker, S. and Klokmose, C. N., 2012. Preparing Students for (Inter-)action with Activity Theory. *International Journal of Design*, Vol. 6, No. 3, pp. 99-111.

Budd, J. and Wang, W., 2017. Industrial Design Education: Taming Technology to Enhance User Experience. *Archives of Design Research*, Vol. 30, No. 3, pp. 17-27.

Churchill, E.F. et al, 2016. The Future of HCI Education: A Flexible, Global, Living Curriculum. *Interactions*, Vol. 23, No. 2, pp. 70-73.

Cockton, G., 2013. Usability Evaluation. In M. Soegaard & R. F. Dam (eds), *The encyclopedia of human-computer interaction (2nd ed.).* The Interaction Design Foundation.

Desmet, P. and Hekkert, P., 2007. Framework of Product Experience. *International Journal of Design,* Vol. 1, No. 1, pp. 13-23.

Deutsch, K.W., 1952. On Communication Models in the Social Sciences. *Public Opinion Quarterly*, Vol. 16, No. 3, pp. 356-380.

Djajadiningrat, T. et al, 2004. Tangible Products: Redressing the Balance between Appearance and Action. *Personal and Ubiquitous Computing,* Vol. 8, No. 5, pp. 294-309.

Faiola, A., 2007. The Design Enterprise: Rethinking the HCI Education Paradigm. *Design Issues,* Vol. 23, No. 3, pp. 30-45.

Faiola, A. and Matei, S. A., 2010. Enhancing Human-Computer Interaction Design Education: Teaching Affordance Design for Emerging Mobile Devices. *International Journal of Technology Design Education,* Vol. 20, pp. 239-254.

Farsides, T., 2004. Cognitive Mapping: Generating Theories of Psychological Phenomena from Verbal Accounts and Presenting Them Diagrammatically. In G. M. Breakwell (ed), *Doing Social Psychology Research.* Wiley-Blackwell, Oxford.

Forlizzi, J. and Battarbee, K., 2004. Understanding Experience in Interactive Systems. Experience, Context-of-use and the Design of Product Usability. *Proceedings of the 2004 Conference on Designing Interactive Systems: Processes, Practices, Methods, and Techniques*. Cambridge, USA.

Frigg, R. and Hartmann, S., 2009. Models in Science. In E. N. Zalta (ed), *Stanford Encyclopedia of Philosophy.* The Metaphysics Research Lab, Center for the Study of Language and Information, Stanford University, Stanford.

Getto, G. and Beecher, F., 2016. Toward a Model of UX Education: Training UX Designers within the Academy. *IEEE Transactions On Professional Communication*, Vol. 59, No. 2, pp. 153-164.

Getto, G. et al., 2013. Teaching UX: Designing Programs to Train the Next Generation of UX Experts. *SIGDOC'13*. Greenville, USA, pp. 65-69.

Gonzalez, C. A. et al, 2014. Perspectives on the Training of Human Factors Students for the User Experience Industry. *Proceedings of the Human Factors and Ergonomics Society 58th Annual Meeting*, Vol. 58, No. 1, pp. 1807-1811.

Gonzalez, C. A. et al, 2017. Are Human Factors Students Prepared for Careers in User Experience Research? A Survey of Predicted and Actual Skill Utilization. *Proceedings of the Human Factors and Ergonomics Society 2017 Annual Meeting*, Vol. 61, No. 1, pp. 1101-1105.

Hanington, B. M., 2010. Relevant and Rigorous: Human-Centered Research and Design Education. *Design Issues*, Vol. 26, No. 3, pp. 18-26.

Hekkert, P. and Schifferstein, H. N. J. (eds), 2008. *Product Experience*. Elsevier, USA.

Holtzblatt, K. et al, 2004. *Rapid Contextual Design: A How-to Guide to Key Techniques for User-Centered Design*. Morgan Kaufmann, San Francisco.

IxDA, 2004-18. *Welcome to the Interaction Design Association*. https://ixda.org (20 March 2018).

Jordan, P.W., 2000. *Designing Pleasurable Products*. Taylor and Francis, UK.

Karahanoğlu, A., 2013. *Exploration of User Experience of Personal Informatics Systems*. PhD thesis, Middle East Technical University, Ankara.

Karapanos, E. et al, 2009. User Experience Over Time: An Initial Framework. *SIGCHI Conference on Human Factors in Computing Systems,* Boston.

Kuru, A., 2015. Cross Impact Analysis: An Alternative Way of Qualitative Data Analysis of Repertory Grid Technique. *Journal of Design Research*, Vol. 13, No. 4, pp. 362-380.

Law, E. L-C. and van Schaik, P., 2010. Modelling User Experience – An Agenda for Research and Practice. *Interacting with Computers*, Vol. 22, No. 5, pp. 313-322.

MacDonald, C. M. and Rozaklis, L., 2017. Assessing the Implementation of Authentic, Client-Facing Student Projects in User Experience (UX) Education: Insights from Multiple Stakeholders. *80th Annual Meeting of the Association for Information Science & Technology,* Washington USA, pp. 268-278.

Miles, M. et al, 2013. *Qualitative Data Analysis: A Methods Sourcebook*. SAGE Publications, USA.

Miles, S. and Rowe, G., 2004. The Laddering Technique. In G. M. Breakwell (ed), *Doing Social Psychology Research*. Blackwell, Oxford.

Pruitt, J. and Adlin, T., 2006. *The Persona Lifecycle: Keeping People in Mind throughout Product Design*. Elsevier, Oxford.

Reynolds, T. J. and Olson, J. C., 2001. *Understanding Consumer Decision Making: The Means-End Approach to Marketing and Advertising Strategy*. Lawrence Erlbaum, Mahwah, New Jersey.

Richardson, A., 2010. Using Customer Journey Maps to Improve Customer Experience. *Harvard Business Review*, Vol. 15, No. 1.

SCAD, 2018. *User Experience Design Programme Page*. https://www.scad.edu/academics/programs/user-experience-design (15 April 2018)

Süner, S. and Erbuğ, Ç., 2016. Evaluation of Construct Elicitation as a Research Method to Obtain Design - Relevant Data from Children. *METU Journal of the Faculty of Architecture*, Vol. 33, No. 2.

Süner, S., 2018. *Elicitation, Prioritisation, Observation: A Research Model to Inform the Early Design Phases with Child-Centred Perspectives.* PhD thesis, Middle East Technical University, Ankara.

Töre Yargın, G., 2013. *Developing a Model for Effective communication of User Research Findings to the Design Process*. PhD thesis, Middle East Technical University, Ankara.

UXPA, 2018. *About UXPA International: Supporting Those Who Advocate for User Experience*. https://uxpa.org/about-us (20 March 2018).

Vorvoreanu, M. and Connoly, P. E., 2015. Using an Experience Design Approach to Curriculum Creation. *122nd ASEE Annual Conference & Exposition*, Seattle.

Vorvoreanu, M. et al, 2017. Advancing UX Education: A Model for Integrated Studio Pedagogy. *CHI 2017,* Denver.

Wansink, B., 2003. Using Laddering to Understand and Leverage a Brand's Equity. *Qualitative Market Research: An International Journal,* Vol. 6, No. 2, pp. 111-118.

White, B. J. and Kapakos, W. A., 2017. User Experience (UX) in the CIS Classroom: Better Information Architecture with Interactive Prototypes and UX Testing. *Issues in Information Systems*, Vol. 18, No. 2, pp. 59-70.

Young, I., 2008. *Mental Models: Aligning Design Strategy with Human Behavior*. Rosenfield, USA.

HOW EMPATHIZING WITH PERSONA HELPS IN DESIGN THINKING: AN EXPERIMENTAL STUDY WITH NOVICE DESIGNERS

Abhishek Dahiya and Jyoti Kumar
Indian Institute of Technology Delhi, New Delhi, India

ABSTRACT

Personas are widely used by HCI designers in design process. From defining target users to explicating user understanding, persona assists designers at various stages of design process of HCI systems. Design literature advocates the use of persona not only as a source of information about users but also as a tool to empathize. This paper reports observations from an experimental study done on novice designers on how empathizing with persona affected their design solutions. A total of 30 novice designers participated in this study. Participants were asked to design a graphical composition for persona. The data collected was analyzed through expert's rating on design solutions on the basis of directness of illustration of persona information and verbal protocols. On the basis of direct illustration of persona information on design solutions it was observed that empathizing with persona helped designers to iterate more on design thinking.

KEYWORDS

User Centered Design, Persona, HCI Design, Design Thinking, Empathy in Design

1. INTRODUCTION

In User Centered Design (UCD) process (Norman,1988) for HCI products, user research is one of the crucial steps (Hong 2009). It has been argued that designer's mental model and users' mental models may be different (Norman 1988) and user research can help in bridging the mental model gap which will lead to designs that will be easier for users (Carroll 2003). There are various user research methods suggested by design practitioners and researchers for HCI design (Steen and Kuijt; Landauer 1988). Some of these methods are usability testing, qualitative interviewing, card sorting, direct observation, paper prototyping, focus groups etc. User data is helpful to designers in taking various design decisions in HCI design process. User data collected through various methods is documented and reported in various formats (Pruitt and Adlin 2006). User data formats could be in form of text (reports, observations etc.), pictures, documentary videos etc. Often in design firms, collection, documentation and presentation of user information is done by user research team.

Persona is one of the form of user data presentation in HCI design. Personas are "fictitious, specific, concrete representations of target users" (Pruitt & Adlin, 2006). A persona represents target users who share common behavioural characteristics (i.e., is a hypothetical archetype of real users) (Pruitt & Adlin, 2006). Introduced by (Cooper,1999), personas were integrated into the design processes to help designers in developing useful and usable designs (Cooper 1999; Pruitt John 2003;Caballero, Moreno, and Seffah 2014). Although persona facilitates designers in many ways like audience prioritization, communication aid, organization of research data, innovative thinking, etc. one of the prime roles of persona is empathy creation, i.e. "creating an understanding of and emotional identification with the users/customers."(Miaskiewicz and Kozar, 2011). Thus, persona is a tool for designers to get informed about and feel empathized with the users. The way a designer uses persona information in his or her design thinking process and the way empathy influences the design thinking may thus be an interesting study to undertake.

Design thinking is a complex process(Newell Allen, 1988). Differences in solution generation approaches between expert designers and novice designers have been studied (Cross, 2001). Novice designers were observed to have difficulty in analyzing width (scope) of the design problem (Atman et al. 1999). Further, novice designers showed less 'cognitive actions' during design thinking (Kavakli and Gero 2001), and used more hit and trial methods for solution generation (Ahmed, Wallace, and Blessing, 2003), etc. This paper reports observations on design thinking process of novice designers under influence of empathy exercise on persona. A total of 30 industrial design students participated in this study. One group of participants had a persona description alone while the other group underwent an empathy exercise along with persona description. Participants in the study were given a persona and graphic design problem to solve. Effect of empathizing with persona on design solution was analyzed using solutions generated by the participants, verbal protocols and expert rating.

2. PERSONA AS A DESIGN TOOL IN HCI DESIGN

Cooper (1999) defines persona as "A precise description of our user and what he wishes to accomplish". Calde, Goodwin & Reimann (2002) describe persona as "fictional, detailed archetypal characters that represent distinct groupings of behaviors, goals and motivations observed and identified during the research phase". Persona are therefore "abstractions of groups of real consumers who share common characteristics and needs" (Pruitt & Adlin, 2006). Persona descriptions includes demographic information, socioeconomic status, occupations, likenesses, possessions etc. of the users. Descriptions in persona helps designers to form an understanding of their target audience which can assist them in design decisions (Cooper, 1999; Manning; 2003; Pruitt & Adlin, 2006). Pruitt (2006) emphasizes on using rigorous user studies to create foundational documents of persona. Personas are therefore a consolidated plot of various user information and understanding developed by user researchers. Generally speaking, persona narratives: (1) aims to provide explicit information and the needs of the users to designers in context of the product to be designed (Long, F. 2009) (2) help designers to empathize with the fictional character and make sense of user's affective and cognitive states (Miaskiewicz and Kozar, 2011)

Although, persona is a buzz word in HCI design, Matthews (Matthews, Judge, and Whittaker 2012) argues that many design practitioners do not use persona in practice. She further argues that in absence of proper training of using persona, designers could not appreciate benefits of using persona to assist in design process. Therefore, there is a need to instill the use of persona to designers so as to aid their design thinking processes. This paper argues that empathizing with persona can be a tool to help designers in design thinking.

2.1 Persona as an Empathy Tool for HCI Design Thinking Process

Persona help HCI designers in design process to create solutions based on the needs of users (Cooper & Reimann, 2002; Grudin & Pruitt, 2002(Caballero, Moreno, and Seffah 2014). One of the roles of persona is to elicit empathy in designers to understand their users. Design literature (Miaskiewicz and Kozar, 2011; Pruitt & Adlin, 2006; Nielsen, 2013) argues that "empathy is part of a process where the reader attempts to understand the feelings of the character by testing various feelings that fit the situation of the character". Persona is given by a name and stories are added to it on the basis of user data collected. Therefore, discrete user data collected from various sources is thus *personified.* The authors posit that *personifying* user data helps for designers to empathize with a character rather than discrete factual data.

Creating persona is an iterative process which includes assimilating and analyzing user data from various user research methods (Pruitt & Adlin, 2006). Once persona is developed, a designer uses this persona to understand and empathize with the user. User insights thus developed help designers to make design decisions while ideating for solutions. Figure 1 illustrates a flowchart of how persona is developed and used in HCI design process.

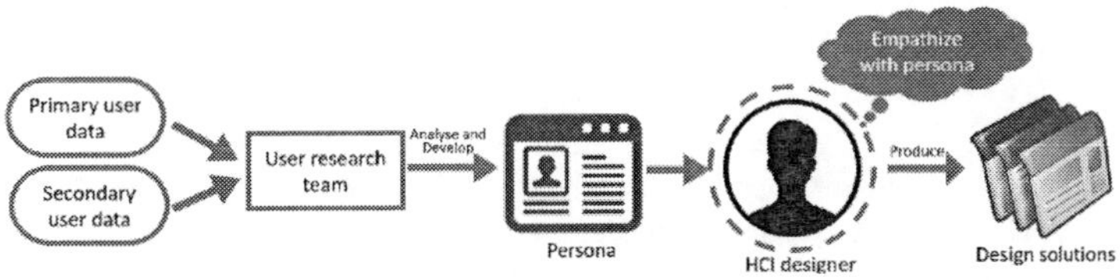

Figure 1. Flowchart illustrating development and using persona in design process

2.2 Influence of Persona on Design Thinking

According to Cooper,(Cooper 1999) human beings are able to predict behavior and mental conditions of other human beings. This ability helps designers to envision how users will behave and respond to their design in any situation (Grudin, J. ,2006). Grudin explains that development of persona as a user understanding tool is based on the fact that people tend characterize other people in terms of traits: these are broad dispositions that predict or explain much of people's behavior. Grudin further argues that "actions and behaviors are predicted by building an internal model of the person. This ability to engage with models of real people is also applicable to the models of fictional people" (in this case, personas). According to Cooper (Cooper,1999,) "The more specific the persona is, the more effective they are as design tools. With more specific, idiosyncratic details, the persona becomes a "real" person in the minds of the developers." Working with persona can be as realistic as working with real users (Grudin, J. ,2006). Hence, representation of user data as fictional people can be as engaging as models of real people.

2.3 Methods to understand Design Thinking

Creative outcomes in design process are influenced by a number of cognitive applications and combinations (Bonnardel, 2000). This is primarily because the characteristics of design activities typically present indefinite criteria and constraints, which makes it difficult to study design thinking(Cross, 2001). There have been various attempts in literature to understand design thinking. Verbal protocol studies have been frequently used in various experiments to examine thinking processes (Cross, 2001).In verbal protocol study researchers provide extracts of protocols, and explained how a segment is encoded along with the meaning of the encoded behaviors (Kim and Kim, 2015). Since using think aloud protocol to study design thinking faces certain challenges on validity of gathered data (Someren, 1994), retrospective verbal accounts (i.e., recalling what one was thinking recently) offer one means of observing cognitive activities (Cross 2001). Verbal protocols are thus analyzed on the basis of frequencies of encoded items and presented in form of tables/charts and matrices. Valkenburg and Dorst used different shapes of figures to represent design activities, and represented the relationships between activities using arrows and boxes(Valkenburg and Dorst, 1998). Linkograph, which was developed by Goldschmidt (Goldschmidt 1990) studies design thinking process by representing a combination of sequential 'design moves', and links between them. Design researchers have also analyzed design thinking processes using sketches developed by designers while ideating for solutions (Tversky and Suwa 2009; Cardoso and Badke-Schaub, 2011). In the experiment, reported in this paper, design solutions were generated by the participants for a given design problem. Literature reports that novice designers tend to perform less cognitive actions during design thinking as compared to experts while solving design problems (Kavakli, M., & Gero, J. ,2001). Authors posit that such a behavior could be a reason why novice designers often tend to 'jump to conclusions' very early while generating solutions for design problems. Further, design thinking includes information retrieval from memory (Dominowski, R.L., & Dallob, P. ,1995). Runco (Runco, 1995) argues that direct retrieval of information from memory is a sign of unoriginality of ideas. For the ideas to be creative, some manipulation of information must be involved. In this paper, to analyze design solutions created by participants 'direct illustration of user information' into design solutions has been considered as a marker of less 'cognitive actions' by novice designers.

3. EXPERIMENT METHODOLOGY

Novice designers were given a graphical design problem along with persona description of the users. Participants were asked to read persona before ideating for solution of the problem provided. Participants were divided into two groups. One group of participants were given persona description and asked to design solutions for the problem (Control group, 16 participants). The other group underwent a 10-minute empathy exercise along with persona description before they were asked to design solutions (Experiment group, 14 participants). Design solutions produced by both the groups along with their verbal protocols were then recorded to analyzed to assess the influence of empathy on design outcomes.

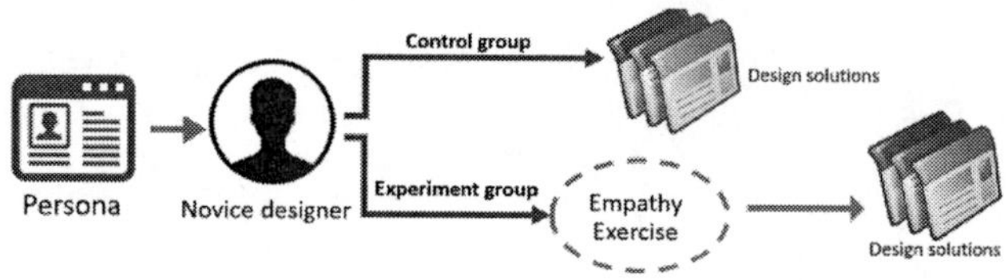

Figure 2. Experiment process for Control group and experiment group

3.1 Persona Description

Participants were provided a persona before the design task was explained to them. Persona included a profile picture of the user and text describing about the user's demographics, interests, hobbies, habits, work profile and family background. The personas provided to the participants is shown in Figure 3 below. In control group, out of 16 participants, 8 participants (P1 to P8) were provided first persona and next 8 participants (P9 to P16) were provided second persona. In experiment group, out of 14 participants, 7 participants (P17 to P23) were provided first persona and next 7 participants (P24 to P30) were provided the second persona. Two personas were used instead of one with an aim to cross validate influence of specific elements of persona on designers' design thinking.

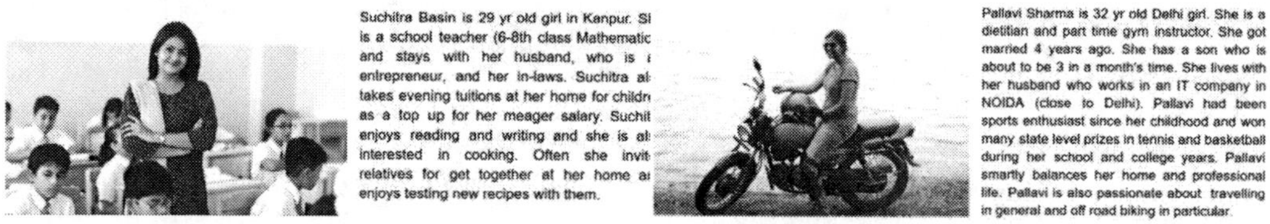

Figure 3. Personas given to the participants: First persona(left), Second persona(right)

3.2 Empathy Exercise

Participants in experiment group were subjected to a 10-minute empathy exercise after reading persona. The aim of this empathy exercise was to help designers take time to think about the user that they are designing for. The empathy exercise included scenario and some task within the scenario that was narrated to the participants by the facilitator. Following was the text narrated to the participants:

"Please close your eyes. Imagine yourself as the persona you just read about. Recall what are the things you like, work you do, activities that interests you. Imagine it is Saturday afternoon and you've just returned to home from your work. Now picture yourself in your (Suchitra/Pallavi) living room. Take your time to look around and see the interiors and objects placed near you. Take a look at the wall clock right in front of you, the photo frame kept on the table next to you, your water bottle, your bag, the painting on the side wall, see the design of on the carpet, lamp on the side of the bed, take a look at the wardrobe, open the wardrobe and go through the dresses you have. Try to observe details of your room for next 10 minutes"

3.3 Design Task

Participants were asked to design "graphical composition for smart phone back cover" for the given persona using stickers of various geometric shapes. The idea of using shapes to design the graphical compositions was to minimize individual differences in ability of sketching/drawing. For example, a participant with low sketching/drawing competency might restrain his/her design ideas due to his/her inability to illustrate the idea. All participants were given equal set of materials required for the task. Participants were instructed to use only the provided materials only for final solution. Participants were free to use colors over the stickers provided to express their design ideas. Materials provided to the participants were: 1. Persona description and Design problem with instructions, 2. A4 size template of smart phone back cover, 3. Stickers: 24 circles, 12 squares, 6 rectangles, 6 rounded rectangles, 6 trapeziums and 6 triangles of various sizes, 4. Rough sheets, 5. Sketch pens, 6. Pencil, eraser and cutter.

3.4 Participants

Participants who volunteered to participate in this experiment were post-graduate students in Industrial Design at Indian Institute of Technology, Delhi. A total of 30 students participated in the study. Participants constituted 16 males and 14 females with age ranges between: 23-27 yrs. (average age: 24.6 yrs., Std. dev.: 1.18 yrs.).

3.5 Experimental Procedure

Experiments were conducted in a controlled environment. Participants were given an isolated desk in a room which was free from any visual cues relevant to problem at hand. It was ensured that there were no visual or auditory disturbances. Participants were first given the persona to read followed by design task followed by instructions. Next, control group participants were provided an envelope consisting of materials required for the task and asked to ideate for solutions after the instructions. Whereas, experiment group participants were subjected to 10-minute empathy exercise after the participants had completed reading persona. Materials required for the task for experiment group participants were provided after empathy exercise session. Participants of both groups were given 40 minutes to ideate and design solutions. Participants were not allowed to use of any sources of inspiration like pictures form internet, magazines, books etc. while designing the graphical composition.

After the design task, participants were given 10-minutes break. Lastly, the experiment was followed by retrospective qualitative interview of the participants explaining how they went about designing the graphical composition.

Figure 4. Pictures showing experimental setup, with Group B participant: 1 reading the persona, 2 during empathy exercise, 3 ideating for solutions, 4 composing final design

4. ANALYSIS METHOD

The design solutions created by participants were analyzed for 'directness in application' of persona descriptions. As discussed in section 2.3, a 'direct illustration of user information' into design solutions has been considered as a marker of less 'cognitive action' by novice designers. The 'directness of application' or 'direct illustration' of persona elements into design outcome was judged by three expert designers. Two of the three experts were industrial designers one of which was an interaction designer having five years of experience in design industry, other had one year' experience in manufacturing industry. Third expert was associated with design academics for more than seven years. Experts were first asked to read the two personas. Next, the experts were asked to evaluate design solutions on the basis of directness of illustration of the textual descriptions written in persona. For example, a sample of directness of illustration from this experiment is illustrated in Figure 5. For persona one, description mentioned persona as 'gym instructor', and the designer illustrated gym equipment in design outcome. This is a direct illustration of persona information. Similarly, for second persona, it was mentioned that the user is a mathematics school teacher, illustrations of a school classroom or arithmetic operations in design is a marker of direct illustration of persona information.

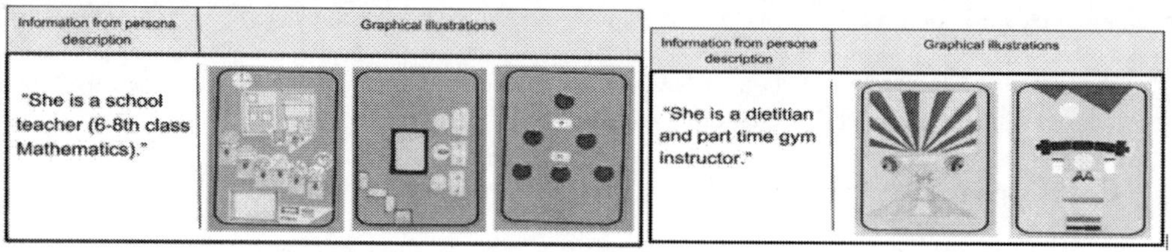

Figure 5. Examples explaining of directness of illustration for persona 1(left) and 2(right)

The ratings were recorded on a 9 point Likert scale ranging from 1 (indirect illustration) to 9 (direct illustration). Judges were kept blind to the existence of the different experimental conditions, and design solutions from the two groups were mixed randomly in the viewing order. The inter-rater reliability of judges' ratings was computed using the Cronbach alpha coefficient. In this experiment the inter rater reliability was found to be 0.920 which is highly significant.

5. OBSERVATIONS AND RESULTS

The main observation was that participants which had undergone empathy exercise had more 'cognitive actions' during design thinking. This section discusses in detail the findings leading to this major observation. It was observed in design solutions that, most of the design solutions generated by participants in control group (without empathy exercise) illustrated the information presented in persona description directly. These illustrations were very direct visual depiction of words or phrases in the persona description. Verbal protocols from retrospective interview showed that participants of this group were influenced by words in persona description (Figure 6).

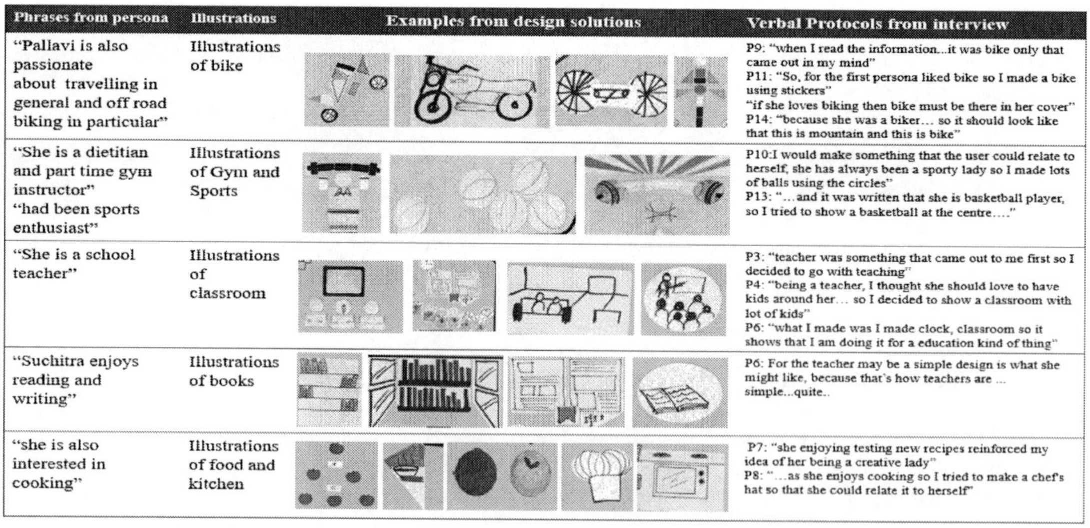

Figure 6. Graphical illustrations by the participants along with verbal protocols

Scores obtained through experts rating on design measuring directness of illustration were analyzed through two tailed t-test at 95 % confidence interval. T-test results indicate that participants in control group (without empathy exercise) illustrated the information provided in persona more directly than the experiment group (with empathy exercise) ($f = 25.716$, $p < 0.01$). It is also evident from the boxplot (Figure 7) that median of control group is much higher than experiment group. This means that majority of participants in control group illustrated the information provided in persona more directly than participants of experiment group. Therefore, a higher degree of directness of illustration of control group shows that novice designers in absence of empathy perform less cognitive actions as compared to the experiment group.

Table 1. Results of t-test measuring *directness of illustration*

Groups	N	Mean	Std. Dev.	Std. Error Mean	Df	F value	Sig.
Control group	48	5.35	1.80	.260	88	25.716	0.001
Experiment group	42	2.33	.845	.130	68.61		

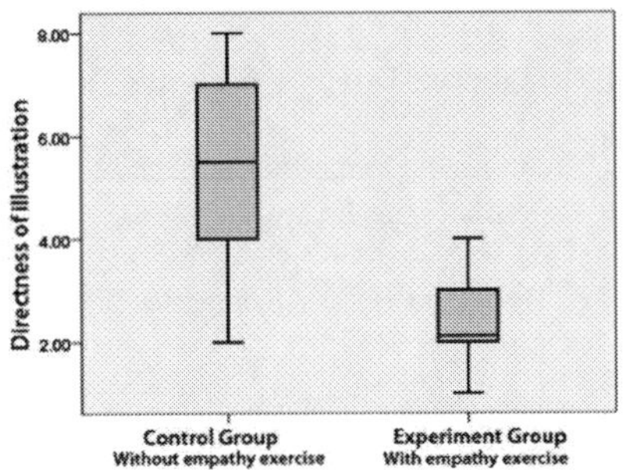

Figure 7. Overall comparison of directness of illustration

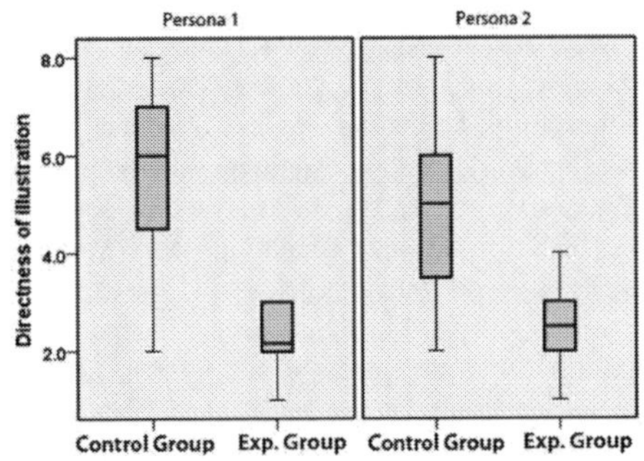

Figure 8. Persona wise comparison of directness of illustration

6. CONCLUSION

While persona description has been known to aid the design thinking process, the way the designers empathize with persona to arrive at design conclusions can be used to understand the design thinking process and the design outcomes. The results from the study reported in this paper argue for a need to train designers through empathy exercises to overcome personal limitations in empathizing with users. The design outcomes, verbal protocols and expert evaluations have suggested that novice designers when using empathy exercise along with persona description were able to generate higher 'quality' of design thinking (more cognitive actions). This finding also implies that there is need to accommodate empathy exercises in the professional design practices along with user research and persona depictions.

7. LIMITATIONS AND FUTUREWORK

The present study was limited to analysis of design solutions on the basis of directness of illustration of user information on design solutions. Further studies studying design thinking can analyze other aspects of design thinking processes creativity, novelty, fixation etc. which will create a holistic framework to understand role of empathy in quality of design outcomes. Further, this study has reported effects of empathy exercise on design thinking. However, this research has not measured the degree of improvement of empathetic ability due to the empathy exercise on different designers. The present study is limited to observation of the effect of empathy on novice designers, further studies with professional designers may give useful benchmarks for comparison of design thinking and empathetic abilities.

REFERENCES

Ahmed, S., Wallace, K. M., & Blessing, L. T. (2003). Understanding the differences between how novice and experienced designers approach design tasks. Research in Engineering

Atman, C., Chimka, J., Bursic, K., & Nachtmann, H. (1999). A comparison of freshman and senior engineering design processes. Design Studies. Retrieved from

Bonnardel, N. (2000). Towards understanding and supporting creativity in design: analogies in a constrained cognitive environment. Knowledge-Based Systems, 13(7–8).

Caballero, L., Moreno, A. M., & Seffah, A. (2014). Persona as a Tool to Involving Human in Agile Methods: Contributions from HCI and Marketing. In Human-Centered Software Engineering (pp. 283–290). Springer Berlin Heidelberg.

Calde, S., Goodwin, K., & Reimann, R. (2002). SHS Orcas: the first integrated information system for long-term healthcare facility management. In Case studies of the CHI2002|AIGA Experience Design FORUM on - CHI '02 (pp. 2–16).

Cardoso, C., & Badke-Schaub, P. (2011). The Influence of Different Pictorial Representations During Idea Generation. The Journal of Creative Behavior, 45(2).

Carroll, J. M. (2003). HCI models, theories, and frameworks: Toward a multidisciplinary science. Morgan Kaufmann. Morgan Kaufmann. Retrieved from

Cooper, A. (1999). The Inmates Are Running the Asylum: Why High-Tech Products Drive Us Crazy and How to Restore the Sanity. Technology. Sams Publishing.

Cross, N. (2001). Design Cognition. In Design Knowing and Learning: Cognition in Design Education (pp. 79–103).

Dominowski, R.L., & Dallob, P. ,1995. Insight and Problem Solving. In R. Sternberg & J. Davidson (Eds.), The nature of insight. (pp. 33 - 62). Cambridge, MA: MIT Press.

Goldschmidt, G. (1990). Linkography: assessing design productivity. In R. Trappl (Ed.), Cyberbetics and System '90 (pp. 291–298). World Scientific, Singapore.

Grudin, J. (2006). Why personas work: The psychological evidence. *The Persona Lifecycle*, 642-663.

Hong, S. M. (2009). User Research and User Centered Design; Designing, Developing, and Commercializing Widget Service on Mobile Handset. In Human Centered Design (pp. 854–861).

Kavakli, M., & Gero, J. (2001). The Structure of concurrent cognitive actions: A case study of novice and expert designers. Design Studies.

Kim, E., & Kim, K. (2015). Cognitive styles in design problem solving: Insights from network-based cognitive maps. Design Studies, 40.

Landauer, T. K. (1988). Research Methods in Human-Computer Interaction. In Handbook of Human-Computer Interaction (pp. 905–928). Elsevier.

Long, Frank. "Real or imaginary: The effectiveness of using personas in product design." In *Proceedings of the Irish Ergonomics Society Annual Conference*, vol. 14. Irish Ergonomics Society, 2009.

Matthews, T., Judge, T., & Whittaker, S. (2012). How do designers and user experience professionals actually perceive and use personas? In Proceedings of the 2012 ACM annual conference on Human Factors in Computing Systems.

Manning, H., Temkin, B., & Belanger, N. (2003). The power of design personas. Forrester Research. http://www.forrester.com/ER/Research/Report/0,1338,33033,00.html

Miaskiewicz, T., & Kozar, K. A. (2011). Personas and user-centered design: How can personas benefit product design processes? Design Studies, 32(5).

Newell, Allen, and H.A. Simon. 1988. "The theory of human problem solving" In Readings in Cognitive Science, 33–51.

Nielsen, L. (2013). Personas - User Focused Design. Springer London.

Norman, Donald A. 1988. The Design of Everyday Things/Emotional Design/Design of Future Things. Basic Books.

Pruitt, J. S., & Adlin, T. (2006). The Persona Lifecycle (pp. 46–65). Elsevier.

Runco, M. A. (1995). Cognition and Creativity. Contemporary Psychology, 44(6).

Steen, M., & Kuijt, L. (1988). Early user involvement in research and design projects–A review of methods and practices.

Van Someren, M. W., Barnard, Y. F., & Sandberg, J. A. C. (1994). The think aloud method: a practical approach to modelling cognitive.

Tversky, B., & Suwa, M. (2009). Thinking with Sketches. In Tools for Innovation (pp. 75–84). Oxford University Press.

Valkenburg, R., & Dorst, K. (1998). The reflective practice of design teams. Design Studies, 19(3).

INVESTIGATING ELEARNING PREFERENCES OF ADULTS WITH INTELLECTUAL DISABILITY

Marian McDonnell, Irene Connolly and Amina Abbes
Institute of Art, Design & Technology, Kill Avenue, Dun Laoghaire, Co Dublin, Ireland

ABSTRACT

Let's Go is an e-learning application that is designed to teach independent life skills. The aim of this study was to investigate the e-learning content (learning-modalities) preferences of adults with ID, and whether their preferences can inform the design of engaging educational content. Mixed methods were used to investigate learning-modality preferences, overall technology experience and opinions of Let's Go, of seven adults with ID. Results indicated a significant preference for the game-based learning-modality, compared to audio, and video. Additionally, there was a significant relationship between what participants preferred, and what they wanted in the application. However, due to ethical reasons, it was impossible to ascertain the levels of ID of the participants, resulting in limited possibility of generalization. Nonetheless, the significant findings support the need for inclusion of individuals with ID in design. This indicates that the preferences/interests of adults with ID should be considered, to ensure the design of adequately engaging content.

KEYWORDS

Intellectual Disability, Technology, User-Centred Design, Education, Preferences, Learning-Modalities

1. INTRODUCTION

1.1 Overview

Let's Go is an eLearning application designed to teach individuals with Intellectual Disabilities (ID) independent life skills, thereby increasing inclusion and reducing stigma. Previous research on Let's Go involved evaluation of the application through the trainers' perspective, yielding information about usability and need for age-appropriate images (McDonnell & Verdes, 2016). However, there is limited research around what makes an application engaging for adults with ID. Therefore, this study aims to investigate the engagement aspect of Let's Go, by investigating what adults with ID prefer in terms of content, specifically the learning-modalities provided in Let's Go.

1.2 Background

ID is characterized by limitations in intellectual and adaptive functioning, affecting social, practical, and cognitive aspects of their lives (American Psychiatric Association [APA], 2013). People with ID still face daily stigma and barriers to inclusivity and independence. These barriers can be reduced by providing better access to education, training, healthcare, structural and technological support,while simultaneously seeking the thoughts and opinions of people with ID to improve such services and supports (Moore & Schelling, 2015).Assistive Technology (AT) has been shown to promote and support inclusivity, better quality of life, independence, and learning for people with ID (Brown et al, 2011; Darcy et al, 2016). The prior emphasis behind AT used to be on specifically designed technology; such as hearing aids and, screen readers. However, this has evolved to also include modern day mainstream technology such as mobiles, and tablets (Brown et al, 2011; Hammel et al, 2002). Research by Darcy et al, (2016) found that mobile technologies increased the quality of life of users with disability, by increasing their confidence, communication, independence, and social participation.

Several studies have explored the educational potential of technology, from training individuals with ID in life skills; such as use of public transport and social behaviours, to teaching literacy and numeracy skills (Feng et al, 2010; Mechling, & O'Brien, 2010; Ortega-Tudela & Gómez-Ariza, 2006). Ramdos et al, (2011), systematically analysed studies in relation to computer-based interventions for teaching life-skills, found promising results in improving areas such as navigating public transport, ordering food, and shopping. Nonetheless, despite the highlighted benefits of modern technology, people with ID are still at risk of being left behind in this age of technology (Chadwick & Wesson, 2016). User-centred design is gaining increased attention, due to the highlighted effects of accessible technology (i.e., inclusivity, education) for people with ID (Mazzone et al, 2010; Dekelver et al, 2015). This is prompting developers, researchers, and designers to include individuals with ID, in the design and evaluation processes (Kramer et al, 2015; Porcino et al, 2015).

1.3 User-Engagement and e-Learning

"Successful technologies are not just usable; they engage users", O'Brien and Toms (2008, p938). User Engagement (UE) is measured in many ways i.e., mixed methods – including both subjective (interviews/focus-groups), and objective (observations) (O'Brien & Lebow, 2013). It is defined as the user's investment (affective, cognitive, and/or behavioural) in the interaction with technology mediated environments such as educational-software (O'Brien & Cairns, 2016). Studies have identified many attributes related to UE; including - challenge, aesthetics, gamification, captivating content, interaction, motivation, and interest (Hamari et al, 2016; Muntean, 2011; O'Brien & Toms, 2008). Additionally, for individuals with ID; Buzzi et al, (2016) found that providing content personalization, and appropriate levels of challenge, are important for designing engaging applications. For example, Cumming and Rodriguez (2013), found that using an iPad increased educational engagement among children with ID; however, this increase eventually declined. Abandonment is problematic, specifically as repetition is important if individuals with ID are to master a skill (Downing, 2010). Therefore, it is crucial to design a learning-environment that motivates and encourages active engagement with content to promote learning and skill mastery (Brown et al, 2011, 2013; Charoenpit & Ohkura, 2013; Kwon & Lee, 2016).

1.4 Preferences/Interests and Engagement

One way to design engaging applications, is by taking into consideration the users' interests and preferences – while controlling for usability, as poor usability can indicate poor engagement (Moshfeghi et al, 2013; O'Brien & Toms, 2008). Interest/preferences are concepts related to engagement – they function by motivating interaction/attention and engagement; thereby keeping the individuals' attention focused on the task i.e., intrinsically motivated (Peters et al, 2009).Including user interests/preferences, positively impacts the users' engagement levels (Hilliard et al, 2014; Milward et al, 2016). Nevertheless, very little studies explore the preferences/interests of people with ID, for design of technology. In terms of learning-modality preferences, Williams (2015), investigated the website preferences of adults with ID, and found that although audio was appreciated, it was rarely used. Additionally, Brown et al., (2013), found that the 'playful', gamified mode of their route-learning application for users with ID, resulted in increased fun and motivation compared to the non-gamified modes. However, none of these studies completely focused on investigating the preferences/interests of adults with ID, in terms of contents within educational-applications. Learning-modality refers to how information is presented, and usually includes - auditory, visual, kinaesthetic and tactile presentations, furthermore – games are increasingly being used as a modality for educational instruction (Buzzi et al, 2016, Kwon & Lee, 2016; Let me be ME [LMBM], 2013). The learning-modality needed, relies on the individuals' learning style which usually differs for everyone depending on a combination of their cognitive ability, their sociological, psychological experiences, and environmental surroundings (Dunn, 1983; LMBM, 2013). Literature supports that teaching learners through learning-modalities that match their learning style can lead to an increase in motivation, academic achievement and decrease in challenging behaviours (Coffield et al, 2004; Winebrenner, 2016). This was also reported for students with disabilities; by providing preferred learning environments – teachers noted increases in academic achievements and self-esteem (Brunner & Majewski, 1990). Therefore, providing learning-modalities in relation to cognitive ability and preferred learning-styles is important when it comes to ensuring engaging learning-environments (Dunn, 1983; Graf & Kinshuk, 2008). Yet no studies have explored this factor in relation to e-learning technology.

1.5 The Present Study

The cognitive abilities (i.e., reading/writing, and fine/gross motor difficulties) of individuals with ID were considered when developing Let's Go (Sharma et al, 2012), resulting in a design focused on usability (McDonnell & Verdes, 2016). However, due to limited literature surrounding content preferences/interests of adults with ID, designing for engagement was difficult.

1.6 Research Aim

The study aims to investigate, whether adults with ID will demonstrate a clear preference for a learning-modality, and if there is a relationship between their preferences and content 'wants' in term of e-learning. The following hypotheses will be tested:

H1: There will be a significant difference for observed preference, based on type of learning-modality (game, audio, video).

H2: There will be a significant difference for reported preference, based on type of learning-modality (game, audio, video).

2. METHOD

2.1 Design

2.1.1 Mixed Methods

A mixed methods design is recommended when investigating user-experience to gather the usability and hedonic aspects of computer-mediated interactions (O'Brien & Lebow, 2013). Part one: Within-subjects design, investigating the effect of one independent variable; learning-modality (K=3, game, audio, video), and one dependent variable; learning-modality preference scores. Part two: Correlational design, analysing the relationship between participant reported modality-preference and content wants.

2.1.2 Observation

Controlled observations, with time sampling was used to gather participants' behavioural and emotional responses to each of the three learning-modalities. This method is often used in computer-related research, and in research with participants with ID (Mansell, 2011; Preece et al, 2015).

2.2 Participants

A gatekeeper was tasked with recruiting the participants, to avoid any possibility of coercion. This method is commonly used when recruiting people with ID (Nind, 2008). Per ethical approval, a maximum of 10-12 participants could be recruited. However, in the end only eight participants could participate. Nonetheless, Borsci et al, (2012) reported that around five-eight users with ID, could identify up to 83% of interface problems. Data was excluded for one participant due to participation in the pilot session. The final sample included seven-participants (4=male, 3=female), between the ages of 18-20 (M=19, SD=0.53).

2.3 Materials

2.3.1 Accessibility

The materials inspired by Maloney (2012), were all designed to be easily understandable by the participants – as recommended by British Psychological Society (2014). Included, the Expression of Interest-Form, Information-Sheet, Consent-Form, Demographic Questionnaire, Focus-Group questions, adapted System-Usability-Scale (SUS), Debrief-Form and lastly, the Task-List.

2.3.2 Tasks

A total of four tasks were included in the task list. Four of them, consisted of the available modules from Let's Go. Only three which presented educational material in three different ways (game, audio, video), were observed. The first, was the 'travel-training', drag-and-drop game, the second, a 'body-language', audio clip and third, a 'manners', video clip. The fourth task was not observed, and only included as entertainment for participants who finished early.

2.3.3 Behaviour-indications and Checklists

The usability-indications, were adapted from the DEVAN usability and fun indications coding-scheme (Macedo & Trevisan, 2013). The 'fun problem' indications were removed, or placed in the preference-indications to avoid duplication and confusion between the final checklists. Additionally, for the preference-indications observation-checklist; a caregiver-survey was issued to gather data on any idiosyncrasies in how the participants express behaviours/emotions. This method is often used when observing preference behaviours among participants with ID (Parsons et al, 2012; Petry & Maes, 2006).

2.3.4 Adapted-SUS

The adapted-SUS, includes ten-items; two open-ended, two multiple-choice, and six Smileyometer questions. The Smileyometer measured on a four-point rating scale, and was included to limit the cognitive load on the participants. This was deemed a sensitive measure by Williams (2015). The Smileyometer-scale was found to have acceptable reliability, with a Cronbach's Alpha of .706 (Kline, 2005).

2.4 Lab Set Up

Computers running Windows-10 OS were used to run the Let's Go application. The computers had touchscreen monitors, for participants more comfortable using touch, however, mice were also provided. Headphones were available for each participant to complete each activity. Additionally, time-sample was adjusted from 5-minute observations per task, to 3-minutes per task.

2.5 Procedure

Two separate, identical test-sessions involving four participants, and one carer, were then run. Effort was made to build rapport with the participants by making them feel welcome and relaxed – a method encouraged by literature for research with individuals with ID (Nind, 2008). The participants then filled out the demographic forms – assistance was provided, as required/requested. Participants were numbered to allow their data to be anonymised. They were introduced to the task sheet and told to take as much time needed to complete each task – assistance was offered as required/requested. As the participants performed each task in the same order, they were observed in two intervals, of 1-minute and 30-second time samples per task, by one researcher and one assistant who stood at each side of the participant. As the tasks were not long, it was not deemed important to control against order-effects. Once all participants finished all tasks, they were invited to complete the adapted-SUS. Assistance was provided as required/requested. This session lasted about forty-five minutes. A fifteen-minute refreshment break was provided for the participants – before commencement of the focus.

2.6 Analysis

2.6.1 Observed-Preferences

Preference scores were obtained by counting positive emotions/behaviours observed, and subtracting the amount of negative emotions/behaviours observed. Observations were categorised to each construct based on initial observations and on researcher/assistant agreement (Sevilla et al, 2007). The Smileyometers were coded in an ordinal manner 1-4, where 1 signified either 'very hard, or dislike a lot', and 4 signified either 'very easy, or like a lot', depending on the questions asked. The two-multiple choice preference/wants questions were coded ordinally, from 1-4. For example, 'Game=4, Video=3, Audio=2, Something-else=1'.

3. RESULTS

3.1 Technology Characteristics

3.1.1 Descriptive Statistics

All participants (N=7) stated that they used the computer. Furthermore, six participants reported owning a smartphone, and five an iPad/Tablet. All the participants (100%) stated that they used the internet.

Participants reported using technology for a variety of activities, including for educational purposes (see Figure 1 for activities). Moreover, (71%) of the participants reported that they did not need help to use the internet, while (28%) stated that they needed help 'sometimes'. Lastly, out of the participants who reported owning/using an iPad/tablet, all stated that they are easy to use.

3.2 Participant Experience of Let's Go

3.2.1 Descriptive Statistics

All participants (100%) stated that they would use Let's Go again (to learn) if certain changes were made to the application (see Figure 2 for participant's recommendations). Furthermore, (75%) of participants said they would recommend the application to their friends.

3.3 Inter-observer Reliability

To determine the level of agreement between the two observers' 'preference/usability behaviour' observations, a Cohen's κ was run. This indicated that there was a good level of inter-observer agreement between the observers, $\kappa=.748$, $p<.001$ (Altman, 1999).

3.4 Observed Learning-Modality Preferences Descriptive Statistics

The independent variable was learning-modality, with three categories (K=3); game, audio, and video. The dependent variable was observed preference-scores. The mean scores indicate that the game-based learning-modality, yielded higher preference scores compared to audio and video-based learning-modalities. See Table 1 for Means (M), and Standard-Deviations (SD).

Table 1. M and SD for Preference Scores of the Three Learning-Modalities

Learning-modality	Preference scores		
	M	**SD**	**N**
Game	**6.43**	**2.07**	**7**
Audio	**3.43**	**.98**	**7**
Video	**2.43**	**2.88**	**7**

4. DISCUSSION

4.1 Overview

Results show that a stronger preference for the game-based learning-modality was observed. However, the results indicate no significant self-reported preference for anyone of the provided learning-modalities. Additionally, analysis was carried out to explore whether participants' self-reported preferred aspect of Let's Go would correlate to what they wanted more of in the application. The results indicate that there is a relationship between what the participants liked and what they wanted more of in Let's Go.

4.2 Learning-Modality Preferences

Results indicate that there was a statistically significant observed preference for the games-based learning-modality, compared to audio, and video-based learning-modalities. These findings are reflected in previous studies in this area which noted that individuals with ID demonstrated more motivational behaviour with games-based modalities, and that audio was rarely used (Brown et al, 2013; Williams, 2015). Therefore, the data indicates that adults with ID demonstrate more engagement-related behaviours when interacting with the games-based content, which is supported by the literature (Brown et al, 2013; Monterrat et al, 2014; Muntean, 2011). In relation to self-reported learning-modality preferences, there was no statistically significant difference between the game, audio, or video-based learning modalities. This does not fall in line with previous research (Brown et al., 2013; Williams, 2015). Therefore, the result should be interpreted cautiously. This result could be due to the following weaknesses during this part of the study, i.e., participant reactivity/acquiescence bias, or small sample size. The need for providing appropriately challenging content is documented in engagement design-guidelines and has also been noted by recent research in technology for people with ID (Buzzi et al, 2016; Muntean, 2011). All participants said they would use the application for educational purposes, and majority said they would recommend it to their friends.

4.3 Conclusion and Implications

This study brings attention to how important the preferences of adults with ID are, as they can increase engagement, and potentially increase motivation to regularly use the application. Additionally, making applications, and technology for people with ID, without their feedback/input can result in applications that are abandoned due to lack of interest, thereby resulting in loss of educational potential and chance for inclusivity and independence (Cumming & Rodriguez, 2013; Monterrat et al, 2014). Research in how technology can positively impact the lives of those with ID is plentiful (Brown et al, 2011; Darcy et al, 2016). However, this has not resulted in an increase in accessible technology. This needs to be rectified, as people with ID are in danger of being left behind, in a society that is becoming more reliant on technology every-day (Chadwick & Wesson, 2016).

REFERENCES

Altman, D. G, 1999. *Practical statistics for medical research*. Chapman & Hall/CRC Press, New York, USA.

American Psychiatric Association, 2013. *Diagnostic and statistical manual of mental disorders.* doi:10.1176/appi.books.9780890425596

Borsci, S. et al, 2012. The Bootstrap Discovery Behaviour Model. *Cognitively Informed Intelligent Interfaces*, pp. 258-279. doi:10.4018/978-1-4666-1628-8.ch015

British Psychological Society, 2014. *Code of Human Research Ethics*. Retrieved from BPS Publication website: http://www.bps.org.uk/publications/policy-and-guidelines/research-guidelines-policy-documents/research-guidelines-poli

Brown, D. et al, 2013. Engaging Students with Intellectual Disabilities through Games Based Learning and Related Technologies. *Universal Access in Human-Computer Interaction. Applications and Services for Quality of Life*, pp. 573-582. doi:10.1007/978-3-642-39194-1_66

Brown, D. J. et al, 2011. Designing location-based learning experiences for people with intellectual disabilities and additional sensory impairments. *Computers & Education*, Vol. 56, No. 1, pp. 11-20. doi:10.1016/j.compedu.2010.04.014

Brunner, C. E., & Majewski, W. S, 1990. Mildly handicapped students can succeed with learning styles. *Educational Leadership*, Vol. 48, No. 2, pp. 21-21. Retrieved from http://www.ascd.org/ASCD/pdf/journals/ed_lead/el_199010_brunner.pdf

Buzzi, M. C. et al, 2016. Learning games for the cognitively impaired people. *Proceedings of the 13th Web for All Conference on - W4A '16*. doi:10.1145/2899475.2899487

Chadwick, D., & Wesson, C, 2016. Digital inclusion and disability. *Applied Cyberpsychology*, pp. 1-23. doi:10.1057/9781137517036_1

Charoenpit, S., & Ohkura, M, 2013. A new e-Learning system focusing on emotional aspect using biological signals. *Human-Computer Interaction. Applications and Services*, pp. 343-350. doi:10.1007/978-3-642-39262-7_39

Coffield, F. et al, 2004. *Learning styles and pedagogy in post-16 learning: A systematic and critical review*. Retrieved from http://sxills.nl/lerenlerennu/bronnen/Learning%20styles%20by%20Coffield%20e.a..pdf

Darcy, S. et al, 2016. I've got a mobile phone too! Hard and soft assistive technology customization and supportive call centres for people with disability. *Disability and Rehabilitation: Assistive Technology*, pp. 1-11. doi:10.3109/17483107.2016.1167260

D'Eath, M. et al, 2005. *Guidelines for researchers when interviewing people with an intellectual disability*. Retrieved from http://www.fedvol.ie/_fileupload/File/Interviewing%20Guidelines%281%29.pdf

Dekelver, J. et al, 2015. Design of mobile applications for people with intellectual disabilities. *Proceedings of* Creativity *in intelligent technologies and data science: First conference, CIT&DS 2015,* Volgograd, Russia, pp. 823–836. doi: 10.1007/978-3-319-23766-4_65

Downing, J, 2010. *Academic instruction for students with moderate and severe intellectual disabilities in inclusive classrooms*. Corwin Press, California, USA.

Dunn, R. (1983). Learning style and its relation to exceptionality at both ends of the spectrum. *Exceptional children*, Vol.49, No. 6, pp. 496-506.

Faber, J., & Fonseca, L. M, 2014. How sample size influences research outcomes. *Dental Press Journal of Orthodontics*, Vol.19, No. 4, pp. 27-29. doi:10.1590/2176-9451.19.4.027-029.ebo

Feng, J. et al, 2010. Computer Usage by Children with Down Syndrome. *ACM Transactions on Accessible Computing*, Vol.2, No. 3, pp.1-44. doi:10.1145/1714458.1714460

Field, A. P, 2013. *Discovering statistics using IBM SPSS* (4th ed.). SAGE, London, United Kingdom.

Genova, A, 2015. Barriers to inclusive education in Greece, Spain and Lithuania: Results from emancipatory disability research. *Disability & Society*, Vol.30, No. 7, pp. 1042-1054. doi:10.1080/09687599.2015.1075867

Graf, S., & Kinshuk, 2008. Technologies linking learning, cognition, and instruction. In J. M. Spector, M. D. Merrill, J. Van Merrienboer, & M. P. Driscoll (Eds.), *Handbook of research on educational communications and technology* (3rd ed., pp. 305-316).

Hamari, J. et al, 2016. Challenging games help students learn: An empirical study on engagement, flow and immersion in game-based learning. *Computers in Human Behavior*, Vol.54, pp. 170-179. doi:10.1016/j.chb.2015.07.045

Hammel, J. et al, 2002. The impact of assistive technology and environmental interventions on function and living situation status with people who are ageing with developmental disabilities. *Disability and Rehabilitation*, Vol. 24, No. 1-3, pp. 93-105. doi:10.1080/09638280110063850

Hilliard, M. E. et al, 2014. User Preferences and Design Recommendations for an mHealth App to Promote Cystic Fibrosis Self-Management. *JMIR mHealth and uHealth*, Vol. 2, No. 4, pp. e44. doi:10.2196/mhealth.3599

Howell, D. C, 2013. *Statistical methods for psychology* (8th ed.). Cengage Learning, Inc, California, USA.

Kline, R. B, 2005. *Principles and practice of structural equation modelling* (2nd ed.). Guilford Press, New York, USA.

Kramer, D. et al, 2015. Developing navigational services for people with Down's Syndrome. *2015 International Conference on Intelligent Environments*, pp. 128-131. doi:10.1109/ie.2015.26

Kwon, J., & Lee, Y, 2016. Serious games for the job training of persons with developmental disabilities. *Computers & Education*, Vol. 95, pp.328-339. doi:10.1016/j.compedu.2016.02.001

Let me be ME! [LMBM], 2013. *Welcome to "Let me be ME!"*. Retrieved from Let me be ME EU website: http://www.letmebeme.eu/pt/toolkit/pt/images/sept13/welcome/welcome.pdf

Macedo, I., & Trevisan, D. G, 2013. A method to evaluate disabled user interaction: *A case study with down syndrome children. Universal Access in Human-Computer Interaction. Design Methods, Tools, and Interaction Techniques for eInclusion*, pp. 50-58. doi:10.1007/978-3-642-39188-0_6

Maloney, M, 2012. *Accessible information: Advocating the Use of technology for individuals with intellectual disability on their Path to individualised services* (Master's thesis, Dublin Institute of Technology, Dublin, Ireland). Retrieved from http://arrow.dit.ie/scschcomdis/45/

Mansell, J, 2011. Structured observational research in services for people with learning disabilities. SSCR methods review, 10. NIHR School for Social Care Research, London, UK. Retrieved from http://eprints.lse.ac.uk/43159/

Mazzone, E. et al, 2010. Involving users in the design of ICT aimed to improve education, work, and leisure for users with intellectual disabilities. *Lecture Notes in Computer Science*, pp. 5-12. doi:10.1007/978-3-642-14100-3_2

McDonnell, M., & Verdes, C, 2016. Designing applications for intellectual disability users to teach independence skills. In *Multi Conference on Computer Science and Information Systems. International Conferences: Interfaces and Human Computer Interaction 2016.* pp. 264-268.

Mechling, L. C., & O'Brien, E, 2010. Computer-Based Video Instruction to Teach Students with Intellectual Disabilities to Use Public Bus Transportation. *Education and Training in Autism and Developmental Disabilities*, Vol.45, No. 2, pp. 230-241.

Milward, J. et al, 2016. User preferences for content, features, and style for an app to reduce harmful drinking in young adults: Analysis of user feedback in app stores and focus group interviews. *JMIR mHealth and uHealth*, Vol.4, No. 2, pp. e47. doi:10.2196/mhealth.5242

Moore, E. J., & Schelling, A, 2015. Postsecondary inclusion for individuals with an intellectual disability and its effects on employment. *Journal of Intellectual Disabilities*, Vol.19, No. 2, pp. 130-148. doi:10.1177/1744629514564448

Moshfeghi, Y. et al, 2013. Influence of timeline and named-entity components on user engagement. *Lecture Notes in Computer Science*, pp. 305-317. doi:10.1007/978-3-642-36973-5_26

Muntean, C. I, 2011. Raising engagement in e-learning through gamification. Retrieved from https://www.researchgate.net/publication/265877898_Raising_engagement_in_e-learning_through_gamification

Nind, M, 2008. *Conducting qualitative research with people with learning, communication, and other disabilities: Methodological challenges*. Retrieved from ESRC National Centre for Research Methods website: http://eprints.ncrm.ac.uk/491/

O'Brien, H., & Cairns, P, 2016. *Why engagement matters: Cross-disciplinary perspectives of user engagement in digital media*. Retrieved from DOI 10.1007/978-3-319-27446-1

O'Brien, H. L., & Lebow, M, 2013. Mixed-methods approach to measuring user experience in online news interactions. *Journal of the American Society for Information Science and Technology*, Vol.64, No. 8, pp. 1543-1556. doi:10.1002/asi.22871

O'Brien, H. L., & Toms, E. G, 2008. What is user engagement? A conceptual framework for defining user engagement with technology. *Journal of the American Society for Information Science and Technology*, Vol.59, No. 6, pp. 938-955. doi:10.1002/asi.20801

Ortega-Tudela, J. M., & Gómez-Ariza, C. J, 2006. Computer-assisted teaching and mathematical learning in Down Syndrome children. *Journal of Computer Assisted Learning*, Vol. 22, No. 4, pp. 298-307. doi:10.1111/j.1365-2729.2006.00179.x

Park, E. et al, 2009. Correct use of repeated measures analysis of variance. *Korean J Lab Med*, Vol.29, No. 1, pp. 1-9. Retrieved from DOI 10.3343/kjlm.2009.29.1.1

Parsons, M. B. et al, 2012. Identifying indices of happiness and unhappiness among adults with autism: Potential targets for behavioral assessment and intervention. *Behavior Analysis in Practice*, Vol.5, No. 1, pp. 15-25.

Peters, C. et al, 2009. An exploration of user engagement in HCI. *Proceedings of the International Workshop on Affective-Aware Virtual Agents and Social Robots - AFFINE '09*. doi:10.1145/1655260.1655269

Petry, K., & Maes, B, 2006. Identifying expressions of pleasure and displeasure by persons with profound and multiple disabilities. *Journal of Intellectual & Developmental Disability*, Vol.31, pp. 28–38. doi:10.1080/13668250500488678

Porcino, T. et al, 2015. A participatory approach for game design to support the learning and communication of autistic children. *Entertainment Computing - ICEC 2015*, pp. 17-31. doi:10.1007/978-3-319-24589-8_2

Ramdoss, S. et al, 2011. Use of computer-based interventions to promote daily living skills in individuals with intellectual disabilities: A systematic review. *Journal of Developmental and Physical Disabilities*, Vol.24, No. 2, pp. 197-215. doi:10.1007/s10882-011-9259-8

Sevilla, J. et al, 2007. Web accessibility for individuals with cognitive deficits. *ACM Transactions on Computer-Human Interaction*, Vol.14, No. 3, pp. 1-25. doi:10.1145/1279700.1279702

Sharma, V. et al, 2012. Down syndrome: good practice guidelines for education. Retrieved from: http://www.ucl.ac.uk/educational-psychology/newsletter/resources/APPGDS_guidelines.pdf

Winebrenner, S, 2016. Teaching students about their own modality strengths can lead to positive learning outcomes. *Learning: Research and Practice*, Vol.2, No. 2, pp. 160-164. doi:10.1080/23735082.2016.1207357

A TECHNOLOGICAL SOLUTION FOR A COLLABORATIVE MOBILE WEB PLATFORM: HIGHER M@T-EDUTUTOR

Pedro Miguel Faria[1, 2], Isabel Araújo[1, 2] and Pedro Vilaça[1]
[1] *School of Technology and Management – Polytechnic Institute of Viana do Castelo*
[2] *ARC4DigiT – Applied Research Center for Digital Transformation*
Portugal

ABSTRACT

It is huge the use of communication technologies in the teaching-learning process, including the use of mobile technologies. Current higher education students belong to the so-called "native digital generation", who constantly access the information, through these same devices. In higher education, there is a week timetable where teachers seek to clarify student's doubts, physically in the teaching institution. However, usually, the students do not use this timetable. Thus, a question arises: how to support students in their studies, namely in clarifying doubts, without being necessary to physically be in the higher education institution. As a possible solution to this challenge a collaborative web platform was developed to be used, with mobile devices, to support tutoring at distance. The platform has data transmission capabilities, in real-time, between two users. This paper presents a learning web platform, developed with the purpose to allow doubts clarification, at distance, between teacher and students, in a collaborative way, in real time. The work accomplished demonstrates to have a potential to increase the clarification of doubts online, between teachers and students, with the objective of promoting the students learning.

KEYWORDS

Mobile Learning, Web Platforms, Collaborative Work, Tutoring

1. INTRODUCTION

We currently live in a knowledge society, strongly signalled by the use of networked technologies (Lucena, 2016). The use of mobile technologies and social digital networks are no exception and put us in constant interaction with (cyber) sociotechnical spaces. The students of the XXI century, known as the native digital generation, are the ones that use those spaces very early, "because they learned from the technologies and the networks, how to interact, to produce and to publish" (Lucena, 2016). They spontaneously access information through these same mobile devices, such as smartphones and tablets. "The mobile phone has reached such an omnipresence that the new generations consider it a product of nature, such as milk or tomato" (Andreoli, 2007: 23).

The increasing access to the Internet through mobile devices (e.g. smartphones, tablets, PCs, game consoles) is remarkable and, inevitably, learning through these devices is a reality in many educational institutions (Attewell et al., 2009; Moura & Carvalho, 2010). It is not possible for education to remain unalterable to this reality. The use of communication technologies in the teaching-learning process is increasing and its relevance has been studied. Several authors defend the pertinence of educational practices that involve the use of communication technologies (Hernandez, 2017; Noor-UI-Amin, 2013). The evolution of mobile technologies emerges as an innovative tool for teachers and students, which triggered new forms of learning in different contexts (Sharples, 2009; Pachler, 2011). Thus, with the use of wireless mobile technologies in education, a new concept emerged – mobile learning (m-learning) – which simplifies the access to content, anytime and anywhere, facilitating a more flexible organization of learning time. For Ismail et al. (2010) there is a relationship between e-learning and m-learning, due the increasing power and sophistication of mobile devices. Ubiquity and context-aware will always be aspects of mobility that will make m-learning a unique and special approach to education.

It is common, in higher education, a weekly schedule in which teachers seek to clarify doubts of their students, physically in the higher institution. However, in general, students do not use this schedule. Thus, an idea emerged, in which a tool could be developed, in order to try to support the students in their studies, more specifically in the clarification of doubts, without the need of a teacher and a student be physically present in the same space. To achieve that the students could use devices that usually have at their disposal, their smartphones. In this way, a prototype of a collaborative web platform was developed, in order to be used with mobile devices, to support tutoring at distance. It is intended to facilitate the interaction between users in the same shared working area, in real-time, between a teacher and his students, in the clarification of doubts, through mobile devices, which students informally use in their daily lives. This paper presents the Higher M@t-EduTutor platform, which allows students to ask questions to his teachers, using their smartphones. In the following section, the theoretical framework of the study is carried out. Then the platform is described, presenting and justifying the options taken and finally the conclusions are presented where it is reflected on the difficulties, limitations found and future development prospects.

2. LEARNING MEDIATED BY MOBILE DEVICES

Currently, education, namely higher education, has a mission to prepare students for the labour market, increasingly so demanding and competitive. Thus, students face major challenges, in addition to managing a large volume of information. Students build knowledge but also need to develop skills to enjoy success in the globally and digitally interconnected world. According to Partnership for 21st Century Skills[1], students' competencies to better address future challenges are: critical thinking, problem solving, communication, collaboration, creativity and innovation.

Technologies, particularly mobile technologies, have fostered the emergence of new opportunities to improve and guide the teaching and learning process. Students acquire a sense of ownership in relation to the learning tasks and technologies used (Waycott, 2005), enhancing motivation and commitment in learning activities. These technologies are an adequate support for the development of individual and collaborative learning strategies, suitable for students training.

For some time, education has been directed towards a new concept: m-learning. There are several definitions, but in this paper we follow the Quinn (2011) definition. He considers that m-learning is any activity that allows an user to be more productive when consuming, interacting or creating information, mediated through a portable compact digital device, small in size, with connectivity and used on a regular basis. Thus, several studies were carried out concerning the use of mobile technologies to support activities in an educational context (Ligi, 2017). However, learning through the use of mobile devices, such as smartphones and tablets, is simply an adjustable part of the educational model, not an autonomous tool in the classroom (Sharples, 2009).

3. MOBILE WEB COLLABORATIVE PLATFORMS

Several mobile devices apps with different functionalities and media support (text, image, audio, video, drawing, among others) have been developed (Arantes et al., 2017). However, not all apps support collaborative work between users, in real-time, an also do not run on browsers. Currently, there are several applications and collaborative platforms available on the internet, many of them having different functionalities, but with the same objective: to allow the access to more than one user, as well as to ensure communication in real time, allowing a collaborative discussion between users, as referred by Palloff and Pratt (2005: 11): "*Collaboration enhances learning outcomes and reduces the potential for learner isolation that can occur in the online environment*".

---

[1] http://www.p21.org

3.1 Specific Web Platforms

Taking into account the initial issue, the target audience (students of the digital generation) and its scope, it was sought to extend the students attendance time, to a virtual environment. In this regard, we considered the development of a technological solution for mobile devices, having a touch screen (e.g. smartphones and tablets), supported on the web, with client-server functionality, and bidirectional communication using technologies such as Node.js and Web Sockets. In this sense, among several collaborative platforms, we sought to analyse their available functionalities.

3.1.1 Google Docs

One of the oldest and most used collaborative platform that allow document sharing and edition by multiple users, in real time, is Google Docs. In order to be able to do that is sufficient to have a Google account. This platform has similar features to Microsoft Word, concerning text creation and edition. Additionally, it has other functionalities such as "Suggestions Edition", concerning the content edited on the shared document, which can be accepted or rejected by the author, promoting the collaboration between users. Another available feature called "Explore" facilitates the search for text and images, relevant to the content to be produced in the shared document. This collaborative platform allows the communication between users, through a text chat. However, this feature is not available to be downloadable in mobile devices.

Another collaborative tool from Google is Google Drawings, which allows the free drawing of some graphic primitives. Some of this tool features are partially available in Google Docs. The full version contains a wide variety of graphic shapes that allow the creation of diagrams and graphics, also allowing free drawing. This tool, besides the insertion of images, also allows the insertion of video, although this functionality is not directly available in the list of tools (Google Slides is used to do that). Unlike many other Google platforms, Drawings is a web platform that does not support mobile devices such as smartphones and tablets. This tool, although it can be accessed through the browsers of mobile devices, is not properly optimized to that, making it practically impossible to use its features.

3.1.2 AWW

AWW is a collaborative platform suitable to work on mobile devices, which has basic drawing/text tools, sharing the drawing area (canvas), "post-it" note creation and chat communication (in the paid plan) through a link share. On this platform the administrator may provide edit or view-only permissions to the invited users, before sharing the workspace. No user registration is required. However, in order to save the work online, you will need to register (free of charge). This platform allows the upload of files of various formats, namely image, .pdf and .pptx files. When the contents of these files consist of more than one page, it is spread across multiple work areas, allowing the user to switch between each of them.

3.1.3 Realtime Board

Realtime Board is a collaborative platform for work teams. It has several predefined templates that facilitate the process of developing a product or service, within its "infinite canvas", allowing the users to comment and to leave notes, and also use a wide selection of tools. A disadvantage of its free plan is to be limited in terms of features available to the user, such as:

- it allows the creation of only up to 5 working areas;
- the voice and video communication is available only in the paid plan;
- it has a lower administrative capacity, namely in the definition of policies of team members invitations, limit on the number of team members, among others;
- project export is allowed, but the images have lower quality and are available with a watermark.

For a better workflow and inclusion of new tools and capabilities, this platform allows the installation of some add-ons/plugins (Souza, 2011) and its a platform used by several companies such as Spotify, Twitter, Netflix and Autodesk.

3.1.4 Web Whiteboard

This platform is a simple and quick alternative to collaboratively draw and/or write on mobile devices. However, the responsiveness of the platform to such devices is not adequate. This platform has only the most basic graphic primitive drawing tools, with only four colours, a rubber and a text tool, with the possibility of inserting notes into "post-its" objects. The Web Whiteboard only requires registration if the user is willing to pay a monthly subscription, from which it becomes possible to save the drawing areas and to manage the permission functionality of the invited users, in order to have, or not, the ability to edit a shared work.

3.1.5 WhiteboardFox

Like the previous described platform, this one is also a collaborative, fast-access platform that does not require user registration. In addition to the basic tools like the brush, the eraser and the text tool, this platform already offers a slightly larger selection of available colours, as well as image upload and zoomIn/zoomOut options. Regarding the "eraser" tool, it completely erases an "object" instead of erasing part of the drawing. Thus, the "eraser" tool has a different operating mode when compared with the AWW, Web Whiteboard and Higher M@t-EduTutor platforms. In addition, these workspaces can be saved and used later, being sufficient to save the document link or to download the work as an image.

3.2 Comparative Analysis

After the survey and selection of some collaborative platforms, a comparative analysis was made, in terms of technical characteristics, considering the following functionalities:

1. Responsive, mobile-friendly
2. Touch support on tactile screens
3. Flexible drawing area size (canvas)
4. "Eraser" tool to delete completely or part of an object
5. File import support (e.g. image, .PDF)
6. Export of drawing canvas as an image
7. Audio communication support between users
8. Spell check and auto-fill
9. Real-time text chat
10. Free version of the platform

Then, in Table 1, the functionalities of the analysed collaborative platforms are presented.

Table 1. Comparison between different collaborative platforms

Functionalities	Google Docs	AWW	Realtime Board	Web Whiteboard	Whiteboard Fox
1	▯	○	▯	✖	▯
2	▯	▯	▯	▯	▯
3	✖	▯	▯	✖	▯
4	✖	○	○	○	▯
5	▯	▯	▯	✖	▯
6	✖	▯	▯	▯	▯
7	✖	▯	▯	✖	✖
8	○	✖	✖	✖	✖
9	▯	▯	▯	✖	✖
10	▯	○	○	○	▯

Caption: ✖ - does not apply; ○ - partially applies; ▯ - applies

From the analysed platforms, it was verified that all have a free version, although some offer a limited set of functionalities, such as the AWW platform, which for e.g. does not provide the audio communication functionality for free. All platforms support tactile screens and allow exporting the desktop as an image, with the exception of Google Docs. It should be noted that this platform does not have the free drawing functionality in the mobile application. Although platforms have touch support on tactile screens, the responsiveness of the Whiteboard Web is not suitable for mobile devices, and it is the platform with fewer features, including a very limited canvas. However, this platform has a feature that enhances commenting on the working area, as does AWW and Realtime Board. The only platforms whose canvas is endless are Realtime Board and WhiteboardFox. Although AWW has a limited canvas, it is the only one that allows the creation of several canvases, allowing to freely switching between them. The analysed platforms, with the exception of Web Whiteboard, allow importing image files. The AWW and Realtime Board platforms allow also importing .pdf and .ppt files. The import of documents in .pdf and .ppt format differs. While in AWW each imported page creates a new canvas, on Realtime Board the document is imported into the same working area, allowing the user to browse all the pages. With the exception of Google Docs, all platforms allow exporting the desktop as an image.

One of the relevant functionalities on these platforms is the ability to write and draw freely on the working area (canvas), as well as to correct or delete the drawings (in whole or in part). On WhiteboardFox and Realtime Board the user cannot partially erase a drawing (it is only possible to completely delete the object(s)). However, in AWW and Web Whiteboard it is possible to delete part of the object. For spell checking and autocomplete, none of the reviewed platforms have this functionality.

In a collaborative platform, the possibility of communication is fundamental. Therefore, the communication functionality via audio or text was analysed. It has been found that on Google Docs, AWW and Realtime Board platforms text communication is possible, and audio communication is only available on AWW and Realtime Board, but with a paid plan. However, text and audio communication was not implemented on Realtime Board mobile devices versions (browser and app).

4. THE HIGHER M@T-EDUTUTOR PLATFORM

4.1 General Purpose

Succinctly, we may classify the Higher M@t-EduTutor project as a prototype of a collaborative, real-time, responsive and mobile-compatible web platform (e.g. smartphones and tablets). One of the main objectives that it is intended to achieve with the development of this platform is to substitute the use of a board like the one that is present in a classroom. This platform has features of an online editor, which includes basic writing and drawing tools, being able to write and draw freely, in real time, with other connected users, having the user at his disposal several tools, among which one text tool, brush, rubber, possibility of loading images, cleaning the drawing area and export the work area as an image.

4.2 Structure of the Collaborative Platform

One of the premises of the development of this platform was the availability of collaborative support to several users. The technological solution found for the implementation of the collaborative functionalities includes the implementation of a server, through the use of the node.js framework (Syed, 2014), along with the use of websockets (Wang, 2013). These sockets allow a real-time connection between two applications, capable of transmitting data between them: "*The WebSocket API enables you to establish full-duplex, bidirectional communication over the Web, between your client application and server-side processes*" (Wang, 2013, p.14). The server receives, through sockets, (x and y) coordinates in a 2D area, in result of user interaction with the canvas, by drawing some object. After receiving these messages on the server, the server shares that information with the other connected users, thus allowing real-time collaboration.

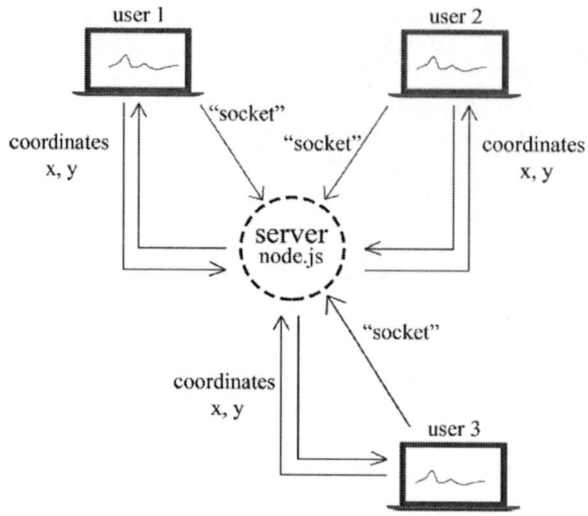

Figure 1. Functional representation between server and users

Figure 1 represents that internal functional structure of the Higher M@t-EduTutor platform, through the connection of users to a node.js HTTP server, using sockets technology. In order the server may receive information about the work performed by users, it is necessary to send the data of all actions performed in the working area (canvas). The server receives the (x and y) coordinates previously transformed into an object, as well as all the information emitted by the users. In this way, the server transmits all data from one user to the remaining connected.

4.3 Front-End

Nowadays, one of several concerns the programmer must pay attention, in the development process of web applications/platforms, is that they must be responsive, in order they can be used on different mobile devices (Shahzad, 2017). In this way, the Higher M@t-EduTutor platform was developed so that it automatically adjusts to different dimensions of the displays in which it is used. When implementing the HTML code and formatting the web page styles, using CSS, it was taken into consideration the purpose of the platform responsiveness.

An HTML element (canvas) was used to create the user's drawing area in which it is possible to draw text and graphic primitives. This drawing functionality results from several x, y points, consecutively represented by the user interaction. Another tool developed similarly to drawing objects is a "rubber". Additionally, the user has the possibility to add text boxes, developed in HTML and using a javascript library (JQuery). In this way, it is possible for the user to write and apply text freely on the working area. Colour, font (Arial) and size were fixed. An import module for image files, locally available, was also developed using the FileReader[2] API. At any time, the user has the possibility to use a "clean/delete" operation of all the content present in the canvas. Another feature available on the prototype allows exporting the canvas as an image file (.jpg) that the user can, for example, save and/or share with someone.

Javascript was chosen as the programming language used in the development of the various functionalities included in the platform. Some of these features, developed in javascript, allow support for user interaction operations with the canvas. This interaction is performed through events (click/pressure and drag/movement) of the pointing system (e.g. the mouse, a pen or the user's finger). The platform continuously collects the 2D x, y coordinates, in result of the pointing system interaction with the canvas, in order to ensure that the drawing is performed in the correct coordinates. Javascript was used also to add support to track events on tactile screens, typically available on mobile devices.

---

[2] https://www.w3.org/TR/FileAPI/#dfn-filereader

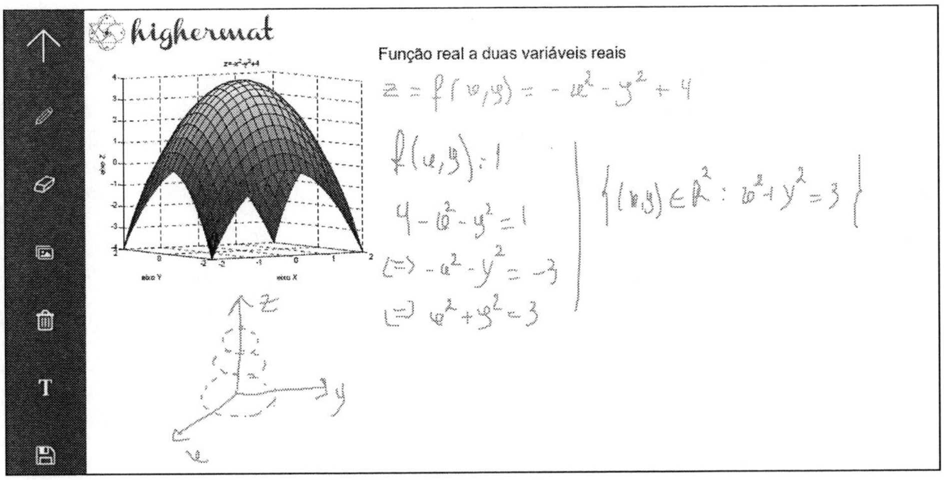

Figure 2. Example of the platform operation

An example of the collaborative use of the Higher M@t-EduTutor platform is shown in Figure 2. Three of the platform features are used, namely free drawing, importing image files and writing text. In this case the figure represents the result of a student who seeks to clarify doubts with a teacher. In this particular example, the student uploaded an image to the canvas. And, using the platform drawing tool, he wrote a mathematical function, in order to simplify the explanation of his doubt to the teacher, who proceeds with the resolution of the exercise. Whenever any user wants, may save on his device a copy of the canvas, as an image. An interesting feature developed in the platform, in order to become easier for users to distinguish between what each one writes/draws on canvas, is the automatic assignment of different objects drawing colour, for each user. Thus, a teacher can more easily distinguish what a student writes/draws on the canvas, from what is written/draw by him or vice versa. Another interesting feature available to the users is the possibility to hide the side tool menu, thus obtaining more free space to draw in the canvas area.

4.4 Analysis

Through the analysis of this platform, in terms of technical features, considering the functionalities considered in the comparative analysis in section 3.2, is verified that the Higher M@t-EduTutor free platform is responsive, suitable for mobile devices, has touch support for tactile screens, the size of the canvas is flexible, has a "rubber" tool to erase part of the drawn object, supports the import of files (e.g. images), and it allows to export the drawing canvas as an image. However, it does not support audio communication between users, does not allow for spell checking and automatic text filling, and does not have real-time text chat, but it possible to the users to simultaneously interact on the same canvas area, supporting communication between users. This platform prototype has already been subject of usability evaluation by students, who had concluded that, the platform is suitable and useful in an educational context, and revealed to be as a possible support in student learning. From the analysis performed to the platform, it is verifiable that most of the students considered that the Higher M@t-EduTutor platform has a high degree of usability (Araújo & Faria, 2017).

5. CONCLUSIONS

Throughout the development of this platform we have encountered some difficulties, namely in the inclusion of the tools in a collaborative way and their compatibility with mobile devices with touch screen. However, it was possible to develop a first relatively stable prototype of a web platform, compatible with several browsers, through the implementation of a server using the node.js framework and connections via websockets, enabling real-time communication.

The Higher M@t-EduTutor platform, at the level of the studied functionalities, lacks in communication support via audio between users, spell check and automatic text filling and text chat in real-time. These functionalities are not simultaneously available in any of the analysed platforms. It should be noted these functionalities, although relevant, could be bridged, by using other parallel platforms specifically for this purpose (e.g. Skype). However, it should be noted that the Higher M@t-EduTutor platform allows interaction between users, simultaneously on the same canvas, since it is possible to draw, to write using handwritten or the text tool, to export images, among other features, enhancing communication between users.

In the future, a number of new features can be implemented, such as allowing users to share their working area through a link, allowing users to collaborate with anyone they want. It would be a plus, the inclusion of text and voice communication among users, since it facilitates the collaboration between them, not having to resort to third-party applications. Another feature to implement will allow users to save their work on the platform itself. This will require the development of a user database support system. In this way, users would be able to access the various interaction sessions, stored through their personal account in the platform, among other features that would enhance the collaborative work between teachers and students.

REFERENCES

Andreoli, V. 2007. *O Mundo Digital*, Lisboa, Editorial Presença.

Arantes, F., Freire, F., Breuer, J., Silva, A., Oliveira, R. & Vascon, L. 2017. Towards a Multisemiotic and Multimodal Editor. *Journal of Computer Science & Technology*, 17(2) 100-109.

Araújo, I. & Faria, P. 2017. Higher M@T-Edututor - A prototype of a platform to support tutoring at distance using mobile devices. *10th annual International Conference of Education, Research and Innovation.* ICERI2017 Proceedings, 6048-6055.

Attewell, J., Savill-Smith, C. & Douch, R. 2009. *The impact of mobile learning examining what it means for teaching and learning*. London, LSN.

Hernandez, R. M. 2017. Impacto de las TIC en la educación: Retos y Perspectivas. *Propósitos y Representaciones*, 5(1), 325-347.

Ismail, I., Mohammed Idrus, R. & Mohd Johari, S., S . 2010. Acceptance on Mobile Learning via SMS: A Rasch Model Analysis. *iJIM - International Journal of Interactive Mobile Technologies*, 4, 10-16.

Ligi, B. & Raja, B. 2017. Mobile learning in higher education. *International Journal of Research Granthaalayah*. 5(4)SE, 1-6.

Lucena, S. 2016. Digital cultures and mobile technologies in education, *Educar em Revista*, Curitiba, Brasil, 59, 277-290

Moura, A. & Carvalho, A. 2010. Twitter: A productive and learning tool for the SMS generation. In C.M. Evans (Ed.), *Internet Issues: Blogging, the Digital Divide and Digital Libraries*. Nova Science Publishers, 199-214.

Noor-Ul-Amin, S. 2013. An effective use of ICT for education and learning by drawing on worldwide knowledge, research and experience: ICT as a change agent for education (A Literature review). *Scholarly Journal of Education*, 2(4), 38-45.

Pachler, N., Pimmer, C. & Seipold, J. 2011. *Work-based mobile learning: concepts and cases*. Bern, Switzerland, Peter-Lang.

Palloff, R. & Pratt, K., 2005. *Learning Together in Community : Collaboration Online*. Jossey-Bass, San Francisco, USA.

Quinn, C. 2011. *Designing mLearning: Tapping into the mobile revolution for organizational performance*. San Francisco: Pfeiffer.

Shahzad, F. (2017). Modern and Responsive Mobile-enabled Web Applications. *Procedia Computer Science* 110 (2017) 410–415.

Sharples, M., Inmaculada, A. S., Milrad M. & Vavoula, G. 2009. Mobile Learning. *Technology Enhanced Learning: Principles and Products*. Nicolas Balacheff, Sten Ludvigsen ,Ton de Jong,Ard Lazonder, Sally Barnes Editors, 233-249.

Souza, M. 2011. *Expert Oracle Application Express Plugins.* Apress, New York, USA

Syed, B. 2014. *Beginning Node.js.* Apress, New York, USA

Wang, V. , Salim, F. & MosKovits, P. 2013. *The definitive Guide to HTML5 WebSocket*. Apress, New York, USA

Waycott, J, Jones, A. & Scanlon, E. 2005. Using a PDA as a learning or workplace tool, Learning, *Media and Technology* , 30(2) 107-130.

EXPLORING AESTHETICS, EMOTION AND USABILITY IN ELEARNING APPLICATIONS FOR USERS WITH INTELLECTUAL DISABILITY

Hannah O' Sheehan, Marian McDonnell and Irene Connolly
Institute of Art, Design and Technology, Kill Avenue, Dun Laoghaire, Co. Dublin, Ireland

ABSTRACT

Despite the abundance of literature in the area of human-computer interaction (HCI), there is limited HCI research about users with intellectual disability. This research project evaluates *Let's Be Safe*, an eLearning application in development at the Institute of Art, Design and Technology, Dun Laoghaire. This application aims to educate young adults with intellectual disability about cyberbullying - an issue prevalent among this population - and cybersafety. Twenty-two individuals with mild to moderate intellectual disability took part in the research. The study employed a mixed-methods design including observational and inquiry methods of usability evaluation. The evaluation investigated the relationships between perceived aesthetics, emotional response and usability for the application. The analyses found no significant relationships between aesthetics, emotional response and usability for this user group. However, the research gathered rich data, which will contribute to the development of *Let's Be Safe*.

KEYWORDS

Intellectual Disability, eLearning, Aesthetics, Emotional Response, Usability, Cyberbullying, Cybersafety

1. INTRODUCTION

1.1 Intellectual Disability

Intellectual disability (ID) is a neurodevelopmental disorder involving impaired intellectual and adaptive functioning. ID is characterised by deficits in three domains; conceptual, social and practical (American Psychiatric Association, 2013). Individuals with ID experience deficits in areas of problem solving, abstract thinking, judgement and learning. Deficits in adaptive functioning result in failing to reach developmental and sociocultural standards for independence and social responsibility (Toth, Lacy & King, 2016).

1.2 Intellectual Disability, Technology and Design

Technology holds much potential for aiding individuals with disabilities within many aspects of their everyday lives (Vicente & López, 2010). The use of information and communication technologies (ICT) can be empowering for individuals with disabilities. It has been suggested that the use of technology has the capability to improve quality of life for those with ID. This is especially true in the case of assistive and support technologies (Tanis et al., 2012). Despite the many benefits, research shows that technology is underutilised by individuals with intellectual disability (Tanis et al., 2012; Vicente & López, 2010). Technology is a beneficial platform, which supports innovative ways to teach and learn. eLearning is learning conducted through technology (Mayes & de Freitas, 2007). The use of eLearning for individuals with ID can expand their opportunities for learning. It also has the potential to reduce the impact of the digital divide amongst this population (Arachchi, Sitbon & Zhang, 2017). In order to design technologies that are accessible for such individuals there are certain requirements. As the need to better integrate this population in society is becoming increasingly recognised, these requirements have become an important goal (Persson, Åhman, Yngling & Gulliksen, 2015). In the area of design, approaches such as Universal Design, Inclusive Design and Design for All have been promoted as ways to increase accessibility of ICT. Such approaches encourage developers to consider the needs of the user throughout the design process (Persson et al., 2015).

1.3 Aesthetics, Emotion and Usability

Hassenzahl (2008) defines aesthetics as "a predominantly affect-driven evaluative response to the visual Gestalt of an object". It is the visual appeal of an interface or product (Hassenzahl, 2008). Users' perceptions of aesthetics comprise of two dimensions: classical and expressive aesthetics. Classical aesthetics represents the extent to which a design is clean and balanced; while expressive aesthetics is reflected by the creativity and originality of design (Lavie & Tractinsky, 2004). Despite being an essential component of user experience, it is only in recent years that emotion in human-computer interaction (HCI) has gained attention in research. During an interaction with an interface, users experience an emotional response (Agarwal & Meyer, 2009). The International Organization for Standardization (1998) define usability as "extent to which a product can be used by specified users to achieve specified goals with effectiveness, efficiency and satisfaction in a specified context of use."

1.3.1 Relationship between Aesthetics, Emotion and Usability

Research suggests that a user's perception of usability can be influenced by the interface aesthetics. It has been found that designs deemed more aesthetically pleasing were also perceived as more usable (Hartmann, Sutcliffe & De Angeli, 2007; Sonderegger & Sauer, 2010; Thüring & Mahlke, 2007). A relationship between aesthetics and emotion has been recognised within HCI research (Sonderegger & Sauer, 2010; Thüring & Mahlke, 2007). The emotion of an individual can be positively influenced by the aesthetic design of an interface (Sonderegger, Zbinden, Uebelbacher & Sauer, 2012). The usability of a system is likely to influence the emotional response of the user (Agarwal & Meyer, 2009). Good usability, leading to a more fluid human-computer interaction, is suggested to increase levels of pleasure (Porat & Tractinsky, 2012). Individuals with ID can have a desire to please those perceived as authority figures, which can lead to inaccurate responses. During usability testing carried out with individuals with Down Syndrome, the most common cause of ID, Cáliz, Martínez, & Cáliz (2017) found that participants are likely to provide "friendly" answers to usability questionnaires in spite of the individual's experience. Subsequently, usability reported by this user group can differ significantly from the observed usability. Although these elements have been the concentration of much research within the area of HCI, there is a paucity of research focusing specifically on users with ID.

1.4 Cyberbullying and Intellectual Disability

With the advancement of technology, cyberbullying has become increasingly pervasive. Cyberbullying is characterised by deliberate and repeated harm towards an individual carried out in an electronic context. As the popularity of social networking rises, it is likely such forms of communication will emerge as platforms for victimisation (Heiman & Olenik-Shemesh, 2015). While research within the area of cyberbullying among those with ID is limited, there is evidence to suggest a high prevalence of victimisation and bullying behaviour among individuals with ID (Kowalski, Morgan, Drake-Lavelle & Allison, 2016). There is heightened concern for young adults with ID and their safety online as they are viewed as more naïve than neurotypical peers (Sorbring, Molin & Löfgren-Mårtenson, 2017). The high prevalence of cyberbullying among individuals with ID suggests the necessity for coping, intervention and prevention strategies (McGrath, Jones & Hastings, 2009). Educational initiatives teaching about cybersafety are pivotal to ensure the safety of individuals with ID online. The implementation of awareness-raising and teaching skills to enable individuals to recognise and report bullying in service environments is vital (McGrath et al., 2009).

1.5 Present Study

Slonje, Smith and Frisén (2013) suggest the use of technologies as mediums for interventions for cyberbullying. *Let's Be Safe* is an eLearning application in development designed specifically for the use of individuals with ID. This application intends to educate young adults with ID about cyberbullying and cybersafety through video, audio, reading activities and games. There is limited research within the area of instructional and educational technologies for individuals with ID. It is becoming increasingly recognised that attention to research in this area is crucial. Furthermore, there is a lack of involvement of people with ID in usability studies, an essential element in the process of designing for users with ID (Caton & Chapman, 2016). The present study intends to investigate the relationship between aesthetics, emotion and usability in an eLearning application for users with ID. The findings aim to contribute to the development of the *Let's Be Safe* eLearning application. Additionally, this research will add to the existing literature within the area of instructional and educational technologies.

1.5.1 Research Questions

1. Is there a relationship between perceived aesthetics and reported usability for this user group?
2. Is there a relationship between observed usability and reported usability for this user group?
3. Is there a relationship between observed emotional response and observed usability for this user group?
4. Is there a common theme in preferred images for individuals within this user group?

2. METHOD

2.1 Design

This study employed a mixed-methods design, using observational and inquiry methods of usability evaluation. Correlational design was used to analyse the relationships between aesthetics, emotion and usability, reported and observed. Qualitative methods were applied to gather rich data related to the usability of the application, the emotional response of the user during the interaction. Qualitative thematic analyses were conducted to examine data collected during the observational evaluations.

2.2 Participants

Purposive sampling was used to recruit participants with mild to moderate intellectual disability. A total of twenty-two participants took part. The individuals recruited were nominated by care staff at Carmona House Services, Glenageary, Co. Dublin. Participants ranged in communication, literacy, cognitive and ICT skills. All participants met the following inclusion criteria:

1. Adults (18 years of age or above) with intellectual disability,
2. Sufficient verbal communication skills to express thoughts and experience of the interaction.

Participants involved were representative of the target user group for the *Let's Be Safe* application.

2.3 Materials and Accessibility

The format of materials must be considered when designing for participants with ID. Simplifying the language used in the materials and the use of shorter sentence structures can alleviate comprehension problems experienced by participants with ID (Jen-Yi, Krishnasamy & Der-Thanq, 2015). As the prevalence of vision impairments is high among individuals with ID, font style and size should be considered (Owens, Kerker, Zigler & Horwitz, 2006). All materials to be used by the participants were adapted to provide an accessible and comprehensive format. These documents were in an easy-to-read format, using simple language and clear font, and included images to aid understanding. An information sheet explained the purpose of the study. An expression of interest form was distributed to interested individuals. Consent forms were provided. A demographic form collected basic information about participants. A debrief form thanked participants and restated the purpose of the study. Contact information of the primary researcher was also provided. Coded observation sheets, extracted from the adapted DEVAN method, were developed to measure usability and emotional response. This method was used successfully in usability tests and observations carried out with children with Down Syndrome (Macedo, Trevisan, Vasconcelos & Clua, 2015). The System Usability Scale (SUS) was adapted for individuals with ID and is considered a suitable satisfaction questionnaire for this user group (Cáliz et al., 2017). This was used to gather opinions from participants of their experience using *Let's Be Safe*. It incorporated Smileyometers used to record participants' opinions on the usability and aesthetics of the eLearning application. The Smileyometers were based on a 4-point Likert scale.

2.4 Apparatus

A desktop computer was set up for each participant in order to conduct the usability testing. All computers were equipped with standard mice and headphones. The *Let's Be Safe* prototype was running on all computers. TechSmith Camtasia screen recording software captured participants' interaction with the application, recording screen activity such as the users' navigation of the interface and errors.

2.5 Procedure

2.5.1 Overview

Prior to recruitment of participants and commencement of the study, ethical approval was granted from the Saint John of Gods Ethics Committee and the Department of Technology and Psychology Ethics Committee. Participants attended one of three sessions at the Institute of Art, Design and Technology, Dun Laoghaire, Co Dublin. Care staff with whom they were familiar accompanied them. Each session took place in a computer laboratory and was two hours in length. On the day of each session, the participants were greeted and shown to the computer laboratory where the study took place. They were each assigned a number with which they would be identified throughout the study. They were introduced to the researchers and seated at a table with their identifying number in front of them. The study was explained and the process was clearly communicated. Participants were reminded they can stop at any stage during the study and were free to withdraw. The demographic form was distributed and completed by each participant. Care staff were present to assist any individuals requiring help.

2.5.2 Usability Testing

Usability testing is the most frequently used method for evaluating the usability of a product or system. This method involves testing a prototype with the intended user group by simulating the interaction under controlled conditions (Dumas & Redish, 1999; Sonderegger & Sauer, 2010). Providing specific tasks for the users to perform while using the system allows the functionality and usability to be explored. The performance of these tasks will suggest the extent to which the system can support the proposed functions (Ruben & Chisnell, 2008). Participants sat individually at a desktop computer on which the *Let's Be Safe* prototype was running. Each participant was given a task sheet and instructed to follow the steps provided to perform the set tasks. The tasks included watching videos, reading information, listening to audio and playing games. Thirty minutes was assigned to complete the usability test.

2.5.3 Observation

The observational method of usability evaluation collects data by observing the users' experience of interacting with the system (Cáliz et al., 2017). Participants were observed as they performed the tasks during their interaction with the application. This observation focused primarily on usability and emotional response. The frequency of behaviours and actions observed were noted on the observation sheets. The context of the observed behaviour/action was also recorded. Researchers observing the interactions recorded any relevant free-form notes. Participants were each observed for ten-minute periods. An assistant researcher timed the observations. After the usability testing, the participants were provided with the adapted SUS to complete. Care staff and researchers were present to assist any individuals that required help. The individuals were thanked for their participation and debriefed before leaving the computer laboratory.

3. RESULTS

3.1 Overview

The present study investigated the relationship between aesthetics, emotion and usability for users with ID. A Spearman's correlation was performed to examine these relationships. Observational analysis was conducted to investigate these relationships further. Thematic analysis examined data collected during the observation.

3.2 Descriptive Statistics

Participants were males and females ranging from 19 to 34 years (M = 22.23 years, SD = 3.72). Participants took part in one of three sessions. Eight individuals participated in session one, nine in session two and five in session three. The demographic form collected data from participants relating to their ICT habits. All participants had experience using technology. Almost two-thirds of participants use technology daily.

The Adapted SUS included a Smileyometer measuring the opinions of participants in relation to the aesthetics and usability of *Let's Be Safe*. The majority of participants reported that they found *Let's Be Safe* very aesthetically pleasing. Half of the participant responses reported that *Let's Be Safe* was very easy to use.

3.3 Inferential Statistics

A Spearman's correlation was conducted to determine the relationship between self-reported factors and observed factors. The correlation between reported aesthetics and reported usability was found to be not significant (r_s (20) = .014, p = .954). The correlation between reported usability and observed usability was found to be not significant (r_s (20) = .310, p = .171). The correlation between observed usability and observed emotional response was also found to be not significant (r_s (20) = .071, p = .754).

3.4 Analysis Procedure

3.4.1 Thematic and Observational Analysis

A combination of both inductive and deductive approaches of thematic analysis is used in this research study. The advantage of this approach is the integration of themes derived from literature with themes that emerge from the data examined (Anderton & Ronald, 2017). The observational method of usability evaluation used in the present research focused on usability and emotional response of users during the interaction. Thematic analysis was conducted on the data collected during the observations. Deductive thematic analysis was applied, using a coding frame from the literature. Prior to the data collection process, ten primary themes were identified. Five themes corresponded to usability and five were representative of the emotional response of users. The inductive approach was utilised when analysing the data collected to identify sub-themes.

3.5 Findings

3.5.1 Observation

The observation applied a coding framework from the literature. This framework identified ten major themes: five responding to usability and five to emotional response. The data collected from the observation were analysed and sub-themes were identified.

3.5.2 Usability

Theme 1. *Errors* (Sub-theme: *Inconsistent layout*): The errors made during the interaction with the prototype were predominantly because of inconsistency in the layout of the interface. The majority of screens placed menu items at the centre of the interface. Errors occurred when menu items were arranged at the top of the interface and users clicked elements at the centre of the screen. Theme 2. *Assistance Required* (Sub-themes: *Reading difficulties*): The majority of the users required at least minor assistance during the interaction due to difficulties encountered. Some participants were illiterate while others struggled with reading. Subsequently, these individuals required assistance throughout the usability testing. Assistance was also required if an error was made and the user was confused. Theme 3. *Confusion* (Sub-themes: *Inconsistency*): Following on from errors due to inconsistent layout, several participants showed confusion with inconsistent layout and design. Users struggled to find menu items arranged at the top of the interface as the majority of menus were arranged at the centre of the screen. Theme 4. *Physical/Motor Problems:* There were no physical or motor problems observed. Theme 5. *Perception Problems:* There were no perception problems observed.

3.5.3 Emotional Response

The themes relating to emotional response captured engagement and enjoyment. These emotional responses create the overall user experience. Theme 6. *Task Completion:* The majority of participants completed all given tasks. Theme 7. *Interest/Boredom:* Most participants showed clear interest throughout the interaction.

The videos and games were observed to be the most engaging elements. A number of participants were disengaged during the listening activity, looking around them or facial expression suggesting boredom. Participants with reading difficulties were unable, or struggled, to engage with the reading activity. Theme 8. *Like/Dislike:* Some participants showed a particular liking towards the game elements of the module. Observed dislike was mostly in response to the topic as opposed to elements of the prototype. Theme 9. *Vocalisation – Positive and Negative* (Sub-themes: *Cheer, Sigh, Frustration*): There was very little vocalisation from participants during the observation. A number of users cheered when answering questions within the game correctly. Some users with reading difficulties let out a sigh when struggling with reading modules. One user expressed frustration when unable to locate the Stories module. Theme 10. *Behaviour – Positive and Negative* (Sub-themes: *Smile, Frown, Upset*): A number of participants showed a positive emotional response when answering questions within the game correctly. Negative behaviours expressed were mostly in response to the topic rather than the elements of the prototype. One participant became upset because of experiencing difficulties using the application.

3.5.4 Image Preferences

The adapted SUS recorded participants' favourite and least favourite image within *Let's Be Safe*. Twenty participants responded to the question recording their preferred image. Overall, the majority of individuals within this user group prefer graphics such as emoticons and cartoons.

4. DISCUSSION

4.1 Discussion of Present Findings

The aims of the present study were to investigate the relationship between perceived aesthetics, emotional response and usability for young adults with mild to moderate intellectual disability during their interaction with the eLearning application, *Let's Be Safe*. Previous research carried out among neurotypical users found significant relationships between perceived aesthetics of an interface, emotional response and usability during human-computer interaction (Porat & Tractinsky, 2012; Sonderegger & Sauer, 2010; Sonderegger et al., 2012). However, the analyses of the data found no significant relationships between perceived aesthetics, emotional response and usability. These factors have been the focus of much research within the area of HCI while the scarcity of research with a focus on users with intellectual disability is evident. The findings of this present research are contradictory to the expectations.

4.1.1 Aesthetics, Emotional Response and Usability

Aesthetics received the highest rating on the self-report measures with the majority of users reporting to like the aesthetic design of the interface a lot. The observation suggested that participants found it difficult to navigate through the interface, yet the interface of *Let's Be Safe* was perceived as very aesthetically pleasing. This is inconsistent with previous research, which has found that impaired usability can impact negatively on perceived aesthetics (Hartmann et al., 2007). Research shows that the usability of a system can influence the emotional response of the user (Thüring & Mahlke, 2007; Sonderegger et al., 2012). Participants who experienced major usability issues were observed showing signs of frustration and upset. However, the analysis found no significant relationship between observed emotional response and observed usability. The findings of the self-reported usability collected in the SUS suggest that users found the application very easy to use. However, the data collected during the usability observation suggest that the majority of users had difficulty using the prototype independently. This contradiction is in line with expectations and consistent with the research, which suggests participants in this user group are likely to provide "desired" responses to usability questionnaires contrary to the individual's experience during the interaction (Cáliz et al., 2017).

4.1.2 Image Preferences

The *Let's Be Safe* application is designed for use by individuals with ID. The interface consists of many images to aid understanding and promote familiarity (Arachchi et al. 2017). The majority of participants reported the graphic images - emoticons and cartoons - as their preferred image. Images of real people were the second favoured style of image. Participants were reluctant to report images they did not like. This may be explained by the pleasing nature of individuals in this population (Cáliz et al., 2017).

4.2 Theoretical and Practical Implications

The current research contributes to the copious amount of literature within the area of human-computer interaction while adding originality through the involvement of users with intellectual disability, a population often disregarded in this research area. The findings of this study will contribute to the development and improvement of the eLearning application, *Let's Be Safe*. The observational analyses have provided rich information regarding the nature of usability difficulties and sources of users' emotional response. The results of this research will be the foundation for recommendations made to the developers of *Let's Be Safe* in order to increase the accessibility of the application for the target users.

4.3 Strengths and Limitations of the Present Study

A major strength is the involvement of individuals with ID in the development process of a system targeting this user group. The quality of data collected during the user testing suggests the importance of involving the target user group in the development process as well as the need for further research with this user group (Caton & Chapman, 2016). Another strength of this study is the large number of participants involved in comparison to previous qualitative research within both the population and research topic (Slonje et al., 2013). A limitation of this research is that the validity of responses is uncertain as it is unknown whether the responses reflect the actual thoughts and experiences of the individuals. Responses collected may be inaccurate due to the tendency of this population to please those perceived as authority figures (Cáliz et al., 2017).

4.4 Future Research

Future studies may benefit from the use of facial recording software during the user testing. Due to ethical constraints, this research was not permitted to use facial recording software during the interaction with the prototype. The use of such devices would capture supplementary material, which would support and contribute to the data collected during observation.

4.5 Conclusion

Although the relationships between aesthetics, emotional response and usability has been extensively researched within the field of HCI, the current study was diverse as it's focus was on a population often overlooked; users with intellectual disability. Contrary to expectations, this research did not achieve significant results in examining the relationship between aesthetics, emotional response and usability for this user group. However, the research gathered rich data, which will contribute to the improvement and development of the *Let's Be Safe* eLearning application. The findings also highlight the significance of further research in the area of HCI for users with intellectual disability and the importance of research into the area of cyberbullying among this same population.

REFERENCES

Agarwal, A., & Meyer, A. (2009). Beyond usability: evaluating emotional response as an integral part of the user experience. In *CHI'09 Extended Abstracts on Human Factors in Computing Systems* (pp. 2919-2930). New York, NY: ACM Press.

American Psychiatric Association (2013). Diagnostic and Statistical Manual of Mental Disorders (5th ed.). Arlington, VA: American Psychiatric Publishing.

Anderton, B. N., & Ronald, P. C. (2017). Hybrid thematic analysis reveals themes for assessing student understanding of biotechnology. *Journal of Biological Education, 1*, 1-12.

Arachchi, T. K., Sitbon, L., & Zhang, J. (2017). Enhancing Access to eLearning for People with Intellectual Disability: Integrating Usability with Learning. In *IFIP Conference on Human-Computer Interaction* (pp. 13-32). Cham, Switzerland: Springer.

Cáliz, D., Martínez, L., & Cáliz, R. (2017). Helping people with down syndrome through a usability testing guide proposal for mobile applications. *International Journal of Computer Science, Engineering and Information Technology, 7*(2), 1-19.

Caton, S., & Chapman, M. (2016). The use of social media and people with intellectual disability: A systematic review and thematic analysis. *Journal of Intellectual & Developmental Disability, 41*(2), 1-15.

Dumas, J. S., & Redish, J. (1999). *A practical guide to usability testing*. Portland, OR: Intellect Books.

Hartmann, J., Sutcliffe, A., & De Angeli, A. (2007). Investigating attractiveness in web user interfaces. In *Proceedings of the SIGCHI conference on Human Factors in Computing Systems* (pp. 387-396). New York, NY: ACM Press.

Hassenzahl, M. (2008). Aesthetics in interactive products: Correlates and consequences of beauty. In H. N. J. Schifferstein & P. Hekkert (Eds.), *Product experience* (pp. 287-302). San Diego, CA: Elsevier.

Heiman, T., & Olenik-Shemesh, D. (2015). Cyberbullying experience and gender differences among adolescents in different educational settings. *Journal of Learning Disabilities, 48*(2), 146-155.

Jen-Yi, L., Krishnasamy, M., & Der-Thanq, C. (2015). Research with persons with intellectual disabilities: An inclusive adaptation of Tourangeau's model. *ALTER-European Journal of Disability Research/Revue Européenne de Recherche sur le Handicap*, *9*(4), 304-316.

Kowalski, R.M., Morgan, C.A., Drake-Lavelle, K., & Allison, B. (2016). Cyberbullying among college students with disabilities. *Computers in Human Behavior*, *57*, 416-427.

Macedo, I., Trevisan, D. G., Vasconcelos, C. N., & Clua, E. (2015, January). Observed interaction in games for down syndrome children. In *48th Hawaii International Conference on System Sciences* (pp. 662-671). Piscataway, NJ: IEEE Press.

Mahlke, S., & Thüring, M. (2007, April). Studying antecedents of emotional experiences in interactive contexts. In *Proceedings of the SIGCHI Conference on Human Factors in Computing Systems* (pp. 915-918). New York, NY: ACM Press.

Mayes, T., & de Freitas, S. (2007). Learning and e-learning: The role of theory. In H. Beetham & R. Sharpe (Eds.), *Rethinking pedagogy for a digital age: Designing and delivering e-learning* (pp. 13-25). London, UK: Routledge.

McGrath, L., Jones, R.S.P., & Hastings, R.P. (2009). Outcomes of anti-bullying intervention for adults with intellectual disabilities. *Research in Developmental Disabilities, 31*(2), 376-380.

Owens, P. L., Kerker, B. D., Zigler, E., & Horwitz, S. M. (2006). Vision and oral health needs of individuals with intellectual disability. *Developmental Disabilities Research Reviews*, *12*(1), 28-40.

Persson, H., Åhman, H., Yngling, A. A., & Gulliksen, J. (2015). Universal design, inclusive design, accessible design, design for all: Different concepts —one goal? On the concept of accessibility — historical, methodological and philosophical aspects. *Universal Access in the Information Society*, *14*(4), 505-526.

Porat, T., & Tractinsky, N. (2012). It's a pleasure buying here: The effects of web-store design on consumers' emotions and attitudes. *Human-Computer Interaction*, *27*(3), 235-276.

Rubin, J., & Chisnell, D. (2008). Handbook of usability testing: How to plan, design, and conduct effective tests. Indianapolis, IN: Wiley Publishing, Inc.

Sonderegger, A., & Sauer, J. (2010). The influence of design aesthetics in usability testing: Effects on user performance and perceived usability. *Applied Ergonomics*, *41*(3), 403-410.

Sonderegger, A., Zbinden, G., Uebelbacher, A., & Sauer, J. (2012). The influence of product aesthetics and usability over the course of time: a longitudinal field experiment. *Ergonomics*, *55*(7), 713-730.

Sorbring, E., Molin, M., & Löfgren-Mårtenson, L. (2017). "I'm a mother, but I'm also a facilitator in her every-day life": Parents' voices about barriers and support for internet participation among young people with intellectual disabilities. *Cyberpsychology: Journal of Psychosocial Research on Cyberspace*, *11*(1), 43-60.

Tanis, E. S., Palmer, S., Wehmeyer, M., Davies, D. K., Stock, S. E., Lobb, K., & Bishop, B. (2012). Self-report computer-based survey of technology use by people with intellectual and developmental disabilities. *Intellectual and Developmental Disabilities*, *50*(1), 53-68.

Thüring, M., & Mahlke, S. (2007). Usability, aesthetics and emotions in human–technology interaction. *International Journal of Psychology*, *42*(4), 253-264.

Toth, K., de Lacy, N., & King, B. H. (2016). Intellectual disability. In M. K. Dulcan (Ed.), *Dulcan's textbook of child and adolescent psychiatry* (2nd ed., pp. 105-134). Arlington, VA: American Psychiatric Publishing.

Vicente, M. R., & López, A. J. (2010). A multidimensional analysis of the disability digital divide: Some evidence for Internet use. *The Information Society*, *26*(1), 48-64.

GOOGLE GLASS AS A LEARNING TOOL: SHARING EVALUATION RESULTS FOR THE ROLE OF OPTICAL HEAD MOUNTED DISPLAYS IN EDUCATION

Georgios Dafoulas, Cristiano Cardoso Maia and Ariadni Tsiakara
Computer Science Department, Faculty of Science and Technology, Middlesex University
The Burroughs, Hendon, London, NW4 4BT, United Kingdom

ABSTRACT

This paper provides an overview of the findings from an evaluation of the role of Google Glass in education over the past three years. The authors have experimented with Optical Head Mounted Displays as a support tool for various learning activities over the past few years. The study described in the paper commenced back in 2014 and continued despite the fact that the development of the Google Glass technology was paused and then shifted towards enterprise clientele. This was a result of our confidence that the future of learning interfaces is aligned to the proliferation of augmented reality and the fact that the Google Glass interface offers an ideal tool for learners due to its light structure and seamless wearing experience. The paper discusses how Google Glass has been used for a range of learning activities and describes the learners' experiences from using the device. The main contribution of the paper is in the form of measuring the success of the specific interface by sharing the results of three years of evaluations. The evaluation results are further analysed taking under consideration a number of profiling techniques of the learners involved including their personality type and learning style.

KEYWORDS

Learning tools, E-learning, Optical Head Mounted Displays, Google Glass, Interface Evaluation, Learning Interfaces

1. INTRODUCTION

This paper discusses the role of Optical Head Mounted Displays (OHMDs) in an educational context. The paper initially describes how the authors engaged in the use of Google Glass as a learning tool for providing student feedback but also offering a technology utilising augmented reality, guiding students in the synthesis of learning portfolios. The work carried out is placed within the context of relevant literature, and the arrangements needed for setting up the necessary infrastructure are discussed in detail. The paper concludes with a presentation of a thorough evaluation with more than 300 participants over two years, focusing on the technology's usability, as well as its suitability for certain learning tasks.

2. BACKGROUND

Our work with OHMDs started more than five years ago when commissioned to participate in the investigation of a project using Google Glass for an international pharmaceutical organisation. The scope of the project was to remote train or guide users in troubleshooting machinery. The concept found a useful application in a number of learning activities as the Google Glass offered an opportunity to provide feedback to students, mentor academics, monitor student activity and also offer a tool to display real time evaluation from students participating in lectures and lab sessions. In this paper we will discuss a number of uses of Google Glass in our research and we will focus on how participating students evaluated the interface for the purpose of their specific learning activity.

There is evidence in the relevant literature of the usefulness of OHMD. Their main strength is their ability to produce and support augmented reality applications. This concept is associated with the integration of information with a live video or even the user's surrounding environment in real time format. One of the key uses of the Google Glass for our research was its capability to merge new information into an existing image. An example of one of the first commercial applications of augmented reality technology is the analysis systems used in televised football games for post match analysis (Kaufmann et al, 2007). OHMD are not designed to provide workstations; therefore, traditional input devices such as keyboards do not support the concept of smart glasses as a wearable device (Scheffel et al, 2012). This was not a limitation for our work, as we focused primarily on the integration of content into pictures taken with the Google Glass, as well as the exchange of pictures with messages between users. For example lecturers could view students' voting on different aspects of their lecture (e.g. pace being too fast, slides being boring), while students were able to receive pictures showing examples of what they have done wrong during their presentations. At the same time students were able to use the Google Glass to take photographs of specific part of their work including social network interfaces as instructed by their tutors in a series of messages displayed through the OHMD.

One of the main capabilities of OHMD is to be able to provide users with a readable, effective interface that can be an information source whilst not distracting there attention from reality. This wearable technology provides users and developers with the opportunity to exploit a new method of computer interaction and enhancing the users level of control over a system. This was the main attraction to our study, as it allowed students to use their computers, while wearing the Google Glass and browsing through a series of instructions displayed. A brief training session was required for the participants to grasp the use of the OHMD interface, which usually lasted less than a couple of minutes. OHMD can provide educators, trainers and professionals with the ability to train, assist and support workplace or classroom learning (Schweizer, 2012). Using OHMD for interactions with students and transmit real-time updates should provide improvements in terms of student performance, learning enhancement and participation in learning activities. Students are not willing to ask questions during seminars with a large number of attendees and thus would miss out on gaining valuable training and education (Kuhn et al, 2015). As we will see later in the paper, the vast majority of the students found the use of this technology not only a rewarding experience but also a useful tool enhancing the way they received feedback for their learning.

There is a lot of literature on the role of OHMD in education. Johnson et al (2011) discuss the many applications of augmented reality in education, focusing on how interactive experiences are likely to appeal to digital native learners. As Bacca et al (2014) identified there are a number of issues that may affect the learning process including "difficulty in maintaining superimposed information" and "paying too much attention to virtual information". There is evidence in relevant literature that the use of augmented reality technology increases willingness to participate, as students feel more engaged and able to participate (Almeida et al, 2014). Montero et al (2013) used the technology to enhance and support communication within presentations and lectures. As Tang (2014) states, Google Glass is generally used to capture pictures, record videos and provide feedback to the individuals. Pardo and Siemens (2014) also report that an early indication of student progress can allow the opportunity for prompt intervention from teachers and a personalisation of teaching, which would benefit all three mentioned stakeholders.

3. GOOGLE GLASS AS A LEARNING TOOL

As mentioned so far, there is evidence of the usefulness of OHMD in education and in particular on the way augmented reality can assist students in a number of learning activities. In our research we did not wish to provide yet another application displaying useful information associated with artefacts that students would handle or a virtual assistant providing information relevant to specific items learners would interact with. Instead we used Google Glass in tow main ways. First we used the display for providing step-by-step guidance to students while they collected evidence of their work for their learning portfolios. The role of the OHM was to provide the information that would otherwise be in the form of guidance sheet or a set of guidelines provided through the e-learning platform. The second use of the Google Glass was for providing feedback to students on their presentations. A series of photographs were taken during the student presentations and informative vignettes were provided to show whether the students did well or not in relation to the content of their presentation, as well as their posture and delivery style. The later part of this paper shares the findings from the evaluation of both uses of Google Glass as an educational tool.

This research study involved two undergraduate modules (i) a first year module covering foundation topics of business information systems and (ii) a third year module covering strategic management in information systems. Both modules used social networks as part of the learning process. Facebook was used in both modules, while the second module involved the use LinkedIn and Twitter. Participants conducted four activity types:

- Reading, social media content relating to specific tasks.
- Writing on social media as required by their coursework.
- Showing, sections of their group report they have created.
- Browsing, though various social media features and explaining their use.

The first task was designed with emphasis on identifying learners' ability to multi-task effectively, as they had to follow the instructions offered on Google Glass, and in parallel to read content from the social media they used for their module. The second task required them to type their contribution to the social media interface they were directed by the Google Glass guide. The third task requested learners to take a photograph of specific sections they created as part of their group report. Finally the learners were requested to provide an explanation for various features and contributions they had in the social media pages used for their module. The scope of the learning activity was to assess whether the experience of using an OHMD has an impact to a range of learning activities and interface tasks.

Figure 1. Lab setting for providing feedback to students

As shown in figure 1, the lab setting for the use of Google Glass for feedback provision is rather simple. The student delivers the presentation, while an instructor observes the sessions taking photographs and adding vignettes from a list of pre-designed feedback messages. A second instructor ensures that there are additional photographs of the student's presentation, as Google Glass is limited in the number of photographs that can be taken due to its battery life, over-heating and speed of capture. A camcorder is also used for providing video recordings to students. These recordings are used for tagging certain delivery messages, as an additional feedback mechanism. The concept of this setting is to provide an additional feedback mechanism to the student taking advantage of the Google Glass ability to create vignettes on captured photographs. This use of augmented reality can be further enhanced if the presenter wears an OHMD that displays in real time the transmitted feedback. Alternatively the feedback messages can be received via a smart phone, table or PC.

Figure 2 shows the lab setting for students using Google Glass while performing the four tasks identified earlier in the paper. To the left there is a photograph showing the student positioned in front of a computer, while wearing the Google Glass. After the training is completed the student begins his/her navigation through the screens displayed on the Google Glass and performs the required tasks. The picture on the right shows the student's view of the task that must be performed and also the picture of the social media interface that must be read as instructed. Some of the simple messages displayed on the Google Glass guidelines include the following:

- Task 1 – Show 3-4 features you have used on your page. Take a photograph of these features.
- Task 2 – Read a post of one of your visitors. Take a photograph of the post.
- Task 3 – Go on the report structure for Element 3 (note: part of the module's coursework). Show which sections you are planning to do. Take a photograph of the report structure.

The video recording of the session is required for additional checks to avoid plagiarism (i.e. students showing others' work as theirs) but also as another way to provide students with their experience of the OHMD interface. The video is also used for assessing difficulties in using the OHMD interface and analysing average times for performing the different tasks.

Figure 2. Lab setting for observing students using Google Glass

Figure 3 shows the feedback students receive following their presentation. There is a range of criteria used for assessing the content and delivery of the presentation. In the examples included we can see positive and negative feedback associated with the content of the specific slides, as well as the body language and posture of the presenter at the moment the photograph was taken. These pictures are overall well received by students as they offer 'rich' feedback and more specific guidance on what has gone wrong and areas for further improvement. We will see in the next section of the paper how students evaluated their experience using Google Glass for these tasks, as well as the usefulness of using the specific OHMD for getting feedback on their presentations.

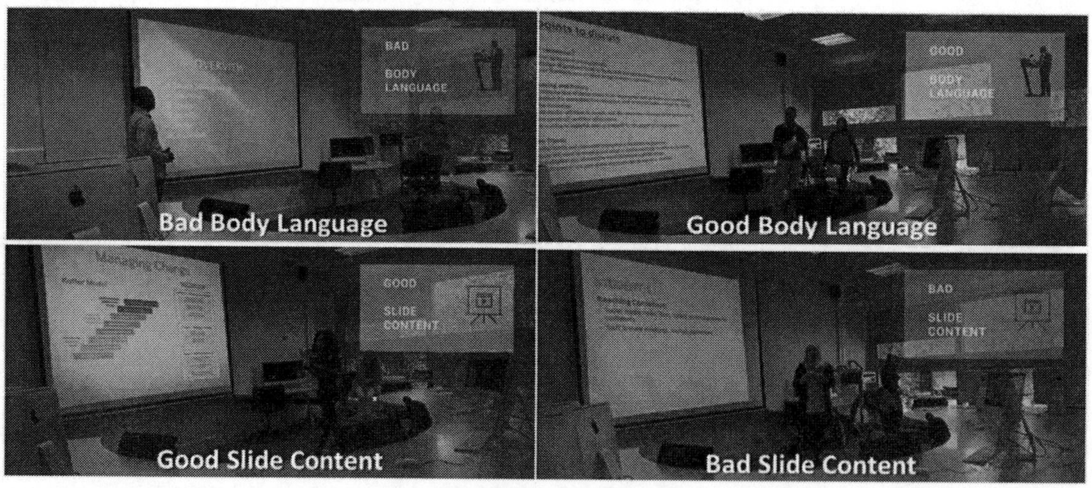

Figure 3. Feedback provided to students via Google Glass

4. EVALUATION RESULTS FOR THE ROLE OF OPTICAL HEAD MOUNTED DISPLAYS IN EDUCATION

Following the completion of both activities using the Google Glass, the research study involved a detailed evaluation on the use of the particular interface. The scope was to assess whether OHMD is suitable for the specific task. The survey conducted included seven questions. The first three questions were focused on the use of Google Glass and in particular, they focused on comfort, navigability and simplicity or ease of use. The second part of the survey included four questions, corresponding to the four tasks students had to complete while wearing the Google Glass, namely (i) browsing, (ii) reading, (iii) writing, (iv) showing.

The survey was in the form of affirmative statements and participants had to use a 10-point scale to indicate whether they disagreed with each statement (i.e. 1 out of 10) or agreed (i.e. 10 out of 10). Before we analyse the responses to the specific questions, it is important to discuss the overall satisfaction of using the technology. As shown in figure 5, the vast majority of the students tend to find the technology very useful. This result is from an earlier study that took place in 2015-16, during a period we were trying to identify whether the positive reaction to the technology is actually associated with the usefulness of its functionality and its ability to play a significant role in learning enhancement. As with all innovative uses of technology, there is likely to be a positive bias towards using such technologies in comparison to more traditional learning environments. It is important to state that at no point incentives were provided for student participants of the study. The task was based on volunteers in both modules. The initial pilot study involved 92 participants of whom 27 were females and 65 males, while 30% of the students were enrolled on the Business Information Systems in Practice (year one) module and 70% were enrolled on the Strategic Management and Information Systems (year three) module.

The overall satisfaction for using the technology was quite high for both modules (74.1% for the final year module and 71.43% for the first year module). However there were different patterns when we see responses according to gender for both modules. It appears that first year female students were the least enthusiastic in using the technology. Nevertheless, female students of the final module seemed to be the most positive in relation to the overall experience of using OHMD in their learning. Despite the fluctuations observed we were able to reflect on the fact that the positive reactions ranged from 65% to 76%, which led to further pilot studies and more evaluations.

As mentioned earlier, the questionnaire consisted of seven questions, where students need to provide a score from 1 (low) to 10 (high) in agreement to the following statements:

(1) The Google Glass was comfortable to wear.
(2) The Google Glass was easy to navigate.
(3) The Google Glass was simple to use.
(4) Ease of use while browsing on the screen.
(5) Ease of use while reading from the screen.
(6) Ease of use while showing content on the screen.
(7) Ease of use while writing on the screen.

The results from both modules were impressive over a two-year period. The cohorts covered were 2016-17 and 2017-18, involving 90 students from year 1 and 276 students from year 3. The average responses across all seven questions were quite similar for both modules with 71.4% and 71.9% for the first and third year modules respectively. The simplicity of the device scored higher for both modules. The most challenging activity was to read from the screen while wearing the Google Glass, as voted from students of both modules.

Our study was not limited on simply assessing the views of our students on the seven questions but also make associations between the students' views on the use of OHMD for supporting their learning and the profiles of the participating students. All students of the two modules undertake a series of profiling exercises at the beginning of their studies. These profiling surveys are concerned (i) management style (Adize's model is used), (ii) team roles (based on Belbin's roles), (iii) personality profiles (using MBTI types) and (iv) learning styles (based on the VARK classification). It is really important to be able to assess whether the views of students are affected by their profiles. This would allow us to make some assumptions on the way these and similar technologies are likely to be received by learners with similar profiles in the future.

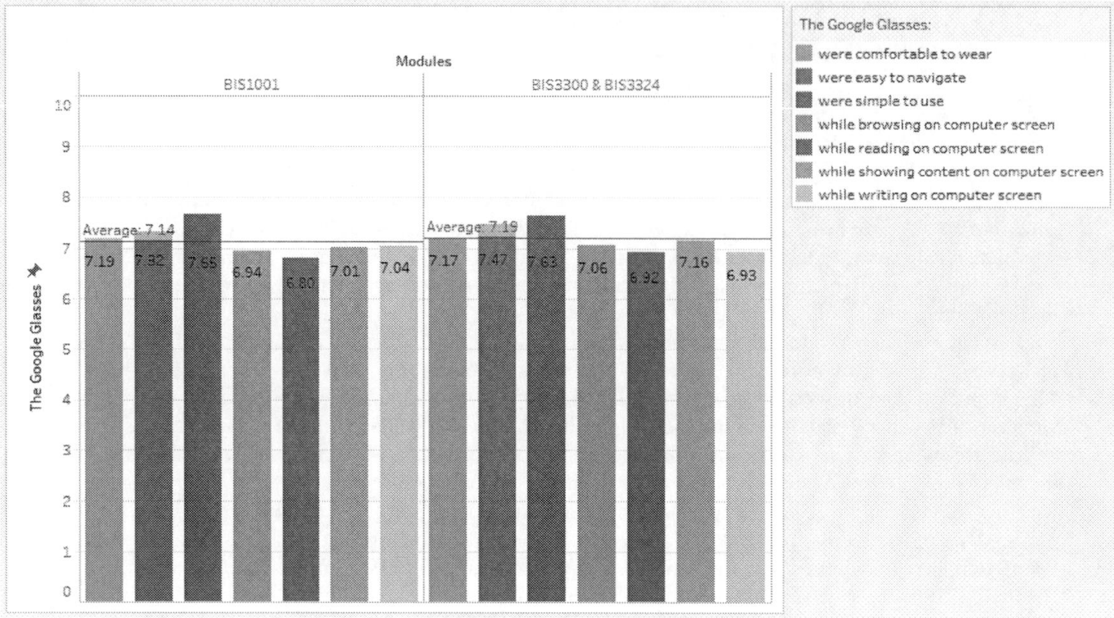

Figure 4. Evaluation responses on Google Glass effectiveness and suitability for the task

As shown in figure 5, there are different responses when we take under consideration the team roles of the participants. According to Belbin we have nine different role profiles in a team. As our students were all studying the same computing topic, we did not take under consideration the 'Specialist' role of Belbin's model. However, when classifying the student responses according to the eight remaining profiles 'Completer Finisher', 'Coordinator', 'Implementer', 'Monitor Evaluator', 'Plant', 'Resource Investigator', 'Shaper', and 'Team Worker' we can observe certain patterns. It is evident that 'Plants' seemto provide the lowest scores in most of the four tasks performed with the help of Google Glass. On the other hand 'Implementers' and 'Monitor Evaluators' seem to find the use of Google Glass quite positive when performing the majority of the tasks. 'Coordinators' were the ones who found that Google Glass were comfortable to wear and easy to navigate more than anybody else, while Shapers were the ones whou found it easier to use.

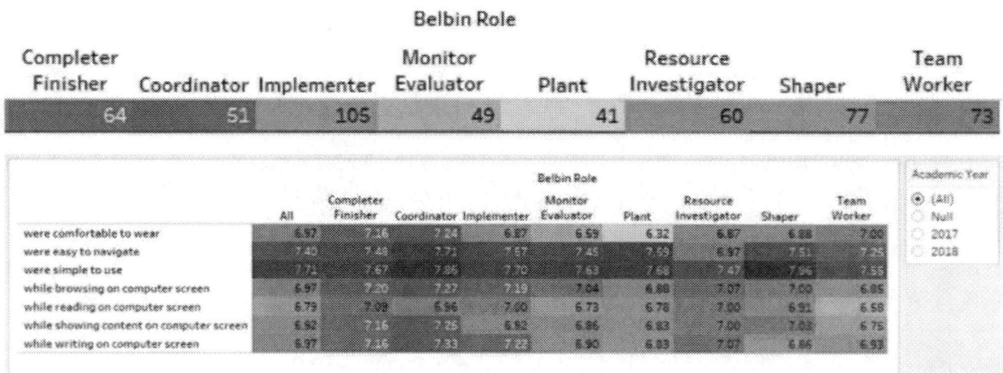

Figure 5. Evaluation responses on Google Glass classified according to Belbin profiles

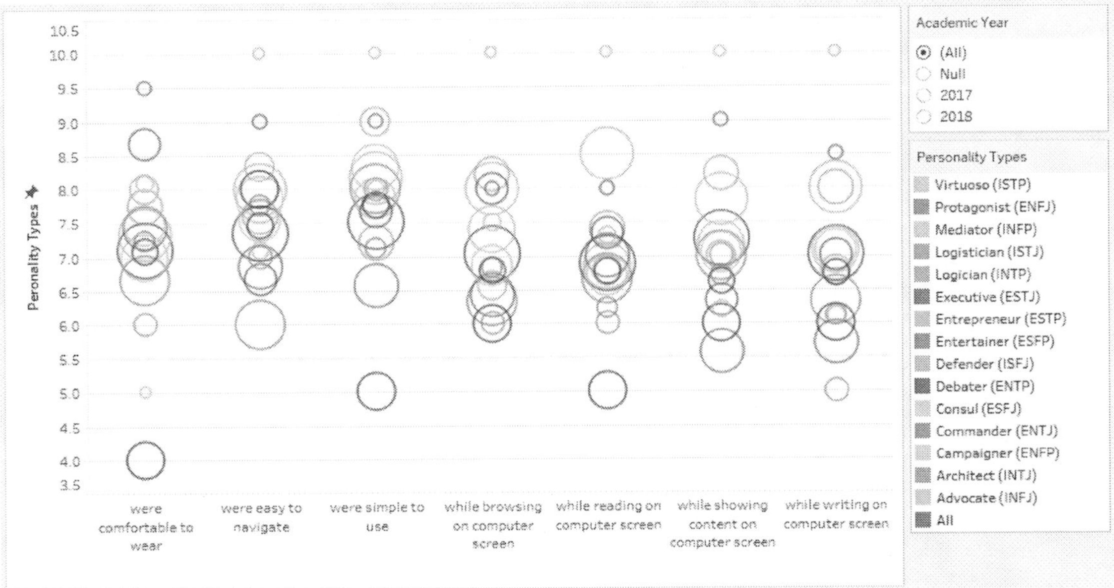

Figure 6. Evaluation responses on Google Glass classified according to MBTI profiles

Similarly interesting findings are provided when reviewing the evaluations categorised according to personality profiles as identified using the MBTI type indicator. Virtuosos, also known as ISTP profiles (Introversion-Sensing-Thinking-Perception) and 'Protagonists' also known as ENFJ (Extraversion-Intuition-Feeling-Judgment) seem to be the types that were really impressed with the technology and found it easy to use and helpful across most tasks. On the other end of the spectrum, the 'Debater' type also known as ENTP (Extraversion-Intuition-Thinking-Perception) are the ones with the most negative response for comfort, ease of use and ability to read while wearing the Google Glass. It is important to note that due to the large number of types included in the MBTI typology, some types have a rather small number of representative students. When observing more common types we see 'Mediators' known as INFP (Introversion-Intuition-Feeling-Perception) being more positive across most questions while 'Commanders' known as ENTJ (Extraversion-Intuition-Thinking-Judgment) provide more negative responses.

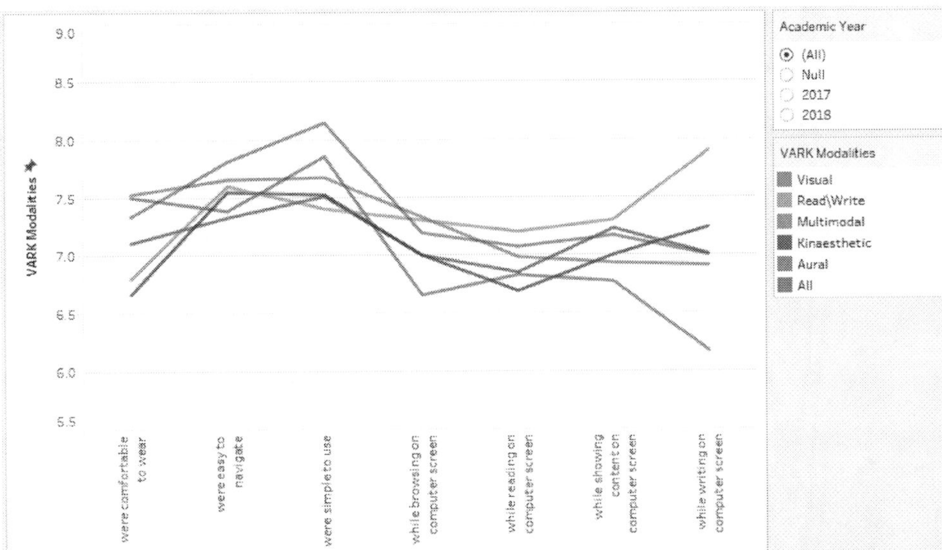

Figure 7. Evaluation responses on Google Glass classified according to VARK profiles

Finally, as shown in figure 7, the VARK classification that distinguishes learners according to their preference to learn as (i) visuals, (ii) aural, (iii) read/write, or (iv) kinaesthetic shows similar response patterns on usability aspects between visual and aural types. Read-write and kinaesthetic profiles tend to provide similar responses on the way Google Glass facilitates the different learning tasks.

5. CONCLUSION

This paper discussed the use of Google Glass as a learning tool and in particular its use for providing feedback, as well as offering guidelines for constructing learning portfolios. The paper's main contribution is by suggesting a lab setting for using OHMD in educational contexts, as well as sharing detailed findings from an extensive evaluation of the technology over a period of two years with more than 300 participants in two undergraduate models. The paper also provides a classification of evaluation responses against different typologies used for participant profiling.

REFERENCES

Almeida, S.D.I., Yamamoto, G, Taketomi, T, Miyazaki, J, & Kato, H. (2014) Increasing Willingness to Communicate in Co-located Presentation Meetings using Augmented Reality. 'The Virtual Reality Society of Japan,' 19 (1), pp. 55-67.

Bacca, J., Baldiris, S., Fabregat, R., Graf, S. & Kinshuk 2014, "Augmented Reality Trends in Education: A Systematic Review of Research and Applications", Journal of Educational Technology & Society, vol. 17, no. 4, pp. 133.

Jonsson, A., Avdelningen för Naturvetenskap, Forskningsmiljön Learning in Science and Mathematics (LISMA), Sektionen för lärande och miljö & Högskolan Kristianstad (2013) "Facilitating productive use of feedback in higher education", Active Learning in Higher Education, 14 (1), pp. 63-76.

Kaufmann, H. and Csisinko, M. 2007. Multiple Head Mounted Displays in Virtual and Augmented Reality Applications . The International Journal of Virtual Reality. 6 (2), p43-50.

Kuhn, J., Lukowicz, P., Hirth, M. and Weppner, J. 2015. Using Google Glass as Experimental Tool for Wearable- Technology Enhanced Learning in Physics. Workshop Proceedings of the 11th International Conference on Intelligent Environments. 1 (1), p212-214.

Montero, A., Zarraonandia, T., Aedo, I. & Diaz, P. 2013, "Uses of Augmented Reality for Supporting Educational Presentations", Advanced Learning Technologies (ICALT), 2013 IEEE 13th International Conference on, pp. 426-428.

Pardo, A. and Siemens, G., 2014. Ethical and privacy principles for learning analytics. British Journal of Educational Technology, 45(3), pp. 438-450.

Scheffel, J. and Kockesen, G. 2012. Wearable Web Technology: Google Glass and the Mirror AP, p1-11.

Schweizer, H. 2012. Smart glasses: technology and applications. Ubiquitous computing . 1 (1), p1-5.

Tang, J. (2014) Beginning Google glass development, Apress, Berkeley.

EXPLORING THE IMPACT OF AMBIGUOUS ICONS IN MOBILE WEB INTERFACES

Waleed AlNuwaiser[1], Stephanie Wilson[1] and George Buchanan[2]
[1]*City, University of London, London, United Kingdom*
[2]*University of Melbourne, Melbourne, Australia*

ABSTRACT

Signs and icons are a fundamental part of the user interface (UI). They are mechanisms of interaction between humans and devices (including mobile devices), and they enable users to achieve tasks. Users typically act on icons as a consequence of their understanding of the icon's visual representation. Meaningful icons enhance users' comprehension, whereas ambiguous icons increase users' confusion. However, little is known about the confusion that may be caused by ambiguous icons in a sequence of interactions. In other words, there is scarce research regarding the effect of the navigational order or interaction sequence that users undertake on their interpretation of ambiguous icons. Thus, this paper explores the impact of ambiguous icons on the accuracy of users' interpretations. Ambiguity is controlled by using pairs of visually identical icons with two different meanings. A semiotic analysis was conducted to investigate users' comprehension of the icons and elicit the causes for their interpretations. We also provide insight into the cognitive processes within working memory and the inherent deliberation, reasoning and comprehension processes that influence users' interpretations.

KEYWORDS

Usability, Ambiguous Icons, Navigation Sequence and Mobile Context

1. INTRODUCTION

The internet and electronic communication have given rise to a wide range of interactive technologies, including mobile devices, and a similarly wide range of usability contexts. User interfaces (UIs) are designed using signs (i.e. graphical representations) that convey important meanings/functions to the users (Ferreira et al., 2005). Due to the centrality of signs in interactive mobile devices, semiotics is key to the study of signs. Such signs consist of three parts: the *object*, the *representamen*, and the *interpretant*. The relationship between these parts is a central notion in semiotics. The object is defined as the actual/physical thing that a sign stands for; the representamen is the user who interprets the meaning of the sign in her/his mind; and the interpretant is the sign created in the mind of the user (Ferreira et al., 2005). Peirce further classified signs into three different categories: icon, index and symbol. The simplest form of these categories is icon, which is considered a visual representation of what it stands for. An index indicates what is being represented or, in other words, it is a graphical representation of the intended meaning. A symbol embodies a conventional and cultural relation between the meaning and the sign. Since symbols have no logical or direct relation to the intended meaning, previous experience or cultural knowledge is required for correct interpretation (Peirce et al., 1931). To distinguish between signs in the Peircean model and the signs in UIs, we will use the term icon in the subsequent sections of this paper.

A significant issue is the extent to which elements of UIs are effective at conveying sufficient information for the user to recognise and understand, or 'map', theories in spite of limited contextual familiarity (Stickel et al., 2014). If the concept that is represented by an icon is not immediately apparent, users may need supportive text tags to accurately interpret an icon's meaning. This highlights the necessity to account for user needs, as well as the connection between physical and cognitive direct design. Icons should be as unambiguous as possible (Bedford, 2014). The polysemic nature of icons – i.e. that an icon suggests multiple meanings/functions in a ***1:m*** relation - implies a subjective measurement that complicates the recognition and comprehension of symbols to arrive at an accurate associative conclusion concerning the symbol's function (Dessus & Peraya, 2007).

In this work, ambiguous icons are defined as icons that are visually identical but have different meanings. Table 1 presents an example of ambiguous icons taken from online holiday booking websites and mobile apps. For instance, from Table 1 it can be seen that two different meanings/functions were used for the same icon on online websites. Inconsistent usage of icons has been found on many online websites and mobile apps, but this study focuses specifically on holiday booking websites due to the current prevalence of booking flights or hotels through online websites or mobile apps.

Table 1. A Pair of Ambiguous Icons

Icon	*Function/Meaning*
	*Scrolls up to the top result*
	*Shares the details of the flight over social media*

This study investigates ambiguous icons in mobile devices. The limited physical screen space on mobile devices means that there is less space available to display icons and therefore there is a greater reliance on sequences of screens. Hence, we specifically investigate the effect of the sequence in which icons are presented on the accuracy of users' comprehension from a semiotics perspective. We first summarise existing semiotic studies. Subsequently, we investigate and critique a number of models and frameworks that utilise semiotics. We then report the design and method of our study. The results are presented and subsequently discussed with regard to users' cognitive processes. Finally, we suggest future directions for this work and conclude the paper.

2. RELATED WORK

A number of semiotic frameworks and models have been proposed for assessing icons in UIs. This section discusses the criteria proposed for developing icons that can be understood by users with no supplementary textual information, and also surveys semiotic frameworks utilised in HCI.

The extant literature places particular focus on the semiotic idea of indexicality, which clarifies the association between user-interface representations and user context (Jesper & Jeni, 2010). This analysis intends to expand the literature with regard to mobile interaction design, and understanding and characterising the dynamics between UI and user context.

Since the semiotic method considers the contextual foundation in the use of icons, it is useful for identifying and comprehending the impediments to accurately recognizing and interpreting the icons (Islam & Bouwman, 2015). Users interact with web interfaces while perceiving the meaning of icons displayed therein.

De Souza et al. (2006) have deconstructed the meta-communication procedure and the messages which explain this interplay; in other words an understanding of who the users are, their needs, preferences, and motives, all of which are encouraged by both the qualitative and interpretative processes utilised by semiotic engineering procedures. Semiotics has been utilised in more novel regions of HCI, such as the MuTable interface and the Multi-touch interface in a Tabletop application platform (Derboven et al., 2012). A comprehensive analysis of this MuTable Interface was conducted by De Souza et al. (2009) using the Communicability Evaluation Procedure (CEM).

It is necessary to analyse the general domain of mobile usability. The change from desktop-based computing to mobile devices embedded in all facets of social- and work life has made it necessary to use frameworks that analyse interactions over a variety of mobile contexts (Oulasvirta, 2004). However, there are several constraints and challenges to HCI practice concerning user perception that have resulted from this change (Zhang & Adipat, 2005). Small display size, screen resolution and regular reversal of interaction order and context (walking/driving) may all have a considerable effect on users' comprehension of display icons.

The limitations of mobile devices have semiotic effects: Since mobile devices have a limited display capability, icons exhibited on these devices will have a diminished volume to match the limited screen space. Thus, the total amount of information (image/verbal) conveyed by the icons to the mobile users is reduced and as a result, users are more likely to be presented with a series of screens on a mobile device. Hence, the users' interpretations might be affected – often adversely – by the mobile context and their working memory might be highly demanded. Conversely, on larger PCs with higher screen resolution, icons are richly exhibited with respect to the quantity of information that can be communicated to users.

The comprehension of icons is part of a cognitive process that is established in visual working memory (VWM) and determined by continual transformations. The acquisition and interpretation of icons and the function of memory are key to understanding the processes connected with icons. Visual understanding processes are explained by the Gestalt principles of group, which include connectedness, similarity, and proximity (Wilson, 2012). Working memory refers to the temporary period during which the mind combines experiences to create meaning, which is then stored in long-term memory (Trogu, 2015). The significance of this dynamic has been explored in a study conducted by Glanzer and Cunitz (1966), which found that free recall was associated with both short-term and long-term memory mechanisms.

The semiotic method of examining UIs provides deeper insight into the improvement of users' interpretations of signs through design. Moreover, differentiating the connection between user's interpretations in semiotics and the cognitive and mental impacts on this illustrates the exchange of information that occurs between designers and users in HCI.

In summary, many techniques (such as usability evaluation techniques) are utilised to enhance usability in the development of web-based and other interactive technologies (Fernandez et al., 2012). However, using semiotic methods on mobile web interfaces and mobile programs requires further investigation. Therefore, it is important to undertake additional research. With regard to the current state of users' interaction with websites and apps, there are several design challenges that must be addressed to enhance the accuracy of users' interpretation of icons. To bridge this gap within the research it is necessary to explore the amount of ambiguity caused by the polysemic nature of icons on a mobile device. Indeed, examining this ambiguity will help determine the impact of the navigation order/sequence on participants' interpretations of ambiguous icons.

3. STUDY DESIGN AND ANALYSIS METHOD

This study explored users' comprehension of ambiguous icons. Twenty participants were recruited for the study. All participants were adults and were aware of smart-phone technology. They were students and were studying at either undergraduate or postgraduate level. Participants were randomly allocated to one of two different groups. Each group consisted of ten participants who performed two tasks on a custom-designed holiday booking website: a flight-booking task and a hotel-booking task. One group navigated the website to search for a flight and then for a hotel. The other group navigated the website in the reverse order (first hotel then flight). All tests were conducted on an I-phone5s running Google Chrome.

Three icons were presented in each task. Table 2 displays the icons that were presented and their designed functions in both tasks. The icons formed three pairs of ambiguous icons, numbered as 1, 2 and 3 in Table 2. For example, pair 1 consisted of a heart icon with the function "likes the hotel" and a heart icon with the function "saves the flight details to the user's favourite list".

Table 2. Tested Icons

Task	***Hotel Booking***			***Flight Booking***		
Icon	1 	2 	3 	1 	2 	3 
Function	*likes the hotel*	*books the hotel*	*scrolls up to the top result*	*saves the flight details to the user's favorite list*	*expands the details of the flights*	*shares the details of the flight over social media*

The study sessions were run as semi-structured interviews. Participants were asked to undertake the tasks and, while doing so, were asked to interpret the meaning of the icons at two points in time: *a) pre-interaction/touching and b) post-interaction/touching*, The following questions were asked to explore participants' comprehension of the icons' functions in the two different interaction phases and to determine to what extent participants were confident about their interpretations in the pre-interaction phase. In the pre-interaction phase, they were asked: *What do you think would happen if you touched this icon? Why do you think that would happen? How confident are you about this interpretation? (Scale 0~100%). Which part of the interface was more helpful to understand this icon's function/meaning? (Icon only, Icon and its Context – percentage % in case of both).* In the post-interaction phase, they were asked: *What happened? Why do you think that happened?*

Sessions were audio-recorded. All the audio-recordings were transcribed into texts. Qualitative and quantitative analyses were applied in four main stages:

A) *Deductive:* the five-scale accuracy coding scheme proposed in Islam and Bouwman (2016) was applied to rate the accuracy of participants' interpretations of the meaning of the icons.

B) *Inductive:* inductive coding of the interview data was used to create relevant codes which justified participants' interpretations as well as the difference between the interpretations of the ambiguous icons in the pairs.

C) *Tracing* changes in participants' interpretations through a pairing process between icons in a sequential interaction. In this process, we compared participants' interpretations in post-interaction for the first icons of the pairs with their interpretations in pre-interaction for the second icons of the same pairs.

D) *Summarising* the results obtained in the aforementioned stages utilising descriptive statistics.

4. ANALYTICAL RESULTS

In the following sections, the results are presented in terms of the accuracy of users' interpretations, icon pairing across interfaces and users' confidence in their interpretations.

4.1 Accuracy of Users' Interpretations

With regard to the accuracy of interpretations between the two groups, there were significant differences between the responses in the pre-interaction stage. The pre-interaction responses were coded on the 5-point accuracy scale *{accurate, moderate, conflicting, erroneous, and incapable}* (Islam & Bouwman, 2016). As Figure 1 indicates for the group-1 interaction sequence, almost three times as many icons were accurately interpreted according to the designers' intended interpretation, compared to the alternative sequence in group-2. No significant difference in terms of the number of icons was found to be conflicting or erroneous. However, almost as many icons were coded as *incapable* in group-2 (i.e. when the user was unable to interpret the meaning of an icon by saying 'I don't know'). In other words, for group-2, a larger number of participants were unable to interpret the icon at all. For the post-interaction sequence, the results indicate that in most cases the participants' interpretations matched the designer's assigned meaning.

In most cases across both groups, the objects represented in the icons were found to be highly recognisable. Figure 2 reveals that the majority of participants responded that icon and context combined were more useful in understanding the icon's function/meaning than the icon alone at the pre-interaction stage.

4.2 Pairing Ambiguous Icons across Web Interfaces

While the previous analysis explores the accuracy of icon interpretations, further analysis was necessary to identify the effect of sequence interactions on participants' interpretations. The data were analysed for each sequence, for each participant, to identify whether different interpretations occurred for a given pair of icons. A total of six icons were used, consisting of three pairs: icons 1 and 4 were identical; icons 2 and 5 were identical but differed in terms of direction; and icons 3 and 6 were identical. Figure 3 illustrates the icon pairing process in a sequence.

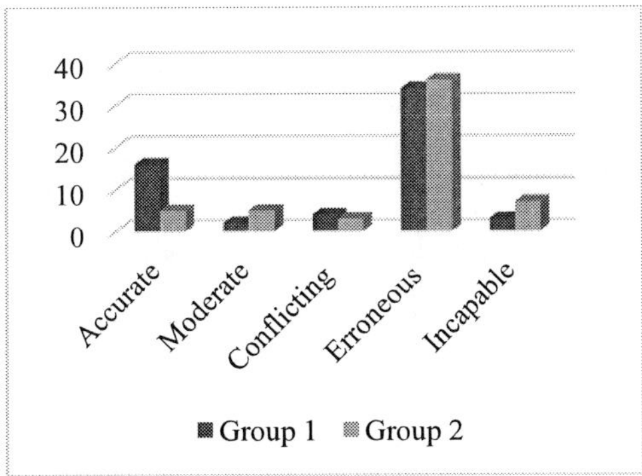

Figure 1. Pre-Interaction Interpretation Accuracy

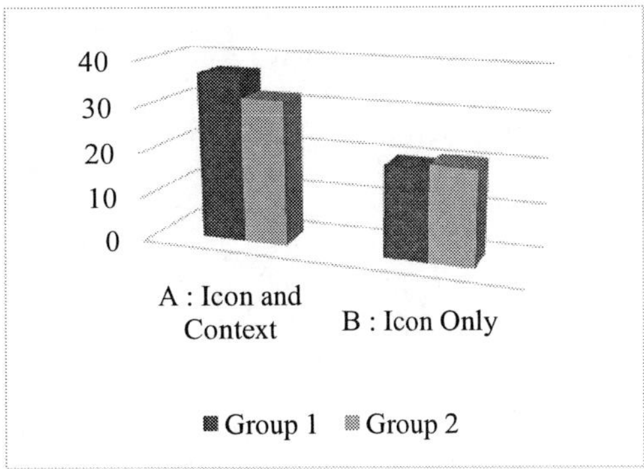

Figure 2. Icon Understandability

In order to analyse the effect of the sequence of interactions on the accuracy of interpretations, the reasons cited by each participant for each icon pair need to be examined. Overall, the results indicate that the interaction sequence was cited as a reason for participant's interpretations more often for icons 1-4 and icons 3-6 in group-2 compared to group-1. Figures 4 and 5 display the results of this analysis. The results strongly indicate that sequence interactions influenced participants' interpretations (multiple contexts refer to responses where the participant attributed the interpretation to more than one context: icon, external context, internal context). Further analysis was undertaken to compare the post-interaction interpretations for one icon with the pre-interaction interpretations for the second icon in the same pair. For each participant, the similarity of the interpretation across the sequence was compared. The reasons were cited to identify the effect of the first icon's post-interaction with the second icon's pre-interaction interpretation. Finally, the accuracy of the interpretations within their respective interaction were also analysed.

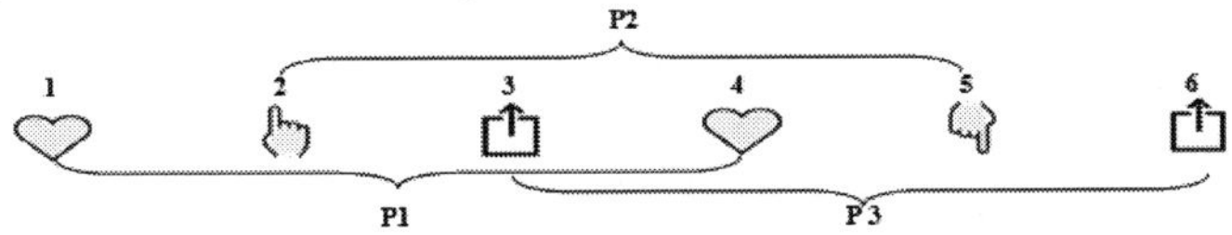

Figure 3. Icon Pairing

For icon pairs (1, 4) and (3, 6) in group-1, the post-interaction interpretations are identical in nearly all cases. The reasons cited for these icon pairs indicate a sequence interaction effect. For icons 1-4, in 80% of cases the previous interaction is cited as the main (50%) or secondary (30%) reason for their pre-interaction interpretation. In terms of accuracy for icon-1, 60% of cases are accurate and 40% are erroneous. However, in the majority of cases for icon-4, the interpretations are erroneous, meaning that they do not match the designers' intended meaning. Based on the reasons cited, it can be seen that sequence interaction had a significant influence on subsequent interpretations. This pattern is reflected in the responses for icons 3 and 6. For icons 2 and 5, where the icons are marginally different, the interpretations were different in 90% of cases.

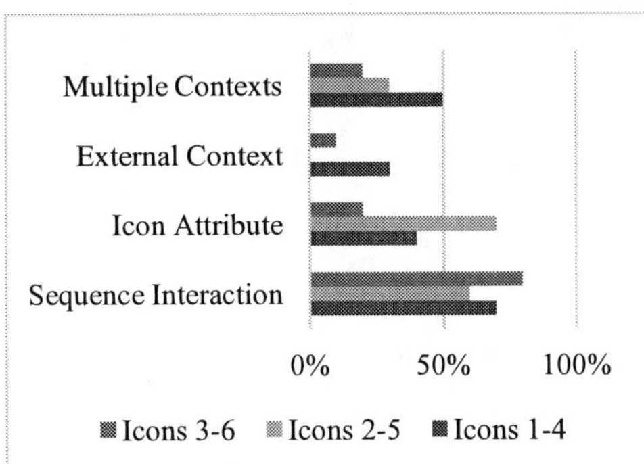

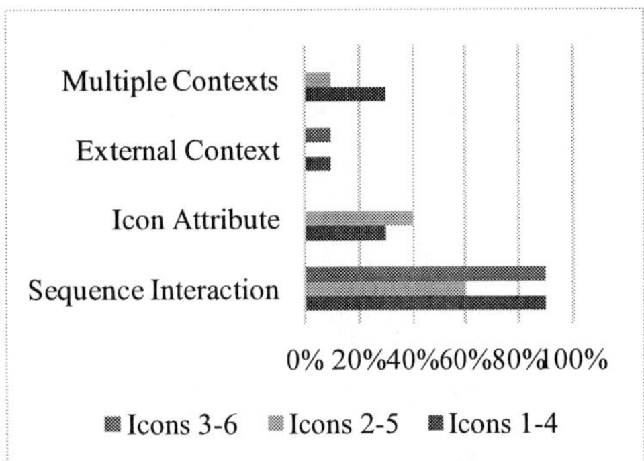

(NB: Percentages reflect the percentage of users that cited this factor. Overlap due to multiple factors cited in each response)

Figure 4. Reasons Cited in Group-1

Figure 5. Reasons Cited in Group-2

These results exhibit a similarity for icon pairings 1 and 4 among both groups in terms of interpretation and accuracy. For icons 1 and 4, and icons 2 and 5, the reasons cited were evenly balanced between previous interaction and icon attributes. For icons 3 and 6, the majority cited previous interaction as the main reason for respondents' interpretations.

Overall, the results indicate that sequence interactions significantly impact the accuracy of users' interpretations. In both groups, sequence interaction either significantly decreases or has no effect on interpretation accuracy. There was no change in the accuracy of participants' interpretations for more than 70% of cases in group-1. The results indicate a decrease in accuracy between icon pairs, with the participants' interpretations of the respective pair changing significantly from Accurate to Erroneous. In 25% of cases, no change was noted. In this instance, participants who had erroneously interpreted the first icon in the pair subsequently adopted the same interpretation for the second icon. Therefore, when sequence interaction is erroneously interpreted, that interpretation is recalled for the next icon in the pair.

The results from group-2 indicate a lower percentage of cases (45%) where accuracy decreased significantly for the icon pairs. Only 20% indicated an increase in accuracy, while roughly 33% of cases recorded no change in accuracy level between the icons. This no change result is similar to group-1, in that in all cases participants who had erroneously interpreted the first icon in the pair then adopted the same interpretation for the second icon.

The largest effects were noted for icon pairs (1, 4), and (3, 6), which were solely influenced by previous interaction events in 60% of participants, who had based their interpretation on a pre-interaction factor. For these icons, sequence interaction was found to be the most significant factor in accuracy of interpretation. The results for icon pair (2, 5) reveal that sequence interaction was cited less frequently by respondents. For this icon pair, a marginal difference in the icon in terms of its orientation led 40% of participants to cite the icon attribute as the primary factor influencing their interpretation. Further analysis was necessary to determine the key characteristics of the responses where significant differences were identified in interpretation accuracy.

4.3 Users' Confidence

In relation to users' confidence, a higher level of confidence in icon interpretation was exhibited by participants in group-1 compared to group-2. In group-1, more than 25% of participants on average cited between 75% and 100% confidence compared to group-2. Icon level confidence results indicate a progression from the first icon to the second icon in each pair. For icons 1 and 4, confidence levels increased from the first icon to the second. In both groups, participants interpreted the icons' meanings with 100% confidence 21 times for the second icon compared to 8 times for the first icon in all pairs. For group-1, participants interpreted the meaning of icon-1 with 100% confidence 3 times compared to 7 times for icon-4. Confidence levels were overall higher for icon-5 compared to icon-2 by a marginal level. The change in confidence from icons 3 to 6 is highest for this pair, with a significantly higher level of confidence for icon-6 compared to icon-3. For group-2, the change of accuracy exhibits a marginal change between icons 2, 5, 3, and 6. Overall, the results indicate that participants become more confident for interpretations in the second icon in each pair suggesting a sequence interaction effect. Confidence levels between icon pairs also support the impact of sequence interaction. For both groups, confidence levels improved progressively during the sequences. When comparing icon pairs in both groups, the results indicate higher overall levels of confidence among the first and second icons in each pair.

5. DISCUSSION

This section provides a summary of the key findings of the study and presents a discussion of the theoretical and practical implications. The results of the study indicate that the accuracy of participants' interpretations varied significantly among icons. The data reveals that accuracy of interpretation decreases from high to low during the sequence. In the majority of cases in both groups, the previous interaction in the sequence erroneously influenced the interpretation of the second icon in a given pair. Thus, this discussion explores the semantic implications of the sequence interactions implemented in the study and on the influence of syntactic, pragmatic, social, and environmental factors that represent the semiotic layers.

The evidence demonstrates that all participants drew on long-term, short-term and working memory when interpreting the icons. Participants in this study especially drew on working memory, consciously retaining information relevant to a given task (Bouissac, 1999).

The subject interviews during the pre-interaction and post-interaction interpretations imply a 'sub-vocalisation' process when participants viewed the icons. Within this process, the participant subconsciously names the objects being viewed in their mind. This allows people to rapidly reach meaningful conclusions when perceiving and understanding a visual or verbal organisation (Noizet & Pynte, 1976; Logie, 1996; Baddeley 2014). This is consistent with Braddley's model (2000; 2014), which characterises the working memory component as playing a central role in binding information from two subsidiary systems: visuo-spatial and phonological. The model implies the interaction of both long-term and short-term memory. This is reflected in the responses of the participants in this study, as they drew from previous knowledge and working knowledge generated from the sequence of tasks, including icon attributes (Atkinson & Shiffrin, 1968; Burgess & Hitch, 2005).

However, while the results of the present study implicate the cognitive processes that bind information from different sources, it is also worth noting that sequence interactions had a significant impact on the accuracy of interpretation. Participants consistently cited information from previous sequence interactions as the primary factor that influenced their interpretations.

In all icon pairs, participants recalled information from the previous icon or interaction elements. Recalling information that has been recently memorised or accessed is known as the 'recency effect' (Murphy et al., 2006). When the icon was recently viewed, participants immediately associated their interpretation with the previous icon. This aligns with the theoretical principle that items which have been recently accessed are easier to remember (Burgess & Hitch, 2005), given that the information from the most recent icon interpretations influenced subsequent interpretations. The results suggest that the order of the icons affects the accuracy of the participants' interpretations, which is consistent with previous studies where the interpretation of the first icon in each pair was recalled (Murphy et al., 2006). Indeed, participants in our study consistently attributed significance to the first interpretation. This serial effect is supported by other studies, which found that immediate free recall for items that were successively recalled often came from nearby serial positions (Howard & Kahana, 1999; Deese & Kaufman, 1957). However, this research is distinct from Howard and Kahana (1999) in several ways. Their primary focus was on contextual variability and the effects of serial position on free recall in relation to words. Furthermore, they employed an experimental analysis based on analytic simulations. Conversely, this research is concerned with the accuracy of interpretations of ambiguous icons and sequence interactions.

In instances where another icon was viewed recently, participants' interpretations were associated with the previous icon. The conversion to long-term memory is evidenced by the learning processes that participants described with regard to their interpretation and confidence levels: *"When I was in the flights page it was like something new; new icons; but when I transfer to the hotels page, I was confident with the icons given";* or *"This icon is new for me; I wasn't expecting this before. If I face it next time, I will expect it"*. This is reflected in the variation in participants' confidence levels. Moreover, the negative change in interpretation accuracy indicates that user interpretations should be maximised through the use of a semiotic analysis. Table 3 lists the codes that were extracted in the inductive stage of the analysis; They are associated with examples from participants' interpretations.

Furthermore, a comparison of the pre-interaction reasons for interpretations between the first and second icons in the pair implicates the sequence interaction effect as a contextual factor. The reasons cited for the interpretation of the first icon of three pairs indicate that participants rely significantly on external context, and icon positing and direction. However, for the second icon in each of the three pairs, participants predominantly cited the previous icon effect or the previous interaction as the main reason for their interpretation. Nevertheless, non-influential sequencing can undermine the interpretation, as the results indicate that working memory may override information from the latest sequence interaction. This is evidenced by the high number of Erroneous responses for the second icon in each pair.

Table 3. Extracted Codes

Code	*Participants' Interpretations*
Confusion	*'Because this hand is pointing upwards the finger, see I'm confused now because with this hand'.*
Consistency	*'The symbol shouldn't be used for different purposes'.*
Co-occurrence effects	*'Mainly three symbols the first one that shows me the favourite of this one. This one I'm not sure but I think it gunna be selecting it; it is because of the neighbour icon functionality'.*
External Context	*'I have seen it in WhatsApp. I have experienced this before in WhatsApp and it's for sharing'.*
Intuitiveness	*'It's very intuitive that heart as a like, I understand what it means I think it doesn't require to be mention interpretation as well'.*
Learning	*'This icon is new for me; I wasn't expecting this before. If I face it next time I will expect it'.*
Personal Context	*'I don't think many people download hotel information'.*
Lack of Familiarity	*'I'm looking at the icon for the first time in my life'.*
Positioning	*In the icon pair (2, 5): 'And even the position because down here in the bottom right I would presume it's for booking a flight or going next'. In the icon pair (3, 6): 'Because it is right to the hand and it is near to the flight details'.*
Previous Icon Effect	*'I feel more confident for this meaning from the last page'.*
Signified	*'For favourite you may use star symbol instead'.*

The positioning or direction of icons was cited multiple times as a factor that affected participants' interpretations. It is possible that a co-occurrence effect occurred in a small number of cases. Participants referred to pop-up messages and neighbouring icon functionality as co-occurrence factors in their interpretation. Furthermore, the intuitiveness of the icons was cited by a small number of participants as an important factor in their interpretation. Maximising this factor can support the interpretation of the icon, particularly for novice users who are not familiar with the icons in question. Users deliberated on the significance of each symbol with regard to its meaning and what it represented. In some cases, syntactic elements were noted in users' deliberations such as position, clarity and presentation of the icon (Islam & Bouwan, 2016).

The interview responses often referenced the importance of personal contexts. Participants cited a range of different personal contexts from their external experiences in interpreting icons: such as previous experience with social media and mobile device applications, and even desktop applications. Some icons were recognised as being widely used in external applications and websites, and associated with common functions such as 'favouriting', liking or sharing. Participants emphasised the importance of text support, where one participant stated it reinforced their interpretation.

Some evidence suggests the importance of consistency between external contexts and internal contexts. Several of the participant narratives noted a significant level of ambiguity in interpreting the icons. One participant's comment emphasises the significance of multiple factors, stating that "the information and the context are not enough and the icon is index finger pointing up; so it's really complicated for me". While the benefit of sequence interaction through the recency and icon effect can support interpretation accuracy, inconsistency or conflicting signals between external and internal contexts generate significant levels of confusion that undermine and mislead participants' interpretations.

Overall, in spite of the quantity of data that supports the effect of participants' personal contexts on interpretation, it is clear that participants attach greater significance to the internal context. The results from this study are in accordance with the contextual representations emphasised by Burgess and Hitch (2005), in contrast to short-term memory models. Users in this model retrieve and evaluate information from contextual items. Burgess and Hitch (2005) have found that the relative significance of different items can be measured by the recency-weighted sum of the context of each item. Consistency was a key theme that emerged from the participant interviews, emphasising that the utilisation of icons throughout the entire sequence should be consistent. Indeed, doing so can minimise confusion and maximise recency effects. Furthermore, subsequent rehearsal and retrieval can promote conversion to long-term memory if the same symbols are used within sequence interactions.

6. FUTURE WORK

This study investigated the impact of sequence on how accurately users interpreted a set of ambiguous icons. The ambiguity was controlled for by distinguishing between the meanings of two visually identical icons. However, the level of inaccuracy and uncertainty in the participant's understanding of an icon also vary by the amount of visual similarity between icons. This was indicated in our study by participants' interpretations of icons 2 and 5. The consideration of how the visual similarity of icons impacts on how well users recognise them, is worthy of future detailed research. The degree of similarity between icons might well influence the level to which similar, but different, icons are recognisable to users. We intend to observe users' behaviour by employing an eye-tracking technique to elicit viewing times of similar icons and thus, quantify the variation in speed with which participants recognise the icons. Users' speed of recognition may vary in accordance with the icons' visual similarity. This work will be conducted on a larger sample of users.

Furthermore, as the capacity of working memory is finite, it limits participants' ability to remember the totality of an interaction. It appears that judgments are often unintentionally based on incomplete memory subsets (Wiswede et al., 2007). Guan et al. (2006) also considered this effect, and to focus on it, measured the degree to which participants failed to report elements they had viewed. That study found that participants did not discuss elements they had viewed in half the cases. To gain a deeper insight into inner emotional states and cognitive processes, researchers should not only rely on objective measures, but also draw on participants' subjective judgments and memory employing think-aloud protocols, questionnaires, and interview: qualitative insights are key to further progress.

7. CONCLUSION

In summary, the findings from this study contribute new knowledge to the existing design perspective that considers diverse, external (social) and contextual factors that influence users' cognitive processes when they interact with a modern graphical user interface. The results suggest that the sequence of interaction is a key factor that affects how accurately users assess the meaning of ambiguous icons. In turn, this naturally impacts on users' comprehension of these icons. Therefore, it might be useful, in a sequence of interaction, to have a design technique to inform the design of a mobile interface, where that technique will help designers increase the accuracy of users' interpretations when the interface is used. Our insights are consistent with Howard and Kahana (1999), who found that context provides a signal or cue that improves users' subsequent recall of icons. Our findings provide evidence that participants drew upon the sequential context of information: when interpreting the second icon in a pair, they drew on their experience of the first in the pair.

REFERENCES

Atkinson, R. C. and Shiffrin, R. M., 1968. Human memory: A proposed system and its control processes. In: Spence, K. W. and Spence, J. T., 1968. *The psychology of learning and motivation (Volume 2)*. New York: Academic Press. pp. 89–195.

Baddeley, A., 2000. The episodic buffer: a new component of working memory? *Trends in Cognitive Sciences*, 4(11), pp. 417-423.

Baddeley, A.D., 2014. *Essentials of human memory*. Hove, UK: Psychology Press Classic Editions.

Bedford, A., 2014. *Icon usability*. NNGroup Usability Report. [online] Available at: <http://www. nngroup. com/articles/icon-usability/> [Accessed May 2018].

Bouissac, P., 1999, Semiotics and the science of memory. In: *Conference on Semiotics and the European Heritage*. Dresden, February 1999.

Burgess, N. and Hitch, G., 2005. Computational models of working memory: Putting long-term memory into context. *Trends in Cognitive Sciences*, 9(11), pp.535-541.

Charles S. Peirce. et al., 1931, *Collected papers of Charles Sanders Peirce*, London: Belknap Press of Harvard U.P.

De Souza, Clarisse Sieckenius. et al., 2006. *The Semiotic Inspection Method*. in *Proceedings of VII Brazilian Symposium on Human Factors in Computing Systems*. New York, NY, USA: ACM.

De Souza, Clarisse Sieckenius and Carla Faria Leitão, 2009, *Semiotic engineering methods for scientific research in HCI.* Synthesis Lectures on Human-Centered Informatics, 2(1): p. 1-122.

Derboven, Jan, et al., 2012, *Semiotic analysis of multi-touch interface design: The MuTable case study*, International Journal of Human-Computer Studies. 70(10): p. 714-728.

Dessus, P. and Peraya, D., 2007. *Cognitive modeling of icon comprehension. Enhancing learning through HCI*. Hershey: Idea Group Publishing.

Deese, J. and Kaufman, R.A., 1957. Serial effects in recall of unorganized and sequentially organized verbal material. *Journal of Experimental Psychology*, 54(3), p.180.

Fernandez, Adrian. et al., 2012, *A systematic review on the effectiveness of web usability evaluation methods*. in *Evaluation & Assessment in Software Engineering (EASE 2012), 16th International Conference on*: IET.

Ferreira, J., et al., 2005. The semiotics of user interface redesign. *Proceedings of the Sixth Australasian Conference on User interface*, 40. Australian Computer Society.

Glanzer, M. and Cunitz, A.R., 1966. Two storage mechanisms in free recall. *Journal of Verbal Learning and Verbal Behavior*, 5(4), pp.351-360.

Guan, Z. et al., 2006. The validity of the stimulated retrospective think-aloud method as measured by eye tracking. In: GRINTER, R., RODDEN, T., AOKI, P., CUTRELL, E., JEFFRIES, R. and OLSON, G. (eds.), *Proceedings of the SIGCHI Conference on Human Factors in Computing Systems*, pp. 1253–1262. New York: ACM Press.

Howard, M.W. and Kahana, M.J., 1999. Contextual variability and serial position effects in free recall. *Journal of Experimental Psychology: Learning, Memory, and Cognition*, 25(4), p.923.

Islam, M.N. and Bouwman, H., 2015. An assessment of a semiotic framework for evaluating user-intuitive Web interface signs. *Universal Access in the Information Society*, 14, pp.563-582.

Islam, M.N. and Bouwman, H., 2016. Towards user–intuitive web interface sign design and evaluation: A semiotic framework. *International Journal of Human-Computer Studies*, 86, pp.121-137.

Jesper Kjeldskov and Jeni Paay, 2010. Indexicality: Understanding Mobile Human-computer Interaction in Context ACM Trans. Comput.-Hum. Interact., Vol. 17, No. 4. (December 2010), doi:10.1145/1879831.1879832

Logie, R.H., 1996. The seven ages of working memory. In: J.T.E. Richardson, R.H. Logie, E.R. Stoltzfus, L. Hasher, R.T. Zacks, and R.W. Engle (eds.), *Working memory and human cognition*. New York: Oxford University Press. pp. 31-59.

Murphy, J., et al., 2006. Primacy and recency effects on clicking behavior. *Journal of Computer Mediated Communication*, 11(2), pp.522-535.

Noizet, G. and Pynte, J., 1976. Implicit labelling and readiness for pronunciation during the perceptual process. *Perception*, 5(2), pp. 217-223.

Oulasvirta, Antti, *Human-computer interaction in mobile context: a cognitive resources perspective.* Unpublished licentiate thesis, University of Helsinki, Finland, 2004.

Trogu, P., 2015. Working memory and background knowledge: Cognitive science in the design classroom. *FORMakademisk*, 8(1), pp.1-17.

Stickel, C., et al., 2014. Cutting edge design or a beginner's mistake? - semiotic inspection of iOS7 icon design changes. In: *International Conference of Design, User Experience, and Usability*. Springer International Publishing. pp. 358-369.

Wiswede, D. et al., 2007. Serial position effects in free memory recall: an ERP-study. *Biological Psychology*, 75, pp.185–193.

Wilson, K.D., 2012. *The effects of gestalt principles on diagram comprehension: an empirical approach*. [online] Available at: <http://dl.acm.org/citation.cfm?id=2521076> [Accessed May 2018].

Zhang, Dongsong and Boonlit Adipat, 2005 *Challenges, methodologies, and issues in the usability testing of mobile applications.* International Journal of Human-Computer Interaction, 18(3): p. 293-308.

EVALUATING SYSTEM ACCESSIBILITY USING AN EXPERIMENTAL PROTOCOL BASED ON USABILITY

Ana Carolina Oliveira Lima[1*], Maria de Fátima Queiroz Vieira[2†], Ronaldo da Silva Ferreira[3‡], Yuska P. C. Aguiar[4§], Moisés Pereira Bastos[5**] and Sandro Laerth Maciel Lopes Junior[6††]

[1]*Center for Innovation in Industrial Robotics and Control, Ave. Darcy Vargas, 1200 - Park Ten, Manaus - AM, 69050-020, Brazil.*

[2]*Federal University of Campina Grande, R. Aprígio Veloso, Street. 882 - University, Campina Grande - PB, 58429-900, Brazil*

[3]*Nilton Lins University, Ave. Prof. Nilton Lins, 3259 - Flowers, Manaus - AM, 69058-580, Brazil*

[4]*Federal University of Paraiba, University City, s/n - Castelo Branco, João Pessoa - PB, 58051-900, Brazil*

[5]*State University of Amazonas, Ave. Darcy Vargas, 1200 - Park Ten, Manaus - AM, 69050-020, Brazil*

[6]*Minho University, Campus de Azurém, 4800-058 Guimarães, Portugal*

ABSTRACT

This article aims to a systematic approach to assess product accessibility and the adapted system of an experimental protocol originally designed to evaluate product's usability. The adapted protocol approach is focused on products and systems for visually impaired. The developed study with the proposed protocol investigates assistive technology adequacy to target users, regardless of their gender, age or previous experience in this technology usage. The tasks performed by 30 users community were categorized as activities of entertainment, learning and social inclusion. The data obtained from the experiment carried out with the protocol application enabled the test of a set of assumptions about the protocol usage.

KEYWORDS

Assistive Technology, Accessibility and Usability

1. INTRODUCTION

Accessibility has become a major concern of computer system developers. However, unlike its counterpart - Usability, it does not have an established protocol to evaluate quality in products and systems developed for users. For many interactive software systems, a large part of the interaction between user and technology depends on the use of visually presented material (ISO, 2008). Individuals, who are visually intact, typically use the keyboard, mouse, or other pointing devices to provide information and various screen types as output devices. On the other hand, blind or visually impaired users employ their auditory and tactile senses as visual sense. In this case, the typical non-visual forms of interface used in interactive software are auditory or tactile (Sodnik, Grega and Tomazic, 2011). Screen readers, software most commonly used by visually impaired users, are based on speech synthesizers that read the contents of computer screen using synthesized artificial speech (V. Raman and S. Yesilada, Y., 2003, Thiessen And Chen, 2008).To evaluate the usability of devices and accessibility systems, it is essential to follow an experimental protocol that provides a script with procedures and it is aided by documents that guide the evaluator during experiments planning and conduct. This research goal is to explain the factors that can lead a prediction on assistive technology impact on the target population.

[*] ana.lima.leal@gmail.com
[†] fatima@dee.ufcg.edu.br
[‡] poncairedk@gmail.com
[§] yuska@dcx.ufpb.br
[**] mpbastos@uea.edu.br
[††] sandrojr2001@yahoo.com.br

In particular, it examines how accessibility can affect the visually impaired users' behavior when using screen readers and Braille keyboards. To support this research, this work proposes an existing experimental protocol adaptation, originally designed to evaluate the interactive products and systems usability, adapting it to evaluate the usability level of accessibility resources available to the visually impaired, thus classifying the accessibility level from the utilitarian point of view. Help resources can consist of specific systems and components designed to increase accessibility levels, such as hardware, software, or input / output devices. The existing experimental protocol for usability evaluation was conceived, formalized and adopted over the years in research and products usability evaluation in the Laboratory of Human Machine Interfaces (LIHM) of the Federal University of Campina Grande (UFCG) (Aguiar and Vieira, 2009), (Lima, Vieira, Aguiar, 2010). The adapted protocol was validated in its suitability to evaluate screen readers accessibility level and Braille keyboard, when used by blind people and visually impaired.

2. BACKGROUND

To evaluate devices usability and accessibility features, an experimental protocol was adopted to provide a set of procedures and related documents to guide the evaluator during experiments planning and conduction. In the research literature, few studies have been found mentioning the adoption of a protocol during the devices usability evaluation and resources for accessibility.

The research, cited in (Hansen, Mislevy, et al., 2005), evaluated internet assistive technology, while (Sanchez and Hassler, 2017) cites an evaluation of speech synthesizers. However, these assessments were qualitative in nature, e.g. based on user opinion and focused exclusively on screen readers and speech synthesizers used to access Internet sites. The evaluation experiments cited did not mention the support of an experimental protocol and were limited to a small number of participants. Samples of users with fewer than 10 participants were not significant to support the reported inferences. In addition, the mechanisms used for data collection and analysis were only superficially addressed. In the researched literature, there were few reports of usability tests applied to evaluate the accessibility of devices for visually impaired users. Here follows a brief presentation of the relevant work found on this subject.

In the research described in (Hansen, Mislevy et al., 2005) a protocol for assessing accessibility features, more specifically the JAWS screen reader, is mentioned, based on observation of task performance followed by a user satisfaction survey. The tasks were designed to assess the user's skills in: reading comprehension, listening comprehension, grammatical structure, and writing and math skills using the tool.

The usability test was performed with fifteen participants: four blinds, two with low vision, three with learning disabilities, two were deaf, two deaf-blind and two without any type of disability. Despite its contribution, this protocol is focused on evaluating a screen reader when accessing the Internet and is not comprehensive enough to be used in the evaluation of other resource types. The need of specific participants during the tests (such as human assistants to act as interpreters) is not mentioned.

In reference (Sánchez and Hassler, 2017), a protocol is described to evaluate the usability of AUDIOMUD; A virtual reality software game for blind users. The game goal is to place the player in the human body in order to cure diseases, based on the listed symptoms, changing the conditions to which the body is subjected. The interaction with this virtual environment is based on a text reader (synthesizer) that guides the player along the navigation allowing interactions with other players, through a system of chat. In (Hansen, Mislevy, et al., 2005), the adopted protocol during the reported experiment is composed by the following steps: game introduction; Observing the user during the interaction, while recording the experiment in photo and video; Applying a questionnaire to raise the user satisfaction level and report the results.

It is important to note that in most of the publications cited, the experiments were designed to evaluate a specific device or help resource designed to improve the accessibility of web browsing activity.

Authors in (Hansen, Mislevy, et al., 2005) propose guidelines to ensure e-commerce sites security for the blind, while in (Borges, 2009) solutions are proposed to ensure accessibility in digital libraries.

From the review, it was clear that in rare cases where an experimental protocol is described, this is too shallow to answer the questions raised about the conditions under which the tests were performed. In addition, the sample size was too small to support the conclusions drawn. Hence the need to propose an experimental protocol to support the usability devices evaluation and systems designed to support the accessibility and accessibility level achieved.

3. MATERIALS AND METHODS

The experiment consisted in evaluating the usability of three accessibility aid features: a Braille keyboard and two voice synthesizers for blind users. The voice synthesizers used were DOSVOX and JAWS. DOSVOX software was developed for Portuguese language and it is available for free for blind people. The software tools evaluated were: text editor, screen reader and e-mail. JAWS is software marketed by Freedom Scientific and the features tested were the screen reader and the internet browser. The version chosen for tests was the most recent one at the time of the test preparation (version 4.1), with a platform developed for DOS environment instead of Windows. The JAWS version was 12.0, also the latest available below. JAWS and DOSVOX were chosen because of their popularity among users of the Institute for Blind People as well as the Braille keyboard.

An experimental usability protocol consists a set of interrelated steps, processes and activities to guide an evaluation team during the experiment phases: planning, conducting, collecting data, analyzing and reporting the results. These steps are presented in (Aguiar and Vieira, 2009). The adapted protocol supported the planning and evaluation phases of usability assessment experiences during which people with visual impairment participated in performing tasks to demonstrate the suitability of specific accessibility features. As the protocol proposed by (Aguiar and Vieira, 2009) has a comprehensive and modular structure, the adaptation implied to accommodate the usability assessment of the accessibility of systems and devices that resulted in small changes in their steps and processes, without changes in their structure. Its application is to verify that a visual support, under evaluation, conforms to an adequate technical standard of accessibility. The adequacy requirements are presented in (Lima, Vieira and Aguiar, 2010).

3.1 Inference of the User's help towards Performance and Motivation Levels

During the experiment, the choice of tasks aimed to investigate the hypothesis of how the aids could interfere in the users' performance and in their motivation level. Three types of activities were planned in the categories: learning, leisure and social inclusion.

Before starting activities, users were asked to express their preferences by choosing the keyboard type (Braille or conventional keyboard) and the desired media on which they wanted to read the script describing the tasks (Ledor, JAWS or DOSVOX system or printed Braille). Likewise, users had the option of answering the questions at the end of each task: writing in Braille, typing on the keyboard, or expressing orally when their voice would be recorded. The following is a description of tasks.

- Task 1 (task category: learning) - consisted of reading, with speech synthesizer support, and understanding a predefined text. Users had to choose between three texts, in different themes (1- World Cup, 2- Brazilian dance festival and 3 - explanations on how to apply for jobs in the public sector). After reading, users answered related questions.
- Task 2 (task category: fun, entertainment) - The user alone or, when needed, with the help of a team member expert, was asked to access a news site; Select and read news; And highlight (orally or in writing) the aspects considered most relevant and interesting.
- Task 3 (task category: social inclusion): The user alone or, when needed, with the help of a team member expert, was requested to access a specific financial website (Caixa Econômica Federal), which is the financial agent from the Brazilian government's program that offers loans to low-income families to buy houses and simulate the application for a loan, filling out the necessary forms.

3.2 User Group Recruitment

Recruitment of participants (users) was carried out through interviews based on the profile of the individuals and their availability and interest in participating in the research. Because of this research, thirty-two people were chosen and agreed to participate in the tests.

The number of participants was the direct result of their perception of relevance and potential impact to their community. Of the recruited group, 30 participants were identified as beginners or frequent users of JAWS and DOSVOX screen readers, who offer similar features. Each task was assigned an estimated period of time. The group of participants consisted of blind individuals, aged between 18 and 60, both genders, with blindness or acquired blindness, from a generalized context (teachers and school students for the blind).

This study focused on participant's computing skills and familiarity with screen readers. According to their abilities they were classified as beginners, intermediate and advanced. Beginners rarely used computers and had poor screen reader skills. Intermediate users were learning to use screen readers, and expert users were highly skilled in using screen readers and computers.

3.3 Group Performance: Testing Criteria

The groups were compared in performance using the ANOVA test, with classification criteria and the Tukey test, to evaluate the conditions of normality and homogeneity necessary for the tests validation. The system used for analysis was Minitab 15 (Minitab - 2012). The ANOVA and Tukey tests were chosen to compare the averages among the three groups of users, depending on the characteristics in the sampling universe (size and homogeneity) and the significance criterion for the two tests. In order to support this analysis, the following metrics were considered: total number of errors, time spent on the task, number of times the request was requested, number of errors due to interpretation of the text; Number of times participants reported difficulty understanding audio and related incorrect actions.

3.4 Group Performance Testing

The usability test followed the steps of the experimental protocol, with preparation of materials followed by a pilot test to validate the adequacy of resources and materials directed to the data collection and analysis of variables of interest. The experiments were carried out at the Laboratory of Human Machine Interfaces (LIHM) of the Federal University of Campina Grande (UFCG), and at the Instituto dos Cegos, Campina Grande. Users and usability specialists followed the procedures specified in the experimental protocol, duly adapted to the specific context of working with visually impaired people.

As specified in the protocol, participants were invited to sign an agreement stating the purpose of the experiment and the rules of participation, including their right to anonymity. You should highlight their right to stop participation at any time during the test. Conditions, accepted, participants were also asked to state otherwise if they agreed to the recording of video images. All participants agreed to video recording. At the beginning of the session, participants received the test script containing a description of each task to be performed. The script was available in Braille printed form and in electronic format, which could be read using a screen reader.

After introducing the participant to the test, they were asked to perform the tasks specified in the script. During the test, participants were filmed, and data were pooled for further analysis.

4. OBJECTIVES

The main objective of this research is to provide a procedure set, oriented by a protocol that can be clear and rigorous, allowing the replication of results regarding the accessibility claims of products and systems, thus validating their robustness.

During this research, the Braille keyboard was evaluated comparatively with the voice synthesizers, due to a generalized opinion that, despite the tactile feedback that facilitates the visual sensorial substitution, its adoption could be weakened by the increasing use of speech synthesizers. The goal during the experiment was comparing user preferences and effectiveness when performing tasks with both.

The performance evaluation was based on the following set of metrics: total time spent performing task; Completion of the task (completed successfully, completed only with help, completed, but failed, aborted); And the number of times the participant has asked for help. The main assumption was that the nature of the task could interfere with the participant's performance.

5. RESULTS

The percentage data presented in table 1 was obtained according to items 3.1 and 3.2, respectively, where the final states of Tasks 1, 2 and 3 are represented by the groups of participants classified as experienced, inexperienced and intermediate, according to with 3.3.

Table 1. Performance levels of participants versus nature of tasks

Participants	Task1: learning (A); Task 2: fun (B); Task3: social inclusion (C). Portion concluded (%)											
	Incomplete			With aid			Successfully			Failed		
	A	B	C	A	B	C	A	B	C	A	B	C
Experienced	0	0	0	0	0	0	13	19	40	19	29	60
Inexperienced	0	43	0	36	0	0	0	0	0	0	9	0
Intermediate	0	0	0	32	0	0	0	0	0	0	0	0

Task 1, most users requested help to run it, e.g. 36% of inexperienced users and 32% of intermediate users, while only the group of experienced users could perform the task, where 13% performed the failed task and 19% successful. In Task 2, it was observed that 43% of the intermediate users did not complete or abandon the task, while a small part of this group (9%) could complete the task, but with errors. Experienced users could complete the task (19% successful and 29% with errors).

And for Task 3, most experienced users completed the task with errors (60% of users), while the other 40% completed the task successfully.

The results reflect the participants' lack of knowledge about the tools, which were overcome, only for Task 1, and with the evaluation team help. On the other hand, the group of experienced users could complete Tasks 1, 2 and 3, although some of them with errors. There was also a strong influence of participants' experience in the outcome of tasks for those who could use JAWS and DOSVOX, regardless the nature of task. Parametric tests were applied to compare the results of the groups. The groups were compared in performance using the ANOVA test, with classification criteria and the Tukey test. The normality and homogeneity conditions required for the validation of the tests were accepted. The system used for analysis was Minitab 15 (Minitab - 2012). The ANOVA and Tukey tests were chosen to compare the averages among the three groups of users, depending on the characteristics in the sample universe (size and homogeneity), the criterion of significance for both tests were 0.5. To support this analysis, the following metrics were considered: total number of errors, time spent on the task, number of times the request was requested, number of errors due to interpretation of the text; Number of times participants reported difficulty understanding audio and related incorrect actions. The results of the statistical test are shown in Table 2.

Regarding the number of requests for assistance and incorrect actions, according to item 3.3, the p-value obtained and used was lower than the criterion of significance adopted for the ANOVA test adopted in 3.3, which allowed rejection of their respective null hypothesis. Thus, Tukey's test was applied, resulting in statistically significant differences between the means of two groups (experienced and intermediate) and (experienced and inexperienced) participants. Therefore, since the value zero does not belong to the confidence interval, it follows that the group of experienced users shows better performance.

About incorrect actions, there are differences between the average results for experienced and inexperienced groups of participants with inexperienced users exhibiting better performances (item 3.3). This result could be explained by considering inexperienced users submitted to a brief training (item 3.4) and being less experienced were more careful in performing their tasks, thus reducing the errors incidence.

Table 2. Results of the ANOVA and Tukey tests and their relevance for the adopted metrics

Metric	Groups	Mean	ANOVA (p-value)	TUKEY
Total Task Time	1	14.6	0.98	?
	2	14.5		
	3	14.2		
Total number of errors	1	2.4	0.9	
	2	3.8		
	3	4.9		
Number of Help Requests	1	0.01	0	Group3= Group2 (0,9 a 1,7)
	2	4.2		Group1 ≠ Group3 (3,1 a 5,8)
	3	4.6		Group1 ≠ Group2 (2,7 a 5,4)
Text interpretation error	1	2.9	0.08	
	2	2.4		
	3	2.9		
Difficulty to understand audio	1	0.2	0.05	
	2	0.9		
	3	0.9		
Number of Incorrect Actions	1	0.5	0.03	Group3= Group2 (0 a 0,8)
	2	0		Group1 = Group3 (0,5 a 0,3)
	3	0.4		Gruop1 ≠ Gruop2 (0,9 a 0,2)

Thus, with the presented inferences, the previous experience of participant with the resource did not interfere with the performance level of Task 1. The analysis of the usability results based on the nature of the task was performed only for the group of participants enabled in the Using the JAWS and DOSVOX systems, since this was the only group able to perform all tasks, considering the null hypothesis for the ANOVA test, referred to in 3.1.

According to 3.1, the hypothesis of the research, there are no significant differences between the means of the groups as to the total number of errors incurred in performing Tasks 1, 2 and 3. It also states that the number of errors is reduced when the Participant Is highly motivated to accomplish the task.

From the ANOVA test, the mean of the total number of errors decreased in the following order: the highest for Task 2 ($\mu T2 = 7.7$); Followed by Task 1 ($\mu T1 = 2,4$) and Task 3 ($\mu T3 = 1,2$). The value of the significance criterion ($p = 0.01$) was lower than the level of significance adopted for the hypothesis test, therefore, the null hypothesis was rejected. From the Tukey test, applied to the second hypothesis, it was verified that:

• The average of total number of errors incurred during Task 1 is equal to that of Task 3, since the confidence interval does not exclude zero (-3.9 to 6.3);

• The average of total number of errors incurred during Task 3 is different from Task 2, since the confidence interval excludes zero (1.3 to 11.6), meaning that the participants achieved a better performance during Task 3, With the mean error A 1.2;

• The mean of total number of errors identified during Task 1 is different from Task 2 because the confidence interval excludes zero (0.1 to 10.4), meaning that the participants achieved a better performance during Task 3, with an error rate equal to 1.2.

The usability of Braille keyboard was evaluated considering the difficulty of the user in locating characters during the evaluation test. As none of the participants had prior experience with the Braille keyboard, the predominant feature during the analysis was the participant's previous knowledge about Braille, rather than previous experiences with the keyboard itself. Among the 30 participants in the test, the clear majority (27) opted for Braille. By focusing on the sample of individuals who chose to use the Braille keyboard, 79% (19) had prior knowledge of the Braille method and 21% did not know.

Table 3. Participant knowledge about Braille versus ability to use the Braille keyboard during the test

Participants Groups		*Task 1 (%)*	*Task2 (%)*	*Task 3 (%)*
Had difficulties to use the keyboard	Knew Braille	22	0	11
	Did not know Braille	33	13	0
Did not have difficulties to use keyboard		45	87	89

Regarding Task 1, it can be inferred that the level of difficulty with keyboard use was higher among participants who did not know the Braille method (33%) when compared to those who knew it (22%), in contrast to Braille 45% Of users did not have difficulty using the keyboard. On the other hand, in Task 2, the difficulty in using the keyboard occurred only among participants who did not know the Braille method (13%). During this task, all participants reported some kind of difficulty in using the keyboard. Finally, few participants were able to perform Task 3, and considering that they had already gained more familiarity with the keyboard, the reported level of difficulty was low.

Given the experimental protocol modularity and scope for usability assessment, the changes needed to adapt it to accessibility assessment consisted of small adjustments in some steps, processes and activities; Mainly in the experiment planning stages to adapt the test environment to specific needs of the group of participants.

The adapted protocol, adopted in item 3.4, proved to be adequate for the purpose of supporting the usability evaluation of the accessibility resources, promoting an ethical treatment appropriate to the participants of the experiment. The results obtained (item 3.3), from usability point of view, indicate that there is no direct influence of previous experience with specific help resources, on the performance of the user, given the metrics: total task time; Total number of errors; Errors in text interpretation due to the difficulty in understanding the audio produced by the synthesizer. According to the results, it was verified that the inexperienced users, in some tasks, presented better performance, which can be explained by an introductory training session, more requests of help of evaluation team besides being less confident and therefore experienced participants. This result is evidenced by the fact that only the experienced participants completed Tasks 1 and 2; The latter being successfully completed only by this group. It is important to mention that, despite the experience of experienced participants with computer systems and accessibility aids, difficulties were observed in the group, which prevented them from performing tasks more efficiently.

On the other hand, inexperienced users could only use the accessibility aid products helping team, without which it would have been impracticable to participate in the experiment. Regarding the Braille keyboard usage, according to results, the difficulties observed in Tasks 1, 2 and 3 were higher among participants who did not know the Braille method. Given the last step of experiment, during participants were encouraged to discuss their experience, the participant's educational background impact on the expectations and opinions on the accessibility aids evaluated was highlighted. The steps to follow in this research are to refine the materials of the experiment and extend its application to an even larger sample that allows more inference between subgroups of participant profiles. The availability of the protocol should facilitate planning and usability testing, hopefully exposing the difficulties faced by the visually impaired community when using accessibility features, as well as their levels of acceptance regarding perception, understanding and ease of interaction. Although the focus of this research has not been evaluated by the JAWS and DOSVOX speech synthesizers, the protocol application results suggest that resource users may benefit from the redesign of some features related to the usability problems found.

6. CONCLUSION

Given the experimental protocol modularity and scope for usability evaluation, the necessary changes to adapt it to the accessibility evaluation consisted in minor adjustments in some steps, processes and activities; mainly in the planning steps of the experiment to adapt the testing environment for the specific needs of the group of participants.

The adapted protocol proved to be adequate for the purpose of supporting the assessment of the usability of accessibility features, promoting an ethical and adequate treatment to participants of the experiment. The results obtained, from the usability point of view, indicate that there is no direct influence of previous experience with specific aid resources, on the user's performance, given the metrics: total task time; total number of errors; text interpretation errors due to the difficulty in understanding the audio produced by the synthesizer. According to the results, it was found that inexperienced users, in some tasks, displayed a better performance, which can be explained by an introductory training session, more numerous requests for help from the evaluation team besides being less confident and therefore more careful than the experienced participants. This result is evidenced by the fact that only the experienced participants completed Tasks 1 and 2; with the latter being completed successfully only by this group. It is important to mention that despite the experience of the experienced participants with computer systems and accessibility aids, difficulties were observed in the group, which prevented them from performing the tasks more efficiently. On the other hand, inexperienced users were only able to use the accessibility aid products with the help of the team, without which would have been unviable the participation in experiment. Regarding the use of Braille keyboard, according to the results, the difficulties observed during Tasks 1, 2 and 3, were higher amidst participants who did not know the Braille method. Given the last step of the experiment, during which the participants were enticed to discuss their experience, it was highlighted the impact of the participant's educational background on the expectations and opinions on the evaluated accessibility aids.

The following steps in this research consist on refining the experiment materials and extending its application to an even bigger sample which allows for more inference between subgroups of participant's profiles. The availability of the protocol should facilitate the planning and performing of the usability tests, hopefully exposing the difficulties faced by the visually impaired community when using accessibility resources, as well as their acceptance levels regarding perception, comprehension and ease of interaction.

Even though the focus of this research was not evaluated the voice synthesizers JAWS and DOSVOX, the results from the protocol application suggest that the resources users can benefit from the redesign of some features related to the usability problems found.

ACKNOWLEDGEMENT

We thank the researchers, Maria de Fátima Vieira, Federal University of Campina Grande, Ronaldo da Silva Ferreira, Nilton Lins University and Yuska Aguiar and Flávio Filho, both from the Federal University of Paraiba, for their collaboration during the researches that originated this research, as well as Nilton Lins University, Generation of investment and investment in their laboratories, leveraging subsequent research.

REFERENCES

A. Lima, M. Vieira, L. Aguiar. 2010. *Experimental Protocol for Accessibility*. In: IADS 2010.IADIS International Conference Interfaces and Human Computer Interaction Experimental Protocol for Accessibility. In: IADIS International Conference Interfaces and Human Computer Interaction. Freiburg, Germany.

Borges, J. A. S. 2009. *Tecnopolicy and the regulation of competition between blind with computer and computer unassisted sighted people in taking exams to get into Brazilian universities*. In: Society for Social Studies of Leuthold Science Annual Meeting, 2009, Washington. 4S'2009 Annual Meeting, 2009.

C. AGUIAR and Q. VIEIRA, 2009. *Proposal of a Protocol to Support Product Usability Evaluation*. International Association of Science and Technology for Development (IASTED), US Virgin Islands.

Hansen, E. G., R. J. Mislevy, et al. (2005). Accessibility of tests for individuals with disabilities within a validity framework.Elsevier, v.33, p.107–133

ISO 9241-171, 2008. *Ergonomics of human-system interaction: Guidance on software accessibility*, London, UK. Part 171.

Sánchez, J. and T. Hassler (2007)."AudioMUD: A Multiuser Virtual Environment for Blind People " IEEE Transactions on Neural Systems and Rehabilitation on Engineering V.15.

S. Loiacono, S. Djamasbi, T. Kiryazov. Factors that affect visually impaired users' acceptance of audio and music websites. J. Human-Computer Studies. 71, 321–334, 2013.

V. Raman, 2003, Specialized browsers. In: Harper, S., Yesilada, Y. 2003, WebAccessibility: A Foundation for Research,1st Edition. Human-computer- Interaction Series. Springer-Verlag, Ch.12, pp.195–213, ISBN:9781-84800-049-0.

A COMPREHENSIVE USABILITY EVALUATION OF AN ONLINE HR SYSTEM

Monerah Al-Mekhlal, Lamis Abu Romman and Bushra Al-Saqer
Department of Information Systems, King Faisal University, P.O. Box:400, Al-Hufof, Al-Hasa, 31982 Saudi Arabia

ABSTRACT

Human resource (HR) systems are now widely recognized as a critical success factor for implementing successful ERP and efficient interaction between employees and their organization. The employees in each organization are considered one of its most valuable resources, and HR systems are considered the backbone of any organization. For an HR system to be efficient, effective, and satisfactory, it is expected to meet various usability criteria. Different usability evaluation methods are available to assess a system's usability. Employing different usability evaluation methods can offer more reliable and interesting results. MenaMe HR is one of the famous HR systems in the Arabian Gulf region that supports the main features of personnel information management such as payroll information, training, career planning, and appraisal management, among others. This paper aims to comprehensively assess MenaMe's usability using four usability methods: heuristics evaluation (HE), cognitive walkthrough, competitive research, and automated self-reporting (through user testing). Each of the them contributed to assessing the MenaMe HR system. The assessment results have yielded that system learnability, navigation, presentation, and task support are associated with more usability problems. Understandability and findability have been also linked with a number of usability issues through competitive research and automated self-reporting methods. This research also explores how each method reveals different types of problems.

KEYWORDS

HR, Heuristic Evaluation, Cognitive Walkthrough, Competitive Research, Automated Self-Report

1. INTRODUCTION

During the last 20 years, technology has had a significant influence on human resource management (HRM) and human resource information systems, which are focused on utilizing technology to support HR functions (Johnson et al., 2016). Recently, the use of information technology (IT) in HR is rapidly growing. There are different web-based systems available that provide easy-to-use HR functions such as managing employees' information, payroll, career development, and training. The utilization of HR technology has improved many sub-functions and enabled the field to enhance efficiency, decrease administrative workload, and provide improved service to employees, retirees, and job applicants (Johnson et al., 2016). Usability constitutes the effective interaction between users and computer technology. It aims to measure a system's learnability, efficiency, memorability, error tolerance, and user satisfaction. These measurements can be assessed through different usability evaluation methods. Usability evaluation consists of different methodologies to measure usability aspects of a system and identify precise problems (Kumar et al., 2015). The MenaMEHR online HR system has been selected as a case study to conduct a usability evaluation. MenaMEHR is a web-based solution that enables employees and managers to edit, modify and view their HR-related information online. It has been widely used in the Arabian Gulf due to its helpful features.

The main goal of this study is to conduct a comprehensive assessment of the selected system and then provide related recommendations based on the assessment's results. In addition, this paper explores the findings of each method and the types of problems found. This paper consists of six sections. Section 2 discusses the related work on HR system usability assessment. In Section 3, the usability methods used in this paper are explored and explained. Section 4 presents the main findings and assessment results in terms of performance in each method and overall. Section 5 highlights limitations and future work.

2. RELATED WORK

Usability is an important factor in HR systems' success. Different studies have been conducted to assess HR systems' usability. Wong et al. (2015) conducted a usability evaluation of one of the most popular business process management software systems (SAP). The focus was on performing a critical analysis of related issues and implications using the System Usability Scale (SUS) and interviews. The results indicated the system's weakness was in learnability, which could be addressed by training sessions (Wong et al., 2015).

Danda (2015) evaluated the usability of the SAP R/3 application, finding its configuration set up and difficulty in use. Additionally, Liu (2014) studied the SAP application's usability at Volvo Group. The study consisted of observation, interviews, and questionnaires. The results showed that the system had issues in customization, presentation, and learnability (Liu, 2014).

Moreover, Scholtz et al. (2013) conducted an empirical study on the usability evaluation of a medium-sized ERP system. The usability evaluation results provided considerable insight into the usability problems encountered by students when using ERP systems in their university courses and provided a valuable contribution to usability theory and in particular frustration theory (Scholtz et al., 2013). In this regard, Singh and Wesson (2009) conducted a usability evaluation on ERP systems. They reviewed several usability studies of ERP systems in order to propose a set of specific usability criteria for ERP systems (Singh & Wesson, 2009). The results obtained were that a set of ERP usability heuristics can identify significantly different usability issues from Nielsen's 10 heuristics for general system usability (Singh & Wesson, 2009).

In addition, a usability assessment was conducted on ERP systems in two countries, Germany and Latvia (Lambeck et al., 2014). A usability survey was distributed among 184 users from Germany and 24 users from Latvia. It aimed to measure usability in different counties and find the common usability problems in the ERP interface. Only minor or medium usability problems were faced (Lambeck et al., 2014). However, questionnaires are usually criticized in usability testing due to the lack of actual interaction with users. Furthermore, Kumar et al. (2015) conducted an in-depth usability assessment of an online human resource information system at Fiji National University. The assessment surveyed 60 users who examined the system for usefulness, satisfaction, and ease of use. The users were divided into three broad categories: academic, service and support, and administration. The results show that usability problems were very few and minor (Kumar et al., 2015). Based on the evaluation results, recommendations were proposed to improve system usability, such as improving the document upload, online video tutorials, and user interface and including an additional SMS notification feature and comprehensive user instructions (Kumar et al., 2015). In addition, Yusuf et al. (2014) conducted a usability assessment to investigate the usability problems of HR in Malaysian e-government. Their study covered qualitative and quantitative data. Usability testing was conducted with five participants performing actual tasks. They found that most participants faced major problems with the system design and required formal training and a manual to perform the given tasks (Yusuf et al., 2014).

It can be noticed that different usability evaluation methods have been adopted and utilized by different researchers. This research aims to employ four usability evaluation methods: heuristic evaluation, cognitive walkthrough, competitive evaluation, and automated self-reported (through user testing). These methods can offer deep insight into system usability and offer reliable and valuable findings and comparisons.

3. RESEARCH METHODS

Usability evaluation can be conducted using one or more evaluation methods. As explained in the previous section, four usability methods will be used to comprehensively assess MenaMEHR's usability. This will also make it possible to compare each method's findings regarding performance and its effectiveness. Each used method will be explained in the next sections.

3.1 Heuristic Evaluation

Heuristic evaluation is one of several usability evaluation techniques for identifying usability problems. It depends on examining and evaluating a user interface against a set of specific usability rules or heuristics. Heuristic evaluation was published by Nielson and Molich (1990), who refined the heuristics based on a factor analysis to derive a set of 10 heuristics (Chen & Macredie, 2005). These 10 heuristics are among the most frequently cited sets of heuristic evaluation tools that provide researchers with a cost-effective and practical means to effectively assess interface designs and usability (Gonzalez-Holland et al., 2017). Novices and experts alike can use heuristic evaluation due to its flexibility, which makes it easy to learn. In addition, heuristic evaluation ensures accurate evaluation of the user interface as well as of most usability problems and allows their severity to be discovered (Chen & Macredie, 2005). Accordingly, heuristic evaluation is particularly of value in circumstances where there are limited time and resources, so skilled experts can yield high-quality results in a short time without the need of concerning end users in the evaluation. On the other hand, it has been criticized because evaluators may focus on certain features during evaluation while ignoring others, which affects the meaningfulness of evaluation results (Jaspers, 2009). This could be due to the general level of the heuristics. This can be improved through detailed heuristics and proper implementation (Gonzalez-Holland et al., 2017).

3.2 Cognitive Walkthrough

The second method in this study is cognitive walkthrough. One of the expert-based inspection methods, it can evaluate system usability in an early system design as an evaluator walks through the selected system using predefined tasks (Jaspers, 2009). This method is cost-effective and fast compared with many other forms of usability evaluation methods such as heuristic evaluation (Blackmon et al., 2002). It can also be implemented prior to development during the design phase, providing rapid insight before budget is spent developing an unusable product or applied to a ready product (Blackmon et al., 2002). Cognitive walkthrough differs from other expert-based methods as it is highly structured and explicitly guided by users' tasks (Jaspers, 2009).

3.3 Competitive Research Usability Evaluation

Competitive usability evaluation is the third method used in this research. It aims to determine a web site's performance in relation to competitors' sites (Nielsen Norman Group, 2013). The comparison can be holistic, ranking sites by overall site-usability metrics (checklists), or it can be more focused, comparing features, content, or design elements across sites (Eustace, 2013; Nielsen Norman Group, 2013). Competitive evaluation assesses the website's design as either better or worse than its competitors' and discovers the relative strengths and weaknesses of competing designs. It allows an in-depth look at how others solve the same design problems. The goal of this evaluation is to see what competitors are doing, how they're doing it, what's working, and what's not (Nielsen Norman Group, 2013). Evaluation can take the form of expert reviews, where an experienced usability practitioner reviews the designs based on his or her expertise and knowledge of usability, or competitive usability testing, where users complete a set of tasks using two or more competing sites (Nielsen Norman Group, 2013). The comparison is based on the Creating Valuable Content Checklist generated by Eustace Consulting, which consists of five matrices that measure findability, understandability, readability, actionability, and sharability (Eustace, 2013). The metrics are as follows:

- The findable metric mainly measures headings' font size, metadata description, links between webpages, and inclusion of "alt" tags on images that describe the pictures for the visually impaired.
- The readable metric measures how long users scan the web content until finding the needed content; pyramid writing style; chunking the content with short paragraphs and content consistency.
- The understandable metric emphasizes selecting the proper content type, creating a user persona that fits different audiences, applying a standard reading level, and providing valuable information.
- The actionable metric measures the inclusion of a call to ensure the users can act on the content, ease of asking questions and commenting, invitation to share the content, and having a list of actionable items.
- The sharable metric highlights emotional responses and measures whether the site includes the benefits of sharing information, asks to share information, makes sharing simple, and personalizes sharing.

3.4 Automated Self-Reported

The automated self-reported data method is also utilized in this research through user testing. It offers the most important information about users' perception of the system and their interaction with it (Hornbaek,

2006). Automated self-reporting evaluation can be applied with five measures, such as the number of keystrokes, number of clicks, number of visited pages, time needed to complete the desired tasks and task success. Such measures are recorded for each task using an automated tool. The importance of the automated self-reporting evaluation is to examine the usability of each task. This method allows evaluators to evaluate the effectiveness of the site's linking structure, including the navigation, to see how users get around the site and complete their intended tasks. The recorded results may allow the owners of the system to develop and improve the effectiveness of their services (Habboub, 2017).

4. USABILITY EVALUATION AND RESULTS

This section contains detailed discussion about how each method has been conducted and its results while evaluating the MenaMEHR HR web system.

4.1 Heuristics Evaluation (HE)

Five experienced evaluators conducted heuristics evaluation using the common 10 heuristics. It can be noticed that more problems are related to visibility of system status, user control and freedom, consistency and standards, and recognition rather than recall, aesthetic and minimalist design, and help and documentation. The heuristics evaluation method usually results in general findings due to its general criteria. However, what this method has revealed in this research is in line with other research such as Wong et al. (2015) and Liu (2014) as learnability and page presentation are common problems in HR and ERP systems. The MenaMEHR system does have a number of good usability aspects such as users are able to follow up their request easily. Evaluators have reported that notification process can be considered as a positive usability aspect. Table 1 shows these heuristics and explanation of the related usability problems.

Table 1. MenaMEHR HE results

Heuristics	Description
H1: Visibility of system status.	• The system status causes some confusion if the user enters incorrect information on the login page. It does not show its status. • The system shows an error message, then a blank page forever. The original page does not notify the user of the system status (having rejected the entered data) and enable him to re-enter the data.
H2: User control and freedom.	• Navigation between system pages is ineffective. If a user wants to move to a previous page, there is no choice or button to return.
H3: Consistency and standards.	• Labels and fields are inconsistent due to their position (links or relation), their font size, and their small volume for the page and large white spaces. • The main sections of the system are poorly designed. The graphic shapes are large, while the labels located next to the graph are small.
H4: Recognition rather than recall.	• There are no guidelines for data. Users are expected to remember the company name and write it in capital letters to be accepted.
H5: Aesthetic and minimalist design.	• The unsatisfactory design layout does not encourage users to use it.
H6: Help and documentation.	• The system sections lack textual or visual guidelines or help.

4.2 Cognitive Walkthrough Method

In order to conduct a cognitive walkthrough, again a different five experienced evaluators attempted to answer four questions, as illustrated in table 2, while performing predefined tasks (login, transaction, inquiry, seeking information). These tasks were selected as the main functions of the MenaMEHR system. If there are positive answers to all four questions for each task, then there are no usability flaws. On the other hand, if there is a negative answer to any of the four questions, that task has usability problems (Jaspers, 2009). Evaluators were expected to report, explain, and, if applicable, recommend action for such issues. The below table 2 shows how the method was conducted by evaluators while performing tasks. It shows how task 1 was formed and how an evaluator performed the given task. This was applied for all the given tasks by all evaluators. Their results were discussed and then aggregated.

Table 2. Cognitive walkthrough method.

Task 1: User login			
Q0: What does the user want to achieve?	A0: The user logs into the system and retrieves/resets his password in case of forgetting.		
Questions for each step	Yes	No	Remarks
Q1: Will the correct action(s) be evident to the users?	√		The process of retrieving a username or resetting a password is clear.
Q2: Will the users connect the label of an action with their goals?		√	There is no connection between an action's label and the user's goal.
Q3: Will the users receive sensible feedback?		√	The process failed. The system was unable to retrieve or reset a user's password.

It can be noticed that cognitive walkthrough found issues related to navigation issues, information organisation, learnability, presentation and system design. This can be justified due to the method's nature, as it guides the evaluators. Yusuf et al. (2014) reported that ERP and HR systems lack system design.

4.3 Competitive Research Method

The competitive research evaluation method was conducted by comparing the site content of MenaMEHR with that of common and popular ERP and HR systems such as SAP, HR.My, HRWeb, PeopleStreme, Peoplesoft, Sage Payroll, PeopleQlik, and Employee Navigator. The websites' selection was based on popularity and functional similarity in the HR domain. The assessment was done by reviewing the associated pages such as the home and login page, payroll page, etc. Then the websites' pages were scored based on the five metrics. The website, that achieves the highest rating, can be described as a usable website as it meets website design standards where the low rating score reflects the poor website design standard achievement.

In figure. 1, the results show that the MenaMEHR web site has the lowest rating in the five metrics (findability, understandability, readability, actionability, and sharability) compared to the other websites. SAP scored the highest mark. Figure. 2 contains the detailed score results for the websites' comparison. MenaMEHR and Peoplesoft scored the lowest in readability and understandability. Sharability can be considered the best metric for MenaMEHR per the achieved results. Further results are related to inappropriate font size on the webpages; a lack of metadata for the web content such as titles, keywords, and description; an inappropriate content scanning sequence; and unclear and indirect actions. These results are in line with heuristic evaluation findings in system visibility and status and user control and freedom in this research. Liu (2014) also reported that presentation is one of the usability issues in ERP and HR systems.

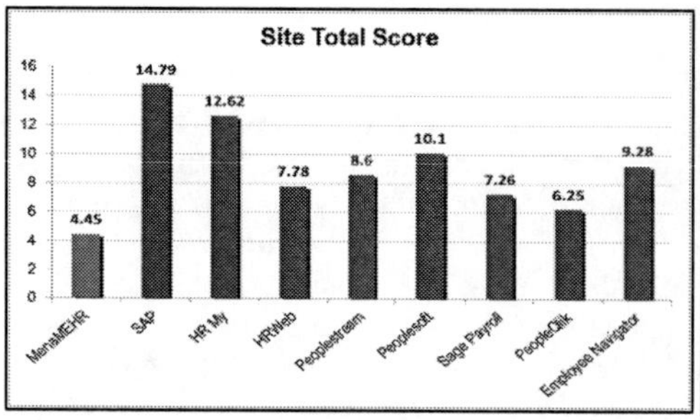

Figure 1. Total scores for competitive research matrices

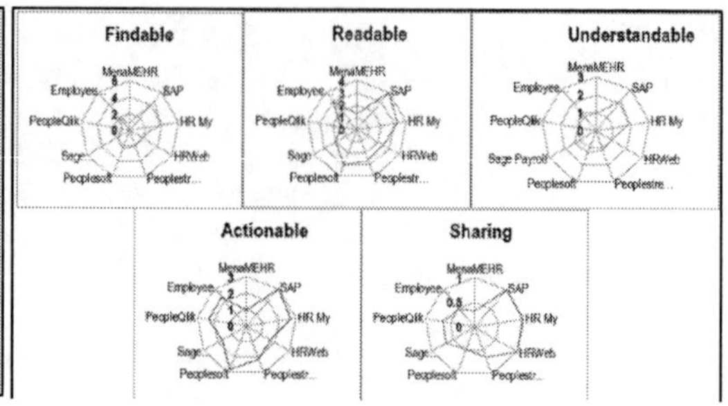

Figure 2. Competitive research metrics

4.4 Automated Self-Reporting Method

The automated self-reporting method was utilized by five users through user testing (three female and two male) who performed four tasks. All of them speak English, have computer skills and previous experience. These characteristics are similar to the actual users of MenaMEHR system. Five measures were used: the number of keystrokes, the number of clicks, the time spent to complete the given task, the number of visited pages to accomplish the task, and task success. These five measures represent the efficiency and effectiveness usability criteria. The Mousotron tool was used in this research (Blacksun Software, 2018). Mousotron is a mouse and keyboard activity monitor that keeps statistics of users' mileage. It calculates how far a user's mouse cursor has travelled on the screen and how many times the mouse buttons have been clicked. It can be noticed that each task required more than one minute to be performed and too many keystrokes for each task. The users needed to visit four pages to perform Tasks 2 and 3. Although such numbers do not clearly point to a clear issue, they can be considered with the results of previous methods such as heuristics evaluation and competitive research, as both methods reported findability as a usability issue in the MenaMEHR system. Other researchers such as Wong et al. (2015) and Liu (2014) reported that learnability is a clear issue with ERP and HR systems. The results for the four tasks are shown in table 3.

Table 3. Automated self-reported results

Task	Keystroke	Click	Time	No. of visited pages
1- Login	78	5	1 min 15 sec	1
2- Transaction task	104	23	2 min 20 sec	3
3- Salary slip	78	20	2 min 40 sec	4
4- View personal profile	79	13	1 min 34 sec	3

One of the important measure is task success. It measures whether or not the users' were able to perform the given task successfully. The following table (Table 4) shows task success data.

Table 4. Task Success Rate

User\task	Task 1	Task 2	Task 3	Task 4
User 1	S (1)	P (0.5)	S (1)	F (0)
User 2	P (0.5)	S (1)	P (0.5)	F (0)
User 3	S (1)	S (1)	F (0)	F (0)
User 4	S (1)	F (0)	S (1)	F (0)
User 5	S (1)	S (1)	P (0.5)	F (0)
Note: S = success, F = failure, P = partial success				

It can be concluded from the above table 3 that 20 attempts were observed to perform the given four tasks by the five users. 9 of these attempts were successful, 5 attempts were fail and 6 were partially successful. Therefore, success rate which is calculated as follows:

$Success\ rate\ =\ (S\ +\ (P\ *\ 0.5))\ /\ total\ number\ of\ attempts$ (Nielsen, 2001)

$Success\ rate\ =\ (9\ +\ (4\ *\ 0.5))\ /\ 20\ =55\%$. This percentage can provide a general picture of how the system supports users and how much the system is required to be improved to work. It has been noticed that although users were not novice, they have been found struggling to perform the task in particular task 4. This again may confirm the achieved results in heuristic evaluation and cognitive walkthrough as learnability is an issue. This percentage is noticeably lower than the public website percentage (65%) (Giselle and Rosemary ,2017). This could be improved through user training, assistant and proposing helpful manual. In addition to that, there were a number of problems related to the given tasks such as unsatisfactory information search results, inadequate navigation, missing descriptive link text to a number of headings, lack of tool tip, unpleasant visual interface such as missing white spaces and font sizes and information availability and accuracy have been also reported as a usability issue.

5. LIMITATIONS AND FUTURE WORK

Current research has emphasized that heuristic evaluation can be more effective as long as the heuristics are customized to a certain domain. Unfortunately, ERP and HR systems do not have customized usability guidelines. This can be seen as providing opportunities for further research. Moreover, involving larger numbers of users could reveal more usability issues. Applying heuristics evaluation and cognitive walkthrough to different HR systems in addition to MenaMEHR could also result in a more robust conclusion about its usability. Future work could also further develop more approaches, such as employing a questionnaire, that may present more issues in the selected system. Usability measures correlations could be an interesting area to be explored in HR usability evaluation. In addition, interviews with users and administrators may be useful, as direct communication may uncover usability issues.

6. CONCLUSION

In this paper, four usability evaluation methods have been applied to evaluate the MenaMEHR HR system. Each of the four usability methods has shown its usefulness to reveal different usability problems. Using different evaluation methods helped to comprehensively assess MenaMEHR's usability, revealing different usability issues. In this paper, most findings for the heuristic evaluation method were related to system visibility, providing error prevention, making the system more consistent, employing recognition rather than recall, and providing help and documentation. Cognitive walkthrough showed that a number of usability issues such as feedback messages are not understandable by users. It can be clearly seen that success rate is below the percentage of public websites. MenaMEHR system has a number of strength such as follow up and notification process. Different evaluators have reported these good usability aspects.

ACKNOWLEDGEMENT

The authors of this research would like to express their acknowledgement to Dr Majed Al-Shamari for his valuable support and contributions during this study.

REFERENCES

Blackmon, M., Polson, P., Kitajima, M. and Lewis, C. (2002). Cognitive Walkthrough for the Web. Association for Computing Machinery (ACM), New York • 20-25 april 2002, 4(1), pp.463-470.

Chen, S. and Macredie, R. (2005). The assessment of usability of electronic shopping: A heuristic evaluation. International Journal of Information Management, 25(6), pp.516-532.

Danda, S. (2015). Application of Modified Agile Methodology toImprove Usability of SAP ECC. Culminating Projects in Mechanical and Manufacturing Engineering.

Eustace, C. (2013). How To: Create Valuable Content | Eustace Consulting. [online] Eustace Consulting. Available at: https://www.eustaceconsulting.com/blog/general/how-to-create-valuable-content/ [Accessed 8 Apr. 2018].

Giselle J. and Rosemary R. (2017). Web Usability: A Literature Review. the DLSU Research Congress, June 20-22, 2017

Gonzalez-Holland, E., Whitmer, D., Moralez, L. and Mouloua, M. (2017). Examination of the Use of Nielsen's 10 Usability Heuristics & Outlooks for the Future. Proceedings of the Human Factors and Ergonomics Society Annual Meeting, 61(1), pp.1472-1475.

Habboub, H. F., (2017). Usability Evaluation of SAP ERP System (UNRWA Case Study), s.l.: s.n.

Hornbaek, K. (2006). Current practice in measuring usability: Challenges to usability studies and research. International Journal of Human-Computer Studies, 64(2), pp.79-102.

Jaspers, M. (2009). A comparison of usability methods for testing interactive health technologies: Methodological aspects and empirical evidence. International Journal of Medical Informatics, 78(5), pp.340-353.

Kumar, B. A., Kumar, I. & Hussein, S., (2015). Usability Study of Online Human Resource Information Systems at Fiji National University: A Case Study. Asian Journal of Information Technology, 14(1), pp. 42-48. Liu, X., 2014. Usability Analysis of Working with SAP Applications in Volvo Group. Uppsala University, p. 41.

Lambeck, C., Muller, R. & Fohrholz, C., 2014. (Re-)Evaluating User Interface Aspects in ERP Systems -- An Empirical User Study. Waikoloa, IEEE.

Liu, X. (2014). Usability Analysis of Working with SAP Applications in Volvo Group. Uppsala University, p.41. S. Danda, "Application of Modified Agile Methodology to Improve Usability of SAP ECC," Culminating Projects in Mechanical and Manufacturing Engineering., 2015.

Nielsen J.(2001). Success Rate: The Simplest Usability Metric, Alertbox

Nielsen Norman Group. (2013). Competitive Usability Evaluations: Definition. [online] Available at: https://www.nngroup.com/articles/competitive-usability-evaluations/ [Accessed 8 April 2018]

R. Johnson, K. Lukaszewski and D. Stone, "The Evolution of the Field of Human Resource Information Systems: Co-Evolution of Tech. and HR Processes," Communications of the Association for Info. Systems, vol. 38, p. 533–553, 2016.

Scholtz,, B., Calitz, A. and Cilliers, C. (2013). Usability Evaluation of a Medium-sized ERP System in Higher Education. The Electronic Journal Information Systems Evaluation, 16(2), pp.148-161.

Singh, A. and Wesson, J. (2009). Evaluation Criteria for Assessing the Usability of ERP Systems. ACM, New York.

Software, B. (2018). Mousotron : Mouse and keyboard usage counter. [online] Blacksunsoftware.com. Available at: http://www.blacksunsoftware.com/mousotron.html [Accessed 29 March 2018].

Wong, W., Veneziano, V. and Mahmud, I. (2015). Usability of Enterprise Resource Planning software systems: an evaluative analysis of the use of SAP in the textile industry in Bangladesh. Information Dev., 32(4), pp.1027-1041.

Yusuf, S., Taslim, J., Adnan, W. and Baharudin, S. (2014). Usability Evaluation of Human Resource Management Information System (HRMIS). 3rd International Conference on User Science and Engineering (i-USEr), pp.204-209.

AN EXPERIMENTAL STUDY TO EVALUATE INFLUENCE OF USABILITY ON LEARNING BEHAVIOUR

Jyotish Kumar, Aarati Prakash Khare and Jyoti Kumar
Indian Institute of technology Delhi, New Delhi, India

ABSTRACT

Usability has been one of the well-established quality measures of HCI systems. Designing an efficient e-learning system is a complex process and requires usability testing at various stages. Unlike conventional HCI systems, e-learning system is not only designed to interact with users but also to facilitate learning to user. In order to develop learner centric system design, there is a need to find the ways in which learning and usability interact. In this study, six learning behaviour markers were identified which can be integrated with conventional usability testing. This paper investigates a relationship between usability attributes and learning behaviour through usability testing of two different e-learning websites with similar in content but different in usability. Other than usability attributes and learning behaviour markers, Galvanic skin response (GSR) of users was also recorded and compared to support the usability testing results. Significant difference ($p<0.05$) was found in learning behaviour marker counts and GSR along with functional usability testing attributes of both websites.

KEYWORDS

Usability testing, E-learning, Galvanic Skin Response (GSR), Learning Behaviour

1. INTRODUCTION

Rise in internet penetration and advancement in human computer interaction (HCI) technologies have led to a rapid expanse in the use of computer supported e-learning systems. Though, e-learning has become a new paradigm for learning and teaching, it still faces challenges like high dropout rates (40-80%) (Rostaminezhad et al. 2013; Levy 2007). Lack of motivation, less interaction, self-regulation, poor satisfaction, less engagement, social presence etc. are some of the factors reported for reason of high dropout rates (Rostaminezhad et al. 2013; Martínez-Caro 2011; El-Masri and Tarhini 2017a). Therefore, it has been a major challenge for designers to address above mentioned problems and improve the quality of e-learning system design. Usability of the system has been one of the well-established quality measures of HCI systems (Nielsen et al. 2005). One way of designing an effective HCI system is iterating the design through conducting usability test at various stages of design process.

According to the ISO 9241-11 standard, usability is defined as the "extent to which a product can be used by specified users to achieve specified goals with effectiveness, efficiency and satisfaction in a specified context of use" (ISO 9241-11, 1998). Various usability testing methods like heuristic evaluation, cognitive walkthrough, thinking aloud, etc. have been used to evaluate HCI systems (Plantak Vukovac, Kirinic, and Klicek 2010). However, prime focus of usability testing has been limited to cognitive functions of the users. as they interact with the e-learning environment (soloway 1994), while learning is a complex phenomenon. Unlike other HCI systems, e-learning system design is not only limited to interact but also to support knowledge dissemination and acquisition (Kukulska-Hulme and Traxler 2013). Usability evaluation of e-learning systems has specific requirements such as the learning process, instructional design, motivation, pedagogical issues etc. that differentiate it from evaluation of other interactive systems. Implications of usability features of educational packages to achieve educational goals have not been considered and there is a need to find a way in which learning and usability interact (Squires and Preece 1996). Therefore, in order to design learner centric e-learning systems, it is important to address both cognitive factor as well as learning behaviour of users which is affected by usability of e-learning systems.

This study explores six different learning behaviour markers and examines their relationship with usability of e-learning systems so that, it takes care of broader faculty including both cognitive and learning behaviour of users while designing an e-learning system. This paper argues the implications of usability problems on learning behaviour and highlights that specific learning attributes need to be considered while conducting usability testing. In this study, a usability testing was conducted on two e-learning systems with same content but different in usability. One of the system was deliberately designed with usability problems while, another was designed and tested with least possible usability issues. Comparative analysis of different learning behaviour markers through ANOVA has been discussed in detail in results section which shows the influence of usability problems on learning attributes.

2. BACKGROUND

There are different usability testing methods used by researchers and professionals based on the nature of task and scenario. In general, usability testing methods are categorized as analytical or empirical. Analytical methods, which is also known as inspection methods, are quick and low-cost used for interface inspection by usability experts. Alternatively, in empirical methods, testing with actual users is performed.

2.1 Existing Usability Testing Methods

Most frequently reported usability testing methods in literature are heuristic evaluation, cognitive walkthrough, thinking aloud and questionnaire based evaluation. Heuristic evaluation is a quick and low cost method to evaluate the interface through some set of design principles and heuristics (Nielsen, n.d.; Holzinger 2005). This method requires an expert who has in-depth knowledge of design principles and heuristics. Cognitive walkthrough methods are task centric evaluation and evaluated by an expert under a given task and scenario. This method mainly focuses on the cognitive issues while performing a given task under a specific scenario(Holzinger 2005)). Cognitive walkthrough method does not provide any guidelines and evaluation order to achieve good results (Hollingsed and Novick 2007). Thinking aloud comes under empirical category of evaluation where actual users verbalize their thoughts while interacting with the systems. It helps evaluator to understand the user's mental model and mark the keywords though user's word. This method doesn't necessarily need an expert but multiple marking is prefered to avoid errors and achieve high reliability(Plantak Vukovac, Kirinic, and Klicek 2010). Questionnaire based evaluation also comes under empirical category and used when the subjective satisfaction of users with the interface is measured. Rather than evaluating the user interface, it evaluates user's opinions, preferences and satisfaction. This method requires a large number of users to participate (Holzinger 2005).

Recent advancement in usability testing softwares enable us to conduct a quick and low cost usability testing through Input Device Parameters (IDP). IDP like time taken per task, mouse clicks, mouse movements, error rate, task success ratio etc. are capable measures to evaluate effectiveness and efficiency of HCI systems (Kortum P. 2016; Steven M.2013). In this study, a combination of input device parameters and thinking aloud technique has been used to evaluate usability of e learning system.

2.2 Markers of Learning Behaviour

There are some of the factors which affect e-learning like, motivation to learn (Martínez-Caro 2011), attention and engagement (Grossberg 2005), self-efficacy (El-Masri and Tarhini 2017b) hedonic motivation (Deci and Ryan 2012) trust (Dzunic et al. 2011) affect (Hudlicka 2003) etc. Self-efficacy is very subjective factor and least correlated with usability of e-learning systems(Rabeb Mbarek et al 2013). Affective dimension is another broad area which need to be integrated in evaluation of e-learning system design (Hudlicka 2003). This study is focused on e-learning behaviour and three major factor including, motivation, attention and trust were considered to develop markers for usability testing of e-learning system.

2.2.1 Attention and Learning

Attention and learning are very different and yet very linked to each other(Grossberg 2005). Learning is the process of memorization, integration and application of new information and concepts (Terenzini, Pascarella, and Blimling 1999). Attention is the process of prioritizing and applying information and concepts and if there is an attention deficit, the brain fails to prioritize information and the student will be unable to apply concepts during learning (Kearsley 1998). In this study, learner's *engagement and distraction* have been used as markers of attention during learning with e-learning websites.

2.2.2 Motivation and Learning

A properly designed interface of e-learning system can motivate learner to interact and achieve their goals (Granić 2008). A usable design brings positive affect to the learning environment which motivates learner and their behaviour (Hornbæk 2006). Hedonic motivation is defined as the fun or pleasure derived from using a technology(Venkatesh, L. Thong, and Xu 2011). Students are self-determining and intrinsically motivated in e-learning systems when they are interested in or enjoying doing it (Deci and Ryan 2012; Al-Gahtani 2016).Therefore, learner's *excitement and boredom* have been used in this study as markers of learning motivation.

2.2.3 Trust and Learning

Trust plays a key role in technology adoption and reflects in user's behaviour while interacting with system(Luo et al. 2010; Venkatesh, L. Thong, and Xu 2011; and Tarhini 2016). While, a usable system creates more trust and facilitate users to interact with more *confidence* (Sharma, Sarrab, and Al-Shihi 2017). Poor usability of website creates *confusion* and fatigue which hampers interaction with system (Davids, Chikte, and Halperin 2014). So, *confidence and doubtfulness* have been used as markers of learning behaviour while evaluation of e-learning system design.

2.2.4 Skin Conductance and Learning

Galvanic Skin Response (GSR) is the change in electrical conductivity of a human's skin caused by environmental events as well as individual's psychological state. The change is caused by the degree to which a person's sweat glands are active and gives direct assessment of arousal (Nourbakhsh et al. 2012). GSR is easy to use, comfortable to wear and low cost technique. Skin electrodes, are placed at the palmer surface because of the more involvement of sweat glands in this area (Lykken and Venables 1971). Skin conductivity and workload are directly associated(Nourbakhsh et al. 2012). Mehler (2009) reported that, skin conductivity increases with increase in task difficulty. In this study, GSR was used to compare the task difficulty level of both the websites and to find correlation with usability metrics and learning behaviour observations.

3. EXPERIMENTAL DESIGN AND PROCEDURE

This study aimed to observe how usability of e-learning website affects learning behaviour of users. Total three input device parameters namely, time spent per task, no of mouse clicks and mouse movements (pixels) were recorded and frustration was marked by observer to compare efficiency and effectiveness of two websites. Total six learning behaviour markers including engagement, distraction, excitement, boredom, confidence and doubtful were created to compare learning behaviour of participants. Further, Galvanic Skin Response (GSR) was also recorded as a measure of stress during the experiment. For this study, two e-learning websites were developed with exactly same content but different in navigation design. Participants were given a task to navigate for a video lesson and watch it to learn. While participants were interacting with the website, observer marked learning behaviour of the participants and input device parameters were recorded using MORAE software. In order to obtain equal number of markers count, behavioural observations were marked by observers at an interval of 30 seconds. Input device parameters and average marker counts of both observers were compared for two e-learning websites to see the influence of usability attributes on learning behaviour. Experimental details have been discussed below.

3.1 Participants

Total of 42 students (29 males and 13 females) from Indian Institute of Technology Delhi participated in this study. 20 participants used website with usability problem and rest 22 used website without usability problem. All participants were master student of industrial design program. Mean age of 21.6 years and standard deviation of 2.7 years were calculated for all the participants volunteered in the study.

3.2 Stimuli Websites

Two e-learning websites were developed with exactly same content but with different navigation design. E-learning websites comprised of two major task. First task was to navigate and find the learning video module as given in the task description. Second task was to watch a 12 minutes' video. The video was about how to draw objects in scale and proportion. Content of the video was prepared and taught by a fine arts teacher having 25 years of prior experience. One website was easy to use, while the another website was deliberately created with inconsistent navigation.

3.3 Experimental Set-up

Experiments were conducted in a lab environment with one-way mirror setup where observer could observe the participants across the mirror while the participants could not see observer. This setup facilitated no distractions to the participants while the experimenters recorded participants' data and observers marked their behaviour in real time. Stimulus was presented to participants on a 21-inch screen, which was equipped with a mouse, keyboard and webcam. At the observer's end, two 15 inch laptops were used to record and mark the real time behaviour of users during experiment. Data recording and behavioural marking was done by MORAE software. A Neulog GSR sensor with sampling rate of 100 Hz was used to record skin response of the users during the experiment. GSR sensor was placed on the bottom of the fingers of the participants.

3.4 Task and Scenario

The task given to participants had two parts. First, participants had to search for a video lesson on scale and proportion under sketching technique module. Second, they had to watch the 12 minutes' video lesson and learn how to sketch with proper scale and proportion. Participants were selected based on their interest to learn the e-learning topic.

Scenario: *You are preparing for a design entrance exam and looking for some tutorial that can help you to improve scale and proportion in sketching. One of your friend suggested you this website to learn sketching techniques. Search for a video lesson on scale and proportion technique to learn and improve your sketching.*

3.5 Experimental Procedure

Experiment started with participants signing the consent form. Participants were taken to the experiment room and briefed about the experiment. GSR sensor was placed on the left hand's finger of the participants. Scenario was narrated to the participants by the experiment facilitator and then participants were asked to complete the task. While user interacted with website and performed the given tasks, two observers in the adjacent room observed user's learning behaviour through one-way mirror and marked independently in MORAE software. Input device parameters like mouse clicks, mouse movement and time spent per task were automatically recorded by the software. The whole experiment duration was around 15 minutes (0.3-2 minutes for navigation and 12.5 minutes for watching video).

4. RESULTS AND DISCUSSION

A comparative analysis was represented through box plot method and two tailed ANOVA was performed at 95% confidence interval to compare the input device parameters and different markers count using SPSS software.

Table 1. ANOVA table for comparison of functional usability testing attributes during navigation

	Without usability problem		With usability problem		ANOVA	
	Mean	**Std. Deviation**	**Mean**	**Std. Deviation**	**F**	**Sig.**
Time spent (Min)	.302	.121	1.267	.705	40.028	.000
No of mouse Click	1.50	.512	5.33	3.181	31.144	.000
Mouse movement (px)	3196.77	2648.91	11108.33	4246.88	51.871	.000
Frustration	2.35	0.462	5.72	2.54	27.214	.001

Table 1 and Figure 1 show comparison of usability parameters and frustration. Time taken by participants to navigate video module was found significantly higher in website with usability problem than website without usability problem. Total no. of mouse clicks and mouse movements were found significantly higher in case of website with usability problem. Marker count of frustration was found significantly higher in case of website with usability problem. In light of the given task to users, this paper argues that higher no. of mouse clicks and mouse movements, longer duration in navigation and higher count of frustration instances indicates difference in usability of the two e-learning websites. These results matched the expectation of researchers as one of the websites was deliberately developed with poor navigation and inconsistent layouts. Purpose to compare these parameters was to confirm the difference between usability of both websites so that interaction between usability and learning behaviour could be identified.

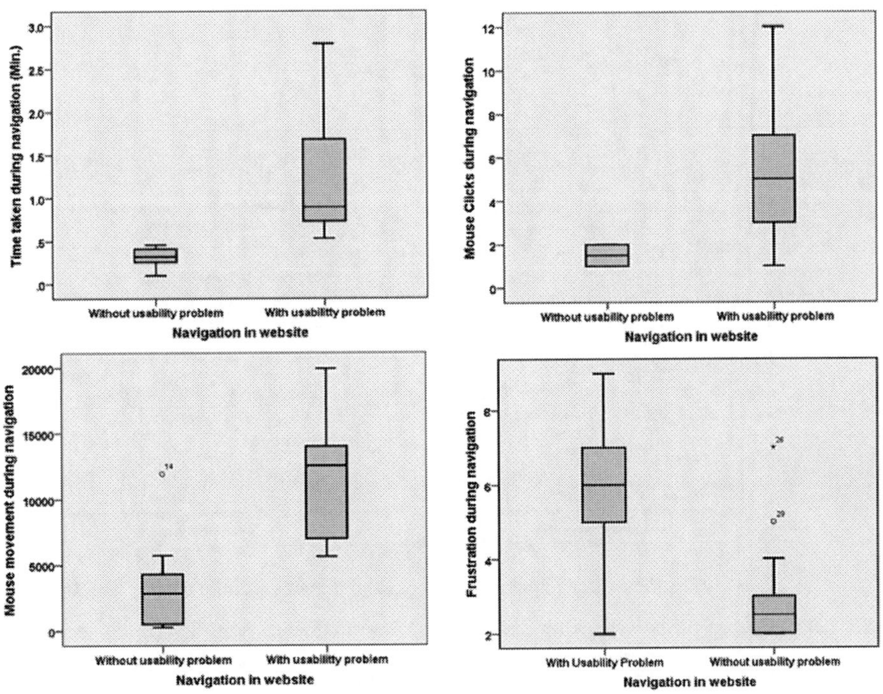

Figure 1. Comparison of usability attributes during navigation

As shown in Figure2 and Table 2, out of six learning behaviour markers, *engagement, distraction, confidence and doubtful* were found to have significant difference in number of counts between both the websites. *Engagement and confidence* were found to have significantly higher number of marker counts for website without usability problem. Which clearly indicates that, efficient usability of e-learning website can draw attention and help the learners to engage more while interacting with system. Effective usability of e-learning website brings more coherence and positive affect to the learning environment which reflects in confidence of user (Hornbaek 2006).

Table 2. ANOVA table for comparison of behavioural markers count during learning

	Without usability problem		With usability problem		ANOVA	
	Mean	Std. Deviation	Mean	Std. Deviation	F	Sig.
Engaged	26.95	9.589	19.61	5.822	8.091	.007
Distraction	3.32	4.487	8.28	5.074	10.755	.002
Excitement	3.55	.858	2.33	.767	2.665	.120
Boredom	2.41	.850	3.94	.918	2.550	.221
Confidence	5.41	1.333	.61	3.973	4.779	.040
Doubtful	2.64	.902	7.28	2.742	7.253	.012

Marker counts of *distraction and doubtful* were found significantly higher for website with usability problem. Which clearly indicates that, poor usability of e-learning website is a serious impediment to learning which adds distraction for users while interacting with the system. An improper designed interfaces brings confusion and doubt which can demotivate learner to achieve their goals. Marker count of *excitement and boredom* didn't show significant difference nevertheless; a small difference was observed which is in good agreement with result of other markers.

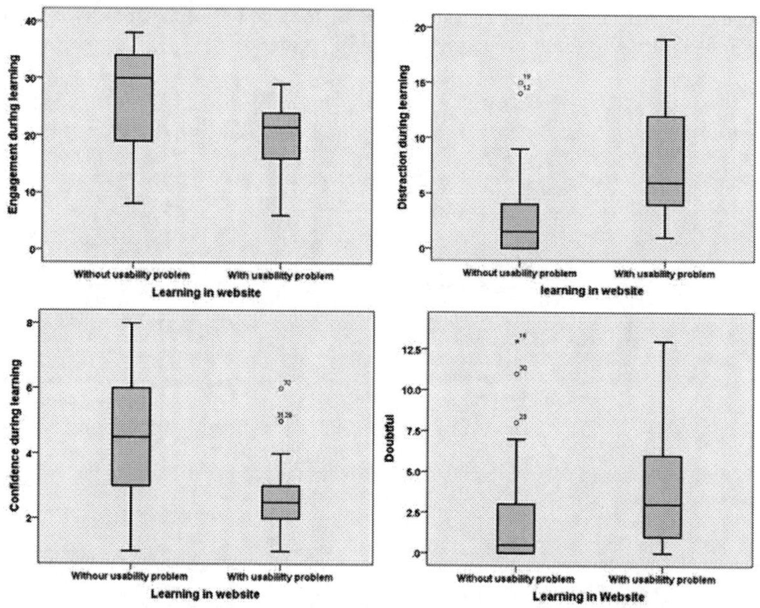

Figure 2. Comparison of behavioural markers count during learning

GSR data was pre-processed using Ledalab incorporated with MATLAB. 10 seconds of both post and prior data was removed and a pre-recorded baseline was subtracted. Time series of skin conductivity data has both slowly varying skin conductance level (SCL) due to overall responses and fast changing skin conductance response (SCR) due to event related responses. In order to separate these two, a de-convolution method was applied in Ledalab (Benedek et al. 2010). Since we are measuring overall responses of websites, SCL was opted as a GSR feature in this paper. Mean of SCL was calculated of all the all 42 participants for both the websites.

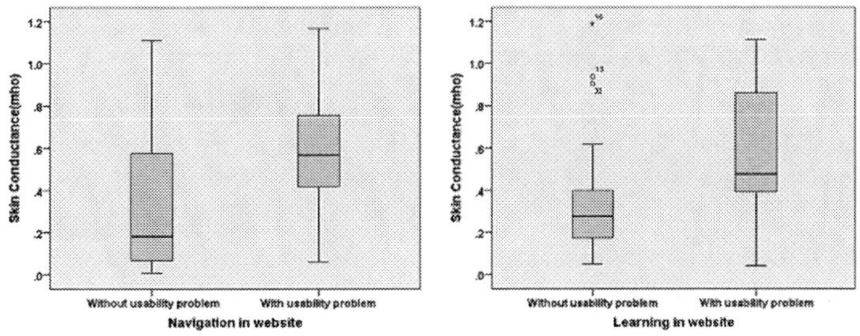

Figure 3. Comparison of skin conductance level during navigation and learning

Skin Conductance Level (SCL) of Galvanic Skin Response (GSR) was compared using two tailed t-test at 95 % confidence interval for navigation and learning phases of users interaction for both the websites. The comparative analysis of GSR showed significantly higher (f=18.63, $p<0.05$) skin conductance level (SCL) for navigation in e-learning website with usability problems (mean = 5.26 µs & std. dev. = 1.51) vs the website without usability problems (mean = 2.16 & std. dev. = 1.57). In light of the results obtained and as discussed in sec 2.4, it is evident that task difficulty while navigating was higher in website with usability problem which is in good agreement with result of input device parameter and marker analysis. Similarly, SCL was compared for learning and website with usability problem (mean= 4.86, std. Dev. = 1.96) was found to have significantly higher (f=13.25, $p<0.05$) value than website without usability problem (mean= 2.57, std.dev. = 0.95). Higher SCL value during learning shows higher stress level of users. These results show that, inconsistent design of interface and poor usability of e-learning websites created extra stress while navigation. Higher SCL during learning shows that stress generated during navigation was carried out during watching the video lesson.

5. CONCLUSION

This paper concludes that; usability of e-learning systems affects user's learning behaviour. Poor usability of websites lowers the *engagement* and adds *distraction* to users which hampers learning. Inconsistent interface design confuses the learner and lowers the *confidence* in the system which reflects in learner's confidence while interacting and learning with system. This paper concludes that, in order to design effective e-learning systems, functional usability testing should expand its dimension and integrate learning behaviour. This study highlights different learning behaviour markers which may be integrated with functional usability testing to support learner centric design. Which will be helpful for a designer to understand and design a better and efficient e- learning system.

6. LIMITATION AND FUTURE SCOPE

This study considered only three major factors of learning namely, *attention, motivation and trust*. Future study can explore more such factors and develop markers for evaluation of e-learning system usability. This study accentuated only navigation and layout design of website. Further study can examine the implications of more such design problems on learning behaviour. Use of advance physiological measures like eye tracker, Electroencephalogram (EEG) and facial expression analysis can further be used to verify these results.

REFERENCES

ISO 9241-11:1998 Ergonomic requirements for office work with visual display terminals (VDTs): Guidance on usability.

Al-Gahtani, Said S. 2016. "Empirical Investigation of E-Learning Acceptance and Assimilation: A Structural Equation Model." *Applied Computing and Informatics* 12 (1).

Davids, Mogamat Razeen, Usuf M. E. Chikte, and Mitchell L. Halperin. 2014. "Effect of Improving the Usability of an E-Learning Resource: A Randomized Trial." *Advances in Physiology Education* 38 (2): 155–60.

Deci, Edward L., and Richard M. Ryan. 2012. "Self-Determination Theory." In *Handbook of Theories of Social Psychology: Volume 1,* by Paul Van Lange, Arie Kruglanski, and E. Higgins, 416–37. SAGE Publications Ltd.

Dzunic, Zeljko, Leonid Stoimenov, and Marija Dzunic. "Trust in eLearning systems based on virtual community of practice." *TECHNICS TECHNOLOGIES EDUCATION MANAGEMENT-TTEM* 6, no. 4 (2011): 1235-1245.

El-Masri, Mazen, and Ali Tarhini. 2017a. "Erratum to: Factors Affecting the Adoption of e-Learning Systems in Qatar and USA: Extending the Unified Theory of Acceptance and Use of Technology 2." *Educational Technology Research and Development* 65

Granić, Andrina. 2008."Experience with Usability Evaluation of E-Learning Systems."*Universal Access in the Information Society* 7 (4).

Grossberg, Stephen. 2005. "Linking Attention to Learning, Expectation, Competition, and Consciousness." In *Neurobiology of Attention,* 652–62. Elsevier.

Hollingsed, Tasha, and David G Novick. 2007. "Usability Inspection Methods after 15 Years of Research and Practice." In *Proceedings of the 25th Annual ACM International Conference on Design of Communication - SIGDOC '07,* 249. ACM.

Holzinger, Andreas. 2005. "Usability Engineering Methods for Software Developers." *Communications of the ACM* 48 (1).

Hornbæk, Kasper. 2006. "Current Practice in Measuring Usability: Challenges to Usability Studies and Research." *International Journal of Human-Computer Studies* 64 (2).

Hudlicka, Eva. 2003. "To Feel or Not to Feel: The Role of Affect in Human–Computer Interaction." *International Journal of Human-Computer Studies* 59 (1–2).

Kearsley, Greg, and Ben Shneiderman. "Engagement Theory: A Framework for Technology-Based Teaching and Learning." *Educational Technology* 38, no. 5 (1998): 20-23.

Kortum, P., and C. Z. Acemyan. 2016. "The Relationship Between User Mouse-Based Performance And Subjective Usability Assessments." *Proceedings of the Human Factors and Ergonomics Society Annual Meeting* 60 (1).

Kukulska-Hulme, Agnes, and John Traxler. 2013. "Design Principles for Mobile Learning." In *Rethinking Pedagogy for a Digital Age,* 244–57. Abingdon: Routledge.

Levy, Yair. 2007. "Comparing Dropouts and Persistence in E-Learning Courses." *Computers & Education* 48 (2).

Luo, Xin, Han Li, Jie Zhang, and J.P. Shim. 2010. "Examining Multi-Dimensional Trust and Multi-Faceted Risk in Initial Acceptance of Emerging Technologies: An Empirical Study of Mobile Banking Services." *Decision Support Systems* 49.

Lykken, D. T., and P. H. Venables. 1971. "Direct Measurement of Skin Conductance: A Proposal for Standardization."

Martínez-Caro, Eva. 2011. "Factors Affecting Effectiveness in E-Learning: An Analysis in Production Management Courses." *Computer Applications in Engineering Education* 19 (3).

Mehler, Bruce, Bryan Reimer, Joseph Coughlin, and Jeffery Dusek. 2009. "Impact of Incremental Increases in Cognitive Workload on Physiological Arousal and Performance in Young Adult Drivers." *Transportation Research Record: Journal of the Transportation Research Board* 2138 (December).

Nielsen, J. n.d. "Usability Inspection Methods." http://dl.acm.org/citation.cfm?id=223730.

Nourbakhsh, Nargess, Yang Wang, Fang Chen, and Rafael A. Calvo. 2012. "Using Galvanic Skin Response for Cognitive Load Measurement in Arithmetic and Reading Tasks." In *Proceedings of the 24th Australian Computer-Human Interaction Conference on - OzCHI '12,* 420–23. ACM Press.

Plantak Vukovac, D., V. Kirinic, and B. Klicek. 2010. "A Comparison of Usability Evaluation Methods for E-Learning Systems." In *DAAAM International Scientific Book 2010.* DAAAM International Vienna.

Mbarek, Rabeb, and Ferid Zaddem. "The examination of factors affecting e-learning effectiveness." *International Journal of Innovation and Applied Studies* 2, no. 4 (2013): 423-435.

Rostaminezhad, M.A., N. Mozayani, D. Norozi, and M. Iziy. 2013. "Factors Related to E-Learner Dropout: Case Study of IUST Elearning Center." *Procedia - Social and Behavioural Sciences* 83 (July).

Sharma, Sujeet Kumar, Mohamed Sarrab, and Hafedh Al-Shihi. 2017. "Development and Validation of Mobile Learning Acceptance Measure." *Interactive Learning Environments* 25 (7). Routledge: 847–58.

Soloway, Elliot, Mark Guzdial, and Kenneth E Hay. 1994. "Learner-Centered Design: The Challenge for HCI in the 21st Century." *Interactions* 1 (2).

Squires, David. 1999. "Usability and Educational Software Design: Special Issue of Interacting with Computers." *Interacting with Computers* 11 (5).

Squires, David, and Jenny Preece. 1996. "Usability and Learning: Evaluating the Potential of Educational Software." *Computers & Education* 27 (1).

Steven M. Manson , Len Kne , Kevin R. Dyke , Jerry Shannon & Sami Eria (2012) Using Eye-tracking and Mouse Metrics to Test Usability of Web Mapping Navigation, Cartography and Geographic Information Science, 39:1, 48-60

Terenzini, Patrick T, Ernest T Pascarella, and Gregory S Blimling. 1999. "Students' out-of-Class Experiences and Their Influence on Learning and Cognitive Development: A Literature Review." *Journal of College Student Development*

Venkatesh, Viswanath, James Y L. Thong, and Xin Xu. 2011. "Consumer Acceptance and Use of Information Technology: Extending the Unified Theory of Acceptance and Use of Technology" 36: 157–78.

Zaharias, Panagiotis. n.d. "Usability in the Context of E-Learning: A Framework Augmenting 'Traditional'' Usability Constructs with Instructional Design and Motivation to Learn.'" *International Journal of Technology and Human Interaction* 5.

EVALUATING USABILITY AND ENGAGEMENT IN A MONEY MANAGEMENT TOOL FOR USERS WITH INTELLECTUAL DISABILITY

Elaine Kavanagh, Marian McDonnell, Ryan Dowler and Irene Connolly
Institute of Art, Design and Technology (IADT), Dun Laoghaire, Co Dublin, Ireland

ABSTRACT

Managing one's own money is important for self-determination and is an area where persons with intellectual disability may need support (Davies et al, 2003). My Money Counts (MMC) is a visual money management application currently in development at Dun Laoghaire Institute of Art, Design, and Technology (IADT) in collaboration with the Money Advice and Budgeting Service (MABS) and Carmona Services. This research project aimed to evaluate the usability and engagement of MMC at its current stage of development. It also aimed to compare observational with self-reported evaluations for both usability and engagement. Participants were ten adults with intellectual disability. A mixed methods approach used controlled observations, qualitative thematic analysis and self-report questionnaires. Findings indicated significant usability issues with the My Money Counts application; engagement was moderately positive. Comparison of self-reported and observed evaluations revealed that observed usability was very poor while self-reported usability was positive; observed engagement was moderately positive while self-reported engagement was very positive. These findings are discussed along with implications, strengths and weaknesses of the study, and suggestions for future research.

KEYWORDS

Intellectual Disability, Money Management, Usability, Engagement

1. INTRODUCTION

1.1 Intellectual Disability and Money Management

Intellectual disability (ID) varies in severity with four levels: mild, moderate, severe and profound (Sulkes, 2016). The most important distinction between persons with intellectual disability (PwID) and the general population is that the former have more intense support needs (Wehmeyer & Thompson, 2016). Research has consistently found that PwID are less self-determined than their non-disabled peers, owing not to any reduced capacity for self-determination but to fewer opportunities for decision-making (Wehmeyer & Abery, 2013).

Managing one's own money is important for self-determination and is an area where PwID may need support (Davies et al, 2003). It requires both decision-making skills and an understanding of financial concepts. Research indicates strong and potentially two-way relationships between decision-making opportunities and both financial decision-making abilities and basic financial understanding for PwID (Suto et al, 2005). Although PwID can learn more effective decision-making skills (Wehmeyer, 2007; Fisher et al, 2012), evidence suggests that money management can present difficulties. A study which examined understanding of basic financial concepts among adults with ID found that success rates decreased as amounts of money increased (Suto et al, 2006). Many persons with Down's Syndrome (DS) have difficulties understanding the concept of money and some may not understand the difference between one euro and one cent (Rus et al, 2017).

1.2 The Role of Assistive Technology

Assistive technology (AT) can be defined as any device which allows a person with a disability to accomplish something they would otherwise find difficult or impossible (Burrow & Brooks, 2012). Recent developments have focused on using mobile technology to assist PwID with independent travel, organisation and planning (Deklever et al, 2015b), social networking (Daems et al, 2016) and employment opportunities (Collins et al, 2014).

There are few ATs aimed at money management. The POSEIDON Project, which develops customisable smart solutions for persons with DS developed a money handling training (MHT) application in response to a survey identifying money management as one of the primary areas needing support (Rus & Braun, 2016). Results were positive: users liked the gamification approach while carers felt that it would help to improve financial understanding and promote safe money handling (Rus et al, 2017). Evaluation of a prototype aimed at helping PwID to balance chequebooks found that users made less errors compared to manual methods (Davies et al, 2003) indicating the potential of a money management application for PwID.

1.3 My Money Counts

My Money Counts (MMC) is a proposed mobile application currently in development at Dun Laoghaire Institute of Art, Design, and Technology (IADT) in collaboration with the Money Advice and Budgeting Service (MABS) and St John of Gods (SJOG) Carmona Services. It aims to provide a visual money management and budgeting application to support independence and self-determination in vulnerable groups. Whilst PwID are the primary target user group, people with a range of other cognitive impairments may also benefit. Mobile technology is a valuable tool for PwID due to its portability and opportunities for inclusion (Borblik et al, 2015) and accordingly it is envisaged that MMC will be a fully responsive mobile application.

1.4 User Centred Design for Persons with Intellectual Disabilities

User Centred Design (UCD) sees users and their goals as the driving force behind product development and is achieved by involving users in the design and/or evaluation process (Rogers et al, 2012). Although UCD involving PwID is not common practice, it is recommended by the Web Accessibility Initiative (Dekelver et al, 2015). In accordance with these recommendations, the principal target users of MMC will form a key element in its evaluation. Their feedback will be assessed in terms of usability and engagement with the results of this evaluation informing the future development of MMC.

1.4.1 Intellectual Disability and Usability

Usability is an attribute which assesses how easy an interface is to use (Neilsen, 2012). Three important principles of usability are effectiveness, efficiency and satisfaction which determine ability to achieve goals, effort used in achieving these goals, and ease of use. (Deklever et al, 2015). Traditional usability evaluations collect data about users' performance on set tasks, task completion time, number of errors and post-test questionnaires (Rogers et al, 2012). Some of these methods are not ideal for PwID (Caliz et al, 2016) although other methods, such as use of an interactive prototype can be particularly important for PwID in facilitating greater engagement in the testing process (Sitbon & Farhin, 2017). Usability is closely related to accessibility, the main feature of which is inclusion of functionality that makes use by PwID possible. Specific mobile interface design guidelines seek to improve usability and accessibility for PwID by making recommendations around navigation, graphic design, text requirements and personalisation (Borblik et al, 2015).

There is no single accepted method for usability testing involving PwID. USATESTDOWN offers a comprehensive usability testing guide of mobile devices for people with DS. Some of its recommendations include use of accessible documentation including an adapted System Usability Scale (SUS), care around anonymity, and careful framing of questions due to users' potential unwillingness to give negative feedback owing to their naturally friendly predisposition (Caliz et al, 2016). POSEIDON's MHT usability evaluation included carers as secondary users who observed primary users, gave feedback and completed usability questionnaires (Rus et al, 2017). Macedo & Trevisan (2013) adapted the Detailed Video Analysis (DEVAN) method for use with children with DS. DEVAN is a coding scheme for detecting usability issues in task-based products for adults by identifying indicators of these issues. The researchers adapted these indicators to reflect behaviour observed in children with DS.

1.4.2 Intellectual Disability and Engagement

Engagement is a complex process involving challenge, aesthetic appeal, novelty, interactivity, awareness, motivation, interest and emotion (O'Brien & Toms, 2008). Engagement with technology can improve user experience (Doherty et al, 2010). Promoting user engagement for PwID should focus on minimizing cognitive load by using graphics, animations, interactivity, choice and auditory output (Lányi et al, 2012). There is no standard measure of user engagement as it differs according to area and demographic although subjective variables (e.g. post-test questionnaire) and objective variables (e.g. using eye trackers) can be examined. (Attfield et al, 2011). However, some of these methods may be unsuitable for PwID. Hookham, et al (2016) suggest that assessing different components of engagement (i.e. behavioural, affective and cognitive) allows for a more targeted measurement of its various aspects: behavioural engagement can be measured by recording time spent focused on a task, affective engagement by observing emotional cues, and cognitive engagement by testing whether the user reaches their goal.

1.5 The Present Study

The main aim of the current study is to evaluate MMC with its principal target users. However, due to the absence of an established method for user testing involving PwID and the possibility that users may report favourably due to a naturally friendly disposition (Cáliz, et al., 2016) this study will also compare observational and self-reported evaluations in order to gain a greater understanding of user testing involving PwID.

1.5.1 Research Questions

1. What are the usability and engagement issues relating to My Money Counts?
2. Is there a similarity between observed and self-reported usability?
3. Is there a similarity between observed and self-reported engagement?

2. METHOD

2.1 Research Design

This study used a mixed methods design with controlled observations and questionnaires. This approach is recommended to facilitate greater understanding in usability research involving PwID (Lepisto and Ovaska, 2004). Furthermore, the use of both observational and questionnaire methods along with analysis of qualitative and quantitative data is advisable in this type of research. (Caliz et al, 2016).

2.2 Participants

Participants were treated in accordance with the ethical standards of the Psychological Society of Ireland. The participants were recruited from a service provider for PwID via purposive sampling. The sample consisted of 10 adults (3 males, 7 females) aged between 20 and 50 years (M=29.2, SD=10.8) with mild to moderate ID. All participants had adequate verbal communication skills to express views during testing. Due to ethical considerations. no information was obtained regarding levels of ID for individual participants.

2.3 Materials

Coded Observation Sheets were developed to measure usability and engagement indicators during the observations. These were informed by Macedo and Trevisan's (2013) adapted DEVAN study which had a 64% Cohens Kappa reliability rating. Two actions in this method were excluded (Impatience and Random Actions) due to limited observation time. Additionally, based on Hookham et al.'s (2016) suggestion that affective engagement can be measured by observing emotional cues, three of the actions (Dislike, Passive, Bored) were considered better suited as measures of engagement along with the addition of codes to measure vocalisations and behaviour. The Observation Sheets comprised five negative usability factors (*error / wrong action; needs help; confused, unsure how to proceed; physical / motor problem; sight / hearing problem*) and five positive usability factors (*no error; no help needed; tasks are clear; no physical / motor problem; clearly see and hear audio*). Also included were five negative engagement factors (*stop before reaching goal; bored – sighing, looking around, passive; dislikes something specific; negative vocalisation; negative behaviour, frown, grimace*) and five positive ones (*task completed; interested, focused; likes something specific; positive vocalisation; positive behaviour*). The researchers awarded a point for each action observed and recorded notes.

2.3.1 Accessible Materials

All materials provided to participants were accessible, including Expression of Interest Form, Information Sheet, Consent, Demographic and Debrief Forms and were based on materials developed by Maloney (2012).

An accessible Task List was developed to test all major features of MMC. As task understanding is an issue when testing with this group (Williams, 2013) the task list included screenshots with relevant areas highlighted.

An Adapted System Usability Scale (SUS) gathered participants' views on MMC. It included fourteen smileyometer questions. Williams (2015) found a smileyometer with a four-point rating scale to be an appropriate measure for people with learning disabilities as a neutral option could be confusing for this population. The smileyometer sought user opinions on each feature tested: seven items related to ease of use and seven items related to likeability. This scale was found to have a Cronbach's Alpha of .706 (Kline, 2005).

2.4 Procedure

Testing took place in a computer lab at IADT. The participants were shown to computers which had been logged into anonymized MMC test accounts and keystroke recordings were activated. Five tasks were included:

1. **Video Task** – participants were required to locate the *Videos* link on the navigation bar, select the *'My Own Money'* instructional video, enable full screen, watch the video and return to MMC.
2. **Budget Task** – participants were requested to select the *Create a Budget* navigation link and watch a help video outlining the budget creation procedure. They were then asked to drag three items (savings, lunches and phone) from an array of predefined expenditure categories into a selection box, select *I'm ready to make my budget* and click *continue* to input budget expenditure. This screen displayed a wheel which rotated to the next field on pressing enter (see Figure 1). The testers were asked to input *test1* into the *Name of Budget* field, 188 into *Money I Have*, 1 into the *Week* field, 10 into *Savings*, 20 into *Lunches* and 20 into the *Phone* field before clicking *Create Budget* to see a pie chart detailing their budget. Next participants were asked to edit their budgets. This required them to find the bills field, click into the amount, delete the zeros, input 30, and reload the page to see a revised pie chart.
3. **Calculator Task** – participants were asked to add up a series of notes and coins using the money calculator (see Figure 2) and circle the correct answer from a choice of three given on the task list.
4. **Game Task** – participants selected the *App Store* navigation link and *Vending Machine Game.* Players were required to choose an item from a vending machine and enter the correct number of coins.
5. **Manage Profile Task** – participants were asked to select the *My Profile* menu option, click *Change This*, enter a new password (moneycounts) into the *Password* field, enter the same password into the *Password Confirmation* field, and finally enter the original password into the *Current Password* field.

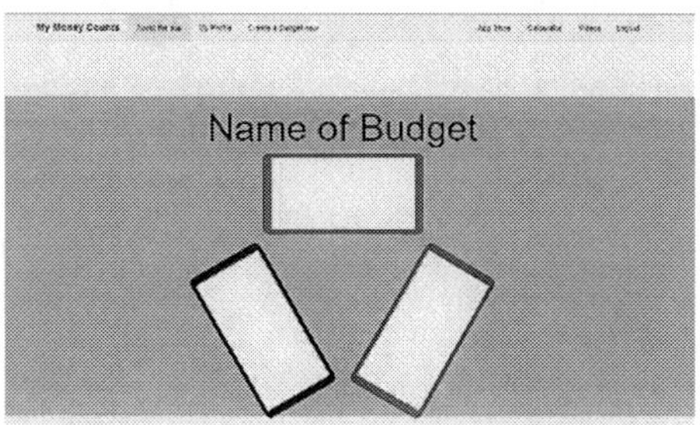

Figure 1. Budget input screen

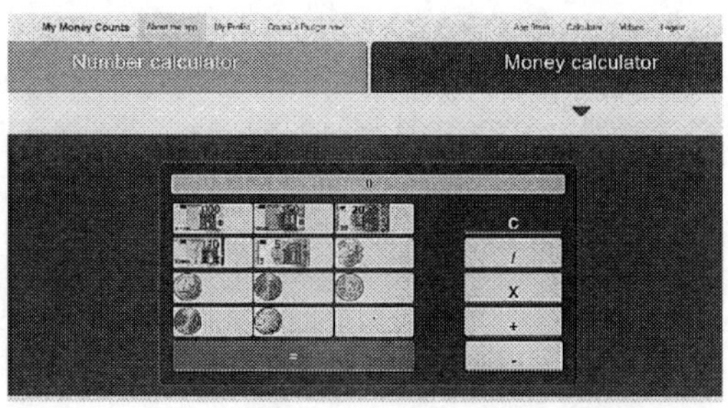

Figure 2. Money calculator

Assistance with tasks was given as required. The researchers and assistant researchers observed each participant for fifteen minutes. After thirty minutes participants were invited to fill out the Adapted SUS with help given as needed. They were debriefed and thanked for taking part in the study.

2.5 Analysis

Reported usability and engagement scores were calculated based on responses to questions in the Adapted SUS relating to ease of use and likeability respectively. These were scored in an ordinal manner from 1 point (very hard / disliked a lot) to 4 points (very easy / liked a lot). Observed usability was calculated by subtracting the number of negative observed usability factors from the number of positive ones. Observed engagement was calculated by subtracting the observed negative engagement factors from the positive engagement factors.

Observed data was also subjected to thematic analysis. This involves examining text-based data in order to identify its major themes (Howitt & Cramer, 2008) and is useful for organizing data while providing rich detail (Braun & Clarke, 2006). As initial analysis indicated the existence of specific task-related issues, data was given a code relative to its specific task. i.e. Video, Budget, Calculator, Game or Password. Data relating to Navigation was coded separately as this posed an issue across tasks. Deeper analysis revealed that underlying issues spanned tasks and themes were identified accordingly.

3. RESULTS

3.1 Usability

A significant number of usability issues were observed, with the most frequently recorded being '*error/wrong action*', '*needs help*' and '*confused, unsure how to proceed*'. Creating a budget was the most problematic task. The calculator, game and password tasks were also difficult. As the number of negative usability observations exceeded positive ones for nine participants, their total observed usability scores were negative which reflects the extent of usability issues observed. See Figure 3 for observed scores. Participants reported fewer negative usability issues than positive, see Figure 4. The most difficult reported task was changing the password.

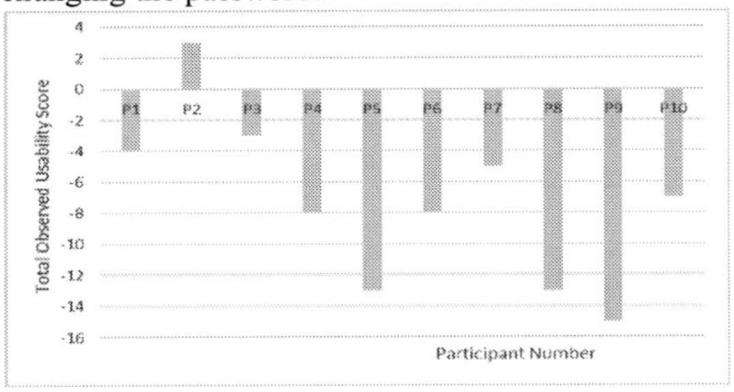

Figure 3. Total observed usability scores

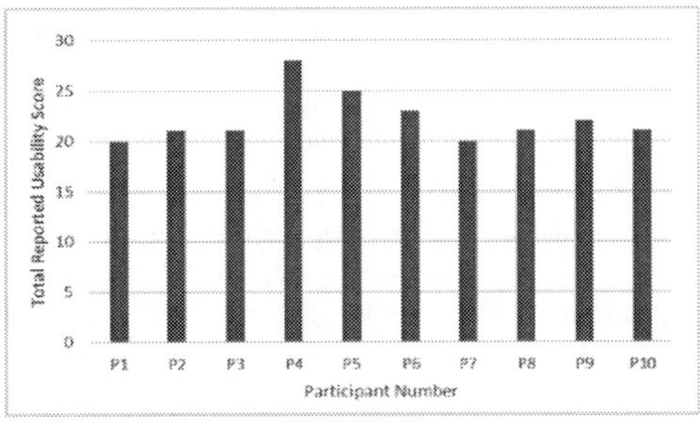

Figure 4. Total reported usability scores

3.1.1 Qualitative Findings

Four main usability themes were identified: Interface Problems, Help Required, Motor Skills and Managing Passwords. The Interface Problems theme included difficulties creating a budget (finding progression buttons and editing the budget), using the money calculator (neglecting to use the calculator '*plus*' button) and navigating. Seven participants experienced navigation difficulties at some stage during the testing.

Help was required in terms of following instructions on the task list, working through tasks, reading, and calculation difficulties. All participants required help to complete at least one task with some needing help throughout. Five participants were helped to create a budget. Significant help was required entering current password once and new password twice into the relevant fields during the password task.

The Motor Skills theme related to difficulties with typing and click and drag functions, observed in four participants. The Managing Password theme summarized the challenging nature of this task, with some participants making two or three unsuccessful attempts before being helped to complete.

3.2 Engagement

Although participants engaged well with MMC, a moderate number of negative observations were recorded. The calculator task was the most engaging for participants. The game, while challenging, also engaged participants well. Several *'bored'* observations were recorded during the video task. Although negative engagement indicators were recorded for the budget task due to frustration, positive indicators were also noted. The Manage Profile Task had the fewest engagement observations due to the quantity of help was required; task completion was largely achieved with support. Total observed engagement was moderately positive, see Figure 5 for individual scores. Reported engagement was very positive, see Figure 6 for reported scores.

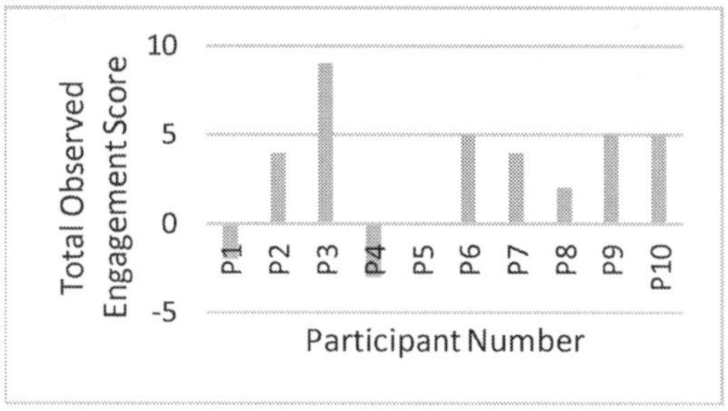

Figure 5. Total observed engagement scores

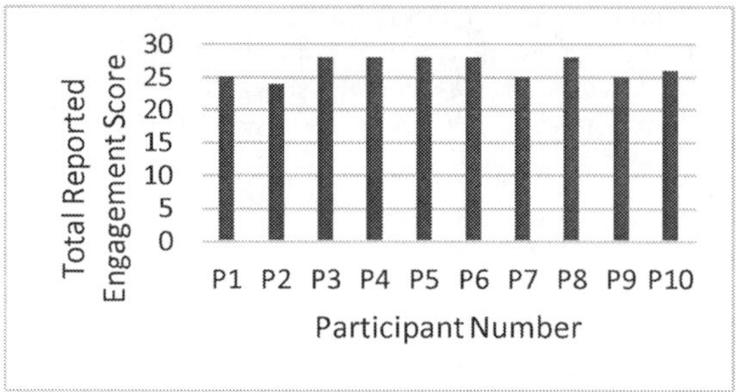

Figure 6. Total reported engagement scores

3.2.1 Qualitative Findings

Two main themes were identified relating to observed engagement: Positive Engagement and Negative Engagement. Positive Engagement reflected interest and appeal shown by participants as well as the number of completed tasks. All participants showed interest in MMC, particularly in the budget creation tool, money calculator and game. The budget and calculation tasks had the highest completion rates. All users created a budget, although many needed help progressing through the steps. The calculation task was completed by eight users, with five of these choosing the correct answer. Only five participants changed passwords successfully.

The Negative Engagement theme included observations of boredom, frustration and tasks stopped. Indicators of boredom (fast-forwarding through content or looking around the room) were noted during the video task. Yawning was observed during the budget creation task when users were unsure how to proceed. Four users showed signs of frustration during the session. Few tasks were stopped, with most participants completing even the difficult tasks with help.

4. DISCUSSION

Observational analysis revealed significant usability issues and moderately positive engagement scores, although these were impacted by the usability issues due to frustration experienced by participants. Developing accessible interfaces in AT software for PwID is challenging (Borblik at al., 2015). For MMC, this challenge lies in balancing accessible interface design with the provision of a tool which simplifies money management. The primary usability issues included the complexity of the budget creation process, problems with navigation and managing passwords, and difficulty finding some progression and calculator buttons. Additionally, significant assistance was required by participants while using MMC indicating that it is not accessible. Stakeholders in the MMC project highlighted difficulties with the budget creation process prior to testing and suggested simplifying language, providing audio links and using icons on the pie chart. This is in line with accessible mobile interface design guidelines which recommend a consistent and simple interface structure and menu, with images and symbols to facilitate recognition, labels or instructions to accompany input, and simple language (Borblik et al., 2015). Implementing these recommendations would resolve many usability issues in MMC and empower the target population to use it independently, thus making MMC truly accessible. Regarding navigation, Williams (2013) found large images with hotspot highlighting useful for menu links. Hotspot highlighting on MMC's menu is not well emphasized – greater emphasis here and inclusion of images along with the text would decrease user errors. Difficulties with password recall may be facilitated by giving an option to retain login details (Davies et al., 2015). However, this would not address initial login difficulties. A pattern-based password is being considered as an alternative.

Participants showed great enthusiasm for MMC and engaged well despite poor usability. According to Deklever et al. (2015) people with disabilities see technology as a gateway to the world and this may explain the participants' interest and enthusiasm. However, engagement was impacted by boredom and frustration. Minimizing cognitive load can improve engagement (Lanyi et al., 2012) and this could be achieved by implementing the guidelines for accessible mobile interface design.

While the differences between observed and self-reported evaluations could be explained by the natural friendliness of the user group (Caliz et al., 2016), the issue of response bias in questionnaires (Hayes, 2000) raises that possibility that the discrepancies in the present study are not limited to the population involved. However, users' enjoyment of an experience may be more memorable than the difficulty of the process, making self-reported usability data crucial as a measure of users' perceptions and feelings (Albert and Tullis, 2013).It must be considered that the participants rated MMC highly despite the observed evaluations.

5. CONCLUSION

The present study has practical implications for the future development of MMC as the findings will inform its next stage of development. This study also underlines the need for caution in interpreting results of self-reported evaluation in usability testing involving PwID. In this respect, this study echoes previous research regarding the importance of using observations and questionnaires to gain a full and thorough understanding when usability testing with PwID (Lepisto & Ovaska, 2004; Caliz et al., 2016). Future research could test with a larger sample to allow for greater quantitative data analysis. Also, as usability lab tests can yield different results to field tests (Rogers et al., 2012), future tests could allow participants to use MMC in their daily lives.

The present study aimed to evaluate usability and engagement in MMC. Findings indicate significant issues, with improvements in terms of both usability and accessibility being required in future iterations. However, users engaged well with MMC indicating good potential for future adoption by its target users. A second aim of this study was to compare observational with self-reported evaluations for both usability and engagement. Inconsistencies between observed and self-reported measures highlight the need for researchers to use a variety of methods when conducting usability testing involving PwID. Finally, this study emphasizes the importance of including PwID in the evaluation process as their input is crucial to success in future developments of MMC.

REFERENCES

Albert, W. and Tullis, T., 2013. *Measuring the User Experience: Collecting, Analyzing, and Presenting Usability Metrics*. Elsevier, Waltham, USA.

Attfield, S. et al, 2011. Towards a Science of User-Engagement (position paper). *Proceedings of WSDM Workshop on User Modelling for Web applications*. Hong Kong, China, pp. 9-12.

Borblik, J. et al, 2015. Assistive Technology Software for People with Intellectual or Development Disabilities: Design of User Interfaces for Mobile Applications. *Proceedings of Information, Intelligence, Systems and Applications (IISA) 6th International Conference*. Corfu, Greece, pp. 1-6.

Braun, V. and Clarke, V., 2006. Using Thematic Analysis in Psychology. *In Qualitative Research in Psychology,* Vol. 3, No. 2, pp. 77-101.

Burrow, S., and Brooks, D., 2012. Atdementia: An Information Resource on Assistive Technologies that Help Support the Independence of People with Dementia. *In Dementia*, Vol. 11, No. 4, pp. 553-557.

Cáliz, D., Martínez, L., Alamán, X., Terán, C., & Cáliz, R. (2016). 'USATESTDOWN' a Proposal of a Usability Testing Guide for Mobile Applications Focused on Persons with Down Syndrome. *Ar-chivo Digital UPM*, *1*, 1-17.

Collins, J. C. et al, 2014. Use of Portable Electronic Assistive Technology to Improve Independent Job Performance of Young Adults with Intellectual Disability. *In Journal of Special Education Technology*, Vol. 29, No. 3, pp. 15-29.

Daems, J. et al, 2016. AbleChat: Development of a Chat App with Pictograms for People with Intellectual Disabilities. *In Engineering4Society 2016*, p. 25.

Davies, D. K. et al, 2003. Utilization of Computer Technology to Facilitate Money Management by Individuals with Mental Retardation. *In Education and Training in Developmental Disabilities*, pp. 106-112.

Davies, D. K. et al, 2015. An Interface to Support Independent Use of Facebook by People with Intellectual Disability. *In Intellectual and Developmental Disabilities*, Vol. 53, No. 1, pp. 30-41.

Dekelver, J. et al, 2015. Design of Mobile Applications for People with Intellectual Disabilities. *In Communications in Computer and Information Science*, Vol. 535, pp. 823-836.

Dekelver, J. et al, 2015. Viamigo: A Digital Travel Assistant for People with Intellectual Disabilities: Modeling and Design Using Contemporary Intelligent Technologies as a Support for Independent Traveling of People with Intellectual Disabilities. *Proceedings of Information, Intelligence, Systems and Applications (IISA) 6th International Conference*. Corfu, Greece, pp. 1-6.

Doherty, G. et al, 2010. Design and Evaluation Guidelines for Mental Health Technologies. *In Interacting with Computers*, Vol. 22, No. 4, pp. 243-252.

Fisher, Z. et al, 2012. Practical Aspects of a Visual Aid to Decision Making. *In Journal of Intellectual Disability Research*, Vol. 56, No. 6, pp. 588-599.

Hookham, G. et al, 2016. Comparing Usability and Engagement Between a Serious Game and a Traditional Online Program. *Proceedings of Australasian Computer Science Week Multiconference*. Canberra, Australia, p. 54.

Howitt, D. and Cramer, D., 2008. *Introduction to Research Methods in Psychology*. Pearson Education Ltd., Harlow, UK.

Kline, R. B., 2005. *Principles and practice of structural equation modeling* (2nd ed.). Guilford Press, New York, USA.

Lanyi, C. S. et al, 2012. Results of User Interface Evaluation of Serious Games for Students with Intellectual Disability. *In Acta Polytechnica Hungarica,* Vol. 9, No. 1, pp. 225-245.

Lepistö, A. and Ovaska, S., 2004. Usability Evaluation Involving Participants with Cognitive Disabilities. *Proceedings of Nordic Conference on Human-Computer Interaction.* Tampere, Finland, pp. 305-308.

Macedo I. and Trevisan D.G., 2013. A Method to Evaluate Disabled User Interaction: A Case Study with Down Syndrome Children. *Proceedings of International Conference on Universal Access in Human-Computer Interaction*. Berlin, Germany, pp. 50-58.

Maloney, M. 2012, 'Accessible Information: Advocating the Use of Technology for Individuals with Intellectual Disability on their Path to Individualised Services', M.Sc. in Computing (Assistive Technology), DIT, Ireland.

Money Counts n.d., Introduction to Money Counts, viewed 10 November 2017, <http://www.moneycounts.ie/>.

Neilsen, J. 2012, *Usability 101: introduction to usability,* viewed 12 November 2017, <https://www.nngroup.com/articles/usability-101-introduction-to-usability/>.

O'Brien, H. and Toms, E.G., 2008. What is User Engagement? A Conceptual Framework for Defining User Engagement with Technology. *In Journal of the American Society for Information Science and Technology,* Vol. 59, No. 6, pp. 938-955.

Rogers, Y. et al, 2012. *Interaction Design: Beyond Human Computer Interaction.* John Wiley & Sons Ltd., Sussex, UK.

Rus, S. and Braun, A., 2016. Money Handling Training-Applications for Persons with Down Syndrome. *Proceedings of Intelligent Environments (IE) 12th International Conference.* London, United Kingdom, pp. 214-217.

Rus, S. et al, 2017. Assistive Apps for Activities of Daily Living Supporting Persons with Down's Syndrome. *In Journal of Ambient Intelligence and Smart Environments*, Vol. 9, No. 5, pp. 611-623.

Sitbon, L. and Farhin, S., 2017. Co-Designing Interactive Applications with Adults with Intellectual Disability. *Proceedings of 29th Australian Conference on Computer-Human Interaction*. Brisbane, Australia, pp. 487-491.

Sulkes, S. B. 2016, *Intellectual Disability*, viewed 16 April 2018, <https://www.merckmanuals.com/en-pr/professional/pediatrics/learning-and-developmental-disorders/intellectual-disability>.

Suto, W. M. I. et al, 2005. The Relationships Among Three Factors Affecting the Financial Decision-Making Abilities of Adults with Mild Intellectual Disabilities. *In Journal of Intellectual Disability Research*, Vol. 49, No. 3, pp. 210-217.

Suto, W. M. I. et al, 2006. Understanding of Basic Financial Concepts Among Adults with Mild Learning Disabilities. *In British Journal of Clinical Psychology*, Vol. 45, No. 2, pp. 261-266.

Wehmeyer, M. L., 2007. *Promoting Self-Determination in Students with Developmental Disabilities.* Guildford Press, New York, USA.

Wehmeyer, M. L. and Abery, B. H., 2013. Self-Determination and Choice. *In Intellectual and Developmental Disabilities*, Vol. 51, No. 5, pp. 399-411.

Wehmeyer, M. L. and Thompson, J. R. 2016, *Intellectual Disability and Support Needs – the Unique Support Needs of People with Intellectual Disabilities,* viewed 12 December 2017, <http://www.apa.org/pi/disability/resources/publications/newsletter/2016/09/intellectual-disability-support.aspx>.

Williams, P., 2015. Eliciting web site preferences of people with learning disabilities. *In Journal of Research in Special Educational Needs*, Vol. 17, No. 1, pp. 49-63.

Williams, P., 2013. Web site Usability Testing Involving People with Learning Disabilities Using Only Images and Audio to Access Information. *In Journal of Research in Special Educational Needs*, Vol. 13, No. 2, pp. 142-151.

BLUEEYES – EASING THE NAVIGATION AND ORIENTATION OF BLIND PEOPLE

Marta Silva, Anabela Gomes, Ana Rita Teixeira and João Orvalho
Master in Human Computer Interaction (HCI), Coimbra Education School, Polytechnic of Coimbra, Rua Dom João III – Solum 3030-329 Coimbra, Portugal

ABSTRACT

As reported by the World Health Organization (WHO), of the 7 billion people alive today, an estimated 253 million live with visual impairment that cannot be corrected with glasses or contact lenses. From these, 30 million blind or partially sighted persons live in Europe. Over the past years, blindness that is caused by diseases has decreased due to the success of public health actions. However, the number of blind people that are over 60 years old is increasing by 2 million per decade. Unfortunately, all these numbers are estimated to be doubled by 2020. With these facts, is necessary to bring awareness and understanding of the challenges blind people face and help to motivate research into new technology to answer those questions. This document starts to identify the challenges people with visual disabilities face in their life. The problem of navigation and orientation as well the different possibilities to deal with the locomotion situation is also addressed in this paper. It describes the traditional navigational solutions as well other which involves more sophisticated technological devices and their multimodal interfaces. The paper ends with the description of the BlueEyes project (Orvalho, 2016), consisting in a solution to help blind people moving in a city. The first phases of the project are described, and the actual research situations is also slightly explained.

KEYWORDS

Beacons, Internet of thinks, Human Computer Interaction, Context-aware mobile computing, Accessibility, Blind

1. INTRODUCTION

The challenges of being blind are in everyday activities like reading, cooking, shopping, going outside, using the internet, withdrawing money from an ATM, determining how much of a liquid is in a glass, handling cash, among others (Andress, 2015). According to the research, "eighty to eighty five percent of our perception learning cognition and activities are mediated through vision" (Politzer, 2015). So, all the corresponding activities represents a challenge for a person with vision disability and the difficulty to overcome it, can lead to isolation, loneliness and bring along emotional, social and financial impacts on her/his life. Within these varied challenges, it is possible to group them in two lifelong challenges: accessing the world of information and navigating through space. Society has done a far better job of opening the world of information but it has just started to identify and analyse the serious navigational limitations the blind travellers normally face. Unfortunately, these limitations are the ones that have a severe and bigger negative impact on their life development (Baldwin, 2015).

Currently, technology is a way to support some of their needs and has the potential of improving in a certain extent their life. In fact, it can be stated that today's infrastructure technology is accessible to facilitate blind people to join school, jobs and in leisure activities on a par with sighted peers. On the other hand, there is no such progress concerning blind navigation and therefore, management of mobility and orientation represents still a big and important challenge which needs to be addressed and supported by technology (Baldwin, 2015). Reduced visual capacity challenges people's spatial problem solving every day and in many ways, e.g. how to obtain, recognise, understand, and process information needed in the environment. Indeed, wayfinding can be very stressful and can cause anxiety and become a strong reason not to leave home if it is necessary to visit unfamiliar or complex places, such as shopping malls, train, metro and bus stations, among others (Saarela, 2015). It is vital that public places and community settings will be designed to be secure, as inclusive as possible and accessible for all.

2. CURRENT TOOLS TO ASSIST BLIND PEOPLE IN NAVIGATION

As mentioned before, one big challenge blind people face in everyday life, is mobility and orientation. Orientation refers to the "ability of understanding the spatial properties of an environment and being aware of one's position and his/her relationship with the surroundings"; on the other hand, mobility indicates the "capability of efficiently and safely moving in an environment (e. g. in a city by using public transport) (Giudice and Legge, 2008). In order to get an overview of the current tools which helps blind people in their navigation, these are grouped in two general categories (Baldwin, 2015):

- Currently established navigational strategies which includes independent travel (using human sensory abilities with no other aids); use of a sighted guide; use of the long cane; and use of dog guides (Baldwin, 2015). These are the simplest and the most inexpensive navigations and available tools (trained dogs and the white cane) (Baldwin, 2003). Even though these tools are very widespread, they cannot offer the blind all information and structures for safe mobility, which are accessible to people with eyesight (Shah et al., 2006).
- Electronic navigational aids - in the last few decades, many portable/wearable technological devices have been developed with the aim of improving locomotion for people with visual impairments:
    - Electronic Travel Aids (ETAs) like Mowat Sensor, Sonic Glasses, Pathsounder or Laser Cane. These are devices that gather information about the surrounding environment and transfer it to the user through sensor cameras, sonar, or laser scanners (Sánchez and Elías, 2007; Liu et al., 2010). The objective is to help the blind to avoid obstacles.
    - Electronic Orientation Aids (EOAs) - these are devices that provide pedestrians with directions in unfamiliar places (Kammoun et al., 2011), and support on finding out the route for the best path, providing mobility instructions and path signs to guide the user and develop her/his brain about the environment. It means it aids the blind in finding their way in an unknown environment. EOA is only for occasional use in unknown environments or for very difficult routes that are not used frequently.
    - Position Locator Devices (PLD) - these are devices that define the exact position of its holder such as devices that use GPS technology (Gaggi, 2016).

The navigational technologies are classified according to their sensor characteristics: sonar-based devices (using sonic sensors), vision-based (using cameras or lasers), infrared (IR) or GPS devices (Nicholas, 2008). Sonar-based devices detect and localize objects in order to offer those people a sense of the external environment using sensors. The sensors also aid the user with the mobility task based on the determination of dimensions, range and height of the objects. Camera or laser-based devices use a technology that converts images from a camera into patterns of vibrations delivered through an array of vibrotactile stimulators on the tongue. Infrared signage are systems consisting of infrared transmitters and a handheld IR receiver. Usually the transmitters are placed in strategic locations in the environment. Each sign sends short audio messages, via a constantly emitted IR beam, which can be decoded and spoken when picked up by the receiver. GPS devices enables the user to know his/her position when navigating outdoors, due to the location's information provided by satellite.

However, these systems present some drawbacks. Sonar-based devices have some limitations. They are not very effective in crowded environments because the signal is prone to reflection errors and the technology is also expensive. Camera-based devices need a high bandwidth. Even though GPS technology has made tremendous advances on outdoor navigating systems, methods for tracking position and orientation in indoor environments are still not reliable. Next, some considerations on the technology currently accepted and used by blind population is made.

2.1 White Canes and Guide Dogs

White canes are principally used to scan user's environment for obstacles or orientation landmarks, but they are also useful for other people to identify the user as blind and take the necessary precautions. The latter is the reason for the cane's famous white colour, which in many jurisdictions is mandatory. Used in combination with normal sensory monitoring (and often with a sighted guide), the long cane allows for travel in both familiar and unfamiliar areas. It is cheap, light, portable, needs little maintenance, and it is easy to use (Baldwin, 2015). There are three types of white canes, depending on a person's visual impairment, age, height and specific needs: Identification Canes, White Support Canes and Long Canes. Identification Canes: lightweight, can collapse to fit in a pocket or briefcase are used by the person to indicate to others that they are blind or visually impaired; they can be used to assist with depth perception on stairs or curbs. White Support Canes: collapsible, or rigid are designed to support a person's weight and to help him or her walk. Long Canes are used as bumpers and probes, mainly for independent travel in the home or unfamiliar places requiring specialized training from an orientation and mobility instructor (FFB, 2018).

The main disadvantage of the white cane is its incomplete resolution. It is a near space tool and it does not recognize spatial position or objects. It doesn´t bring blind travellers closer to the abilities obtainable by sight (Baldwin, 2015). The guide dog is also a "mobility aid" that can assist blind people so they can travel safely. They can guide people around obstacles and through crowds, stop at curbs and stairs, and sometimes even be trained to find a limited number of objects that are within sight when given orders. The guide dog user can also train the dog to find frequently used landmarks, such as a bus stop pole or a mailbox (Noriega, 2018). But it is necessary to be aware that guide dogs are expensive as well their maintenance and care. Also, people misinterpret their use: the person who is blind or has low vision directs the dog; the function and purpose of the dog is to merely guide the person around obstacles and indicate the location of steps and curbs. For example, a guide dog cannot know when to cross a street since it is colour blind.

Studies relating different mobility aids (Whitmarsh, 2001) highpoint the diverse purposes, advantages and disadvantages of guide dogs and other aids, such as long canes. For example, guide dogs mobility are more likely to be considered more relaxing than long cane mobility, since the previous implicates obstacle prevention and the latter obstacle detection. A guide dog also offers more advantages than long canes in unfamiliar surroundings or in unknown routes. On the other hand, long canes do not need the care and domestic space of a guide dog (Miner, 2001). Still, the cane and guide dog have similar limitations. "They are most effective for detection of proximal cues, are limited in detecting overhanging or non-ground-level obstructions and do not provide much in the way of orientation information about the user's position (Giudice, 2008).

2.2 Accessible Pedestrian Signals - APS

As mentioned, blind people encounter several difficulties when walking and crossing roads, especially in big cities where traffic jams are more intense. APS support blind pedestrians by using a device that communicates information about pedestrian timing in non-visual format such as audible tones, verbal messages, and/or vibrating surfaces (Harkey et. al., 2007). There are different types of APS´s within different countries which provide different information (audible and vibrotactile signals). It can be about the existence and location of the push button that activates a "Walk" signal; the beginning of the walk interval; the direction of the crosswalk and the location of the destination curb; intersection street names in braille, raised print, or speech messages, intersection signalization with a speech message, and intersection geometry through tactile maps and diagrams or through speech messages (Harkey et. al., 2007).

2.3 Global Positioning System – GPS

As within APSs the orientation on crossing streets is very helpful for blind pedestrians, but still they are not aware of the street name or their position in order to reach a certain destination. With the support of a global positioning system (GPS), the user is able to know his position when navigating outdoors, due to the location's information provided by satellite. This information is displayed on various smartphone applications, for instance Google Maps or dedicated GPS devices (Ruffa et al., 2015). "GPS-based navigation systems are a true orientation aid, as the satellites constantly provide updated position information whether or not the pedestrian is moving" (Giudice, 2008).

There are several GPS-based navigation systems available on the market which use visual display (and some that even provide coarse speech output for in-car route navigation), but they cannot be used fully by blind navigators. Examples of available GPS devices for blind people are the Wayfinder system (Wayfinder, 2005), the Trekker system and the GPS Braille note (Denham et al., 2004).

The information provided by a GPS is "expected to greatly improve blind orientation performance and increase user confidence in promoting safe and independent travel. No other technology can provide the range of orientation information that GPS-based systems make available" (Giudice, 2008). There are nevertheless certain limitations on this technology: although the accessible software is not expensive, the indispensable software is quite costly. Additionally, the user needs to periodically buy new maps and databases of commercial posts of interest. But the most significant disadvantage of GPS is that it cannot be used indoors and is also unable to tell a user about the presence of drop-offs, obstacles, or moving objects in the environment, such as cars or other pedestrians (Hersh, 2006).

3. IBEACON TECHNOLOGY

As stated before, indoor navigation technology still needs further development. There are several devices for specific daily needs, but it is missing a stable accepted technology that provides information about the user's immediate surroundings. This can be in a shopping-mall, a grocery store, airport, train station etc. So, the path of technology development on mobility and orientation tools for visual disabled people should be towards the enhancement of the potential for smarter interaction and accessibility, by adding multisensory features into environments, and by developing multisensory way-finding solutions.

iBeacon can be used as a possible solution, because it is a technology which its potential can be exploited for multisensory and mobility in order to facilitate the tracking, routing and mapping solutions. An iBeacon is a small-scale network transmitter that instead of using latitude and longitude to define the location uses a Bluetooth low energy signal, which iOS devices detect (Gilchrist, 2014). In other words, it's a tiny device with low power consumption that can be placed in a wall or another part of a building. It transmits constantly an identification number via Bluetooth to enable devices which are around and use the corresponding application. BLE beacons-based indoor navigation apps can help visually-impaired and blind people understand the surrounding world in a similar way as GPS technology already does. BLE Beacons (also called Bluetooth Smart or Version 4.0+ of the Bluetooth specification) is the power and application-friendly version of Bluetooth that was built for the Internet of Things (IoT) (Apple, 2018).

One example of a project that builds up a smart environment was developed in Helsinki in a Shopping Mall. The environment was tagged with iBeacons that communicated with blind people's smartphone and BlindSquare App. iBeacons were set on locations that had landmark recognized by blind or visually impaired people (Saarela, 2015). Another project from Indoo.rs whose target was to develop a solution for Terminal 2 at Los Angeles Airport and designed as a mobile app with a voice assistant that helps visually-challenged travellers find their way to any location at the terminal. Another project is an indoor navigation solution for the London tube called Wayfindr. It has been designed by the "ustwo studio in close collaboration with the Royal London Society for Blind People. The developers successfully tested the new system in the Pimlico station in the spring of 2015. They launched Wayfindr as the first open navigation standard for blind people in October 2015" (Suddia, 2018).

For successful navigation, users need at least a "smartphone with BLE (Bluetooth Low Energy) onboard (iOS 7, Android 4.3 or later) and a pre-installed app. The app contains maps of the facility and it guides people via voice directions. This might not be comfortable for other people so the users need bone-conduct earbuds or Google Glass. This will make the directions inaudible for others, but the app's users will still hear what is going on outside. Another option is a smart watch which receives directions from a smartphone application and transmits them as tactile signals" (Suddia, 2018).

4. BLUEEYES PROPOSAL (ORVALHO, 2016)

The aim of this project (Orvalho, 2016) is to help the blind to be aware of the environment in which they live, where navigation and way finding is crucial to guarantee their mobility and to improve their quality of life. We also know that people with visual disabilities in new environments usually feel totally disoriented and isolated. It is not easy for blind people to move independently, therefore it is urgent to ensure easy mobility for them. According to the World Health Organization, nowadays, there are 285 million people with visual impairment, of which 39 million are completely blind and 246 million have low visibility disabilities. Therefore the aim is to improve the social inclusion of these citizens, with novel mobility solution to assist the visually impaired in their daily journey, using a smartphone, without the need for any special hardware, and Bluetooth Low Energy (BLE) technology. Thus, a practical scientific research is proposed supported by three Beacon's Living Labs, in Coimbra, Caldas da Rainha and Tábua.

Another aim is to determine a good architectural model for context-aware mobile apps that leverage Beacons and determine their strengths and limitations for context-awareness for real-world settings. These applications will act like a city guide with accurate tracking and micro-location context-aware on a mobile device with BLE. Each Living Lab network contains iBeacons (Apple) and Eddystone (Google) beacons.

In the city of Coimbra the living lab will be at SMTUC line 5 (25 bus stops and 5 buses) to support the mobility of blind citizens in the city of Coimbra. The system will assist the visually impaired to the proximity of a stop and inform the number of buses and their route. Additionally, it can calculate the best route for their destination. In the event of routine alterations, customers will be informed. Blind customers can interact and determine decisions of SMTUC (a Portuguese acronym for Municipal Transport Services of Coimbra) services, especially those that are intended to function. Inside the bus, the blind may have access to more usable audio information from these stops, the current stop, as well as additional information to support route and the following, such as route change to move to the desired destination.

In the city of Caldas da Rainha the living lab will be at the Bordaliana Route, to support the mobility of blind citizens. This is a cultural route dedicated to Rafael Bordallo Pinheiro, with his giant works of art to integrate a urban street art project. Designed for walking, Bordaliana Route offers a longer route, which approximately takes two hours to be completed, to see unique toponymic parts, human scale and read about episodes of Rafael Bordallo Pinheiro's life and a bit of history of the city.

In the city of Tábua the living lab will be at the centre of the town, to help the pedestrian movement of visually impaired people to access services at public buildings.

The first phase of the project is ready. A survey for an exact number of beacons for each Living Lab network with iBeacons (Apple) and Eddystone beacons (Google), the study of the points of their placement and the acquisition of beacons from different manufacturers was already made. Its facilities, tests and validation are already in working mode. Also underway is the creation of a public web site with georeferenced information of the location of each beacon and technical information inherent in the operation and the maintenance plan.

Understanding our Users and their HCI needs is a crucial aspect of BueEyes project. Our primary users are blind people. UX projects typically consist of three main phases, a research phase, a design phase and a further research phase, designed to test and validate the designs, including the prototypes. The target audience will be distributed in the 3 aforementioned cities. UX studies will be developed in the context of usability lab IPC (Polytechnic of Coimbra)/ESEC (Coimbra Education School), with Masters students in HCI and bachelor's in communication and Multimedia Design. All case studies, creation of personas, wireframes and prototypes involve the blind citizens of the towns of living labs and their association (ACAPO - a Portuguese acronym for Association of the Blind and of Portugal). Now, we are starting to define a set of procedures to start interviewing and observing blind people in their day to day, studying and researching multimodal interactions that should have a crucial role in this project. Therefore, some considerations are described in the following section.

5. MULTIMODAL INTERACTION DESIGN

When it comes to building interfaces for blind people, it is necessary to explore multimodal interfaces. How is it to navigate without seeing? Finding such Human Computer Interface (HCI) concepts from augmentative and alternative communication can serve designers, engineers or educators in various ways in order to reduce social disability.

Multimodal human-computer interaction refers to "interaction with the virtual and physical environment through natural modes of communication" (Bourguet, 2013). Multimodal systems can offer a flexible, efficient and usable environment allowing users to interact through input modalities, such as speech, vibration or hand gesture, and to receive information from the system through output modalities, such as speech synthesis, smart graphics and other modalities, opportunely combined. Voice message is a speech channel used either through an input or output modality generally considered self-sufficient, carrying most of the informational content in a multimodal interface. There are significant advantages such as (Orvalho, 2016):

- "Creates a time-efficient interaction. Just as we try to limit the number of clicks a user must make to complete an action, limit the amount of voice interaction needed.

• Keep messages short and allow interruptions. Don't force a user to listen to long messages or lists of choices without a way to continue forward.

• Let users control the speech rate. "Many blind users of screen readers can listen to text as exceedingly fast speeds." Designers should recognize this enhanced skill and design accordingly.

• Make it discoverable. Consider how the ability to speak with a device is conveyed. If it is expected that a user speaks to a device, make sure that user knows it exists and can open a dialog" (Campbell, 2018).

Unfortunately, speech input typically uses a limited vocabulary, forcing the user to recall a particular command syntax. Ambiguities can appear as a result of recognition errors as well as erroneous language constructs (Campbell, 2018).

Voice Vision substitution is similar to vision enhancement, yet the result constitutes non-visual display, which can be vibration, auditory or both, based on the hearing and touch senses that can be easily controlled and felt by the blind user. For example, a smart cane uses a special vibrator glove which has a specific vibration for each finger, and each one has a specific meaning (Elmannai, 2017). Another example is the "Path Force Feedback belt" to help blind people navigate outside. It uses three components: "the main unit (the process) with two dual video cameras, power supply which is packed into a pocket and the belt to be worn around the user's waist. The belt has a number of cells that gives feedback to the user" (Oliveira, 2013). The corresponding cells will vibrate around the belt and show the user the right path. The system is designed such that each feature has its own signature use of the vibration pattern. So, each vibration frequency differentiates a specific feature or obstacle, e.g., the sidewalk's border marked in some way.

Hand gesture was extensively studied as an efficient input modality. Gesture languages with different levels of complexity (starting from grasp-release commands to Sign Language) were proposed for various applications (Popescu et al., 2002). In addition to input modalities, emerging technologies such as indirect sensing of neural activity (e.g., brain–computer interfaces) may become practical components of multimodal interaction systems in the near future (Turk, 2013). As shown, there are different possibilities of multimodal interfaces that describe interactive systems that seek to leverage natural human capabilities to communicate via speech, gesture, touch, facial expression, and other modalities, bringing more sophisticated pattern recognition and classification methods to human–computer interaction. While these are unlikely to fully displace traditional desktop and GUI-based interfaces, multimodal interfaces are growing in importance due to advances in hardware and software, the benefits that they can provide to users, and the natural fit with the increasingly ubiquitous computing environment (Cutugno, 2012).

Multimodal interfaces can increase task efficiency, and Humans may process information faster and better when it is presented in multiple modalities (Turk, 2013).

6. CONCLUSION

This paper provides information related to problems blind people are facing, starting from the challenges that are beyond their daily life and then emphasises one of the most complex and important challenge, that is navigation and orientation in indoor and outdoor environments. Specially, mobility challenges in large complex buildings concerns almost everyone. It is critical that public places and community settings will be designed to be safe, as inclusive as possible and accessible for all. There are several technologies in development with multimodal human-computer interaction that can turn these indoor locations into smart environments. The future of new solutions, brings us to the world of the artificial intelligence and intelligent machines through smaller and cheaper solutions. These navigational tools will be personalized, prescribed appliances, designed to satisfy individual tastes as well as needs. These tools will be part of clothing, unseen, but probably not unheard. The device will be linked to the internet, to a powerful server computer specifically tailored to the blind traveller. In the age of technology, people with disabilities have certainly new hope coming in waves year after year, like never before in history.

In this paper we described the idea underlying the BlueEyes project, consisting in a useful system for the orientation and navigation of blind people. The project is being implemented in 3 Portuguese cities with different needs and realities.

ACKNOWLEDGEMENT

Project BlueEyes – Beacons and HCI: Making the Invisible Visible
Project N.º 23797, AAC N.º 02/SAICT/2016 – Projetos IC&DT Politécnicos, do Portugal 2020
Cofinanciado por:

REFERENCES

Andress, J. 2015. Privacy Concerns and Behaviors of People with Visual Impairments, April 18–23, 2015, Seoul, Republic of Korea. Available online: https://www.ranker.com/list/obvious-things-blind-people-have-to-deal-with/justin-andress

Apple, 2018,iBeacon for developers.Available online: https://developer.apple.com/ibeacon/

Baldwin, C. 2015. The Future of Blind Navigation Available online: http://www.wayfinding.net/navigation.html.

Baldwin, D. 2003. Wayfinding technology: A road map to the future. In *J. Vis. Impair. Blind.* Vol. 97, pp. 612–620.

Blattner, M.M. and Glinert, E.P. (1996). Multimodal integration. In *IEEE Multimedia*, Vol. 3, No. 4, pp. 14–24.

Bourguet, M. L. 2003. Designing and Prototyping Multimodal Commands. *Proceedings of Human-Computer Interaction (INTERACT'03)*, pp. 717-720.

Brady et. al. 2013. Visual Challenges in the Everyday Lives of Blind People, University of Rochester, Computer Science1 Rochester, NY 14627 USA, Copyright 2013 ACM 978-1-4503-1899-0/13/04...$15.00.

Campbell, B. 2018. UX Design Collective. Tips for Designing Accessibility in Voice User Interfaces. Curated stories on user experience, usability, and product design. Available online: https://uxdesign.cc/tips-for-accessibility-in-conversational-interfaces-8e11c58b31f6

Cutugno, F., Leano, V. A., Rinaldi, R. and Mignini, G. 2012. Multimodal framework for mobile interaction. *International Working Conference on Advanced Visual Interfaces*, Naples, Italy, pp. 197–203.

Dandona L. and Dandona R. 2006. Revision of visual impairment definitions in the International Statistical Classification of Diseases. In *BMC Med.* Vol. 4, No. 7. doi: 10.1186/1741-7015-4-7.

Denham, J., Leventhal, J., and Heather, McComas. 2004. Getting from Point A to Point B: A Review of Two GPS Systems : Trekker and GPS Braille Note, AccessWorld, AFB Press, American Foundation for the Blind, November 2004 Issue Vol. 5, No. 6.

Duffy, M. 2018. Low Vision and Legal Blindness Terms and Descriptions. Copyright © 2018 American Foundation for the Blind. All rights reserved. Available online: http://www.visionaware.org/info/your-eye-condition/eye-health/low-vision/low-vision-termsand-descriptions/1235.

Elmannai, W. and Elleithy, K. 2017. Sensor-Based Assistive Devices for Visually-Impaired People: Current Status, Challenges, and Future Directions. In *Sensors (Basel)*, Vol. 17, No. 3, pii: E565. doi: 10.3390/s17030565.

Filipe, V., Fernandes, F., Fernandes, H., Sousa, A., Paredes, H. and Barroso, J. 2012. Blind navigation support system based on Microsoft Kinect. In *Procedia Computer Science,* Vol. 14, pp. 94-101.

Foundation fighting blindness (FFB). 2018. Mobility & orientation packet. Available online: http://www.blindness.org/sites/default/files/pages/pdfs/Mobility%20%26%20Orientation%20Packet.pdf.

Gaggi, O, Manzoni, P., Palazzi, C., Bujari, A. And Marquez-Barja, J. M. 2016. Smart Objects and Technologies for Social Good. *Proceedings of the Second International Conference, GOODTECHS*, Venice, Italy.

Gilchrist, C. 2014. Learning iBeacons. Packt Publishing Limited. Birmingham, United Kingdom

Giudice, N. A. and Legge, G. E. 2008. Blind Navigation and the Role of Technology. University of California, Santa Barbara University of Minnesota. The Engineering Handbook of Smart Technology for Aging, Disability, and Independence, Edited by A. Helal, M. Mokhtari and B. Abdulrazak Copyright 2008 John Wiley & Sons, Inc.

Giudice, N. A., Bakdash, J. Z., Legge, G. E. 2007. Wayfinding with words: Spatial learning and navigation using dynamically-updated verbal descriptions. In *Psychol Res.* Vol. 71, No. 3, pp. 347–358.

Giudice, N. A., Legge, G. E. 2008. Blind navigation and the role of technology. In *Eng. Handb. Smart Technol. Aging, Disabil. Indep.*, pp. 479-500, 10.1002/9780470379424.

Harkey et. al. 2007. Accessible Pedestrian Signals: A Guide to Best Practices. Contractor's Guide for NCHRP Project 3-62.

Hersh, M. A. 2006. Electronic travel aids and electronic orientation aids for blind people: technical, rehabilitation and everyday life points of view. *Conference & Workshop on Assistive Technologies for People with Vision & Hearing Impairments Technology for Inclusion CVHI*, X (ed.).

Kammoun, S., Marc, J.-M., Oriola, B. and Christophe J. 2011. Toward a better guidance in wearable electronic orientation aids. *Proceedings of the IFIP Conference on Human-Computer Interaction*, Lisbon, Portugal.

Liu J., Liu J., Xu L., Jin W. 2010. Electronic travel aids for the blind based on sensory substitution. *Proceedings of the 2010 5th International Conference on Computer Science and Education (ICCSE)*, Hefei, China.

Marion, A. H., Michael, A. J. 2008. Assistive technology for Visually-impaired and Blind People. Springer; London, UK: 2008.

Miner, R. J. 2001. The experience of living with and using a dog guide. In *Re View*, Vol. 32, No. 4, pp.183-190.

Noriega, D. Q. 2018, Dog Guides for People with Vision Loss. Available online: http://www.visionaware.org/info/everyday-living/essential-skills/an-introduction-to-orientation-and-mobility-skills/dog-guides-for-people-with-vision-loss/1234.

Oliveira, F. J. 2013. The path force feedback belt. *Proceedings of the 2013 8th International Conference on Information Technology in Asia (CITA)*, Kuching, Malaysia.

Orvalho, J. 2016. *Project BlueEyes – Beacons and HCI: Making the Invisible Visible, N.º 23797, submetido ao AAC N.º 02/SAICT/2016 – Projetos IC&DT Politécnicos, do Portugal 2020, Politechnic of Coimbra; FCT - The Portuguese national funding agency for science, research and technology. Co-financed by Centro2020, Portugal2020 and UE-Fundo Europeu de Desenvolvimento Regional; Partners Instituto Politécnico de Viseu; Monsters and Company – Solução de Comunicação, Lda; Stakeholders: Municipality of Coimbra, Municipality of Caldas da Rainha, Municipality of Tábua and ACAPO (Portuguese Association of the Blind and Poorly-sighted).*

Politzer, T. (n.d.). Introduction to Vision and Brain Injury. Available online: https://nora.cc/vision-a-brain-injury-mainmenu-64.html.

Popescu, V., Burdea, G. and Trefftz, H. 2002.Chapter 25: Multimodal interaction modeling. Department of Electrical and Computer Engineering, Rutgers University, Piscataway, NJ 08854 USA.

Ruffa, A. J. et al. 2015. Assessing iBeacons as an Assistive Tool for Blind People in Denmark. An Interactive Qualifying Project Denmark Project Center May 2, 2015.

Saarela, C. 2015. Solving way-finding challenges of a visually impaired person in a shopping mall by strengthening landmarks recognisability with iBeacons. Ed.D (Special Education), Multi-sensory and Assistive Technology (MATEC). Häme University of Applied Sciences (HAMK), in Finland.

Sánchez J. and Elías M. 2007. Guidelines for designing mobility and orientation software for blind children. *Proceedings of the IFIP Conference on Human-Computer Interaction*, Rio de Janeiro, Brazil.

Scheiman, M., Scheiman, M., & Whittaker, S. G. (2007). Epidemology, history and clinical model for low vision rehabilitation. In M. Scheiman, M. Scheiman, & S. G. Whittaker, Low Vision Rehabilitation: A Practical Guide for Occupational Therapists (pp. 5-11).

Suddia, A. 2018. Indoor Navigation Apps Designed For the Visually Challenged: Why Does The Market Need Them? Available online: https://itechcraft.com/indoor-navigation-for-blind/

Thorofare, NJ: Slack Incorporated.Shah, C., Bouzit, M., Youssef, M. and Vasquez, L. 2006. Evaluation of RUNetra tactile feedback navigation system for the visually-impaired. *Proceedings of the International Workshop on Virtual Rehabilitation*, New York, NY, USA, pp. 72–77.

Turk, M. 2013. Multimodal interaction: A review. Department of Computer Science, University of California, Santa Barbara, CA 93106-5110, United States.

Whitmarsh, L. 2005.The Benefits of Guide Dog Ownership Guide Dogs, Hillfields, Burghfield, Reading RG7 3YG, UK

Whitmarsh, L. and Nzegwu, F. 2001. Client Satisfaction Survey 2001. Unpublished report. Reading: Guide Dogs for the Blind Association; 2001.

World Health Organization (WHO). 2017.Vision impairment and blindness. Fact sheet. Updated October 2017. http://www.who.int/mediacentre/factsheets/fs282/en/ .

USABILITY ASSESSMENT OF FACIAL TRACKING FOR USE IN CLINICAL OUTCOMES AND APPLICATIONS

Francesco Luke Siena[1], Bill Byrom[2], Paul Watts[1]and Philip Breedon[1]
[1]*Nottingham Trent University, 50 Shakespeare Street, Nottingham, NG1 4FQ, UK*
[2]*CRF Health, Brook House - 3rd Floor, 229-243 Shepherds Bush Road, Hammersmith, London, W6 7AN, UK*

ABSTRACT

There is an ever-growing body of facial tracking assessment applications available within the health and wellness sector. One of the most prominent areas is the use of 3D cameras and processing technologies in the development of rehabilitation interventions and in the measurement of health outcomes. Recent advancements in facial tracking applications within mobile platforms and cloud computing analytics suggests that new clinical assessment and human computer assessment technologies have significant future potential for pervasive in-clinic and field-based health assessment solutions. This paper reviews the technical capabilities of three facial tracking platforms with a focus on the common issues relating to clinical measurement considerations required for patient-facing systems. Key factors are assessed in relation to 3D camera platforms, mobile applications and cloud computing applications including camera position, lighting and shadows, eye detection and common obstructions or features that affect tracking. Published examples of facial tracking clinical and health wellness applications are presented in relation to human computer interaction interfaces. This paper aims to demonstrate the potential for future applications being developed relating to each of these technologies for clinic-based applications.

KEYWORDS

3D Camera Tracking, Clinical Outcomes, Clinical Endpoints, Cloud Computing Facial Analytics, Facial Tracking, Mobile Applications

1. INTRODUCTION

Facial tracking assessment applications are becoming increasingly prominent within the clinical and health and wellness sector. Human computing interfaces and patient facing systems are two areas where systems have been developed to assess the health status of a patient or provide a method of rehabilitation. There are many examples of systems within the health and wellness sector that focus on the measurement of gait and balance, upper extremity movement, chest wall motion, etc., however all these solutions rely upon robust and validated methodologies to measure health status and track changes in status over time. This paper explores the key issues associated with accurate facial tracking and assessment within the clinical assessment sector.

An ever-increasing number of 3D camera-based technologies available in today's market enables applications within 3D scanning, motion capture, gaming, wellbeing applications or clinical and healthcare research to be created. The rapid development of 3D cameras and processing technologies has resulted in a market with numerous options, all with varying strengths and weaknesses. Within facial tracking and analytics, recent advancements in mobile platforms and cloud computing applications provide new and innovate alternative solutions that can be applied to the clinical assessment of patients within human computing interfaces and patient-facing systems.

1.1 Facial Tracking Application to Clinical Research

Facial tracking may provide the opportunity to learn more about the status, progression and treatment of certain disease indications, in particular those affecting the central nervous system (CNS). There are a number of attributes that might be possible to measure using facial tracking technologies that may provide opportunities for novel objective clinical outcome measures, these include expression detection, facial symmetry and movement, blink detection and eye tracking, facial muscle strength and tongue dexterity.

1.1.1 Expression Detection

The relative positioning of facial landmarks enables the determination of expression. Conditions such as autism are developmental disorders associated with impairments in social interaction. A source of those impairments is difficulty creating facial expressions of emotion. In young children, autism is difficult and time consuming to diagnose by healthcare professionals. Researchers at Duke Medicine have developed an app-based solution to identify a child's facial expression using video captured using the front-facing camera while watching short video clips designed to generate an emotion such as laughter or surprise (Autism and Beyond, 2014).

1.1.2 Facial Symmetry

Facial paralysis is a common component of conditions such as stroke and Bell's palsy, which can improve through regular conduct of exercise regimens. Longitudinal changes in aspects of facial paralysis in these conditions could be tracked by measuring aspects of facial symmetry and distortion based on relative distances between specific facial landmarks. Numeric measures of facial symmetry enable the tracking of temporal improvements arising from pharmacological or physical therapy treatment.

1.1.3 Blink Detection and Eye Tracking

Identifying eye opening and closure events may facilitate the measurement of blink rate. Blink rates are believed to reflect the activity of the central dopaminergic systems (Karson, 1983). Patients with Huntingdon's disease or schizophrenia show higher blink rates than normal subjects; patients with Parkinson's disease and progressive supranuclear palsy show lower blink rates (Grandas et al, 1994). Understanding the scan patterns associated with eye movements can be useful in the study of certain neurological diseases and brain injury. Altered fixation stability and saccadic movements (rapid eye movements that abruptly change the point of fixation) are associated with several CNS disorders such as Huntington's disease, progressive supranuclear palsy and Parkinson's disease (Termsarasab et al, 2015). In the early stages of dementia, saccadic eye movement recordings may help discriminate between different types of the disease (Mosimann et al, 2005). Eye tracking is also gaining increased interest as a potential biomarker for brain injury (Samadami, 2016).

1.1.4 Facial Muscle Strength

Facioscapulohumeral muscular dystrophy may present as a weakness of the facial muscles. For example, a patient's eyes may remain slightly open when asleep, or they may be unable to tightly close their eyes. Patients may also experience difficulty pursing their lips. Using the tracking points around the mouth and lips it may be possible to use facial tracking technology to instrument a lip pursing test, along with other tests of facial muscle strength, which could provide valuable outcome measures in these and other disease indications.

1.1.5 Tongue Dexterity/Agility

Patients with Huntingdon's Disease are often assessed using the Unified Huntington's Disease Rating Scale (Kieburtz et al, 2001), an assessment conducted and rated by clinicians. One component of the assessment considers measurement of aspects of motor impersistence, specifically difficulty keeping the tongue fully protruded upon command. The scale's tongue protrusion task is performed by asking the patient to hold the tongue extended for 10 seconds and rating the response on a 5-point verbal response scale. Facial tracking approaches may enable instrumentation of tests such as these, with increased precision of measurement and greater richness of information collected.

2. CAPABILITIES OF FACIAL TRACKING

Facial tracking technological solutions are becoming more common within the healthcare sector. The most common hardware utilised to track the face and its movements are 3D Depth cameras using inbuilt infrared LED's to illuminate the subject. Background objects can be ignored as the computer can accurately isolate individual objects based upon their detected distance from the camera. Accurate 3D tracking of facial landmarks enables the tracking and measurement of many aspects of facial movement such as facial paralysis recovery after stroke/Bell's palsy. Camera tracking has been utilised for many years, however this has often focused on 2D camera tracking due its low setup costs. 2D camera tracking uses contrasting colours to pick out facial features in normal lighting conditions. However, lighting conditions and skin tone can dramatically affect the results when there are significant contrast changes, however Raja et al (1998) and Kjeldsen and Kender (1996) discuss segmentation approaches to overcome these issues. Background colours can also affect the ability for the camera to track features as the objects in the picture merge into one another. Variable lighting conditions can adversely affect the quality of tracking and can affect the accurate tracking of facial landmarks; this has been especially noted with the Microsoft Kinect (Shires et al, 2013). 2D depth tracking has severe limitations with expression recognition. Table 1 provides a brief comparative analysis of the advantages and disadvantages of 2D v 3D depth camera facial tracking.

Table 1. 2D vs 3D Camera Solutions - Facial Tracking Comparative Assessment

2D Facial Tracking Advantages	3D Facial Tracking Advantages
– Lower Bandwidth Requirements. – Lower Cost (Hardware). – No Specialised Hardware Required.	– Three Dimensional Measurements. – Unaffected by head orientation. – High accuracy/ increased range of depth data. – Increased accuracy of pose recovery. – Fast and accurate facial feature ID and tracking. – High detection rate and sampling rates. – Accurate expression recognition.
2D Facial Tracking Disadvantages	**3D Facial Tracking Disadvantages**
– Limited by lighting levels. – Limited by occlusions. – Image processing limitations. – CPU intensive for reduced outputs. – Limited emotion tracking capabilities. – Limited facial feature tracking & identification. – Limited expression recognition. – Limited by scene clutter. – Limited by skin tone.	– Increased setup costs (hardware and software). – Complexity of programming. – Increase in initial calibration complexity. – Restrictions can exist with lighting levels. – Some limitations by occlusions. – Unknown response to facial feature deformities. – Some limitations for facial feature detection. – Minor limitations caused by laser refraction during tracking.

Recent advancements in facial tracking technologies suggests there are three key areas where they will be utilised within the clinical and healthcare sector. The current state of the art focuses on 3D camera tracking modules; however, a rapidly developing area focuses on mobile platforms, such as the Apple© iPhoneX® that utilises Face ID which is described as an intuitive and secure authentication method enabled by a state-of-the-art TrueDepth camera system (Apple Inc., 2017). Visage Technologies© (Linköping, Sweden) also offer FaceTrack, FaceAnalysis and FaceRecognition packages (Visage Technologies, 2018).

Cloud-computing data analytics focusing on facial tracking applications also provides a solution with significant future potential. Vinay et al (2015) demonstrates innovation with a cloud based big data analytics framework for face recognition in social networks using machine learning and Hossain and Muhammad (2015) present a cloud-assisted speech and face recognition framework for health monitoring.

2.1 3D Camera Tracking Modules

3D Camera modules are computer add on devices; the two best known are the Microsoft Kinect and Intel RealSense camera ranges. These camera modules use 3D depth camera technology paired with a RGB & IR camera. Signals from these are combined and passed into a tracking algorithm to identify objects within a captured image. Both the Intel RealSense and Microsoft Kinect camera ranges utilise freely available SDKs (Software Development Kits) that allow third party developers to build upon existing libraries developed by the manufacturers. Table 2 presents the advantages and disadvantages associated with 3D camera modules.

Table 2. 3D Camera Modules Advantages & Disadvantages

Advantages	Disadvantages
– Fast and reliable tracking is achievable.	– Limited to selected device/manufacturers.
– Camera modules can be positioned as required.	– Additional hardware required (PC/Screen).
– SDK's are typically free to download.	– Camera modules are often bulky.
– High resolution	– Some SDK's do require a licence fee which can be quite expensive.
– Fast processing of live camera frames.	

3D Camera modules require additional hardware such as a PC/workstation and visual display. The camera modules are relatively cheap (~US $270), however the additional hardware significantly raises the costs. The 3D camera modules tracking quality excels due to the high-resolution colour cameras and the use of depth camera technology to extract faces from a photo frame. The camera can be positioned as required to capture the targets face from any desired angle within the camera's field of view (FOV).

Table 3 provides a brief overview of the technical capabilities of the Microsoft Kinect 2.0 (Microsoft Corp., Redmond, Washington, USA), the Intel® RealSense™ SR300 and D435 (Intel Corp., Santa Clara, CA, USA) and the CREATIVE® BlasterX SENZ3D (Creative Technology Ltd., Jurong East, Singapore). The Microsoft Kinect Sensor V2/2.0 has however ceased manufacture potentially signalling the end of Microsoft's involvement in this sector (Good OS, 2017). The Intel RealSense camera range is best placed to take advantage in the clinical and healthcare sector (Siena et al, 2018); RealSense technology is utilised in many other camera modules including the CREATIVE® SENZE3D.

Table 3. Comparison Of 3D Camera Tracking Modules

Specification/Function	Intel® RealSense™ SR300	Intel® RealSense™ D435	Microsoft Kinect® 2.0	CREATIVE® BlasterX SENZ3D
RGB Camera (Pixel)	1080 at 30 FPS, 720 at 60 FPS	1920 x 1080 at 30 FPS	1920×1080 at 30 FPS	720p at 60 FPS, 1080p at 30 FPS
Depth Camera (Pixel)	Up to 640 x 480 at 60 FPS	Up to 1280 x 720 at 90 FPS	512×424 at 30 FPS	Up to 640 x 480 at 60 FPS
Range (m)	0.2-2	0.11 - 10	0.7-6	0.2-1.5
Facial Tracking & Recognition	Yes	Yes	Yes	Yes
Facial Tracking Points *	78	78	87	78
Expression Recognition	Yes	Yes	Yes	Yes
Connectivity (USB)	3.0	3.0	3.0	3.0
Release Date	Q1 2016	Q1 2018	Q4 2013	Q4 2016
Approximate Price (US$)**	80	180	30	270

* SDK Version Dependant ** Prices as of March 2018

2.2 Mobile Based Camera Tracking

Mobile application SDK's utilise the existing cameras on mobile platforms. The application developer captures an image from the mobile device and passes it into a tracking SDK. If a face is detected, the SDK outputs face coordinates and landmark points of key facial features. Mobile application SDK's often utilise a software licensing system, either on a number of devices using the SDK or licences per developer working on the solution. It is often the case that a separate licence is required for each platform being targeted (IOS/Android). This can prove to be costly and requires payment throughout the lifetime of the product. Table 4 presents key advantages and disadvantages associated with mobile camera tracking solutions.

Table 4. Mobile Based Camera Tracking Advantages & Disadvantages

Advantages	Disadvantages
– Integrated into existing products owned by patients	– Offset camera will affect results. Camera may not sit centre to the screen.
– Fast processing of live camera frames	– Support for multiple devices required in solution (Camera resolutions/Quality)
– Platform is designed for mobility	– Speed is dependent on device specifications
	– SDKs and licensing can be expensive
	– Cross platform development needed to support all common devices (IOS/Android)
	– Poor or excessive lighting can cause issues

2.3 Cloud Computing Facial Tracking

Cloud computing facial tracking uses a web API system to process an image on a web server; the web server runs the facial tracking algorithms on the image and returns the results in either an XML or JSON format. The results contain a set of coordinates for each face located along with landmark points for each. The system requires access to the internet as all cloud-based solutions are hosted on the World Wide Web (WWW). The speed of the call is dependent on the connection speed and the latency of the connection. Cloud computing solutions are not suitable for video streams due to the latency, they are however capable of providing results to any device capable of connecting to the WWW.

Cloud computing solutions are very reliable and are often linked to artificial intelligence (AI) systems that continuously improve their algorithms to improve accuracy. Cloud computing solutions are priced on the number of calls to the API; many services offer a free level of access for low volume calls. Cloud computing offers a reliable system which has low implementation and setup costs due to API implementation which can take hours not days/weeks/months, unlike other solutions. With variable pricing which adapts to usage, this provides a low-cost solution accessible from any platform and can use any camera, mobile, web or photograph. However, drawbacks include slow frame-by-frame processing rates over the Internet and incompatibility with live video.

3. PERFORMANCE ASSESSMENT OF FACIAL TRACKING

Facial tracking performance was assessed utilising a 3D camera-tracking module (Intel RealSense), cloud computing (FacePlusPlus) and a mobile platform (Visage Technologies). Through assessment, key considerations have been identified that will be important when developing future clinical applications. The use of glasses, positioning of the camera, lighting conditions and the lighting position around the target subject can all have a considerable effect on the ability for any tracking system to detect key facial features accurately.

3.1 Glasses

Glasses can present many issues with facial tracking systems. The first common issue is with the frames of the glasses being indistinguishable from the subject's face and therefore being tracked by the system as an area of interest such as the eyebrows or the eyes themselves. The second issue is with the frames or lenses of the glasses obstructing important facial features such as the eyebrows or eyes. If the feature is not visible, then the facial tracking system will estimate the position of the landmark points based upon the known features currently successfully being tracked. The third is the magnification of the eyes. Strong lenses in glasses will magnify the eye of the subject and increase the size of the eye relative to the rest of the face (Figure 1).

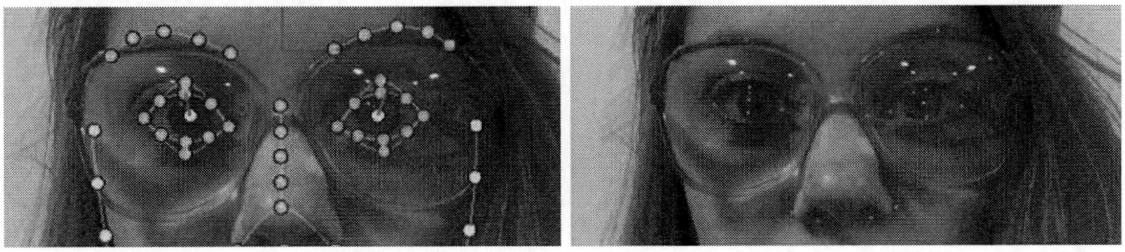

Figure 1. Glasses Amplifying the Eye. (Left - Visage Mobile Tracking, Right – FacePlusPlus Cloud)

3.2 Shadows

Shadows can play a significant role in altering the accuracy of the facial tracking algorithms and will alter areas of contrast and obstruct the facial tracking systems ability to track facial features. Shadows created by a pair of glasses for example can cause algorithms to track the incorrect region of the face. The landmarks highlighted on Figure 2, show the tracking algorithm has incorrectly identified the frame, shadow of the frame or reflections within the frame as eyebrow landmarks. To avoid these issues, uniform lighting is advised to be applied across the subject's face, preferably with the light source in front of the subject to prevent shadows from forming around the eye sockets, nose and lips. This will also remove shadows created by the frames of glasses.

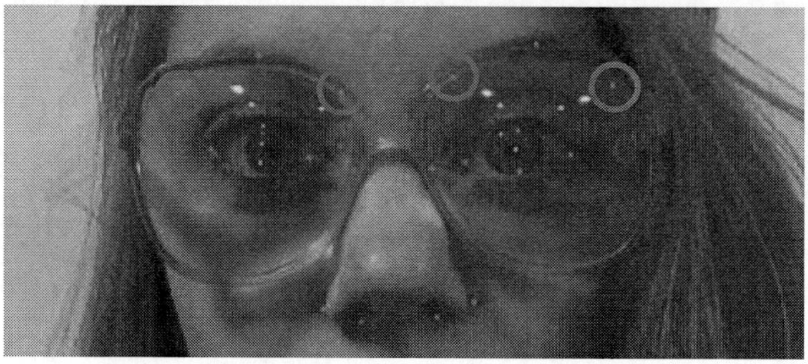

Figure 2. Inaccurate Eyebrow Tracking – Glasses & Shadows

3.3 Iris

Current eye tracking algorithms suffer from incorrect identification of the iris at the bottom of the subject's eye. This is very noticeable should the subject be performing a rehabilitative exercise that aims at widening the eyes, thereby revealing the lower white portion of the eye. Incorrect identification is also noticeable when the patient is required to look up and above the camera. On FacePlusPlus, this tracks as the bottom of the eye (Figure 3. Left) and on the Intel RealSense camera the bottom of the iris is tracked as the centre of the iris (Figure 3. Right). If accurate tracking of the eye is required, it is advised the activity does not require the subject to look away from the camera and that the focus point remains in a fixed location throughout the activity.

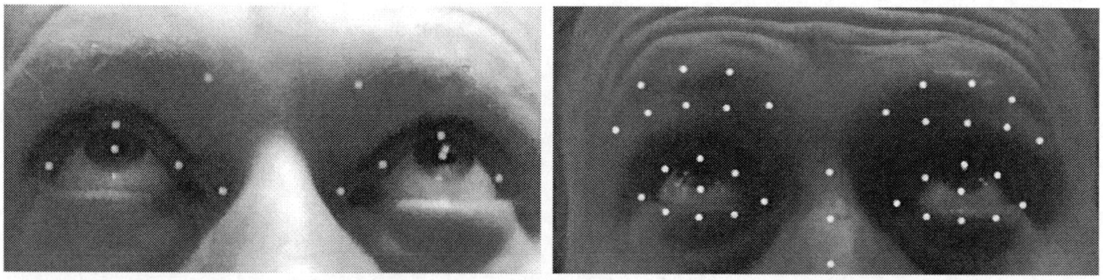

Figure 3. Iris Tracking (Left – FacePlusPlus Cloud Processing, Right – Intel RealSesnse)

3.4 Camera Positioning

The position of the camera relative to the desired user focus point can have an adverse impact on measurements, especially if high accuracy measurements are required. If the camera is located to the left or right of the centre then the user will visibly appear to look away from the camera, this will affect horizontal measurements as the user's face will be rotated slightly off-centre. If the camera is located above or below the focus point, this will cause the user to rotate their head up or down, thus vertical measurements will be affected. This can also affect measurements of the eyes due to the iris interfering with the tracking. This is especially important to consider when using mobile platforms (i.e. smartphones/tablets) or other hand-held devices. Different devices will place the camera in various locations in relation to the centre of the user interface (Figure 4).

Figure 4. Camera Location of Three Mobile Platforms

3.5 Lighting

Lighting can have a substantial impact on facial tracking. It affects the contrast of the subject's face in the image data being assessed. Facial tracking algorithms often use this contrast to identify regions of interest and to find the lines that make up the outline of the facial tracking feature. If the line cannot be distinguished, then the tracking either will fail or will track to the first line it can locate. Figure 5 shows FacePlusPlus tracking the same face in three different lighting conditions.

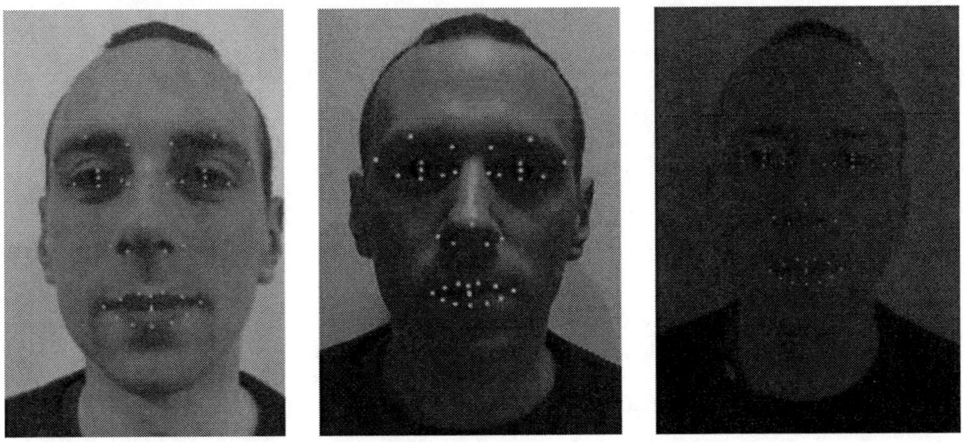

Figure 5. Normal Lighting (Left), Lighting Above (Centre), Poor/Low Lighting (Right)

The tracking in the centre and right images is enhanced by the prediction algorithms within the tracking libraries to compensate for the low lighting. This is good for functionality, as this does not require a high level of accuracy; however, it is important to note that this can have an impact when performing measurements requiring high precision. It is advised that the subject be in a well-lit area with uniform light across the face. Some landmarks within the eyes, eyebrows and lips can be slightly altered by the low contrast in the images; this will have an adverse effect on any accurate measurements made.

4. PUBLISHED FACIAL TRACKING CLINICAL APPLICATIONS

The Face to Face solution (Breedon et al, 2014), funded by the UK NIHR Invention for Innovation Programme, is a rehabilitation system for facial paralysis in stroke patients. It recognizes facial expressions by tracking movement across the face, applying the recognized motion onto an onscreen representation of the user using the Microsoft Kinect. The user performs a series of facial exercises assessed by the system and scored according to how well the user can undertake each of the defined set of expressions. This will enable shorter consultations through the presentation of quantified improvement, in addition to optimizing the performance of the exercises. Numeric measures of facial expression and symmetry enable the tracking of temporal improvements arising from pharmacological or physical therapy treatment. Other researchers have also explored methodological aspects of using depth images provided by Microsoft Kinect to accurately recognise specific facial exercises performed in rehabilitation for patients suffering from dysfunction of facial movements (Lanz et al, 2013).

González-Ortega et al (2014), produced a system to track and monitor cognitive rehabilitation exercises performed by patients suffering from left-right confusion, a cognitive condition in which subjects are unable to name or point to the right or left sides of objects, including their own body. This condition is seen in Gerstmann's syndrome (Lebrun, 2005), and can be observed in some dementia patients (Fischer et al, 1990). This system combined skeletal and facial tracking using the Microsoft Kinect in the assessment of various exercises such as touching the right eye with the left hand, touching the nose with the right hand, and touching the left ear with the right hand etc. The system was able to identify and record when the subject was able to perform each requested movement correctly, along with reaction times and movement completion times. This may aid the monitoring of longitudinal change in left-right confusion.

Youssef et al (2013) used the Microsoft Kinect system to classify six facial expressions and a neutral expression, with moderately successful results. They identified that a possible application of the work would be to help children with autism to recognize emotions and suggested that expression recognition combined with a computer animation may provide an engaging feedback and training tool. Tang et al (2017), used the Intel RealSense camera to detect emotional response to cartoon clips to assess spontaneous emotion production in children with autism.

The Microsoft Kinect has been used to detect heart rate by detecting changes in colour intensity of the facial skin due to blood flow movement resulting from heart beats. This approach has been shown to produce favourable results (Gambi et al, 2017). Other researchers have used facial tracking using depth cameras to explore fatigue detection (Anggraini et al, 2016), and tracking of articulatory movements during speech and non-speech tasks that could aid the assessment, diagnosis and treatment of motor speech disorders such as amyotrophic lateral sclerosis, Parkinson's disease (PD) and stroke (Bandini et al, 2017).

5. CONCLUSION

This assessment of facial tracking approaches has highlighted several issues that need to be considered when developing clinical applications and solutions. By careful monitoring of the user interface (UI), many of the problems with iris tracking and camera location can be avoided or minimised. Careful monitoring of the environment around the subject should also be carefully considered to prevent interference from changing light conditions and shadows; this will ensure accurate and consistent results across multiple sessions and subjects.

The selection of the optimal facial tracking platform between the three types discussed in the paper inevitably relates to factors including the availability of hardware, the price of the final product solution and the requirement for video or static tracking of facial features. Each platform offers its own advantages and disadvantages that will ultimately guide the development and the design of the product. If all these factors are taken into consideration, facial tracking can offer a solid and reliable solution for use within clinical applications.

Caution is however advised if a clinical application requires a high level of accuracy, especially when considering factors such as tremor detection. Simply based on the applications discussed within this paper alone, continued development of facial tracking algorithms, improvements in accuracy and the speed of calculations suggests there is a strong case for developing further clinical solutions including rehabilitative patient facing systems.

REFERENCES

Anggraini, N. et al, 2016, November. Facial recognition system for fatigue detection using Intel Realsense Technology. *In Information and Communication Technology for The Muslim World (ICT4M), 2016 6th International Conference* (pp. 248-253). IEEE.

Apple Inc. (2017). About Face ID advanced technology. Available at: https://support.apple.com/en-gb/HT208108 Accessed 2 March 2018.

Autism and Beyond. (2014). About The Study. Available at: https://autismandbeyond.researchkit.duke.edu/study Accessed 9 March 2018.

Bandini, A. et al, 2017. Video-based tracking of jaw movements during speech: Preliminary results and future directions. *Proc. Interspeech 2017*, pp.689-693.

Breedon, P. et al, 2014. First for Stroke: using the Microsoft 'Kinect'as a facial paralysis stroke rehabilitation tool. *International Journal of Integrated Care*, 14(8).

Fischer, P. et al, 1990. Right-left disorientation in dementia of the Alzheimer type. *Neurology*, 40(10), pp.1619-1619.

Gambi, E. et al, 2017. Heart Rate Detection Using Microsoft Kinect: Validation and Comparison to Wearable Devices. *Sensors*, 17(8), p.1776.

González-Ortega, D. et al, 2014. A Kinect-based system for cognitive rehabilitation exercises monitoring. *Computer methods and programs in biomedicine*, 113(2), pp.620-631.

Good OS (2017) Kinect is officially dead. Really. Officially. It's dead. In: Polygon. https://www.polygon.com/2017/10/25/16543192/kinect-discontinued-microsoft-announcement Accessed 2 March 2018.

Grandas, F. et al, 1994. Eyelid motor abnormalities in progressive supranuclear palsy. *In Progressive Supranuclear Palsy: Diagnosis, Pathology, and Therapy* (pp. 33-41). Springer, Vienna.

Hossain, M.S. and Muhammad, G., 2015. Cloud-assisted speech and face recognition framework for health monitoring. *Mobile Networks and Applications*, 20(3), pp.391-399.

Intel. (2017) Intel® RealSense™ Camera SR300 Product Data Sheet. https://software.intel.com/sites/default/files/managed/0c/ec/realsense-sr300-product-datasheet-rev-1-0.pdf Accessed 2 March 2018

Karson, C.N., 1983. Spontaneous eye-blink rates and dopaminergic systems. *Brain*, 106(3), pp.643-653.

Kieburtz, K. et al, 2001. Unified Huntington's disease rating scale: reliability and consistency. *Neurology*, 11(2), pp.136-142.

Kjeldsen, R. and Kender, J., 1996, October. Finding skin in color images. In Automatic Face and Gesture Recognition, 1996., Proceedings of the Second International Conference on (pp. 312-317). IEEE.

Lanz, C. et al, 2013, February. Automated Classification of Therapeutic Face Exercises using the Kinect. *In VISAPP* (1) (pp. 556-565).

Lebrun, Y., 2005. Gerstmann's syndrome. *Journal of Neurolinguistics*, 18(4), pp.317-326.

Mosimann, U.P. et al, 2005. Saccadic eye movement changes in Parkinson's disease dementia and dementia with Lewy bodies. *Brain*, 128(6), pp.1267-1276.

Raja, Y. et al, 1998, April. Tracking and segmenting people in varying lighting conditions using colour. In Automatic Face and Gesture Recognition, 1998. Proceedings. Third IEEE International Conference on (pp. 228-233). IEEE.

Samadani, U., 2016. Will eye tracking change the way we diagnose and classify concussion and structural brain injury?. Concussion, 1(1), pp.1-3.

Shires, L. et al, 2013, May. Enhancing the tracking capabilities of the Microsoft Kinect for stroke rehabilitation. *In Serious Games and Applications for Health (SeGAH), 2013 IEEE 2nd International Conference on* (pp. 1-8). IEEE.

Siena, F. et al, 2018. Utilising the Intel RealSense Camera for Measuring Health Outcomes in Clinical Research. *Journal of Medical Systems*, 42(3), p.53.

Tang, T.Y. et al, 2017, Emotion Recognition via Face Tracking with RealSense (TM) 3D Camera for Children with Autism. *In Proceedings of the 2017 Conference on Interaction Design and Children* (pp. 533-539). ACM.

Termsarasab, P. et al, 2015. The diagnostic value of saccades in movement disorder patients: a practical guide and review. *Journal of clinical movement disorders*, 2(1), p.14.

Vinay, A. et al, 2015. Cloud based big data analytics framework for face recognition in social networks using machine learning. Procedia Computer Science, 50, pp.623-630.

Visage Technologies. (2018). FaceTrack - Visage Technologies. [online] Available at: http://visagetechnologies.com/products-and-services/visagesdk/facetrack/ [Accessed 2 Mar. 2018].

Youssef, A.E. et al, 2013. Auto-optimized multimodal expression recognition framework using 3D kinect data for ASD therapeutic aid. *International Journal of Modeling and Optimization*, 3(2), p.112.

GAMER TYPOLOGY BASED ON PERSONALITY AND MOTIVATIONAL FOOTPRINTS

Castulus Kolo and Niklas Lüst
Macromedia University of Applied Sciences, Sandstraße 9, 80335 Munich, Germany

ABSTRACT

This proposed contribution discusses to what extent the choice of particular video games mirrors a player's personality with gaming motivations as an intermediate variable. Based on an online survey (n=1612) we first confirm the applicability of the five-factor (OCEAN) model on personality types in a German speaking gamers' context. Gaming motivation is then introduced as a psychological concept contrasting motives and incentives. A recent empirical study by Yee on gaming motivations with a US perspective is generally replicated with our sample. Motivations are analogously derived from a principal component analysis of over 40 items referring to diverse aspects of gaming motivations. A cluster analysis suggests clusters of motivations that could in turn be correlated with specific personality aspects. Furthermore, with certain "motivational footprints" and "gamer personalities" respectively certain games are favoured. Knowing particularly enticing combinations of motivations met may guide the development of future games targeting specific personalities.

KEYWORDS

Media Psychology, Audience Research, Personality, Gaming Motivation, Media Choice

1. INTRODUCTION AND RATIONALE

Over the past few decades, video games have evolved from subsidiary gimmicks, to a multi-billion-dollar entertainment industry. With an estimated global revenue of $108.9 billion in 2017, video games have long surpassed the music industry and are getting close to the movie industry. Today, video games are being played by all age groups and the ratio of male to female players is more or less balanced (ESA, 2017). In 2017, more than 2.2 billion worldwide played video games of which over 1 billion online. This corresponds to almost one third of the global internet population (Newzoo, 2017).

From the economic importance and the far-reaching media effects a better understanding of the motivations to play video games as well as investigating a potential connection with player personality and how those factors ultimately lead to the choice of particular games appears to be a rewarding endeavour. In the following we will first give an overview on how player motivations have been categorized in earlier studies, as well as how according to theoretical concepts, personality may affect these motivations and in turn possibly also game choice. From such theoretical constructs we derive the following hypothetical model (Figure 1):

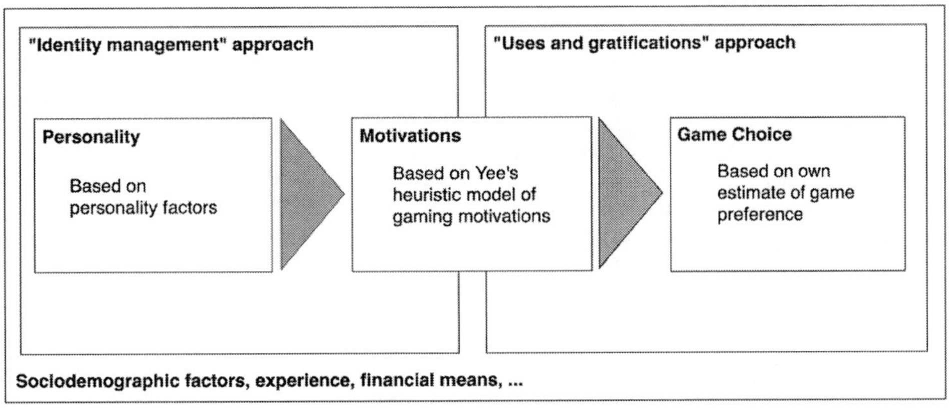

Figure 1. Overall model for forming gaming motivations and game choice

It is assumed that the core personality traits of a person mirror in the motivations to play video games which in turn dictate the choice of games. The "identity management "approach implies that the motivations and actions of a gratification-seeking individual are determined by their personality. The "uses and gratifications" theory is an audience-centred approach which focuses on the question "Why do people become involved in one particular type of mediated communication or another, and what gratifications do they receive from it?" (Ruggiero, 2000, p. 29). In order to verify or falsify this theoretical model we formulated the following research questions and hypotheses:

RQ1: Do the motivations to play video games reflect in game choice?

- H1: The gaming motivation model is reproducible in the German speaking region.
- H2: Motivations to play video games are correlated with preference of certain games.

RQ2: Is there a relationship between player personality and gaming motivations?

- H3: Gaming motivations can be related to specific personality types.

RQ3: Is there a relationship between player personality and game choice?

- H4: Inferences about game choice can be made based on player personality.

After discussing the results of a quantitative online survey among German players to test the latter we will conclude in this proposed contribution with some considerations of the limitations of our study and an outlook on further research.

2. PRIOR RESEARCH RESULTS AND THEORETICAL UNDERPINNINGS

2.1 Yee's Typology of Gaming Motivations

American researcher Nick Yee launched the "Quantic Foundry" in 2015, a long-term survey project aiming to further understand gaming behaviour. The 50-item questionnaire polls about in-game preferences using Likert scales. Through factor analyses, motivational drivers were derived. Since its launch, over 300,000 gamers have participated and a new taxonomy was established, comprising a total of twelve motivations clustering into six main groups (see Table 1).

Gamers scoring high in the action cluster enjoy fast-paced gameplay using weapons. The social cluster is comprised of competitive and community-oriented gamers who thrive to either benchmark themselves against others or interact with fellow gamers. Mastery-driven players seek to constantly improve their gaming abilities and are not daunted by time-consuming and difficult challenges. Achievement hunters are interested in constant character progression, becoming as powerful as possible and the acquisition of all in-game collectibles. High scores in the immersion cluster indicate an avid interest in the game lore, the story and its characters. Discovery-oriented players enjoy expressing their individuality through customisation and try to find the boundaries of what is possible in the game world (Yee, 2016).

Table 1. Yee's gamer motivation model (Yee, 2016)

Action "Boom!"	**Destruction** Guns. Explosives. Chaos. Mayhem.	**Excitement** Fast-Paced. Action. Surprises. Thrills.
Social "Let's play together"	**Competition** Duels. Matches. High on ranking.	**Community** Teamwork. Chatting. Interacting.
Mastery "Let me think"	**Challenge** Practice. High difficulty. Challenges.	**Strategy** Thinking ahead. Making decisions.
Achievement "I want more"	**Completion** Get all collectibles. Complete all missions.	**Power** Powerful character. Powerful equipment.
Immersion "Once upon a time"	**Fantasy** Being someone else, somewhere else.	**Story** Elaborate plots. Interesting characters.
Creativity "What if?"	**Design** Expression. Customization.	**Discovery** Explore. Tinker. Experiment.

White: Action-Social Grey: Mastery-Achievement Dark grey: Immersion-Creativity

While the motivations within each of the main groups are highly correlated, patterns could also be found to link the six categories. Through multidimensional scaling, the twelve motivations can be mapped into three overarching clusters (see different shades of grey in Table 1): "action-social" (white), "mastery-achievement" (grey), and "immersion-creativity" (darker grey). The motivation "power" can be considered a bridge between the mastery-achievement and action-social clusters, while the "discovery" motivation is a bridge between the "mastery-achievement" and "immersion-creativity" clusters. This scaling method was conducted for all geographical regions and remained consistent throughout (Yee, 2016). Conclusions could also be drawn by looking at the collected socio-demographic data. From a gender perspective, motivational drivers for women were much more likely to be "fantasy", "design" and "completion", while men scored higher for "destruction", "competition", "strategy" and "challenge". The significance of these gender differences was however dwarfed by age differences. The competition motivation, which had the biggest gender difference at an early age (15-35) showed little to no difference at the ages (35-55). It was shown that age accounts for twice the variance that gender does. The "action-social" cluster varied the most dramatically with age (Yee, 2016). Yee therefore suggests that game developers should focus more on designing games adjusted to different age groups than to gender.

2.2 Distinguishing Personality Types

One of the most established models to categorize personality traits is the five-factor model of personality, which splits personality into five dimensions. The model assumes that all aspects of human personality can be described through existing adjectives in most languages. By factor-analysing large quantities of personality survey data, reoccurring denominations were found and a taxonomy of five traits was developed (Goldberg, 1990). The model has been proven to be replicable cross-culturally (McTear, Callejas and Griol, 2016) and is often used in empirical studies to connect personality with behaviour. McRae and John (1992) coined the term "OCEAN" model due to the initials of the five dimensions, which they describe as follows:

- Openness: The tendency to appreciate art, new ideas, values, feelings and behaviours.
- Conscientiousness: The tendency to be careful, on-time, to follow rules and to be hardworking.
- Extraversion: The tendency to be talkative, sociable and to enjoy others; the tendency to have a dominant style.
- Agreeableness: The tendency to agree and go along with others rather than to assert one's own opinions and choices.
- Neuroticism: The tendency to frequently experience unpleasant emotions such as anger, worry, and sadness, as well as being interpersonally sensitive.

Based on these five factors, an individual's personality can thoroughly be illustrated. When performing a five-factor personality test, participants receive an individual score for each dimension. The score determines how pronounced each trait is in the participant's psyche (McRae & John, 1992).

2.3 Game Choice

Apart from long term motivations, motives and incentives are further components that lead to action. A motive is defined as a single impulse that leads to an action. It is not ongoing and pursues one acute purpose. Motives occur individually and do not follow a bigger agenda. They can however create the basis for the development of a motivation. In order to explain a behavioral difference of two people exposed to the same situation, motives can be used (Heckhausen & Heckhausen, 2010). An incentive on the other hand, is the stimulus that leads a person to become active. It is synonymous with the reward that ultimately grants gratification (Franzoi, 2011). Incentives are used to get people to display or discontinue certain behaviours. This however only works if the individual places value in the reward as well as seeing it within reach. The value of an incentive can change over time and in different situations. Incentives are also always external triggers for action (Franzoi, 2011).

While an individual's personality influences the manifestation of motivations, motives and incentives, other factors like mood, physiological condition and social context also contribute. According to the uses and gratification theory, individuals actively seek to satisfy their needs. The choice of media is dependent on the recipient's current needs as well as his or her expectations towards the respective media format (Ruggiero, 2000). The assumption can therefore be made that game choice is largely dependent on an individual's own perception of how well a certain game is able to satisfy their needs.

3. METHODOLOGY

In order to test the interplay of personality, gaming motivations and game preference given certain socio-demographic circumstances, the online survey was accordingly divided into four parts. In total, the questionnaire comprised 92 items in random order within their thematic block. Because of a focus on the German speaking region, all questions were asked in German. Negatively and positively formulated items were used to counteract acquiescence bias. Before the survey went online, it was pre-tested to ensure intelligibility.

In order to conceptualise the fiver-factor model of personality, a suitable scale had to be found that would not be overwhelming for respondents and still provide valid data. Cooper, Smillie and Corr (2010) tested a Mini-IPIP (International Personality Item Pool) comprised of a total of 20 items with four of them designated for each of the five dimensions of the OCEAN model. Results showed that the Mini-IPIP was suitable as a short form for the five-factor model. The items are formulated as first-person statements which respondents should apply to their self-assessed personality (not at all accurate, somewhat inaccurate, neither inaccurate nor accurate, somewhat accurate, fully accurate). The applicability of the Mini-IPIP as a functional measurement tool was also confirmed by Donnellan, Oswald, Baird and Lucas (2006) across five studies with consistencies at or well above 0.60 (Cronbach's α).

Concerning motivations, we referred to the original but translated questions from Yee (2016). Each item in Yee's original item set refers to one of twelve motivational drivers (see Table 1). Respondents were asked to rate the importance of game elements and in-game activities on a five-level Likert scale (not at all important, slightly important, somewhat important, very important, extremely important). Based on these motivations a "motivation profile" or "motivational footprint" respectively for each respondent could be derived.

An additional aim of the online questionnaire was to inquire about game preferences and investigate whether gaming motivations also reflect in the games respondents usually play. This part of the survey comprised a list of ten video games from various genres. A diverse spectrum of games attempts to cover a broad range of preferences. Criteria for the choice of games were popularity, contemporary relevance, and publisher specifications about the main in-game activities. GameSpot's annual Video Game Rankings for each genre were used as a guideline (2016). Respondents were asked to report about which games they have already played and to what extent (game unknown, not played before, played before, frequently played, intensively played). The chosen games were: League of Legends (LoL), Diablo III (D3), Counter-Strike: Global Offensive (CS:GO), The Witcher 3: Wild Hunt (W3), Hearthstone (HS), Grand Theft Auto V (GTA5), Civilization VI (CIV6), World of Warcraft (WoW), Minecraft (MC) and Heavy Rain (HR).

4. STUDY RESULTS

4.1 Yee's Model Revisited and Replicated

In order to replicate the motivation model, reliability tests were conducted for each of the twelve motivational factors. According to theory, a Cronbach's α value above 0.7 suggests a reliable model. The results show strong similarities and all values have acceptable to good internal consistencies. The only exception is the factor "power" with a value of 0.65 meaning limited consistency.

To further investigate whether all twelve motivational factors can be reproduced in the German speaking region, a factor analysis of the 48-item inventory was conducted. The Kaiser-Meyer-Olkin measure of sampling adequacy was 0.92 and therefore well above the recommended value of 0.60. Bartlett's test of sphericity was highly significant ($p < 0.001$), and all 48 items correlated >0.3 with at least one other item. A principle components analysis was applied because the primary purpose was to identify and compute composite coping scores for the factors underlying the motivation item inventory (see Table 2). As deviation from Yee (2016), only ten factors could be identified. The initial eigenvalues show that the first component explained 20.8% of the total variance, component two 12.8%, component three dropped down to 5.7%, component four explained 4.9%, component five 4.6%, component six 3.2%, component seven 3%, component eight 2,8%, component nine 2.6% and component ten 2.2%. Component eleven and twelve had eigenvalues just below one and do therefore not justify the creation of new factors. The ten resulting factors were examined using a varimax rotation.

Table 2. Gaming motivations component variance output

Total Variance Explained

Component	Initial Eigenvalues			Extraction Sums of Squared Loadings			Rotation Sums of Squared Loadings		
	Total	% of Variance	Cumulative %	Total	% of Variance	Cumulative %	Total	% of Variance	Cumulative %
1	9,9	20,8	20,8	9,9	20,8	20,8	4,4	9,3	9,3
2	6,1	12,8	33,6	6,1	12,8	33,6	3,2	6,7	16,1
3	2,7	5,6	39,3	2,7	5,6	39,3	3,1	6,6	22,7
4	2,3	4,9	44,2	2,3	4,9	44,2	3,0	6,2	29,0
5	2,1	4,5	48,8	2,1	4,5	48,8	2,9	6,2	35,2
6	1,5	3,1	51,9	1,5	3,1	51,9	2,8	6,0	41,2
7	1,4	3,0	54,9	1,4	3,0	54,9	2,7	5,6	46,9
8	1,3	2,7	57,7	1,3	2,7	57,7	2,6	5,6	52,5
9	1,2	2,5	60,3	1,2	2,5	60,3	2,5	5,2	57,7
10	1,0	2,2	62,5	1,0	2,2	62,5	2,2	4,7	62,5
11	,9	1,9	64,5						
12	,9	1,9	66,4						

Extraction Method: Principal Component Analysis.

When looking at the factor loadings of each item and comparing them to Yee's original model of twelve factors, it becomes apparent that the found components resemble eight of Yee's motivational factors quite closely. The items of the motivations that could not be allocated distinctively to their respective components can be summarised into two categories. "Challenge" and "strategy" items both loaded mainly into the same component creating the previously mentioned "mastery" cluster and "design" and "discovery" merged into a "creativity" cluster (see Table 1). This makes sense as the motivations in each group are closely related and the findings agree with Yee's cluster analysis (2016). To further verify this notion, a hierarchical cluster analysis showed a cluster dendogram which supports the relationship of the motivation factors. "Challenge" and "strategy" as well as "design" and "discovery" are both linked directly with one another, indicating a strong relationship. One possible explanation for the assembly of four factors into two could be the relatively small sample size. Apart from that, the other motivations also show strong resemblance with Yee's original findings (cf. Table 1). The "action" cluster ("excitement" and "destruction") could only be partly replicated as the two motivations are further apart on the cluster dendogram and share no direct links. The "immersion-creativity" cluster is clearly visible in the bottom part of the dendrogram. While not all items loaded perfectly into their respective component, the results suggest that overall, Yee's gamer motivation model and hence hypothesis 1 (H1) is supported in the German speaking region. On these grounds, the following analyses will be based on Yee's original motivational factors.

4.2 Socio-Demographic Differences in Motivations

Various non-parametric comparison of means tests were conducted which focused on gender, age and educational background.

In order to analyse the interplay between gender and gaming motivations, a Mann-Whitney U test was calculated. Only male and female responses were taken into consideration ($n = 1601$). Results showed that there was a significant difference in mean ranks for each of the twelve gaming motivations (p not higher than .006). "Power", "challenge", "strategy", "excitement", "community", "destruction" and "competition" all had higher mean ranks for men than for women. Female gamers scored higher for "completion", "story", "design", "discovery", and "fantasy". The Mann-Whitney U test indicated that the biggest difference in mean ranks was for the "competition" motivation (male rank = 881.62, female rank = 596.05, $p < .001$). It becomes apparent that male motivations were more likely to be part of the "action-social" as well as the "mastery" cluster, while female gamers pursued motivations in the "immersion-creativity" cluster. Overall, motivations to play video games were higher for men than for women. Many of these gender differences align with existing stereotypes that men are more competitive and thrill-seeking, while women prefer creative and immersive game elements.

Furthermore, it was investigated how educational attainment affects the motivations to game. A Kruskal-Wallis test was conducted ($n = 1612$), which found significant differences in mean ranks for "power" ($Chi^2(6) = 12.917$, $p = .044$), "challenge" ($Chi^2(6) = 19.916$, $p = .003$), "completion" ($Chi^2(6) = 19.870$, $p = .003$), "design" ($Chi^2(6) = 25.271$, $p < .001$), "excitement "($Chi^2(6) = 21.819$, $p = .001$), "community" ($Chi^2(6) = 67.474$, $p < .000$) and "destruction" ($Chi^2(6) = 46.399$, $p < .001$). Overall, gaming motivations were higher for respondents with a lower educational background. Biggest difference in mean ranks was found for the "community" motivation. Literate gamers attribute less importance to gaming motivations in general. No significant differences could be found for the "story", "strategy", "discovery", "fantasy" and "competition" motivations. According to this, it can be assumed that the "immersion-creativity" cluster is less affected by the educational background of the gamer. Mean rank differences did however not cross a value of 300, thus suggesting that educational background has a moderate effect on gaming motivations.

Lastly, the relationship between age and gaming motivations was examined. A correlation analysis was conducted to understand how age correlates with the motivational factors. Significant negative correlations were found for "power" ($r = -.082$, $p = .001$), "challenge" ($r = -.129$, $p < .001$), "strategy" ($r = -,076$, $p = .002$), "design" ($r = -.093$, $p < .001$), "fantasy" ($r = -.050$, $p = .046$), "excitement" ($r = -.184$, $p < .001$), "community" ($r = -.129$, $p < .001$), "destruction" ($r = -.084$, $p = .001$), and "competition" ($r = -.232$, $p < .001$). "Competition" showed the strongest correlation. No significant correlations were found for "completion", "story" and "discovery". When analysing these results, it becomes apparent that all significant correlations were negative. The statement can therefore be made that overall gaming motivations decrease with age. The influence of age on the motivations to game were found to be more impactful than gender.

4.3 Influence of Personality on Gaming Motivations

In order to verify a potential relationship between player personality and gaming motivations, correlation analyses were calculated. Due to the non-normal distribution of the data, a non-parametric Spearman's rank correlation test was used. Firstly, the interplay between personality and gaming motivations was analysed. All twelve motivations were correlated with the factors of the five-factor personality model. The following results answer RQ2 (Is there a relationship between player personality and gaming motivations?) and support H3 (Gaming motivations can be allocated to specific personality types). Significant correlations (p) and their coefficients (r) were found as follows.

- Extraversion: Extraversion correlated positively with "power" ($r = .131$, $p < .001$), "strategy" ($r = .135$, $p < .001$), "excitement" ($r = .174$, $p < .001$), "community" ($r = .187$, $p < .001$), "destruction" ($r = .080$, $p = .001$) and "competition" ($r = .248$, $p < .001$). A negative correlation was found for "story" ($r = -.141$, $p < .001$). "Competition" showed the strongest correlation.
- Agreeableness: Agreeableness correlated positively with "story" ($r = .074$, $p = .003$), "design" ($r = .085$, $p = .001$), discovery ($r = .074$, $p = .003$) and "community" ($r = .142$, $p < .001$). A negative correlation was found for "destruction" ($r = -.144$, $p = .001$). "Destruction" showed the strongest correlation.
- Conscientiousness: Conscientiousness correlated positively with "challenge" ($r = .055$, $p = .026$), "completion" ($r = .134$, $p < .001$) and "strategy" ($r = .097$, $p < .001$). A negative correlation was found for "fantasy" ($r = -.078$, $p = .002$) and "destruction" ($r = -.077$, $p = .002$). "Completion" showed the strongest correlation.
- Neuroticism: Neuroticism correlated positively with "challenge" ($r = .135$, $p < .001$), "strategy" ($r = .154$, $p < .001$), "excitement" ($r = .068$, $p = .006$), "community" ($r = .082$, $p = .001$) and "competition" ($r = .094$, $p < .001$). A negative correlation was found for "design" ($r = -.120$, $p < .001$) and "fantasy" ($r = -.145$, $p < .001$). "Strategy" showed the strongest correlation.
- Openness: Openness correlated positively with "challenge" ($r = .088$, $p < .001$), "story" ($r = .203$, $p < .001$), "strategy" ($r = .154$, $p < .001$), "design" ($r = .169$, $p < .001$), "discovery" ($r = .228$, $p < .001$) and "fantasy" ($r = .101$, $p < .001$). A negative correlation was found for "destruction" ($r = -.064$, $p = .010$) and competition ($r = -.101$, $p < .001$). "Discovery" showed the strongest correlation.

When interpreting these results, it becomes apparent that certain gaming motivations correlate stronger with certain personality traits than with others. A pattern can be identified for each of the five dimensions.

Players scoring high in "extraversion" act out motivations in the "action-social" cluster. They are outgoing, social and thrill-seeking. "Community", "competition", "destruction" and "excitement" are all motivations that reflect these properties. "Story" correlated negatively with "extraversion", suggesting that extraverts are more interested in immediate gratification than feeling the need to dive deep into another world and its story. Correlations for "agreeableness" were weaker but still provided significant insights. A positive correlation with "community" is coherent as "agreeableness" high scorers are considered friendly and compassionate. They strive for the approval of others and like to play in groups. A negative correlation with the "destruction" motivation further underlines this notion. "Conscientiousness" matched with the "mastery-achievement" cluster. Gamers are invested in "strategy", "completion" and "challenge". Conscientious people are organised and effective. They aim to complete their in-game collections and optimise their gameplay and success strategies. Furthermore, neurotic people are considered emotional and sensitive. According to the results they are less interested in "fantasy" and "design" aspects and prefer "challenge"- and "strategy"-based games. Lastly, "openness" could be allocated to the "immersion-discovery" cluster. Open minded people are curious and imaginative. They tend to indulge in "story" and "fantasy" elements of a game and want to discover the game world. Table 3 shows all significant correlation results.

Table 3. Gaming motivations and five-factor personality correlation results (only with $p<0.05$)

	Extraversion	Agreeable-ness	Conscientiousness	Neuroticism	Openness
Power	.131				
Challenge	.169		.055	.135	.088
Completion			.134		
Story	-.062	.074			.203
Strategy	.135		.097	.116	.154
Design		.085		-.120	.169

Discovery		.074			.228
Fantasy	-.141		-.078	-.145	.101
Excitement	.174			.068	
Community	.187	.142		.082	
Destruction	.080	-.144	-.077		-.064
Competition	.248			.094	-.101

The correlation coefficients in the table are quite low. Several other factors will probably determine the motivations to play video games. Nevertheless, the correlations exhibited in Table 3 are all significant and H3 is therefore verified. Gaming motivations can be allocated to certain personality types and allow inferences about game choice to be made.

4.4 Gaming Motivations and Game Choice

Multiple linear regression analyses were calculated to predict game choice based on gaming motivations. The games were treated as dependent variables and the twelve gaming motivations as independent variables (predictors). The following results answer RQ1 (Do the motivations to play video games reflect in game choice?) and support H2 (The motivations to play video games are confirmed by game preference). Because a relationship between player personality and gaming motivations has already been proven, these results also answer RQ3 (Is there a relationship between player personality and game choice?) and confirm H4 (Inferences about game choice can be made based on player personality). Furthermore, motivational footprints could be derived and mapped to the selected games. In the following we summarize the significant predictors and their standardized coefficients (β).

- League of Legends: A significant regression equation was found ($F(12, 1599) = 13.693$, $p < .001$), with an adjusted-R^2 of .086. Significant predictors were “completion” ($\beta = -.078$, $p = .005$), “design” ($\beta = .092$, $p < .001$), “destruction” ($\beta = -.143$, $p < .000$) and “competition” ($\beta = .203$, $p < .001$). “Competition” had the strongest positive influence.
- Diablo III: A significant regression equation was found ($F(12, 1599 = 8.359$, $p < .001$) with an adjusted-R^2 of .052. Significant predictors were power ($\beta = .081$, $p = .009$), “design” ($\beta = .129$, $p < .001$), “community” ($\beta = .061$, $p = .036$) and “competition” ($\beta = -.098$, $p = .004$). “Design” had the strongest positive influence.
- Counter-Strike: Global Offensive: A significant regression equation was found ($F(12, 1559 = 25.875$), $p < .001$) with an adjusted-R^2 of .157. Significant predictors were “power” ($\beta = -.104$, $p < .001$), “strategy” ($\beta = .100$, $p = .004$), “excitement” ($\beta = .090$, $p = .008$) and “competition” ($\beta = .323$, $p < .001$). “Competition” had the strongest positive influence.
- The Witcher 3: Wild Hunt: A significant regression equation was found ($F(12, 1599) = 11.577$, $p < .001$) with an adjusted R^2 of .073. Significant predictors were “power” ($\beta = .074$, $p = .014$), “story” ($\beta = .143$, $p < .001$), “design” ($\beta = .075$, $p = .010$) and “discovery” ($\beta =.086$, $p = .008$). “Story” had the strongest positive influence.
- Hearthstone: A significant regression equation was found ($F(12, 1599) = 7.560$, $p < .001$) with an adjusted R^2 of .047. Significant predictors were “completion” ($\beta = -.071$, $p = .013$), “strategy” ($\beta = .081$, $p = .028$), “design” ($\beta = .069$, $p = .020$), “discovery” ($\beta = .081$, $p = .013$), “excitement” ($\beta = -.077$, $p = .032$), “destruction” ($\beta = -.088$, $p = .003$) and “competition” ($\beta = .190$, $p < .001$). “Destruction” had the strongest negative influence.
- Grand Theft Auto V: A significant regression equation was found ($F(12, 1599) = 18.609$, $p < .001$) with an adjusted R^2 of .116. Significant predictors were “excitement” ($\beta = .124$, $p < .001$) and “destruction” ($\beta = .219$, $p < .001$). “Destruction” had the strongest positive influence.
- Civilization VI: A significant regression equation was found ($F(12, 1599) = 8.610$, $p < .001$) with an adjusted R^2 of .054. Significant predictors were “completion” ($\beta = -.092$, $p < .001$), “strategy”

(β = .258, p < .001), "discovery" (β = .114, p < .001) and "community" (β = -.090, p = .002). "Strategy" had the strongest positive influence.

- World of Warcraft: A significant regression equation was found ($F(12, 1599) = 6.231$, $p < .001$) with an adjusted R^2 of .038. Significant predictors were "power" (β = .080, p = .010), "completion" (β = -.108, p < .001), "design" (β = .131, p < .001) and "destruction" (β = -.094, p < .001). "Design" had the strongest positive influence.
- Minecraft: A significant regression equation was found ($F(12, 1599) = 8.852$, $p < .001$) with an adjusted R^2 of .055. Significant predictors were "challenge" (β = -.101, p = .014), "design" (β = .072, p = .015), "discovery" (β = .203, p < .001) and "community" (β = .099, p < .001). "Discovery" had the strongest positive influence.
- Heavy Rain: A significant regression equation was found ($F(12, 1599) = 11.328$, $p < .001$) with an adjusted R^2 of .071. Significant predictors were "completion" (β = -.061, p = .032), "story" (β = .176, p < .001), "design" (β = .064, p = .028) and "community" (β = -.063, p = .028). "Story" had the strongest positive influence.

When comparing the positive predictors from each regression analysis with the stated motivational specifications of each game, it becomes apparent that multiple accordance exist. Negatively polarised predictors additionally reinforce the genre propositions and content-related emphases of the tested games. The only motivational driver which could not be proven as a predictor for any of the games was "fantasy". The rather low R^2 can be attributed to the fact that gaming motivations are not the most determining predictors for game choice and many other factors have influence. As these analyses solely focused on the influence of gaming motivations on game choice, the results still support H2 and it can be assumed that the motivations to play video games do reflect in the game choice of respondents. Table 4 shows the regression results for each of the tested games and their respective predictor polarisations. A '+' stands for a positive influence and a '-' for a negative one.

Table 4. Regression analysis results for motivational drivers and game choice (only values with p<0.05)

	LoL	D3	CS:GO	W3	HS	GTA5	CIV6	WoW	MC	HR
Power		+	-	+				+		
Challenge									-	
Completion	-				-		-	-		-
Story				+						+
Strategy			+		+		+			
Design	+	+		+	+			+	+	+
Discovery				+	+		+		+	
Fantasy										
Excitement			+		-	+				
Community		+					-		+	-
Destruction	-				-	+		-		
Competition	+	-	+		+					

5. CONCLUSION

The results of this study have shown that Yee's motivation model is a stable construct to determine gaming motivations also in the German speaking region. Eight of the twelve motivations ("destruction", "excitement", "competition", "community", "completion", "power", "story" and "fantasy") were directly replicable. The "design" and "discovery" motivations merged together to create an "immersion" factor, while "challenge" and "strategy" fused to form a "mastery" factor. Both of these superordinate groups have already been identified by Yee (cf. Table 1). It was also illustrated that the item inventory can be used to define specific motivational footprints related to games preferences of various genres. Overall gaming motivations decreased with age as well as with higher education level and revealed gender-specific differences. By correlating the gaming motivations with John and McRae's five-factor model of personality, it was proven that gamer personality has an impact on the motivations to play and therefore also on the choice of games. A new and more refined model can therefore be proposed which combines an identity management approach and the uses and gratifications theory to explain gaming motivations (see Figure 1). The personality of a person will have direct effect on the motivations to play video games and therefor also on their choice of games.

Marketing strategies of many of today's video game publishers often depict games as fundamentally escapist tools, enabling players to take on entirely new identities and perform tasks, they would normally not be able to experience in their everyday life. The results of this study however suggest, that an opposite approach may be more beneficial. As Yee (2016) already pointed out, games should be considered as identity management tools. Gamers gravitate towards gameplay that aligns with their core personality traits.

A limitation of this study is the fact that data was mainly provided by dedicated players who actively seek information about gaming online. As the study was only posted in gaming related Facebook groups as well as on game websites and forums, exposure was primarily directed towards more engaged players. The socio-demographic distribution does however suggest that a large part of the overall player base could be covered.

The non-normal distribution of the data implies that many answers leaned towards one extreme (i.e. either not at all important or extremely important) and fewer towards a more neutral answer option (i.e. somewhat important). The risk of interference or deliberate fraud always exists with online surveys and cannot be fully ruled out. Moreover, the translation of item sets from English into German may have led to inadvertent discrepancies as some statements may have been understood differently than intended.

Additionally, the list of games correlated with motivations only comprised successful and well-known titles with contemporary relevance. Many gamers do however enjoy playing video games that are over 10 years old. Nostalgia was not yet considered as a motivational factor at all, although it is often expressed as a substantial inducement to play "historic" games.

Further, the scale used to measure game preference by play duration may also only give a one-sided view. Someone who is interested in a certain game has not necessarily invested a lot of time in it.

The motivations according to Yee's model have proven to be a reliable and valid construct, which is applicable for different cultures and demographic contexts. However, socio-demographic circumstances and player personality are by far not the only factors that deserve an investigation when conducting gaming-specific motivational research in the future. The role of an individual's social conditions, especially in problematic contexts is worthy of further analysis and is assumed to have comparable impact on gaming motivations and game choice as personality. The fact that the social environment directly influences an individual's personality reinforces this notion.

REFERENCES

American Psychological Associaton. (2015). *Resolution on Violent Video Games*. Online: http://www.apa.org/news/press/releases/2015/08/violent-video-games.pdf. Accessed: 04.07.2017.

Andreasen, E., & Downey, B. (2001). The Bartle Test of Gamer Psychology. *The Mud Companion* (1).

Bartle, R. (1996). Hearts, Clubs, Diamonds, Spades: Players Who suit MUDs. *The Journal of Virtual Environments, 1*(1). Online: http://mud.co.uk/richard/hcds.htm. Accessed: 12.06.2017.

Bartle, R. (2004). *Designing virtual worlds*. Indianapolis, Indiana: New Riders Pub.

Brown, S. [Ahoy]. (2014). Pixel pioneers: A brief history of graphics, part one. Online: https://www.youtube.com/watch?v=dzN2pgL0zeg. Accessed: 08.05.2017.

Comelli, G., & von Rosenstiel, L. (2009). Führung durch Motivation. Mitarbeiter für Unternehmensziele gewinnen. Munich, Germany: Vahlen.

Cooper, A., Smillie, L., & Corr, P. (2010). A confirmatory factor analysis of the Mini-IPIP five-factor model personality scale. *Personality and Individual Differences,* 48(5). Online: http://www.sciencedirect.com/science/article/pii/S019188691000022X. Accessed: 28.06.2017.

DeCamp, W. (2015). Impersonal agencies of communication: Comparing the effects of video games and other risk factors on violence. *Psychology of Popular Media Culture, 4*(4).

Donnellan, M.B., Oswald, F.L., Baird, B.M., & Lucas, R.E. (2006). The mini-IPIP scales: tiny-yet-effective measures of the Big Five factors of personality. *Psychological Assessment 18*(2). Online: https://www.ncbi.nlm.nih.gov/pubmed/16768595. Accessed: 03.07.2017.

ESA. (2017). *Essential facts about the computer and video game industry. ESA.* Online: http://www.theesa.com/wp-content/uploads/2017/04/EF2017_FinalDigital.pdf. Accessed: 24.05.2018.

Festl, R., Scharkow, M., & Quandt, T. (2013). Problematic computer game use among adolescents, younger and older adults. *Addiction, 108*(3). Online: https://www.ncbi.nlm.nih.gov/pubmed/23078146. Accessed: 15.06.2017.

Franzoi, S. (2011). *Psychology: a discovery experience*. Australia Mason, Ohio: South-Western Cengage Learning.

Goldberg, L. (1990). An Alternative "Description of Personality": The Big-Five Factor

Structure. *Journal of Personality and Social Psychology, 59*(6). Online: http://projects.ori.org/lrg/PDFs_papers/Goldberg.Big-Five-FactorsStructure.JPSP.1990.pdf. Accessed 20.05.2017.

Heckhausen, J., & Heckhausen, H. (2010). *Motivation und Handeln*. Berlin Heidelberg, Germany: Springer-Verlag.

Hellström, C., Nilsson, K., Leppert, J., & Aslund, C. (2012). Influences of motives to play and ime spent gaming on the negative consequences of adolescent online computer gaming. *Computers in Human Behavior, 28*(4). Online: http://www.sciencedirect.com/science/article/pii/S0747563212000659. Accessed: 17.06.2017.

Kolo, C., & Baur, T. (2004). Living a Virtual Life: Playing Patterns and Social Dynamics in Online Games. In: *Game Studies, 4*(1).

Kolo, C., & Müller, J. (2010). Sind Spielerinnen anders? Eskapismus und andere Motivationskomponenten in verschiedenen Games und sozialen Kontexten im Geschlechtervergleich. In Swertz, C.; Wagner, N. (Eds.), Game Play Society. Contributions to contemporary Computer Game Studies. sModels explaining gaming behavior: A theoretical review and empirical study across different games. *Proceedings of the International IADIS Conference "Gaming and Entertainment Technologies 2013"*, Praha

McDonald. E. (2017). The global games market will reach $108.9 billion in 2017 with mobile taking 42%. *Newzoo.* Online: https://newzoo.com/insights/articles/the-global-games-market-will-reach-108-9-billion-in-2017-with-mobile-taking-42/. Accessed: 04.05.2017.

Newzoo. (2017). Newzoo's 2017 Report: Insights into the $108.9 Billion Global Games Market. *Newzoo.* Online: https://newzoo.com/insights/articles/newzoo-2017-report-insights-into-the-108-9-billion-global-games-market/. Accessed: 24.05.2018

McRae, R., & John, O. (1992). An Introduction to the Five-Factor Model and Its applications. *Journal of Personality 60*(2).

McTear, M., Callejas, Z., & Griol, D. (2016). *The Conversational Interface: Talking to Smart Devices*. Bern, Switzerland: Springer.

Rickey, D. (2013). Let the Gears Begin. Engines of Creation 1. *Skotos*. Online: http://www.skotos.net/articles/engines01.shtml. Accessed: 23.05.2017

Ruggiero, T. E. (2000). Uses and gratifications theory in the 21st century. *Mass Communication and Society, 3*(1). Online: http://citeseerx.ist.psu.edu/viewdoc/download?doi=10.1.1.547.5879&rep=rep1& type=pdf. Accessed: 23.05.2017.

Yee, N. (2002). *Facets: 5 motivation factors for why people play MMORPGs*. Online: http://www.nickyee.com/facets/facets.PDF. Accessed: 21.05.2017.

Yee, N. (2004*). Motivations of Play in MMORPGs: Results from a factor analytic approach.* Online: http://www.nickyee.com/daedalus/motivations.pdf. Accessed: 22.05.2017.

Yee, N. (2006). *Motivations for Play in Online Games. Cyberpsychology & Behavior, 9(6)*. Online: https://pdfs.semanticscholar.org/794e/ 19fe40a3207ae29eec4ddf4f2feeb773a3ff.pdf. Accessed: 24.05.2017.

Yee, N. (2016). Gamer motivation model. *Quantic Foundry*. Online: http://quanticfoundry.com/wp-content/uploads/2016/03/Gamer-Motivation-Profile-GDC-2016-Slides.pdf. Accessed: 25.05.2017.

PURCHASE INTENTIONS IN LEAGUE OF LEGENDS – THE ROLE OF INDIVIDUAL AND CULTURAL DIFFERENCES FOR EXPLAINING SOCIAL IDENTIFICATION

Bastian Kordyaka, Katharina Jahn and Bjoern Niehaves
University of Siegen, Kohlbettstraße 15, 57072 Siegen, Germany

ABSTRACT

Multiplayer Online Battle Arena (MOBA) is a computer game genre with increasing popularity and leaping revenues. The MOBA phenomenon is particularly interesting from an economic perspective since the majority of purchases consists of virtual items with hedonic value. Although research has already identified meaningful explanations, an answer to the question what motivates players to purchase virtual items in the specific context of the most successful MOBA game League of Legends (LoL) is still scarce. We build upon the assumptions of the social identity approach to explain purchases of virtual items. Additionally, we investigate individual and cultural antecedents of social identification. Results of our survey (n=181) indicate that social identification holds the potential to explain the intention to purchase virtual items and that cultural (patriotism) as well as individual (psychosocial development) factors predict social identification.

KEYWORDS

Social Identification, Cultural Differences, Patriotism, Individual Differences, Age, Purchase Intention

1. INTRODUCTION

Looking at the realms of video gaming from an economic perspective and connected to the emergence of the new game genre Multiplayer Online Battle Arena (MOBA) a remarkable revolution went on within the last decade. Specifically, a meaningful shift in potential sources of revenue for video games can be observed. A unique feature of MOBAs with pivotal significance is that they follow a free-to-play business model. Thus, every player can play a fully functional game without the need to invest any (real) money, which can explain the rapid dissemination of the game genre. MOBAs make the biggest share of revenue by selling virtual items, whereby a surprising effect can be observed that the majority of them possesses only hedonic value (opposed to functional value). Therefore, rather psychological (opposed to technological) drivers for purchase decisions of virtual items are indicated and open an innovative field for researchers.

Human-Computer Interaction (HCI) and Information Systems (IS) research already investigated potential drivers for purchase decisions of virtual items using psychological and technological perspectives (e.g. Guo and Barnes 2007; Kim et al. 2012; Kim and Chan 2007; Musabirov et al. 2017). Looking at the context of MOBAs, purchase behavior can be informed by research on marketing and psychology, which have shown that social identification can be a relevant predictor of purchases (e.g. Madrigal 2000). HCI and IS research already made use of social identification as an indirect predictor of purchases (Kim et al. 2012) but no study illustrated a direct effect up to now. Furthermore, a recent meta-analysis indicated that purchases of virtual items follow a platform-specific path in MOBAs (Hamari and Keronen 2017). One particularly noteworthy example of an economic successful MOBA game is League of Legends (LoL), which has up to 100 million monthly users and had the highest revenue within the framework of computer games in 2017 ("LoL Global Revenue 2017 | Statistic" 2018).

The purchase decision of a player is not holistically captured in the context of LoL and the reason for purchase decisions remain an open question up to now. Building on the assumptions of the social identity approach (Tajfel and Turner 2004), we postulate a meaningful role of social identification with the LoL community as a potential driver for purchases of virtual items. In addition, we want to provide a more concrete starting point to address and better understand social identification in the context of LoL. Therefore, we investigate antecedents holding the potential to explain social identification. On a cultural level, we want to test the effect of different levels of patriotism as an antecedent of social identification. On an individual level, we propose that the level of psychosocial development of a player influences the perception of social identification. Conclusively, the paper is guided by the following two research questions (RQs):

RQ1: *What effect does social identification have on purchases of virtual items in League of Legends?*
RQ2: *Which individual and cultural differences can explain social identification in League of Legends?*

2. RELATED WORK

2.1 Social Identification in Video Games

According to the social identity approach (Tajfel and Turner 2004), the identity of an individual can be divided into a personal and a (group dependent) social identity. Personal identity refers to the individual and identifies them as different from others, whereas social identity identifies the individual as a member of a group and different from other groups. In general, individuals strive for a positive self-concept. To achieve this, they use social comparisons on the level of individuals as well as on the level of (social) groups to maintain or enhance a positive self-concept (McLean and Syed 2014). Research already illustrated that the saliency of a social identity can have a meaningful effect on attitudes and behavior of an individual in a specific situation (Haslam et al. 1999).

From the perspectives of HCI and IS research and related to the context of video games, a corresponding construct that already caught the interest of researchers is online identity (Carter et al. 2014; Haimson et al. 2015; Kim et al. 2012). Kim et al. defined online identity as a configuration of the defining characteristics of a person in an online space (Kim et al. 2012). One noteworthy feature in contrast to the offline world is that it is much easier to portray a desired identity in an online context since characteristics can be selectively changed or hidden without high transaction costs between different groups. Taking the assumptions of the social identity approach into account, online identity consists of a personal and a social identity as well. Additionally, it is not necessarily tied to an offline identity and can be quite divergent. For the purpose of our study, we focus on the social (group-related) part of the online identity, representing the degree that an individual feels to be a member of the community of a MOBA game (i.e. LoL community).

2.2 Antecedents of Social Identification

2.2.1 Patriotism

Patriotism is defined as an attachment to a country, either accompanied by the intention of positive change by criticism and questioning (constructive patriotism) or by the inability to tolerate criticism and an unconditionally positive evaluation of the country (blind patriotism) (Schatz et al. 1999). Patriotism has been shown to influence consumer preference for domestic products in contrast to foreign products (Knight 1999). With regard to social identity theory, this finding can be explained by the positive self-concept that emerges for individuals high in patriotism when they evaluate domestic products more positive than foreign products (Verlegh 2007). With 41% of individuals in the US believing that their country is the best of the world, and only 5-11% of Western European countries agreeing to this statement (YouGov 2016), patriotism in North America can be regarded as more pronounced than in Western Europe. We therefore assume that regional differences can play a major role for identification with a virtual online gaming group when the game is originated in a region with high patriotism. For these individuals, identification with domestic games can contribute to positive self-concept because the game is strongly related to the best country of the world, and belonging to such a group enhances self-concept.

2.2.2 Stages of Psychosocial Development

The theory of psychosocial development postulates eight stages an individual has to undergo in order to develop its identity and self-concept between birth and death (Erikson 1963). Within the framework of our study, we focus on differences between the two psychosocial stages of *fidelity* (adolescence 13-19 years) and *love* (early adulthood 20-39 years) because they seem particularly meaningful in the context of LoL as they represent the stage of first intensive contact with MOBA games and the subsequent stage. In the adolescent stage of fidelity, the individual explores and experiments a sense of identity depending on relevant peer groups to answer the questions "who am I" and "what can I be" (Stevens 1983). Nowadays, online contexts like video games are an important place for self-exploration and self-presentation. Within the stage of love in early adulthood, the young adult establishes more autonomy and searches for role models outside the previous peer groups. The concept of identity shifts away from family or school by the ongoing development of identity regarding job and partnerships to answer the question "can I love" (Stevens 1983).

Referring to the context of video gaming, findings from neighboring contexts can shine light on effects of the different stages of psychosocial development. Chaplin and Lowrey (2010) looked at consumer based technologies and found out that individuals in their late adolescence (15 to 19 years) start to develop more flexible constellations of their self-concept. These finding suggests that older adults experience a richer self-concept compared to adolescents. Accordingly, we assume that the formerly more important feeling of belonging to a virtual group decreases over time by the ongoing development of competing possible identities.

2.3 Purchase Behavior as a Consequence of Social Identification

Looking at consequences of social identification like purchase behavior, different academic perspectives can be exploited. First, a consumer research approach can be detected. Cornwell and Coote (2005) discovered a positive relationship between consumers' identification and product purchases and Wu and Tsai (2008) found empirical indices that the degree of social identification positively influences purchases. Additionally, research explains purchases with the aid of advancement in status, keeping up with others, experience new content, customization, and self-expression (Cha 2011; Lehdonvirta 2009). Second, a perspective dealing with technical affordances to explain purchases can be detected (Hamari and Lehdonvirta 2010; Oh and Ryu 2007; Wohn 2014). Oh and Ryu looked at the connection between game mechanics and showed a sustained demand for virtual items (Oh and Ryu 2007). We focus on the first described perspective to better understand purchases. Transferring these findings to our context of interest, we expect that the purchase of virtual items is influenced by the level of perceived social identification.

Research already illustrated that virtual items have attributes capable of generating emotional or hedonic responses for individuals, which are associated with purchases. Lehdonvirta classified attributes of virtual items into three general categories, which are functional, hedonic, and social (van Dick 2001). Against the background of LoL as a context, we focus on the hedonic meaning of virtual items because within the game the majority of available items is of hedonic nature and includes no functional meaning. Babin et al. (1994) defined hedonic as the value individuals receive based on the subjective experience of fun and playfulness.

3. CONTEXT AND AIMS OF THE STUDY

To test effects of individual and cultural antecedents of the perceived social identification and its effect on the intended purchase of virtual items, we use the context of League of Legends (LoL). The game is part of the growing Multiplayer Online Battle Arena (MOBA) game genre and follows a free-to-play business model in which every player has the chance to experience a fully functional game without the need to invest any money. One remarkably unique feature LoL possesses is its economic potential. In 2017, the game showed the highest revenues for video games in general ("LoL Global Revenue 2017 | Statistic"). The portfolio of available virtual items consists of champions, skins (clothing of a champion), and accessories (mostly ward skins and summoner icons), whereby the majority of those items possesses no functional but rather hedonic values (skins and accessories). Thus, players cannot significantly enhance their chances of winning games with the aid of the majority of their purchases. Interestingly, the question if social identification with the virtual group holds the potential to explain purchase intentions in LoL remains unanswered so far.

From a social identity perspective (Tajfel and Turner 2004) social identification can be used to explain purchases. Since LoL has the largest footprints of any video game on digital platforms and in streaming media communities (e.g. YouTube, Twitch.tv), a relevance for players' self-concept to be part of a virtual group is indicated (Kerr, 2017). Therefore, we propose social identification as a driver for purchases because virtual items are one way to portray a desired image of oneself towards an important group for the self-concept. Additionally, we assume that the context of LoL is particularly suitable to test cultural differences as antecedents of social identification because LoL players come from all over the world, which indicates a meaningful cultural variance. Since LoL is developed and published by the American company Riot Games, we expect different expressions for the self-concept of players in different regions of play. Additionally, regarding individual differences, past surveys have discovered that the average age of players in LoL is around 20 years ("Average Age in Esports vs. Major Sports" 2017). This suggests a connection to different stages of psychosocial development and varying levels of significance for the perception of the self-concept and social identification of a player (Erikson and Erikson 1998).

The aims of our study are twofold. First, we want to test if social identification (operationalized as identification with the virtual group) increases purchase intentions for virtual items in the context of LoL (Hypothesis 1). Second, we intend to examine individual and cultural antecedents on the perception of identification with the virtual group. Specifically, we assume that players from North America show higher social identification with the virtual group than players from Western Europe (Hypothesis 2). Additionally, we hypothesize that younger players identify more strongly with the virtual group than older players (Hypothesis 3). The research model and the corresponding hypotheses are illustrated in Figure 1.

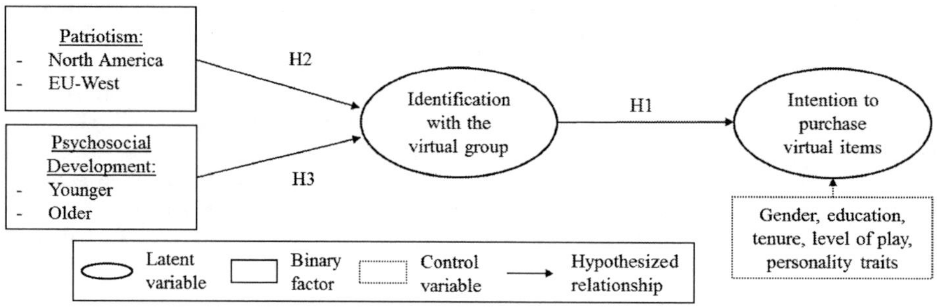

Figure 1. Research model

4. RESEARCH METHODOLOGY

4.1 Data Collection and Participant Characteristics

We conducted a cross-sectional survey using a digital questionnaire which we disseminated through official community boards, gatekeepers, and social media platforms (i.e. Facebook and Reddit). To increase the motivation for people to participate, incentives for survey attendance were given out in the form of a lottery comprising five in-game currency vouchers. After cleaning the data regarding missing cases, the final sample of our study consisted of 181 participants. The age of the participants had an average of close to 21 years (M=20.70, SD=3.71) and ranged from 14 to 38 years. The vast majority of our sample consisted of males (168 males, 13 females). Most participants (76%) started to play LoL more than three years ago (M=3.29, SD=1.69). Participants stated that the highest academic degree they currently held was a high school diploma (110) or bachelor's degree (49). The majority of participants played either on the silver (20%), gold (30%), or platinum (25%) level of play.

4.2 Measures of Variables

To develop our survey instruments and operationalize the variables of interest, we adapted validated scales from existing literature. Wherever possible, we asked participants to indicate their perception on a 7-point Likert-scale ranging from 1 ("strongly disagree") to 7 ("strongly agree").

Intention to purchase digital items. To measure the intention to purchase digital items (M=4.29, SD=2.08, α=.96, skew=-.29, kurtosis=-1.27), we adapted three items (e.g. "The probability that I would consider buying Riot Points within the next six months is high.") taken from Kim et al. (2012).

Identification with the virtual group. We captured identification with the virtual group (M=5.05, SD=1.32, α=.87, skew=-.82, kurtosis=-.67) using four adapted items (e.g. "Participating in League of Legends is important to me.") from Kyle et al. (2004).

Patriotism. To capture the level of patriotism, we used the variable region of play which can be considered a valid proxy to the independent variable of interest (see for example Beauchamp 2014). As regards to content, we collected data from North America (125 players) and Western Europe (56 players).

Stages of psychological development. To assess the ages of psychological development, we used the variable of age (e.g. "How old are you?") and computed a new variable splitting our dataset between the stages of fidelity (< 20 years) and love (> 20 years) (Erikson and Erikson 1998). After doing so, the fidelity stage consisted of 91 players (M=17.88, SD=1.69) and the love stage of 90 players (M=23.56, SD=2.93).

Personality Traits. To protect our results from potential confounding effects, we used the Ten Item Personality Measure ("TIPI") which is a brief and longtime validated measure of the Big-Five personality dimensions. The TIPI consists of ten statements representing the personal traits openness (e.g. "conventional", M=3.31, SD=1.38), conscientiousness (e.g. "self-disciplined", M=4.38, SD=1.15), extraversion (e.g. "extraverted", M=4.90, SD=1.31), agreeableness (e.g. "critical", M=5.21, SD=1.39), and neuroticism (e.g. "anxious", M=4.68, SD=1.24) with two items each.

5. RESULTS

To answer our first hypothesis, we proceed in two subsequent steps. First, we wanted to control our results from potential confounding effects. Therefore, we carried out a multiple linear regression analysis using sociodemographic (gender, education, tenure, level of play) and control variables (personality traits) as predictors to explain the intention to purchase digital items. The regression equation illustrated a non-significant result ($F(9,171) = 1.59$, $p = .12$) and explained 3% of the variance of the intention to purchase digital items. Furthermore, the data met the necessary assumptions of independent errors ($d = 1.92$) and multicollinearity was not a concern (Tolerances $\geq .79$, VIFs ≤ 1.27). To avoid the problem of multiple comparisons, we adjusted our p-values using the false discovery rate. After doing so none of the regression weights showed a significant effect ($p \geq .18$). Thus, we recorded that none of the inserted independent variables directly explained the intention to purchase digital items.

Second, we wanted to test the effect of identification with the virtual group as an independent variable on the dependent variable intention to purchase digital items. Additionally, we took into account the independent variables patriotism and stages of psychological development to control for unwanted effects. Therefore, we carried out a multiple regression analysis. The regression equation showed a significant result ($F(3,177) = 7.81$, $p < .001$) and explained 11% of the variance of intention to purchase digital items. Furthermore, the data met the necessary assumptions of independent errors ($d = 1.93$) and multicollinearity was not a concern (Tolerances $\geq .95$, VIFs ≤ 1.05). After controlling our p-values using the false discovery rate, only the regression weight of identification with the virtual group showed a significant effect ($p < .001$). The other two independent variables did not reach statistical significance ($p \geq .37$). Thus, we assumed that we found empirical support for hypothesis 1.

To answer our second and third hypotheses, we proceed one more time in two steps. First, we looked for potential confounds regarding the dependent variable identification with the virtual group. Therefore, we ran a multiple regression analysis inserting sociodemographic (gender, education, tenure, level of play) and control variables (personality traits) as predictors of identification with the virtual group. The regression equation illustrated a non-significant result ($F(9,171) = 2.00$, $p < .05$) and explained only 5% of the variance of the dependent variable. Furthermore, the data met the necessary assumptions of independent errors (d = 1.79) and multicollinearity was not a concern (Tolerances $\geq .79$, VIFs ≤ 1.27). To avoid the problem of multiple comparisons, we adjusted our p-values using the false discovery rate. After doing so none of the regression weights showed a significant effect ($p \geq .29$). Thus, we recorded that none of the inserted independent variables directly explained identification with the virtual group.

Second, we wanted to test the divergent effects of patriotism and stages of psychological development on the variable identification with the virtual group. Therefore, we carried out a 2x2 ANOVA with the two factors patriotism (North America vs. Western Europe) and stages of psychological development (stage of fidelity vs. stage of love). The analysis yielded a significant overall model test ($F(3,177) = 5.11$, $p < .01$) and significant main effects for the factors patriotism ($F(3,177) = 4.42$, $p < .05$) and stages of psychological development ($F(3,177) = 6.33$, $p < .05$) as well as a significant interaction effect of patriotism and stages of psychological development ($F(3,177) = 5.76$, $p < .05$). Players from North America (M = 5.41, SD = 1.27) showed significantly higher levels of identification than players from Western Europe (M = 4.89, SD = 1.31) and younger players (M = 5.24, SD = 1.33) showed higher levels of identification than older players (M = 4.86, SD = 1.28). In addition, the effect of patriotism was greater for younger players (M = 5.83, SD = .98 vs. M = 4.90, SD = 1.39) compared to older players (M = 4.82, SD = 1.40 vs. M = 4.87, SD = 1.25, Figure 2).

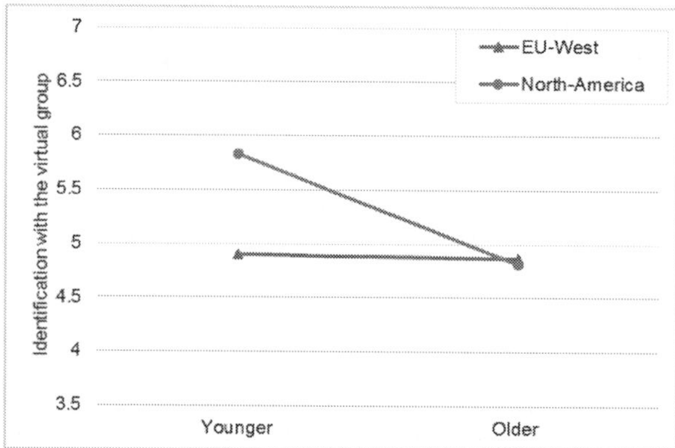

Figure 2. Interaction effect patriotism x stages of psychological development

6. DISCUSSION

In light of the approval of Hypothesis 1 (social identification is positively connected to purchase intentions), we extended existing findings from HCI and IS domains (Cha 2011; Lehdonvirta 2009) using psychological affordances to explain hedonic driven purchases. Additionally, our result constitutes an expansion of the external validity of existing findings from marketing research stating that social identification is a significant predictor of purchases (Cornwell and Coote 2005; Wu and Tsai 2008) in the new context of MOBAs. On a theoretical level, our findings exhibit several promising avenues, since social identification is a long time explored phenomenon in social psychology (e.g. Tajfel and Turner 2004) so that it is possible to transfer existing findings to shine further light on the interdependencies of consequences of social identification in the context of MOBAs. On a practical level, our finding illustrates the meaningfulness of the communication strategy of a game developer and the indirect effect it can have on revenues.

Additionally, we found support for Hypothesis 2 stating that cultural differences have an effect on the perception of social identification (i.e. patriotism). Thus, we expanded the assumptions of Knight (1999) that individuals tend to prefer domestic products by showing that players from North America tend to identify higher with the virtual group of the game LoL provided by the American game developer Riot than players from Western Europe. On a level of theory, we understand this finding as a reference that the empirical picture is more multifaceted than simple cause and effect relationships. Furthermore, this empirical statement could be useful to use and reevaluate findings from the rich literature of cross-cultural differences from neighboring disciplines. On a practical level, we interpret the effect of patriotism as a call for different foci of communication depending on the different servers of the game and cultural independent advertisements.

Approving the content of Hypothesis 3 (younger players show higher levels of social identification than older players), we conclude that older people possess a more flexible (Chaplin and Lowrey 2010) and richer self-concept (Chasteen 2005) which reduces the social identification with the LoL community. On a theoretical level, this finding validates the assumptions of the model of stages of psychosocial development (Erikson 1963) for the first time in the context of MOBAs and specifically, in LoL. On a practical level, the finding illustrates the enormous potential of socialization of younger people when playing LoL.

Furthermore, with the explorative finding that identification with the virtual group decreases only for older North American individuals but not for older Western European individuals, we found an interaction effect we did not hypothesize. One explanation for this unexpected finding might be that for younger Western European players, identification with LoL does not play a major role for their identity development because LoL is a game that is originated in North America. Therefore, they cannot profit as much as North American players from enhancing their self-concept by identifying with LoL in the fidelity phase of their development. Correspondingly, their level of identification equals the level of older North American and older Western European individuals, for whom this phase of development is already finished. This implies and further validates the conclusions that communication strategies to address players' intention to buy virtual items should be adopted to different development stages and different cultural backgrounds. For this, it might be a successful route to address European adolescent players' identification with virtual items related to Europe or content relevant in adolescence (e.g. music). On the other hand, for older adults' it might be efficient to emphasize that the desire for belonging to specific friends can be satisfied, regardless of culture.

7. LIMITATIONS AND OUTLOOK

Since the interpretation of our findings is subject to certain limitations, we will illustrate some of them and show potential ways to deal with them in the following. First, regarding the external validity, it would be useful to further revise the robustness of the contributions of our study attempting to replicate them in neighboring contexts. One fruitful way for future research could be to include other MOBA games (such as DotA 2) and explore potential commonalities and differences to better evaluate our findings. Second, on the level of internal validity, we had to deal with a balancing act between efficiency and comprehensive insights. In future studies, we recommend to use more direct measurements of patriotism and scales of self-disclosure and desirability to control for possible confounds. Third, regarding the level of the design, participants in our study self-selected themselves, which might have caused an undesired effect of selection. However, the demographics of our participants showed rather ordinary values for a stereotypical LoL player. Future studies could still try to use the technique of quota samples to ensure a representative sample. Fourth, future research could investigate identification effects of Western Europeans with games not originated in North America as well as the role of privacy for social identification and online purchases.

REFERENCES

"Average Age in Esports vs. Major Sports." 2017. *ESPN.Com*, September 17. (http://www.espn.com/esports/story/_/id/20733853, accessed June 5, 2018).

Babin, B. J., Darden, W. R., & Griffin, M. (1994). Work and/or fun: measuring hedonic and utilitarian shopping value. Journal of consumer research, 20(4), 644-656.

Beauchamp, Z. 2014. "Where People Love Their Nation & Where They Don't," *Vox*, May 18. (https://www.vox.com/2014/5/18/5724552/patriotism-pride-global-world, accessed May 25, 2018).

Carter, M., Downs, J., Nansen, B., Harrop, M., and Gibbs, M. 2014. *Paradigms of Games Research in HCI: A Review of 10 Years of Research at CHI*, ACM Press, pp. 27–36.

Cha, J. 2011. "Exploring the Internet as a Unique Shopping Channel to Sell Both Real and Virtual Items: A Comparison of Factors Affecting Purchase Intention and Consumer Characteristics," *Journal of Electronic Commerce Research* (12:2), p. 115.

Chaplin, L. N., and Lowrey, T. M. 2010. "The Development of Consumer-Based Consumption Constellations in Children," *Journal of Consumer Research* (36:5), pp. 757–777.

Cornwell, T. B., and Coote, L. V. 2005. "Corporate Sponsorship of a Cause: The Role of Identification in Purchase Intent," *Journal of Business Research* (58:3), pp. 268–276.

van Dick, R. 2001. "Identification in Organizational Contexts: Linking Theory and Research from Social and Organizational Psychology," *International Journal of Management Reviews* (3:4), pp. 265–283.

Erikson, E. H. 1963. *Childhood and Society (Rev. Ed.)*, New York: Norton.

Erikson, E. H., and Erikson, J. M. 1998. *The Life Cycle Completed (Extended Version)*, WW Norton & Company.

Guo, Y., and Barnes, S. 2007. "Why People Buy Virtual Items in Virtual Worlds with Real Money," *ACM Sigmis Database* (38:4), pp. 69–76.

Haimson, O. L., Brubaker, J. R., Dombrowski, L., and Hayes, G. R. 2015. *Disclosure, Stress, and Support During Gender Transition on Facebook*, ACM Press, pp. 1176–1190.

Hamari, J., and Keronen, L. 2017. "Why Do People Buy Virtual Goods: A Meta-Analysis," *Computers in Human Behavior* (71), pp. 59–69.

Hamari, J., and Lehdonvirta, V. 2010. *Game Design as Marketing: How Game Mechanics Create Demand for Virtual Goods*.

Haslam, S. A., Oakes, P. J., Reynolds, K. J., and Turner, J. C. 1999. "Social Identity Salience and the Emergence of Stereotype Consensus," *Personality and Social Psychology Bulletin* (25:7), pp. 809–818.

Kerr, C. (2017). "Twitch's 10 Most-Watched Games of 2015." (/view/news/265668/Twitchs_10_mostwatched_games_of_2015.php, accessed March 27, 2018).

Kim, H.-W., and Chan, H. C. 2007. "Why People Pay for Digital Items? Presentation Desire of Online Identity," *PACIS 2007 Proceedings*, p. 7.

Kim, H.-W., Chan, H. C., and Kankanhalli, A. 2012. "What Motivates People to Purchase Digital Items on Virtual Community Websites? The Desire for Online Self-Presentation," *Information Systems Research* (23:4), pp. 1232–1245.

Knight, G. A. 1999. "Consumer Preferences for Foreign and Domestic Products," *Journal of Consumer Marketing* (16:2), pp. 151–162.

Kyle, G., Graefe, A., Manning, R., and Bacon, J. 2004. "Predictors of Behavioral Loyalty Among Hikers Along the Appalachian Trail," *Leisure Sciences* (26:1), pp. 99–118.

Lehdonvirta, V. 2009. "Virtual Item Sales as a Revenue Model: Identifying Attributes That Drive Purchase Decisions," *Electronic Commerce Research* (9:1–2), pp. 97–113.

"LoL Global Revenue 2017 | Statistic." (2018). *Statista*. (https://www.statista.com/statistics/806975/lol-revenue/, accessed April 29, 2018).

Madrigal, R. 2000. "The Influence of Social Alliances with Sports Teams on Intentions to Purchase Corporate Sponsors' Products," *Journal of Advertising* (29:4), pp. 13–24.

McLean, K. C., and Syed, M. U. 2014. *The Oxford Handbook of Identity Development*, Oxford Library of Psychology.

"Most Popular Core PC Games | Global." (2018). *Newzoo*. (https://newzoo.com/insights/rankings/top-20-core-pc-games/, accessed April 24, 2018).

Myers, D. 2012. *Social Psychology*, McGraw-Hill Education. (https://books.google.de/books?id=O1bpXwAACAAJ).

Oh, G., and Ryu, T. 2007. "Game Design on Item-Selling Based Payment Model in Korean Online Games.," in *DiGRA Conference*. (http://www.lmc.gatech.edu/~cpearce3/DiGRA07/Proceedings/085.pdf).

Schatz, R. T., Staub, E., and Lavine, H. (1999). "On the Varieties of National Attachment: Blind Versus Constructive Patriotism," *Political Psychology* (20:1), pp. 151–174.

Stevens, R. 1983. *Erik Erikson: An Introduction*, Open University Press.

Tajfel, H., and Turner, J. C. 2004. *The Social Identity Theory of Intergroup Behavior.*

Verlegh, P. W. J. 2007. "Home Country Bias in Product Evaluation: The Complementary Roles of Economic and Socio-Psychological Motives," *Journal of International Business Studies* (38:3), pp. 361–373.

Wohn, D. Y. 2014. *Spending Real Money: Purchasing Patterns of Virtual Goods in an Online Social Game*, ACM Press, pp. 3359–3368.

Wu, W., and Tsai, C.-H. 2008. "The Empirical Study of CRM: Consumer-Company Identification and Purchase Intention in the Direct Selling Industry," *International Journal of Commerce and Management* (17:3), pp. 194–210.

YouGov. 2016. (https://d25d2506sfb94s.cloudfront.net/cumulus_uploads/document/emt4t4eijk/International%20Toplines_W.pdf).

INTEGRATING CHALLENGE BASED LEARNING APPROACH INTO THE STAGES OF THE GAME DESIGN THINKING

Isabel Cristina Siqueira da Silva
UniRitter Laureate International Universities, Porto Alegre, RS, Brazil

ABSTRACT

Game design thinking is a constantly evolution process and challenges professionals to proposing new products that involve innovation and creativity to achieve their goals and satisfy their target audience. New methodologies are being proposed and tested in order to establish design patterns that aid in the development stages of games during the game design process. In this sense, the methodology challenge based learning, unlike project and problem based learning, proposes the replacement of the question or the problem by a challenge. This is an important proposal in a game designer's learning, which looks for the ability to analyze and evaluate real open-ended nature problems, leading to more experiential perspective. Thus, this methodology present to the learners (and future professionals) a challenge scenario asking them to think about a number of possible solutions using a variety of interactive tools. This work presents the experiences and reflections related to the challenge based learning methodology applied to the process of game design thinking in undergraduate game classes. The results, obtained from cases study, are analyzed and discussed highlighting insights on the combination of both methodologies challenge based learning and game design thinking.

KEYWORDS

Game Design Thinking, Challenge Based Learning, Education, Innovation, Creativity

1. INTRODUCTION

Many authors propose the development of games as resources during the implementation of active methodologies. However, what methodology should be used when is the game not the way, but the end, the goal to be achieved?

The area of game design still requires discussions involving the proposal of active methodologies for teaching and developing. In this sense, it is noticed that new proposals of methodologies can increase, in a significant way, the sense of creativity, innovation and inspiration for the different stages of game design. Thus, innovative education models are needed to develop professionals that are more creative in order to explore new possibilities for game proposals.

The game design can focus on two main purposes: (1) entertainment and (2) education or training. While the first has a primary purpose of pure entertainment, and need to find a place on the game market, the second is related to "serious games", developed for explicit learning goals, simulations of realistic situations, training, safe failures, etc.

According to Gestwicki e McNely (2012), design thinking applied to game design is adequate for providing immersive and research-based learning, approaching the academic goals of business environments. In addition to immersion, the generation of ideas, the analysis of possibilities, the selection of solutions and the implementation are characteristics of design thinking that can be adapted for the game developing. Game design thinking (GDT) concepts can contribute significantly to the methodology adopted in the classroom, especially in higher education institutions. This methodology makes learning more dynamic, persistent and interesting, and assists students in the development of autonomy and critical sense.

On the other hand, challenge-based learning (CBL) extends the classroom environment and access to communication tools and real-world project management, encouraging studies beyond the school day. CBL uses strategies focused mainly on student autonomy that converge to the solution of the challenge identified and elaborated by the student himself. Binder et al. (2017) highlight the flexible and open character of the

CBL that generates a need for integration with other methods and techniques in any of its phases. In this context, these authors propose to apply CBL to mobile software development teaching. Similarly, Marin et al. (2013), Santos et al. (2013), Gabriel (2014) and Silveira (2016) discuss the integration of CBL with different methodologies as design thinking, scrum, biochemistry and flipped classroom respectively.

Thus, this work proposes to combine both GDT and CBL methodologies in order to investigate the convergence between these concepts and the gains in student engagements and game design results. The main goal is to encourage future game designers to think about the game design process broadly and effectively, to continually reflect on the content and process, and to understand the importance of the user-centric approach. The results are discussed from case studies performed in classrooms of an undergraduate game course.

The text is organized as follows. In addition to this introductory section, section 2 presents the background of this paper, presenting the main guiding themes: CBL and GDT, as well as related works. Section 3 discusses the proposed methodology and the case studies. Finally, section 4 presents the discussion of the results and the final considerations.

2. BACKGROUND AND RELATED WORKS

In this section, we present the characteristics of the methodology challenge based learning (CBL) and the stages of game design thinking (GDT), and, at the end, related works to the game design process.

2.1 Challenge Based Learning

The CBL approach emerged as a byproduct of a collaborative initiative that began in 2008, called "Apple Classroom of Tomorrow - Today" (Apple, 2008), whose goal was to identify the key principles for designing educational environments in the 21st century, helping schools come closer to this generation of students in order to increase the engagement of these in the school. According to Nichols et al. (2016), CBL is a learning framework initiated at Apple, Inc. that empowers learners to address challenges while acquiring content knowledge in diverse fields. Through CBL, students and teachers proving that learning can be deep, engaging, meaningful, and purposeful.

CBL can be described as extended problem based learning (PBL) and project based learning (PjBL) which are usually focused on a driving question or problem but, different these methodologies, in CBL the practical activity (the challenge) defines the content that must be studied (Jonassen, 1999) (Baloian et al., 2004) (Johnson et al., 2008) (Robinson, 2013) (Binder et al., 2017). Then, the question or the problem is replaced by a challenge. The CBL framework is shown in the Figure 1.

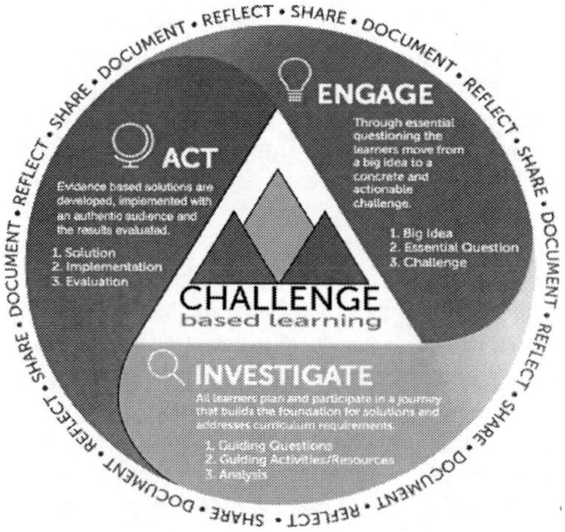

Figure 1. CBL Framework - reproduced from (Nichols, 2016)

The CBL methodology presents three main steps: (1) engage, (2) investigate, and (3) act. These three steps are interconnected in a process where the student is responsible for his/her learning based in a challenge. Each step prepares the learners to move to the next stage, encouraging them to use technologies of their daily lives to solve real world problems by creating a space where students can direct their own research, using critical thinking about how to apply what they learn. Thus, the learning does not follow the passive approach and the teacher is a collaborator.

As can be seen in the framework of Figure 1, the engage step is related to three main issues: big idea, essential question, and challenge. An essential questioning, allows the learners to contextualize and personalize the big idea (broad concept), moving from this to a concrete and actionable challenge, that is immediate and actionable.

In the investigate step, according to Nichols et al. (2016), the learners plan and participate in a journey that builds the foundation for solutions and addresses academic requirements. For this purpose, the survey of guiding questions, guiding activities and resources are carried out. At the end, the analysis of the lessons learned through the guiding questions and activities is performed, allowing the identification of solutions.

The last step of CBL is the act, where a solution is developed, applied in a real environment, and evaluated.

2.2 Game Design Thinking

The Game Design Thinking (GDT) methodology considered in this work was proposed by Silva and Bittencourt (2016) and aims to develop games based on design thinking and lean and agile concepts of project development. The GDT is divided into four main stages: team definition, conception, prototyping and validation. These steps are described below and are summarized in the schematic of Figure 2.

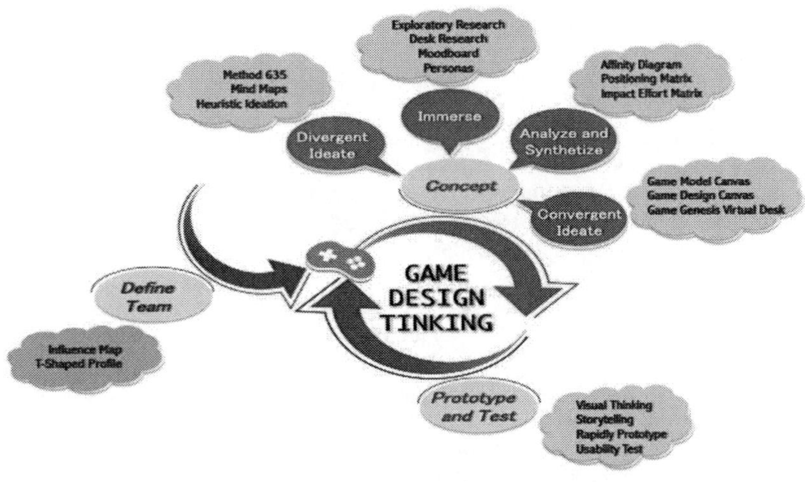

Figure 2. Game Design Thinking methodology - adapted from (Silva, 2016)

The definition of the team that will work in a game development is a fundamental step to reach the objectives of the game given the interdisciplinary characteristic involved in the different stages of conception and prototyping. Team members should interact, identify opportunities and come up with creative and innovative solutions to the problems of game development. Generally, game design teams need members who play at least the roles of game designer, programmer, 2D/3D artist, sound producer, etc. For this first stage, two strategies are proposed: influence map and T-shaped profile (Glushko, 2008).

The game conception depends on four phases of conception: divergent ideation, immersion, analysis and synthesis, and convergent ideation. It is noted, therefore, that the conception begins and ends based on the creative process and its two types of thinking: divergent and convergent.

Divergent ideation seeks to create options, from a significant quantity and diversity of ideas, in order to promote a variety of options for the immersion phase. Different brainstorming techniques can be applied in this stage, as the method 635 (Rohrbach, 1969), the mental map (Buzan and Buzan, 2006) and the heuristic ideation technique (Gray at al., 2010). After divergent ideation, where ideas about the game are raised, the immersion step starts, where the identification of needs and opportunities that will guide the generation of solutions in the next phase of the project are carried out. For the development of a game, four techniques are suggested at this stage: exploratory research, desk research, moodboard and empathy maps or personas (Vianna, 2012) (Gray at al., 2010).

In the analysis and synthesis step, definitions related to the game must make. In addition to considering the data gathered in the exploratory survey and the moodboard panel, cards created in the desk research can be arranged in an affinity diagram to identify similarities and patterns between them. The positioning and impact matrices are other tool proposals for this phase. The first is the definition of criteria such as time, complexity, innovation, costs, team members' abilities, motivation among others, while the impact matrix can be used after the positioning matrix and represents another analysis technique.

The convergent ideation closes the game design phase and is characterized by making choices based on existing alternatives related to it. In this step, the ideas generated in the previous steps are critically analyze so as to select them based on previously defined criteria, expanding the original ideas. Two tools can be used to the convergent ideation: the game model canvas (Jiménez, 2013) and game design canvas (Vekony, 2013) is suggested. Besides, to help generate new ideas while the canvas is being filled, it may be interesting to use the game genesis virtual deck (Gehling, 2016).

During prototype and tests step, four major actions should be considered: rapidly prototype, publish the game for feedback and evaluation, feedback analyze and make improvements if necessary. However, before proceeding to prototyping itself, is important to align the development process with the team members to facilitate understanding of the flow of the game. In this context, two resources can be applied: visual thinking and storytelling. Once the process is clear to team members, game implementation is started.

2.3 Related Works

Currently, there are few studies addressing CBL and/or GDT as a methodology to aid the game design process. However, some relevant works specifically related to the game design are discussed in this subsection.

More than a decade ago, Hunicke et al. (2006) proposed the MDA framework - mechanical, dynamic and aesthetic. According to the authors, MDA is a formal approach to understanding the game, bridging the gap between design and development, critique and research on games. In this way, the authors seek to reinforce the iterative processes of game developers, academics and researchers, helping study and design games and artifacts. In the same year, Gurgel et al. (2006) discussed the importance of assessing the games usability describing the process of developing a serious game focusing on testing the graphical interface and player interaction. The authors point out that the performance of usability tests with specialists should be tested throughout the entire process of developing a game, with special emphasis between the pre-production and production phases.

Gestwicki e McNely (2012) present a case study involving the development of an educational game about curatorial and museum operations. This development was based on Kembel's design thinking model (Kembel, 2009), consisting of five steps: empathy, problem definition, ideation, prototyping and testing. The authors point out that immersive learning provides a differential for students as it is combined with regular empathy, which stems from a deep understanding of stakeholders and their needs, and the interactive approach.

Bem et al. (2014) discuss the importance of the game design process and affirm that the alternatives for this issue are still in the process once is a relatively recent area of study. The work explores possibilities of methodologies for generating alternatives, creative techniques and tools. The authors do not relate this process to design thinking alternatives, but rather to generic design methods such as subject research, object research, generation and selection of alternatives, and prototyping.

Murakami et. al (2016) followed the traditional steps of design thinking for the development of a serious game: immersion, analysis and synthesis, ideation and prototyping. In the proposed methodology, the analysis and synthesis phase starts from the compilation of the information obtained in the immersion phase in a game design document (GDD), shared via the web with the study participants. Next, in the ideation phase, the authors represented the ideas of the gameplay in a gameplaybrikcs. From GDD and gameplaybricks, the concept and other aspects of the game were refined and implemented in the prototyping phase in the following sequence: definition of conceptual art, generation of graphic elements, definition of graphic interface, search for programming solutions and generation of versions of the game.

Jewell (2016) uses the term game design as a synonym for gamification and discusses the development of serious games and applications in higher education and in business. The author argues that the concept of serious games, as well as providing fun and entertainment for players, involves important aspects of different sciences, thus providing great benefits for people who have access to a learning environment and/or training. Still in relation to gamification, Kristiansen and Rasmussen (2014) point out that the use of Lego blocks aid in training and creative learning. This method is known as Lego serious play (2018) and features similarity to design thinking, combining descriptive, creative and challenging imagination to form strategic imagination. Thus, Lego blocks help participants to apply descriptive imagination, followed by the challenging imagination, where images are formed to interfere in different situation and, finally, the imagination is used creating a new scenario in order to advance the solution of the initial problem.

From these presented works, its noticed that the game design still requires specific methodologies, in order to give developers the understanding of the design process of a complete project. In this sense, the GDT methodology seeks new ways for game innovation from a user-centered approach where multidisciplinarity, collaboration and tangibilization of thoughts and processes lead to innovative solutions. Besides, CBL aims the acquisition of skills by developing a solution to a real problem identified and proposed by the student. Thus, the contents that must be studied arise from the needs of this proposed challenge.

3. CHALLENGE BASED LEARNING APPLIED INTO GAME DESIGN THINKING

This section presents the proposed combination of the GDT and CBL methodologies, highlighting the benefits that can be achieved in the learning process of game design students.

3.1 Methodology

In order to combine both GDT and CBL approaches, the Table 1 presents the proposal of mapping between concepts. As presented in the Table 1, this proposal starts with the CBL engage step and the first stage is the GDT team's definition.

Table 1. GDT and CBL approaches correspondence

Challenge Based Learning	Game Design Thinking
Engage: Big Idea, Essential Question, Challenge	Team Define; Concept: Divergent Ideate
Investigate: Guiding Questions, Guiding Activities/Resources, Analysis	Concept: Immerse, Analyze and Synthesize
Act: Solution, Implementation, Evaluation	Concept: Convergent Ideate; Prototype and Test

The definition of the team has a crucial importance because the team components must know each other, focusing on the personality of the members as well as their professional aptitude. It is necessary to give these team members autonomy so that they can think creatively and make associations. With the teams already formed, the GDT conception phase began with the divergent ideation based on brainstorming involving initial big ideas about the game. Thus, the big idea, the essential question and the challenge, proposed in CBL methodology, emerge.

After the divergent ideate step completed, starts the CBL investigate, whose correspondent stages in the GDT are immerse, analyze and synthesize. Then, once the ideas about the game are raised, GDT's immersion begins with the identification of needs and opportunities that will guide the generation of solutions in the next phase of the project. This phase enables the proposition of CBL guiding questions, that point towards the knowledge the learners will need to develop a solution to the challenge, activities and resources, used to answer the guiding questions.

The CBL investigate step ends with the analysis of the lessons learned through the guiding activities that provides a foundation for the identification of solutions. The possibilities previously raised can be analyzed in order to identify similarities and patterns between them. Thus, ideas and information are grouped to stimulate creativity, facilitating the conception of new ideas and favoring their convergence in the next stage. Many of these groupings can be evaluated considering how much effort will be required to implement them.

The last phase of CBL is the act, where evidence-based solutions are projected, implemented and evaluated with an authentic audience. In GDT, we have the last stage of concept, with convergent ideate, followed by prototype and tests. It is time to critically analyze and judge the ideas generated in the previous steps so as to select them based on previously defined criteria, expanding the original ideas. The developing of the prototype is initialized focusing in the tangibilization of the big idea, promoting the passage from the abstract to the physical in order to represent reality and provide validations, considering the optics of the player and the developer. At the end, tests are performed and, according to Nichols et al. (2016), provide the opportunity to assess the effectiveness of the solution, make adjustments and deepen subject area knowledge.

3.2 Case Studies

The proposed methodology was applied to three final classes of an undergraduate games course in a period of four months, reaching around sixty students. Initially, the students presented their influence maps and T-shaped profile in order to know each other better in terms of personal preferences and professional profile. The size of the teams varied between three and five members.

Once the teams are set, the students propose the big idea of the game in the conception phase, from the divergent ideation based on the brainstorming of the initial ideas about the games (entertainment or serious games). Each team was responsible for generating the big idea of their own game, although colleagues from other teams collaborated with the essential questions during the brainstorming. For this, method 635 was used in this work, where, at the end, the students presented their original ideas, the ideas suggested by the colleagues, which would be included in their work, and the ideas discarded, justifying the choices. Starting from the big idea, a set of questions that reflect current global problems related to the theme was elaborate. After reflection and dialogue, team members reduced these issues to just one that, when resolved, gave rise to the challenge.

Once the challenge is clear and definite, a set of guiding questions is raised to better understand the problem and what skills are needed to solve it. In order to do that, the immersion in the challenge, the analysis and the synthesis stages start through the two techniques: desk research and moodboard elaboration. For the desk research, the items surveyed were summarized in insight cards containing title, brief description, source and date of the researched data. The analysis and synthesis of the information collected during the immersion phase was used to construct affinity diagrams, identifying clusters from the insight cards, moodboards, and big pictures (Figure 3 (a)).

The convergent ideation (solution design) is the last stage of the conception and synthesizes ideas in game model canvas and game design canvas (Figure 3 (b)). Thus, both the business model and the game concept could be sketched in an agile way, intensifying details of definition of the scope of the game and design concepts.

(a) (b)

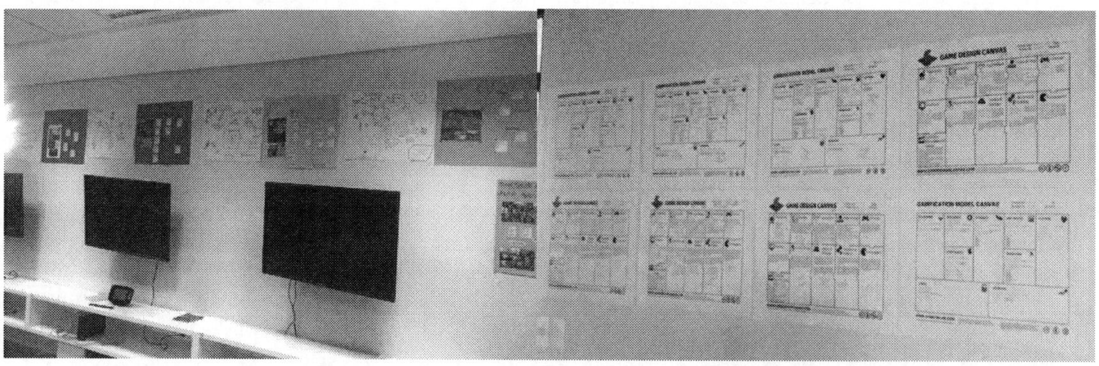

Figure 3. Challenges: (a) Affinity diagrams and big pictures; (b) game model canvas and game design canvas

To finish the process, visual thinking and board game concepts are to visualize the game flow and test the mechanics. At the end, before the prototype step, the team members were invited to fill a chronogram clearly indicating the roles and responsibilities of each member. Then, the proposals implementations were started following, in a first moment, the methodology rapidly prototype, where games toys were presented in a video, for colleagues and professors, and tested, with the target audience, in order to find some concept problems and get initial insights. After that, the complete implementation was started.

The tests with the prototypes was performed by usability tests (face to face and remote), where subjects (target audience) completed a pre-test questionnaire, a questionnaire in a likert scale format, with five assertions: "strongly agree", "agree", "undecided", "disagree" and "strongly disagree", and a post-test questionnaire where they could express suggestions and criticisms. For this study, design cycle was applied, where the students prototype, test and refine their solution concepts.

4. DISCUSSION AND CONCLUSIONS

Nowadays, the game market needs professionals with profiles of game designers who, although they can act in a specific activity like programming, modeling, animation, audio production among others, need to know the entire process of developing a game. In this sense, undergraduate game courses require that their teachers adopt methodologies to assist the student in understanding the process as a whole, encouraging him in the interdisciplinary training that the area in question demands.

This work presents the proposal to combine game design thinking and challenge based learning methodologies in order to engage the future game designer to think the process of a game design in a more innovative, creative and effective way. Through an empirical analysis, it can be observed that the classes that applied the methodologies of game design thinking and challenge based learning allowed the groups of students to work in a more "free" way, without the initial concern with the programming language and the modeling of scenarios and characters for example, but focusing on high-level concepts.

Thus, as the flow of the methodologies progressed, it was noticed that the students had more creative ideas, connecting points not so obvious from the initial premises, as well as trying to serve segments of different consumers. It was noticed that the phase of divergent ideation allows the teams an enriching brainstorming, "opening the mind" for the generation of game concepts. In the immersion stage, there is an evolution in the students' original ideas while the analysis stages and convergent ideation allow the synthesis of the game concept in an agile and efficient way. In order to do that, the teams summarize the models, business, and game design in panels which facilitate the identification of trends, creativity, inspiration and innovation among team members.

During the prototype step, the adoption of visual thinking and/or storytelling allows the entire visualization of the game flow and mechanics, visualizing the narrative of the game. Later, the construction of a game toy based on rapidly prototype promotes the insights about mechanics and interaction before the realization of a complete prototype developing, avoiding the well-known pitfall of cascade methods, where errors can be detected only at a final stage.

At the end, this case studies allowed to conclude that the fact of the student can choose his challenge related to the game design is an additional motivation factor, as it encourages the freedom and, especially, the possible personal projects that many students have when starting a game course. Thus, the future professionals of game design can be better prepared in proposing new products that involve innovation and creativity to achieve their goals and satisfy their target audience.

REFERENCES

Apple. 2008. *Apple Classrooms of Tomorrow - Today*. Technical Report, Apple Inc., Cupertino, USA.

Apple. 2012. *Challenge Based Learning: A Classroom Guide.* Technical Report, Apple Inc., Cupertino, USA.

Baloian, N., Breuer, H., Hoeksema, K., Hoppe, U. and et Milrad, M. 2004. Implementing the Challenge Based Learning in Classroom Scenarios. In Proceedings of the Symposium on Advanced Technologies in Education. Argostoli, GRE.

Bem, R. F. S., Alquete, T. and Martins, V. F. 2014. Proceedings of XIII Brazilian Symposium on Computer Games and Digital Entertainment (SBGames), Porto Alegre, BRA.

Binder, F. V., Nichols, M., Reinehr, S. and Malucelli, A. 2017. Challenge Based Learning Applied to Mobile Software Development Teaching. In *IEEE 30th Conference on Software Engineering Education and Training (CSEE&T)*, Savannah, USA.

Buzan, T. and Buzan, B. 2006. *The Mind Map Book.* New York: BBC Active.

Gabriel, S. E. 2014. A modified challenge-based learning approach in a capstone course to improve student satisfaction and engagement. Journal of Microbiology & Biology Education, Vol. 15, Nro. 2, pp. 316–8.

Gehling, M. 2016. Game Genesis Virtual Deck: uma ferramenta para criar ideias de jogos. Proceedings of XV Brazilian Symposium on Computer Games and Digital Entertainment (SBGames), São Paulo, BRA.

Gestwicki, P. and Mcnely, B. 2012. A case study of a five-step design thinking process in educational museum game design. In Proceedings of Meaningful Play.

Glushko, R. J. 2008. Designing a Service Science Discipline with Discipline, IBM Systems Journal, Vol. 47, No. 1, pp. 15-38.

Gray, D., Brown, S. and Macanufo, J. 2010. Gamestorming. *A Playbook for Innovators, Rulebreakers, and Changemakers.* O'Reilly Media. Massachusetts, USA.

Gurgel, I., Arcoverde, R. L., Almeida, E. W., Sultanum, N. B. and Tedesco, P. A. 2006. A importância de avaliar a usabilidade dos jogos: a experiência do Virtual Team. Proceedings of V Brazilian Symposium on Computer Games and Digital Entertainment (SBGames), Recife, BRA.

Hunicke, R., Leblanc, M. and Zubek, R. 2004. MDA: A Formal Approach to Game Design and Game Research. Proc. AAAI workshop on Challenges in Game, AAAI Press.

Jewell, D. 2016. Game-Design Thinking in Education and Beyond. Available in: <http://www.pearsoned.com/education-blog/game-design-thinking-in-education-and-beyond/>. Last access: 16 abr. 2018.

Jimenéz, S. 2013. Gamification Model Canvas. Available in: <http://www.gameonlab.com/canvas/>. Last access: 16 abr. 2018.

Johnson, L., Smith, R., Smythe, J. and Varon, R. 2008. *Challenge based learning: An approach for our time.* The New Media Consortium, Austin, USA.

Jonassen, D. H. 1999. Designing Constructivist Learning Environments. In *Instructional-Design Theories and Models: A New Paradigm of Instructional Theory.* Lawrence Erlbaum Associates, Vol. 2. C.M. Mahwah, USA.

Kembel, G. *Awakening creativity.* Available in: <http://fora.tv/2009/08/14/George_Kembel_Awakening_Creativity>. Last access: 16 abr. 2018.

Kristiansen, P. and Rasmussen, R. 2014. Building a Better Business Using the Lego Serious Play Method. John Wiley & Son. New Jersey, USA.

Lego Serious Play. 2018. The Method. Available in: <https://www.lego.com/en-us/seriousplay/the-method> Last access: 16 abr. 2018.

Marin, C., Hargis, J. and Cavanaugh, C. 2013. iPad learning ecosystem: Developing challenge-based learning using design thinking. Turkish Online Journal of Distance Education, Vol.14, No. 2, pp. 22-34.

Murakami, L. C., Leite Jr, A. J. M., Sabino, R. F. S. and Macedo, D. A. 2016. Design Thinking como metodologia alternativa para o desenvolvimento de jogos sérios. Nuevas Ideas en Informática Educativa 2014. Memorias del XIX Congresso Internacional Informática Educativa (TISE), Fortaleza, Brasil. Available in: <http://www.tise.cl/volumen10/TISE2014/tise2014_submission_200.pdf>. Last access: 16 abr. 2018.

Nichols, M., Cator, K. and Torres, M. 2016. *Challenge Based Learner User Guide*. Digital Promise, Redwood City, USA.

Rohrbach, B. 1969. *Kreativ nach Regeln – Methode 635, eine neue Technik zum Lösen von Problemen: Creative by rules - Method 635, a new technique for solving problems*. Absatzwirtschaft 12, pp. 73-53.

Robinson, J. K. 2013. Project-based learning: improving student engagement and performance in the laboratory. In *Analytical and Bioanalytical Chemistry*, Vol. 405, Issue 1, pp 7-13.

Santos, A. R., Fernandes, P., Sales, A. and Nichols, M. 2013. Combining Challenge-Based Learning and Scrum Framework for Mobile Application Development. *ACM Conference on Innovation and Technology in Computer Science Education*, pp. 189-194.

Silva, I. C. S. and Bittencourt, J. R. 2016. Proposta de Metodologia para o Ensino e o Desenvolvimento de Jogos Digitais Baseada em Design Thinking. *Proceedings of XII Brazilian Congress on Design Research and Development, Blucher Design Proceedings,* v. 9, n. 2, São Paulo: Blucher, pp. 2317-2328.

Silveira, I. 2016. A Game Development-based strategy for Teaching Software Design Patterns through Challenge-Based Learning under a Flipped Classroom approach. *In 24º Workshop sobre Educação em Computação.* Porto Alegre, BRA.

Vekony, D. 2013. Game Design Canvas – Seu projeto de jogo em uma página! Available in: <http://www.marketingegames.com.br/game-design-canvas/>. Last access: 16 abr. 2018.

Vianna, M., Vianna, Y., Adler, I., Lucena, B. and Russo, B. 2012. Design Thinking: inovação em negócios. MJV Press, Rio de Janeiro, BRA

A PROPOSAL FOR AN ARM FRAMEWORK FOR F2P MOBILE GAMES

Marisardo Bezerra de Medeiros Filho[1], Farley Millano de Mendonça Fernandes[2], Felipe Matheus Calado Oliveira de Souza[3] and André Menezes Marques das Neves[4]

[1]*Design, Universidade Federal de Pernambuco, Brazil / Faculdade Estácio da Paraíba, Brazil*

[2]*UNIDCOM/IADE - Unidade de Investigação em Design e Comunicação, Av. D. Carlos, I, 4, 1200-649 Lisboa, Portugal*

[3]*Jogos Digitais, Universidade Católica de Pernambuco, Brazil*

[4]*Design, Universidade Federal de Pernambuco, Brazil*

ABSTRACT

The mobile game market grows year after year through new distribution methods, design techniques and specific trends. The free-to-play (F2P) business model has been standing out in mobile app stores showing to be currently the most profitable way to monetize mobile games. User acquisition, retention and monetization are the main categories of an analytic business model framework, called ARM. However, the strategies used to acquire, retain and monetize users are spread throughout multiple sources, which makes the work of game designers and companies more difficult when developing the ARM strategy for a game. In this work, we present an ARM framework for F2P mobile games, which list and organize these strategies in a single source, considering categories, subcategories and specific elements. In this paper, we present the first version of the framework with a set of forty-five elements, eight subcategories, and three main categories.

KEYWORDS

Game design, Free-to-Play, Mobile Games, Acquisition, Retention, Monetization

1. INTRODUCTION

To make profitable Free-to-Play (F2P) games, there are some elements used to promote new players acquisition, retain them playing and drive them to monetize the game. Acquisition - Retention - Monetization (ARM) strategies are an important tool to help game developers to understand elements and relations between such stages, increasing the chances to make more profitable F2P games (Fields and Cotton, 2012; Lovell, 2013; Luton, 2013; Thibault, 2013).

However, these ARM strategies are dispersed throughout various sources such as websites, academic works and books. During this research we could not find any source that listed or tried to organize, formally, a set of ARM F2P game elements. We believe that such listing can be important for knowledge development about free-to-play mobile game design and help game development professionals and researchers to formally identify possibilities and opportunities related to such games.

The general objective of this work is to organize common ARM F2P game strategies in an unique framework, describing and organizing the content of ARM related elements and strategies. It can be used by to design acquisition, retention and monetization features on F2P games and also be used as a foundation to further academic researches on the subject. The specific objectives of this research are:

- Review the academic and professional literature regarding Acquisition, Retention, Monetization, and ARM Funnel, applied to F2P mobile games, this being the aim of this paper;
- Propose the elements and an architecture to organize an ARM framework for F2P mobile games;
- Evaluate the proposed ARM framework with F2P mobile games experienced professionals;
- Based on the evaluation conducted, make the adjustments needed for the final version of the framework.

This paper is organized with the following structure: The next chapter covers the main aspects about ARM in F2P mobile games; the third chapter lists and presents the main elements regarding user acquisition, retention and monetization; and the fourth chapter presents the conclusions and discussions of this work.

2. ARM IN F2P MOBILE GAMES

The term ARM refers to an analytic framework, often used to describe a business model, in mobile game industry. As an acronym, it means Acquisition, Retention, and Monetization. It could be useful as an aid to understand the business models used by F2P mobile games, and also as a guide for developers when applying the concepts at their own games. Acquisition strategies are used to attract new users to the game; Retention strategies aims to keep them playing and lastly, Monetization strategies are used to make users generate revenue for the game (Kuusisto , 2014; Tao, 2014).

However, games that are not F2P use a different framework, named B2P (buy-to-play), where its users first buy the game (Monetization), then discover the gameplay (Acquisition), and finally can repeat the experience (Retention) (Davidovici-Nora, 2014). In this context, the retention is at the end of the process and does not have a direct connection with monetization. On the other hand, F2P games business model architecture is way more complex and can generate multiple interactions among stages and not only a one-to-one relationship.

In F2P games, the monetization stage is pushed to the end of the process as payment is optional to a certain extent. Games with F2P business model put emphasis on experience before monetizing it, in order to accumulate a huge user base and make them engaged. Considering that the price to acquire a F2P game is zero, acquisition stage seems to be an easy and automatic stage in such model when compared with B2P ones (Davidovici-Nora, 2014).

The following structure (figure 1), initially proposed by Kontagent (2011), presents ARM funnel.

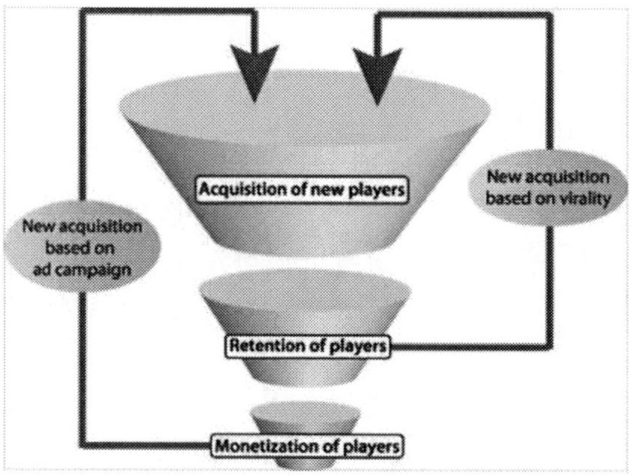

Figure 1. Illustration of ARM funnel for video games (THIBAULT, 2013, p.21)

These three stages are strictly linear and act more like a recurring cycle within the overall framework, it can be explained as (Fields & Cotton, 2012):

- First, the game acquires a large player base (acquisition);
- Then it should retain some of these players (retention), keeping enough of them coming back so that they will like the game enough to invest their money into it (monetization).
- Some of the players you retain will spread the word about your game and make it viral. They will raise the brand awareness of your game and attract new players (acquisition).
- Game´s profits from monetization can be invested into acquiring more users (advertising campaign).
- The cycle repeats.

Katkoff (2012a) explained an example (figure 2) that helps understanding how these stages are connected. In his example, the player starts building a house, but in order to finish it, she needs some specific items. At this point, the player knows that getting these items require several play sessions and a lot of grinding (retention). The player can skip grinding simply by asking friends to gift these items (something that generates new players acquisition), or, as a third option, just paying to proceed (monetization).

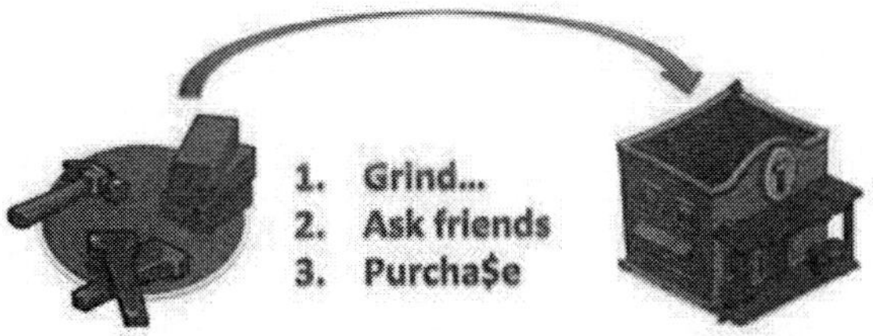

Figure 2. Most common virality formula (KATKOFF, 2012a)

The next chapter of this paper will explain separately every element of the ARM framework applied to F2P mobile games, considering the specific aspects of each one and relations among them.

3. ARM STRATEGIES

This chapter presents elements used to acquiring, retaining and monetizing through players in F2P games.

3.1 Acquisition

In F2P games, player acquisition is the first one to take place, since it is not necessary to buy the game to have it. F2P games have to convince users to spend money after they have already made the acquisition decision. Then, it is usually necessary a large number of players in order to make this model profitable (Alha, et al., 2014; Davidovici-Nora, 2014; Nguyen, 2014).

Askelöf (2013) explains that, in the ARM model, user acquisition sources are classified as being either viral or non-viral. Viral user sources refer to new players which have been generated by existing users. Whereas non-viral sources are those that are not generated by existing users, such as: advertising, cross-promotion and offer walls.

Based on this research, it was selected a proposal of elements, indicated by professionals and academic researchers as directly related with acquisition in F2P games. Based on Askelöf (2013) explanation, acquisition was divided in two main subcategories: Viral and Non-Viral. The selected categories and subcategories are not excluding among themselves, then an element could also represent, sometimes, more than one of these categories. The selected subcategories are organized below:

3.1.1 Viral Strategies

The Viral strategies are:

- *Invitation Mechanics*: There are a lot of mechanics to encourage users to invite their friends to try the game, where the player will usually be rewarded with some gifts for every invited person that installs the game (sometimes it is not necessary to install it). This is a way to reward users for sharing the game with some form of free content. This technique is often used by game designers as an incentive for users to invite their friends, increasing the virality. Also, there are some mechanics that encourage players to ask for help to quickly reach some objective, which could attract new players and help their retention as well. Some common examples of invitation rewards are: Boosts, power-ups and gacha tickets (Askelöf, 2013; Katkoff, 2012a; Morel, 2012; Paavilainen, et al., 2017);
- *Timeline Social Features Sharing*: Social features like leaderboards and achievements that players can share on their timeline. It can also increase user base retention and growth (Askelöf, 2013; Maiberg, 2013; Paavilainen, et al., 2017);
- *Word of Mouth*: Here we will assume it is just like what does not involve mechanics from the game, but things like natural invitations by players without using actions on the game. If a game is engaging and brings a good experience, it should make more players tell their friends about it (Askelöf, 2013; Kuusisto, 2014; Narinen, 2014; Williams, 2012);
- *Chart Position in Market Places*: Better chart position in marketplaces will provide more visibility, then it would help a game to gain more installs (Kuusisto, 2014);

3.1.2 Non-Viral Strategies

The Non-viral strategies are:

- *Natural Organic Installs*: We have decided to use this term to represent organic installs that do not take influence by consume of previous players or cross-promotions, like the pure store exposure - without considering charts - or trending news when an updated version of a game is in the store (Kaniel, 2012). Some authors present all organic installs as viral (Khalil, 2016; Williams, 2012), but we decide to do not do that, because viral is always about players bring more players, in the definition we are using;
- *Cross-promotions (within other games or Apps)*: Some companies provide the ability to cross-promote a game with others in their network, allowing reach large audiences at a relatively inexpensive cost basis by mutually advertising. Another example of cross-promotion is to redirect players between other games of the same company. This way, all of the company´s games can get a better chance of exposure (Askelöf, 2013; Luton, 2013; Morel, 2012; Williams, 2012);
- *Offer Walls*: Through Offer Walls, players can earn in-game currency by performing certain tasks. Examples of such tasks are installing an app or game. However, since the player is often only interested in getting the reward and not in using the offer they signed up for, players obtained through this method tend to quickly abandon. Offer Walls are a common method for monetizing users, but can also be used for player acquisition, by giving offers to players of competitor games (Askelöf, 2013; Morel, 2012);
- *Off Game/App Advertising*: We are considering, in this element, advertising that not occurs through other games or apps. This includes advertisements on websites or on social networks, banners on online stores, or e-mail campaigns (Askelöf, 2013; Kaniel, 2012; Khalil, 2016; Morel, 2012; Nguyen, 2014);

3.2 Retention

The second level of the ARM funnel is known as retention. For Thibault (2013), this category is about how to keep players involved into the game and what should be done to retain them on a mid and long-term basis.

Basically, retention is a measure of how many players keep playing the game after their initial play session. Since resources have been spent to acquire players, it is important to make them engaged. Then, it is directly linked to player engagement (Narinen, 2014). In a similar way, Luton (2013) explains, as related to retention, that the number of players who are retained over a given time period in a game, indicating how sticky the game is, or how effective it is at keeping players playing.

Askelöf (2013) presents three categories of game mechanics and dynamics used to make a player engage in Social Network Games (SNGs):

- *Progress Systems*: It is about the common mechanics used in SNGs to manage progress, and how this progress is communicated to the player;
- *Social Aspects*: These are mechanics that support social interactions;
- *Time-Based Limitations*: A set of techniques used in SNG to control the length of game sessions.

Then, we have selected a set of elements, indicated by professionals and academic researchers, as directly related to retention in F2P games. We divided them into three subcategories, as the division proposed by Askelöf (2013) for SNGs. We have decided to use the following subcategories since they are self-explanatory and fit better with the selected elements. We also changed the name of the subcategory Time-Based Limitations to Space and Time-Based Limitations, to bear the Location Triggers element. The selected categories and subcategories are not mutually excluding, then an element can represent, sometimes, more than one of these subcategories.

3.2.2 Progress Systems Strategies

The Progress System strategies are:

- *Achievements*: Often referred to as badges, achievements provide the feeling to reach something, rewarding players who fulfill some required conditions (Askelöf, 2013; Katkoff, 2012b; Lovell, 2013; Maiberg, 2013; Thibault, 2013);
- *Points*: Players can collect them to reach some task, challenge, better competition position, in-game richness, or more. The following divisions were found in the literature: experience points; redeemable points (or game coins); skill points; karma points; reputation points; progress points (or levelling up) (Askelöf, 2013; Kuusisto, 2014; Lovell, 2013);

- *Leaderboards*: A leaderboard, sometimes called *scoreboard*, is a competitive return trigger and its purpose is to make comparisons among players (Askelöf, 2013; Lovell, 2013; Luton, 2013; Nguyen, 2014). In our framework, this element is part of progress system subcategory, as well as social aspects subcategory, because it is about how the player is progressing in relation to others;
- *Levels*: It is an indication of how far has the player progressed in a game. It is not just about challenge progression, but also about new places and challenges to explore (Askelöf, 2013; Davidovici-Nora, 2014; Luton, 2013; Narinen, 2014);
- *Tutorial*: Sometimes called onboarding, it is the act of guiding players during specific moments of the game when they need to do something new (Askelöf, 2013; Luton, 2013; Narinen, 2014);
- *Objective*: An objective is a task, mission, quest or challenge that the player can reach in the game. By giving the player an objective, depth and meaning can be added to the game, creating variety to gameplay and adding constant rewards (Askelöf, 2013; Kuusisto, 2014; Salen and Zimmerman, 2004).

3.2.2 Social Aspects Strategies

The Social Aspects strategies are:

- *Leaderboards*: Leaderboards are an important social element to keep players competing against each other, while exposing their individual ranking position. Leaderboards can also help monetization when players willing to overcome others pay to do that easier and faster (Askelöf, 2013; Lovell, 2013; Luton, 2013; Nguyen, 2014). As explained before, this element is also part of progress system subcategory and social aspects subcategory as well;
- *Achievements sharing*: It is a social aspect tool that allows competitive and exposure interactions (Askelöf, 2013; Katkoff, 2012b; Maiberg, 2013; Thibault, 2013);
- *Socializing*: Also known as goal change, this element refers to a player's willing to play with other friends or teammates, making their goal socialized (Fukada, 2011, apud Askelöf, 2013; Nguyen, 2014);
- *Help request*: Using invitation mechanics to complete some task or goal in a game, the player can ask for help from their friends. This system encourages players to bring new players in (acquisition) and existing players come back to the game. (Askelöf, 2013; Katkoff, 2012a; Luton, 2013; Morel, 2012; Paavilainen, et al., 2017);
- *Gifting*: That is the possibility to spontaneously give gifts to others, who are notified, and then they are encouraged to join (acquisition) or come back to the game to return the favor. Reciprocity strengthens the social ties between the players, reminding them to keep playing (Luton, 2013; Paavilainen, et al., 2017; Radoff, 2011);
- *Challenges*: players can invite others to compete with them (Luton, 2013);
- *Competition sense*: It is about any other kind of situation players competing against the machine, against oneself and against others (Radoff, 2011; Salen and Zimmerman, 2004);
- *Cooperation sense*: It is about any other kind of situation players interact with each other in a noncompetitive way. Like social commitment, based on the sense that makes players return to complete some waiting action for another player, or helping their guild with some of their specific abilities. The willing to cooperate is the basis of this element (Luton, 2013; Radoff, 2011; Salen And Zimmerman, 2004).

3.2.3 Space and Time-Based Limitations Strategies

The Space and Time-Based Limitations strategies are:

- *Energy System*: These are common techniques used to limit the length of players′ sessions. Each action the player takes consumes energy and, as her energy drains to zero, she needs to wait until her energy bar is restored before it is possible to continue (Askelöf, 2013; Katkoff, 2012b; Luton, 2013);
- *Time to Complete*: Also known as construction time, it is about the time taken to build some object, learn a new ability or complete any other waiting bar that allows new resources in the game, forcing the player to wait or spend money to avoid it (Askelöf, 2013; Narinen, 2014; Luton, 2013);
- *Cooldown*: It is a time limit on how often certain actions can be used in game. (Askelöf, 2013);
- *Reward for Replaying*: Also known as incentivize appointment, or reward retention, they are mechanisms that reward player for returning to the game (Askelöf, 2013; Luton, 2013; Narinen, 2014; Nguyen, 2014);

- *Punishment for Absence*: It is, in some way, opposite of the reward for replay element. The player receives some penalty for not returning to the game for some specific period of time (Askelöf, 2013);
- *Limited-Time Events*: Also known as limited time campaigns, these are seasonal events that offer something special for a short period (Askelöf, 2013; Luton, 2013);
- *Come Back Message*: Also known as nudge triggers, that is appointed as one of the weakest return triggers. These are messages that remember the player about the game when they have not played the game for some time (Luton, 2013; Nguyen, 2014);
- *Location Triggers*: It is about when the game provides rewards for players playing in some specific places (Luton, 2013).

3.3 Monetization

Narinen (2014) explains that, in F2P games, monetization is the act of selling optional services and virtual resources to players within the game. The player can buy these resources with real money, which usually include things like cosmetic changes, virtual items and virtual currencies. Morel (2012) argue it is necessary be prepared to invest money to acquire users, since 2-6% of F2P players pay for something. Regarding free social mobile games, Nguyen (2014) says that two of the most notable ways to monetize them are selling advertisement and virtual items.

F2P model lets players play the game without paying up-front, but incentives are constantly given to the user to invest some money in order to further improve their gaming experience. By spending money in the game, a player can boost its abilities, advance quicker and overcome time limitations. About this issue, selling virtual items is consider the main method for monetization in F2P games. Then, instead of requiring players to pay in order to keep playing a game, a F2P one prefers to rely on specific game mechanics to incentivize players to naturally spend money in it (Askelöf, 2013).

Appels et al. (2017), explain that such products rely on revenues from two sources: paying consumers, and paying advertisers. For Luton (2013) the ways to monetize F2P games are:

- *In-app Purchases (IAP)*: Also known as microtransactions, they are purchases made by a player to acquire virtual goods or virtual currencies, items or usable resources in a game;
- *Advertising*: Ads provided by third-party suppliers that pay publishers on the number of impressions made in-game (interactions or exhibitions);
- *Product placement*: It is the practice to insert a real product in a game and reinforce the product estimate among its players by their association. It can be also considered a subtler way of advertising;
- *Merchandise*: The act of selling of physical goods associated with the game;
- *Store Cards*: These are physical cards with a code that can be redeemed for credits to be spent in the game. This item can be seen as an alternative to IAPs.

Based on this research, we have selected a set of elements, indicated by professionals and academic researchers, as directly related to monetization in F2P games. They were also divided into three subcategories, following the division proposed by Luton (2013), with some adaptations. Store cards were inserted into IPA subcategory since it is another way to monetize by in-app purchases. Furthermore, product placement was inserted into advertising subcategory, because it is just a subtler way of advertising. The selected categories and subcategories are not mutually excluding, then an element can represent, sometimes, more than one of these categories. The subcategories are following bellow.

3.3.1 In-app Purchase Strategies

The In-App Purchase Strategies are:

- *Virtual Currencies*: These are virtual money that allow players buy things in the game. There are basically two types of them: hard currency and soft currency. Hard currency is rewarded on a finite number of or low frequency of actions and it is commonly purchased, whereas a soft currency is infinitely rewarded through a core loop and commonly earned in large quantities. Hard currencies usually are more used for premium functions (Askelöf, 2013; Kuusisto, 2014; Luton, 2013);
- *Content*: It consists of more content to explore within the game, such as: maps, levels, new abilities, characters or similar that give players more things to do (Luton, 2013; Radoff, 2011);

- *Play Accelerators*: Also known as convenience, it consists of the purchase of anything that allows players skips ahead, providing them with something that would usually need time and dedication to reach it (Luton, 2013; Radoff, 2011);
- *Competitive Advantage*: Stands as anything that provides players with any competitive advantage against the game or other players (Luton, 2013; Radoff, 2011);
- *Customization*: It is how the game lets players customize their avatar or the game's world, making changes just for vanity or expressive reasons, or changes that could also make difference in gameplay (Askelöf, 2013; Davidovici-Nora, 2014; Kuusisto, 2014; Luton, 2013; Nguyen, 2014; Radoff, 2011);
- *Collectibles*: These items belong to a set of items that exists only to be collected (RADOFF, 2011);
- *Gifts*: They can help player-to-player interaction, but sometimes also can be acquired by hard currency (Luton, 2013; Paavilainen, et al., 2017; Radoff, 2011);
- *Store Cards*: Physical cards with codes that can be redeemed for credits to be spent in the game.

3.3.2 Advertising Strategies

The Advertising strategies are:

- *Banner Ads*: It is a thin strip that usually is shown at a top or bottom of the screen (Luton, 2013);
- *Interstitial Ads*: These are ads that appear between the transition of two screens and usually are presented full screen. They monetize better than banner ads (Luton, 2013);
- *Video Ads*: Video ads are one of the most effective ads, but often the most intrusive (Luton, 2013);
- *Offer Walls*: As a monetize method, offer walls make money through actions that players need to do, as installing another game or signing up for a service. This method is a common way for monetizing users, rewarding players with some limited in-game resources and publishers with monetization (Askelöf, 2013; Luton, 2013; Morel, 2012);
- *Affiliate Linking*: It is a link to a store, which tracks the player and pays out a percentage of any sales made. For example, the ad takes the player from the game to a store, and if they make some purchase in that store it monetizes for the publisher (Luton, 2013);
- Product Placement: As explained, it is the use of real products within the game as a way to advertise;
- Merchandise: As explained, it is the act to sell physical goods associated with the game.

4. CONCLUSION

The free mobile game design has specific characteristics that demand an investigation. The proper understanding of these characteristics can allow game professionals to create more profitable and successful mobile games. For example, a set of acquisition, retention, and monetization mobile free-to-play game elements, schematically organized, could be helpful to turns these elements formally accessible to be consciously designed on real games.

In this research we have organized a framework for F2P mobile games, assembling a set of forty-five elements, eight subcategories, and three main categories. These elements were put together through a research focused on professional and academic literature. We believe this framework can be very useful for free-to-play game design and game production professionals, as well as researches related to this subject. A formally organized list of applicable elements could turn the selection of F2P solutions more effective. Game designers and producers, while using this framework, can verify if they are forgetting any element or consider alternatives that could help the game to be successful. We should also consider the use of the proposed framework as the basis for more research about ARM strategies in games.

As a future work, we are going to evolve this framework, validating and modifying its structure and elements, as well its labels. It will be done through surveys with F2P mobile game professionals.

REFERENCES

Appel, G. et al, 2017. Retention And The Monetization Of Apps. Available at: <http://www.hitechmarkets.net /files/appellibaimullershachar2017.pdf > accessed: December 27, 2017.

Askelöf, P., 2013. Monetization Of Social Network Games In Japan And The West. Thesis, Master of Science degree. Lund University, Sweden.

Alha, K. et al, 2014. Free-To-Play Games: Professionals' Perspectives. *Proceedings of Nordic Digra*, v. 2014. Visby (Gotland), Sweden.

Davidovici-nora, M., 2014. Paid And Free Digital Business Models Innovations In The Video Game Industry. *Digiworld Economic Journal*, no. 94, 2nd q. 2014, p. 83.

Fields, T. and Cotton, B., 2012. *Social Gamer Design: Monetization Methods And Mechanics.* Elsevier: United States of America.

Kaniel, O., 2012. Events Tracking Technology. U.S. Patent application n. 13/649,402, 11 out. 2012.

Katkoff, M., 2012a. From Players To Payers. Available at: <https://www.deconstructoroffun.com/blog//2012/05/from-players-to-payers-4-steps-to.html> Last access: December 25, 2017.

Katkoff, M., 2012b. Mid-Core Success Part 2: Retention. Available at: <https://www.deconstructoroffun.com/blog//2013 /10/mid-core-success-part-2-retention.html> last access: December 30, 2017.

Khalil, H., 2016. Engineering Viral Growth. Thesis, Master of Science degree. Aalto University, Finland.

Kontagent, 2011. The Top 7 Metrics Of High Successful Social Companies. Available at: <http://static.kontagent.com /whitepaper/knt_wp_top7metrics_p3_finalx.pdf> last access: July 12, 2017.

Kuusisto, M. et al., 2014. Evaluating Free-To-Play Monetization Mechanics In Mobile Games: Case: Improvement Proposal To Supersonic-Game. Thesis, Bachelors' degree. Tampere University of Applied Sciences, Finland.

Lovell, N., 2013. The Pyramid Of Free-To-Play Game Design. Available at: <https://www.gamasutra.com/blogs/ nicholaslovell/20130919/200606/the_pyramid_of_freeto> last accesse: January 03, 2018.

Luton, W., 2013. *Free-To-Play: Making Money From Games You Give Away*. New riders, San Francisco, USA.

Maiberg, E., 2013. Pearl's Peril Is Wooga's Fastest-Growing Game To Date. Available at: < http://www.adweek.com/ digital/pearls-peril-is-woogas-fastest-growing-game-to-date/ > last access: December 23, 2017.

McClure, D., 2007. Startup Metrics For Pirates: Aarrr!. 500 Hats. Available at: <http://500hats.typepad.com/500blogs /2007/09/startup-metrics.html> last access: January 28, 2018.

Morel, R., 2012. Choosing The Right Business Model For Your Game Or App. Available at: <https://www.adobe.com /devnet/flashplayer/articles/right-business-model.html> last access: December 20, 2017.

Narinen, A., et al, 2014. How Player Retention Works In Free-To-Play Mobile Games: A Study Of Player Retention Methods. Thesis, Bachelors' degree. Tampere University of Applied Sciences, Finland.

Nguyen, H., 2014. Monetization For A Free-To-Play Mobile Game. Thesis, Bachelors' degree. Kajaani University of Applied Sciences, Finland.

Radoff, J., 2011. *Game On: Energize Your Business With Social Media Games*. Wiley Publishing, Inc. Indianapolis, USA.

Salen, K. and Zimmerman, E., 2004. Rules Of Play: Game Design Fundamentals. The MIT Press. Massachusetts, USA.

Tao, Z. et al., 2014. Item Recommendation Using Collaborative Filtering In Mobile Social Games: *A Case Study. Big Data And Cloud Computing (bdcloud). IEEE Fourth International Conference*. IEEE, 2014. P. 293-297.

Paavilainen, J. et al., 2017. A Review Of Social Features In Social Network Games. *Transactions of the digital games research association*, v. 3, n. 2, 2017.

Thibault, C., 2013. *Game Data Analysis–Tools And Methods*. Packt Publishing ltd. Birmingham, United Kingdom.

Think Gaming, 2018. Top grossing all devices-games. Available at: <https://thinkgaming.com/> last access: January 28, 2018.

Williams, J., 2012. Applying Lessons Learned On Facebook To Mobile App Development. Available at: <https://www.gamasutra.com/blogs/joshwilliams/20120117/90918/applying_lessons_learned_on_facebook_to_mobil e_app_development.php> last access: December 25, 2017.

CAMPUS EXPLORER: FACILITATING STUDENT COMMUNITIES THROUGH GAMING

Benjamin Bürgisser[1], Fabio Zünd[2], Renato Pajarola[1] and Robert W. Sumner[2]
[1]*University of Zurich, Switzerland*
[2]*ETH Zurich, Switzerland*

ABSTRACT

University students are often highly focused on their current lectures and imminent exams and thus neglect to interact with students across departments and to engage in campus life. To facilitate a more closely-knit community of university students, we evaluate a set of suitable core game mechanics, social features, and reward systems to motivate students to explore their university and to meet other students. Our prototype mobile application implements a location-based approach and includes game mechanics such as building check-ins, meeting other students, campus expeditions, and campus events. We evaluate the potential of our approach using both qualitative and quantitative data collected during an initial playtesting phase. Our analysis has shown that our location-based mechanics and a focus on social features were well received by students. Players engaged in exploring the campus and see potential in location-sharing and future collaboration features.

KEYWORDS

Gamification, Location-based, Game Design, Social, Community Building

1. INTRODUCTION

Despite extracurricular activities offered by most universities, interacting with students across departments and engaging in campus life can be challenging for students. Between lectures, projects, exercises, and exams, time to meet new people and to explore the campus is often scarce. On larger campuses, many students visit lectures affiliated with a specific department. Such lectures are typically held at only a small subset of all university buildings. The hurdle for cross-department interactions can, therefore, be high. To approach these problems, we evaluate solutions based on *gamification* and *location-based mobile gaming*. In a university context, gamification is often used as a tool to motivate learning behavior and for educational purposes (Seaborn and Fels, 2015). However, the objectives of our gamified experience targeted at university students are to gamify campus life and community building. Moreover, we intend to spark a feeling of belonging to the university.

For successful gamification, game mechanics need to be chosen with care. Deterding (2012) argues that implementing simple components of complex modern games cannot only fail to engage players but actually damage their interest. Successful gamification requires a deep understanding of the users and their motivators. This allows for utilizing and amplifying their intrinsic motivation for a certain task, rather than trying to force behavior for which the users have no motivation.

Based on our objectives, we have identified a set of tasks for which to motivate students. Those tasks are exploration and discovery, communication and participation in campus activities. In order to determine whether those tasks are interesting to players and what game mechanics could be used to amplify that interest, we have implemented a concept for a mobile game called *Campus Explorer*. As a pilot implementation, it focuses on the design and evaluation of a location-based base mechanic allowing check-ins to locations in the real world and on creating a feeling of belonging to the university through exploration, communication, and location-sharing features. It lays the groundwork for future work in this area to further explore this approach to gamify community building and collaborative tasks to motivate students to meet in the real world.

We carefully selected game mechanics and reward systems found in social media platforms and existing mobile games to evaluate their suitability as motivators for each task. The mechanics are implemented as points of interest (POIs) displayed on a virtual map (Figure 1), which the player can explore by moving in the real world. Real-life location changes are adopted by an avatar representing the player. The game features quick and simple gameplay. Thus, it may be played before and after lectures, while commuting between university buildings or during breaks. We implemented our prototype as a mobile game for the Android and iOS platforms using the Unity[1] game engine in the front-end and Amazon Web Services (AWS)[2] in the back-end. We evaluated Campus Explorer in a playtesting session of four weeks testing the location-based concept and the selected game mechanics with respect to our objectives.

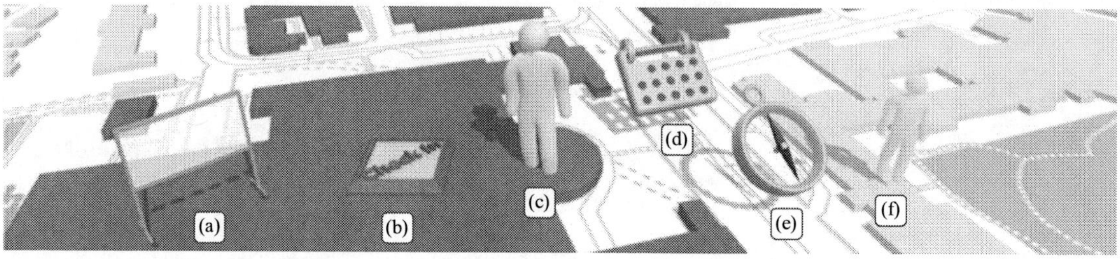

Figure 1. Variations of the point of interest base-mechanic: (a) blackboards, (b) building check-ins, (c) the player's avatar, (d) event check-ins, (e) expedition check-ins and (f) player check-ins displayed on the game map

2. RELATED WORK

Deterding (2012) created an achievement system for students in interactive games and media. Students could receive collectible cards for playful or creative interactions with staff and faculty as such interactions have proven to increase student retention rates. Moreover, an achievement was given to everyone playing the game, if more than 90% of the freshmen would pass the introductory programming class. In response, juniors and seniors organized study session for the freshman, and instead of the usual 85%, the passing rate was at 91%.

For Campus Explorer we decided to focus more on interactions between students and on exploring the campus, rather than interactions with staff and academic achievements, thus gamifying extracurricular activities and campus life. We tried to adhere to the findings of Deterding creating challenges and mechanics which would engage students in fun and interesting tasks and amplify their motivation to take part in campus life.

Fitz-Walter et al. (2012) implemented Orientation Passport, a gamified application pursuing similar objectives to ours. The authors' main goals include introducing students to the campus, encouraging exploration and participation in events as well as socializing among students and simplifying the transition from school to the university environment.

Whereas Campus Explorer is meant to enrich the student experience throughout the whole semester, Orientation Passport is specifically targeted at new students in their first few weeks at the university. Another significant difference in their approach is Orientation Passport not being designed as a game first. Instead, their application offers a number of functionalities helpful for students attending university orientation. The achievement system and game elements were later introduced to create a more motivating and fun experience.

The results achieved with Orientation Passport are promising, and the gamification of Orientation Passport was well received by students. The location-based functionality offered by utilizing QR codes was favored by most students over other game elements and the interactive map added to the application was considered among the most useful features. These findings show that the game mechanics we selected for Campus Explorer, which are mainly based on exploring an in-game world map, may in fact be well received by students.

[1] https://unity3d.com/
[2] https://aws.amazon.com/

3. GAME DESIGN

We designed Campus Explorer as a mobile social and exploration game targeting smartphones and tablets (Android and iOS). Running on mobile devices, the game can easily be played in-between lectures or while exploring the campus. Moreover, this approach allows us to use the built-in GPS of such devices to implement a location-based approach. Utilizing the real-life location of the player enables us to show players interesting locations on the campus in close proximity and to verify visits using our POI mechanics (Section 3.2).

Location-based social media applications specifically targeted at students have proven the potential of location-based services in a university context. Examples include Yik Yak, once valued at $400 million (Statt, 2017), and Jodel[3] with 1.5 million active users and 5 million messages being posted each day (Kreuter, 2017). Campus Explorer evaluates similar social functionality implemented as blackboards (Section 3.2).

The core concept of Campus Explorer relies on three basic steps:

1. **Exploring the map:** The players explore the game map by moving in the real world.
2. **Visiting locations:** Tasks and challenges based on our POI system.
3. **Receiving rewards:** For visiting POIs, a player is rewarded with points and achievements.

3.1 Player Motivation

According to Aparicio et al. (2012), successful gamification requires the identification of intrinsic motivators or objectives interesting to people before the appropriate mechanics can be determined. We specifically selected our game mechanics to cater to the four player types as defined in Bartle's taxonomy (Bartle, 1996). Bartle identifies four groups of players, each responding to different motivators: Achievers, Explorers, Socializers, and Killers.

While the reward systems discussed in Section 3.3 offer mechanics designed for achievers and killers, our building and expedition check-ins offer exploration and our blackboards, event and player check-ins are meant to intrigue socializers.

To motivate players regardless of their player type, Csikszentmihalyi (1975) argues that players need to be challenged according to their skills. Thus, as a player's skills increase while playing the game, challenges need to increase as well. For this reason, we offer increasingly more complex variants of our POI system, which are unlocked during the course of our game. When users start the game for the first time, they are confronted with only two simple POI variants: Building check-ins to acquire points and blackboards to communicate with other players. The remaining mechanics unlock as the player progresses.

3.2 Points of Interest

The mechanics and features we evaluate with Campus Explorer are based on variations of a POI-based core-mechanic. This concept is similar to Pokémon Go[4], which has previously shown the potential to motivate students to walk to POIs in the real world (Barkley et al., 2017). As shown in Figure 2, our POI system allows us to place tasks, events, and locations to explore as well as other students on a map representing a player's actual surroundings. Each POI provides some functionality to confirm a visit to the location. For each visit, the player is rewarded according to Section 3.3 and the POI is added to the player's collection of completed activities.

Building Check-ins. As the simplest variation of our POI system, building check-ins allow players to check into university buildings by the press of a button displayed on the game map. The building check-in is a very simple task on purpose. We intend the feature to encourage players to open the application whenever they are on campus to receive some quickly earned points and to motivate them to explore and discover buildings. For this reason, we allow daily check-ins for each building. Thus, the feature should serve as a catalyst for players to try out the more complex POIs of our application.

Blackboards. Campus Explorer features virtual blackboards that allow players to anonymously communicate with each other in a location-based manner. Our virtual blackboards are inspired by the idea of actual physical blackboards which are usually bound to a certain location and are sometimes used by students

[3] https://www.jodel-app.com/
[4] https://www.pokemongo.com/

to leave their own anonymous messages and drawings. A visit is performed by posting a message on the board. Due to our blackboards allowing an unlimited amount of posts, we have decided against rewarding points for each visit and thus removed a major extrinsic motivator for this task. Instead, we allow the players to upvote and downvote messages and sort the messages based on their score. We intend postings well-liked by other players to be rewarded through a higher placement on the list of top messages as it has been done previously in applications such as Yik Yak and Jodel.

Expedition Check-ins. Since the building check-ins may provide little challenge for advanced players, we introduce expedition check-ins as a more complex exploration-based task. They require a player to find a specific location on the campus based on a description and optionally an image. Due to a potentially large number of different expeditions, they can be accepted at expedition hubs in a similar fashion to accepting a quest in a role-playing game. This allows players to select an expedition they deem interesting and to solve it when it is most convenient for them. Thus, an expedition comprises two types of POIs: A hub to accept the expedition and an expedition goal to confirm the check-in.

Event Check-ins. Similar to the approach chosen for the expedition check-ins, players can choose from different events accessible through an event hub and confirm a visit at the event destination. However, due to the nature of events, there is an added time constraint. The exact location of the event is communicated to the player through the description of the event and a navigation line displayed on the map optionally guides the player to the event location. To confirm the check-in, an additional code can be defined, which could be communicated by the event organizer during the event.

Player Check-ins. Player check-ins are POIs that are created from player data and allow for location-sharing among players. They are represented on the map by color-coded avatars. Once checked into, a player can schedule a meeting with the other player to receive additional points. To confirm that two players have indeed met, they each input a code that is displayed on the other player's phone.

Due to potential privacy concerns, player check-ins are a voluntary feature. A player check-in is placed at the player's current location only if they press a radar button displayed at the bottom of the screen. This POI will be available to other players for a predefined number of hours. In exchange for activating the radar, the player check-ins based on the other players' avatars are made visible and allow for check-in. Otherwise, no avatars are shown apart from the player's own avatar.

(a) (b) (c) (d)

Figure 2. (a) Check-in buttons placed on the map allow check-ins to buildings, (b) the description of an expedition check-in enables players to find locations at the university, (c) a navigation line guides the player to an event location, (d) location-sharing functionality allows finding other players on the map

3.3 Reward Systems

Schell (2014) states that the most important rule of any game is its goal or its sequence of goals. Goals should be concrete, achievable and rewarding. We try to meet these requirements by focusing on one basic game mechanic, our POI system, which allows progressively more challenging variations, and on well-established reward systems such as points, leaderboards, and achievements.

Points are the core of our reward system. Campus Explorer rewards points for checking into POIs and for unlocking achievements. The number of awarded points depends on the complexity of the task. For instance, checking into a building is rewarded with a minimal number of points, whereas expeditions reward the highest number. Based on the number of points collected, the player is ranked on a leaderboard. This allows players of the killer player type in Bartle's taxonomy to compete and impress their peers. For achievers, it sets the goal to reach high rankings.

In addition to receiving points for the goals set by the POI mechanic, an achievement system provides extrinsic motivation to complete specific meta-goals, which might intrigue the achiever and the explorer player types. We created achievements for reaching certain numbers of check-ins (such as an "explorer" achievement for checking into multiple buildings), for checking into players from multiple different university departments, and for acquiring certain amounts of points.

3.4 Tutorial

To teach players our game mechanics and clearly define goals for the player to reach, we provide a comprehensive tutorial mode and help buttons available in the header bar of most panels. The tutorial starts automatically when playing the game for the first time and continues automatically after unlocking each feature. For the duration of the tutorial, the player's avatar is placed on the campus close to the POIs relevant to the tutorial. Thus, it is playable from outside of the campus and does not depend on the player's current location.

4. IMPLEMENTATION

We developed Campus Explorer as a cross-platform mobile Unity application for Android and iOS. In the back-end, we employ a NoSQL database provided by AWS and utilize serverless lambda functions to operate on the data. Storing all player and POI data in the NoSQL database enables us to add new tasks and challenges without changing the application binaries, to analyze and visualize player behavior, to adjust the game rules to better balance the game, and to add new achievements when some players have progressed further than we have originally planned. As Campus Explorer is a location-based application, we use the services provided by Mapbox[5] to display map data in the Unity game client.

5. EVALUATION

We evaluated our first prototype implementation in the form of a playtest at the campuses of two local universities. We collected both quantitative data stored by our game and qualitative data based on a survey.

5.1 Test Setup

We released our game in the beta programs of the official distribution platforms of our supported operating systems Android and iOS. This allowed our selected participants to download the game to their own devices and to play it on their own terms and in multiple sessions throughout a given test period. Participants were given a basic description of the game, as it would be found in the application stores native to each supported OS. During the playtest, the participant's goal was to unlock as many features of the app as time permitted and to rank as high as possible on the leaderboard. The playtesting session lasted four weeks, and we continuously added participants.

To realistically evaluate our game, we created more than 200 POIs at the two campuses and at additional locations convenient for our participants. To create interesting expeditions, we scouted the campus areas our participants would be most likely to visit. We photographed attractions, art pieces, statues, and buildings as visual aids and as additional motivation for the participants to find the locations.

[5] https://www.mapbox.com/

As our evaluations happened on a small scale and within a short time frame, we did not yet have the opportunity to work together with the universities to include real-life events in our prototype. This is an important constraint to consider with respect to the results of our playtest. Instead, we created event check-ins located at canteens, allowing check-ins during lunchtime, and at train stations, allowing check-ins each morning and evening. Additionally, we created two events at the university sports center representing real sports lessons.

5.2 Playtest Results

During our playtest, 49 individual players started the Campus Explorer application at least once. We received 29 answers to our survey, which we sent to each participant four days before the end of the playtest. Of the 29 participants responding to our survey, 14% were female and 86% were male. 90% of the participants were students with a background in computer science or technology. 41% did not attend any lectures during the playtesting phase and were therefore rarely on campus. This is due to many of the participating students working on projects, such as their master's thesis. Due to a disproportionately large number of our participants being male and visiting only a few or no lectures, they represent only a subgroup of students we are targeting with Campus Explorer. Further testing with students of different demographics could gain valuable additional insights in the future.

5.2.1 Player Activities and Performance

Out of 49 players, 96% checked into buildings and accumulated a total of 784 building check-ins. In comparison, other POI variations were only used by between 22% and 31% and the number of accumulated check-ins is considerably lower. However, while only 31% of the players posted messages on the blackboard, 92% looked at the messages posted on the blackboards a total of 339 times.

Our numbers show that most testers played the first lecture of the tutorial introducing them to the building check-in. 96% of the players checked into the building that can be checked into during the tutorial phase. Many players decided not to continue playing shortly after the tutorial with half the players (49%) starting the game less than five times during the test phase. This might explain lower numbers for checking into other POI types than the ones initially unlocked (visualized in Figure 3) and for receiving at least one achievement (55% of the players unlocked achievements leading to a total of 116 achievements). This retention rate might be partially due to many testers not attending lectures during the playtesting phase and thus rarely visiting the campus.

(a) (b) (c)

Figure 3. Heatmaps visualizing (a) 784 building check-ins, (b) 91 expedition check-ins, (c) 46 event check-ins

5.2.2 Survey Results

The first part of our survey contained questions about games for students in general, before focusing specifically on our implementation. For each of these questions, the participants could select exactly one given option or suggest their own answer.

Asked about the genre that would fit a student-oriented mobile game the most, 38% of the playtesters would prefer a social or party game and 34% chose location-based exploration. In addition, more than half of the testers (55%) favored social features as the main focus such a game should have. Gaming features (17%), competition (14%) and exploration (7%) had priority for a minority of the testers. When asked specifically about whether the location-based mechanic works as the base for a game for students, only 10% of the participants would have preferred a different base mechanic. Thus, our location-based game with social features seems to be in line with our tester's preferences towards a game for students.

In the second part of the survey, we focused specifically on our prototype. First, we asked our playtesters what they thought of the mix of gaming, social and exploration features in Campus Explorer. A majority of 59% of the testers selected the option stating that the mix enriches the experience. 41% were of the opinion that there should be a clearer focus. None of the participants stated that Campus Explorer should be a game only or not a game at all. While a future prototype could focus more on a specific mechanic, overall, offering a mix of features satisfying different styles of playing seems to be a promising solution.

Despite the numerous features and variations of POIs, most participants found the game to be easy to understand with an average rating of 3.9 on a scale from 1 ("complicated") to 5 ("easy to understand").

For different types of features, we asked the playtesters whether they would like to see more of them, if the current implementation offers enough of those features or if there should be less of them. The results are shown in Figure 4 and suggest that while the amount of exploration and social features in our prototype is satisfying to a majority of testers, future iterations might profit from more gaming and collaborative features.

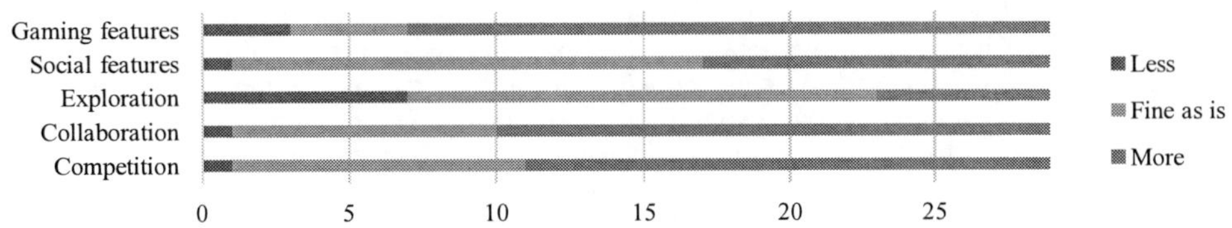

Figure 4. Feature categories rated by whether there should be more or less of them

For each of our five POI variations, we asked participants to rate them in their current state on a scale from 1 ("didn't like") to 5 ("loved") and to rate their future potential on the same scale from 1 ("should be removed") to 5 ("has a lot of potential"). For simplicity, we average the rating for each functionality in Figure 5. The ratings suggest that all of the aforementioned features were generally liked more than they were disliked, yet there was also no feature that was outstandingly well received by players. This is a result we expected for a first prototype as no previous balancing or polishing based on actual player feedback had been performed. We can detect a tendency for features with lower ratings based on their current state to be attributed with a higher potential and vice versa. Based on the results, player check-ins would benefit the most from further polishing. This feature could be extended to allow to manage friends lists, to facilitate communication and to enable collaboration between nearby players for future collaborative tasks.

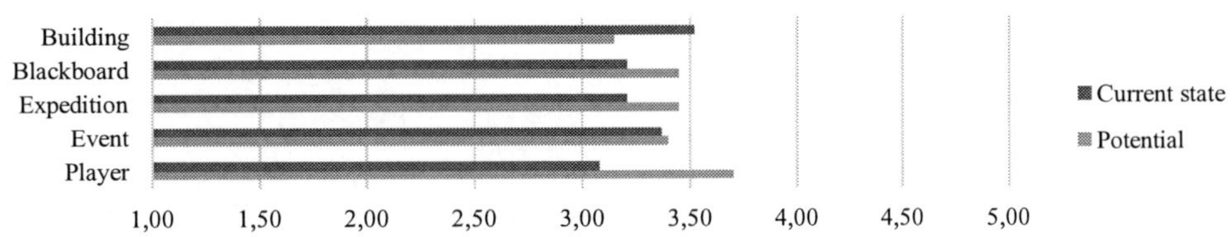

Figure 5. The average rating of the current state and potential of each POI variant on a scale from 1 to 5

We asked to rate a number of functionalities in our game based on how motivating they are. The average ratings on a scale from 1 ("demotivating") to 5 ("very motivating") are shown in Figure 6. Despite a majority of players answering in favor of social features in the first part of the survey, the social aspect of our prototype was not especially motivating for players. Points as an extrinsic motivator were rated highest with an average of 4.0. This indicates a potential for future work to redesign the social and exploration features to be more motivating on their own for the game to rely less on extrinsic motivators such as points, achievements, and leaderboards.

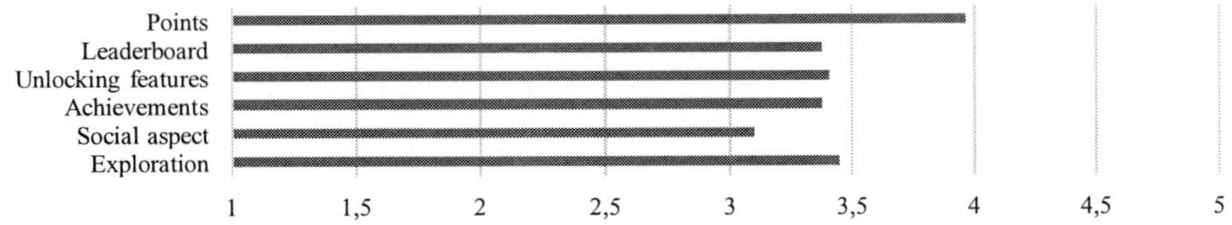

Figure 6. The average motivation rating of the features in Campus Explorer from 1 to 5

When asked if any feature led the playtesters to meet other players, only 7% answered positively. However, they all reported to having previously known the players they met. We hope to facilitate more player meetings in the future with real-life events represented in the game and with the addition of collaborative gameplay elements.

Creating a feeling of belonging is an important goal we tried to achieve with Campus Explorer. 52% of the playtesters believe that the game could spark such feelings if there were more players and 17% already felt closer to their university using our current prototype. 14% of the playtesters reported that the game provoked no such feelings. Those are very promising results as they suggest that the current prototype of Campus Explorer could already spark a feeling of belonging if it was widely deployed.

6. CONCLUSION

We designed and implemented a mobile location-based game, Campus Explorer, with the intention to gamify campus life, to facilitate community building, and for students to develop a feeling of belonging to their university. Five POI-based game mechanics, that is, building check-ins, blackboards, expedition check-ins, event check-ins, and player check-ins, contribute to a rich and promising gaming experience.

In a playtesting session of four weeks with 49 active players, we evaluated the game mechanics in terms of their suitability to provide motivation for students to explore and to discover, to communicate, and to participate in campus activities. Asked about games targeted at students, a vast majority of our playtesters are in favor of the location-based approach and appreciate a strong focus on social features. The mix of features made possible by our POI system was generally well received. The number of exploration features was satisfying to most players and building check-ins were performed at particularly high rates. Most players agreed that our approach has the potential to spark a feeling of belonging to the university if more students played the game.

For future work, players see potential in the location-sharing feature in the form of player check-ins and would appreciate more gaming and collaborative features. To facilitate community building, the player check-ins could be used to form groups of players that collaborate and compete with each other. Furthermore, our POI system could be varied to incorporate puzzles, quiz-questions, and collaborative mini-games to complete check-ins.

REFERENCES

Aparicio, A.F. et al., 2012. *Analysis and application of gamification*. In Proceedings of the 13th International Conference on Interacción Persona-Ordenador (p. 17). ACM.

Barkley, J.E., Lepp, A. and Glickman, E.L., 2017. *"Pokémon Go!" May promote walking, discourage sedentary behavior in college students*. Games for health journal, 6(3), pp.165-170.

Bartle, R., 1996. *Hearts, clubs, diamonds, spades: Players who suit MUDs*. Journal of MUD research, 1(1), pp.19.

Csikszentmihalyi, M., 1975. *Beyond boredom and anxiety*. Jossey-Bass.

Deterding, S., 2012. *Gamification: designing for motivation*. interactions, 19(4), pp.14-17.

Fitz-Walter, Z., Tjondronegoro, D. and Wyeth, P., 2012. *A gamified mobile application for engaging new students at university orientation*. In Proceedings of the 24th Australian Computer-Human Interaction Conference (pp. 138-141). ACM.

Fullerton, T., 2008. *Game design workshop: a playcentric approach to creating innovative games*. CRC press.

Gåsland, M., 2011. *Game mechanic based e-learning*. Science And Technology, Master Thesis (June 2011).

Krasner, G.E. and Pope, S.T., 1988. *A description of the model-view-controller user interface paradigm in the smalltalk-80 system*. Journal of object oriented programming, 1(3), pp.26-49.

Kreuter, S., 2017. *Die "Jodel"-App: Frust und Fun für alle*. Available at: http://www.faz.net/aktuell/stil/leib-seele/jodel-app-anonym-lokal-und-lustig-kommunizieren-15126386.html [Accessed 9 May 2018].

Schell, J., 2014. *The Art of Game Design: A book of lenses*. AK Peters/CRC Press.

Seaborn, K. and Fels, D.I., 2015. *Gamification in theory and action: A survey*. International Journal of human-computer studies, 74, pp.14-31.

Statt, N., 2017. *Yik Yak, once valued at $400 million, shuts down and sells off engineers for $1 million*. Available at: http://www.proquest.com/products-services/ProQuest-Research-Library.html [Accessed 9 May 2018].

DESIGN AND EVALUATION OF SMARTPHONE-BASED TRAINING FOR MINDFULNESS AND OPENNESS TO EXPERIENCE

Jacek Sliwinski, Mary Katsikitis and Christian Martyn Jones
University of the Sunshine Coast, Queensland, Australia

ABSTRACT

In this study a modified version of an app for training mindfulness and the mindfulness factor openness to experience, is presented. This study also extends the utility of an existing app, Positive Activity Jackpot. The Positive Activity Jackpot app uses gamified micro-tasks, by developing and integrating mindfulness-specific tasks. An evaluation of the app's subjective and objective efficacy is reported from the findings in the following two studies: firstly, an expert review and secondly, a between subjects experiment. The newly created/modified app was rated by experts as a suitable tool for inducing the state mindfulness in the first study and demonstrated a significant training effect for state mindfulness in the second study, but failed to reach significance for the openness to experience measure. In conclusion, micro-tasks using mindfulness apps may fit current busy schedules, as well as engaging users through playful audio-visual feedback. The validity of the openness to experience sub-scale in this study, as well as the lack of appropriate state mindfulness instruments for evaluating digital mindfulness apps, were identified as main limitations.

KEYWORDS

Gamification, Mobile App, mHealth, Mindfulness, Meditation, Openness to Experience

1. INTRODUCTION

After the invention of PCs and brain imaging, smartphones are believed to transform psychology research profoundly (Miller, 2012). The great spread of smartphones along with its technological capabilities makes it a promising tool and platform for researchers. At the same time, there is a growing interest and application of mindfulness within medicine and other areas (Black, 2014). Practising mindfulness as attention and emotion regulation training has been shown to improve psychological wellbeing, especially by alleviating stress, anxiety, depression and other mood disorders (Khoury, Sharma, Rush, & Fournier, 2015). Naturally, the interest in smartphone-based mindfulness interventions as a convenient method to deliver these benefits is growing as well.

A literature and software review of smartphone-based mindfulness interventions by Plaza, Demarzo, Herrera-Mercadal, and García-Campayo (2013) found 50 mindfulness-based mobile applications (apps) out of >1000 hits related to mindfulness and meditation on the Google Play store and concluded that there is "a complete lack of evidence to support the usefulness of those apps" (Plaza et al., 2013, p.13). Another review by Mani, Kavanagh, Hides, and Stoyanov (2015), that focused on iPhone apps, identified 23 mindfulness apps that were mostly guided-meditation apps only (thus limited in interactivity) and of poor quality. Interactivity is the key element to build experiential knowledge, which fosters the cultivation of mindfulness (Sliwinski, Katsikitis, & Jones, 2015). In terms of quality, the aspects of engagement and aesthetics and information were particularly low, which translates to a lower intention and motivation to use the apps and practise mindfulness. Although mindfulness re-search is growing rapidly, with the benefits of the practice being more and more confirmed (Sedlmeier et al., 2012), the current state of art for mobile-based mindfulness interventions is lacking innovation and research.

Before developing mindfulness technology and evaluating its efficacy, however, the issue that must be addressed is that there appears to be no consensus in the scientific community about the concept of mindfulness itself. There is a great number of questionnaires that claim to measure mindfulness, with great conceptual differences (Bergomi, Tschacher, & Kupper, 2013a). One of the most recent operationalisations of mindfulness is the Comprehensive Inventory of Mindfulness Experiences (CHIME) by Bergomi et al. (2014), which was developed to unify other available questionnaires and provide a comprehensive measure of mindfulness. Nine aspects of mindfulness were identified that are covered by previous operationalisations of mindfulness (2013b; 2014). Those aspects were factor analysed and reduced to eight factors, forming the final structure of mindfulness and resulting measurement instrument.

This current study aims to present an accessible and interactive method to train one mindfulness factor, that is openness to experience, which to date has not been addressed by scientific in the context of mindfulness training. The factor expresses a non-avoidant (confrontational) attitude towards experiences that are characterised by openness and curiosity (Bergomi et al., 2013b, 2014). People scoring high on this dimension try to perceive all the richness of stimuli in their environment and do not suppress their emotions or distract themselves but deliberately direct their attention to all of them (including pain and other negative experiences). As such, openness to experience is a crucial aspect of mindfulness for the process of emotional regulation, by bringing experiences into attention to be addressed by the self-regulatory processes of mindfulness meditation (Chambers, Gullone, & Allen, 2009).

The outcome of this study is to present a smartphone-based app for improving mindfulness and openness to experience, which can be used anywhere, by anyone. In the following, the design of the mobile app is described, including the proposed custom modifications. In two evaluation studies the suitability of this app is tested in the context of improving mindfulness. Finally, relevant implications are discussed, along with recommendations for future studies.

2. DESIGN

To improve the mindfulness factor openness to experience, the existing Android app Positive Activity Jackpot (National Center for Telehealth and Technology; T2, 2014) was chosen, which is available for free on the Google Play Store. It is designed like a slot machine, where players press a lever, which spins a wheel of fortune, representing various activities. During the spin, an intriguing sound is played, together with pulsing vibrations. The resulting activity can be chosen to be performed, or an-other spin can be made. After selecting an activity, the app provides the opportunity to invite friends and to schedule the activity in the phone's personal calendar.

In its original form, this app features 375 activities (e.g. "watch TV", "go to a muse-um", "buy clothes"), which are not suitable for this study, because they provide a distraction of inner experiences, particularly internal discomfort. For this reason, custom activities were developed (see Table 1) and integrated in this app. The activities were designed based on existing validated questionnaires and theory about openness to experience (Bergomi et al., 2014; Cardaciotto, Herbert, Forman, Moitra, & Farrow, 2008; McCrae, Costa, & Martin, 2005; Walach, Buchheld, Buttenmüller, Kleinknecht, & Schmidt, 2006). The beneficial key mechanic of this app is encouraging users to perform novel tasks in a playful (gamified) way. By using the custom developed activities, it is targeted at improving the mindfulness aspects openness to experience.

2.1 Activities

The openness to experience is a subject of investigation in personality psychology and is measured by established instruments. Although there are a few questionnaires that claim to measure a construct called openness to experience (e.g. Big Five, HEXACO), only one questionnaire was found that measures it as intended in this study within the context of mindfulness, namely the NEO-Personality Inventory-3 (NEO-PI-3; McCrae, Costa, & Martin, 2005), in particular its sub-scale openness to inner feelings and emotions. Available items from validated questionnaires are taken as theoretical basis to develop activities that increase openness to experience, as well as items from other mindfulness questionnaires, which were used to develop this CHIME factor (Bergomi et al., 2014), namely the Freiburg Mindfulness Inventory (FMI; Walach et al., 2006) and the Philadelphia Mindfulness Scale (PHLMS; Cardaciotto et al., 2008).

Based on these items, activities were developed to improve the mindfulness factor openness to experience (see Table 1). The central theme of all available items was identified as non-avoidance of feelings and sensations, especially negative ones, which was used as the theoretical design guideline for constructing the activities. To achieve an increased non-avoidance to inner experiences, activities were developed that focus attention on this particular aspect. To sustain engagement, a variety of activities targeting different parts of body and mind were chosen. For practical reasons, some the activities make use of physical resources (paper, pen, stop watch), however, digitalizing all activities is possible (e.g. by implementing a drawing and countdown function in the app).

Table 1. Openness to experience activities

#	Activity description
1	On a piece of paper, describe your current feeling(s) with as many adjectives as possible.
2	On a piece of paper, draw your current feeling(s).
3	Sit still for 1 minute and concentrate on what you feel (use the stop watch).
4	Choose a random part of your body. Focus on it for 1 minute and observe curiously what you feel (use the stop watch).
5	Touch the paper sheet. Explore it slowly and observe what you feel.
6	Touch the pen. Explore it slowly and observe what you feel.
7	Close your eyes for 1 minute and investigate what you currently feel (use the stop watch).
8	On a piece of paper, describe what you currently smell.
9	On a piece of paper, write down what you are currently aware of (e.g. sounds, smells, tactile sensations, etc.).
10	For 1 minute, focus on the feeling of air on your skin (use the stop watch).
11	Focus on something that is difficult in your life. Curiously observe the sensations in your body for 1 minute (use the stop watch).
12	On a piece of paper, draw a tree with your non-dominant hand. Observe how you feel.
13	Sing something! Curiously observe how you feel during and after.
14	Balance on one leg, while curiously observing how you feel.

3. EVALUATION

To evaluate this app and its activities, two studies were conducted. In stage 1, domain experts were consulted to evaluate the feasibility of this app for improving openness to experience. Stage 2 tested the app's efficacy experimentally.

3.1 Stage 1: Expert review

The first stage aims to validate the subjective efficacy of the modified version of the Positive Activity Jackpot for improving the mindfulness factor openness to experience. Following ethics approval (S/15/762), seven domain experts (3 males, 4 females) with a median age of 44 years (range 23-52 years) participated in this experiment. All experts had prior meditation experience (active meditators for at least three years; median 11 years), and prior game experience (including experience in academic game studies). Participation was voluntary and not incentivized. To gather feedback from the experts and their opinion on the fit of openness to experience to the proposed app, an offline survey was created, which was distributed via email. A demographic sheet asked for the experts' gender, age, and prior gaming and meditation experience. The evaluation sheet provided some basic information about the study's purpose along with instructions to score and answer each question honestly. A detailed definition of openness to experience was presented, followed by a description of the proposed app, with a link to the game on the app store. On a 7-point scale (anchor points: not feasible at all, neutral, very feasible), participants were asked "In your expert opinion, how feasible is it that this game can improve openness to experience?". After scoring the feasibility of the game for openness to experience, participants were asked to explain their judgement. The Positive Activity Jackpot app was scored for its fit with openness to experience with a mean of 5.6 (SD: 0.9, range 5-7), which supports its choice as a mindfulness game for training openness to experience. Two participants were excluded from analysis, as they did not give a definite score, stating to have no opinion.

3.2 Stage 2: Experimental evaluation

The aim of the second stage is to evaluate the modified version of the Positive Activity app for its efficacy based on empirical user testing.

3.2.1 Participants

For this stage, a total of 20 participants from a convenience sample were used, who were recruited via social networks, radio advertisement, posters, flyers and face-to-face promotion on the campus of the University of the Sunshine Coast, Queensland, Australia. Participants had no prior meditation experience and sufficient gaming experience to be familiar with touch controls. Interest in mindfulness was used as a selection criterion to minimise a priori differences in disposition, which is a methodological concern for one-shot studies (Sedlmeier et al., 2012). One participant was excluded from analysis due to prior meditation experience. The remaining participants were 12 males and 7 females with a median age of 26 (range 19-44). Participation was incentivized with a $20 voucher for a large retailer. The study was completed with ethics approval from the University of the Sunshine Coast (S/15/788).

3.2.2 Design

A between subjects factorial design was applied, where each participant interacted with the app. Mindfulness was measured before and after a 20 minute intervention and at follow-up. In a pre- and post-test and one-week follow-up, the State Mindfulness Scale (SMS; Tanay & Bernstein, 2013) measured the participant's state mindfulness and immediate effect of the app (instructing the participant to focus on the past 15 minutes). To measure the effect on the individual mindfulness aspect as hypothesized, CHIME (Bergomi et al., 2014) was administered in pre-test and one-week follow-up (instructing the participant to focus on the past two weeks).

3.2.3 Measurement

The SMS with its two factors, State Mindfulness of Mind and State Mindfulness of Body, both taking traditional Buddhist scholarship as a conceptual foundation. The 21 questionnaire items were generated based on the feedback from mindfulness researchers and instructors. Participants rate their agreement with each statement on 5-point Likert scale. Example items are "When my mood changes, I notice it right away" and "I see my mistakes and difficulties without judging myself". The CHIME scale measures eight individual mindfulness factors with 37 items to which participants answer on a 6-point Likert scale.

To investigate the reliability of the measurement instruments, we conducted reliability analyses on the current sample, which revealed a Cronbach's α=.94 for the SMS total and a Cronbach's α=.84 for the CHIME total. Both SMS sub-scales had also good to excellent reliability (Mind, α=.92; Body, α=.86). The CHIME sub-scale for openness to experience demonstrated a poor reliability of α=.49. A further analysis of the openness to experience sub-scale showed that deleting any individual item would not increase the reliability above .53. No gender effects were found for the openness to experience sub-scale. Game experience had no effect on scale reliability.

3.2.4 Procedure

Participants were greeted and presented with a research project information sheet explaining the purpose and procedure of the experiment, as well as a consent form before the start of the experiment. Then, a pre-test questionnaire was administered, which included CHIME, SMS, and a self-assessment about mindfulness and game experience, as well as demographics. For the time of the intervention the participant was left alone, with the instruction to keep on playing until the experimenter comes back. Participants were instructed to perform the chosen activity immediately or to pull the lever again to draw another activity if so desired. The play session was stopped by the experimenter (entering the room) after exactly 20 minutes, after which the SMS was applied as a post-test questionnaire. Seven days later, participants were contacted by email to complete the follow-up questionnaire, which included CHIME and SMS. After completion of the study, the incentive was sent out.

3.2.5 Analysis

Descriptive statistics were used to explore individual differences between participants. Reliability statistics were conducted for all scales and sub-scales used. Experimental data obtained from mindfulness questionnaires (pre-test, post-test, follow-up) were analysed by means of repeated measure ANOVA. Post-hoc tests were applied to highlight where differences occur. Two participants did not finish the follow-up questionnaire, which was treated as missing data. One participant did the follow-up one day later than instructed (after eight days instead of seven), one participant completed it five days later, and one participant was 12 days late. The follow-up time was coded as a variable and tested for interactions.

3.2.6 Results

Repeated measures ANOVAs were applied to test the effects of time on mindfulness. The modified Positive Activity Jackpot had a statistically significant effect on state mindfulness, as measured by the SMS total scores, ANOVA, $F(2, 32) = 16.8$, $p < .01$. This effect was pre-sent for both SMS sub-scales, Mind, $F(2, 32) = 17.9$, $p < .01$, and Body, $F(2, 32) = 13$, $p < .01$. No interaction effects for gender, age, follow-up time, and group, were revealed for any of the conducted tests. As shown in Figure 1, SMS scores increase significantly from pre- to post-test, $F(1, 18) = 34.8$, $p < .01$., and then drop again at follow-up, while still being higher compared to the pre-test, though not significant.

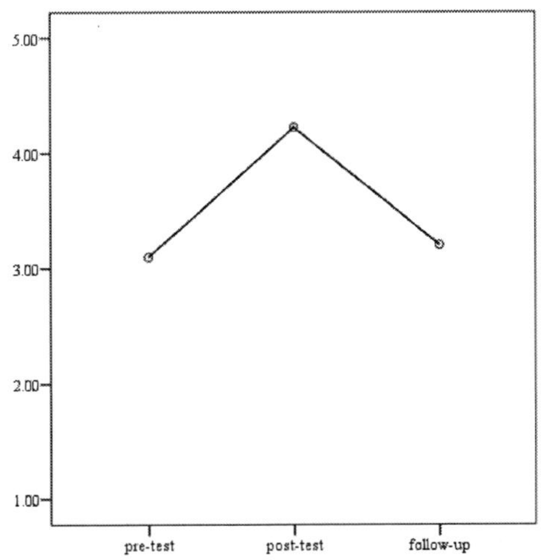

Figure 1. SMS total scores across all points in time for the modified version of the Positive Activity Jackpot app

No significant increase of trait mindfulness, as scored by the CHIME total and the CHIME openness to experience sub-scale, was observed between pre-test and the one-week follow-up. No interaction effects for gender, age, follow-up time, and group, were revealed for any of the conducted tests. Correlating the total scores of SMS and CHIME at both, pre-test and follow-up, revealed significant correlations in both cases (.585 and .487) at the .01 level and .05 level respectively. Correlations between individual factors of SMS and CHIME are shown in Table 2.

Table 2. Correlation matrix between CHIME and SMS total scores and individual factors at pre-test

	CHIME	Openness	SMS	Mind	Body
CHIME	-	-	-	-	-
Openness	.264	-	-	-	-
SMS	.585**	-.206	-	-	-
Mind	.653**	-.013	.927**	-	-
Body	.453	-.351	.943**	.75**	-

Note. ** $p \leq .01$.

At the end of the experiments, after the debriefing, participants shared their feedback about their experience unprompted. Besides the variety of tasks, participants liked the gong sound (programmed by the stop watch), which "was very helpful to let go". Two participants found the sound of pulling the lever (quickly alternating high pitched tones) annoying. From all activities, the tree-drawing task was liked the most, whereas the least liked (and most skipped) activities were standing on one leg, and singing, because they triggered embarrassment and because they were perceived as unsuitable for public environments.

4. DISCUSSION

The aim of this study was twofold: firstly, to modify an existing smartphone app so as to in-corporate a mindfulness factor within it, namely openness to experience; and secondly, to evaluate its efficacy in achieving a state of mindfulness for the participants engaged with the game. Stage 1 investigated the subjective suitability of a modified version of Positive Activity Jackpot app for improving the mindfulness factor openness to experience. Domain experts stated their agreement that this gamified app has the potential of training mindfulness in the context of openness to experience. Stage 2, tested empirically the efficacy of the app on a state and trait mindfulness scale, including the specific factor openness to experience. The app showed a significant effect on state mindfulness, as measured by the SMS, confirming its efficacy for training mindfulness. This was furthermore supported by positive comments about its subjective efficacy in form of participants' informal feedback at the end of the study. Some participants even resisted ceasing the game when the experimenter came in to conclude the play session. The Positive Activity Jackpot allows for quick play sessions on the go that can be easily integrated into the daily routines of its users. The use of short micro-tasks is especially suitable for the context of modern busy lives, which was identified as a core concern of mindfulness app users (Laurie & Blandford, 2016).

A study by Vacca and Hoadley (2016), describes the design and evaluation of a mindfulness app which also features micro-tasks, though with a focus on self-reflection and non-reactivity. Activities included several tracking exercises such as noticing one's mood, thoughts, as well as recent experiences of compassion and gratitude. After each activity, the user is redirected to a screen with the instruction to not react. The app's general design and functionality is similar to our modified version of the Positive Activity Jackpot, which makes the implications by Vacca and Hoadley (2016) applicable to our app. The author's found that a daily commitment by the user (prompted by the app) of a maximum of three activities in-creased engagement, which was further promoted by check-ins in the form of notifications (Vacca & Hoadley, 2016).

This app's custom activities for openness to experience were not effective in improving their target mindfulness factor. Besides the methodological challenges of measuring their efficacy (see Limitations), it is unclear if the chosen activities are feasible for training open-ness to experience. No other study to date focused on approaches to improve openness to experience, which might be attributed to its common definition of being a personality trait (McCrae, Costa, & Martin, 2005), which cannot be trained. The app's positive effects on state mind-fulness, however, confirm its positive influence on mindfulness. Yet, it is unclear how a non-digital application of these activities would compare against this digitalized approach.

In the case of the mindfulness app AEON, a non-digital control group, where participants had to imagine the same task revealed to be equally effective for improving the mindfulness skill of thought-distancing (Chittaro & Vianello, 2014), therefore it may be that drawing these activities on paper cards will yield similar benefits. While mindfulness meditation is some-times perceived as a daunting task (Lomas, Cartwright, Edginton, & Ridge, 2014), the advantage of this digital app is that it provides a more motivating method through its gamification elements, that might strengthen the daily mindfulness practice and achieve more stable benefits.

A valuable addition to the existing app mechanics would be presenting more information about mindfulness to educate the user, integrating more context-dependent tasks, providing progress feedback and rewards for spotting and enduring experiential states, as well as using digital timers and drawing tools to replace the physical aids that were used in this study. To keep users motivated and engaged (i.e. to use the app daily to maintain bene-fits), social features are recommended that make them part of a community. In addition to that, opportunities to collect in-game rewards by doing daily challenges can increase the long-term engagement with the game. As a general design implication for apps that aim to improve openness to experience, it is recommended to gamify activities that stimulate inner exploration. The use of gambling elements such as a wheel of fortune or a slot machine mechanic, intriguing sound effects and tactile stimuli (vibrations) enhance the motivation and engagement in use.

Finally, mindfulness is intended to be practised regularly and continuously. For this study, the app was used only once for 20 minutes, which already revealed significant effects on a state level. This supports the regular use of this app by users to improve mindfulness and associated health benefits. Although training effects for state mindfulness were demonstrated, as a stand-alone app it does not do justice to the whole concept of mindfulness, which includes at least seven other factors (Bergomi et al., 2014). It is not meant to be a substitute for meditation, but rather an additional support tool and a way of getting people into a routine for practising mindfulness.

For evaluating digital health apps and serious games, objective physiological measures (e.g. galvanic skin response, heart rate variability) are recommended, which can be correlated with the participant's subjective experience. Biometrics can continuously measure during use of the app and allow pinpointing of relevant events and their effects to further investigate effective mechanisms of action. This would be especially helpful to assess the distinct influence between the general app design such as its user interface and its content (in this case the activities). Within apps for mindfulness, new opportunities of the technology can be exploited to develop alternative methods of measurement that are less dependent on self-assessment (like questionnaires) and more reliable. For example, the user's behaviour within an app or digital game can be tracked and classified in mindful and mindless behaviour to assess the user's state.

5. LIMITATIONS

No significant effects were found for openness to experience, as measured by the CHIME. This may have resulted due to measurements for openness to experience being undertaken only at pre-test and follow-up. The impact of the app on openness to experience could not be measured directly after the intervention, because CHIME is a trait questionnaire, which ad-dresses the last 2 weeks (contrary to the SMS, which refers to the last 15 minutes). To minimise history effects, the break between intervention and measurement was shortened to one week only, however this may have been still too long to track any benefits. On the other hand, addressing the participant's experience of the last two weeks, while only one week passed, may have decreased the instruments sensitivity.

Furthermore, the poor reliability of the CHIME sub-scale for openness to experience undermines the correct measurement of the app's efficacy. It is unclear what accounts for the poor reliability, investigating CHIME and its relationship with individual factors revealed that its total score does not correlate significantly with openness to experience, which demonstrates a weakness of the scale in this study. Openness to experience correlates negatively with the SMS (total and all sub-scales) in this study, which underlines the methodological weakness of this CHIME factor.

Both questionnaires, SMS and CHIME were found to correlate significantly. This shows that CHIME results might have been in support of the app's efficacy if the instrument had been also administered at the post-test level. However, the variance between the correlations of SMS and CHIME scores from pre-test to follow-up highlights the conceptual differences between both instruments. The principle challenge is to measure individual mindfulness factors, as defined by CHIME, on a state level.

Future studies on mindfulness-based interventions need to find a way to assess all mindfulness factors directly after an intervention. For the context of apps, it would provide additional value to add measurement points in-between the intervention. Especially short questionnaires would be suitable as process measures, in this case one item on a visual-analog scale per CHIME factor would be feasible. However, any item should be consistent with the overall design of the app. Being an integral part of the app, this method would provide the least detrimental effect on engagement (not breaking the "magic circle") and may overcome some of the biases associated with self-report questionnaire (e.g. Hawthorne effect).

6. CONCLUSION

Mindfulness apps have become popular, however, they offer little or no interactivity. In this study, we tested a modified version of the Positive Activity Jackpot, which has potential for engaging users by incorporating gamification in the form of slot machine mechanics. Based on existing validated scales for openness to experience, we have created activities to be used by the app. Two studies validated the app for its subjective and objective efficacy, confirming its feasibility for the context of training mindfulness plus delivering a general positive experience. This study and the associated modified Positive Activity Jackpot app presents an original contribution to the landscape of mindfulness apps and mobile interventions. The value of such an app lies in the flexibility and cost-efficacy of self-administered mindfulness treatment to improve health and wellbeing. Moreover, the activities of the app can be conveniently adjusted to fit the training need.

REFERENCES

Bergomi, C., Tschacher, W., & Kupper, Z. (2013a). The assessment of mindfulness with self-report measures: existing scales and open issues. Mindfulness, 4(3), 191-202.

Bergomi, C., Tschacher, W., & Kupper, Z. (2013b). Measuring mindfulness: first steps towards the development of a comprehensive mindfulness scale. Mindfulness, 4(1), 18-32.

Bergomi, C., Tschacher, W., & Kupper, Z. (2014). Construction and first validation of the Comprehensive Inventory of Mindfulness Experiences. Diagnostica, 60(3), 111-125. doi:10.1026/0012-1924/a000109

Black, D. S. (2014). Mindfulness-based interventions: An antidote to suffering in the context of substance use, misuse, and addiction. Substance Use & Misuse, 49(5), 487-491.

Cardaciotto, L., Herbert, J. D., Forman, E. M., Moitra, E., & Farrow, V. (2008). The assessment of present-moment awareness and acceptance the Philadelphia mindfulness scale. Assessment, 15(2), 204-223.

Chambers, R., Gullone, E., & Allen, N. B. (2009). Mindful emotion regulation: An integrative review. Clinical Psychology Review, 29(6), 560-572.

Chittaro, L., & Vianello, A. (2014). Computer-supported mindfulness: Evaluation of a mobile thought distancing application on naive meditators. International Journal of Human-Computer Studies, 72(3), 337-348.

Khoury, B., Sharma, M., Rush, S. E., & Fournier, C. (2015). Mindfulness-based stress reduction for healthy individuals: A meta-analysis. Journal of Psychosomatic Research, 78(6), 519-528.

Laurie, J., & Blandford, A. (2016). Making time for mindfulness. International journal of medical informatics.

Lomas, T., Cartwright, T., Edginton, T., & Ridge, D. (2015). A Qualitative Analysis of Experiential Challenges Associated with Meditation Practice. Mindfulness, 6(5), 848-860.

Mani, M., Kavanagh, D. J., Hides, L., & Stoyanov, S. R. (2015). Review and Evaluation of Mindfulness-Based iPhone Apps. JMIR mHealth and uHealth, 3(3), e82.

McCrae, R. R., Costa, J., Paul T, & Martin, T. A. (2005). The NEO–PI–3: A more readable revised NEO personality inventory. Journal of personality assessment, 84(3), 261-270.

Miller, G. (2012). The smartphone psychology manifesto. Perspectives on Psychological Science, 7(3), 221-237.

Plaza, I., Demarzo, M. M. P., Herrera-Mercadal, P., & García-Campayo, J. (2013). Mindfulness-Based Mobile Applications: Literature Review and Analysis of Current Features. JMIR mhealth and uhealth, 1(2), e24.

Sedlmeier, P., Eberth, J., Schwarz, M., Zimmermann, D., Haarig, F., Jaeger, S., & Kunze, S. (2012). The psychological effects of meditation: A meta-analysis. Psychological Bulletin, 138(6), 1139-1171.

Sliwinski, J., Katsikitis, M., & Jones, C. M. (2015). Mindful Gaming: How Digital Games Can Improve Mindfulness. Human-Computer Interaction–INTERACT 2015 (pp. 167-184): Springer.

T2. (2014). Positive Activity Jackpot [Mobile app]. Retrieved from https://play.google.com/store/apps/details?id=t2.paj

Tanay, G., & Bernstein, A. (2013). State Mindfulness Scale (SMS): Development and Initial Validation. Psychological Assessment, 25(4), 1286-1299.

Vacca, R., & Hoadley, C. (2016). Understanding the Experience of Situated Mindfulness Through a Mobile App That Prompts Self-reflection and Directs Non-reactivity. International Conference on Universal Access in Human-Computer Interaction (pp. 394-405): Springer.

Walach, H., Buchheld, N., Buttenmüller, V., Kleinknecht, N., & Schmidt, S. (2006). Measuring mindfulness—the Freiburg Mindfulness Inventory (FMI). Personality and Individual Differences, 40(8), 1543-1555.

FORTUNE8: EMOTIVE FAMILY ENTERTAINMENT

Anthony Ku
Arizona State University, Tempe, Arizona, USA

ABSTRACT

The onset of aging heath is a transition in an individual's lifetime that can become as vexatious as it is inevitable. The human body gradually weakens as arthritis, blindness, heart disease and multitudes of other ailments begin to take root. Examining the present product market, nearly all products catered towards the elderly user demographic consist of tools designed to assist the various physical limitations that heighten with age. Products such as canes, hearing devices, and monitors have established a dominant presence in the user market to provide elders with the aid they require to effectively cope with their respective maladies. Despite this, a significant portion of the elder demographic struggles daily with debilitating cognitive disorders. Mental illnesses pose as much of a crippling impact on elders as do physical ailments, but the current market struggles to offer any solutions for these issues beyond psychological counseling and prescribed medicine. Looking beyond disorders such as Alzheimer's and dementia, research studies outline the shocking prevalence of underlying mental stigmas such as anxiety and loneliness in elders. Fortune8 is a conceptual entertainment console designed to help elucidate the needs of elderly users who suffer from cognitive stigmas and attend to their specific requirements by attempting to innovate an overshadowed market demographic. The project's background, research, and conceptualization are detailed in this paper as well as descriptions and features of the final product that were presented to a panel of judges at Arizona State University.

KEYWORDS

Elder, Mental Stigmas, Cognitive Needs, Loneliness, Anxiety, Underlying Needs, User-Oriented Design, Social Interaction, Families, Ubiquitous Entertainment, Immersive Engagement, Cultural Play, Poker

1. INTRODUCTION

To address the research question of alleviating mental stigmas in elders, understanding the different types of environments elders find themselves in was key to understanding the obscure nuances of these ailments. One salient consequence of old age is the gradual loss in independence where a weakening physical state renders an elder to their home for most of the day. As conditions worsen, the elder's decreasing quality of life becomes exacerbated as they become incapable of completing tasks on their own. As a result, many elders are forced into one of two options; relocate to a care facility or live dependently with a loved one, in most cases of the latter an adult child of the elder. In both scenarios, elders struggle with accepting their loss of independency or become deeply invested in those surrounding them and start to develop intense feelings of attachment. Two of the most common mental stigmas, loneliness and anxiety, were chosen as focal points over the course of this project as the ubiquitous nature of these disorders existed as a paradox to the lack of designed solutions aimed towards relieving them.

2. BACKGROUND

2.1 Inspiration

Inspiration for this study was derived from the researcher's personal experiences with his grandmother Ya-Chao who immigrated from Taiwan to live with her son's family after her husband passed away in 1998. Attempting to adjust from her life in Taiwan to living in America proved to be an excruciating transition. Due to a poor grasp of the English language and no friends to interact with besides her surrounding family, Ya-Chao felt extremely isolated. Because her son was her only child, Ya-Chao developed a fervent bond to him and his family that resulted in amplified negative sentiments when she was left alone. Encumbered by feelings of anxiety and loneliness, her constant attempts to reach out often went unheard due to the family's busy and stressful schedules. Ya-Chao's story and passing inspired memories of her personal struggles and questioned what solutions could be devised to help other elders in similar predicaments.

2.2 Conceptual Framework

The conceptual framework conceived as the foundation of the study references the three components of successful aging as proposed by Rowe and Kahn: avoiding disease and disability, active engagement with life, and high cognitive and physical (Kahn, & Rowe, 1997). In understanding the model of successful aging in relation to the practical needs of the elderly demographic, a Venn diagram composed of three topics displays the proposed feedback relationship between mental stigmas affecting the elderly, living dependently with family, and intuitive recreational activities. These three topics were chosen as recurring themes among elders that connected to one another through an abundance of interactions. These three topics are further substantiated by Rowe and Kahn as through twin studies and randomized, controlled prospective trials, there is growing evidence that risk factors for diseases in older populations can be associated with external factors – environmental and behavioral factors should be further emphasized in the treatment of diseases such as the three topics chosen. Each topic was studied in the context of the user demographic to brainstorm potential needs. By studying the relationships between these chosen topics, research questions were formed to help gain insight towards solutions. These questions provided the researcher with a solid foundation to build upon as the investigative process progressed towards the interview phase.

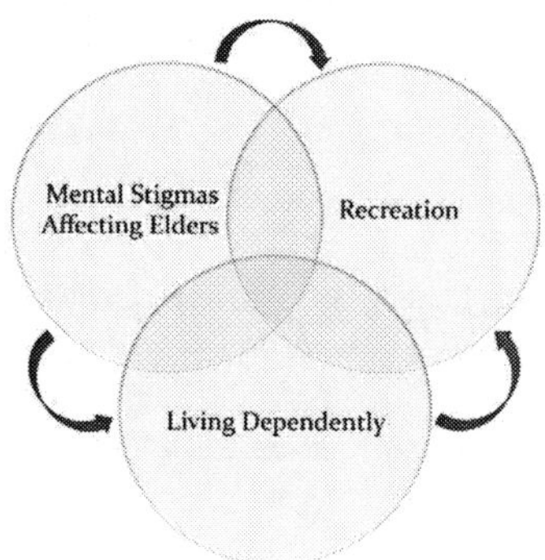

Figure 1. The Fortune8 conceptual framework

3. RESEARCH

3.1 Preliminary Online Research

The initial step of the research process encompassed general data collection using the internet as a gathering source. A multitude of websites relayed information regarding the commonality of mental illness in elders, as well as profound definitions of cognitive neglect and abuse. According to the National Council on Aging, nearly 43% of elders suffer from varying degrees of loneliness, and seniors over the age of 60 are 45% are more likely to experience fatal risks. The NCOA also states that in nearly 60% of elder abuse or neglect incidents, the individual resides with their family. A phenomenon found to be particularly impactful was the notion that loneliness is contagious. This stigma delineates how individuals who feel isolated and as a result develop negative emotions tend to pollute the environment with their hampered mood, eventually leading to surrounding residents feeling negatively as well. In addition, research shows that there is an inverse relationship between mental health stigma and treatment, with mental health stigma being primary concern for older adults who choose to not seek mental health services (Conner, et al., 2011). The stigma obstacle is further exacerbated when looking at marginalized, aging populations due to their exposure to racism, discrimination, prejudice, poverty, and violence – aspects of life that highlight experiences faced by minorities and the underprivileged.

In a different study looking at the aging population in Japan, the research shows how participants who described themselves as healthy and poor felt cognitively younger than those that considered themselves as unhealthy but wealthy (Chéron, & Kohlbacher, 2011). The results of this study ultimately showed how feeling good was correlated to a greater difference between actual and cognitive age, supporting the idea of the importance of external factors on one's health. The individual who were sampled also converged in their personal values; they assigned a greater score to values such as "warm relationship with others," "fun and enjoyment in life," and "self-respect" over "excitement," and "sense of belonging." The researchers of this study also point out how while the study only focuses on one culture and its people, the results should be cross-culturally applicable.

3.2 Poker Cards

As aforementioned, the topics of mental stigmas, recreation, and dependent living situations were studied in relation to each other in the context of the elderly user. After analyzing the relationships corresponding between these themes, poker cards were chosen as the focal point for developing a product that would answer the research question of how to alleviate cognitive stigmas in elders living with family. Poker was chosen as playing cards are a ubiquitous outlet of entertainment worldwide. A plethora of different game types exist across a multitude of cultures and poker itself is seen as symbol of fun competition. Studies strongly demonstrated that elders who participated in card games have proven to stave off diseases such as dementia by sharpening their mental acuity through regular mental activity. Herbert asserts that skills such as "psychological acuity and the ability to leverage uncertainty" are "separated from the game itself" (Whybrow,, 2005). Traditionally, poker games also exist as a popular pastime for family members of all ages to share, compete, and bond with one another.

The current competitive market for poker products encompasses a narrow range of products. Beyond the traditional physical deck of cards and other products such as game sets which include cards, chips, and other accessories, all other poker-related products on the market currently exist of video-game-like applications in some form or another. Games on consoles such as the Sony™ PlayStation™, apps on smart phones and tablets, as well as versions of poker adapted for trending virtual reality systems are commonplace. Although there is a great abundance in digital poker applications, these types of adaptations seldom achieve much success among elderly consumers. For elderly consumers, the consensus corroborated feelings of confusion, frustration, and disinterest towards modern poker software. Elders communicated that digital poker gaming was vastly less desirable to playing a traditional game of bridge or blackjack with their loved ones using authentic playing cards they know and cherish.

It is important to note that the gaming industry can appeal to older consumers by capitalizing on the desire to remain cognitively young; nevertheless, companies must recognize the diverse needs of the elderly (Chéron, & Kohlbacher, 2011). Companies such as Nintendo™ have illustrated how brain training and sports games assist in improving cognitive age while still prioritizing entertainment and fun. Older consumers identify a motley of values that can be applied to all age groups. In creating digital or virtual gaming system for elderly consumers, all aspects of their lives must be considered to provide an addictive but productive experience.

3.3 User Interviews

The methodology of the user needs research was comprised of two types of data collection, survey respondence and in-person/over the phone interviews. Survey distribution was conducted at Archstone Care Center located in Chandler, Arizona. 20 interview queries were synthesized into a survey which was distributed by caretakers and staff to 22 elders residing at the facility. Many of the residents at Archstone had previously lived dependently with family before eventually transferring to the facility. The method of survey distribution was implemented because many of the elders felt unsafe with speaking with a stranger. The questions asked were developed over the course of the research process and stimulated respondents to respond to what activities were most valuable to them, what types of living situation they were in before receiving hospice, and how they interacted with family during visitation times.

Personal interviews were conducted via phone calls and in-person meetings. As aforementioned, due to the safety concerns of many elders, only a handful of personal interviews took place. These methods of investigation were chosen for individuals who were familiar with the researcher and were at ease with a more personal interaction. Respondents consisted of elders living with family and individuals living with an elder, including Yao-Chao and her son who participated in the research process before her passing. During the in-person interviews, participants responded positively to playing cards as a form of recreational activity among activities such as gardening and reading. To record the elder's habits and preferences as well as attain a better understanding of the nuances of various game modes, elders interviewed personally were invited to play poker with the researcher to simulate a more intimate and enjoyable interview process. Elders relished the opportunity to teach their favorite games through play and distinctly eased into a more unreserved attitude during questioning. These interviews were invaluable towards moving onto the conceptualization phase as the elders who chose to participate in the teaching games elicited the sincerest replies and disclosed specific instances where they felt disassociated from their family.

4. USER NEEDS

4.1 Physical Activity

The predominance of respondents in both surveys and interviews conveyed the necessity of regular physical activity to remain content. Although their weakened physicality makes it difficult for them to participate in physical exercises done in the past, elders relayed that keeping active, at least to some extent, was crucial to feeling uplifted. In the surveys distributed, caretakers and elders alike described motion video games such as those found on the Nintendo™ Wii™ as light-hearted activities that were effective in keeping the degree of physical strain low while creating an easily comprehendible and enjoyable simulation. Researchers Jung, Li, Janissa, Gladys, and Lee of Nanyang Technological University deduced in a study of elders who played the Wii™ regularly that "apart from having a sense of well-being, the other two most desirable conditions in order for the elderly to enjoy life is good physical health and social contacts" (Jung, et al., 2009). Although the Wii was a common source of recreation for many of the elders interviewed, some individuals confessed that they still felt lonely playing by themselves. Elders who lived with family reported that although they usually went on walks with family members, they would sometimes feel confined in their residence and that watching television or resting in bed for most of the day tended to exacerbate unpleasant emotions of unfulfillment.

4.2 Generational Gap

Elders interviewed divulged that they were ecstatic to spend time with grandchildren and other young family members but were hindered by an apparent generational gap that has grown to become a significant rift between today's children and their grandparents. As previously mentioned, the modern product market for poker-related products consists absolutely of digital gaming devices. These types of products are tools that today's children commonly use as toys. Khoo and Cheok concluded that most children deeply enjoy playing games on computers and other devices through the childhood and as such, are less inclined to feel excited about "elderly-styled" activities such as chess and fishing (Khoo et al., 2007). Although data collected strongly supported that elders were not averse to technology, personal interviews corroborated that they found more value in simpler products. Smart phones, tablets, and gaming consoles are always within the grasp of the recent generation but provide no real connection or value to their grandparents. "Moreover, most of current computer and video games do not involve physical body movements and social interactions which are proven to be essential for the enjoyment of life" (Khoo et al., 2007). Many elders relayed that when attempting to spend time with grandchildren, many times the child would ask to play video games which the elder did not understand. In other situations, elders would reach out to children only to feel rejected as they were preoccupied with new age devices. Several surveys studied during the data collection conveyed a discrete trepidation of playing or gambling online as ill-intentioned outsiders often took advantage of elders to scam them for money and private information. These phobias only reinforced aversity which many elders felt towards video games and online gaming that consequently create rifts between generations.

4.3 Feeling Like A Burden

After analyzing the surveys collected from Archstone Care Center, the data presented supported that many elders who lived with family before felt the same emotions that Ya-Chao felt. Respondents disclosed that they longed for loved ones to come and visit them at the facility but often felt that they might be a burden to them. Akin to Ya-Chao's predicament, many elders had sons or daughters with their own families living nearby but were embattled by demanding careers and hectic schedules consisting of taking their children to school or extracurricular activities. Caretakers at the facility relayed that phone calls were made available for elders but were kept limited as to prevent potentially anxious elders from disturbing their family.

Elders living with family imparted similar messages but were much more positive in their attitudes. Speaking with both family members and elders living in the same home, the general message was that the principal rule to follow was to always make time during the day to communicate and interact. During a personal interview with a family, a daughter and her elderly mother described their habit of settling down in the evening to talk about each other's day and engage each other in recreational activities such as games of bridge or crossword puzzles. The elder admitted that although she would feel anxious when lonesome, she understood her daughter's obligations and upheld a promise to never hold grudges. She communicated that for some elders in her situation, anxiety and loneliness tends to take control and they begin to harbor grudges over time that only leads to disputes, anger, and unresolved feelings of disassociation. Elders who regularly communicated with their families with a calm, positive mentality achieved more effective success towards soothing their negative emotions and sustaining benevolent relationships.

4.4 Key Emotive Interactions

During the data collection process, each elderly respondent circulated a recurring answer that homed in on a central need that was paramount to elders; key emotional interactions with their loved ones. The need to communicate and interact with loved ones was essential, however the way the elder connected with them was equally as crucial. Several respondents relayed that it was not the amount of time spent with family that was most impactful on them, but rather the frequency of emotional feedback they received from them. Elders cherished moments where laughter, competition, or even debate occurred between them and members of their family and conveyed these types of interactions moved them the most and helped them feel more of a part of their family. An interview with an elder residing at Archstone Center confided the joy she felt when her daughter and grandchildren came to visit and shared stories of their recent activities. Additionally, elders surveyed at the facility corroborated that experiencing key emotional expressions and interactions during family visitations eased their minds and allowed them to feel content and secure and less anxious. These types of emotional communication were placed as the ceiling of the user needs hierarchy as the project moved onto the conceptualization phase as the implications of this need as a necessity were unanimous.

5. DESIGN PROCESS

5.1 Conceptualization

Conceptualization began by conducting preliminary sketching exercises that allowed the researcher to sift through numerous design directions in short amounts of time. Per the project directive, emerging and future technologies were kept in mind to explore options that would diversify and innovate the product market. After analyzing the total mass of sketches with mentors and peers, the theme of emulating the archetypical variety game set which holds traditional game pieces such as cards, chips and dice was pointed out and discussed. This theme was met was with positive feedback as the concept of a modular unit with classic inspiration was nostalgic, functional, and aesthetically intriguing. One of the design directions the researcher saw abundant potential in was creating a console unit that would merge familiar physical playing pieces such as cards and chips with a digital gaming experience. RFID technology has become increasingly popular amongst current products such as the Skylanders™ line of children's toys which allow the user to play as various characters by placing their respective action figure onto a playing surface that recognizes unique electronic signatures embedded in the figure's base. The idea of physically playing a game of poker on a device while translating the gameplay into a technological interface shed light onto potential solutions where advances in technology could be utilized to broaden and enhance communication between individuals while retaining the physical experience of playing cards.

Examining current trending and developing technologies, the age-old method of connecting to a screen such as a television was concluded to be unimaginative. Many elders had relayed in the research process that they felt a large portion of their time was spent in front of the television and yearned for more captivating and interactive outlets. To combat this concern, immersive technologies such as virtual reality, augmented reality, and even emerging developments in hologram projection were analyzed in context to their potential effects on bringing the elder closer to their family. Among these channels, virtual reality has become a widely well-received form of entertainment for elders who have shown to become instantly immersed in a new environment and felt at ease at their enrapturement. Augmented and virtual reality methods have also shown great potential within the past two decades as rehabilitation and assistive tools for elders suffering from cognitive diseases. Cherniack relayed in his study that when elderly patients suffering from mental illnesses such as dementia, stroke and Parkinson's disease are exposed to various virtual reality applications showed "enhanced ability to perform daily activities" (Cherniack, 2010).

Such improvements can also be seen in treating phobias through VR exposure therapy. In a case study looking at a survivor of 9/11 with PTSD, exposure therapy through VR showed promise over traditional imaginal exposure therapy (Difede, & Hoffman, 2002). Through 1-hour virtual reality sessions of planes flying over the World Trade Center, jets crashing, and people jumping to their deaths, the treatment was extremely successful in reducing acute PTSD by 90% of symptoms according to the Clinician Administered PTSD Scale. While case studies are not representative of the population or even other PTSD patients, VR showed potential to treat PTSD patients, with both positive results and patient feedback.

In another study of 33 patients suffering acrophobia, VR served as not only an equally beneficial form of exposure therapy, but also a potentially safer treatment option (Emmelkamp, 2002). The study looked at the effectiveness of specifically low-budget VR compared to in vivo exposure therapy. Patients responded similarly regarding the benefits of both treatments in terms of the Acrophobia Questionnaire, Attitude Towards Height Questionnaire, and the Behavioral Avoidance Test. Conducted in 2002, virtual reality, despite being a nascent treatment, already illustrated the equality in in-vivo and VR exposure therapy - at the very least, virtual reality could be an alternative as it could provide a completely controlled setting devoid of extraneous variables that could offset patients and lead to unwarranted behavior.

As the use of virtual reality gains more prominence in psychological therapy due to its effectiveness, researchers are beginning to study the reasons as to why it is successful on the human psyche. According to one study, virtual reality's success can be attributed to its target of "presence" as defined by social richness, realism, immersion, social actor within medium, and medium as social actor. There is undeniably inaccuracy in measuring presence through questionnaires; however, the results suggest that the inherent design of VR allows users to go beyond the interface of traditional games and in many ways their own mind (Krijn, et al., 2001). The idea of VR is to integrate real-time computer graphics, body tracking devices, visual displays, and other sensory inputs to immerse individuals in a virtual environment.

The immersion of virtual reality (and thus augmented reality) with a physical poker set resonated most positively to user feedback as it signified the product would allow elders to play in their home environment while adding immersive and exciting features through AR features.

5.2 Prototyping

After concept sketches were reviewed, a phase of prototyping was conducted to attain a realistic perspective of size, ergonomics, and aesthetic value. To retain the value of playing poker cards, each prototype featured a flattened surface. Using a deck of cards, the researcher simulated playing games on foam study models to analyze the most efficient dimensions for the console. A 12" by 12" surface was concluded to be enough room to comfortably play cards without creating a bulky size and silhouette. To break away from monotonous rectilinear forms, circular shapes were explored and met with receptive feedback as they emulated the curved contours of poker tables found in casinos. Although a flat surface would be mandatory to provide a surface to play cards on, the prototypes showed that developing a one-piece product with a leveled surface would limit visual and functional values as many early models strongly resembles common objects such as electronic tablets. To combat this, the idea of a two-piece gaming console was suggested that would keep the necessary flatness, but also fabricate a product that would have different functions, appearances, and levels of interaction.

5.3 Branding

The primary focus of the brand strategy for Fortune8 was to create an experience as opposed to a single product. The primary objective of the product was to bring elders closer to their families and alleviate stigmas such as loneliness, but it was also crucial to create a poker gaming experience that was exciting, familiar, and immersive. Takamura states: "Regardless of the messages companies try and send to consumers, the identity of the brand is ultimately controlled by the interpretation of the consumer base" (Takamura, & Ragland, 2009). The moniker of Fortune8 was conceptualized by alluding to the mantra of good fortune the number eight is seen as a symbol of luck and prosperity across various Asian cultures and is especially revered by Chinese audiences who traditionally display strong devotion towards taking in parents and other aging relatives when they can longer take care of themselves.

It was critical that the materials chosen for the product aligned with elders' preferences. During the research phase, elders communicated that when buying products, they mainly considered four aspects; materials, texture, functionality, and quality. Sustainable hardwood and metal were chosen to be the two principal materials to construct the console with. Lastly, the material used for the playing surface was finalized to be green felt, a combination whose texture and appearance has cemented itself as a hallmark among poker venues.

6. FINAL CONCEPT FEATURES

6.1 Concept Overview

Fortune8 is an augmented reality-integrated game console that fuses the traditional game of poker with modern technologies. The console is constructed of two sections, a lid that functions as the main gaming interface and a charging base that houses the internal components within a felt mold. The console's form was refined to keep ergonomics optimal for elder users in mind. Smooth beveled curves allow the console to be comfortably and easily gripped and moved. To incorporate additional auditory aspects of gameplay, the hollowed base functions as a speaker. Familiar sounds of coins jingling, cards being flipped, and ambient casino noises help to further immerse the user with a nostalgic ambiance. Widget noises such as cheering after a win establish a lively experience that also guides the user via auditory cues. 3D-printed Polymagnet tracks located on both the bottom of the lid and lip of the base interact effortlessly to fluidly rotate and lift off from each other when the lid is rotated away from the locked magnetic position to create a user experience that accommodates elders suffering from limitations such as arthritis. To set up for gameplay, the lid is removed, flipped over, and placed onto the base where the spherical curvatures align.

Figure 2. The Fortune8 console in its resting position

Figure 3. Changing the console to active orientation via reconfiguring the lid. Inner contents nestled in base

6.2 RFID-Integrated Components

To retain the physical experience of playing poker, radio-frequency encrypted playing cards and chips connectively identify with the responding electronic playing felt surface to transmit gameplay information into the AR interface. These familiar pieces emulate the feel of playing high-stakes poker on the familiar felt surface of a casino table. Physical details in the slicked coating of the cards, textured plastic chip cores and ridged outer lining of the chips pique the user's curiosity to persistently pick up, feel, and play with the objects. The elder playing on the console against a loved one playing with a mobile device deals out cards and chips for both players. The AR interface divides the surface into a section for each player to guide the elder when dealing cards and awarding rewards. As cards are laid down, the mobile player can see the cards appear on their screen. These cards feature a unique electronic signature on both the face and backside to signify to the mobile player when cards are facedown and flipped up. This interaction allows the elder's opponent to see the positions of the deck, active cards, and discard pile in a real time digital interface. Chips are dealt out to both sides of the playing surface as each player's rewards and resources. Traditional one, five, twenty, fifty, and hundred-dollar values are denoted by the indicative corresponding colors and textures of the respective chips that also feature unique frequencies. During gameplay, the mobile player proceeds to select various actions such as "hit me" or "pass" which signal the elder to perform a corresponding action.

When both players are satisfied with their results a "ready" command is selected to signify to the elder to reveal all cards on the table and the elder can then proceed to move the anted chips to the winner's side of the table.

Figure 4. The RFID encrypted playing cards, poker chips, and electronic felt playing surface

6.3 Mobile App

By downloading the Fortune8 app on their mobile device, loved ones seeking to interact with the elder are enabled to play against them at their own convenience. This service helps to prevent the elder from feeling like a burden to their family as loved ones can freely invite the elder to play wirelessly without the elder having to feel anxious about reaching out or disturbing their family. Adult family members can open the Fortune8 app and enjoy spending time playing games with their elder during idles times such as a break at work. Younger generations such as the elder's grandchildren can become more excited about playing games on their smartphone or tablet and are enabled to bond with their elder through a channel they are more accustomed to. Being able to interact with their grandparents using a mobile device creates a more inviting and convenient opportunity for younger generations while enabling elders to more frequent interactions with younger family members.

The mobile app relays information regarding the elder's game activity and indicates when they were last active. The app can monitor elements of the elder's gameplay that include the types of games they have been playing, which game modes are most popular to them, and generate an overview of their weekly activity to report days where they feel liveliest and others where their mood is gloomy. By checking up on the elder through real-time updates, family members can feel at ease knowing how active the elder has been and utilize that information to anticipate times where negative mental stigmas may be overbearing. Crucially, the Fortune8 app enforces private security to strictly allow only family and loved ones access to the elder's information. This eliminates the common phobia of playing online with strangers and potentially being taken advantage of as incidents of intentional abuse have become conventional behavior for online deviants. Protecting elders from malicious experiences and guaranteeing a safe online gaming experience helps to dissolve any fears or anxieties they may have of prior mischances.

Figure 5. The Fortune8 app checks on the elder's activity and allows loved ones to invite the elder to play

6.4 Emotive Augmented Reality Interactivity

Understanding the need for emotive interaction as the principal need of elders living dependently, augmented reality presented itself as a solution for palliating the effects of loneliness and anxiety by connecting elders with their loved ones in an immersive experience. By using a real-time AR interface that is easy to use, the elder is enabled to feel closer to their family as if playing right across the table from them through a channel where the key emotive interactions elders value as most meaningful are plentiful.

When playing together, players can create video-game styled avatars which they can customize and unlock rewards for to promote a fun sense of competition. Using facial recognition software present in modern smartphones, the mobile player's facial expressions and bodily movements are translated onto a lifelike hologram of their avatar which is viewable through the AR eyewear. These characters embody a wide range of charismatic personas such as the high-stakes gambling cowboy and the sultry secret agent. Potential collaborations with famed franchises such as Star Wars™, Disney™, and Nintendo™ allow both children and elders to play as their favorite iconic characters. The AR intercommunication incorporates the famous "poker face" interaction which fun facet of competitive strategy that is usually left out in other poker video games. In the context of the traditional game of blackjack, players can attempt to detract one another from predicting the strength of their cards by reacting expressively when receiving a low "hit" hand or reserving their emotions to play it cool after being dealt a game-winning "21". Interacting with these animated avatars and capturing key expressions creates a non-verbal channel of communication that reinforces consistent interactions through creative, visual play.

Figure 6. Using the AR eyewear, the elder can view the opposing player's expressions and movements captured through smartphone facial recognition software

7. EVALUATION

Post-conceptualization, evaluation review sessions were conducted with the user demographic. A presentation showcasing the research findings, design process, and images of the final concept features was shown to both elders who participated in the initial research process as well as new participants. A full-scale model of the Fortune8 console was constructed and brought to each meeting to help participant(s) gain a better understanding of the concept's nuances. Participants were fond of the console's circular form and appreciated the visual language of the product and its components. Using the model's parts, participants explored various physical functions of the concept such as reorienting the lid, removing the inner components from the base, and gripping the handles. Using the nestled deck of cards, the experience of playing on the felt surface was demonstrated. After playing several games, elders relayed that the provided space created a safe atmosphere that allowed for a more intimate experience between themselves and their opponent. Elders remarked that the space provided felt appropriate for two-player games and for games involving additional players, that a much wider space would be required. A common sentiment concurred that the console created a personal feel that diminished the surrounding environment and captured a gameplay experience that focused solely on the two parties involved.

Because a fully-functioning prototype was unavailable, some participants struggled with understanding how the RFID and AR technology operated. Many were under the impression that these devices would require a complex and difficult user process. To help elucidate the user experience of these mechanisms, the researcher brought similar appliances in existing RFID-integrated games and contemporary smart glasses to exhibit the functionality of these channels. To simulate the augmented reality experience, Oculus Rift™ headwear was used in relation with telecommunication applications that allowed elders to see and communicate with another individual in virtual reality. RFID video games and mobile apps were presented to demonstrate the interconnectivity between physical objects and an electronic interface which delighted many of the participants. For several of the elders, the experience of playing a video game by manipulating familiar objects instead of the traditional game controller or keyboard was a welcome surprise. Overall, users had trouble visualizing several aspects of the concept's technological functionality but were able to attain a better understanding of these processes after being exposed to similar existing products that they found intriguing and enjoyable.

8. CONCLUSION

Design for elders tends to cater towards assisting the alleviating physical and biological needs that naturally intensify with age. Designers often fall into a paradigm of emphasizing the consequences of ailing physical health and omitting lesser-known cognitive needs which torment a significant portion of the elder population. The goal of the Fortune8 project was to attentively investigate the stories and experiences of elders who find themselves feeling helpless and dejected after transitioning to dependent living. The subject of gaming presented itself as a prospective genesis to originate from as the pastime of playing games has always helped to bond loved ones together. These outlets have helped generations of families to connect with each other through learning, listening and laughing. Studying potential solutions on how to mitigate the negative stigmas of elders living with family, the goal of the Fortune8 project was to create a solicitous and emotive experience by creating a new age gaming experience that adheres to the specific underlying needs of the elder user demographic.

REFERENCES

Chéron, Emmanuel & Kohlbacher, Florian (2011). Understanding "silver" consumers through cognitive age, health condition, financial status, and personal values: Empirical evidence from the world's most mature market Japan. Journal of Consumer Behavior

Conner, Kyaien O. et al. (2011). Mental Health Treatment Seeking Among Older Adults with Depression: The Impact of Stigma and Race. 531 – 543

Difede, J & Hoffman, H. G. (2002). Virtual Reality Exposure Therapy for World Trade Center Post-traumatic Stress Disorder: A Case Report, 529 - 534.

E. Paul Cherniack (2010) Not just fun and games: applications of virtual reality in the identification and rehabilitation of cognitive disorders of the elderly,Disability and Rehabilitation: Assistive Technology, 6:4, 283-289, DOI: 10.3109/17483107.2010.542570

Emmelkamp, P.M.G. (2002). Virtual reality treatment versus exposure in vivo: a comparative evaluation in acrophobia.

Jung, Y., Koay, J. L., Ng., J. S., Wong, G. L. C., & Lee, K. M. (2009). Games for a better life : effects of playing wii games on the well-being of seniors in a long-term care facility. Proceedings of the 6th Australasian Conference on Interactive Entertainment 2009 (IE 2009), Australia.

Kahn, Robert L. & Rowe, John W. (1997). Successful Aging. Proceedings from The Gerontological Society of America. 433 -440.

Khoo E.T., Merritt T., Cheok A., Lian M., Yeo K. (2007) Age Invaders: User Studies of Intergenerational Computer Entertainment. In: Ma L., Rauterberg M., Nakatsu R. (eds) Entertainment Computing – ICEC 2007. ICEC 2007. Lecture Notes in Computer Science, vol 4740. Springer, Berlin, Heidelberg

Krijn, Merel, Schuemie, Martijn J, Van der Mast, Charles, & Van der Straaten, Peter (2001). Research on Presence in Virtual Reality: A Survey, 183 – 185.

Takamura, J. & Ragland, T. (2009). The Simplicity Mantra: A Paradigm Shift in Consumer Response to Branding. [CD-ROM]. Proceedings from the International Association of Societies of Design Research (IASDR09), Seoul Korea, October 2009

Whybrow, Peter D. (2005.) *American Mania: When More Isn't Enough*. New York, NY: Norton, p. 57.

LOCAL TERNARY DESCRIPTOR FOR 3D MODEL MATCHING AND RETRIEVAL

Wen-Hung Liao, Chong-Ming Wang and Yi-Chieh Wu
Dept. of Computer Science, National Chengchi University, Taipei, Taiwan

ABSTRACT

Qmodel Creator is a software for designing block (LEGO) style 3D models using intuitive drawing methods. The produced models are composed of cubes, which are conveniently encoded using voxel-based representation. To support content-based search and retrieval for models generated with Qmodel Creator, we proposed a feature descriptor defined as 3D local ternary descriptor (3DLTD) in this paper. To begin with, we partition the bounding box of each model into cubes and then divide cubes into voxels. Weights are assigned to each voxel according to its distance to the boundary. We randomly select 64 pairs of voxels in each cube and generate a ternary code based on the relationship between each pair of voxels. Weighted bipartite matching is employed to compute the similarity between two models. Experimental results indicate that 3DLTD is suitable for comparing and searching voxel-based 3D models. Compared with 3DBRIEF, our proposed framework is more robust and efficient thanks to the two-level partition. Ternary encoding also promotes feature representativeness and noise immunity while maintaining overall efficacy.

KEYWORDS

Qmodel Creator, Block-Style Model, Local Ternary Descriptor, 3D Model Retrieval

1. INTRODUCTION

Qmodel Creator is a software developed for K-12 students to create 3D models intuitively without prior knowledge of 3D geometry (Hu *et al.* 2015). As shown in Figure 1, students can construct 3D Lego-style models easily by simple sketching. When students finish their modeling, they can upload their work by the in-App function to a database on the 3D Model Co-Learning Space (3DMCLS) established by (Lin *et al.* 2017). The user interface of the website is depicted in Figure 2.

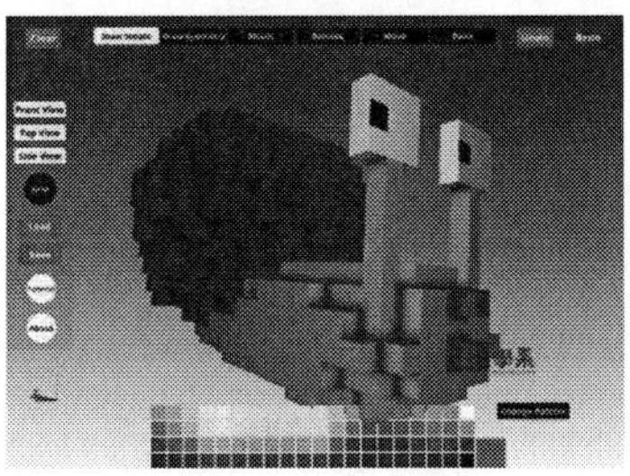

Figure 1. User interface of Qmodel Creator

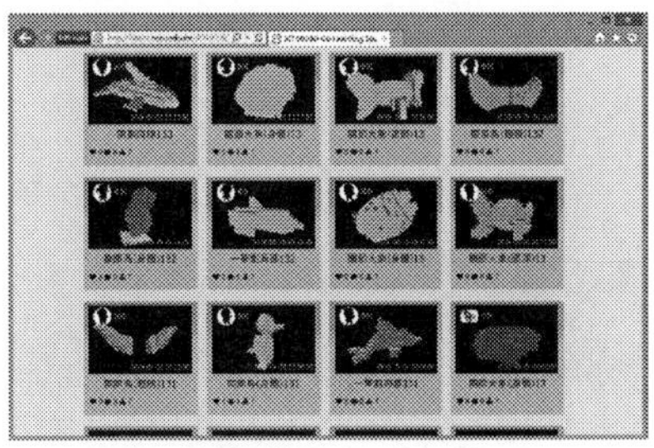

Figure 2. Uploaded models made by Qmodel Creator on 3DMCLS

It is important to provide effective content-based search functions for Qmodel Creator so that peer students can inspect and evaluate them in an organized manner. However, we face the following issues when attempting to construct such a system using existing approaches:

● Search using deep neural networks: K-12 students sometimes do not follow instructions to create models of a certain type, indicating that it is difficult to obtain high quality labeled data. Besides, there exist no cubic style model dataset currently, and the amount of models on our system are insufficient for training deep neural networks.

● Search based on 2D view: The main concept of this kind of methods is to take several snapshots of a model from different perspectives, and then extract 2D descriptor from each snapshot (Chen *et al.* 2003). These descriptors are thus combined to form the features of the 3D model. Since Qmodels are cubic style, too many similar structures will render such methods unsuitable to discern Qmodels effectively.

● Search based on local 3D features: (Matsuda *et al.* 2015) extended the concept of 2D local binary descriptors to 3D and proposed methods such as 3DLBP, 3DBRIEF, and 3DORB for 3D model retrieval. Not all these descriptors satisfied rotational invariance. Moreover, accuracy is sometimes compromised in exchange for computational efficiency.

In this paper, we propose a feature defined as 3D local ternary descriptor (3DLTD) to accomplish model retrieval task with the following desirable properties:

1. Achieving both robustness and efficiency by extending the extended local ternary pattern (ELTP) descriptor for image matching we have developed in (Liao, 2010).
2. Satisfying rotation invariance by introducing weighted bipartite matching.
3. Incorporating weight adjustment based on voxel location to gain higher accuracy for model search.

The rest of this paper is organized as follows. In Section 2 we elucidate the proposed retrieval and matching methodology, as well as experimental design. Section 3 presents and analyzes the experimental results. Section 4 concludes this paper with a short summary.

2. THE PROPOSED METHODOLOGY

In this section, we elucidate the workflow (refer to Figure 3) of retrieving models created by K-12 students using QModel Creator on the 3DMCLS. The proposed framework is divided into two phases, namely, 3DLTD feature extraction and matching strategy. We design several experiments to evaluate the search performance with respect to different parameter settings.

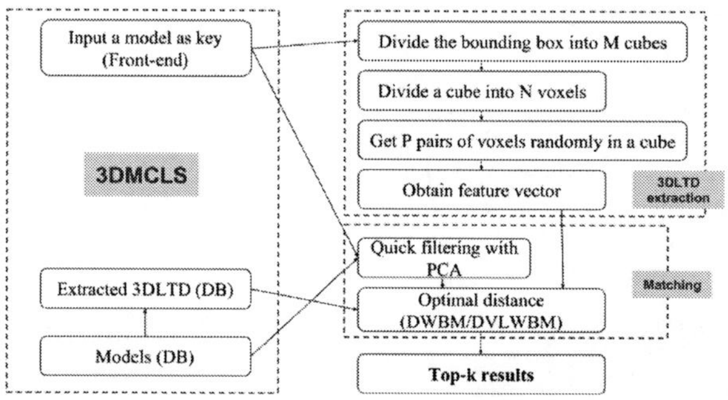

Figure 3. Model Retrieval on 3DMCLS

2.1 Feature Extraction

The proposed feature for Qmodel Creator is built upon the 2D local binary descriptor (LBD) used for image analysis (Liao, 2010). A main difference between 3D Qmodel and 2D image is that the former lacks intensity information. As the encoding in LBD is achieved by comparing average intensity values in an image patch, to extend this concept for 3D models, we must find a way to characterize local structures in a 3D neighborhood.

2.1.1 From 2D to 3D Representation

Firstly, we obtain the bounding box of a model. We then divide it into M cubes. Figure 4-(a) gives an example for $M=27$ cubes. Here a 'cube' is equivalent to a 'patch' in 2D feature extraction. In the next step, we partition a cube into N voxels. The total number of vertices in a voxel is employed to represent the voxel value. Figure 4-(b) shows an example for setting N to 27. Using this setting, each model will contain a total of 729 voxels. Since Qmodels are block-based, the above partition strategy is well-suited for describing local structures.

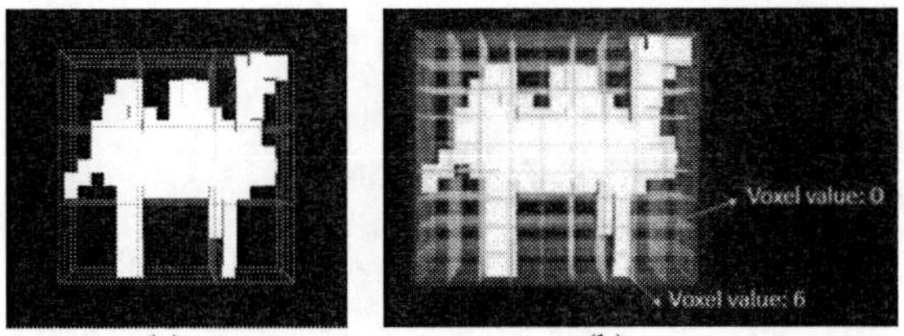

Figure 4. Representing 3D Information. (a) Cube (b) Voxel

2.1.2 3D Local Ternary Descriptor (3DLTD)

We propose 3D local ternary descriptor as a fundamental feature to represent cubic models defined as follows:

$$3DLTD(i,j) = \begin{cases} 2, & \text{if } v(i) - v(j) > \theta \\ 1, & \text{if } |\, v(i) - v(j) \,| \le \theta \\ 0, & \text{if } v(i) - v(j) < -\theta \end{cases} \tag{1}$$

where *v(i)* and *v(j)* are a voxel pair in a cube, and $\theta = log_{10}$ *(Total number of vertices in a model)*.

We choose *P* voxel pairs at random in each cube and then extract feature according to Eq. (1). The same sampling scheme will be employed for all models. Figure 5 illustrates the procedure for feature extraction.

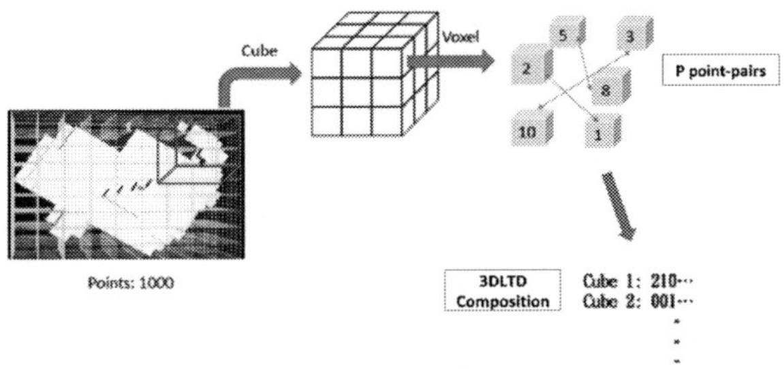

Figure 5. An Example of 3DLTD Extraction

For each model, we will obtain a feature of $P \times N$ dimensions. When *P=64* and *N=27*, the proposed 3DLTD will have 1728 dimensions. Obviously, some dimensional reduction techniques need to be applied to alleviate storage and computational requirements.

2.2 Matching Approach

Model matching calls for translation, scale and rotation invariance. The former two can be addressed with pre-processing. In this section, we consider the rotation invariance issue for Qmodel comparison. For a given query model, we first filter irrelevant based on the orientation of two major axes using PCA. We then set cubes of a model as nodes in a graph, and find the optimal correspondence using weighted bipartite matching. The weight for a voxel (or node) is assigned according to its location in the model.

2.2.1 Quick Filtering

Due to the large number of models on 3DMCLS, we start with quick filtering to speed up the search process. This stage will exclude the most dissimilar models from the candidate list, and therefore reduce the amount of models to be analyzed subsequently. To this end, we apply PCA to obtain the two largest eigenvalues, which are the projection values on two major axes. We compute the difference between two Qmodels according to Eq. (2).

$$Diff(i,j) = |\lambda_{i1} - \lambda_{j1}| + |\lambda_{i2} - \lambda_{j2}| \tag{2}$$

where λ_1 refers to the projection value on the first major axis, and λ_2 refers to the second. We set a threshold of 0.3. That is, when the difference is greater than the threshold, the model will be excluded.

2.2.2 Distance Weighted Bipartite Matching

Previously, we have partitioned the model into N cubes. For each cube, a 3DLTD vector will be generated. Therefore, we can cast the model retrieval task into a $N \times N$ weighted bipartite matching problem. Suppose a cube is a node of one set in the bipartite graph, and nodes a and b belong to model A and B respectively, we can calculate weight of edge $\overline{ab}$ using Eq. (3).

$$W_{a,b} = D_H(\, 3DLTD(a), 3DLTD(b)\,) \tag{3}$$

In Eq. (3), the distance between two 3DLTD vectors is calculated using Hamming distance, denoted as D_H. The distance between two models can be obtained by solving the weighted bipartite matching problem with minimum overall sum. Figure 6 depicts a simple example illustrating how we obtain the minimum distance of two models.

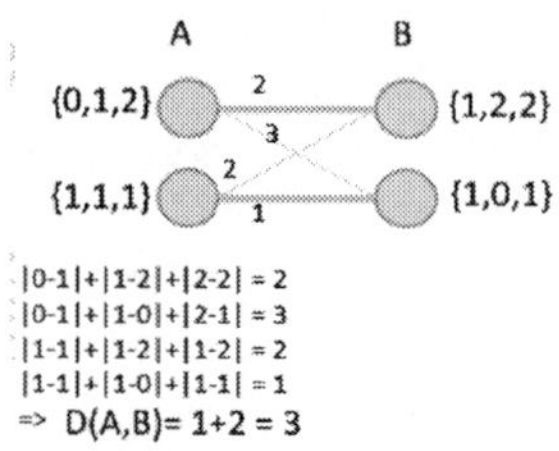

Figure 6. An Example Illustrating the Process of Distance Weighted Bipartite Matching

2.2.3 Distance and Voxel Location Weighted Bipartite Matching

Since Qmodels are cubic style, we expect that the inner part of a model is filled with voxels and thus contains few distinct structures. On the contrary, the distribution of voxel value near the boundary can better capture the model appearance. Therefore, 3DLTD can better represent a model by assigning weights according to the location of a voxel. Eq. (4) presents the rules for weight assignment, which are related to the position of the voxel. Figure 7 shows the detailed settings of voxel weight.

$$VW(voxel) = \begin{cases} 1, & \text{if } voxel \text{ is located at the bounding box} \\ 1/2, & \text{others} \\ 1/3, & \text{if } voxel \text{ lies in the center of the model} \end{cases} \tag{4}$$

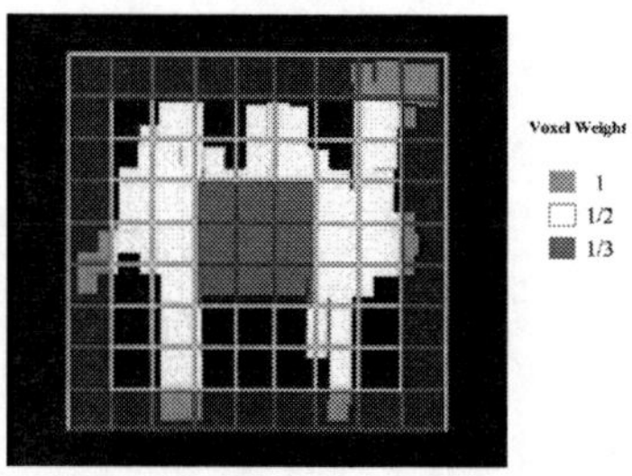

Figure 7. Illustration of Voxel Weight Assignment

During the feature extraction stage, we can get a weight value associated with each voxel according to its position. Therefore, a voxel weight vector can be obtained along with a 3DLTD extracted in each cube. Figure 8 demonstrates the matching procedure after introducing voxel weights. In the bipartite graph matching problem, we compute composite voxel weight vector VW_{ij} of every two cubes belonging to two models respectively by Eq. (5) to fine-tune 3DLTD. The weights in the bipartite graph are calculated by Eq. (6) instead.

$$VW_{ij} = \frac{2}{\frac{1}{VW_i} + \frac{1}{VW_j}}$$

(5)

$$W_{a,b} = D_H\left(\frac{3DLTD(a)}{VW_{ab}}, \frac{3DLTD(b)}{VW_{ab}}\right)$$

(6)

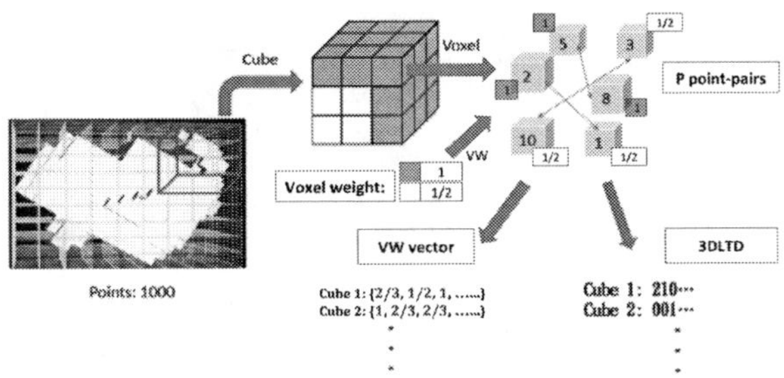

Figure 8. The Modification after Introducing Voxel Weight

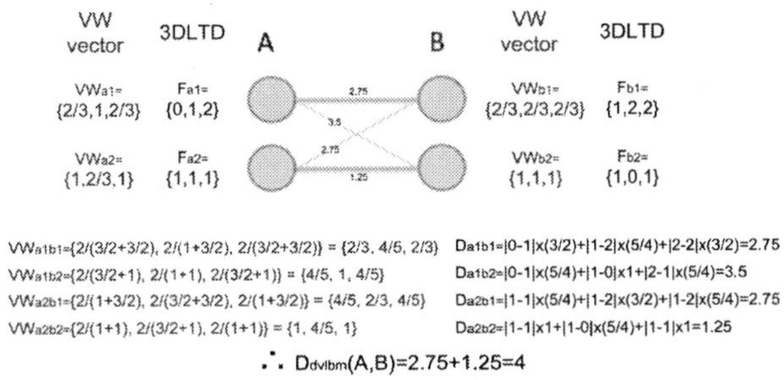

Figure 9. An Example of Distance and Voxel Location Weighted Bipartite Matching

Suppose we have two models A and B to be compared. Let a and b be two cubes from A and B respectively, and VW_{ab} be the result of Eq. (5). Figure 9 extends the example in Figure 6 to illustrate the changes in the distance and location weighted bipartite graph matching process after incorporating VW.

2.3 Dataset

We collected 616 models made with Qmodel Creator on 3DMCLS. We generated more samples by adding or subtracting 5%, 10%, 20% and 30% of voxels to all models at random. For each K% modification, we produce five models. Consequently, there are a total of 12936 models in our experimental dataset.

2.4 Similarity Measure

As discussed previously, the distance between two models can be obtained by solving minimum sum bipartite matching problem. The calculated distance can then be converted into to a similarity measure using Eq. (7),

$$Similarity(A,B) = e^{-\left(\frac{D(A,B)}{\sigma^2}\right)} \quad (7)$$

where $D(A, B)$ is the distance between model A and B, and σ is the standard deviation of the distribution obtained by the mutual distance between any two models in the dataset, as summarized in Table 1.

Table 1. The Statistics for Σ in Similarity Measure

Matching Approach	Number of Point-pair	σ
Hamming Distance	16	7
	32	14
	64	27
DWBM	64	21
DVLWBM	64	41

2.5 Experiments

We design five experiments to investigate the performance of the proposed method with different parameter settings.

2.5.1 Effect of the Number of Voxel Pairs

Since each cube contains 27 voxels, there are $C_2^{27} = 351$ possible combination of voxel pairs in a cube. If too many pairs are taken into consideration, computational requirements will increase. If too few pairs are chosen, there will be only a small amount of significant features present. In this study, we experimented with 16, 32, and 64 voxel pairs. We then choose a parameter that generates stable results for subsequent experiments.

2.5.2 Stability with Random Sampling of Voxel Pair

Once the number of voxel pairs is fixed, we wonder if we can obtain consistent performance when a set of voxel pairs is selected randomly. Three sets of P point pairs (P is chosen based on previous result) have been created randomly to examine their performance accordingly.

2.5.3 Performance of Distance Weighted Bipartite Matching

Based on the result of the first experiment, one set of P-voxel pair is determined randomly and then fixed for further use. Each cube produces a 3DLTD string, and one string represents a node. As a result, we are dealing with a 27×27 minimum distance weighted bipartite matching problem. In next section, we will compare this result with those calculated by Hamming distance directly.

2.5.4 Performance of Distance and Voxel Location Weighted Bipartite Matching

In this experiment, we introduce voxel location weighted scheme and revisit our minimum weighted bipartite matching problem.

2.5.5 3DBRIEF vs. 3DLTD

We will compare our result with the performance of 3DBRIEF (Matsuda *et al.* 2015), which is also a 3-D descriptor extended from 2-D. To obtain 3DBRIEF, we take each voxel as a center, set its neighboring $5 \times 5 \times 5$ voxels as a patch, and then select 64 voxel pairs in the area to generate the 64-bit binary descriptor.

3. RESULTS AND DISCUSSION

This section reports the experimental results and discussed whether the proposed framework can be applied to effective search of models made by Qmodel Creator. For each experiment, we adopt two cases for evaluation:

1. Original model with its augmenting models: The index of the original model is one. The indices of other augmenting models are listed in Table 2. We calculate the similarity between each one of the original 616 models and its augmenting models.

Table 2. Augmenting Models and Corresponding Indices

K% modification	*5%*	*10%*	*20%*	*30%*
Model index	2~6	7~11	12~16	17~21
Color label	Cyan	Green	Yellow	Orange

2. Average similarity: We use each one of the original 616 models on 3DMCLS as the input, apply quick filtering, and calculate the similarity with the remaining models by referencing to Table 1. All results are sorted and then averaged.

3.1 Effect of the Number of Voxel Pairs

Figure 10 shows the result of choosing different number of voxel pairs for the two cases. From the graph 10-(a), we can observe that all sets can reflect the different degree of augmenting models correctly. In Figure 10-(b), the results for 16 and 32 point pairs are relatively flat in Top 80-100, suggesting that the similarity of ranking from #80 to #100 of many input models are almost the same. Meanwhile, the result for using 64 voxel pair shows a steady decline in the ranking, indicating that its describility is more stable. Therefore, we adopt 64 pairs for all subsequent experiments.

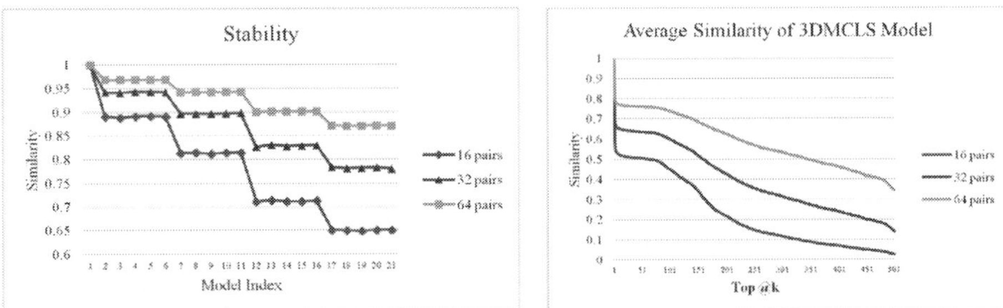

(a) (b)

Figure 10. Result #1: Test with Different Number of Voxel Pairs. (a) Single Model (b) Average Similarity on 3DMCLS

3.2 Stability with Random Sampling of Voxel Pairs

We generate three sets of 64 voxel pairs at random. Results for the two test cases are depicted in Figure 11, which indicates that the matching performance is consistent not only in the single model case, but also in the average similarity test. That is, we can arbitrarily create a sampling set of 64 voxel pairs for extracting 3DLTD on the query and database models, as long as both contain the same sampling voxel pairs.

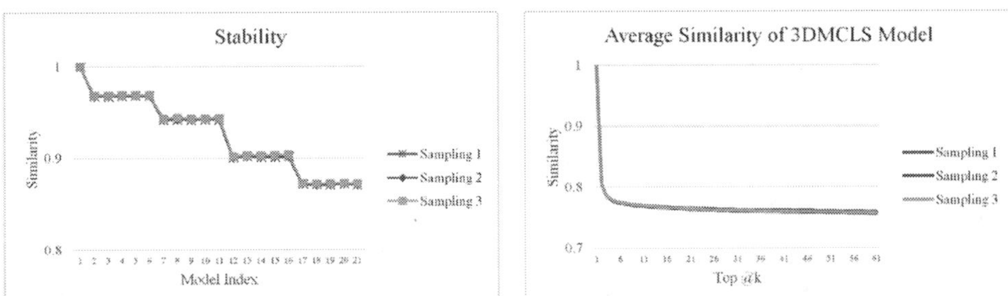

(a) (b)

Figure 11. Result #2: Three Different Sampling Sets of 64 Voxel Pairs. (a) Single Model (b) Average Similarity on 3DMCLS

3.3 Performance of Distance Weighted Bipartite Matching

Figure 12 compares the performance of distance weighted bipartite matching and Hamming distance for the two test cases. Although there is no significant difference between the two approaches in single model test, the result of distance weighted bipartite matching is slightly better than that of Hamming distance on Average similarity test. However, we still need to verify whether model similarity can be related to its appearance in actual applications. For that purpose, we choose two models shown in Figure 13 and obtain the Top10 matches. The result is summarized in Table 3.

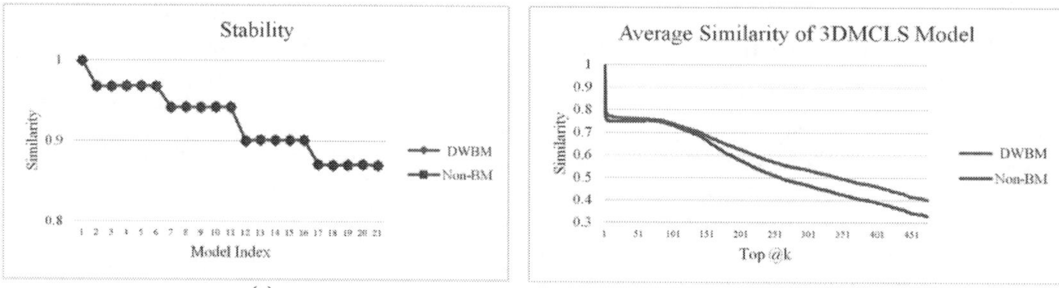

(a) (b)

Figure 12. Result #3: Comparison of DWBM and Hamming Distance. (a) Single Model (b) Average Similarity on 3DMCLS

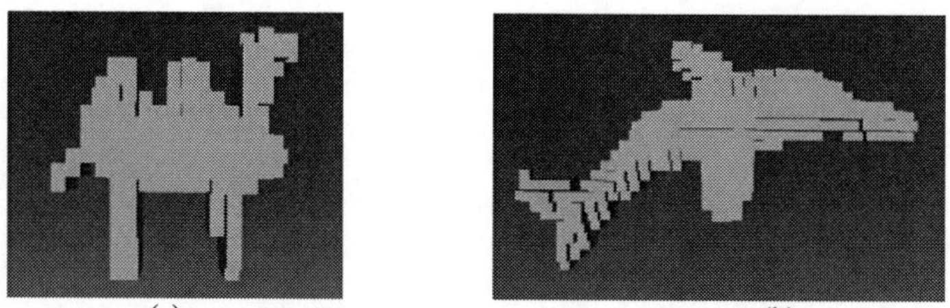

(a) (b)

Figure 13. Two Sample Models for Qualitative test. (a) Model #1 (b) Model #131

Table 3. Comparison of DWBM and Hamming Distance on Top 10 Matches of Two Queries

	DWBM		***Non-BM***	
Rank	#1	#131	#1	#131
#1	1	1	1	1
#2	0.926	0.917	0.963	0.741
#3	0.898	0.896	0.926	0.704
#4	0.889	0.864	0.926	0.704
#5	0.889	0.864	0.889	0.667
#6	0.883	0.858	0.889	0.630
#7	0.877	0.827	0.852	0.593
#8	0.870	0.809	0.852	0.370
#9	0.870	0.769	0.815	0.296
#10	0.864	0.736	0.815	0.259

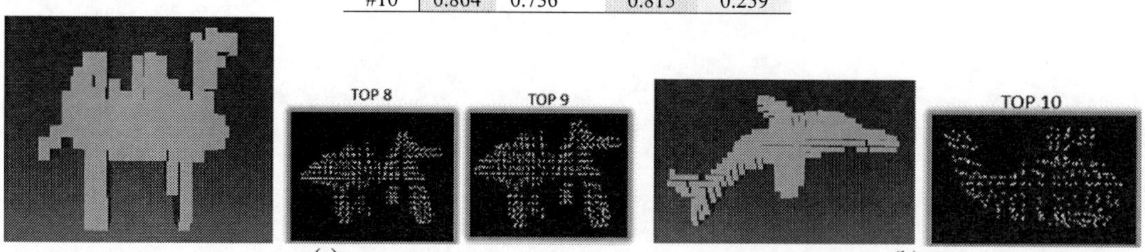

(a) (b)

Figure 14. Top Results Obtained by Distance Weighted Bipartite Matching. (a) Model #1 (b) Model #131

All the Top1 matches in Table 3 are the queries themselves. Additionally, unlabeled models those not augmented from the query. These models are listed in Figure 14. Based on the above results, we can conclude that distance weighted bipartite matching approach not only makes more consistent similarity for augmenting models, but also retrieve other models which are similar in appearance. Moreover, from the results of Figure 14, distance weighted bipartite matching approach is more robust with respect to changes in pose.

3.4 Performance of Distance and Voxel Location Weighted Bipartite Matching

Firstly, Table 1 shows that distance weighted bipartite matching after introducing voxel weight makes the similarity variation between each two models larger. Similar effect can also be observed in Figure 15-(a). Compared with the distance weighted bipartite matching strategy, the more divergent augmenting models are, the less similarity when using distance and voxel location weighted bipartite matching approach. In contrast, performance of weighted bipartite matching on Average Similarity test is better, as shown in 15-(b). To further understand the effect of voxel weight settings, we also investigate the two models shown in Figure 13. The results are listed in Table 4. The non-augmenting models in Top10 matches are also included in Figure 16.

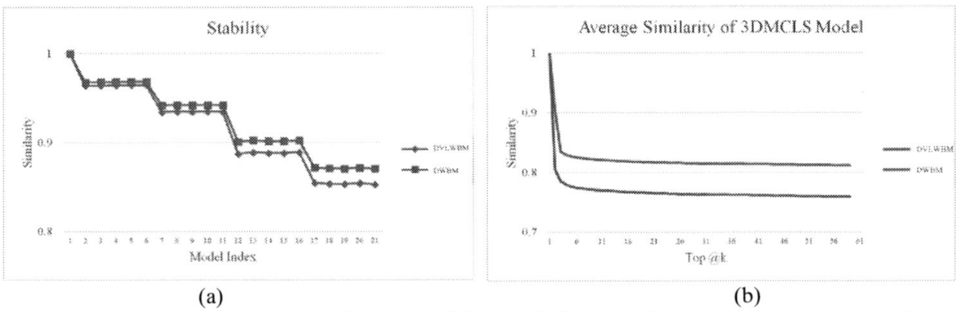

Figure 15. Result #4: Comparison of DVLWBM and DWBM. (a) Single model (b) Average similarity on 3DMCLS

Table 4. Comparing DVLWBM and DWBM on top 10 of Two Input Models, With Color Labels Of Listed Models

	DVLWBM		***DWBM***	
Rank	#1	#131	#1	#131
#1	1	1	1	1
#2	0.957	0.957	0.926	0.917
#3	0.957	0.932	0.898	0.896
#4	0.926	0.914	0.889	0.864
#5	0.909	0.914	0.889	0.864
#6	0.907	0.901	0.883	0.858
#7	0.889	0.895	0.877	0.827
#8	0.884	0.883	0.870	0.809
#9	0.883	0.883	0.870	0.769
#10	0.864	0.877	0.864	0.736

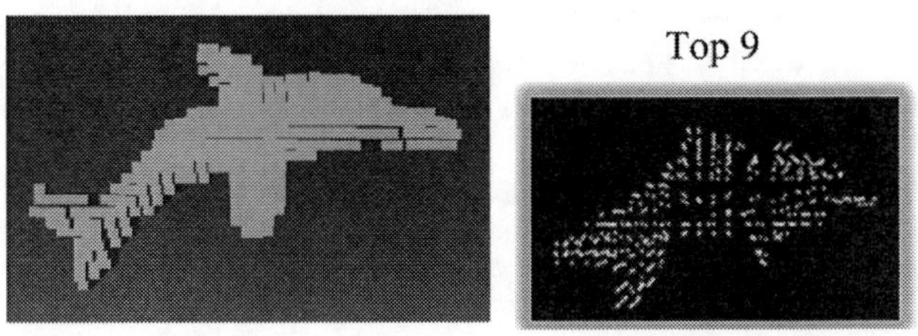

Figure 16. Top Matches Obtained by Weighted Bipartite Matching

3.5 3DBRIEF vs. 3DLTD

In this experiment, we compare 3DBRIEF and 3DLTD in terms of the processing speed. The results are shown in Table 5. Since 3DBRIEF is extracted sequentially, feature extraction or matching require more computations. In a model search system, feature extraction can be processed offline, therefore only matching time matters. 3DLTD plus DVLWBM is much better than 3DBRIEF in matching time due to the drastic reduction of dimension after using weighted bipartite matching approach and the limited number of cubes in a model.

Table 5. Computation time for 3DBRIEF and 3DLTD+DVLWBM

	Feature Extraction		***Matching***	
Number of Models	3DBRIEF	3DLTD	3DBRIEF	3DLTD
31	≈ 2.7s	≈ 1.8s	≈ 4.5s	≈ 0.06s
357	≈ 24s	≈ 29s	≈ 53s	≈ 0.39s
616	≈ 42s	≈ 58s	≈ 89s	≈ 0.6s

4. CONCLUSION

In this paper, we propose a novel descriptor named 3DLTD to characterize 3D models built with QModel Creator. The local descriptors can be efficiently computed from a given model, and the model retrieval process is cast into a weighted bipartite matching problem with modest computational complexity. Experimental results indicate that the proposed framework can be applied to perform 3D model search and retrieval with low latency, making it a feasible solution for implementing the search function in 3DMCLS.

ACKNOWLEDGEMENT

This work is supported by the Ministry of Science and Technology, Taiwan under MOST-105-2218-E-004-002.

REFERENCES

Hu, Chen-Chi, *et al*, 2015. Intuitive 3D Cubic Style Modeling System. *In: SIGGRAPH Asia 2015 Posters.* ACM, 2015. p. 27.

Lin, I-Sheng, *et al*, 2017. A Collaborative Learning System for Sharing 3D Models: 3D Model Co-learning Space. *In: Advanced Learning Technologies (ICALT), 2017 IEEE 17th International Conference on. IEEE.* pp. 502-506.

Chen, Ding-Yun, *et al,* 2003. On Visual Similarity based 3D Model Retrieval. *In: Computer graphics forum*. Blackwell Publishing, Inc. pp. 223-232.

Matsuda, Takahiro, *et al*, 2015. Lightweight Binary Voxel Shape Features for 3D Data Matching and Retrieval. *In: Multimedia Big Data (BigMM), 2015 IEEE International Conference on. IEEE.*

Liao, Wen-Hung, 2010. Region Description Using Extended Local Ternary Patterns. *In: Pattern Recognition (ICPR), 2010 20th International Conference on. IEEE.* pp. 1003-1006.

Tan, Xiaoyang, and Bill Triggs, 2010. Enhanced Local Texture Feature Sets for Face Recognition Under Difficult Lighting Conditions. *IEEE transactions on image processing 19.6*: pp. 1635-1650.

DESCRIBING CLOTHING IN HUMAN IMAGES: A PARSING-POSE INTEGRATED APPROACH

Yanghong Zhou[1,2], Runze Li[1,2], Yangping Zhou[1,2] and Pik-Yin Mok[1,2,*]
[1] *The Hong Kong Polytechnic University Shenzhen Research Institute, Shenzhen, China*
[2] *Institute of Textiles & Clothing, The Hong Kong Polytechnic University, Hunghom, Hong Kong*

ABSTRACT

With the advent of information technology, digital product information grows exponentially. People are exposed to far too much information, and information overload can slow down, instead of speeding up, a simple decision-making process like searching for suitable clothing online. Traditional semantic-based product retrieval may not be effective due to human subjectivity and cognitive differences. In this paper, we propose a method by integrating the state-of-the-arts deep neural models in pose estimation, human parsing and category classification to recognise from human images all clothing items and their fine-grained product category information. The proposed fine-grained clothing classification model can facilitate a wide range of applications such as the automatic annotation of clothing images. The effectiveness of the proposed method is validated through experiment on a real-world dataset.

KEYWORDS

Clothing Retrieval, Clothing Recognition, Fine-Grained Classification, Pose Estimation, Human Parsing, Deep Learning

1. INTRODUCTION

With the rapid growth of digital information online, people can easily share almost everything of their daily life with friends and peers via social networks, but at the same time people also face a new challenge of mass information retrieval. Clothing product retrieval is an attractive research area to both academia and the fashion industry because it improves the users' experience and promotes sales of online shopping. Typically, users search for products at online stores by inputting keywords such as the attributes and styles of clothing. Semantic-based product retrieval is efficient, and the method is widely used by online shopping sites (Egozi et al., 2011). A same category of goods, however, often can be expressed by different text vocabularies, and each clothing attribute is assigned a semantic description according to the type of clothing attributes (such as type, brand, etc.). Because of human subjectivity and cognitive differences, clothing attributes do not have standard definitions, and the accuracy of textual and semantic-based product recommendations is not high.

Another group of researchers proposed to recognise clothing attributes from images. Clothing items are soft and do not have a fixed form, however; thus, clothing classification is a challenging computer-vision problem due to possible deformation and occlusion, and always requires correct localisation of clothing regions in the input images. There are mainly three classes of method to estimate clothing location: pose estimation (Chen et al., 2012), clothing parsing (Yamaguchi et al., 2012; 2013; Arbelaez et al., 2011; Simo-Serra et al., 2014) and clothing detection (Bossard et al., 2012; Eichner et al., 2012). Chen et al. (2012) used the pose estimation method, extracted image features from different human body parts and trained a classification for each attribute using the extracted images features. Considering the natural relationship between clothing attributes, a conditional random field (CRF) is employed on the classification predictions to produce more reasonable attribute lists. Pose provides only the location of human joints, whereas the detail locations of the clothing region remain missing.

Some researchers proposed to take advantage of the clothing segmentation to improve the clothing prediction and treat the clothing classification problem as an image parsing problem, which predicts the clothing type on a pixel level. To do this, Yamaguchi et al. (2012) built a clothing parsing Fashionista

[*] Corresponding author: P.Y. Mok, tracy.mok@polyu.edu.hk

dataset, consists of 685 photos which label the clothing or body clothing on a pixel level. They segmented the image to super-pixels using an image segmentation algorithm (Arbelaez et al., 2011) and exploited a CRF model to predict the clothing labels for each segmented super-pixel. To improve the parsing performance, they used a clothing retrieval approach to predict the clothing items, namely tag prediction, and then combined the tag prediction into the parsing model (Yamaguchi et al., 2013). Considering the complex dependencies between clothing and human pose, Simo-Serra et al. (2014) proposed a pose-aware CRF model for clothing parsing.

In addition, some researchers focused on clothing detection and applied the detection results to predict clothing classification. For example, Bossard et al. (2012) used the Calvin upper-body detector (Bossard, et al., 2012) to estimate the location of upper-body clothing and then trained the classification model based on the detected clothing. With the development of deep learning technology, deep learning technique then was applied for the fast and accurate fashion item detection. Hara et al. (2016) used RCNN (Girshick et al., 2014) to generate object proposals and extract features from each object proposal. Smirnov et al. based on fast-RCNN (Girshick, 2015) and switch selective search to MultiBox (Szegedy et al., 2014) to further improve the detection accuracy.

In this paper, taking advantages of pose estimation and clothing parsing, we design a framework that detects all the clothing items presented in an input human image and classify the clothing type and fine-grained category of each identified clothing item. To distinguish 'dress' and 'upper-clothing and skirt', we combined an image-type classification model with human parsing. The framework is shown in Figure 1. The main contributions of this paper include:

- A novel dataset consisting of 79,153 images annotated with a structure clothing category.
- A new framework for accurate clothing classification combining image type classification, human parsing and pose estimation.
- A coarse attention-based neural network to predict the fine-grained clothing category.

Our fine-grained clothing classification can facilitate a wide range of applications, such as the automatic annotation of clothing images, similar clothing product retrieval, fashion coordination rule mining from online images and fashion trend analysis.

2. METHOD

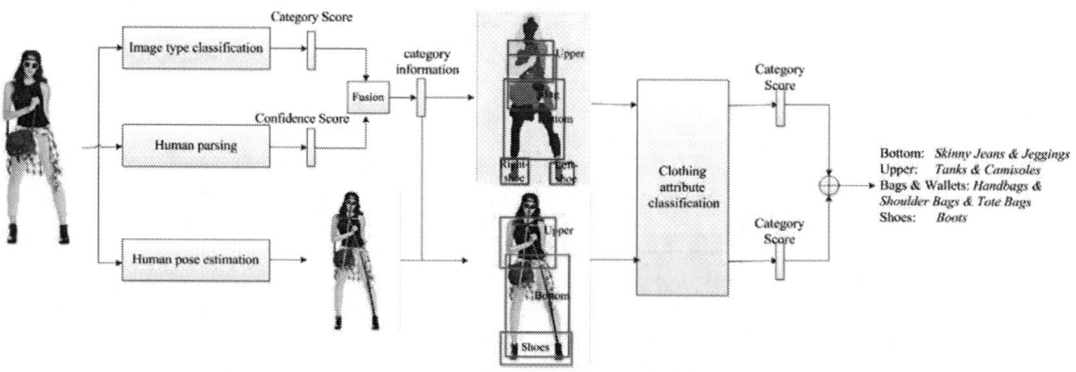

Figure 1. Framework of Fine-Grained Clothing Recognition

Figure 1 shows our framework to recognise the fine-grained category of clothing that the human is wearing. We collected about 10,000 full-body fashion images. As there is no dataset that can recognise all the clothing items and their fine-grained clothing category in the full-body image, we proposed to detect the clothing items in the image first and train fine-grained clothing category classification models to analyse the fine-grained category of these detected clothing items. To do so, we built a dataset labelling with fine-grained clothing categories to train the clothing category classification models for various clothing items. Finally, the detailed category of detected clothing items will be given.

2.1 Clothing Item Detection

In our method, both human parsing and pose estimation were used to detect the clothing region, and image category information was injected to refine the detection result. The clothing type classification then was used to complement the global feature of the image.

We employed Fully Convolutional Networks (FCN) method (Long et al., 2015) and used the ATR dataset to train a human parsing model (as shown in Figure 2). The model can segment the human body into 18 different classes (background, hat, hair, sunglasses, upper-clothing, skirt, pants, dress, belt, left shoe, right shoe, face, left leg, right leg, left arm, right arm, bag, and scarf). If z denotes the confidence score of the last layer of the network, the output of z provides a probability for each label through the softmax function. Given image I, we denote $z^I_{k,i,j}$ the probability of pixel (i, j) belongs to the k-th label and $k^* = argmax\ z^I_{k,i,j}$ will be the predicted label of pixel (i,j). We denote the number of pixels having the predicted label k^* as $N(k^*)$ and compute $z^I_{k^*}=\sum_{k^*} z^I_{k^*,i,j}/N(k^*)$, and regard the mean probability $z^I_{k^*}$ as the probability that the image have the k^* label.

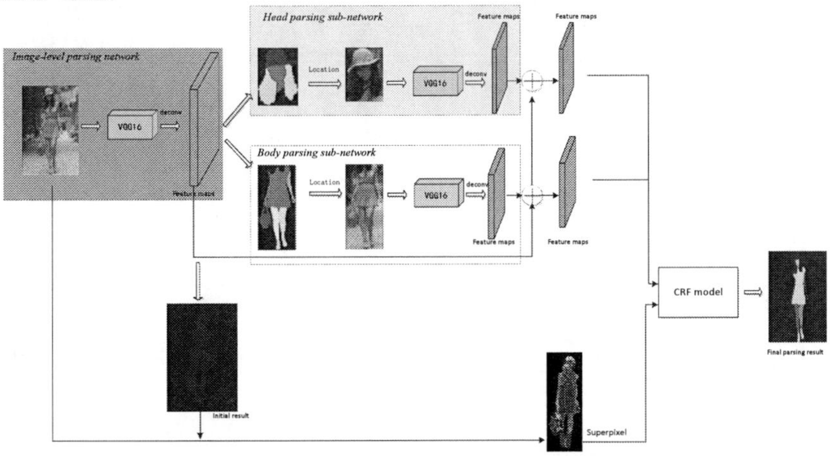

Figure 2. Human Parsing Model

Since human parsing model provide pixel-to-pixel annotation with little global context information, we proposed to train an image-classification model to predict the image category – such as upper clothing, bottom clothing, dress, bag, shoes, sunglasses and overalls – to provide global context information.

Given image I, we denote the classifier score as C^I_k and $k^* = \text{argmax}\ C^I_k$ as the predicted label of image I.

Firstly, we put the image I into the image classification model which is a Resnet-34 classification model and determine its category. If the predicted label is 'dresses' or 'overalls', there will be no skirts in the image and the probability of having upper clothing in the image also is low.

To crop out the corresponding clothing region, we proposed an algorithm which exploits the human parsing model and the image classification model. The image classification model gives the image category (such as dress, upper clothing, bottom clothing (skirt, pants), hat, belt, bag and scarf) and the human parsing model gives the pixels having these labels. The proposed algorithm is shown as follows:

Input Image I
Extract the probability $z^I_{k,i,j}$ of pixel (i, j) belonging to the k-th label for all the pixels via human parsing
Extract the classifier score C^I_k for the image
If $k^* = \text{argmax}\ C^I_k$ is "dresses" or "overalls" do
    $k^* = argmax\ z^I_{k,i,j}$
  For $k^* = argmax\ z^I_{k,i,j}$ is skirt do
    k^* = "dresses" / "overalls"
  If k^* = "upper clothing" and $z^I_{k^*} < 0.8$:
    Eliminate k^*
  Else do
  If k^* = "dress" and $z^I_{k^*} < 0.8$:
    Eliminate k^*
Output: k^*

Moreover, the accuracy of pose estimation model has substantial improvements recently, we used the pose estimator proposed by (Cao et al., 2017) to compute the 2D locations of human joints. The pose estimator has satisfactory performance across the dataset. We proposed an algorithm, which exploits the location of human joints to define the locations of upper clothing, bottom clothing, glasses, dress and shoes as follows:

Input the location of joints using pose estimator

Neck (x_neck, y_neck), Nose (x_nose, y_nose), Right-ear (x_rear, y_rear), Left-ear (x_lear, y_lear), Right-eye (x_reye, y_reye), Left-ear (x_leye, y_leye), Right-shoulder (x_rshoulder, y_rshoulder), Left-shoulder (x_lshoulder, y_lshoulder), Right-hand (x_rhand, y_rhand), Left-hand (x_lhand, y_lhand), Right-hip (x_rhip, y_rhip), Left-hip (x_lhip, y_lhip), Right-knee (x_rknee, y_yknee), Left-knee (x_lknee, y_lknee), Right-shoe (x_rshoe, y_rshoe), Left-shoe (x_lshoe, y_lshoe)

Glasses = [[max(0, y_reye - (y_neck - y_nose) / 6), y_reye + (y_neck - y_nose) / 6, x_rear, x_lear]]

Upper-clothing = [max(y_rshoulder - (y_rsholder - y_neck) /4, 0), max(y_lhand, y_rhand, y_rhip), min(x_rhand, x_rshoulder),max(x_lhand, x_lshoulder + (y_lshoulder - y_neck) / 3)]

Bottom-clothing = [max(y_rhip - (y_rsholder - y_ neck) / 3, 0), max(y_lshoe, y_rshoe, y_rhip), min(x_rhip - (y_rsholder - y_ neck) / 2, x_rshoe - (y_rsholder - y_ neck) / 2), max(x_lshoe, x_lhip + (y_lshoulder - y_ neck) / 2)]

Dress = [max(y_rshoulder - (y_rsholder - y_ neck) / 3, 0), max(y_lshoe, y_rshoe, y_rhip), min(x_rshoulder - int((y_neck - y_nose)) / 2, x_rshoe - (y_rsholder - y_ neck) / 2), max(x_lshoes, x_lshoulder + (y_lshoulder - y_ neck) / 2)]

Shoe = [y_rknee, max(y_rshoe + (y_rshoe - y_ rknee)/3, y_lshoe + (y_rshoe - y_ rknee)/3), min(x_rshoe - (y_rshoe - y_ rnkee)/ 3, x_lshoe -(y_rshoe - y_ rnkee)/ 3), max(x_lshoe +(y_rshoe - y_ rnkee)/3, x_rshoe + (y_rshoe - y_ rnkee)/ 3)]

Output: glasses, upper-clothing, bottom-clothing, dress, shoe

---

Therefore, we obtain the clothing detection using human parsing and pose estimation, respectively.

2.2 Fine-grained Clothing Category Classification

Our goal is to recognise the correct category information and fine-grained attributes of all the clothing items presented on the input image. After detecting the clothing regions, we can build a big fine-grained clothing dataset and train Convolution Neural Netwroks (CNNs) to predict category and fine-grained attributes for given clothing regions.

2.2.1 Datasets

We built the dataset by crawling images from several online shopping websites. As the text description of clothing on different websites is quite different, we defined the clothing category and attribute and relabelled these images. Each image was annotated with a fine class and the corresponding coarse label. Each fine class belongs to exactly one coarse class. Table 1 shows all the clothing classes defined in this work. There are 15 coarse labels and 111 fine clothing labels. The dataset contains 79,153 images, which include 19,520 full-body clothing images, 23,579 upper clothing images and 8,414 bottom clothing images. The number of images for each fine-grained clothing category is shown in Figure 3.

Table 1. A list of Clothing Categories Considered in this Work

Image type	Clothing Category	Subclasses
Full-body clothing	Dresses	'Layered Dresses' (1), 'A-line Dresses' (2), 'Mini Dresses' (3), 'Midi Dresses' (4), 'Maxi Dresses' (5), 'Evening Dresses' (6), 'Bodycon Dresses' (7), 'T-shirt Dresses' (8), 'Wrap Dresses' (9), 'Slit Dresses' (10), 'Shirt Dresses' (11), 'Oversized Dreses' (12), 'Mid-length Dresses' (13)
	Overalls	'Dungarees' (14), 'Jumpsuits' (15), 'Playsuits' (16), 'Bodysuits' (17)
Upper clothing	Tops	'Cropped Tops' (1), 'Shirts' (2), 'Short-sleeved Blouses' (3), 'Long-sleeved Blouses' (4), 'Sleeveless/Short-sleeved Shirts' (5)
	Tanks & Camisoles	'Tanks' (6), 'Singlets' (7), 'Camisoles' (8)
	T-Shirts	'Short-Sleeved T-shirts' (9), 'Long-sleeved T-shirts' (10), 'Polo T-shirts' (11)
	Shirts	'Formal Shirts' (12), 'Short-sleeved Shirts' (13), 'Denim Shirts' (14), 'Polo Shirts' (15)

	Outerwear	'Bombers & Blousons' (16), 'Trench Coats & Pea Coats' (17), 'Jackets' (18), 'Sweaters & Jumpers' (19), 'Hoodies & Sweatshirts' (20), 'Cardigans' (21), 'Denim Jackets' (22), 'Coats' (23), 'Parkas' (24), 'Gilets' (25), 'Blazers & Suits' (26), 'Waistcoats & Vests' (27), 'Down Jackets' (28), 'Capes & Ponchos' (29), 'Leathered Jackets & Coats' (30), 'Overcoats' (31), 'Knitted' (32)
Bottom Clothing	Shorts	'Denim Shorts' (1), 'Casual Shorts' (2), 'Running Shorts' (3), 'Tailored Shorts' (4), 'Cargo Shorts' (5), 'Beach Shorts' (6), 'Culottes' (7), 'Pyjama Shorts' (8)
	Pants & Trousers	'Sweat Pants' (9), 'Slim-Fit Pants' (10), 'Chino Pants' (11), 'Cropped Pants' (12), 'Skinny Pants' (13), 'Wide-Leg Trousers' (14), 'Leggings' (15), 'Flared Trousers' (16), 'Peg Trousers' (17), 'Straight-Leg Pants' (18)
	Skirts	'Slit skirts' (19), 'Pencil skirts' (20), 'Mini Skirts' (21), 'Maxi Skirts' (22), 'Wrap skirts' (23), 'Layered skirts' (24), 'Pleated skirts' (25), 'Midi Skirts' (26), 'Panel skirts' (27), 'A-line Skirts' (28)
	Jeans	'Slim-Fit Jeans' (29), 'Boyfriend Jeans & Causal Jeans' (30), 'Skinny Jeans & Jeggings' (31), 'Cropped Jeans' (32), 'Trumpet Jeans' (33)
Others	Bags & Wallets	Wallets & Card Holders, 'Messengers & Laptop Bags', 'Clutches', 'Purses & Small Item Bags', 'Backpacks', 'Duffle Bags', 'Hangbags & Shoulder Bags & Tote Bags', 'Waist/Chest Bags', 'Bag Accessories', 'Satchels & Sling Bags', 'Luaggages & Storage Bags'
	Shoes	Slip-ons', 'Sandals', 'Flip-flops & Slippers', 'Boots', 'Brogues', 'Boat Shoes & Loafers', 'Trainers & Sneakers', 'Heels & Platforms & Wedges', 'Flats'
	Belts	'Leather Belts', 'Non-leather Belts'
	Sunglasses & Glasses	Squared Sunglasses', 'Round Sunglasses', 'Retro Sunglasses', 'Aviator Sunglasses', 'Oversized Sunglasses', 'Wayfarer', 'Cat Eye Sunglasses'

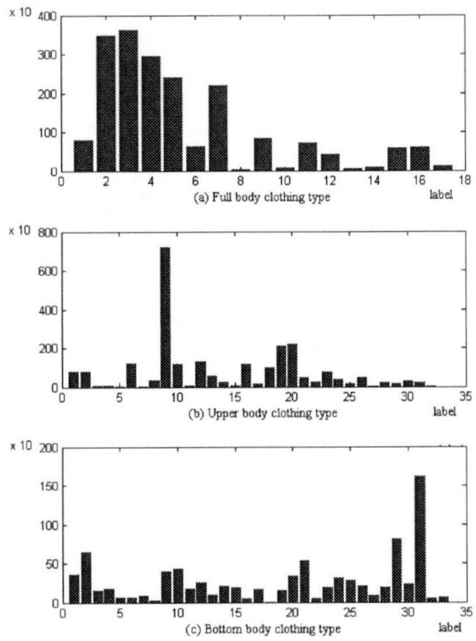

Figure 3. Number of images for each fine-grained category

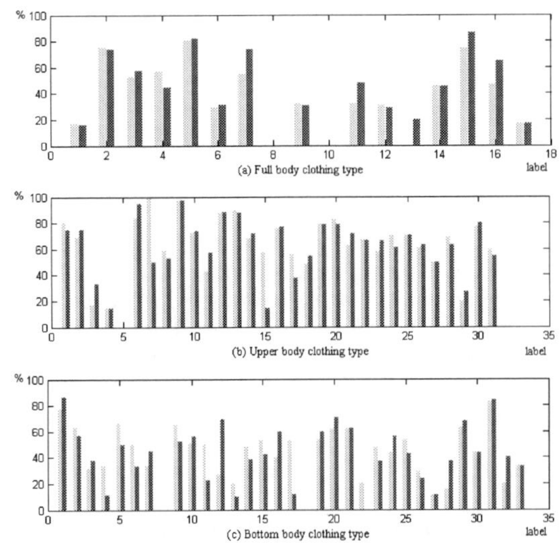

Figure 4. Comparison of per class accuracy between basic Resnet (blue) and our method (red)

2.2.2 Coarse attention-based neural network

Considering the hierarchical relationship between coarse and fine labels, we proposed a new model which jointly learns the coarse and the fine-grained classifiers in a cascaded manner. The proposed coarse attention-based network architecture is depicted in Figure 5 (a). Given image I, we use a feature extractor to obtain the low-level feature

$$x_l = \text{Extractor}(I, W_{\text{extractor}}) \tag{1}$$

where $W_{\text{extractor}}$ represents the feature extractor's parameters. Secondly, based on the low-level feature x_l, we design the coarse and fine-grained classifiers, respectively. We formulate the coarse classification process as follows:

$$\hat{y}_{\text{coarse}} = \text{Predictor}_{\text{coarse}}(x_l, W_{\text{coarse}}) \tag{2}$$

where W_{coarse} indicates the parameters of the coarse classifier and $\hat{y}_{\text{coarse}}$ indicates the category score of coarse category. To take advantage of the hierarchical relationship between the coarse and fine-grained labels, we also designed a coarse information injection module, which enabled the coarse information providing prior knowledge for the fine-grained category classification. Figure 5 shows the overall architecture of the coarse attention-based neural network.

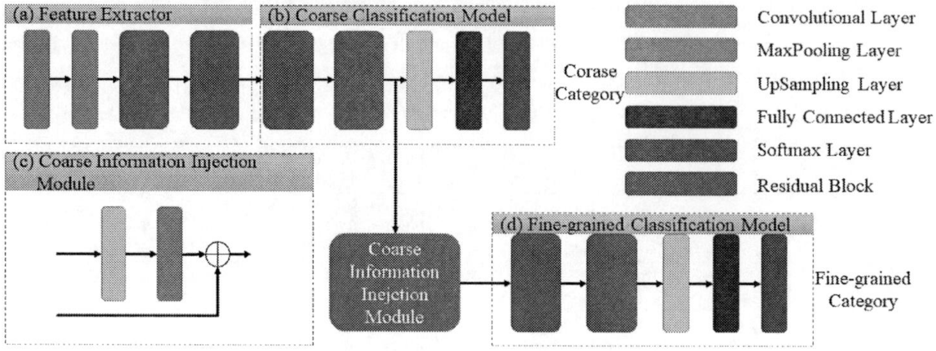

Figure 5. Coarse Attention-based Neural Network

a) Coarse information injection module

We realized the coarse information injection from low-level feature to the fine-grained classifier by designing a coarse information injection module (Figure 5(b)). As the high-level features have semantic information, the coarse information injection module injects the high-level features from the coarse classifier into the low-level features to provide prior knowledge to the fine-grained classifier. Let x_s be the high-level features with semantic meaning and x_l be the low-level features; we pass x_s and x_l through the coarse information injection module (Figure 5(c)) to obtain the features with semantic information as:

$$x_{\text{fusion}} = \text{Injector}(x_l, x_s) \tag{3}$$

The injection module merged the low-level features and the high-level features with semantic meaning using an element-wise addition operation. To match the spatial size of x_l, we performed a bi-linear up-sampling on the high-level features and then added a 1×1 convolutional layer on the up-sampled features. As such, the output of coarse information injection module represents the fused feature maps characterized by high-level semantic knowledge embedding as the learning guidance of the coarse classifier. As shown in Figure 6, in shirt images, semantic prior knowledge of coarse predictor highlights the shirt part features.

Finally, we put the fused feature maps into the fine-grained classifier (Figure 5(d)). and obtain the fine-grained category score as follows:

$$\hat{y}_{\text{fine}} = \text{Predictor}_{\text{fine}}(x_{\text{fusion}}, W_{\text{fine}}) \tag{4}$$

where W_{fine} indicates the parameters of fine label predictor.

b) Loss function

For the model training, we adopted cross-entropy loss for both the coarse and fine-grained classifiers. We deployed a separate loss function at the output of each classifier. The cross-entropy loss is defined as:

$$L(y, \hat{y}, m) = -\sum_{c=1}^{m} y_c \log(\hat{y}_c). \tag{5}$$

where m is number of labels. The loss function for our proposed model is formulated as:

$$L = L(y_{\text{coarse}}, \hat{y}_{\text{coarse}}, m_{\text{coarse}}) + L(y_{\text{fine}}, \hat{y}_{\text{fine}}, m_{\text{fine}}) \tag{6}$$

where m_{coarse} and m_{fine} denote the number of coarse labels and the number of fine-grained labels, respectively.

3. EXPERIMENT

In this section, we firstly evaluate the performance of proposed coarse attention-based neural network on our fine-grained clothing dataset. For comparison purposes, the broadly applied state-of-the-art network Resnet (He et al., 2016) is used as the baseline method. As our goal is to recognise all the fine-grained clothing categories on the full-body images, we used the proposed network to train specific models on full-body clothing images, upper clothing images and bottom clothing images (shown in Table 1). We selected full-body images and detected all the clothing regions using the method in Section 2.2. We then input the detected clothing regions into the corresponding models and obtained the fine-grained clothing category of detected clothing regions.

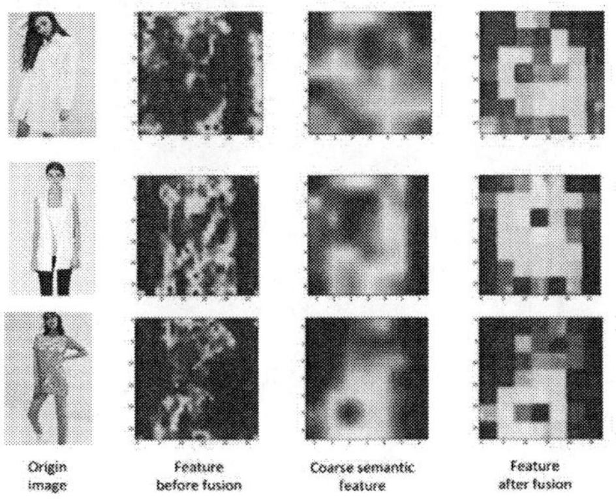

Figure 6. Some Examples of Feature Maps Before Fusion and After Fusion

Figure 7. Some Failure Examples, the Classification Result of our Model (Red) And Ground-Truth (Blue)

3.1 Evaluation of Fine-grained Classification

To evaluate the performance of our method, we trained three models on full-body clothing images, upper clothing images and bottom clothing images. All the datasets were split into three parts: 70% for training, 10% for validation, and 20% for testing. The training implementation set was the same. Input images were resized into 256×256 images. The network was trained with a mini-batch stochastic gradient descent with a momentum of 0.9, and weight decay of 0.0005; the learning rate was set to fixed 0.001. The final model was trained on pytorch for 100 epochs on GPU gtx 1080Ti.

Table 2. Accuracy Comparison of Basic Resnet and Our Model on Full-Body Clothing Type Images, Upper-Body Clothing Type, and Bottom-Body Clothing Type Images

Image type	Accuracy of basic Resnet	Accuracy of our model
Full-body clothing type	56.28%	58.88%
Upper-body clothing type	80.22%	81.12%
Bottom-body clothing type	56.95%	58.88%

We measured performance based on the top-1 accuracy. Table 2 shows the top-1 accuracy of our model and the basic Resnet on image type classification. Compared to basic Resnet-34, our model performed better on these three image types. In particularly, the accuracy of our model on full-body clothing type increased by more than 2%.

We also compared the per-class accuracy of our method with that of basic Resnet. Figure 4 illustrates that our method outperformed basic Resnet on most of categories. The class accuracy of basic Resnet exceeded our method because the number of images was very limited most of the time. To illustrate, the basic Resnet accuracy for Polo Shirts (15) was greater by about 43% and for Trench Coats & Pea Coats (17) by about 21%, but the number of images were 70 and 160, respectively, and the number of images for validation were only 7 and 16. As the number of images were so limited, their effect can be ignored. By filtering out classes with fewer than 1,000 images, there are 4 classes in which the accuracy of our method outperformed basic Resnet in a total of 6 classes for full-body clothing type images, and 6 classes in which the accuracy of our method outperforms basic Resnet in a total of 7 classes for upper-body clothing type images. Therefore, when the number of images is large enough, our method performs better than the basic Resnet.

3.2 Fine-grained Clothing Category Recognition on Full-Body Images

To recognise the fine-grained clothing category of all presented clothing regions in an input human image, we trained a human parsing model on the ART dataset (Liang et al., 2015) to parse the human image, and we estimated the location of human joints using OpenPose (Cao et al., 2017). Based on the human parsing result and estimated human pose, we detected all the clothing regions and input these regions into the corresponding classifiers. For example, the detected upper clothing region was input into the upper clothing classifier and bottom clothing region into the bottom clothing classifier. Figure 8 shows some clothing recognition of our methods.

Figure 8. Examples of Clothing Recognition on Full-Body Images

Figure 7 also shows some failure examples. Some failures were caused by vague clothing definitions. To illustrate, some Short-sleeved T-shirts were mistaken as Long-sleeved T-shirts. Actually, these T-shirts were not exactly Short-sleeved T-shirts and seem to be the Middle-sleeved T-shirts, which are not defined in our clothing categories. Also, when a clothing image has multiple category features, our model can recognise only one and fail to recognise another correct category. For example, some Long-sleeved T-shirts were recognised as Sweaters & Jumpers or Hoodies & Sweatshirt, and Layered Dresses were recognised as Maxi Dresses. Similarly, when one person wears multiple pieces of clothing, like a T-shirt and a jacket, our model can recognise only one article. In addition, when the clothing features are very similar, our model may have difficultly recognising the correct one, such as Tanks and Camisoles, skinny pants and leggings, and casual shorts and running shorts.

4. CONCLUSION

In this paper, we have studied the problem of reinforced clothing category and fine-grained attributes recognition. We developed a new method that integrates human parsing, pose estimation and category classification to segment all clothing regions on input image and carry out fine-grained category and attributes recognition for each clothing region. Using this approach, we can obtain the fashion coordination information of all clothing items on input images.

ACKNOWLEDGEMENT

The work described in this paper was partially supported by a grant from the Research Grants Council of the Hong Kong Special Administrative Region, China (Project No. PolyU 5218/13E). The supports from Guangdong Provincial Department of Science and Technology (Project No. R2015A030401014) Shenzhen Science and Technology Innovation Commission (Project No. JCYJ20170303160155330), are gratefully acknowledged.

REFERENCES

Arbelaez P., M. Maire, C. Fowlkes, and J. Malik, 2011. Contour detection and hierarchical image segmentation, *IEEE Transactions on Pattern Analysis and Machine Intelligence,* vol. 33, pp. 898-916.

Bossard L., M. Dantone, C. Leistner, C. Wengert, T. Quack, and L. Van Gool, 2012. Apparel classification with style, in *2012 Asian Conference on Computer Vision*, pp. 321-335.

Cao Z., T. Simon, S.-E. Wei, and Y. Sheikh, 2017. Realtime multi-person 2d pose estimation using part affinity fields," in *Proceedings of the IEEE conference on Computer Vision and Pattern Recognition (CVPR)*, p. 7.

Chen H., A. Gallagher, and B. Girod, 2012. Describing clothing by semantic attributes, in *European Conference on Computer Vision (ECCV)*, pp. 609-623.

Egozi O., S. Markovitch, and E. Gabrilovich, 2011. Concept-based information retrieval using explicit semantic analysis, *ACM Transactions on Information Systems (TOIS),* vol. 29, p. 8.

Eichner M., M. Marin-Jimenez, A. Zisserman, and V. Ferrari, 2012. 2d articulated human pose estimation and retrieval in (almost) unconstrained still images, *International Journal of Computer Vision,* vol. 99, pp. 190-214.

Girshick R., J. Donahue, T. Darrell, and J. Malik, 2014. Rich feature hierarchies for accurate object detection and semantic segmentation, in *Proceedings of the IEEE conference on Computer Vision and Pattern Recognition (CVPR)*, pp. 580-587.

Girshick R., 2015. Fast r-cnn, *arXiv preprint arXiv:1504.08083.*

Hara K., V. Jagadeesh, and R. Piramuthu, 2016. Fashion apparel detection: the role of deep convolutional neural network and pose-dependent priors, in *2016 IEEE Winter Conference on Applications of Computer Vision (WACV),* pp. 1-9.

He K., X. Zhang, S. Ren, and J. Sun, 2016. Deep residual learning for image recognition, in *Proceedings of the IEEE Conference on Computer Vision and Pattern Recognition (CVPR)*, pp. 770-778.

Liang X., S. Liu, X. Shen, J. Yang, L. Liu, J. Dong, *L. Lin and S. Yan*, 2015. Deep human parsing with active template regression, *IEEE Transactions on Pattern Analysis and Machine Intelligence,* vol. 37, pp. 2402-2414.

Long J., E. Shelhamer, and T. Darrell, 2015. Fully convolutional networks for semantic segmentation, in *Proceedings of the IEEE conference on Computer Vision and Pattern Recognition (CVPR)*, pp. 3431-3440.

Simo-Serra E., S. Fidler, F. Moreno-Noguer, and R. Urtasun, 2014. A high performance CRF model for clothes parsing, in *2014 Asian Conference on Computer Vision*, pp. 64-81.

Szegedy C., S. Reed, D. Erhan, D. Anguelov, and S. Ioffe, 2014. Scalable, high-quality object detection, *arXiv preprint arXiv:1412.1441.*

Yamaguchi K., M. H. Kiapour, L. E. Ortiz, and T. L. Berg, 2012. Parsing clothing in fashion photographs, in *2012 IEEE Conference on Computer Vision and Pattern Recognition (CVPR),* pp. 3570-3577.

Yamaguchi K., M. H. Kiapour, and T. L. Berg, 2013. Paper doll parsing: Retrieving similar styles to parse clothing items, in *2013 IEEE International Conference on Computer Vision (ICCV)*, pp. 3519-3526.

A REAL-TIME FACIAL EXPRESSION RECOGNITION FOR ONLINE EMBEDDED DEVICES REQUIRING USER'S EMOTIONAL INTERACTION

Mi Ra Jeong, Duyoung Heo, Jae-Yeal Nam and Byoung Chul Ko
Department of Computer Engineering, Keimyung University
1095 Dalgubeol-daero, Dalseo-gu, Daegu 42601, S. Korea

ABSTRACT

Currently, much of the automatic facial expression recognition (FER) research focuses on the use of deep-learning algorithms beyond classic pattern classifiers. However, deep-learning based FER approaches require more computing resources to analyze the large amounts of data and the massive number of parameters associated with this approach. Because of this demand on computing resources, deep-learning based FER approaches are not appropriate for real-time embedded applications with limited computing resources. To address this problem, we propose using hierarchical boosted random forest (BRF) classifier instead of deep network algorithms for various embedded devices. For FER, we first detect the face region and facial landmarks from input images and extract geometric feature descriptors considering the spatial position between landmarks. We then apply these feature vectors to proposed hierarchical BRF classifiers and classify facial expressions for the input image. To estimate the performance, we applied the proposed algorithm to the extended Cohn-Kanade (CK+) dataset. The accuracy was 91.6%. Through experiments, the proposed algorithm yielded similar performance compared to deep learning FER algorithms, with a significantly reduced processing cost. Our hierarchical BRF approach is more suitable for real-time embedded systems requiring user emotional interaction like virtual reality (VR) gaming.

KEYWORDS

Facial Expression Recognition, Emotion, FER, Low Specification System, Embedded System, Random Forest

1. INTRODUCTION

Interest in facial expression recognition (FER) technology has been rapidly increasing in various industries such as HCI (human-computer interaction), customer marketing and advertising, virtual reality (VR) and augmented reality (AR) based game, education, medical care, and criminal investigation. Although automatic FER has been studied for more than ten years, it still faces many challenges in of the complexity of facial expressions, changes of facial pose, and various lighting environments. FER performance is not satisfactory when applied to actual applications.

FER research is divided into two groups according to whether the features are handcrafted or generated through the output of a deep neural network (DNN). Conventional FER approaches are composed of three major steps: face and facial component detection, feature extraction, and expression classification. Expression classification utilizes pre-trained FE classifiers, such as a support vector machine (SVM) (Shan et al., 2009; Suk & Prabhakaran, 2014; Carcagni et al., 2015), AdaBoost (Wang et al., 2004), and HMM (Hidden Markov Model) (Uddin et al., 2009), to produce the recognition results using the extracted features. DNN-based FER has emerged as a general approach to machine learning, yielding state-of-the-art results in many computer vision studies with the availability of big data (Ko et al. 2018). The most popular network models among the DNN models available are deep-learning models that are capable of learning long-term dependencies, like the convolutional neural network (CNN) and long-short term memory (LSTM).

Although very deep or wide networks based FER approaches usually perform reasonably well, they still have a few problems with processing time and memory consumption associated with the multitudinous parameters in the training and inference processes. Moreover, the aforementioned CNN trackers mainly pay attention to the accuracy of the FE, giving little consideration for running speed that is a key factor for real-time applications.

Therefore, we propose a FER algorithm based on modified conventional random forest (RF) instead of DNN that is capable of operating in low specification device while preserving comparable FER performance with fast speed in various applications.

2. PROPOSED FACIAL EXPRESSION RECOGNITION

2.1 Overview of the System

To reduce the burden of feature extraction in a real-time system, we propose a concise geometric feature descriptor based on spatial relation between face important positions using distance and angle ratio. As the FE classifier, we propose the hierarchical boosted random forest (BRF) classifier that is an ensemble of boosted randomized decision trees to classify FE accurately. The major contributions along with overall procedures of this paper are shown in Figure 1. We first detect the facial region and landmarks from an input image. The geometric features are constructed based on the spatial relation between the facial landmarks, and the facial expression is recognized with the BRF that is hierarchically constructed using the feature vector. In this paper, we evaluate the performance of our proposed algorithm using a well-known extended Cohn-Kanade (CK+) (Lucey et al., 2010) dataset which includes six basic expressions (anger, disgust, fear, happiness, sadness, and surprise).

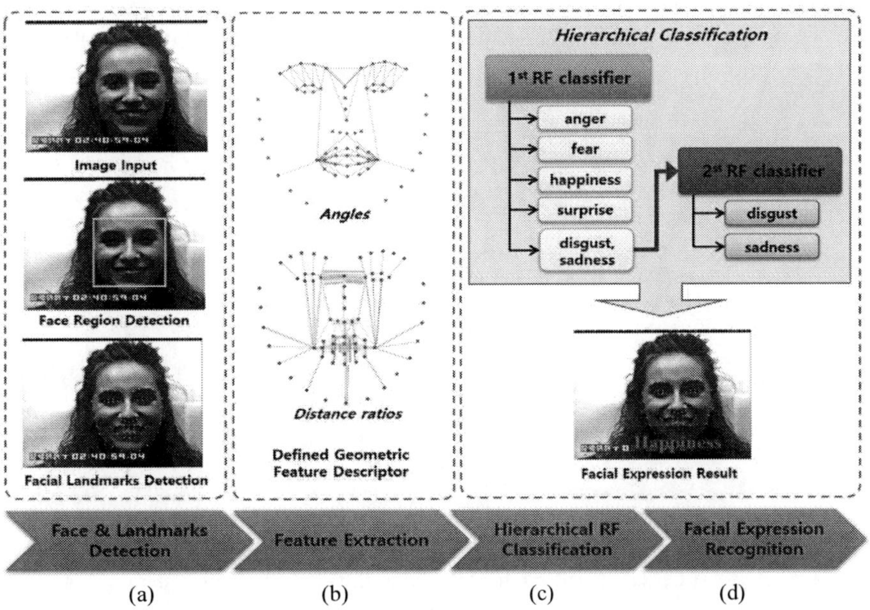

Figure 1. Overview of the proposed method for the facial expression recognition:
(a) face region and facial landmarks are extracted from face regions, (b) two geometric features are extracted based on the distance and angle relations, (c) hierarchical BRF used for detailed facial recognition

2.2 Geometric Feature Extraction

In a real-time system, low processing cost is an essential factor. Although hand-crafted appearance features such as histogram of oriented gradients (HoG) (Orrite et al., 2009; OuYang and Sang, 2013), local binary pattern (LBP) (Shan et al., 2009; Carcagni et al., 2015; Barroso et al., 2013), scale invariant feature transform (SIFT) (Carcagni et al., 2015; Barroso et al., 2013), provide better performance than the geometric feature, they require more memory and computational time because of their high dimension compared to the geometric features. Therefore, our method uses only geometric feature descriptor with low feature dimension without using appearance feature.

The geometric feature descriptor is defined based on facial expression using the spatial relations between the relative positions of facial landmarks. For the spatial relation, we use the distance ratio feature and the angle feature between the relative positions of pairs of landmarks. As the distance ratio feature, we define the individual vector $v_{i,j}$ of pairs of landmarks {i, j} and $v_{m,n}$ of pairs of landmarks {m, n}, as shown in Figure 2 (a). To complement the spatial relation caused by face rotation or face size, the spatial distance ratio is calculated

$$\text{dist}_{\text{ratio}} = \mathbf{v}_{i,j}/\mathbf{v}_{m,n} \tag{1}$$

The angle feature is extracted between three landmarks as shown in the Figure 2 (b). The angle feature of three landmarks $\{a, b, c\}$ is modeled as the angle difference

$$\text{angle}_{diff} = \theta(\mathbf{v}_{a,b}/\mathbf{v}_{b,c}) \tag{2}$$

where $v_{a,b}$ and $v_{b,c}$ are vectors that point from landmark a to landmark b and landmark b to landmark c. The angle difference is robust enough to adjust to changes of face rotation or face size. We extract the 84 dimensional distance ratio features and the 88 dimensional angle distance features. These features are applied to hierarchical BRF, respectively. In this study, facial region and facial landmarks are detected using the DLib (King, 2009) which has higher performance than the openCV detector. The DLib is an open source machine library that provides face detectors and landmark detectors to detect 68 landmarks.

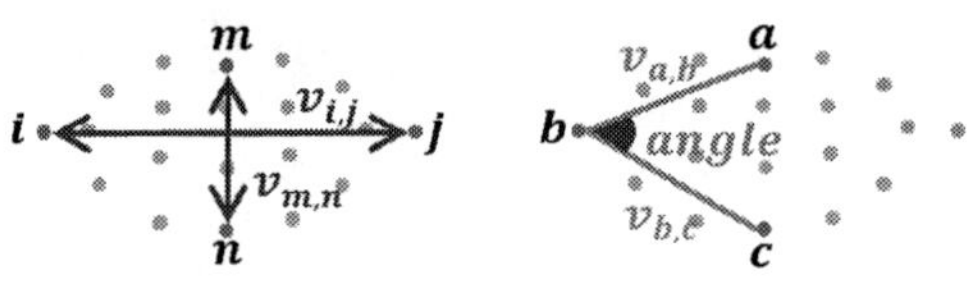

(a) (b)

Figure 2. Geometric feature extraction from mouth region.
(a) an example of distance ratio, and (b) an example of angles between three points

2.3 Facial Expression Classification using Hierarchical Random Forest

The random forest (RF) classifier is an ensemble learning method with a number of decision trees (Ko et al., 2014). As in previous research Ko et al. (2014) and Ko et al. (2013), a random forest classifier has superior generalization performance compared with SVM or an AdaBoost based method. The RF has an advantage of fast processing time since it is based on a simple arithmetic operation. However, RF depends on the number of decision trees and requires a certain amount of memory and CPU capacity. Therefore, BRF (Mishina et al., 2014) and Weighted RF (Li et al., 2010) are introduced to the classification system to maintain the generality with a small number of decision trees when considering the fact that sequential training constructs complementary decision trees for the training samples (Ko et al., 2012).

In this paper, we use the BRF classifier with hierarchical structure for more accurate recognition. As shown in Figure 1 (c), we classify anger, fear, happiness, surprise and other facial emotions including disgust and sadness in the first level because disgust and sadness have similar facial feature. In the second level, the BRF classifies only disgust and sadness from other facial emotions groups for a more precise classification. In this study, two types of BRF classifiers are learned separately using two different feature vectors instead of aggregating as one feature according to the experimental results of Ko et al. (2012).

After a set of BRFs is learned using the positive and negative training data, two feature vectors are extracted from every pixel of test data as shown in Figure 3. These vectors are used as input to the corresponding learned BRF. The probabilities of a FE class using distance ratio and using the angle vector are computed by ensemble averaging of each probability distribution of all trees $L = (l_1, l_2, \ldots, l_T)$ using equations (3) and (4).

$$P_{dist_{ratio}}(C_{FE}|L) = \frac{1}{T}\sum_{t=1}^{T} P(C_{FE}^{dist_{ratio}}|l_t) \quad (3)$$

$$P_{angle_{diff}}(C_{FE}|L) = \frac{1}{T}\sum_{t=1}^{T} P(C_{FE}^{angle_{diff}}|l_t) \quad (4)$$

Then, the final probability of a FE class is estimated by weighted combination of each BRF's probability,

$$\mathrm{P}(C_{FE}|L) = w_1 \cdot P_{dist_{ratio}}(C_{FE}|L) + w_2 \cdot P_{angle_{diff}}(C_{FE}|L) \quad (5)$$

The appropriate coefficient of weight w_1 and w_2 can be adjusted according to the characteristics of FE data type. We set two weights to 0.5 based on the experimental results. When the test image is input, the features for distance ratio and angle difference are extracted, and each feature vector is applied to each BRF classifier to estimate probabilities for each facial expression class. Then, the probabilities for two classifiers are combined by the linear weighted sum method to obtain the probabilities for each expression. After the overall processes of two levels are complete, the class with the highest probability is determined as the final FE for the input image.

3. EXPERIMENTS AND RESULTS

To evaluate the proposed method, we performed experiments using the CK+ dataset (Lucey et al., 2010) which is the most popular database related to FER consisting of 2D video sequences. The CK+ dataset has 327 image sequences from 118 subjects. These image sequences start with a neutral expression and end with a peak expression. All sequence images include the facial landmarks. The peak expressions for each sequence have the FACS code and emotion label. The emotion labels are categorized into seven emotions (anger, contempt, disgust, fear, happy, sadness, and surprise). In our experiment, six emotions are used, omitting the contempt emotion. To evaluate the FER, we performed 5-fold cross validation and measured accuracy as the ratio of true outcomes (both true positive to true negative) to the total number of cases. The number of decision tress for BRF is set to 200 in terms of speed and accuracy.

3.1 Facial Expression Recognition of CK+ dataset

Table 1 shows the confusion matrix for the proposed method using accuracy. Based on the confusion matrices, most of the FEs had a similar classification performance with the exception of 'Anger' and 'Sadness'. The main reason for the lower accuracy rate for these two FEs was that the two FEs have similar facial appearance and spatial relations between landmarks. The overall accuracy of the proposed method was 91.6 %.

Table 1. Confusion Matrix of Proposed Method (%)

	Anger	Disgust	Fear	Happy	Sadness	Surprise
Anger	**80.0**	8.9	0.0	2.2	8.9	0.0
Disgust	1.7	**94.9**	1.7	0.0	0.0	1.7
Fear	0.0	0.0	**92.0**	4.0	4.0	0.0
Happy	1.4	2.9	0.0	**95.7**	0.0	0.0
Sadness	14.3	7.1	3.6	0.0	**75.0**	0.0
Surprise	1.2	0.0	1.2	0.0	0.0	**97.6**

3.2 FER Comparison with State-of-the-arts using CK+ Dataset

To show the robust performance of the proposed method, we compared our algorithm with four state-of-the-art approaches using either the conventional algorithm or DNN: 1) real-time mobile FER (Suk et al., 2014) implemented in a mobile environment using conventional features with SVM classifier, 2) AlexNet based on FER approach (Mollahosseini et al., 2016), 3) deep neural networks based FER approach that used inception layer of the GoogLeNet (Mollahosseini et al., 2016), and 4) 3D CNN based approach that used Inception-ResNet and LSTM together (Hasani et al., 2017).

As shown in Table 2, the results confirmed that the accuracy of the proposed method is much higher than that of Suk et al. (2014) and similar to that of DNN based approaches. In regards to the number of required parameters for each approach, the proposed method requires only approximately two million parameters, compared to AlexNet's 61 million required parameters—which is the smallest number of parameters required among the three DNN based methods. Therefore, the proposed method is more appropriate for real-time embedded systems than deep learning methods.

Table 2. Comparisons with State-of-the-art methods: Accuracy using CK+ Dataset

State-of-the-art methods	Accuracy (%)
Real-time mobile FER (Suk et al., 2014)	85.5
AlexNet (Mollahosseini et al., 2016)	92.2
Deep Neural Networks (Mollahosseini et al., 2016)	93.2
3D convolutional neural networks (Hasani et al., 2017)	93.2
Propose method	91.6

3.3 Applications of Proposed FER

- *FER on mobile phones*: As one of the real-time applications, we applied the proposed FER to mobile phones. As shown in Figure 3, the FER mobile app can recognize facial expressions in real-time input images even in a mobile environment. The mobile app is running on LG G6 model with 5fps.

- *Other embedded devices*: Current FER methods require a large amount of memory and high computational complexity, and thus their application range has been limited. The proposed FER method was also applied to various embedded devices like a smart mirror (Figure 3 (a)), an education smart device (Figure 3 (b)), and facial expression mimicking (Figure 3 (c)) on an embedded system. The education smart device (Figure 3 (a)), which incorporates the FER technology as an educational tool, analyzes the concentration and satisfaction of child while the child is playing with an education device. The smart mirror recognizes the emotion of a user and provides cosmetics, music, videos and images according to user's emotion. Because the FER can be applied in a limited hardware device, the application fields are expected to be more varied.

(a) (b) (c) (d)

Figure 3. Applications being implemented using FER: (a) FER on mobile phone, (b) smart mirror, (c) education smart device, (d) mimicking facial expression on Latte-panda board system

4. CONCLUSION

In this paper, we proposed a FER algorithm based on the geometric feature and hierarchical BRF classifier for running in low specification systems embedded systems and mobile phones. The geometric feature descriptor used the spatial relation among important landmarks of a face to define each facial expression. In addition, this study used the hierarchical BRF classifier that had good generalization performance and fast processing time instead of deep network. From the experiment, we showed that the proposed FER performance had the similar accuracy compared with the method using deep learning algorithm, while the processing cost is considerably lower. As the proposed method was designed to operate in a limited hardware system, the proposed FER can be applied to the various application fields. However, the proposed method should consider the temporal feature in video to improve the performance and recognition of micro expressions. Therefore, we plan to improve the performance by considering temporal feature.

ACKNOWLEDGEMENT

This research was supported by the Scholar Research Grant of Keimyung University in 2018.

REFERENCES

Barroso, E. et al, 2013. Facial expressions: Discriminability of facial regions and relationship to biometrics recognition. *Proceedings of IEEE Workshop On Computational Intelligence in Biometrics and Identity Management (CIBIM)*. Nanyang, Singapore, pp 77–80.

Carcagnì, P. et al, 2015. Facial expression recognition and histograms of oriented gradients: a comprehensive study. *In Springer Plus*, Vol. 4, No. 1 , pp. 645.

Hasani, B. and Mahoor, M. H., 2017. Facial Expression Recognition Using Enhanced Deep 3D Convolutional Neural Networks. *Proceedings of IEEE Conference on Computer Vision and Pattern Recognition Workshops (CVPRW)*. Honolulu, Hawai, USA, pp. 2278-2288.

King, D.E., 2009. Dlib-ml: A machine learning toolkit. *In Machine Learning Research*, Vol. 10, pp. 1755–1758.

Ko, B.C. et al, 2012. Wilefire smoke detection using temporal-spatial features and random forest classifiers. *In Optical Engineering*, Vol. 51, pp. 017208-1-017208-10.

Ko, B.C. et al, 2013. Three-level cascade of random forests for rapid human detection. *In Optical Engine*, Vol. 52, No. 2, pp. 1-11.

Ko, B.C. et al, 2014. Fast human detection for intelligent monitoring using surveillance visible sensors. *In Sensors*, Vol. 14, No. 11, pp. 21247–21257.

Ko, B.C. et al, 2015, Classification of potential water body using Landsat 8 OLI and combination of two boosted random forest classifiers. *In Sensors*, Vol. 15, No. 6, pp. 13763-13777.

Ko, B.C. et al, 2018. A Brief Review of Facial Emotion Recognition Based on Visual Information. *Sensors*, Vol. 18, pp. 1-20.

Li, H. B. et al, 2010. Trees weighting random forest method for classifying high-dimensional noisy data. *Proceedings of IEEE International Conference on E-Business Engineering. Shanghai, China,* pp. 160-163.

Lucey, P. et al, 2010. The extended cohn-kanade dataset (ck+): A complete dataset for action unit and emotion-specified expression. *Proceedings of IEEE Conference on Computer Vision and Pattern Recognition Workshops (CVPRW). San Francisco, CA, USA,* pp. 94–101.

Mishina, Y. et al, 2014. Boosted Random Forest. *Proceedings of the International Conference on Computer Vision Theory and Applications (ICCVTA)*. Lisbon, Portugal, pp. 594–598.

Mollahosseini, A. et al, 2016. Going deeper in facial expression recognition using deep neural networks. *Proceedings of IEEE Winter Conference on Applications of Computer Vision (WACV)*. Lake Placid, NY, USA, pp. 1–10.

Orrite, C. et al, 2009. Hog-based decision tree for facial expression classification. *Proceedings of Iberian Conference on Pattern Recognition and Image Analysis*. Póvoa de Varzim, Portugal, Vol 5524, pp 176–183.

OuYang, Y. and Sang, N., 2013. Robust automatic facial expression detection method. *In Software*, Vol. 8, No. 7, pp. 1759-1764.

Shan, C. et al, 2009. Facial expression recognition based on local binary patterns: A comprehensive study. *In Image and Vision Computing*, Vol. 27, No. 6, pp. 803–816.

Suk, M.H. and Prabhakaran, B., 2014. Real-time Mobile Facial Expression Recognition System – A Case Study. *Proceedings of IEEE Conference of Conputer Vision and Pattern Recognition Workshops(CVPRW).* Ohio, USA, pp. 132-137.

Uddin, M.Z. et al, 2009. An enhanced independent component-based human facial expression recognition from video. *In IEEE Transactions on Consumer Electronics*, Vol. 55, No.4, pp. 2216–2224.

Wang, Y. et al, 2004. Real time facial expression recognition with adaboost. *Proceedings of International Conference on Pattern Recognition (ICPR).* Cambridge, UK, pp. 1-4.

RECONSTRUCTION OF GEOMETRICALLY PROCESSED SURFACE FROM COMPUTED TOMOGRAPHY DATA

Mikhail Novozhilov and Mariya Dubrovskaya
Lobachevsky State University of Nizhni Novgorod
Russian Federation, Nizhni Novgorod, 23 Prospekt Gagarina (Gagarin Avenue)

ABSTRACT

Within this work we consider a problem of isosurface polygonizing by it`s reconstruction from scalar field, obtained from computed tomography data. Proposed method allows to get polygonal surface, convenient for further geometric processing. Firstly, for the problem solving, we build a minimal (this allows to reduce ambiguities) graph, nodes of which represent target surface`s vertices. Secondly, we triangulate the graph by it`s faces traversal. Thirdly, during geometric postprocessing we process the graph in order to improve the surface quality (resolving ambiguities, surface smoothing, holes triangulation). Declared problem can also be solved by Marching Cubes algorithm. However, our approach allows to obtain surface of higher quality and less time spent. Similarly to Marching Cubes algorithm, in our approach we test a condition that is aimed to check for presence of the surface between two nodes with known scalar field values. In our heart CT-scans experiments we examined various forms of our conditions and reconstructed more surfaces than we did using classical Marching Cubes implementation. In addition, our method is fully automatic and doesn`t demand usage of supercomputers, but runs normally on desktop computers. Finally, our method is parallelized at all stages and possesses linear acceleration, relative to the number of processors, that is confirmed by theoretical estimates and experiments.

KEYWORDS

Surface Reconstruction, Marching Cubes, CT-scans, Segmentation, Graph

1. INTRODUCTION

Many applications for medical visualization, computer graphics and surface modeling imply reconstruction of surface from a sequence of contours allocated at parallel planes. Here is still pretty complicated problem without definite solution. Differences in contours` topology and layers` sparseness mean unlimited set of surfaces satisfying these contours.

The approach, proposed here, is an expansion of our previous (Novozhilov, 2016) method, which in it`s turn inherits from classical Marching Cubes algorithm. The latter method subdivides space into rectangular parallelepiped cells and reconstructs surface for each of them independently.

Our algorithm runs on CT data and reconstructs target surface through building contour-wise structures in all three dimensions. The surface is directly reconstructed in form of graph, that`s why we don`t have to join surface pieces into a single surface and to use postprocessing for ambiguities resolving and sharp angles elimination.

Input of our reconstruction algorithm is composed of CT-scans, represented by regular tomography grid, points of which have values, namely densities. Using these points and linear interpolation, scalar field values might be calculated for arbitrary point. Ensemble of points with the same value C, taken from the scalar field, form an abstract surface $f(x, y, z) = C$, *isosurface* we approximate, where C is an *isovalue*.

For the purpose of heart boundaries detection we use a number of conditions. The simplest of them (3.3.1) achieves it`s result our previous work alike (Novozhilov, 2016) and like classical implementation of Marching Cubes as well. For every edge we compare the scalar field values in it`s incident nodes with the isovalue, chosen in advance. The isovalue may be chosen by the user, that makes the method flexible and up to every possible CT-scans, despite their specifics, which can appear from one tomogram to another, cause every CT scanner might inherently differ from the others within CT scanning standards. In case the isovalue is bigger than one of the values and less than another, we say that a target surface point intersects this edge.

In the beginning of the paper we give on overview of related work, then we describe the reconstruction algorithm itself with it`s theoretical description, parallelization together with performance, triangulating of surface graph, surface quality experiments and performance experiments. Finally, we make a conclusion for our work.

2. RELATED WORK

Here in our work Marching Cubes (Lorensen, 1987) algorithm, which is popular nowadays, has been chosen as a base. The algorithm subdivides space into parallelepiped cells and reconstructs surface inside them independently. For every cell look-up table is used, that improves performance. The cells also provide an ability for good parallelization. Nevertheless, this method has ambiguities, which can lead to topology blackouts. Sample ambiguity appears when surfaces join one another in neighbor cells. The decision was proposed by Nielson and Hamann (Nielson, 1991). Another ambiguity presents for allocation of surface inside a cell, which Chernyaev (Chernyaev, 1995) studied in detail. Solutions, found by him, are amplified by Lewiner (Lewiner, 2003), where correct topology of target surface is guaranteed. Etiene (Etiene, 2012) introduced similar detailed survey of topology verification methods.

Further development of Marching Cubes algorithm is aimed at sharp features triangulation improvement. One of approaches implies usage of nonuniform grid. A parallelepiped cell is subdivided according to surface allocation inside. Detailed survey of such algorithms based on Marching Cubes is represented by Sreevalsan-Nair (Sreevalsan-Nair, 2007).

One more examined analogue named DELISO (Tamal, 2008) constructs adaptive Delaunay triangulation of isosurface. Method, where extended look-up table (Sundaresan, 2008) is used, allows to get rid of triangles with sharp angles and is more efficient than Sreevalsan-Nair`s (Sreevalsan-Nair, 2007). However, both DELISO (Tamal, 2008) and SnapMC (Sundaresan, 2008) might create duplicate triangles or vertices.

As a result, neither of studied papers presents an efficient algorithm for merging acquired surface`s patches into a single connected surface.

3. RECONSTRUCTION ALGORITHM

Our reconstruction algorithm consists of graph building and it`s triangulation.

3.1 Building Surface Graph

Here we firstly give theoretical description for our algorithm, then we describe it`s performance.

3.1.1 Theoretical Description

For our approach description let the sample tomogram be the one that is represented like a 3D rectangular grid of size $6 \times 5 \times 5$ with known scalar field values in it`s nodes. Building the model, we first process 2D regular grids orthogonal to Z axis.

Current 2D grid has the following enumeration for it`s nodes (Figure 1, A), which coincides with vertical edges enumeration (excepting the last raw of grid nodes` indices), and for horizontal edges (Figure 1, B).

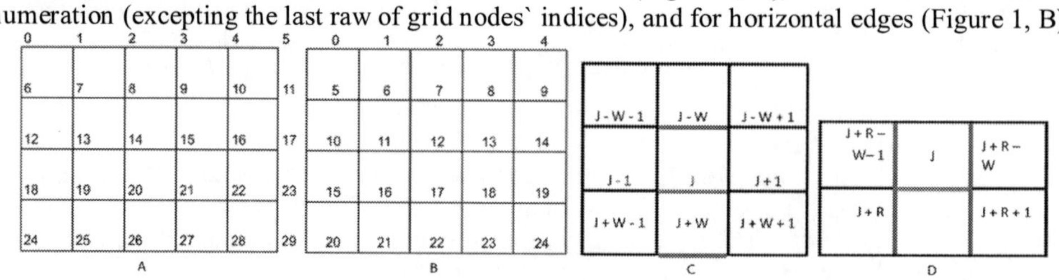

Figure 1. Grid nodes enumeration **(A)**; edges enumeration **(B)**; calculation of top and bottom edges` numbers **(C)**, where $W$ is width of the grid; and of left and right edges` numbers **(D)**, where $R = J / W$

For now the decision whether a point belongs to the target surface is made by our surface condition procedure (or just Surface Condition). Surface Condition can make a decision using distinct conditions. If we detect the point, the vertex position is interpolated (Figure 3, A, middle row).

Thus our algorithm deals with three types of vertices: 1) those lying on horizontal grid lines, 2) others, lying on vertical grid lines, 3) and remaining, lying on grid nodes. Together with the vertex type, appropriate edge number defines it`s grid position. Further, the number will be used in neighbor vertices calculation.

In neighbor vertices calculation we use criterion, according to which vertices allocated at the nearest edges are bound. There are three probable combinations of neighbors allocation for *horizontal* (which lie on horizontal edges, Figure 2A) and *vertical* (lying on vertical edges, Figure 2B) vertices.

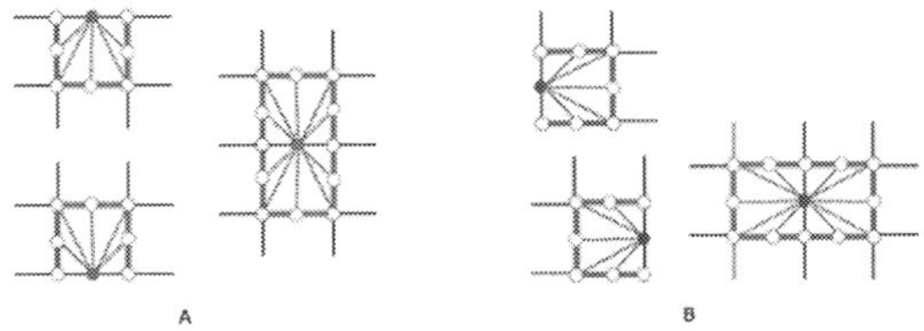

Figure 2. Calculation of vertices` connections. For each vertex we designate neighborhood, which borders upon probable neighbor vertices. Horizontal edges on the left, vertical edges on the right.

Appropriate edges are accessed in order to check for neighbor vertices located at them, using enumeration, suggested by us for vertical (the same for *central*) and horizontal vertices. Example of such vertices` numbers calculation is presented in Figure 1, C and D for edge *J*. The example is given concerning our assumption for the grid to be of size $6 \times 5 \times 5$.

The actions above allow us to build a contour consequence, orthogonal to Z axis (Figure 3A, top and middle rows).

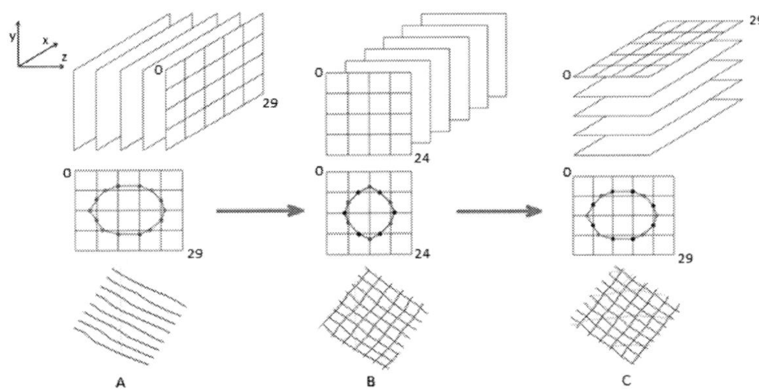

Figure 3. Top row: tomography grid. Middle row: current layer of tomography grid. Bottom row: result surface graph. Sequence of contours, orthogonal to Z axis (**A**, top and middle rows); sequence of contours, orthogonal to X axis (**B**, top and middle rows); sequence of contours, orthogonal to Y axis (**C**, top and middle rows)

Vertical and central vertices, that belong to grids, orthogonal to Z axis, belong also to grids, orthogonal to X axis. These vertices, along with their connections` information, are carried into grids, orthogonal to X axis (we suppose usage of a vertex index), and are correspondingly vertical or central. For the transfer we access appropriate edges using their enumeration. We also calculate new vertices (horizontal on Figure 3B, top and middle rows). After that the previously described algorithm of neighbor vertices calculation in every grid is applied.

At the last stage we don`t have to calculate new vertices, cause they are already calculated during previous stages. We just need to transfer them correctly: vertices, calculated at the first stage will remain horizontal; vertices, calculated at the second stage were firstly horizontal, but will become vertical. Connections calculation algorithm is then applied for each grid.

During vertices processing for a current layer they are saved in an appropriate local array. Then vertices connections` within a layer are calculated. After each layer processing new vertices are saved in a global array with theirs types and numbers, and the memory for a local array is released. Thus for CT-scans of size $N * N * N$ memory usage is about $O(N * N)$.

As a result we have surface graph, for which triangulation exists (Figure 3, A, B, C, bottom row). Sample graph had been reconstructed from CT-scans of a human head.

3.1.2 Parallelization and Performance

All the calculations are divided into independent parts. In our algorithm the most independent parts include layers processing within a single direction, as for each layer processing local buffers are used. These buffers are used in connections calculations, and newly calculated vertices (for the first and the second axes) or indices (for the second and the third axes) are added to the global buffer.

Taking into consideration the source data peculiarity (CT-scans), we suppose, that considerable difference of vertices quantity within two neighbor layers is unlikely to present, that guarantees minimal probability of standing idle. The maximal quantity of processors used is limited to tomogram size along appropriate axis, that is usually about some tens or hundreds layers.

In case the quantity of processors is less than tomogram size, one of possible decisions is to process a group of neighbor layers, which size is equal to accessible processors number. Then the less the group is, the higher is the probability of uniform load. However when processors quantity comes closer to tomogram size, the load can appear non-uniform.

3.2 Triangulating of Surface Graph

After reconstruction we have a minimal representation of surface in form of surface graph. In common case, the faces of this graph are not triangles, but the degree of a face is less or equal to six. If degree of face is bigger, we consider this face as external. Avoiding such faces we achieve an easy enough way of graph triangulation. Examples of surface graph faces are shown in Figure 4A.

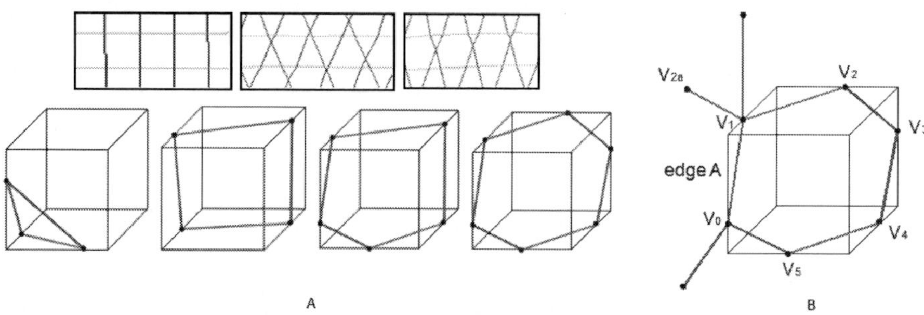

Figure 4. Faces of surface graph with degree from 3 to 6 and their 3D representation **(A)**; scheme of nodes of graph face collection **(B)**

In terms of axes` mutual orthogonality, let`s name layers, ejected from source tomography data, as planes. Since each edge of a face belongs to corresponding plane, orthogonal to appropriate axis, each face of degree from 3 to 6 lies on the cube surface as shown in Figure 4A. In order to triangulate surface graph we need to process all such graph faces. The algorithm consists of steps below:

1. Extract surface polylines that belong to a single surface graph plane,
2. On the current polyline, consider the edges in the order they follow (edge A in Figure 4B),
3. Collect nodes of a graph face. We can uniquely add V_0 and V_1,
4. Then we must collect nodes of two faces started from $\{V_0, V_1, V_2\}$ and $\{V_0, V_1, V_{2a}\}$. At all stages of the face formation we add a node, edge of which lies on the plane orthogonal to the plane of the current edge,
5. It is necessary to check the current three nodes for the presence on a single face, for example, by checking the list of face identifiers of each node. In case of positive result of the test, we say that this face already presents and finish this face traversal,

6. Choose the next node V_n, the one that lies on the same side of the edge plane (V_{n-1}, V_{n-2}) like a node V_{n-3},

7. When V_n is equal V_0, algorithm terminates successfully. Otherwise it exits when number of iterations is above six,

8. Obtain the graph face of degree from 3 to 6, which can be easily triangulated to the end.

3.3 Surface Quality Experiments

Preprocessing of our method includes scalar field denoising, that implies blurring of tomography grid values.

3.3.1 Simple Surface Condition

To calculate vertex position where isosurface $f(x,y,z) = C$ intersects the edge E of tomography grid, we use Surface Condition:

$$Scond(E) = \begin{cases} 1, \ if \ V_1 < C < V_2 \ or \ V_2 < C < V_1 \\ 0, otherwise \end{cases}, where$$

$$V_1, V_2 - values \ of \ scalar \ field \ at \ ends \ of \ edge \ E$$

If $Scond(E) = 1$, isosurface intersects the edge E of tomography grid. Then, we calculate vertex position P by linear interpolation:

$$P = P_1 + t * (P_2 - P_1), \qquad where$$

$$t = \frac{C - V_1}{V_2 - V_1},$$

$$P_1, P_2 - points \ of \ scalar \ field \ at \ ends \ of \ edge \ E$$

This condition usage results in surface in Figure 6, A and B.

This surface condition is also used in classical Marching Cubes algorithm.

3.3.2 Surface Condition for the Range of Isovalues

Sometimes usage of a single isovalue is not enough. In this case we consider isosurface $C_{min} < f(x,y,z) < C_{max}$ instead of $f(x,y,z) = C$. The example of such surface with isovalues range 40...100 is shown in Figure 5A.

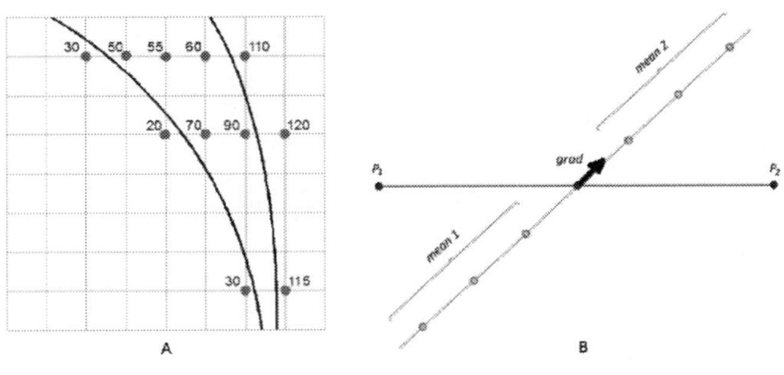

Figure 5. The surface of isovalue range **(A)**; calculations along gradient (edge $P_1 P_2$), where $k = 3$ **(B)**

As shown in Figure 5A, $Scond(E) = 1$ when field value of the one point of edge E belongs to the range, and another does not. To detect this surface we change the surface condition in reconstruction algorithm:

$$Scond(E) = \begin{cases} 1, \ if \ (V_{min} > C_{max} \ or \ V_{min} < C_{min}) \ and \ V_{max} < C_{max} \ and \ V_{max} > C_{min} \ or \\ (V_{max} > C_{max} \ or \ V_{max} < C_{min}) \ and \ V_{min} < C_{max} \ and \ V_{min} > C_{min} \ or \\ V_{min} < C_{min} \ and \ V_{max} > C_{max} \\ 0, otherwise \end{cases}, where$$

$$V_{min}, V_{max} - minimal \ and \ maximal \ scalar \ field \ values \ of \ end \ points \ of \ edge \ E$$

The vertex position is calculated similarly to the simple surface condition.

As shown in Figure 6D, we found more surfaces than using simple surface condition. However at triangulation stage (Figure 6C) we obtain a bigger quantity of ambiguities as well. In future work, we are going to improve our method to get better surface quality.

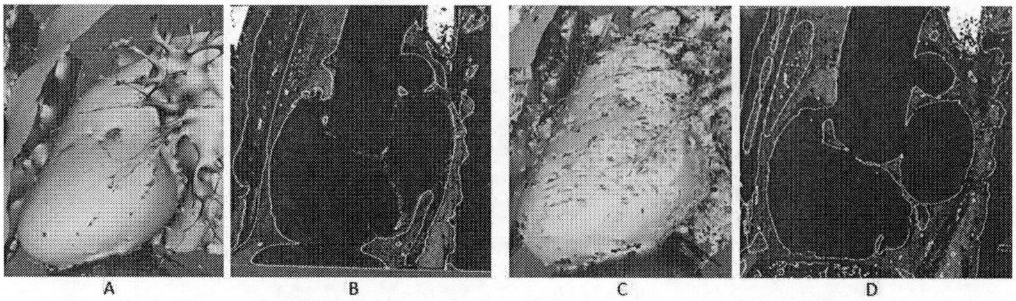

Figure 6. Heart surface **(A)** and sample projection **(B)** (vertical cut, lateral view) with surface points (white), reconstructed using simple surface condition; heart surface **(C)** and sample projection **(D)** with surface points (white), reconstructed using surface condition with isovalue range

3.3.3 Surface Condition with Gradient Used

The third variant of Surface Condition works using gradient, calculated in points of edge E, which is divided into some equal segments. For every edge`s point we compute gradient as 3D vector, which is estimated using central differences:

$$grad = \left(\frac{f(x+\Delta,y,z) - f(x-\Delta,y,z)}{2\Delta}, \frac{f(x,y+\Delta,z) - f(x,y-\Delta,z)}{2\Delta}, \frac{f(x,y,z+\Delta) - f(x,y,z-\Delta)}{2\Delta}\right),$$

where Δ is the same for all three dimensions. This parameter shouldn`t be neither too small (in order to cross over CT noise), nor too large (to not overlap inter-tissues` passages).

As this implementation of Surface Condition is gradient-based, after calculation of the gradient, we pace along gradient forth and back with the same steps` number (k) and the same step size. For each side we calculate arithmetical means (Figure 5B) and compare them in a way, similar to the simple surface condition.

This condition usage results in surface in Figure 7.

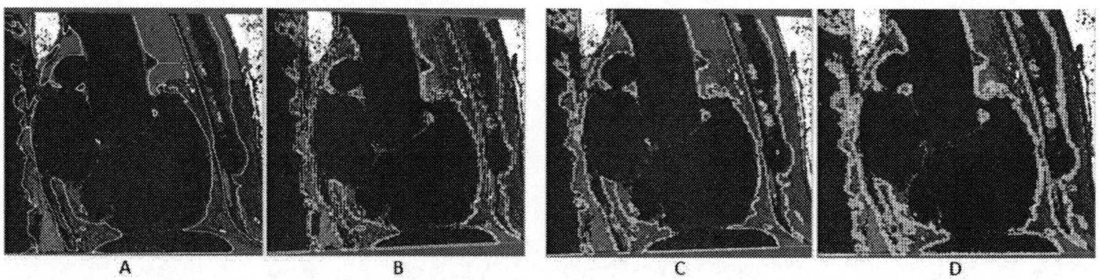

Figure 7. Contours, achieved using 2D gradient **(A, B)** and 3D gradient **(C, D)**, $k = 1$ for two left images, $k = 3$ for two right images

3.4 Performance Experiments

The results below were achieved on Intel®Core™i5 750 2.66 GHz processor. We present performance of surface reconstruction (graph building and triangulation) in Table 1 to compare our algorithm with Marching Cubes (Lorensen, 1987) implementation (Bourke, 1994), amplified with optimized procedure of searching for common vertices for neighbor 3D rectangular cells. The results below repeat those from our previous work (Novozhilov, 2016). We used one of the simplest implementations of Marching Cubes (Bourke, 1994) in order to show the difference between surfaces merging procedure in neighbor cells in Marching Cubes and our algorithm appropriately. Nevertheless, our method is applicable for more complicated algorithms.

Table 1. Comparison with Marching Cubes Implementation

Graph building and triangulation, using Marching Cubes		Graph building and triangulation, using our approach	
Number of nodes	Time	Number of nodes	Time
44188	5,940	40617	2,423
75174	13,100	83458	6,117
109627	20,083	118574	8,560
177577	43,046	176668	12,112
242750	59,804	259546	17,301

Below (Table 2) the last performance results of surface reconstruction are represented. G is graph building stage, T is triangulation stage.

Table 2. Efficiency of graph building and triangulation, the 1st dimension of dataset is represented in the first column, the 2nd and the 3rd are appropriately equal to 512 and 554

Size	Number of nodes	Number of primitives	Time, 1 core			Time, 2 cores			Time, 4 cores			Speed-up, 2 cores	Speed-up, 4 cores
			G	T	G+T	G	T	G+T	G	T	G+T		
100	40617	79175	1,35	0,176	1,526	0,703	0,167	0,87	0,388	0,142	0,53	1,754	2,879
150	83458	164399	2,119	0,375	2,494	1,089	0,335	1,424	0,59	0,29	0,88	1,751	2,834
200	118574	234291	2,852	0,505	3,357	1,492	0,463	1,955	0,82	0,362	1,182	1,717	2,840
250	176668	348229	3,734	0,776	4,51	1,902	0,663	2,565	1,022	0,562	1,584	1,758	2,847
300	259546	511675	4,618	1,152	5,77	2,396	1,047	3,443	1,322	0,872	2,194	1,676	2,630
350	300297	593264	5,495	1,34	6,835	2,815	1,17	3,985	1,5	0,995	2,495	1,715	2,739
400	345159	682275	6,316	1,561	7,877	3,238	1,329	4,567	1,712	1,118	2,83	1,725	2,783
450	391994	776147	7,101	1,741	8,842	3,597	1,49	5,087	1,931	1,287	3,218	1,738	2,748
500	408058	807901	7,863	1,79	9,653	3,99	1,589	5,579	2,173	1,312	3,485	1,730	2,770

As it is represented in Table 2, processing of different numbers of nodes and primitives gives almost the same acceleration. Also, our algorithm doesn`t significantly differ from SnapMC (Sundaresan, 2008), launched at almost equivalent processor.

4. CONCLUSION

We improve our previous method (Novozhilov, 2016) by implementing parallelized triangulation and new surface condition that allows to find higher quantity of surfaces. Besides, we don`t get repeating triangles or vertices.

The proposed approach is applicable for such cases as well, where the output must contain not only triangles set, but also information about vertices and their connections. Such information may be significantly useful for further processing.

Comparing three types of Surface Condition with one another, we can announce, that all the three show results, that are expected in terms of real heart boundaries and are relevant to one another, that proves their correctness.

Moreover, in our reconstruction method we investigated a common case, where we were looking for a surface point along gradients` directions built on an edge of tomography grid, and a particular case, where we were searching for a surface point at the edge itself. We discovered, that results of these both cases almost coincide. Hence, we can state, that going through tomogram`s native points is sufficient for surface vertex search.

The main directions of future research include surface quality improvement and algorithm optimization for approximating to real-time mode, necessity of which is claimed by real clinical conditions. For clinical practice it`s also vital to provide possibility of real-time parameters tuning, in order to allow specialists to search for the best of them, so that the reconstructed surface fits tissues` boundaries on CT-scans precisely enough.

REFERENCES

Bourke Paul. 1994. Polygonising a scalar field:. URL: http://paulbourke.net/geometry/polygonise/, (accessed: 19.04.2018).

Chernyaev E.V. 1995. Marching Cubes 33: Construction of Topologically Correct Isosurfaces. *CERN*. Technical Report No. CN/95-17.

Etiene T. et al, June 2012. Topology Verification for Isosurface Extraction. *IEEE Trans. Visualization & Computer Graphics*. Vol. 18, no. 6, pp. 952-965.

Lorensen W. E. and Cline H. E. 1987. Marching Cubes: A high Resolution 3D Surface Construction Algorithm. *Computer Graphics.* Vol. 21, No. 4. pp. 163–169

Lewiner T. et al, 2003. Efficient Implementation of Marching Cubes' Cases with Topological Guarantees. *Graphics Tools*. Vol. 8, No. 2. pp. 1-15.

Nielson G.M. and Hamann B. 1991. The Asymptotic Decider: Resolving the Ambiguity in Marching Cubes. *Proc. 2nd conference on Visualization (VIS' 91).* San Diego, California. pp. 83–91.

Novozhilov M.M. and Kochukov M.P. 2016. Parallel reconstruction method in orthogonal planes. *Proceedings of the 10th Annual International Scientific Conference on Parallel Computing Technologies.* Arkhangelsk, Russia, pp. 629-641.

Sundaresan Raman and Rephael Wenger, May 26-28, 2008. Quality Isosurface Mesh Generation Using an Extended Marching Cubes Lookup Table. *Proceedings of the 10th Joint Eurographics / IEEE - VGTC conference on Visualization.* Eindhoven, The Netherlands, pp. 791-798.

Sreevalsan-Nair et al, 2007. Topologically Accurate Dual Isosurfacing Using Ray Intersection. *JVRB - Journal of Virtual Reality and Broadcasting*. 4(2007), no. 4.

Tamal K. Dey and Joshua A. Levine, May 2008. Delaunay meshing of isosurfaces. *The Visual Computer: International Journal of Computer Graphics.* Vol. 24, No. 6, pp. 411-422.

A BLIND WATERMARKING METHOD FOR CITYGML

Dayou Jiang[1] and Jongweon Kim[2]
[1]*Dept. of Copyright Protection, Sangmyung University, Seoul, Korea*
[2] *Corresponding author, Dept. of Electronics Engineering, Sangmyung University, Seoul, Korea*

ABSTRACT

We propose a blind watermarking method for CityGML in this paper. Firstly, we parse the CityGML text file and select the virtual 3D city model for watermarking. Secondly, we transform the model by using geometric invariance. Then, we transform the Cartesian coordinate to the Spherical coordinate to obtain the sphere radii of each vertex. Finally, we insert the watermark by altering the DCT coefficients of the sphere radii segment. We conduct several experiments using different parameters to explore the watermark payload. The method can embed 64 bits watermark into a CityGML model. In addition, it shows good robustness against adding noise, rotation, uniform scaling, translation, and vertices reordering attacks. However, it still has drawbacks under cropping and simplification attacks.

KEYWORDS

CityGML, Watermarking, Geometric, Spherical, DCT

1. INTRODUCTION

CityGML is a common semantic information model for 3D urban object representation. Unlike other virtual 3D city models, it can not only be used for visualization but can for thematic queries, analysis tasks, and spatial data mining. What is more, it enables lossless information exchange between different geographic information system and users (Gröger et al., 2012). With the increasing demand of virtual 3D city models for applications like urban planning, tourism, and environmental simulations from a large number of cities and companies, CityGML is especially important with respect to the cost-effective sustainable maintenance of 3D city models.

Although CityGML is an open data model, it can be shared over different commercial applications. So far, there have been no researches on the CityGML model copyright protection. Thus, the development of a copyright protection technology for CityGML models is an urgent problem to be solved.

In the work, we present a blind watermark method for protecting the copyright of CityGML model. The method applies the geometry transformation invariance and embeds the watermark by altering the DCT coefficient of sphere radii in each partition.

The remainder of this paper is organized as follows: Section 2 reviews the related works; Section 3 presents the watermark embedding and extraction procedures; Section 4 presents some experimental results; Section 5 concludes the paper and proposes future working directions.

2. RELATED WORKS

2.1 Feasible Information for Watermarking

CityGML is an application schema based on a number of standard formats from ISO 191xx family, the Open Geospatial Consortium (OGC), the W3C Consortium, the Web 3D Consortium, and OASIS (Gröger et al., 2012). CityGML stores different kinds of objects in the City. It not only includes Building, LandUse, CityFurniture, but also includes Bridge, Transportation, Tunnel, Vegetation, WaterBody and more. It defines the geometrical, topological, semantical, and appearance properties of objects and also stores the relationships between relevant objects. The new classes and attributes of core modules can be extended by defining Application Domain Extension (ADEs).

The objects are stored by using a set of text files and some accompanying images. The text file can represent a specific region, object or a predefined Level Of Detail (LOD). CityGML supports five different LODs. LOD0 is the coarsest level and LOD4 requires the highest 3D point coordinates accuracy. Different each object can have a different representation for every LOD. Different LODs are used for different application requirements.

We have analyzed the feasible information of CityGML for watermarking in reference (Jiang and Kim, 2017). The classical watermarking method likes using the images with a high content of textures because they provide more capacity for data hiding than the one without textures. However, most of the texture images for CityGML are simplex and the brightness difference between pixels is extremely little. The location and size of texture maps are not fixed. For example, the whole grass texture image or part of it may be used several times and mapped according to the locations of LandUse objects. Thus, it is quite complex to extract and recover the watermark in those texture images. XML as a markup language, naturally, can be as a carrier for watermark likes other markup languages. What is more, the attacks on CityGML dataset will bring spatial information changes and the markup language will not be affected. The XML watermarking method by altering the case of letters in the XMLtags is time-consuming. The spatial information of CityGML must be parsed through those markups. Consequently, changing the standard structure of XML file for watermarking is not conducive to parse XML.

After parsing the XML file, the spatial information of mass points, lines, faces, and topologies can be obtained. Therefore, the good ideas and approaches of watermarking methods for 3D models can be borrowed for CityGML models.

2.2 Watermarking Methods for 3D Models

Most of the watermarking methods for 3D models are targeted geometric shapes of 3D polygonal meshes. A few are based on the vertexes, curves, surfaces and mesh spectra.

(Ohbuchi et al., 2001) embedded the watermark into a 3D polygonal mesh in the mesh's spectral domain. The mesh spectra are computed from the eigenvalue decomposition of a Laplacian matrix by using the connectivity of the mesh. The method is robust to common geometric transformation attacks. The method requires much computational cost and it is not blind. (Yu et al., 2003) embedded the watermark via perturbing the length of the vectors that extend from a surface vertex to the center of the model. The watermarking strength is adaptive with respect to the local geometry of the model and it is applicable to models that have a relatively small number of meshes. The method is withstood to mesh simplification and cropping attacks. However, it also needs original models for watermark extraction. (Uccheddu et al., 2004) proposed a wavelet-based blind watermarking of the 3D model. The work firstly using the PCA to normalize the model mesh and then embedding the watermark by perturbing the wavelet coefficient according to the value of the watermarking map indexed by the polar coordinates of the application point of the wavelet coefficient. The high-resolution polygons are decomposed into a low-resolution part and a detail part, while the detail parts are expressed as the wavelet coefficient vectors. The model meshes are designed as semi-regular meshes, thus they are can be decomposed with applying wavelet idea. Nonetheless, the work is not applicable to the CityGML model. (Abdallah et al., 2007) proposed method is not blind and similar to (Ohbuchi et al., 2001). But the work embedded the watermark into the smaller sub-meshes. The work embedded 16 bits watermark and showed a perfect resiliency against cropping and smoothing attacks. (Huang et al., 2013) and (Wang et al., 2014) proposed fragile watermarking schemes for 3D models respectively used the spherical coordinates and hamming code. Both of them can protect the integrity of 3D models and without the problem of embedding holes. (Zhan et al., 2003) proposed method is based on the vertex curvature. The work firstly calculates the root mean square curvature fluctuation of a vertex and then those reordered vertices are divided into some bins. The fluctuation value of vertex in each bin is normalized. Finally, the mean fluctuation values are modulated for embedding watermark. The work can resist several attacks. For that reason that the polygons of CityGML are irregular, the root mean square curvature values of the vertexes are hard to compute. (Abdallah et al., 2015) proposed a blind watermarking scheme. The work is based on vertex distribution and skewness measure. The vertices are divided into separate intervals with an equal range according to the radial distances and then the skewness measure in each interval is modified. The work shows a great resiliency against the most common attacks for models that consist of a large number of vertices and faces. For cropping attack, (Konstantinides et al., 2009) divided the mesh surface into many discrete continuous regions and then sampled and mapped the regions onto oblate spheroids. (Mun et al., 2015) used the surface diameter function segmentation to get partitions and then inserted the watermark into each bin of the histogram of vertex norm distribution in each pair. The watermark payload is 16 and the watermark can be extracted properly even under the cropping ratio of 40%. (Rolland-Neviere et al., 2015) proposed a novel synchronization strategy devised to resist cropping attacks based on landmark vertices. The work relocates the neighboring vertices via active-set optimization to reach the positive detection subspace. Recently, (Wang et al., 2017) proposed a watermark scheme based on the area of the local set of vertex against geometric attacks. The work classified the vertices into three groups (low-resolution, medium-resolution, high-resolution) by controlling the number of vertices in each group. The vertices in the low-resolution group are used to establish the invariant coordinate system. The watermarked vertices are determined by the area of the two-ring neighborhood and the embedding strength is based on the curvature of the vertices. However, the work is not blind because high-resolution vertices are reserved for resisting simplification and smoothing attacks. (El Zein et al., 2017) proposed method used the Fuzzy C-Mean clustering technique to determine the location of the vertices to secret watermark data in 3D mesh models. The statistical measurements like the average and standard deviation are used to alter the value of watermarked vertices. Nevertheless, the work needs original models to achieve high robustness. (Liu et al., 2017) proposed method also used the partition idea. The work used the multi-resolution adaptive parameterization of surface (MAPS) approach to categorizing the vertices into two levels. The vertices at the coarse level are used to establish an invariant space. The vertices of the fine level are selected as feature vertices to secret the watermark.

3. PROPOSED WATERMARKING METHOD

Although the CityGML data consist of huge vertices and polygons, some watermarking algorithms that can be applied to the normal 3D model are not suitable for CityGML a model watermarking.

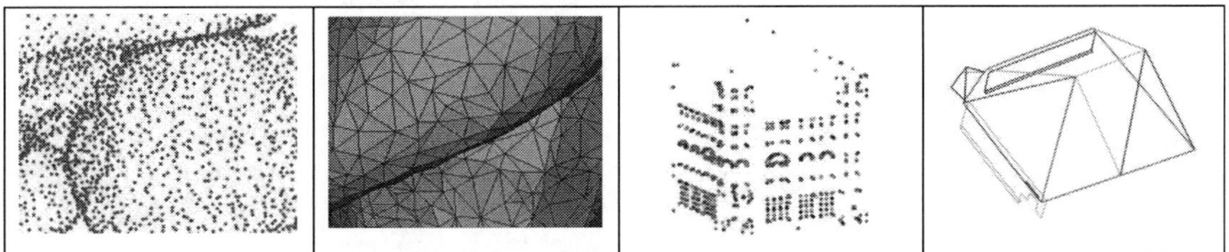

(a) Vertices- normal model | (b) Meshes - normal model | (c) Vertices - CityGML | (d) Polygons - CityGML

Figure 1. Comparing Examples of Spatial Information between CityGMLand Normal Model

As shown in Figure 1, the vertices in normal 3D models are nearly evenly distributed and its faces are all triangles. The area differences between those faces are not big. However, in CityGML model, the numbers of vertices are smaller, the distance difference between adjacent vertices is relatively larger and the shape of the face is not uniform.

Compared to the faces, the vertices can carry much more watermark information. Embedding the watermark by perturbing the coordinate values is relatively simpler than using faces and lines information. The normal, curvatures, and areas will not be used due to the irregular faces of CityGML models. Accordingly, in the work, we proposed a blind watermarking based on the vertices. To resist several common attacks, we normalize the model and embed the watermark in the DCT domain.

3.1 Watermarking Embedding

The watermark embedding procedure is as follows:

Step 1: Parsing the CityGML text file to obtain the spatial information of vertices and faces. The set of unique vertices of the object is expressed as

$$V = \{v_i \in R^3 \mid 0 \le i \le N_v - 1\} \tag{1}$$

N_v is the number of vertices. Vertex $v_i = (x_i, y_i, z_i)$ represents the coordinates in CityGML coordinates. And v_c is the center vertex which is calculated

$$v_c = (s_c, y_c, z_c) = (\sum_0^{N_v-1} v_i) / N_v \tag{2}$$

Step 2: Calculating the Scale factor F_s by using

$$F_s = \frac{1}{N_v}\sqrt{(\sum_0^{N_v-1}(x_i - x_c)^2 + \sum_0^{N_v-1}(y_i - y_c)^2 + \sum_0^{N_v-1}(z_i - z_c)^2)/3} \tag{3}$$

The vertices set after applying uniform scaling is set as

$$VS = V / F_s \tag{4}$$

Step 3: Calculating rotation matrix T_r. Using the PCA algorithm. The set of absolute vertex value after PCA normalization is *VSR*. Hence, T_r is defined as

$$T_r = VSR^T / VS^T \tag{5}$$

Step 4: Calculating the center vertex of *VSR* and obtain the translation invariance vertices set *VSRT* by

$$VSRT(x', y', z') = VSR - \frac{1}{N_v}\sum_0^{N_v-1} VSR \tag{6}$$

Step 5: Transforming the Cartesian coordinate's vertices set *VSRT* to the spherical coordinate's vertices set $SpVSRT(r,\phi,\theta)$. Here, r, ϕ, and θ are computed by

$$r = \sqrt{x'^2 + y'^2 + z'^2}, \phi = a\cos(z'/r), \theta = a\tan(y'/r) \tag{7}$$

Step 6: Reordering the sphere radius at the ascending order to resist the vertices reordering attack. The reordering sphere radius set is *Rr*.

Step 7: Divided the *Rr* into blocks with equal size, the size is set N_b. The partition set is *PRr*. The j th partition is defined as

$$PRr_j = [Rr_{N_b*(j-1)+1}, Rr_{N_b*(j-1)+2}, \ldots, Rr_{N_b*j}], 1 \le j \le floor(N_v / N_b) \tag{8}$$

Step 8: Applying DCT transform for each partition *PRrj* and obtain the first DCT coefficient $DctPRr_j$.

Step 9: Inserting watermark Wm to the CityGML model by altering the value of $DctPRr_j$ using Quantitative Investment Management (QIM) algorithm (Chen and Wornell, 2001). The step size is set *Ds*. The number of watermark bits to be inserted is N_w. The quotient m_j and remainder r_j can be calculated by

$$m_j = floor(DctPRr_j / Ds), r_j = DctPRr_j - m_j * D_s \tag{9}$$

For example, if the watermark value is 1, altering $DctPRr_j$ as follows:

If the watermark value is 1, altering $DctPRr_j$ as follows:

$$DctPRr_j = \begin{cases} (m_j + 0.5) * Ds & if \bmod(m_j, 2) == 0 \\ (m_j - 0.5) * Ds\ if \bmod(m_j, 2) == 1 \& \mid r_j \mid \le 0.5Ds \\ (m_j + 1.5) * Ds\ if \bmod(m_j, 2) == 1 \& \mid r_j \mid \mathrm{f}\ 0.5Ds \end{cases} \tag{10}$$

If the watermark value is -1, altering $DctPRr_j$ as follows:

$$DctPRr_j = \begin{cases} (m_j + 0.5) * Ds & if \bmod(m_j, 2) == 1 \\ (m_j - 0.5) * Ds\ if \bmod(m_j, 2) == 0 \& \mid r_j \mid \le 0.5Ds \\ (m_j + 1.5) * Ds\ if \bmod(m_j, 2) == 0 \& \mid r_j \mid \mathrm{f}\ 0.5Ds \end{cases} \tag{11}$$

Step 10: Inversing the DCT transform. Replacing the original first coefficient values with the watermarked coefficient $DctPRr_j'$. Obtaining the watermarked sphere radius R_r'.

Step 11: Transforming the spherical coordinate to the Cartesian coordinate. Obtaining the watermarked vertices *WVSRT(Wx, Wy, Wz)*.

$$WVSRT = \begin{cases} Wx = Rr'\sin\phi\cos\theta \\ Wy = Rr'\sin\phi\sin\theta \\ Wz = Rr'\cos\phi \end{cases} \tag{12}$$

Step 12: Reversing the watermarked vertices set WV by using the transformation matrix

$$WV = (T_r^{-1} * (WVSRT + \sum_0^{N_v} VSR / N_v)^T) * F_s \tag{13}$$

3.2 Watermark Extraction

The extraction procedure is as follows:

Step 1-8: The processes are the same as watermark embedding.

Step 9: Extracting watermark EWm' from the value of $DctPRr_j''$ of the test CityGML object by using QIM algorithm. The step size is set D_s. The number of watermark bits is N_w. The quotient m_j' and remainder r_j' can be calculated by

$$m_j' = floor(DctPRr_j'' / D_s), r_j' = DctPRr_j'' - m_j' * D_s \tag{14}$$

Then, we use the inverse transform to extract the watermark based on the value of $DctPRr_j''$, m_j', and r_j'.

Step 10: Obtaining each binary watermark bit by adding the watermark value from each N_w length part. The length of the extracted watermark EWm' is N_{wl}. The number of watermark part is N_p. Where $N_p = floor(N_{wl} / N_w)$ and the final k th extracted watermark Wm'_k is defined as

$$Wm'_k = sign(\sum_{d=1}^{d=N_p} EWm'_{(d-1)*N_w+k}) \mid 0 \le k \le N_w - 1 \tag{15}$$

4. EXPERIMENTAL RESULTS AND ANALYSIS

4.1 Evaluation Methods

The Vertex Signal-to-noise Ratio (VSNR) (Soliman et al., 2013) is used to determine the perceptual variations between the original and watermarked models. Where Nv is the number of all unique vertex, (X_j, Y_j, Z_j) and (X_j*, Y_j*, Z_j*) are the original and altered Cartesian coordinates of the vertices.

$$SNR = \frac{\sum_{j=1}^{Nv} X_j^2 + Y_j^2 + Z_j^2}{\sum_{j=1}^{Nv}\left[(X_j - X_j^*)^2 + (Y_j - Y_j^*)^2 + (Z_j - Z_j^*)^2\right]} \tag{16}$$

$$VSNR = 10\log_{10}(SNR) \tag{17}$$

The correlation coefficient (Wang et al., 2011) Cor is used to estimate the robustness of the method. Where Wm' and Wm are the extracted watermark and original watermark, respectively. Nw is the length of the watermark, $\overline{Wm'}$ and $\overline{Wm}$ are the mean value of Wm' and Wm, respectively.

$$Cor(Wm', Wm) = \frac{\sum_{i=1}^{Nw}(Wm_i' - \overline{Wm'})(Wm_i - \overline{Wm})}{\sqrt{\sum_{i=1}^{Nw}(Wm_i' - \overline{Wm'})^2 \sum_{i=1}^{Nv}(Wm_i - \overline{Wm})^2}} \tag{18}$$

4.2 Experimental Results

We conduct experiments on several objects in a CityGML model. The building object No.1 has 1895 vertices and 1194 faces. The visualized Object is shown in Figure 2(a), its vertices and faces are shown in Figure 2(b) and Figure (c), respectively.

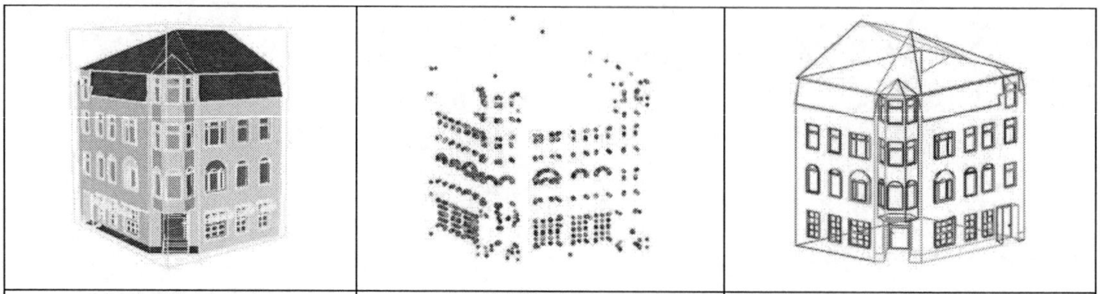

(a) Visualized model | (b) Vertices | (c) Faces

Figure 2. Example of an Object in CityGML Model

The building object No.2 has 878 vertices and 587 faces. The building object No.3 has 1251 vertices and 884 faces. The Vegetation object No.1 has 535 vertices and 378 faces. The CityFurniture object No.1 has 1038 vertices and 815 faces. The visualized Objects of them are respectively as shown in Figure 3(a) ~ Figure 3(d).

(a) Building No.2 | (b) Building No.3 | (c) Vegetation No.1 | (d) CityFurniture No.1

Figure 3. Example of Sample Objects in CityGML Model

In the experiments, the QIM step size is 0.02. Watermarks' lengths L-wm are 16, 32 and 64. The block sizes L-dct for DCT are 4, 6 and 8. The VSNR values of watermarked models are listed in Table 1.

Table 1. Results of VSNR of Watermarked Models under Different Embedding Parameters

Conditions	L-wm 16			L-wm 32			L-wm 64		
	L-dct 4	L-dct 6	L-dct 8	L-dct 4	L-dct 6	L-dct 8	L-dct 4	L-dct 6	L-dct 8
VSNR	183.05	184.89	186.44	182.61	184.86	185.95	182.07	184.35	185.88

We add the noise with different strength to the watermarked models. Firstly, we calculate the maximum distance of the sphere radius and then add the noises onto the randomly selected vertices with different strength. Figure 4 shows watermarked models under different noise attacks. Here, L-dct is 4, L-wm is 64.

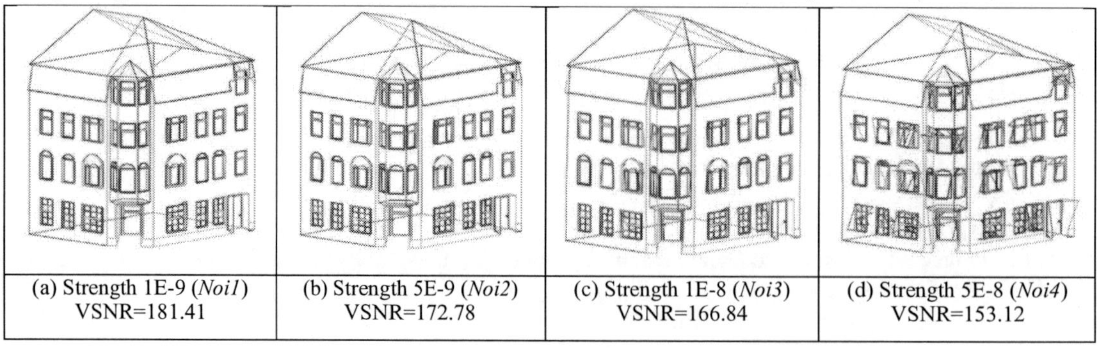

(a) Strength 1E-9 (*Noi1*) VSNR=181.41 | (b) Strength 5E-9 (*Noi2*) VSNR=172.78 | (c) Strength 1E-8 (*Noi3*) VSNR=166.84 | (d) Strength 5E-8 (*Noi4*) VSNR=153.12

Figure 4. Example of Noised Watermarked CityGML

The watermarks used are shown in Figure 5.

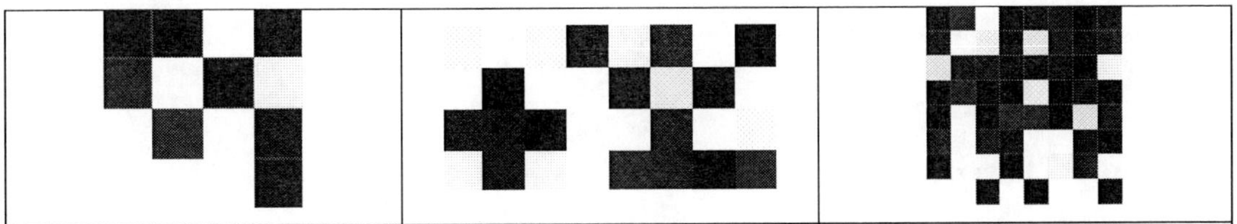

(a) Length 16 | (b) Length 32 | (c) Length 64

Figure 5. Watermarks with Different Lengths

The experimental results are listed in Table 2, here, Noi0 represents without noise.

Table 2. Results of Cor Under Noise Attack of Building No.1

L-dct	L-wm	Noi0	Noi1	Noi2	Noi3	Noi4
4	16	1	1	1	1	0.126
	32	1	1	1	0.8246	0.1697
	64	1	1	0.8606	0.5767	-0.063
6	16	1	1	1	0.8819	0.2582
	32	1	1	1	0.4497	-0.055
	64	1	1	0.6818	0.2806	0.0861
8	16	1	1	1	0.7746	0
	32	1	1	0.777	0.5983	0.1525
	64	1	0.9656	0.5315	0.1741	0.0274

We find that the block size of 4 for DCT has better robustness than other sizes. The method can insert 64 bits watermark with good robustness. For the next attack experiments, we use the L-dct with 4 and L-wm with 32 bits. We set the threshold of 0.5. If the Cor value is larger than 0.5, thus, the test model will be regarded as the copyrighted model.

Stretching the model in X, Y and Z direction in respectively, the corresponding Cor values are 0.012, -0.1156 and -0.2471. Stretching the model in X, Y and Z direction with the same scale factor 2 at the same time, the corresponding Cor value is 1. Therefore, the method can resist uniform scale attacks.

Rotating the model in X, Y and Z direction with the same angle 30° respectively, the corresponding Cor values are 0.749, 0.8246 and 0.886. Rotating the model in X, Y and Z direction with the same angle 30° at the same time, the corresponding Cor value is 0.6314. So the method can resist uniform rotation attacks.

Because before the watermark embedding and extraction process, the sphere radii of vertices are sorted in the ascending order, consequently, the method can resist vertices reordering attacks.

Nevertheless, the method is not robust against the cropping and simplification attacks. Even when 10% the vertices have been deleted, the Cor value is -0.2426. Since that the topology of CityGML faces is differed to the normal 3D models, the detected watermark from the cropping and simplification CityGML model inevitably has much more errors. In this case, the topology of the original and the geometry of the attacked object for resampling should be obtained, but the method will not be blind.

5. CONCLUSIONS

In the paper, a blind watermarking method based on geometric invariance and DCT for CityGML models has been presented. The geometric invariance can resist geometric transformations. Embedding the watermark in the spherical coordinates can simplify the embedding process. What is more, the sphere radius has good stability. DCT coefficient is used to resist the noises. However, the method is fragile to the cropping and simplification attacks without using the original models. We intend to develop an anti-cropping watermarking method by using salient points of CityGML.

ACKNOWLEDGEMENT

This work was supported by Ministry of Culture, Sports and Tourism (MCST) and Korea Creative Content Agency (KOCCA) in the Culture Technology (CT) Research & Development Program 2017

REFERENCES

Abdallah et al., 2007) Abdallah, E. E., Hamza, A. B., and Bhattacharya, P. 2007. Spectral graph-theoretic approach to 3D mesh watermarking. In Proceedings of graphics interface 2007, pp. 327-334. ACM,

(Abdallah et al., 2015) Abdallah, A. E., Abdallah, E. E., Bsoul, M., Al–Khasawneh, A., and Amer, L. 2015. A blind 3D watermarking technique using spherical coordinates and skewness measure. International Journal of Security and Networks, Vol.10, No.1, pp.1-8.

(Chen and Wornell, 2001) Chen, B., and Wornell, G. W. 2001. Quantization index modulation methods for digital watermarking and information embedding of multimedia. Journal of VLSI signal processing systems for signal, image and video technology, Vol. 27, No.1-2, pp.7-33

(El Zein et al., 2017) El Zein, O. M., El Bakrawy, L. M., and Ghali, N. I. 2017. A robust 3D mesh watermarking algorithm utilizing fuzzy C-Means clustering. Future Computing and Informatics Journal. pp.148-156

(Gröger et al., 2012) Gröger, G., Kolbe, T. H., Nagel, C., and Häfele, K. H. 2012. OGC City Geography Markup Language (CityGML) Encoding Standard, https://www.citygml.org/

(Huang et al., 2013) Huang, C. C., Yang, Y. W., Fan, C. M., and Wang, J. T. 2013. A spherical coordinate based fragile watermarking scheme for 3D models. In International Conference on Industrial, Engineering and Other Applications of Applied Intelligent Systems, Springer, Berlin, Heidelberg. pp. 566-571.

(Jiang and Kim, 2017) Jiang, D. Y., and Kim, J. W. 2017. A Zero-Watermarking Scheme for CityGML. 2017 International Workshop on Convergence Information Technology (IWCIT), Busan, Korea, pp.19-22, December 2017

(Konstantinides et al., 2009) Konstantinides, J. M., Mademlis, A., Daras, P., Mitkas, P. A., and Strintzis, M. G. 2009. Blind robust 3-D mesh watermarking based on oblate spheroidal harmonics. IEEE Transactions on Multimedia, Vol.11, No.1, pp. 23-38.

(Liu et al., 2017) Liu, J., Wang, Y., Li, Y., Liu, R., and Chen, J. 2017. A robust and blind 3D watermarking algorithm using multiresolution adaptive parameterization of surface, Neurocomputing, 237, pp. 304-315.

(Mun et al., 2015) Mun, S. M., Jang, H. U., Kim, D. G., Choi, S., and Lee, H. K. 2015. A robust 3D mesh watermarking scheme against cropping. In 2015 International Conference on 3D Imaging (IC3D), pp. 1-6.

(Ohbuchi et al., 2001) Ohbuchi, R., Takahashi, S., Miyazawa, T., and Mukaiyama, A. 2001. Watermarking 3D polygonal meshes in the mesh spectral domain. In Graphics interface, Vol. 2001, pp. 9-17.

(Rolland-Neviere et al., 2015) Rolland-Neviere, X., Doërr, G., and Alliez, P. 2015. Anti-cropping blind resynchronization for 3D watermarking. In 2015 IEEE International Conference on Acoustics, Speech and Signal Processing (ICASSP), pp. 1702-1706.

(Soliman et al., 2013) Soliman, M. M., Hassanien, A. E., and Onsi, H. M. 2013. Robust watermarking approach for 3D triangular mesh using self-organization map. 2013 8th International Conference on Computer Engineering & Systems (ICCES), pp. 99-104.

(Uccheddu et al., 2004) Uccheddu, F., Corsini, M., and Barni, M. 2004. Wavelet-based blind watermarking of 3D models. In Proceedings of the 2004 workshop on Multimedia and security, pp. 143-154.

(Wang et al., 2011) Wang, K., Lavoué, G., Denis, F., and Baskurt, A. 2011. Robust and blind mesh watermarking based on volume moments. Computers & Graphics, Vol. 35, No.1, pp. 1-19

(Wang et al., 2014) Wang, J. T., Chang, Y. C., Yu, C. Y., and Yu, S. S. 2014. Hamming code based watermarking scheme for 3D model verification. Mathematical Problems in Engineering

(Wang et al., 2017) Wang, Y., Liu, J., Yang, Y., Ma, D., and Liu, R. 2017. 3D model watermarking algorithm robust to geometric attacks. IET Image Processing, Vol. 11, No.10, pp. 822-832

(Yu et al., 2003) Yu, Z. Q., Horace, H. I., and Kwok, L. F. 2003. A robust watermarking scheme for 3D triangular mesh models. Pattern recognition, Vol. 36, No. 11, pp.2603-2614.

(Zhan et al., 2003) Zhan, Y. Z., Li, Y. T., Wang, X. Y., and Qian, Y. 2014. A blind watermarking algorithm for 3D mesh models based on vertex curvature. Journal of Zhejiang University SCIENCE C, Vol.15, No.5, 2014, pp. 351-362.

A MOBILE AUGMENTED REALITY-BASED ASSEMBLY GUIDANCE APPLICATION FOR LEGO

Anne Marielle Bagamaspad, John Israel Caingles, Kingston Anthony Koa,
Juan Lorenzo Simeon and Conrado Ruiz Jr.
College of Computer Studies, De La Salle University, Manila, Philippines

ABSTRACT

Usually LEGO structures are created by following an instruction manual in paper or digital form that depicts the LEGO model at different stages of assembly. Some instructions can be very complex and difficult to represent using plain illustrations. Consequently, this makes it difficult to follow and assemble a LEGO structure. Augmented reality (AR) is a technology that adds perceptual information into the physical world and it has recently been gaining popularity. This study explores the use of AR for assembly through ARGO, a mobile application for Android smartphones that serves as an assembly guide for LEGO structures. It can enhance instructions and provide more details that assist users during the construction process. The system can recognize the current step of the LEGO assembly using data captured via Microsoft Kinect while providing visual feedback through the mobile application. To identify the current step, the system obtains the color and depth data from the Kinect camera and converts the data into a point cloud. The point cloud undergoes segmentation to isolate the physical LEGO model and compares it to the point clouds of a preloaded model to check if the brick is placed correctly. The system was evaluated using 3 models and can recognize when to advance to the next step during assembly and estimate the orientation of the step differing an average angle of 48.27 degrees. For each step, it takes an average of a few seconds to decide on the recognition, leading to a short delay for the feedback to appear on the phone.

KEYWORDS

Augmented Reality, Computer-Assisted Instruction, Object Recognition, Object Tracking

1. INTRODUCTION

LEGO is a toy brick system used to create physical models. Its construction is relatively easy utilizing interlocking plastic bricks that could potentially have applications in prototyping. To build more complicated models however requires instruction manuals that usually come in traditionally printed or digital forms. They guide the user through descriptive, sequential instructions and photos of steps or figures of the model being assembled. However, there are some cases where the model being built is complex, or when the instruction set being followed seems to be unclear and it is difficult for the user to follow and correctly assemble the structure. An alternative to these assembly manuals is the use of Augmented Reality (AR).

Augmented reality (AR) is a technology in which information is added or modified into the real physical world, usually through devices like head-mounted displays or mobile devices (Craig, 2013). The effectiveness of this medium to aid in LEGO assembly guidance was tested in experiments conducted at Curtin University. It was revealed that an animated AR system yielded shorter task completion times, less assembly errors, and lower total task loads. When the participants relied on their memory and an instruction manual to complete an assembly, they were more prone to making errors (Hou et al., 2015). One of the most recent applications that also aids in LEGO assembly is an application that shows either an animated partial wireframe of the next, or side-by-side with the next step (Khoung, Kiyokawa, Miller, La Viola, Mashita & Takemura, 2014). Other similar studies include an application that shows the animated parts while showing their connections (Tang et al., 2003), and an application that shows on screen the next step in real-time (Gupta, Fox, Curless & Cohen, 2012).

The studies mentioned above all use either a head-mounted display or a computer monitor to show visual feedback. There is still no context-aware augmented reality mobile phone application that guides the user to build a LEGO structure. Augmented reality applications running on mobile phones have a potential of leveraging a large user base, together with their devices (Shmalstieg and Wagner, 2008).

This paper focuses on the development of ARGO, a system that uses augmented reality to show visual feedback to guide users to build LEGO models and is able to recognize when users complete a certain step and move on to the next itself. The the mobile application guides the user using AR elements by processing color and depth data from Microsoft Kinect camera to recognize the current LEGO model being built. The mobile application communicates and continuously requests data on the current state from the server which interacts with the Kinect camera directly. In order to compare the physical model to steps, the Viewpoint Feature Histogram (VHF) is used (Rusu et al., 2010).

2. RELATED WORK

Hou et al. (2015) investigated if the use of AR can cognitively help in manual assembly. They conducted experiments to compare the inclusion and exclusion of AR as a substitute for paper-based manuals. Results from this study indicated a positive effect of the cognitive facilitation when using an animated AR system. Specifically, the learning curve of trainees significantly improved, and fewer errors were made.

AR-based manuals provide immediate feedback and visual instructions. Showing the visualization of the current state of the object reduces the search time in assembly. In addition, AR would lessen the effort of the user in reading textual information. The amount of attention switching is also minimized and, as such, increases productivity. Furthermore, AR could possibly resolve ambiguities through indicators that shows the proper location of a certain component (Khoung et al., 2014).

In order to save time and resources on conducting trainings, the number of tools that help guide manual assembly continue to increase since studies prove it improves the efficiency of manual assembly (Wang, Ong & Nee, 2016). Nasihara and Okamoto (2015) implemented an augmented reality system that guides users in assembly tasks using image processing techniques to recognize the pieces and guide the piece placement with graphic signs. The system of Pathomaree and Charoenseang (2005) was designed to be a guiding tool that helped users assemble objects and structures. Its implementation involved using a camera and augmented reality concepts to compute the interaction and hand gestures made by the user, which represented specific types of commands on navigating through the steps of the assembly of the object.

There are different types of setups for specifically LEGO assembly guidance using AR. They used either an external camera or head-mounted display to view or input the physical model being built by the user. The AR elements or the output are then shown in a separate monitor, visual display or head-mounted display. None of the past studies have yet to consider the use of a mobile phone to display the feedback (Tang et al., 2003).

Context-aware approaches are systems which take into consideration the current state of the physical model, checking for errors and showing the next state. Gupta et al., (2012) developed a real-time guidance program that checks the correct color and position of a LEGO block. Their program then gives feedback to the user. It automatically moves to the next step if the block is correct and informs the user if there is an error so that the user may fix the mistake. Khoung et al. (2014) developed and tested the effectiveness of an AR-based context-aware assembly support system. They stated that context-related visualization of information helps to reduce search time in assembly. They created two AR context-aware visualization modes for their study. One displayed guidance information directly overlaid on the physical model and another featured a virtual model adjacent to the real model. The result was that the visualization mode that rendered guidance information separate from the physical model was preferable over the overlaying visualization mode.

3. SYSTEM DESIGN

ARGO is a LEGO assembly guidance mobile application that uses augmented reality to show the bricks that the user must place onto the model that he is building. The system is able to recognize the current stage of assembly and shows the next step. ARGO is also able to detect errors during the assembly phase and notifies the user accordingly. It makes use of a client-server architecture. The client is a mobile application and the server is a desktop where data from a Kinect sensor is processed to track and determine the next step of the model.

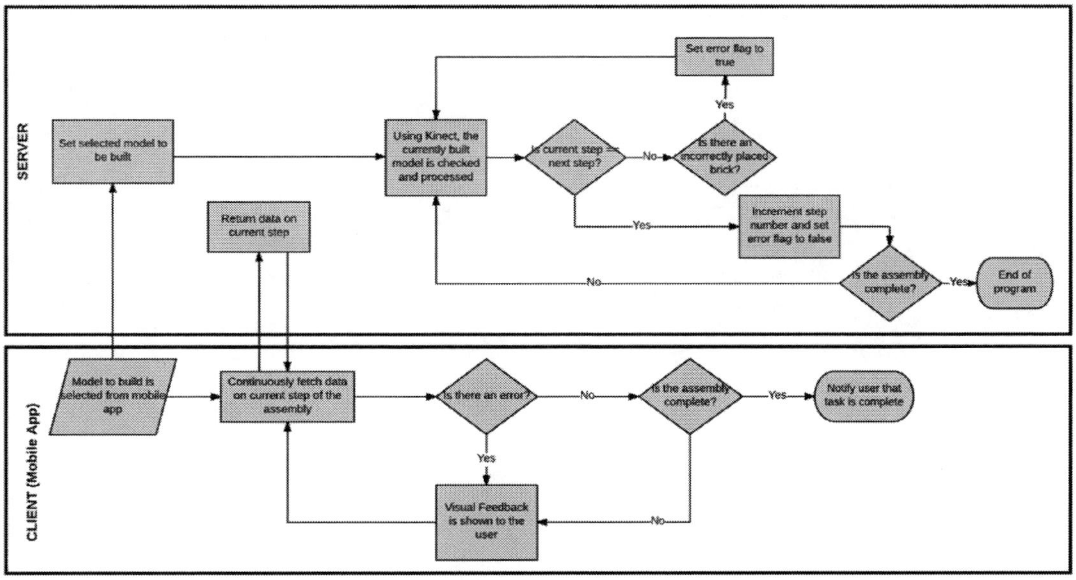

Figure 1. System Flow

3.1 Architectural Design

3.1.1 Client

The task of the mobile application is to provide visual feedback for the user based on the information processed by the server. It accomplishes this through the use of AR elements, specifically showing the next brick or a misplaced brick. The only information being processed on the side of the mobile application is the location on where to display the AR LEGO bricks based on the information sent by the server.

3.1.2 Server

The server, implemented on a desktop computer connected to a Kinect camera, accomplishes the task of processing the current state of the model. This point cloud is compared to the preloaded next step of the model which is being built using the Viewpoint Feature Histogram (Rusu et al., 2010).

Figure 1 shows a summary of the system process flow and how the two components communicate with each other during the assembly process. As the user chooses a model to build from the mobile application, the mobile application communicates this choice to the server while requesting for the next step. The server-side of the system will then take input using the depth sensor of the model. After processing the input, the server then determines the current state of the model as well as the next step using information from the database for the stored LEGO model. As the mobile application obtains this information, it then displays the appropriate visual feedback. The server then waits for any updates in the configuration and then processes the updates accordingly. If it is a correct addition, it moves to the next step; otherwise, it shows an error message. This information is then relayed to the mobile application that displays it to the user.

3.2 Physical Set-up

The physical setup is shown in Figure 2. The system requires the use of an augmented reality marker board, on which the model is being built. The marker board serves as the location where the virtual model would be displayed in the mobile application. The Microsoft Kinect camera is placed at a fixed distance, 45.72 cm away from the marker board, 55.88 cm above the table surface, and tilted 30 degrees, overseeing the assembly area. During the assembly process itself, the physical model must be in range of the Kinect and there must be no other objects that may block the Kinect's view or that may be detected as part of the model. The model must also be on a flat tabletop surface using an augmented reality marker board. The area must also be brightly lit for the sensor to recognize the colors in the area accurately.

Figure 2. Physical Setup of ARGO, as Viewed from Different Perspectives, Top View (Left), Eye Level View (Right); Seen in the Picture is the Placement of the Marker Board, Mobile Device and the Kinect Camera

4. IMPLEMENTATION DETAILS

This section describes the implementation issues of the mobile phone application, the desktop server and how the information of the Microsoft Kinect depth camera was processed.

4.1 Mobile Application

The researchers used the software LeoCAD to virtually represent the LEGO bricks. LeoCAD uses models from the LDraw's Parts Library. It is also used to generate the *.ldr* files of the virtually built models. This file contains the brick type, step number and coordinates of each brick in the building instructions (Bliss, 2012). The .ldr file is parsed by the mobile app, which acts as the instruction manual and a reference for the phone to know what to show next and guide the user in the building process, The *.3ds* files were also generated by this software used to represent the different types of LEGO bricks for the AR of the application.

Using the *.ldr* files and *.3ds* files produced by LeoCAD, ARGO can accurately augment the virtual LEGO bricks along with their realistic dimensions and correct positions in 3D space through the smartphone's camera (Figure 3, left) based on the current step of the assembly fetched from the server. This is implemented using ARToolkit. It also notifies the user of a misplaced brick (Figure 3, middle). The user can also go back to a previous step or move forward to the next step by double tapping the corresponding section of the mobile screen as seen in (Figure 3, right).

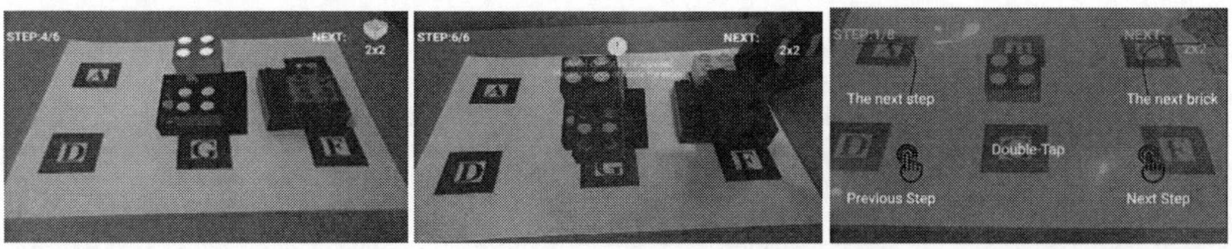

Figure 3. Visual Feedback Elements in ARGO. ARGO Showing the Next Step Through an Animated AR LEGO Brick (Left). Error Message is Shown for a Misplaced Brick (Middle). ARGO's Other Options to Move to the Next or Previous Step (Right)

4.2 Server

The server is accessed by the mobile application to obtain data on the current step. The server is implemented using the Django web framework and the database using MySQL. The main purpose of the server's database is to store the list of models that could be built using ARGO. As the user selects a model to assemble on the mobile app, the server receives this and acts as a mediator for the mobile app and the Kinect data processing part of the system.

4.3 Kinect Data Processing

The application which processes the Kinect data was implemented in C++ and makes use of the Point Cloud Library, which is a large scale, open project for point cloud processing (Rusu and Cousins, 2011).

4.3.1 Segmentation

The depth and RGB data from the Kinect camera were first converted to 3D colored point clouds. The area that is visible to the Kinect was lowered by using a passthrough filter on both the camera point cloud's *x*- and *z*- axis. This is to decrease the amount of points that would need to be processed in the later steps. The table or plane surface of the assembly area is detected using RANSAC. The largest plane in the physical scene's point cloud was assumed to be the plane that is being built upon. This plane was then aligned to the XZ plane, along with the physical model. The color of the point cloud is then normalized to reduce the effect of the intensity of light on the point cloud. After which, the points which contain colors of the LEGO bricks (red, green, blue, yellow) are isolated by using a color filter on the RGB color space, refer to Figure 4. This leaves only the physical LEGO model, removing points of the hands, table and marker board. Then, outliers are removed, these are the points which are farther from the other points based on a distance threshold. This is to account for the presence of some noise in the Kinect camera data, as well as the presence of other colors which were detected but not part of the physical model.

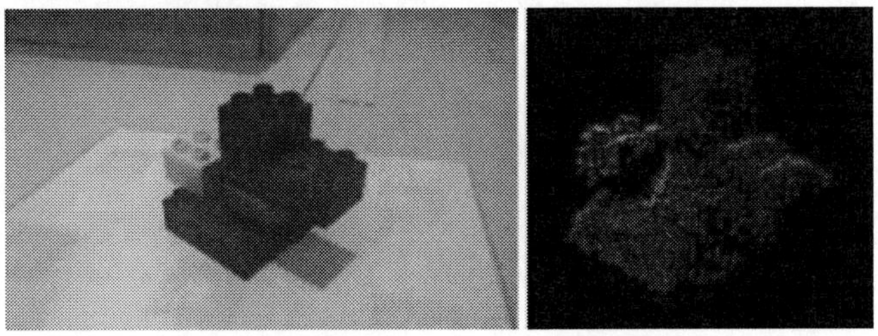

Figure 4. Output Point Cloud from the Segmentation Phase

4.3.2 Feature Estimation using Viewpoint Feature Histogram

After segmentation, features are computed that are used to compare the physical scene to the virtual point clouds. The Viewpoint Feature Histogram (VFH) is used as a descriptor for point clouds. Both the geometry and the viewpoint of the point cloud is encoded into this descriptor. The descriptor has been successfully used to differentiate objects with similar shapes, which is similar to the consequent steps in LEGO assembly, where configurations have only minimal difference with each other. VFH uses purely the 3D features of the point cloud and does not take into account the color or 2D features (Junemann 2012; Ruso and Cousins, 2011).

4.3.3 Training

For the physical model's histogram to be compared to the next step, the application must be trained with templates of the point clouds at different steps. ARGO was trained with all the steps in the assembly, each with different poses to account for rotation invariance. A step went through the previous stages, segmentation and feature estimation, and was then saved to a local file for later use. It was then rotated by 20 degrees and then underwent the processing and saved. This was repeated until the physical model was completely rotated. This meant that each step was composed of 18 point clouds, each representing a pose 20 degrees apart.

4.3.4 Feature Matching using Chi-Square Distance

The application was trained with models and their steps including poses. During runtime, the physical model undergoes the same segmentation and VFH estimation. The physical model's histogram is then matched with the stored histograms of the current step and the next step which were obtained during the training of the system. As each histogram can be measured as a feature vector composed of floating point values, a distance metric can be calculated. The chi-square distance normalizes each bin of the histograms and is computed by:

$$d_{Chi}(\vec{a}, \vec{b}) = \sqrt{\sum_{i=1}^{m} \frac{(a_i - b_i)^2}{a_i + b_i}}$$

where a and b are vectors composed of floating point values $(a_1, a_2, \ldots a_m)$ and values $(b_1, b_2, \ldots b_m)$ respectively.

4.3.5 Evaluating when to Move to the Next Step

The Kinect camera's data is usually noisy, as such, the results of the chi-square distance computation per frame were inconsistent. Instead of using the results of a single frame, the system takes the moving average for each potential pose and take the one with the least average distance at the end of the number of frames/iterations. From preliminary experiments, 30 iterations/frames was found to be a good balance between accuracy and time. After this, the best candidate would then be checked if it was less than the distance threshold, which was set as 45 from preliminary experiments. The distance threshold is also increased to 60, at lower point cloud sizes. The second best candidate is also recorded as if the system is about to update the step, and the first and second candidates differ in step, the second best is checked if it was within 5 units of the first, and if it is, the system would not update the step. To lower the number of false positives/negatives, the distance (result of the chi-Square distance) was increased or decreased whether they met the following criteria: point cloud size and perceived number of brick clusters segmented by color.

The size of the point cloud of the candidates of the recognition was compared to the size of the physical model. This is to make it less prone to accept configurations of an earlier step. The perceived number of brick clusters segmented by color was found by using a similar technique as done in the segmentation process, which was segmenting the model to its red, green, blue and yellow components. After which the point cloud data was clustered by distance, leaving several point clouds. Assuming that there are no adjacent colored bricks, this may give an accurate number of the bricks present in the scene. However, this is still reliant on the orientation of the physical model with respect to the Kinect camera and may be prone to errors due to occlusions. The justification for using this feature is the fact that the number of number of brick clusters between the best candidate in the training data and the physical model must be similar.

5. RESULTS

The system was evaluated by building 3 models, namely "Duck," "Letter J," and "Heart," composed of 6 bricks, 8 bricks and 12 bricks respectively, seen in Figure 5. The threshold used for the chi-squared distance was empirically obtained and was set to 45. The devices used in testing the system were: a Microsoft Kinect 2.0 (sensor), Google Nexus 6P with a Qualcomm Snapdragon 810 processor and 3GB of RAM (client), and a Dell XPS 15 9560 with a 2.8GHz Intel Core i7-7700HQ processor and 8GB of RAM (server).

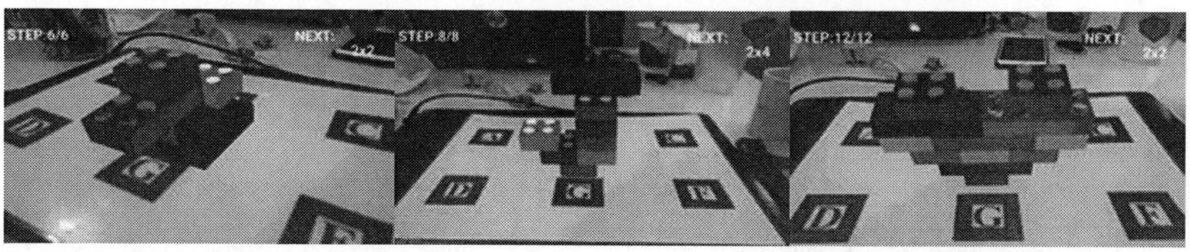

Figure 5. The Models that were used to Evaluate the System: Duck (Left), Letter J (Middle), Heart (Right)

5.1 Accuracy

The accuracy was evaluated by measuring the difference in the angle as recognized by the system to the actual angle physically. The testing was performed by completing the models 3 times each and measuring the angle difference for each step. The results are shown in Table 1.

Table 1. Average Angle Difference of Recognized Pose to Actual Pose and Average Number of Seconds per Cycle per Model

Model	Average Angle Difference (degrees)	Average Seconds per Cycle
Duck	38.89	3.66
Letter J	53.33	3.70
Heart	52.50	4.51
Average	*48.27*	*3.96*

After the evaluation using all 3 models, the system could recognize each step and estimate its orientation differing an average angle of 48.27. From the tables above, both the letter J and heart models have a larger and similar average angle difference compared to the duck model, 53.33 and 52.50 respectively. This is possibly due to how the models are structured, as they are more 2-dimensional as opposed to the duck model. As the system is unable to differentiate bricks misplaced over a small distance, it may have mistaken some steps to be the inverse of themselves. Another difference is that the side view of the letter J and heart is only 1 brick wide, which means that at certain angles, there are less points and therefore less features for the system to use to describe the point cloud, which leads to an inaccurate recognition of the pose.

5.2 Latency

Aside from accuracy, the latency of the system was also measured. The speed influenced by the number of iterations/frames it must average data from to arrive at a decision. The number of iterations based on previous experiments was set to 30. The average number of seconds per recognition cycle or per 30 frames for each model is shown in the Table 1. The testing was performed by completing the models 3 times each and measuring how many seconds it took for each cycle. As seen in the table, the latency is shown to be higher for the model with more steps, possibly due to the higher point cloud size. The average number of seconds for all 3 models is 3.96 or almost 4 seconds, which after testing, is still an acceptable amount for assembling a model.

5.3 Error Detection

The system could detect incorrect steps or configurations. The study has identified three main classes of errors: wrong brick, wrong orientation and wrong position, which may be identified to be as near (1-2 bricks from supposed location) or far (more than 3 bricks from supposed location). Each step was then tested for these different classes of error. From these, the application could reject these errors in most cases and prevent them from moving to the next step, except for some wrong position type errors. This can be attributed to the low resolution of the Kinect camera which is unable to determine the small distances from small objects.

6. CONCLUSION AND FUTURE WORK

This paper proposed a substitute for a paper-based assembly manuals in the form of a smartphone application. The application makes use of augmented reality and an AR marker board to visually guide the user by showing a moving brick attaching to a virtual representation of a LEGO model in each step of the assembly process. To check whether the assembler has correctly built a step in the assembly process, the server compares data obtained from the Kinect camera and data which was preloaded with the different poses of the steps of the models to be assembled. This is done by computing a Viewpoint Feature Histogram (VFH) for the physical model and templates and then comparing them to each other using chi-square distance. The next step is recognized by searching for the template with the nearest average distance for 30 iterations.

The issue of occlusion is one of the major challenges faced by the system. Occlusions create problematic poses for the physical LEGO model that can lead to false positives and false negatives during step recognition. To solve this, other methods may be explored such as 3D reconstruction of the model before recognition or using concave hulls. Another option would be to take advantage of the image obtained from the mobile phone to aid in the recognition as well, instead of only using the mobile phone for visual feedback. This would help in addressing the problem of occlusions by trying to recognize the current step through reconstructing the model from different viewpoints using 3D registration of features from both the Kinect and mobile phone images.

In today's advancing technology, there are companies that have released smartphones that already have a built-in depth camera, making the development of AR-based apps more feasible in the near future. Given that one of this study's main objectives is to develop a LEGO assembly guidance system through an AR-based mobile applications, another recommendation would be for future researchers to explore these types of technology, and eliminate the need for a separate depth sensor like the Kinect camera. The potential of the system to be a collaborative assembly system with many concurrent users may be also explored, as the current implementation already allows this using the client-server architecture.

REFERENCES

Bliss, T., Pobursky and Howard. (2012). LDraw.org Standards: File Format 1.0.2. Available at: www.ldraw.org/

Craig, A. (2013), "Chapter 1 - what Is augmented reality?,". Understanding Augmented Reality, A. Craig (Ed.) and M. Kaufmann, Boston, pp. 1 – 37.

Gupta, A., Fox, D., Curless, B. and Cohen, M. (2012). Duplotrack: a realtime system for authoring and guiding duplo model assembly. Proceedings of the 25th Annual ACM Symposium Adjunct on User Interface Software and Technology. ACM, New York, NY, USA, 13.

Hou, L., Xiangyu, W., Leonhard, B. and Love, P. (2015). Using animated augmented reality to cognitively guide assembly, Master's thesis. Curtin University of Technology, Bentley, Australia.

Junemann, M. (2012). Object detection and recognition with Microsoft Kinect. B.S. Thesis. Freie Universitat Berlin, Germany.

Khuong, B., Kiyokawa, K., Miller, A., La Viola, J.J., Mashita, T. and Takemura, H. (2014). The effectiveness of an ar-based context-aware assembly support system in object assembly. Proc. of 2014 IEEE Virtual Reality (VR). 57–62.

Nishihara, A. and Okamoto, J. (2015). Object Recognition in Assembly Assisted by Augmented Reality System. doi: 10.1109/IntelliSys.2015.7361172.

Pathomaree, N. and Charoenseang, S. (2015). Augmented reality for skill transfer in assembly task. ROMAN 2005. IEEE International Workshop on Robot and Human Interactive Communication, 2005. 500–504.

Rusu, R.B., Bradski, G., Thibaux, R., and Hsu, J. (2010). Fast 3D recognition and pose using the viewpoint feature histogram. Procceedings of 2010 IEEE/RSJ International Conference on Intelligent Robots and Systems. 2155–2162. doi:http://dx.doi.org/10.1109/IROS.2010.5651280

Rusu, R. and Cousins, S. (2011). 3D is here: point cloud library (pcl). Proceedings of IEEE International Conference on Robotics and Automation (ICRA). Shanghai, China.

Schmalstieg, D. and Wagner, D. (2018). Mobile Phones as a Platform for Augmented Reality. Graz University of Technology. Available at: https://data.icg.tugraz.at/~dieter/publications/Schmalstieg_135.pdf

Tang, A.,Owen, C., Biocca, F. and Mou, W., (2003). Comparative effectiveness of augmented reality in object assembly,. Proceedings of the SIGCHI Conference on Human Factors in Computing Systems (CHI '03). ACM, New York, NY, USA, 73–80.

Wang, X., Ong, S.K., and Nee, A.Y.C. (2016) "Multi-modal augmented-reality assembly guidance based on bare-hand interface," Advanced Engineering Information. 30, 3, 406-421. doi:http://dx.doi.org/10.1016/j.aei.2016.05.004.

TOWARDS PARAMETER FREE GROUPWISE NON-RIGID IMAGE ALIGNMENT

Ahmad Aal-Yhia[1], Paul Malcolm[2], Reyer Zwiggelaar[3] and Bernard Tiddeman[3]
[1]*Computer Science Department, Aberystwyth University, Aberystwyth, SY23 3DB, UK*
Post-Graduate Institute for Accounting & Financial Studies, University of Baghdad, Baghdad, Iraq
[2]*Department of Radiology, Norfolk Norwich University Hospital, Norwich NR4 7UY, UK*
[3]*Computer Science Department, Aberystwyth University, Aberystwyth, SY23 3DB, UK*

ABSTRACT

Groupwise non-rigid image alignment is a difficult non-linear optimisation problem, involving many parameters and often large datasets. Previous methods have explored various metrics and optimisation strategies. Good results have been previously achieved with simple metrics, but requiring complex optimisation, often with many unintuitive parameters that require careful tuning for each dataset. In this paper we restructure the problem to use a simpler, iterative optimisation algorithm, with very few free parameters. We demonstrate how to incorporate a stiffness constraint and how to tune the few remaining parameters. Results show that the method reliably aligns various datasets and demonstrates efficiency in terms performance and reduction of the computations.

KEYWORDS

Non-rigid Image Alignment, Groupwise Registration

1. INTRODUCTION

Non-rigid alignment of a group of images is required for many applications such as analysis of face images (Cootes, et al., 2005) and constructing anatomical atlases from medical images (Twining, et al., 2004). Analysing the structure of the alignment across groups of images can be used for building statistical models of appearance and shape, such as Active Appearance Models (AAMs) (Cootes, et al., 2001) (Matthews & Baker, 2004) which can then be used for interpreting those and other images. When building such models from large databases, automation is essential for avoiding using manual annotation that is time consuming and prone to error. Using the statistical model in training with a set of images provides a set of deformation fields across this group without manual intervention (Cootes, et al., 2005).

Previous methods have integrated three main components: representation of the deformation fields between images, an objective function, and a suitable optimisation algorithm (Cootes, et al., 2010). For the deformation field, there are three common ways for representing the deformation fields. A composition of simple warps (Cootes, et al., 2004), (Lotjone & Makela, 2001), dense fields representing the movement of each pixel (Jones & Poggio, 1998) or a sparse set of control points that control a set of splines (Twining, et al., 2004) or the nodes of a triangulated mesh (Cootes, et al., 2005). Optimisation of dense warp fields, or high resolution meshes is computationally expensive. Multi-resolution meshes, going from low resolution to high can help reduce the computational complexity in the early stages, but optimisation over many parameters is still required in the later stages where detail is required. (Sidorov, et al., 2009) showed that complex warps can be built from a set of simpler warps, reducing the need for high dimensional optimisation, which we exploit in this paper.

Optimisation of the alignment requires the selection of a suitable error metric. The Minimum Description Length (MDL) metric was proposed by (Davies, et al., 2001) to align similar 2D shapes and has been extended to image and surface alignment (Twining, et al., 2004) (Davies, et al., 2008). MDL is mathematically well motivated, but can be very expensive in terms of computations for image alignment, as it requires repeatedly rebuilding PCA models (Twining, et al., 2004). Other work has demonstrated that good results can be achieved on image sets with much simpler metrics, such as minimisation of the sum of squared errors from the current estimate of the mean (Cootes, et al., 2010) (Sidorov, et al., 2009).

The final element is selection of a suitable optimisation strategy. Previous work has used gradient descent, line minimisation or simultaneous perturbation stochastic approximation (SPSA). Gradient descent is known to be expensive and requires the selection of a suitable step size. Line minimisation can also be slow and expensive, only optimising along a single direction in the high dimensional space. SPSA requires as many steps as gradient descent, but each step is cheaper as it requires fewer function evaluations. These and other optimisation algorithms require selecting good parameters for getting efficient and accurate performance (Yang, et al., 2013) which is well known to be a difficult problem (Ridge E., 2007) (Yang, et al., 2013). Therefore, performance of the optimisation algorithm relies on solving the problem of parameter tuning for the optimisation algorithm (Ridge E., 2007).

AAMs (Cootes , et al., 2001) (Matthews & Baker, 2004) are an efficient way to optimise a shape and appearance model (usually based on PCA derived models) to an image. The fitting of the AAM model is achieved by minimising an objective function to find the model shape update parameters δp, which comes from a Taylor series approximation. The AAM style optimisation is not suitable for large numbers of parameters, as it requires inverting an N^2 matrix for minimising N parameters. Nevertheless, if a way can be found to reduce the number of parameters involved in the minimisation, AAM style optimisation represents an efficient alignment strategy, with a very few parameters to tune.

The proposed method is based on using a very small number of control points per iteration and using AAM style optimisation. Image derivatives and matrix inversion only needs to be calculated once for each iteration over the set. More complex warps can be built up over iterations (Sidorov, et al., 2009) by concatenation (Tiddeman, et al., 2001). The main contributions of our method are:

- We develop a novel optimisation approach for doing groupwise alignment with no complex parameter tuning required.
- We present an elastic constraint that can be included in the groupwise algorithm.
- We propose a novel simulation method that can be used for estimating the stiffness parameter for the elastic constraint.

2. METHODS

This section describes the algorithmic details of the proposed method that consists of two phases. The first phase is for initialisation by registration of all images in the dataset to a reference image. The second phase uses the resulting images and their warps to achieve a groupwise alignment algorithm to update these warps. Each of these phases is described in more detail in the following sections.

2.1 Initialization of Groupwise Registration

For initialisation, an image is selected at random to use as an initial reference. Pairwise registration is performed between all training images with the initial reference (Cootes, et al., 2004) by using demons registration (Kroon & Slump, 2009) for getting the warp fields to each image. An average of the resulting warp fields is computed and then we invert that average warp. The inverse average of the warp fields is concatenated (Tiddeman, et al., 2001) with the warp field of each training image, which provides initial warps of all training images to the initial estimate of the average shape. The original training images are warped with their new warp fields in order to obtain the initial aligned training images and mean image.

2.2 Groupwise Registration Approach

The resulting images and their warp fields are then used with the groupwise alignment algorithm. We do the whole process in a multiresolution way so that an image starts blurry and gradually gets sharper. An average of all images is computed to get an average image which is recomputed over iterations. The proposed groupwise registration method proceeds as follows:

Groupwise registration algorithm overview
***Inputs**: Pairwise registered images and initial warp functions, stiffness parameter for each resolution*
***Outputs**: Updated warps for each image*
For each resolution from lowest to highest
    For k iterations (or until happy)
        Compute average image.
        Calculate new random control points.
        Calculate derivatives of average image (A)
        Calculate $A^TA+\beta D^TK^TKD$
        For each image, in turn:
            Warp the current image using the current warp
            Set up the control points on the average image and warped image.
            Find update to the control points using Levenberg-Mardquart algorithm
            Warp using new control points
            Concatenate the previous and new warps
        End for
    End for
End for

In each iteration we aim to minimise an objective function by updating the location of the control points on the target image. The objective function we use is given in vector form by:

$$x^2 = \beta(K(w(p+\delta p)) + c)^2 + (S + A\delta p - T)^2 \tag{1}$$

Where β is the stiffness parameter, K is the stiffness matrix that calculates the vector difference between each control point's movement and the average of its neighbours, S is the average image, T is the target image, $w(p+\delta p)$ is the vector of warped control points, $\delta p=\{\delta p_j\}$ is the vector of control point location updates, p is the current estimate of their movement, c is the offset vector which is computed using $-k*w(p)$ only of the first iteration, and we have used a first order Taylor series approximation for $S(p+\delta p)$ using the matrix of derivative images A. The stiffness parameter is required to avoid large distortions that may not reduce the error much, particularly in featureless parts of the image. We approximate $w(p+\delta p)$ by its first order Taylor series per control point and derivatives only need to be evaluated at that point. The error function can be rearranged to:

$$x^2 = \beta(K(w(p) + D\delta p) + c)^2 + (S + A\delta p - T)^2 \tag{2}$$

Where D is a block diagonal matrix, with each block a 2x2 matrix of the derivatives of the warp from the previous iteration at the corresponding point. Taking the derivative of the above with respect to the update parameters and setting the result to zero gives the update equation:

$$2\beta D^TK^T(KD(w(p) + \delta p) + c) + 2A^T(S + A\delta p - T) = 0 \tag{3}$$

Rearranging gives:

$$(\beta(D^TK^TKD) + A^TA)\delta p = -\beta D^TK^T(Kw(p) + c) - A^T(S - T) \tag{4}$$

In line with the usual Levenberg-Marquardt procedure, we modify the above equation to vary smoothly between the Gauss Newton version (above) and the gradient descent method, via the inclusion of a damping term:

$$(B + \lambda diag\{B\})\delta p = -\beta D^TK^T(Kw(p) + c) - A^T(S - T) \tag{5}$$

Where $B = (\beta(D^TK^TKD)+A^TA)$ and λ is the damping term. In each iteration across the set, the (random) control points are fixed, as is the average and its derivatives, and so only involve an update of the matrix according to the damping parameter and inversion of a small matrix. The damping term λ is initialized with the value 10 and decreased by a factor of 10 for steps that improve the error. For steps where the error worsens, the damping factor is increased by a factor of 10 and the step is discarded.

2.3 Initialise Grid of Control Points

The deformation fields are represented by a set of control points that parameterize Thin Plate Splines (TPS) (Bookstein, 1989). The grid of control points consists of 25 points. The locations of the control points are changed in random order within 25 areas for the current and average image per iteration across the set as shown in figure 1.

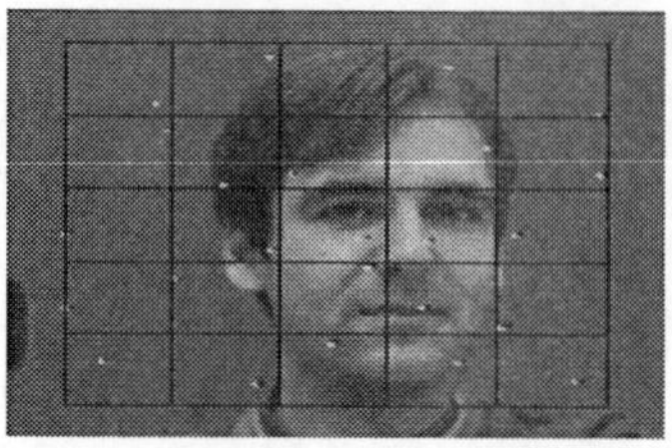

Figure 1. Locations of the Control Points are changed in Random Order within 25 Areas

2.4 Calculation of Derivatives

The partial derivatives of the average with respect to movement of each control point are calculated using a finite difference approximation. For every control point on the average image, the x or y value is modified by δp. The control points without change and the control points with one point changed in x or y are input to a TPS function to create a warp for the image. As a result, the derivative images will be obtained by subtracting the warped image from the average image as shown in the figure 2, the resulting value is divided by δp.

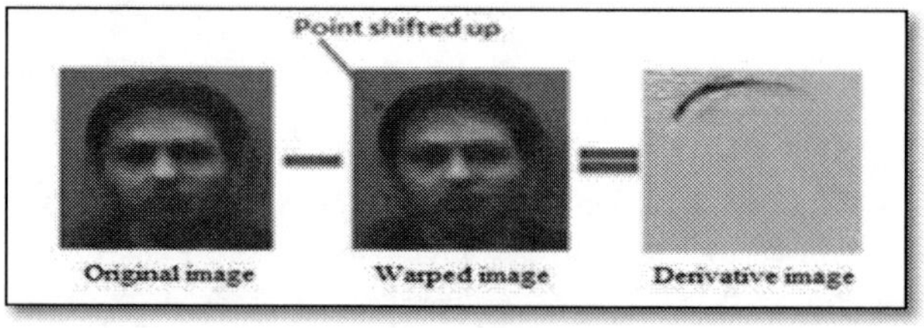

Figure 2. Subtracting a Warped Image from an Original Image for getting a Derivative Image

2.5 Optimisation Algorithm

The derivative images (δS^0, δS^1, δS^2, ... ,δS^N) are saved as a matrix A. Then, a matrix A^TA is computed by applying the dot product operator between all pairs of derivatives contained in matrix A. The step size δp is varied with the resolution, going from 4, 3, 2 and 1 from lowest to highest respectively. The resolution parameter (r) controls a Gaussian blurring and its values are selected according to values of the step size (s) by using the formula $r= 2^{s-1}$. So, values of the resolution parameter are with widths 8, 4, 2 and 1 respectively.

It is difficult to minimise an objective function by searching a space for all deformation fields of images (Sidorov, et al., 2009). Cootes et al. (Cootes, et al., 2010) and (Sidorov, et al., 2009) built a model for performing an optimisation of control points to minimise the objective function. Previous studies (Cootes, et al., 2004), (Sidorov, et al., 2009), (Cootes, et al., 2010), (Davies, et al., 2001) found that optimisation of the deformation fields for one image at a time is sufficient. In (Cootes, et al., 2010) the number of control points used was large (320 points) in fixed locations and indicated that performance is poor when using a small number of them. However (Sidorov, et al., 2009) used a small number of control points in randomised locations per iteration and achieved good alignment. (Cootes, et al., 2004), (Cootes, et al., 2010), (Davies, et al., 2008) used non-linear optimisation and they are expensive in computations and slow in performance.

In the proposed optimisation method, we use some advantages of the previous techniques mentioned above and avoid some their disadvantages. The use of a small set of feature points to build up a complex warp is taken from (Sidorov, et al., 2009). This allows an AAM style optimization, which can be further optimized by only updating the derivative images A and dot product matrix A^TA once per iteration over the set of images. Leave-one-out optimization and alignment to the mean have been proved effective and efficient in previous work, and we use them here. The use of Levenberg-Marquardt provides stability and automatic tuning of the damping term. The key to the power in our method is that we develop an iterative linear optimisation approach for doing groupwise alignment with no complex parameter tuning required as is the case using some optimisation algorithms such as the SPSA algorithm. The only remaining free parameter is the stiffness parameter that controls the relative contribution of the image pixel error and the stiffness. In the next section we show how to estimate this.

2.6 Estimation of Stiffness Parameter

This section presents a simulation method that can be used to tune the stiffness parameter β. Our experiments use the control points on three different datasets of face and prostate images and each of them varies in terms of brightness and contrast, and so requires a different value for β. The method we propose creates synthetic images with known update as the ground truth, which can be used to calculate an optimal value for β. In theory, this approach could be used to estimate a unique value for each image pair, but for efficiency we approximate a single value for each dataset.

The synthetic training data is created by applying a small random warp to each target image, according to a set of random control points placed in the same way as for the main update algorithm. To make the problem more closely match the real data, we also apply a histogram equalisation step, based on matching the histogram of the warped target image to another image in the set, selected at random.

We assume the previous warp to be the identity *(I)*, so only a small update is needed, hence $D = I$. So, the first term of equation (3) is replaced by $2\beta(K^TK(p+\delta p))$ and the stiffness parameter is estimated from this equation, solved for β in the least-squares sense over a set of synthetic example training images i.e. the following equation is minimised.

$$x^2 = \sum_{i\in\Omega}(\beta a_i - b_i)^2 \qquad (6)$$

Where $a_i = (K^TK(\delta p_i))$ is the stiffness vector term given by the stiffness matrix and known required update for the ith example, and $b_i = A_i^T(S_i + A_i\delta p_i - T_i)$ is the vector corresponding to the image error and derivatives from the ith example. The solution is given by:

$$\beta = \frac{\sum_{i\in\Omega} a_i \cdot b_i}{\sum_{i\in\Omega} a_i \cdot a_i} \qquad (7)$$

We estimate a different value of β for each image set and each resolution. The random offset of each control point is limited to twice the step size for that resolution. Example synthetic images are shown in figure 3.

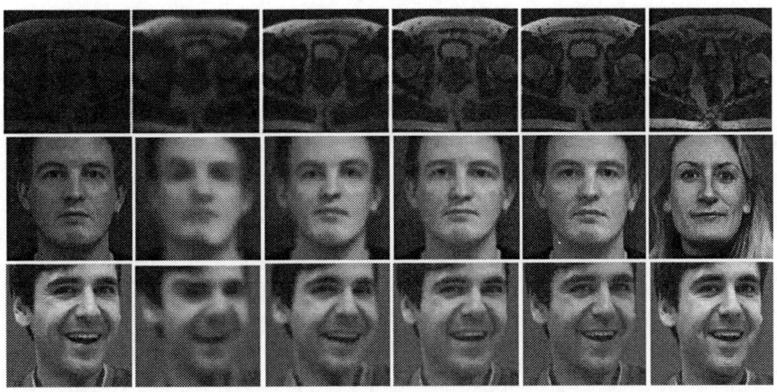

Figure 3. Examples of the original prostate MRI, IMM, and FGNET images with example synthetic images created using a random warp and offset of each control point. From left to right, the original target image, synthetic images at 4 different scales, with their histograms mapped to a target image, the target image used to provide the histogram

3. RESULTS

We have tested our model on a set of 100 frames (every 10th frame) of the FGNET "franck" dataset (FGNET, 2004), a set of 37 front-facing faces from the IMM database (Nordstrøm, et al., 2004) and our set of

38 prostate T2-Weighted MRI images from different patients, where every image represents a slice from a patient.

To assess our model we use the specificity measure as described in (Cootes et al., 2005). By using the aligned images and warps obtained from the groupwise approach, we have used PCA method to build appearance and shape models. The affine part is removed from the aligned warps before building the shape model. The appearance and shape model distributions are used to construct a set of random images - 1000 images were generated for each dataset. We apply the estimate of the affine transformation obtained from the aligned warps to the original training images to produce the affine registered images. We use the random images and the affine registered images for computing the specificity measure. The results are 0.028, 0.084 and 0.098 for PGNET, IMM and prostate MRI datasets respectively. These results indicate a good performance of our method. PGNET dataset has low specificity value while IMM and Prostate MRI datasets have higher specificity value. Also, these results are better than the results in (Tiddeman & Hunter, 2011) for IMM dataset that it was ranged (0.157 - 0.196). The results are shown in figure 4.

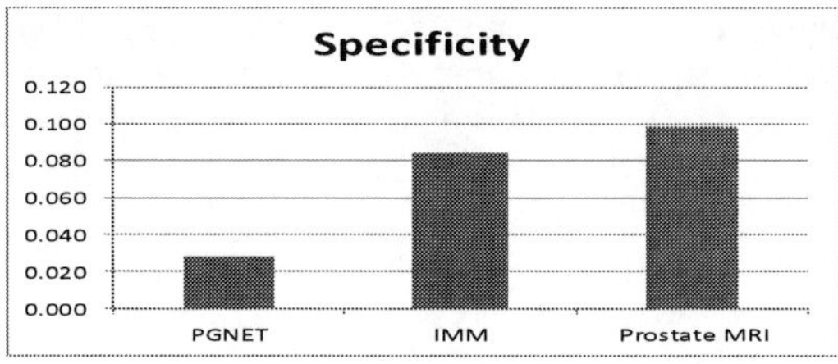

Figure 4. Results of specificity comparison indicate a good performance of our method. PGNET dataset has low specificity value while IMM and Prostate MRI datasets have higher specificity value

We have calculated two types of error for evaluating the performance of the model, the errors of the pixels' intensity and the errors of feature points. Firstly, the errors on pixels are performed for three datasets by computing the error between the average image and a groupwise registered image. Mean and standard deviation of the errors are shown in figure 5(a). The results are as follow: PGNET dataset is 0.0286 (0.0072), IMM dataset is 0.0658 (0.0122) and prostate MRI dataset is 0.0935 (0.0228).

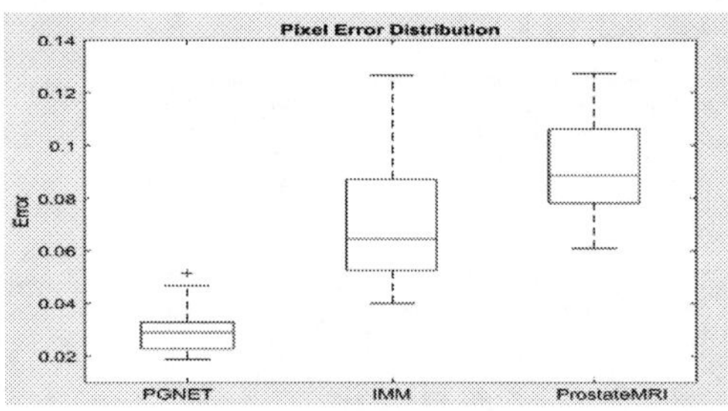

(a)

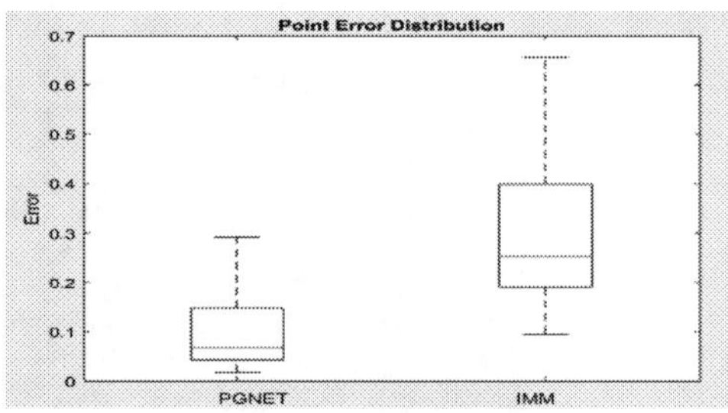

(b)

Figure 5. (a) The distribution of pixel errors for three datasets PGNET, IMM and prostate MRI. (b) The distribution of errors from points manually placed on two datasets PGNET and IMM

Secondly, the errors on feature points are performed for PGNET and IMM datasets by using the manual ground truth points which are used and available publicly (FGNET, 2004) (Nordstrøm, et al., 2004). The evaluation metric of the errors on feature points used in this study is similar to that described by (Cootes, et al., 2010). The feature points used for each image are twenty points as shown in figure 6. The warps fields of the groupwise registered images are used for computing a mean each point for all images on the final average image to estimate the true position of the feature point. Then the warps fields are used to project those mean reference points back to each groupwise registered image for comparing them with the actual positions of the ground truth points. The results are as follow: PGNET dataset is 0.1028 (0.087), IMM dataset is 0.3121 (0.2155). The results of point error distribution are shown in figure 5(b). Figure 7 shows the evolution of the mean of the prostate MRI, PGNET and IMM datasets using our model.

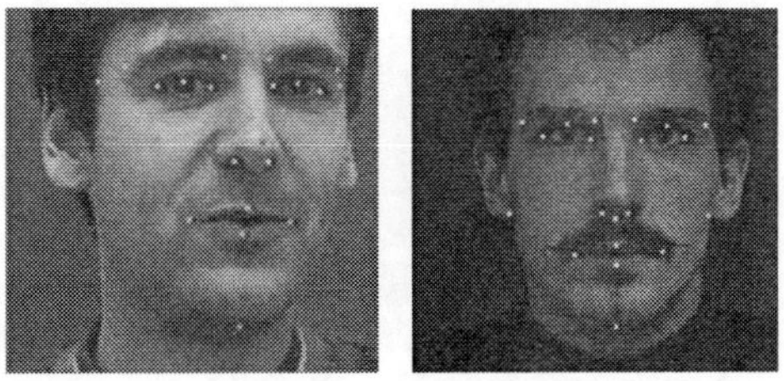

Figure 6. Twenty Ground Truth Points used for Evaluation

Figure 7. Evolutions of the Mean for the Three Datasets Prostate MRI, PGNET and IMM

4. CONCLUSION

In this paper we have developed an iterative linear optimisation approach for doing groupwise alignment with no complex parameter tuning required. The elastic constraint has been presented to be included in the proposed groupwise method. Also, we have proposed a simulation method for estimating the stiffness parameter for the elastic constraint. Our model has been tested on three different datasets of faces and medical images and indicates good results and demonstrates the efficiency of the performance and reduction of the computational requirements. Future work will be to extend the proposed method to 3D images and explore its performance with additional and more complex medical images.

ACKNOWLEDGEMENTS

Ahmad Aal-Yhia thanks Iraqi Ministry of Higher Education and Scientific Research for funding his PhD.

REFERENCES

Bookstein, F., 1989. Principal Warps: Thin-Plate Splines and the Decomposition of Deformations. *IEEE Transactions on Pattern Analysis and Machine Intelligence,* Vol. 11, No. 6, pp. 567–585.

Cootes, T. et al., 2001. Active Appearance Models. *IEEE Transactions on Pattern Analysis and Machine Intelligence,* Vol. 23, No. 6, pp. 681–685.

Cootes, T. et al., 2004. Diffeomorphic Statistical Shape Models. *Proceedings of British Machine Vision.* London, United Kingdom, Vol. 1, pp. 447–456.

Cootes, T. et al., 2004. Groupwise Diffeomorphic Non-Rigid Registration for Automatic Model Building. *In Proc. ECCV.* Prague, Czech Republic, pp. 316–327.

Cootes, T. et al., 2010. Computing Accurate Correspondences Across Groups of Images. *IEEE Transactions on Pattern Analysis and Machine Intelligence,* Vol. 32, No. 11, pp. 1994-2005.

Cootes, T. et al., 2005. Groupwise Construction of Appearance Models Using Piece-Wise Affine Deformations. *In Proceedings of 16th British Machine Vision Conference.* Oxford, United Kingdom, pp. 879-888.

Davies, R. et al., 2001. A Minimum Description Length Approach to Statistical Shape Modelling. *Information Processing in Medical Imaging.* Davis, CA, USA, pp. 50–63.

Davies, R. et al., C., 2008. Groupwise Surface Correspondence by Optimization: Representation and Regularization. *Medical Image Analysis,* Vol. 12, No. 6, pp. 787–796.

FGNET, 2004. Face and gesture network: talking face database. *Available at: http://www-prima.inrialpes.fr/FGnet/data/01-TalkingFace/talking_face.html*

Jones, M. and Poggio, T., 1998. Multidimensional Morphable Models., *In 6th International Conference on Computer Vision.* Bombay, India, pp. 683–688.

Kroon, D. and Slump, C., 2009. MRI Modalitiy Transformation in Demon Registration. *IEEE International Symposium on Biomedical Imaging: From Nano to Macro.* Boston, MA, USA, pp. 963-966.

Lotjone, J. and Makela, T., 2001. Elastic Matching Using a Deformation Sphere. *In MICCAI.* Utrecht, The Netherlands, pp. 541–548.

Matthews, I. and Baker, S., 2004. Active Appearance Models Revisited. *International Journal of Computer Vision,* Vol. 60, No. 2, pp. 135-164.

Nordstrøm, M. et al., 2004. The IMM Face Database - an Annotated Dataset of 240 Face Images. *Technical report, Informatics and Mathematical Modelling,* University of Denmark, DTU.

Ridge, E., 2007. Design of Experiments for the Tuning of Optimisation Algorithms. Department of Computer Science, The University of York, York, United Kingdom.

Sidorov, K. et al., 2009. An Efficient Stochastic Approach to Groupwise Non-rigid Image Registration. *In IEEE Conference on Computer Vision and Pattern Recognition.* Miami Beach, FL, USA, pp. 2208-2213.

Tiddeman, B. et al., 2001. A General Method for Overlap Control in Image Warping. *Computers and Graphics,* Vol. 25, No. 1, pp. 59–66.

Tiddeman, B. and Hunter, D., 2011. Groupwise Non-Rigid Image Alignment-Results of a Multiscale Iterative Best Edge Algorithm. *In VISAPP.* Vilamoura, Portugal, pp. 22-29.

Twining, C. et al., 2004. Groupwise Nonrigid Registration of Medical Images: The Minimum Description Length Approach. *In Medical Image Analysis and Underdtanding.* pp. 81-84.

Twining, C. et al., 2004. Groupwise Non-Rigid Registration: The Minimum Description Length Approach. *BMVC.* London, United Kingdom, pp. 417-426.

Yang, X. et al., 2013. Framework for Self-tuning Optimization Algorithm. *Neural Computing and Applications, Vol.* 23, No. 7-8, pp. 2051–2057.

CHOICE OF THE REGULARIZATION PARAMETER FOR TOTAL VARIATION IMAGE DENOISING USING NO-REFERENCE METRIC

Nikolay Mamaev, Andrey Krylov and Dmitry Yurin
Lomonosov Moscow State University
GSP-1, Leninskie Gory, Moscow, Russia
+7 (495) 939 1000

ABSTRACT

An automatic method for total variation denoising parameter calculation has been proposed. Parameter optimization is performed in the ridge areas of the difference image between original noisy and filtered images (so-called method noise image). Appearance of regular components on method noise is controlled using mutual information closely connected with conditional entropy. Images corrupted with Gaussian-like noise with small correlation radius are considered. Hessian matrix eigenvalues analysis is used for estimation of sizes and directions of image characteristic details. FISTA optimizer was used for the minimization of the regularizing total variation functional. Images with added controlled Gaussian noise from retinal DRIVE and general image BSDS500 databases, and biomedical images of nuclei of HL60 cell line were used for testing.

KEYWORDS

Total Variation Denoising, Image Denoising Quality Assessment, Mutual Information

1. INTRODUCTION

Image denoising using prior models is very important for different practical problems. The prior models can be roughly classified (Zhang, K. et al, 2017) in nonlocal self-similarity models, sparse models, gradient models and Markov random field models.

The above prior model methods preserve intrinsic image structures like edges, ridges and blobs while suppressing additive Gaussian noise, but as one of their main drawbacks we can underline the problem of the method parameters choice. It is a difficult task and too often the parameters are chosen manually. To compete with deep learning methods a solution of this task is necessary.

One of the most popular methods of image denoising is "gradient" model method based on minimization of the total variation (TV) (Rudin, L. I. et al, 1992; Osher, S. et al, 2005). It is one of the classical methods and it had a big influence on the progress of image processing science. The theme "Constrained total-variation image de-noising and restoration" had been selected in 2013 by Thomson Reuters as the highest Top-Ranked Speciality in the area of Mathematics, Computer Science and Engineering in the period 2007-2012 (King, C. and Pendlebury, D. A, 2013).

A denoised image here is obtained by regularization method (Tikhonov, A. and Arsenin, V. Y., 1977) solving variational problem with total variation stabilizer. The method can provide a high quality of the denoised image but it needs an effective procedure for regularization parameter choice. There are many gradient-based optimizers for solving the variational problem for fixed regularization parameter including iterative shrinkage thresholding algorithm (ISTA) (Daubechies, I. et al, C., 2004) and its fast verison (FISTA) (Beck, A. and Teboulle, M., 2009).

Last time deep learning methods show competitive results comparing with different image prior modeling approaches (Zhang, K. et al, 2017; Jin, K. H. et al, 2017). Nevertheless in many cases self-similarity and gradient methods are more stable to the change of the noise type than deep learning methods. One of the ways to solve this problem is to incorporate model based approach into deep learning like using TV regularized L2 loss (Wang T et al, 2017).

In this paper we suggest a method for automatic choice of the regularization parameter for total variation minimization denoising. The method is based on the approach (Mamaev, N. et al, 2017), where image denoising quality assessment method for Non-local Means (NLM) and Local Jets based Non-local Means (LJNLM-LR) methods had been suggested.

Image denoising methods depend on filtering strength parameters. In the ideal case, an optimal parameter is chosen basing on optimization of some metric (for example, PSNR) between filtered image and the source image without noise (or, reference image). Nevertheless in practice we need to use methods that work without reference image (no-reference methods).

Methods to estimate image denoising quality compute a no-reference image quality assessment value. These methods usually calculate image local spatial statistics (Mittal, A., et al, 2012; Moorthy, A. K. and Bovik, A. C., 2011) or statistics in the frequency domain (Saad, M. A. et al, 2012). However, these methods do not take into account the condition of image structure preserving. To control these structures by ridge based approach we calculate image denoising quality using difference between noisy and filtered images (so called method noise (Buades, A. et al, 2005)).

Presence of regular structures in ridge areas of the method noise image shows ridge smoothing or suppression by the testing denoising algorithm. We suppose that sizes of these structures are larger than the noise correlation radius. This regularity can be numerically estimated using entropy, mutual information, etc. Method (Storozhilova, M. et al, 2013) uses an entropy measure of the directed differences of the method noise.

Ridge detection problem is one of the classical problems of image processing. The first basic paper on ridge detection is (Haralick, R. M., 1983). Its approach is based on the transition from discrete pixel grid view to continuous using bicubic interpolation and brightness surface analysis using differential calculus. The method can be applied for detection of thin lines only. Directional derivative analysis is used to classify edges, ridges and valleys, saddles and blobs. A more detailed mathematical definition of ridges is given in book (Eberly, D., 1996). Ridges are considered in multidimensional Euclidean and Riemann spaces and manifolds, a tensor description is also provided. Compact but fairly strict and full analysis and multiscale problem statement are given in (Lindeberg, T., 1998). We note that for the ridge detection problem a multiscale approach is essentially needed unlike edge detection (Canny, J., 1987) or corner detection. This is because the detecting filters for ridges are based on Laplacian or other combination of Hessian matrix eigenvalues and have a significant response only for the scale that is close to the scale of the ridge. In paper (Frangi, A. F. et al, 1998) along with a simplified multiscale consideration a quite interesting mathematical definition of ridges and functionals for their detection are given. Also a three-dimensional case is considered and ridge detection is applied to vessel detection and CT and MRI image analysis. An alternate approach for ridge detection is based on anisotropic diffusion (Direkoglu, C. et al, 2012; Perona P. and Malik, J., 1990) that can be adopted to ridge detection and also allows to take into account information from different scales.

In this paper a method for no-reference image denoising quality assessment to choose regularization parameter of total variation minimization denoising method is proposed. Unlike method (Storozhilova, M. et al, 2013) this method uses mutual information of joint distribution of method noise brightness values at ridge points and values in direction of ridge.

2. TOTAL VARIATION IMAGE DENOISING

Rudin, Osher, and Fatemi (Rudin, L. I. et al, 1992) proposed to obtain a denoised image $\tilde{u}$ as a solution of the following variational problem:

$$\tilde{u} = \arg\min_u \left\{ TV(u) + \frac{\lambda}{2}\|u - f\|_2^2 \right\}, \quad TV(u) = \int_\Omega |\nabla u| dx \tag{1}$$

where f is a noisy image, $TV(u)$ is the total variation of image u and Ω is the image definition area. We can rewrite the minimization problem (1) as:

$$\arg\min_u \{ g(u) + h(u) \}, \tag{2}$$

where $g(u)$ is convex non-differentiable function and $h(u)$ is convex differentiable function. For solving this type of variational problems there exist effective gradient-based algorithms. In our work we use for the functional minimization FISTA algorithm (Beck, A. and Teboulle, M., 2009).

The minimization problem (1) depends on regularization parameter λ that controls the filtering strength. If λ is too high then the regularization term has high impact on the objective function and denoising strength is low and vice versa. So we need an effective method to choose the regularization parameter for fully automated denoising.

3. MULTISCALE IMAGE RIDGE DETECTION

Laplacian filter can indicate the presence of ridge. We define:

$$L^{\sigma}(x,y) = \sigma^2 \cdot I(x,y) * G_{\sigma}(x,y),\ G_{\sigma}(x,y) = \frac{1}{2\pi\sigma^2} e^{\frac{x^2+y^2}{2\sigma^2}} \tag{3}$$

where $I(x,y)$ is intensity of the source image. We note that the differentiation of $L^{\sigma}(x,y)$ is equivalent to convolution of the source image $I(x,y)$ with corresponding Gaussian function derivative. Let $L^{\sigma}_{xx}(x,y)$, $L^{\sigma}_{xy}(x,y)$, $L^{\sigma}_{yy}(x,y)$ be second derivatives of $L^{\sigma}(x,y)$ by the corresponding variables multiplied by σ^2. This multiplication by σ^2 is used to equalize Laplacian filter response at different scales. So, if we increase both the image and σ by same factor the filter response will be same for the corresponding points. Modulus of Laplacian $\Delta L^{\sigma}(x,y)$ has maximum in the central point of ridge of 2σ width. To find ridge direction we build a Hessian matrix:

$$H^{\sigma}(x,y) = \begin{pmatrix} L^{\sigma}_{xx}(x,y) & L^{\sigma}_{xy}(x,y) \\ L^{\sigma}_{yx}(x,y) & L^{\sigma}_{yy}(x,y) \end{pmatrix}, \tag{4}$$

Then eigenvector $\overrightarrow{v^{\sigma}}(x,y)$ corresponding to the smallest by absolute value eigenvalue of $H^{\sigma}(x,y)$ will be directed along the ridge (Lindeberg, T., 1998).

For multiscale ridge detection we use different values of $\sigma \in \{\sigma_1,...,\sigma_n\}$, $\sigma_i = \sigma_0 \cdot v^i$. Calculating $\Delta L^{\sigma_i}(x,y)$ and $\overrightarrow{v^{\sigma}}(x,y)$ corresponding to σ_i, we find the characteristic ridge size $s(x,y)$ and direction $\vec{v}(x,y)$ as:

$$s(x,y) = \arg\max_{\sigma_i}(|\Delta L^{\sigma_i}(x,y)|),\ \vec{v}(x,y) = \overrightarrow{v^{s(x,y)}}(x,y). \tag{5}$$

To eliminate false responses of the Laplacian produced by noise for small σ we use the following scheme:

1. Apply thresholding to $\Delta L^{s(x,y)}(x,y)$:

$$B(x,y) = \begin{cases} 1, |\Delta L^{s(x,y)}(x,y)| \geq T_l \\ 0, otherwise \end{cases}. \tag{6}$$

   The threshold value T_l was set to 0.1 in all tests.
2. Find connected components in $B(x,y)$ image and remove components that have less than 5 pixels.
3. Apply binary mask $B(x,y)$ to $|\Delta L^{s(x,y)}(x,y)|$ to obtain filtered Laplacian responses:

$$F(x,y) = B(x,y) \cdot |\Delta L^{s(x,y)}(x,y)|. \tag{7}$$

The images of $F(x,y)$ and $|\Delta L^{s(x,y)}(x,y)|$ for $\sigma = 2$, $\sigma = 4$ and $\sigma = 8$ computed for synthetic image of nuclei of HL60 cell line (Svoboda, D. et al, 2009) are shown in figure 1.

4. IMAGE DENOISING QUALITY ASSESSMENT USING METHOD NOISE ANALYSIS

We use "method noise" image analysis for image denoising quality assessment. Method noise I_d for image I is defined as the difference between image I and image I_f after application of a denoising method:

$$I_d = I - I_f. \tag{8}$$

In the ideal case, a method noise contains only noise. The presence of details that are also presented on the source image means that these details have been smoothed or wiped out with noise after application of a denoising method, while we want to retain them. The main characteristics indicating that the method noise contains only noise is absence of correlation of nearby pixel values. The presence of regular structures results in the presence of correlation of nearby pixel values at least in area where these structures appear. Method noise image with uncorrelated pixel values indicates that image denoising had not distorted ridges in image. If after image denoising some ridges have been distorted (smoothed of wiped out) the method noise image will contain contours of distorted ridges that results in presence of correlation of intensities of method noise image along these ridges.

To evaluate the correlation of intensities on method noise I_d along ridges we build a joint distribution $p(k,m)$ of the following random variables: let K be a value of method noise in point (x,y) and M be a value of method noise in point $\overrightarrow{(x,y)+s(x,y)\cdot\vec{v}(x,y)}$. Only points where $F(x,y)>0$ are used to take into consideration only points belonging to ridges. At the same time values of the method noise image are quantized to N levels so the nearby values are interpreted as same event. We use bicubic interpolation to find values in the points outside the pixel grid. So $p(k,m)$ is defined as follows:

$$p(k,m) = \frac{1}{P}\cdot\left|\left\{(x,y): \left\lfloor\frac{I_d(x,y)\cdot N}{I_{\max}}\right\rfloor = k \left\lfloor\frac{I_d(\tilde{x},\tilde{y})\cdot N}{I_{\max}}\right\rfloor = m, F(x,y)>0\right\}\right|, \tag{9}$$

$$\tilde{x} = x + s(x,y)\cdot\vec{v}(x,y)_x, \tilde{y} = y + s(x,y)\cdot\vec{v}(x,y)_y, \tag{10}$$

there $I_{\max}$ is the maximal allowed pixel intensity value and P is normalizing constant such that $\sum_{k=1}^{N}\sum_{m=1}^{N} p(k,m) = 1$. We note in the case $s(x,y)=s\equiv const$, $\vec{v}(x,y)=\vec{v}\equiv const$, and $F(x,y)>0$ $\forall(x,y)$ the joint distribution represents a co-occurrence matrix (Haralick, R. M. et al, 1973) built for the direction $s\cdot\vec{v}$.

A mutual information can be used to evaluate independence of random variables in joint distribution. For random variables K and M it is defined as:

$$\mu(K;M) = \sum_{k=1}^{N}\sum_{m=1}^{N} p(k,m)\log\left(\frac{p(k,m)}{p(k)p(m)}\right), \tag{11}$$

there $p(k)$ and $p(m)$ are marginal probability distribution functions:

$$p(k) = \sum_{m=1}^{N} p(k,m),\ p(m) = \sum_{k=1}^{N} p(k,m). \tag{12}$$

The less is the value of μ the less brightness values of the method noise image along ridges are correlated. The values that differ less than $I_{\max}/N$ will be interpreted as single event. If N is too low then small fluctuations of pixel values will be interpreted as different events that can lead to mutual information instability. If N is too high then even fluctuations caused by noise will be considered as the same event and this can lead to poor denoising quality assessment using mutual information.

The Laplacian $\Delta L^{s(x,y)}(x,y)$ has also a response in the points that belong to edges and blobs. This means that the μ value also takes into account pairs of pixels belonging to these edges and blobs. This does not contradict to the condition of ridge preserving since edges, blobs and ridges are distorted in the same time after denoising.

Eventually, the image denoising quality assessment is given by the value of μ calculated for the method noise image I_d. The values of characteristic scales, Laplacian responses and directions of ridges are computed from the source noisy image I. Minimal value of μ from (11) will correspond to the optimal denoising parameter:

$$\lambda_{est} = \arg\min_{\lambda}(\mu). \tag{13}$$

We found the minimal value of μ using an algorithm based on golden section search and parabolic interpolation (Forsythe, G. E. et al, 1977).

We note that the μ value will be unstable or even undefined in the case if the Laplacian does not contain enough values larger than T_l. It also means that the image almost does not contain ridges, edges or other complex structures so edge-preserving denoising is not required. We estimate amount of detected ridges counting the number of points as:

$$S = \left|\{(x, y) : F(x, y) > 0\}\right|. \tag{14}$$

If S value is less than threshold $T_r = \max(100, 0.01 \cdot R \cdot C)$ then denoising is not required and denoising quality assessment is not performed. Here R and C is the number of rows and columns in image respectively. We also note that in the case if there is no noise in source image the μ value will be monotonically increasing with the increase of the filtering strength since the method noise will not contain noise and denoising should not be performed. To avoid this we estimate noise level in image using PCA-based noise level estimation method (Pyatykh, S. et al, 2013). If estimated noise level is lower than ε then denoising is not performed. The proposed denoising quality assessment pipeline is shown in figure 2.

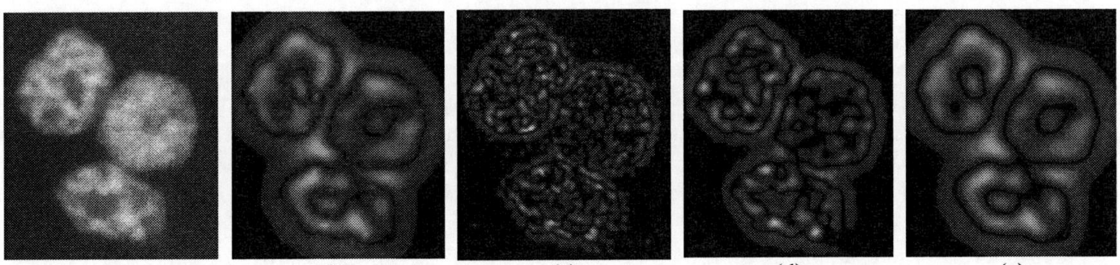

(a) (b) (c) (d) (e)

Figure 1. (a) Synthetic image of nuclei of HL60 cell line, (b) $F(x, y)$ image. $\left|\Delta L^{s(x,y)}(x, y)\right|$ images for $\sigma = 2$ (c), $\sigma = 4$ (d) and $\sigma = 8$ (e)

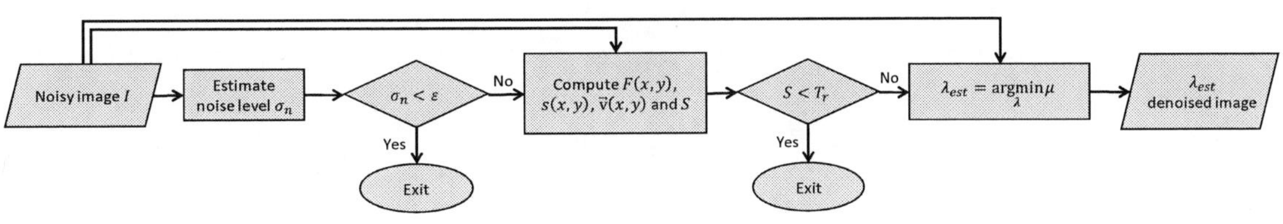

Figure 2. Denoising Quality Assessment Pipeline

5. RESULTS

We tested the proposed method with 2 databases. The first is DRIVE (Staal, J. et al, 2004) database of 40 retinal 565x584 images. These images contain many ridges of different scales and directions to be a good testing set for our method. The second database is BSDS500 (Arbelaez, P. et al, 2011) of 500 481x321 images. The image intensity values from both databases are between 0 and 255. The testing procedure is defined as follows:

1. To each database image a Gaussian noise is added with different standard deviations σ_{noise}. So for each image I we will get image $I_{\sigma_{noise}}$. We use values of $\sigma_{noise} \in \{2i, i = 1,...,10\}$.
2. Total variation minimization with different regularization parameters $\lambda \in \{\lambda_1,...,\lambda_L\}$ is applied to image $I_{\sigma_{noise}}$ producing an image I_{f_λ}. Now we have a set of denoised images $I_{f_{\lambda_i}}$.
3. μ values are calculated for the denoised images. Since we know that the noise is additive Gaussian then PSNR values for source image without noise and denoised images are suitable for testing. The maximal value will correspond to the optimal denoising parameter. We used the following parameters for ridge detection: $\sigma_0 = 1$, $\nu = \sqrt{2}$ and $n = 8$. We have tested different numbers of quantization levels $N \in \{2^i, i = 2,...,7\}$ and observed that the best value is $N = 16$.
4. Optimal parameter $\lambda_{opt} = \arg\max_{\lambda_i}(PSNR(I, I_{f_{\lambda_i}}))$ and estimated parameter $\lambda_{est} = \arg\max_{\lambda_i}(\mu(I_{f_{\lambda_i}}))$ are found. Finally we calculate a relative error for the estimated parameter and the optimal parameter:

$$e = \frac{|\lambda_{est} - \lambda_{opt}|}{|\lambda_{opt}|} \tag{15}$$

The described procedure has been also performed for no-reference image quality assessment methods BRISQUE (Mittal, A., et al, 2012), BLIIDNS-2 (Saad, M. A. et al, 2012) and DIVINE (Moorthy, A. K. and Bovik, A. C., 2011) replacing computation of μ value by computation by the corresponding method at step 3. Quality scores were maximized instead of minimizing used in mutual information based method. Mean values of relative error e for the above methods are given in the figure 3 for DRIVE and BSDS500 databases. It can be seen that for both DRIVE and BSDS500 images the proposed denoising quality assessment method using μ value works better than no-reference image quality assessment methods for all noise levels. An example of image from BSDS500 database and plots of μ and PSNR values per regularization parameter λ are shown in figure 4. A result of application of total variation denoising method with the estimated optimal parameter λ to synthetic image of nuclei of HL60 cell line (Svoboda, D. et al, 2009) is shown in figure 5.

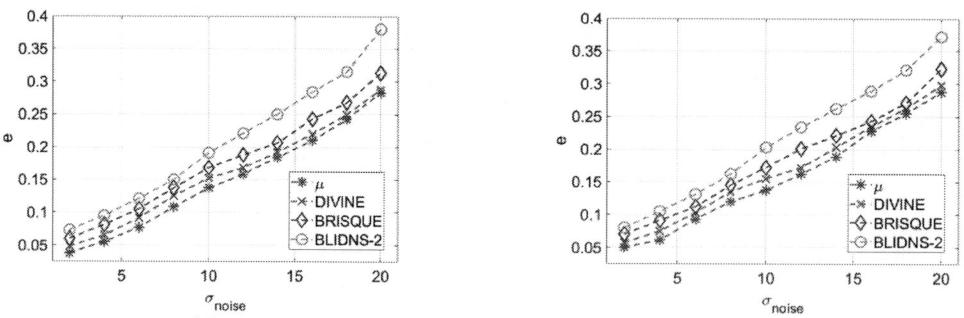

(a) (b)

Figure 3. Plots of mean of relative error e (15) depend on added noise level σ_{noise} for DRIVE (a) and BSDS500 (b) image databases

6. CONCLUSION

We have proposed a method for image denoising quality assessment to be used for selection of optimal regularization parameter for total variation denoising. The usage of mutual information for joint distribution of pixel values of method noise image along ridges looks preferable for this purpose comparing to other denoising quality assessment methods. The future direction of the work will be concerned with analysis of other image structures like textures, etc. and their consideration in a generalized parameters optimization framework.

ACKNOWLEDGEMENT

The work was supported by Russian Science Foundation grant 17-11-01279.

(a)

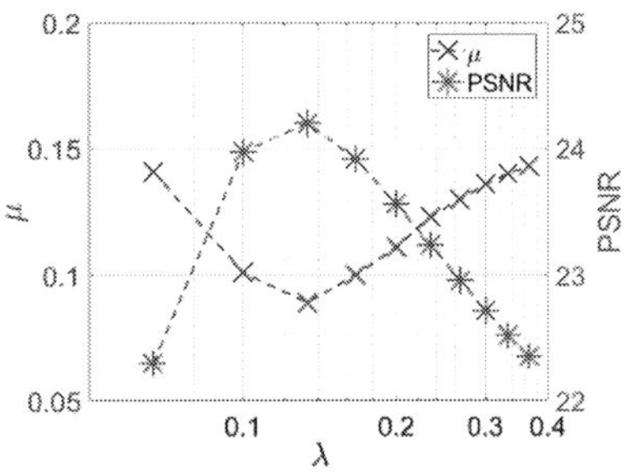

(b)

Figure 4. (a) An image from BSDS500 database, (b) plot of μ and PSNR for I and I_{f_λ} images per regularization parameter λ, $\sigma_{noise} = 15$

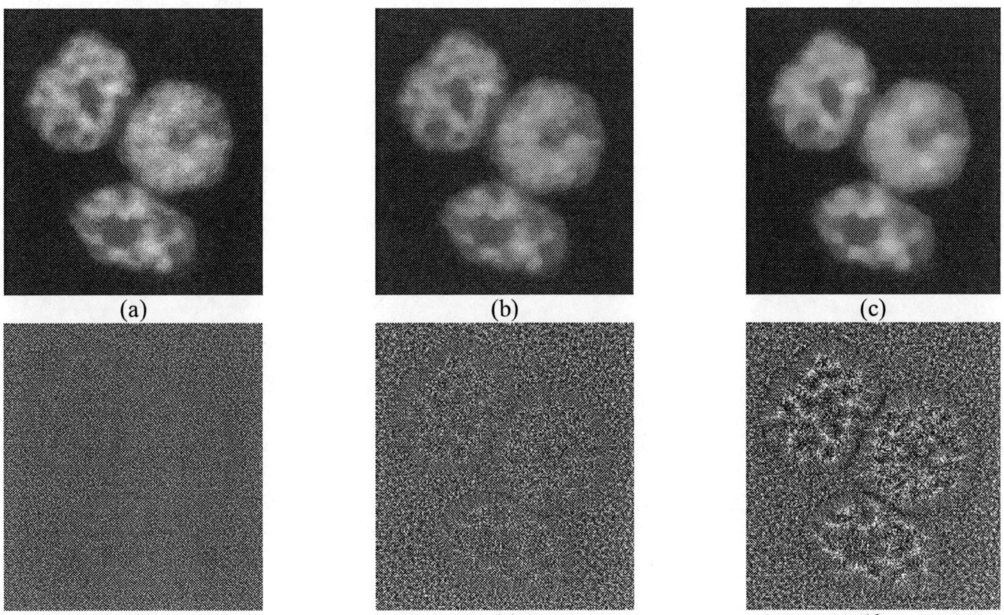

(a) (b) (c)

(d) (e) (f)

Figure 5. Denoising result and method noise for figure 1a. (a) denoising result with regularization parameter lower than optimal, (b) denoising result with optimal regularization parameter, (c) denoising result with regularization parameter bigger than optimal. μ values for images (a) and (c) are 1.4 times larger than μ for optimal regularization parameter. (d-f) method noise for images (a-c). Contrast for images (d-f) is adjusted for better view

REFERENCES

Arbelaez, P. et al, 2011. *Contour detection and hierarchical image segmentation*. IEEE Trans. Pattern Anal. Mach. Intell., vol. 33, no. 5, pp. 898–916.

Beck, A. and Teboulle, M., 2009. *Fast gradient-based algorithms for constrained total variation image denoising and deblurring problems*. IEEE Transactions on Image Processing, vol. 18, no. 11, pp. 2419–2434.

Buades, A. et al, 2005. *A review of image denoising algorithms, with a new one*. Multiscale Modeling & Simulation, vol. 4, no. 2, pp. 490–530.

Canny, J., 1987. *A computational approach to edge detection*. Readings in Computer Vision. Elsevier, pp. 184–203.

Daubechies, I. et al, C., 2004. *An iterative thresholding algorithm for linear inverse problems with a sparsity constraint*. Communications on pure and applied mathematics, vol. 57, no. 11, pp. 1413–1457.

Direkoglu, C. et al, 2012. *On using anisotropic diffusion for skeleton extraction*. International journal of computer vision, vol. 100, no. 2, pp. 170–189.

Eberly, D., 1996. *Ridges in Image and Data Analysis*. Springer Science & Business Media, vol. 7.

Frangi, A. F. et al, 1998. *Multiscale vessel enhancement filtering*. International Conference on Medical Image Computing and Computer-Assisted Intervention, Springer, pp. 130–137.

Forsythe, G. E. et al, 1977. *Computer methods for mathematical computations*. Prentice-Hall.

Haralick, R. M. et al, 1973. *Textural features for image classification*. IEEE Transactions on systems, man, and cybernetics, no. 6, pp. 610–621.

Haralick, R. M., 1983. *Ridges and valleys on digital images*. Computer Vision, Graphics, and Image Processing, vol. 22, no. 1, pp. 28–38.

Jin, K. H. et al, 2017 *Deep convolutional neural network for inverse problems in imaging*. IEEE Transactions on Image Processing, vol. 26, no. 9, pp. 4509–4522.

King, C. and Pendlebury, D. A, 2013. *Research Fronts 2013. 100 Top-Ranked Specialties in the Sciences and Social Sciences*. Thomson Reuters.

Lindeberg, T., 1998. *Edge detection and ridge detection with automatic scale selection*. International Journal of Computer Vision, vol. 30, no. 2, pp. 117–156.

Mamaev, N. et al, 2017. *Image ridge denoising using noreference metric*. International Conference on Advanced Concepts for Intelligent Vision Systems. pp. 591–601.

Mittal, A., et al, 2012. *No-reference image quality assessment in the spatial domain*. IEEE Transactions on Image Processing, vol. 21, no. 12, pp. 4695–4708.

Moorthy, A. K. and Bovik, A. C., 2011. *Blind image quality assessment: From natural scene statistics to perceptual quality*. IEEE transactions on Image Processing, vol. 20, no. 12, pp. 3350–3364.

Osher, S. et al, 2005. An iterative regularization method for total variation-based image restoration. *Multiscale Modeling & Simulation*, vol. 4, no. 2, pp. 460–489.

Perona P. and Malik, J., 1990. *Scale-space and edge detection using anisotropic diffusion*. IEEE Transactions on pattern analysis and machine intelligence, vol. 12, no. 7, pp. 629–639.

Pyatykh, S. et al, 2013. *Image noise level estimation by principal component analysis*. IEEE Transactions on Image Processing, vol. 22, no. 2, pp. 687–699.

Rudin, L. I. et al, 1992. *Nonlinear total variation based noise removal algorithms.* Physica D: nonlinear phenomena, vol. 60, no. 1-4, pp. 259–268.

Saad, M. A. et al, 2012. *Blind image quality assessment: A natural scene statistics approach in the dct domain*. IEEE transactions on Image Processing, vol. 21, no. 8, pp. 3339–3352.

Staal, J. et al, 2004. *Ridge-based vessel segmentation in color images of the retina*. IEEE transactions on medical imaging, vol. 23, no. 4 pp. 501–509.

Storozhilova, M. et al, 2013. *Methods Of Noise Filtering Quality Assessment For CT Images*. The 15-th International Conference Digital Signal Processing And Its Applications, vol. 2, pp. 85–88.

Svoboda, D. et al, 2009. *Generation of digital phantoms of cell nuclei and simulation of image formation in 3D image cytometry.* Cytometry part A, vol. 75, no. 6, pp. 494–509.

Tikhonov, A. and Arsenin, V. Y., 1977. *Methods for solving ill-posed problems*. John Wiley and Sons, Inc.

Wang T et al, 2017, *An ELU Network with Total Variation for Image Denoising.* International Conference on Neural Information Processing, pp. 227-237.

Zhang, K. et al, 2017. *Beyond a gaussian denoiser: Residual learning of deep cnn for image denoising.* IEEE Transactions on Image Processing, vol. 26, no. 7, pp. 3142-3155.

EXTRACTION METHOD OF KEYPOINT DESCRIPTOR FOR OBJECT RECOGNITION IN SONAR IMAGE

Jeong Mun Park[1], Wan-Jin Kim[2] and Kun Su Yoon[3]
[1]*Department of Informatics, Gyeongsang National University, 501, Jinju-daero, Jinju-si, Gyeongsangnam-do, Republic of Korea, 52828*
[2]*Agency for Defense Development, Jinhae PO Box #18, Jinhae-gu, Changwon-si, Gyeongsangnam-do, Republic of Korea, 51678*
[3]*Department of Aviation Control System, Aviation Campus of Korea Polytechnic, 46 Daehak-gil, Sacheon-si, Gyeongsangnam-do, Republic of Korea, 52549*

ABSTRACT

In sonar images, the object shape is often distorted by the external conditions such as sedimentation, pulse repetition interval, ship speed, and redirection, which is generally modeled as the affine transform. Scale invariant feature transform(SIFT) and pyramid-SIFT(p-SIFT) are known as a good solution to the scale and rotation variance. However, these methods are vulnerable to the shearing problem. To solve the affine problem in sonar imaging systems, we propose a new keypoint descriptor extraction method. The proposed method generates multiple keypoint descriptors based on affine transformed images, and picks out effective keypoint descriptors. Test results show that the proposed method, in terms of recognition rate, has better accuracy than those of the conventional methods for scaling of *x*, *y*-axis, rotation, and shearing cases. The average improved accuracy rate of SIFT and p-SIFT is 7% and 4%, respectively.

KEYWORDS

Object Recognition, Keypoint Descriptor, Scale invariant Feature Transform

1. INTRODUCTION

Recently, acoustic imaging sonars are widely used to naval field such as marine exploration and geological survey. Compared with an optical device, the advantage of the imaging sonar is operational robustness and wide swath. Acquired sonar images are generally analyzed by the system operator but the need of automatic image processing has been raised by a huge increase in data and an introduction of unmanned vehicles. Especially, in time critical mission such as military operation, computer assistance is essential to detection and recognize object [Langner, F., & Knauer, C. 2009].

Many researches have been performed to develop computer-aided detection(CAD) and automated recognition(AR) in the air but it is not easy to directly apply the recent achievement on the acoustic imaging sonar system. Since the ocean always changes by environmental conditions of the wind and the current, it yields to unpredictable distortions combined with operational conditions such as pulse repetition interval(PRI), the vehicle speed and movements [Klaucke, I. 2018]. These distortions affect the object detection and recognition.

The conventional algorithms such as SIFT and p-SIFT are well known to overcome undesired object scale variation and rotation [David G. Lowe 2004, Seidenari, L. & Serra, G. 2014]. However, sonar images generally suffer from affine problem due to a difference resolution of the along and the across track, the geometrical slant, and the bottoming and sedimentation condition. To solve the affine problem, we analyzed various sonar images and found out a clue in the keypoint descriptor.

When an image experiences the affine transform, keypoint descriptors remain or disappear. The remained descriptors are considered as having affine invariance and they influence the object recognition performance. To select affine invariant one, we generate several descriptors, which reflect various affine characteristics. Comparing them to the given descriptor of p-SIFT, we choose to have minimum Euclidian distance. To verify the performance of the proposed method, we test for three sonar images.

2. BACKGROUND

2.1 Scale Invariant Feature Transform

The SIFT algorithm was originally proposed by David G. Lowe in 1999. It has been widely used in the digital image recognition due to its invariance property on the scale, and the rotation. The algorithm is consisted of four steps as shown in the figure 1 and is known to have robustness to noisy and imbalanced illumination environments [David G. Lowe 2004].

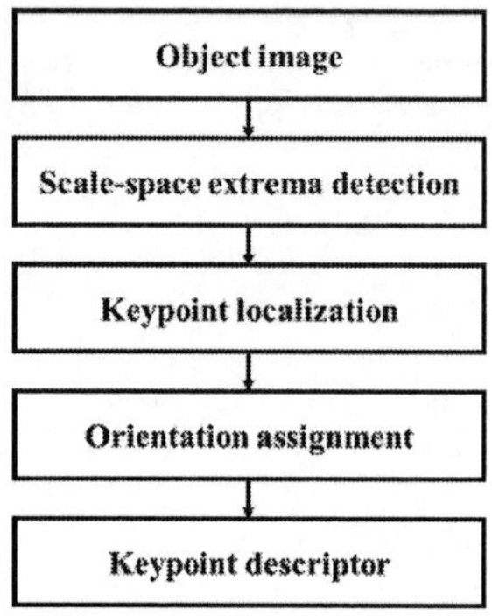

Figure 1. Procedure of the SIFT

2.1.1 Scale-space Extrema Detection

To reduce the calculation, the SIFT algorithm uses a Difference of Gaussian(DoG) method instead of the Harris-Laplace method [David G. Lowe 2004]. The input image is convolved with the Gaussian function, which has different variance levels and the scale-space is constructed to extract keypoint candidates. The DoG is defined as follows

$$D(x, y, \sigma) = L(x, y, k\sigma) - L(x, y, \sigma), \tag{1}$$

where $D(x, y, \sigma)$ is DoG image and $L(x, y, k\sigma)$ and $L(x, y, \sigma)$ are Gaussian blur images with different variance level.

Based on the pyramid, the center pixel marked to the black color is compared to the adjacent 26 pixels as shown in figure 2. If the center pixel has the maximum or minimum value, it is determined to the candidate. This process is repeatedly performed to the intermediate Gaussian images, which are down-sampled in the scale-space.

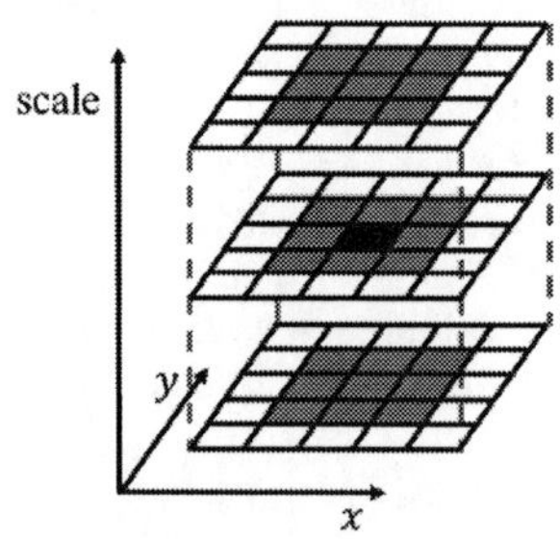

Figure 2. Extracting Keypoint Candidates

2.1.2 Keypoint Localization

In the scale-space extrema detection step, Taylor series and thresholding are used to determine a stable point among the obtained keypoint candidates. This is defined as follows

$$D(\hat{x}) = D + \frac{1}{2}\frac{\partial D^T}{\partial x}\hat{x}, \tag{2}$$

where $\hat{x}$, D, and $D(\hat{x})$ are the location of extremum, DoG image, and the function value at the extremum, respectively. For refining keypoint candidates, the Taylor series is applied to the DoG image. The binary image is approximated to the continuous image and it has a different keypoint. If the distance difference in any direction is greater than or equal 50%, it moves to another position and performs refinement. After the refinement process, contrast pixels lower than the given threshold are eliminated.

2.1.3 Orientation Assignment

For the rotation invariance, the directionality is calculated using the high contrast pixels. The original image is divided into the 16x16 regions and each region represents the directionality as follows

$$m(x,y) = \sqrt{\left(L(x+1,y) - L(x-1,y)\right)^2 + \left(L(x,y+1) - L(x,y-1)\right)^2}, \quad (3)$$

$$\theta(x,y) = \tan^{-1}\left(\frac{L(x,y+1) - L(x,y-1)}{L(x+1,y) - L(x-1,y)}\right), \quad (4)$$

where $m(x,y)$ and $\theta(x,y)$ are the gradient magnitude and the azimuth, respectively. The orientation is quantized to 36 angles along the azimuth direction. After calculating the vector sum, the azimuth with the maximum magnitude becomes the keypoint and the others greater than or equal 80% of the maximum are also chosen as the keypoint.

2.1.4 Keypoint Descriptor

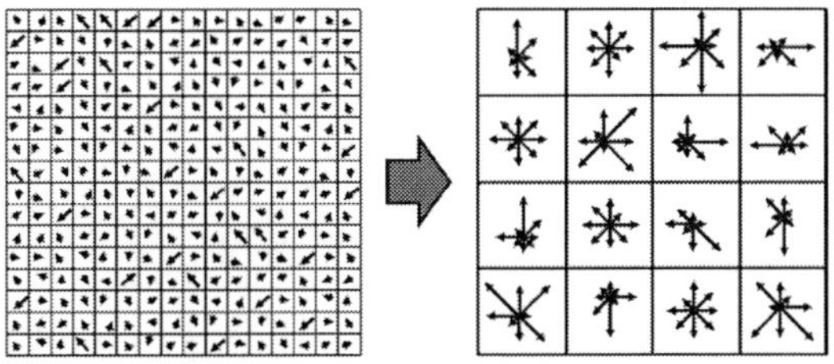

Figure 3. Generating keypoint descriptor.

The rotation invariance is the normalization process to summarize 16x16 region to 4x4 region as shown in figure 3. In 4x4 region, magnitudes are normalized to the maximum value of the vector sum of 16x16 region and the rotation is quantized to eight angles. Each set of the magnitude and angle corresponding to the 4x4 region becomes the keypoint descriptors.

2.2 Pyramid-SIFT

The p-SIFT algorithm had been introduced to reduce miss matching cases of the SIFT. The keypoint detection technique of the p-SIFT is the same as SIFT but it adopts the multi-resolution descriptors as shown in figure 4 [Seidenari, L. & Serra, G. 2014].

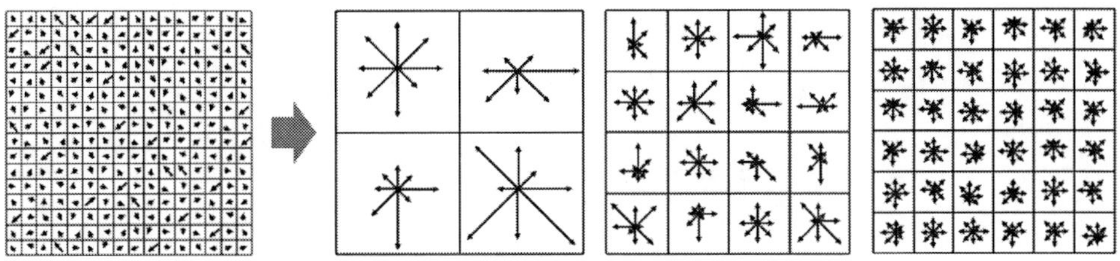

Figure 4. Generating Descriptor of p-SIFT

3. PROPOSED METHOD

The conventional algorithms, the SIFT and the p-SIFT, extract descriptor invariant to the scale and the rotation. However, these methods are not effective the geometric invariance such as the difference scaling of x, y-axis and shearing. For the object detection and classification in sonar images, it is necessary to consider the affine characteristics. We propose a method to extract effective keypoints by comparing affine based keypoint descriptors to the original key descriptor of the p-SIFT. The figure 5 describes the procedure of the proposed method(PM).

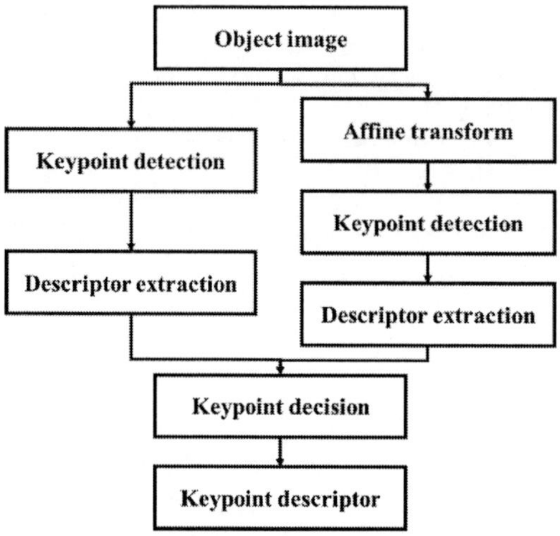

Figure 5. Procedure of the PM

3.1 Analysis about Object Characteristics in Sonar Images

In sonar image, the object may be distorted by change of PRI, ship speed, and redirection. The across track(x-axis) of the object shape is proportionately changed by PRI and the along track(y-axis) is inverse proportional to the ship speed. These change yields to image distortion problem as shown in figure 6.

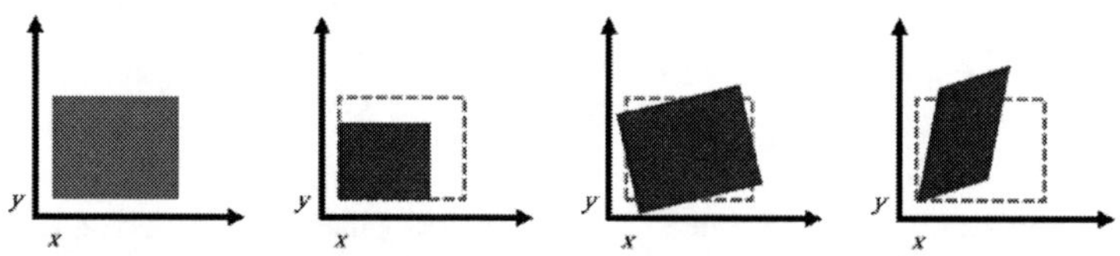

Figure 6. Example of Image Distortion: (a) Original, (b) Scale, (c) Rotation, and (d) Shearing

This problem is modeled as the affine transform and it is defined as follows

$$\begin{bmatrix} x' \\ y' \end{bmatrix} = \begin{bmatrix} p_1 & p_2 \\ p_3 & p_4 \end{bmatrix} \begin{bmatrix} x \\ y \end{bmatrix} + \begin{bmatrix} t_1 \\ t_2 \end{bmatrix}, \tag{5}$$

where p_1, p_2, p_3, and p_4 are corresponding to the rotation and the scale and t_1 and t_2 make the translation [Nomizu, K. & Sasaki, T. 1994]. If we have information on the original and affine image, the solution is to find the parameter values or compare all possible cases. However, in imaging sonar system, it can be hardly to get the original image and we can get just the affine image. The goal of this paper is to find out the same or similar object in other images, which have different perspective or affine characteristic. To overcome this problem, we regard the affine image as the original image and, using equation (5), make another of affine images as shown in figure 7. This makes it possible to generate multiple keypoint descriptors with various affine characteristics and we compared them to that of the p-SIFT.

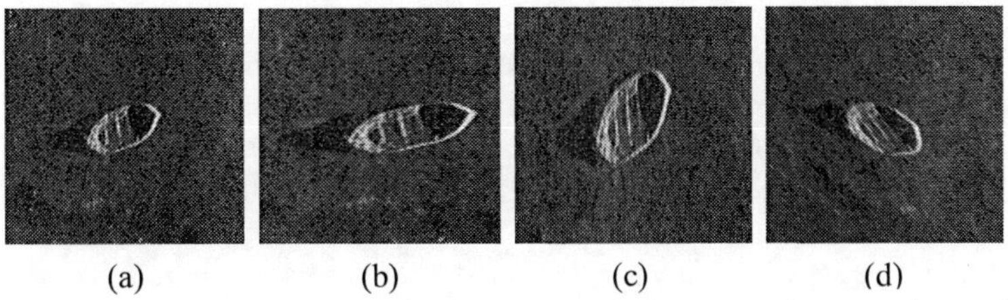

Figure 7. Example of the affine transformed small boat: (a) original, (b) increased PRI(p_1=1, p_4=0.5, p_2=p_3=0), (c) decreased ship speed(p_1=0.5, p_4=1, p_2=p_3=0), and (d) redirection(p_1=1, p_2=0.3, p_3=0.5, p_4=1)

3.2 Keypoint Descriptor Decision

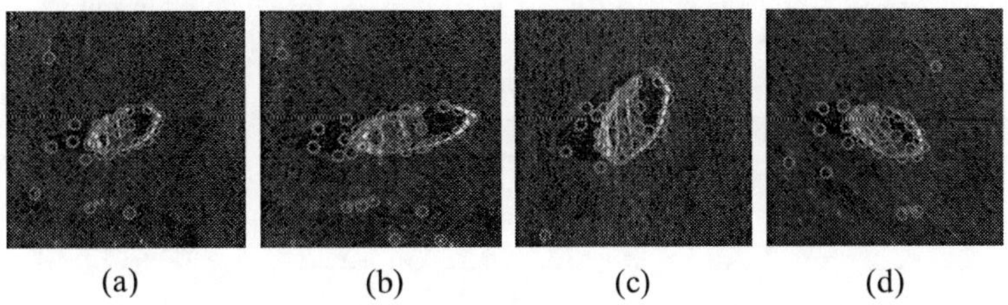

Figure 8. Keypoint of Boat: (a) Original, (b) Increased PRI, (c) Decreased Ship Speed, and (d) Redirection

The keypoint decision is second step of the PM for extracting the affine invariant descriptor. As shown in figure 8, all images have similar keypoint descriptors but they are not perfectly matched due to the distortion. The decision is performed by comparing the keypoint descriptor of the original sonar image and those of the affine transformed images. Example of the decision process is presented in figure 9. Figure 9(b)-(d) show the multiple keypoint descriptors of figure 8(a) corresponding to the white rectangle area in figure 9(a). For all window size, Euclidean distance is calculated and it is defined as follows

$$d_E^2(i,j) = \sum_{k=1}^{MN} (i^k - j^k)^2, \qquad (6)$$

where $i = (i^1, i^2, \ldots, i^{MN})$ and $j = (j^1, j^2, \ldots, j^{MN})$. Notation M, N, i, and j denote image size and image pixels, respectively.

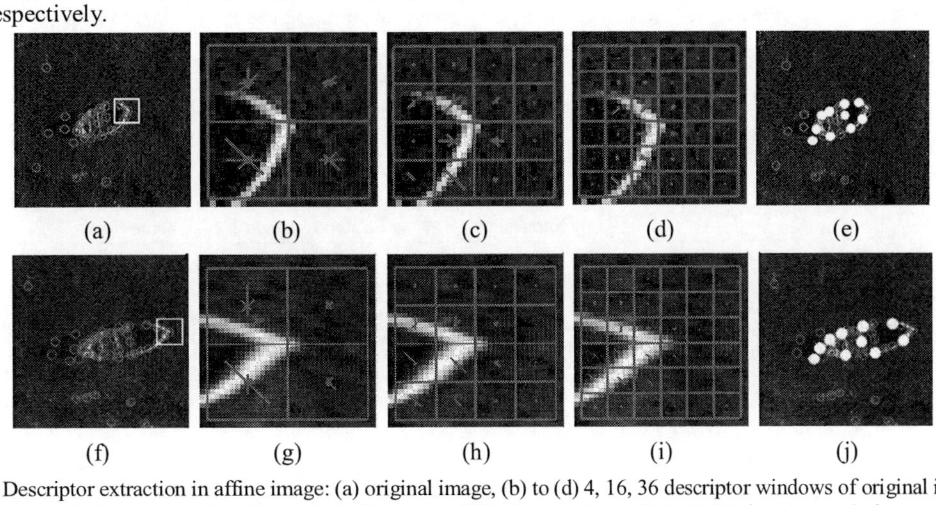

Figure 9. Descriptor extraction in affine image: (a) original image, (b) to (d) 4, 16, 36 descriptor windows of original image, (e) decision result of figure 8(a), (f) increased PRI image, (g) to (i) 4, 16, 36 descriptor windows of figure 9(f), and (j) decision result of figure 8(b)

Keypoint descriptors, which simultaneously satisfy $d_E^2(i,j) \leq 0.3$ comparing all window size of figure 9(b)-(d) with figure 9(g)-(i), are selected. As shown in figure 9(e) and (j), some selected keypoint descriptors(marked by white circle) still remain after affine transform and this means that some keypoints have affine invariance or tolerance. The number of decided keypoint depends on the similarity of object shape between the original image and the affine transformed images and influence the recognition performance.

4. EXPERIMENTAL RESULT

In order to verify the accuracy of the PM, we performed several tests. For the SIFT and the p-SIFT, matching method is adopted [Alhwarin, F. & Wang, C. 2008]. We used three test images(naval mine, artificial reef, drum) with 512x512 resolution as shown in figure 11 and made four affined transformed images for each test image. Test evaluation measure was the recognition rate accuracy and we adopted the binary classification method, which is commonly used to determine accuracy [Zhang, C. T., & Wang, J. 2000]. As shown in figure 12, test results are classified four cases, true positive(TP), false positive(FP), true negative(TN) and false negative(FN). The accuracy is defined as follows

$$\mathrm{ACC} = \frac{TP + TN}{TP + TN + FP + FN}. \tag{7}$$

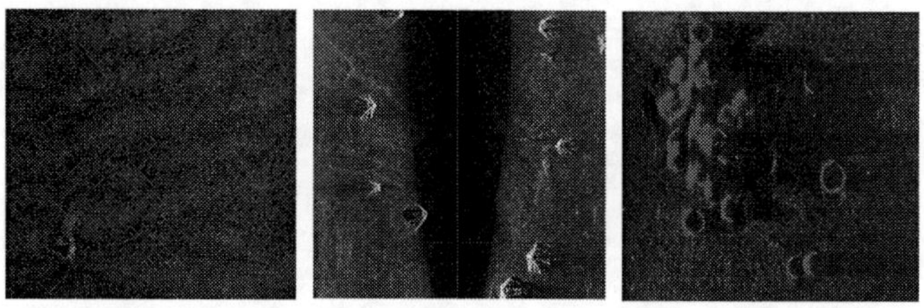

(a) (b) (c)

Figure 11. Three Test Images: (a) Naval Mine, (b) Artificial Reef, and (c) Drum

		Predicted condition	
	Total population	Predicted positive	Predicted negative
True condition	Condition positive	True Positive(TP)	False Negative(FN)
	Condition negative	False Positive(FP)	True Negative(TN)

Figure 12. Four types of Accuracy

TP and TN are chosen when the same feature information is determined. FP comes out when matched feature is different and FN is selected when there is no feature match. Test results are summarized in the Table 1.

Table 1. Accuracy of Recognizing Objects

Object shape	Object	SIFT	p-SIFT	PM
Both coordinates of half scale	Naval mine	90%	92%	**93%**
	Artificial reef	84%	86%	**91%**
	Drum	92%	**93%**	**93%**
x-coordinate of half scale	Naval mine	89%	91%	**92%**
	Artificial reef	83%	85%	**90%**
	Drum	90%	90%	**92%**
Rotation 45°	Naval mine	86%	89%	**92%**
	Artificial reef	84%	85%	**91%**
	Drum	91%	**92%**	**92%**
Shearing	Naval mine	77%	83%	**88%**
	Artificial reef	69%	73%	**84%**
	Drum	80%	84%	**90%**
Average	Naval mine	86%	90%	**91%**
	Artificial reef	73%	82%	**89%**
	Drum	88%	89%	**92%**

The SIFT and the p-SIFT show similar performance to scale and rotation. However, for shearing, the p-SIFT is superior to the SIFT because it uses the multi-resolution keypoint descriptors. The PM has the best performance in most cases, and especially remarkable differences about shearing by using affine invariant keypoint descriptor.

Figure 13 shows the result of naval mine recognition for each algorithm. The left(big one) and the right(small one) side describe the affined and original images, respectively. FP, TP, and FN are denoted by white, gray, and dark gray circles. We can see that the PM has only TP cases compared to the other cases and this means the PM is invariant or tolerant to the affine problem.

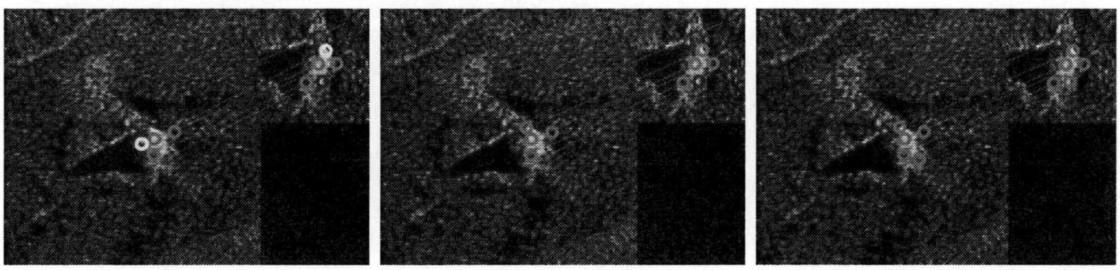

(a) (b) (c)

Figure 13. Recognition Image of Naval Mine: (a) SIFT, (b) p-SIFT, and (c) PM

5. CONCLUSION

In this paper, we proposed the new extraction method of keypoint descriptor for affined sonar images. The proposed method adopts multiple keypoint descriptors to solve affine problem and test results show that it works well all test cases. It is expected to contribute the performance improvement of the object detection and classification and the development of automated sonar system.

ACKNOWLEDGEMENT

This research was supported by the Agency for Defense Development, South Korea, under Grant (UD160014DD).

REFERENCES

Alhwarin, F., Wang, C., Ristic-Durrant, D., & Gräser, A. (2008). Improved SIFT-Features Matching for Object Recognition. *In BCS Int. Acad. Conf.*, London, UK (pp. 178-190).

Danielsson, P. E. (1980). Euclidean distance mapping. Computer Graphics and image processing, 14(3), 227-248.

David G. Lowe (2004), Distinctive Image Features from Scale-Invariant Keypoints, International Journal of Computer Vision, v.60 n.2, p.91-110.

Klaucke I. (2018) Sidescan Sonar. In: Micallef A., Krastel S., Savini A. (eds) Submarine Geomorphology. Springer Geology. Springer, Cham.

Langner, F., Knauer, C., Jans, W., Middelmann, W., & Jans, W. (2009). Image processing in side scan sonar images for object detection and classification. *In Proceedings of the 3rd International Conference and Exhibition on Underwater Acoustic Measurements: Technologies and Results* in Nafplion, Greece (pp. 311-318).

Nomizu, K., & Sasaki, T. (1994). Affine differential geometry: geometry of affine immersions. Cambridge University Press.

Seidenari, L., Serra, G., Bagdanov, A. D., & Del Bimbo, A. (2014). Local pyramidal descriptors for image recognition. *IEEE transactions on pattern analysis and machine intelligence*, 36(5), 1033-1040.

Zhang, C. T., & Wang, J. (2000). Recognition of protein coding genes in the yeast genome at better than 95% accuracy based on the Z curve. Nucleic acids research, 28(14), 2804-2814.

REACTION-DIFFUSION ALGORITHM DESIGNED FOR IMAGE EDGE DETECTION AND ITS PERFORMANCE EVALUATION

Atsushi Nomura[1], Koichi Okada[2] and Yoshiki Mizukami[3]
[1]*Faculty of Education, Yamaguchi University, Yoshida 1677-1, Yamaguchi 753-8513, Japan*
[2]*Center for the Promotion of Higher Education, Yamaguchi University, Yoshida 1677-1, Yamaguchi 753-8511, Japan*
[3]*Graduate School of Science and Technology for Innovation, Yamaguchi University*
Tokiwadai 2-16-1, Ube 755-8611, Japan

ABSTRACT

The present paper proposes image edge detection algorithm utilizing a reaction-diffusion network. The network consists of two-dimensionally coupled FitzHugh-Nagumo type neurons, whose behavior is described by a set of time-evolving partial differential equations. The neurons' non-linearity and their interconnection give the image edges through an iterative computation. The proposed algorithm differs from its previously-proposed one (Nomura et al., 2016) on the pre-processing for initializing the neurons' state and the post-processing for thinning edges. The performance of the proposed algorithm is discussed with three image data-sets and two error measures, in comparison with performance of two other algorithms including Canny's edge detection method.

KEYWORDS

Edge Detection, Reaction-Diffusion, Fitzhugh-Nagumo Type Model, Initial Condition, Edge Thinning

1. INTRODUCTION

There are several approaches for image edge detection, and one of them is the partial differential equation (PDE) approach (Aubert and Kornprobst, 2006). Marr and Hildreth (1980) originally applied a Laplacian of Gaussian (LoG) filter and a difference of two Gaussians (DoG) filter to edge detection, where the Gaussian filter was employed to remove image noise. Koenderink (1984) showed that applying the Gaussian filter to the input pattern is equivalent to an iterative computation of a diffusion equation on the state initialized by the input pattern, where the diffusion coefficient corresponds to standard deviation of the Gaussian function. Since the diffusion coefficient or the standard deviation controls degree of image blurring, it should be large in noisy and featureless image area, and it should be small in noiseless and feature-rich one; a large diffusion coefficient eliminates features points. According to the above consideration on the diffusion coefficient, the idea of employing anisotropic diffusion was introduced into the PDE approach, where the diffusion coefficient is automatically adjusted depending on structure of image brightness distribution for preserving feature points (Perona and Malik, 1990).

The PDE approach was further developed by introducing reaction-diffusion equations, which consist of a diffusion equation and a reaction function; the reaction functions control a rate of state change and they are described by ordinary differential equations. FitzHugh-Nagumo type equation is one of the most interesting reaction-diffusion equations, and provides a mathematical model of a signal propagation phenomenon along nerve axon (Murray, 1989); the behavior of a pair of the reaction function is called FitzHugh-Nagumo nonlinearity. Thus, researchers, who intend to develop bio-inspired algorithm, have applied FitzHugh-Nagumo type equation to image processing tasks (e.g., Morfu, 2009). Several researchers proposed edge or contour detection algorithm by utilizing a discretized version of FitzHugh-Nagumo type reaction-diffusion system (Comte et al., 2001; Nomura et al., 2003; Li et al., 2015). However, the performances of these bio-inspired edge detection algorithms have not been evaluated quantitatively.

The purposes of the present paper are the following two points: (1) improving quantitative performance of a previous reaction-diffusion algorithm designed for image edge detection with FitzHugh-Nagumo nonlinearity (Nomura et al., 2016), and (2) evaluating quantitative performance of the algorithm in comparison with the representative edge detection algorithm of Canny and another one.

In the proposed algorithm, we introduce a pre-processing for initializing the state in FitzHugh-Nagumo type equations and a post-processing for thinning edges. We evaluate the quantitative performance of the proposed algorithm with three well-known image data-sets having the ground-truth data on the basis of two error measures: distance-based and statistical ones.

2. THE ALGORITHM

2.1 FitzHugh-Nagumo Nonlinearity

A pair of time-evolving ordinary differential equations having FitzHugh-Nagumo nonlinearity (FitzHugh, 1961; Nagumo et al., 1962) is described by

$$\frac{du}{dt} = \frac{1}{\varepsilon} f(u,v) = \frac{1}{\varepsilon}[u(u-a)(1-u)-v], \qquad t > 0\#(1)$$

$$\frac{dv}{dt} = g(u,v) = u - bv, \qquad t > 0\#(2)$$

in which $(u(t), v(t))$ denotes the state on time t which is a pair of membrane potential and recovery variables in a neuron, and a, b and ε are constants ($0 < \varepsilon \ll 1$). Figure 1 shows a phase-plot illustrating how the solution (u, v) traces a trajectory according to Eqs. (1) and (2). For example, if a solution (u, v) is initially given in the area satisfying $\frac{du}{dt} = f(u,v)/\varepsilon > 0$ and $\frac{dv}{dt} = g(u,v) > 0$, it goes to an excited state ($u \simeq 1, v \simeq 0$), and then goes back to a resting state ($u \simeq 0, v \simeq 0$) according to the arrows shown in Figure 1. In this paper, we call the pair of Eqs. (1) and (2) 'FitzHugh-Nagumo element'.

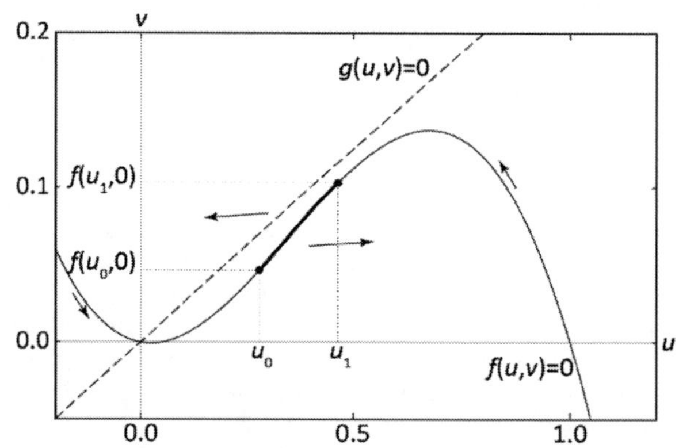

Figure 1. Phase plot of the FitzHugh-Nagumo nonlinearity described by Eqs. (1) and (2), and initial conditions given for image edge detection. The solid curve shows the null-cline of $f(u,v) = 0$, and the broken one does that of $g(u,v) = 0$. Initial conditions of u and v are set on the thick solid curve of $f(u,v) = 0$ in the range of u_0 and u_1. Arrows show temporal changes of solutions

2.2 Reaction-Diffusion Network and Image Edge Detection Algorithm

FitzHugh-Nagumo type reaction-diffusion network refers to a system of discretely coupled FitzHugh-Nagumo elements. Nomura et al. (2016) previously proposed a network designed for image edge detection, and described by

$$\frac{du_{i,j}}{dt} = C_u\left[\sum_{(k,l)\in\ell} u_{k,l} - 4u_{i,j}\right] + \frac{1}{\varepsilon} f(u_{i,j}, v_{i,j}), \qquad t > 0\#(3)$$

$$\frac{dv_{i,j}}{dt} = C_v\left[\sum_{(k,l)\in\ell} v_{k,l} - 4v_{i,j}\right] + g(u_{i,j}, v_{i,j}) + \mu|\nabla G * I|_{i,j} \times (1 - U(t)), \qquad t > -\tau\#(4)$$

in which $(i,j) \in M \times N$ (image grid) denotes a grid position of the network as shown in Figure 2, and C_u and C_v are coupling strength among the target position (i,j) and its nearest neighboring ones in $\ell = \{(i+1,j), (i-1,j), (i,j+1), (i,j-1)\}$; $|\nabla G * I|$ denotes absolute gradient of Gaussian filtered image $\nabla G * I$, and $|\nabla G * I|_{i,j}$ denotes its sampled value at (i,j) and is normalized so as to satisfy $u_0 \leq |\nabla G * I|_{i,j} \leq u_1$; μ is a negative constant and $U(t)$ denotes the step function giving 0 in $t < 0$ and 1 in $t \geq 0$. Note that Eq. (3) is defined in $t > 0$, and Eq. (4) is defined in $t > -\tau$ $(\tau \geq 0)$.

Initial conditions given for image edge detection are

$$u_{i,j}(t) = |\nabla G * I|_{i,j}, -\tau \leq t \leq 0, \qquad v_{i,j}(-\tau) = f(u_{i,j}, 0).\#(5)$$

Equation (5) imposes the time difference on Eqs. (3) and (4); $v_{i,j}(t)$ is defined only at $t = -\tau$ and then $v_{i,j}(t)$ is computed by Eq. (4) with the fixed $u_{i,j}(t)$ in $-\tau < t < 0$. Thus, we can consider that the time range of $-\tau < t \leq 0$ is the pre-processing stage.

After the computation of Eqs. (3) and (4) in finite duration of time L_t, FitzHugh-Nagumo elements are expected to autonomously enter excited state at edge positions. Thus, an edge map E is tentatively obtained by

$$E = \{\, (i,j) \mid u_{i,j} > 1/2 \,\}.\#(6)$$

Since the tentatively obtained edges have more than one-pixel width, the following edge thinning is employed in the post-processing stage. If an edge pixel $(i,j) \in E$ has the maximum value of $v_{k,l}$, $(k,l) \in E$ along the direction of $(\nabla G * I)_{i,j}$, as shown in Figure 3, the pixel remains in the final edge map, otherwise the pixel is eliminated from E.

The above proposed algorithm differs from the previous one (Nomura et al., 2016) on the following two points. The first one is on the initial condition. The proposed algorithm utilizes the absolute gradient of blurred image $|\nabla G * I|_{i,j}$, which is given to the initial condition of the network in Eq. (5). On the other hand, the previous algorithm utilizes the raw image $u_{i,j} = I_{i,j}$ as the initial condition. The second one is on the edge thinning in the post-processing. The previous algorithm does not employ any edge thinning, therefore edges having more than one-pixel width remain in edge detection results.

Finally, the proposed algorithm is summarized as Algorithm 1.

Algorithm 1. Proposed reaction-diffusion algorithm. Time t is discretized with a finite difference δt and the floor function $\lfloor\cdot\rfloor$.

Compute $G * I$ with a diffusion equation.
Compute Eq. (5).
$k = -\lfloor\tau/\delta t\rfloor$
while $k < 0$ **do** /* pre-processing */
  $u_{i,j}^{k+1} = u_{i,j}^{k}$
  Compute $v_{i,j}^{k+1}$ with Eq. (4).
  $k = k + 1$
end while
while $k < L_t/\delta t$ **do**
  Compute $u_{i,j}^{k+1}$ and $v_{i,j}^{k+1}$ with Eqs. (3) and (4).
  $k = k + 1$
end while
Compute E with Eq. (6).
Edge thinning on E. /* post-processing */

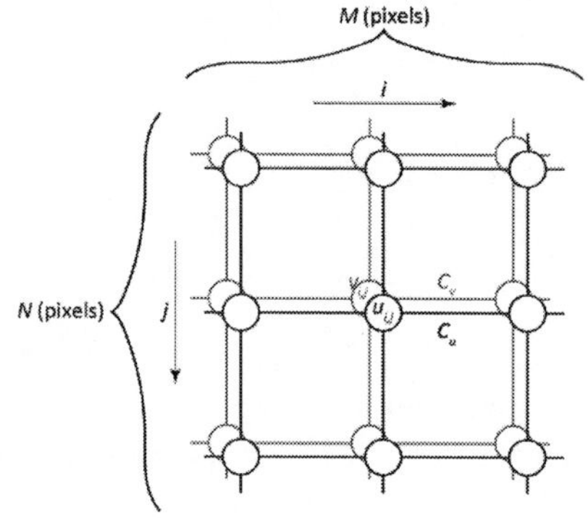

Figure 2. Network of coupled elements of FitzHugh-Nagumo nonlinearity, in which $M \times N$ denotes the image grid and its size, $(i, j) \in M \times N$ is the position, and C_u and C_v are coupling strength

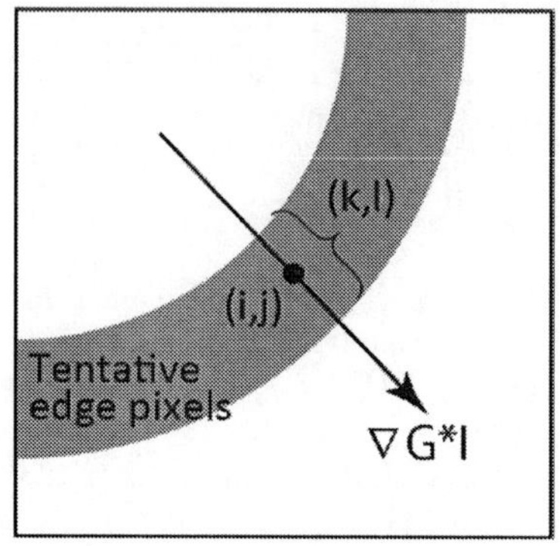

Figure 3. Edge thinning on tentative edge pixels denoted by dark area. The pixel (i, j) having the maximum of $v_{k,l}$ in the direction of $\nabla G * I$ remains as the finally detected edge pixel

3. EXPERIMENTS AND DISCUSSIONS

The present section demonstrates quantitative performance of the proposed algorithm by utilizing three image data-sets and two error measures, in comparison with two other competitive algorithms. The three data-sets are

- UFSo consisting of 50 images, most of which are capturing artificial objects (Bowyer et al., 1999; see the website pointed by http://figment.csee.usf.edu/edge/roc/),
- USFa consisting of 10 aerial images provided on the above website, and
- RuG consisting of 40 images, most of which are capturing animals (Grigorescu et al., 2003; see the website pointed by http://www.cs.rug.nl/~imaging/) and which are collected for performance evaluation of contour detection algorithms.

All images are gray scale. Ground-truth edge maps provided by human are also included in the data-sets. On the three data-sets the following three edge detection algorithms were tested.

- Canny algorithm built in the software package MATLAB 2013a. There are three parameters: σ, two threshold levels (higher and lower). The parameter $\sigma \in \{1.0, 1.1, 1.2, \cdots, 10.0\}$ was chosen for the best score of the F-measure (later shown); the two threshold levels were automatically chosen by the package.
- BGTG algorithm proposed by Martin et al. (2004) and provided on the BSDS300 website pointed by https://www2.eecs.berkeley.edu/Research/Projects/CS/vision/grouping/segbench/. Parameters of the algorithm were chosen at the default values (not optimized). Edge detection results of BGTG have edge gradient, which was binarized with a threshold level $\theta \in \{128, 150, 192, 224, 255\}$ for evaluation, and was chosen for the best score of the best F-measure.
- Reaction-diffusion (RD) algorithm proposed in this paper. Parameter settings were chosen for the best score of the F-measure, and were shown in Table 1.

Table 1. Parameter settings of the three algorithms: Canny, BGTG and RD for each image data-set. In RD, Gaussian filtering was computed by a diffusion equation with a unit diffusion coefficient during time ℓ_t

	Canny	BGTG	RD		
Algorithm	σ	θ	C_u, C_v	a, b, ε	$u_0, u_1, \tau, \mu, \ell_t$
USFo	2.4	224	4, 12	$0.10, 4.0, 1.0 \times 10^{-3}$	$0.2, 0.5, 0.01, -2.0, 0.10$
USFa	2.2	224	4, 12	$0.10, 1.0, 1.0 \times 10^{-3}$	$0.2, 0.5, 0.01, -2.0, 0.05$
RuG	4.4	224	16, 12	$0.10, 4.0, 1.0 \times 10^{-3}$	$0.2, 0.5, 0.05, -2.0, 0.05$

An obtained candidate edge map E_c is quantitatively evaluated with two error measures: F-measure and SD (Lopez-Molina et al., 2013). The F-measure is derived from the measures of Precision (P) and Recall (R) with their equal balance, and is defined by

$$F = \frac{2PR}{P+R}, \quad P = \frac{|E_c \cap E_{gt}|}{|E_c|}, \quad R = \frac{|E_c \cap E_{gt}|}{|E_{gt}|}, \#(7)$$

in which E_{gt} is the ground truth edge map; $|E|$ denotes the number of edge pixels contained in E. The measure P evaluates how much detected edge pixels are correct, and R does how much edge pixels of the ground truth are detected. The F-meausre denotes the higher the better. In this paper, three-pixel distance between E_c and E_{gt} is tolerated. The other measure SD evaluates distance between E_c and E_{gt}, and is defined by

$$SD = \frac{\left[\sum_{(i,j)\in E_c} d_{i,j}(E_{gt}) + \sum_{(i,j)\in E_{gt}} d_{i,j}(E_c)\right]}{|E_c \cup E_{gt}|}, \#(8)$$

where $d_{i,j}(E)$ denotes Euclidian distance between the position (i, j) and its nearest point in E; more than 50 pixels in the distance is truncated at 50 pixels. The SD measure denotes the lower the better.

Table 2 shows the average scores on the three algorithms and the three data-sets. On the data-set USFo, the RD algorithm works much better than the others; on USFa, although Canny works better than the others, RD also works as well as Canny; on RuG, the BGTG algorithm works much better than the others.

Figure 4 shows scores on the three algorithms and all the images. On USFo, the RD algorithm provided much better results, for example, on the images '110', '126', '138', '203', '220', 'egg'; on USFa, the Canny did that on the image 'airfield'; the BGTG algorithm did those on the bear and goat images. Figure 5 shows edge detection results on the three images 'USFo-110', 'USFa-airfield' and 'RuG-bear_8'.

Let us discuss the results. The RD algorithm detects very small and sharp edges, and achieves better performance on artificial objects. This is a merit of the RD algorithm, in comparison with the other two algorithms. This is supported by the average scores on the USFo data-set in Table 2 and the results of 'USFo-110' shown in Figure 5; the data-set contains many artificial objects. Detected small and sharp edges were brought by the FitzHugh-Nagumo nonlinearity. The demerit of the RD algorithm is to fail in detecting blurred or low contrast edges. In Figure 5 this demerit can be easily confirmed by comparing the results of Canny and RD in the left upper area of 'USFo-110', and low contrast straight lines in 'USFa-airfield'. The results for 'RuG-bear_8' show that the small edges within the head of the bear were detected, while the contour of the bear's head was not detected.

In the experiments, we had difficulty on choosing the optimal parameter settings of the RD algorithm. The other two algorithms have only one parameter, and it was easy to optimize them. Thus, the difficulty of the RD algorithm is also a demerit, which is caused by many parameters and nonlinearity of the FitzHugh-Nagumo elements of the RD algorithm. In particular, the nonlinearity is difficult for the users to handle, and any further optimization or learning algorithm on choosing the parameter settings of the RD algorithm will be required.

Finally, Figure 6 shows an example of edge thinning on the image 'USFo-pitcher'; the proposed edge thinning processed the tentative edge map of Figure 6(a) and provided the final edge map of Figure 6(b). The one-dimensional distributions of (u, v) are plotted around detected edge pixels in Figure 6(c). This result demonstrates that the tentative edge map obtained by the RD algorithm was improved by the edge thinning.

Table 2. Performance evaluation results on the edge detection algorithms: Canny, BGTG and RD on the three data-sets: USFo, USFa and RuG with the two measures F and SD. The best score for each data-set is indicated in bold

Algorithm	Canny	BGTG	RD
USFo	F=0.570, SD=17.6	F=0.521, SD=19.3	F=**0.640**, SD=**16.9**
USFa	F=**0.697**, SD=**12.2**	F=0.579, SD=15.0	F=0.683, SD=13.3
RuG	F=0.353, SD=24.0	F=**0.505**, SD=**20.5**	F=0.421, SD=26.0

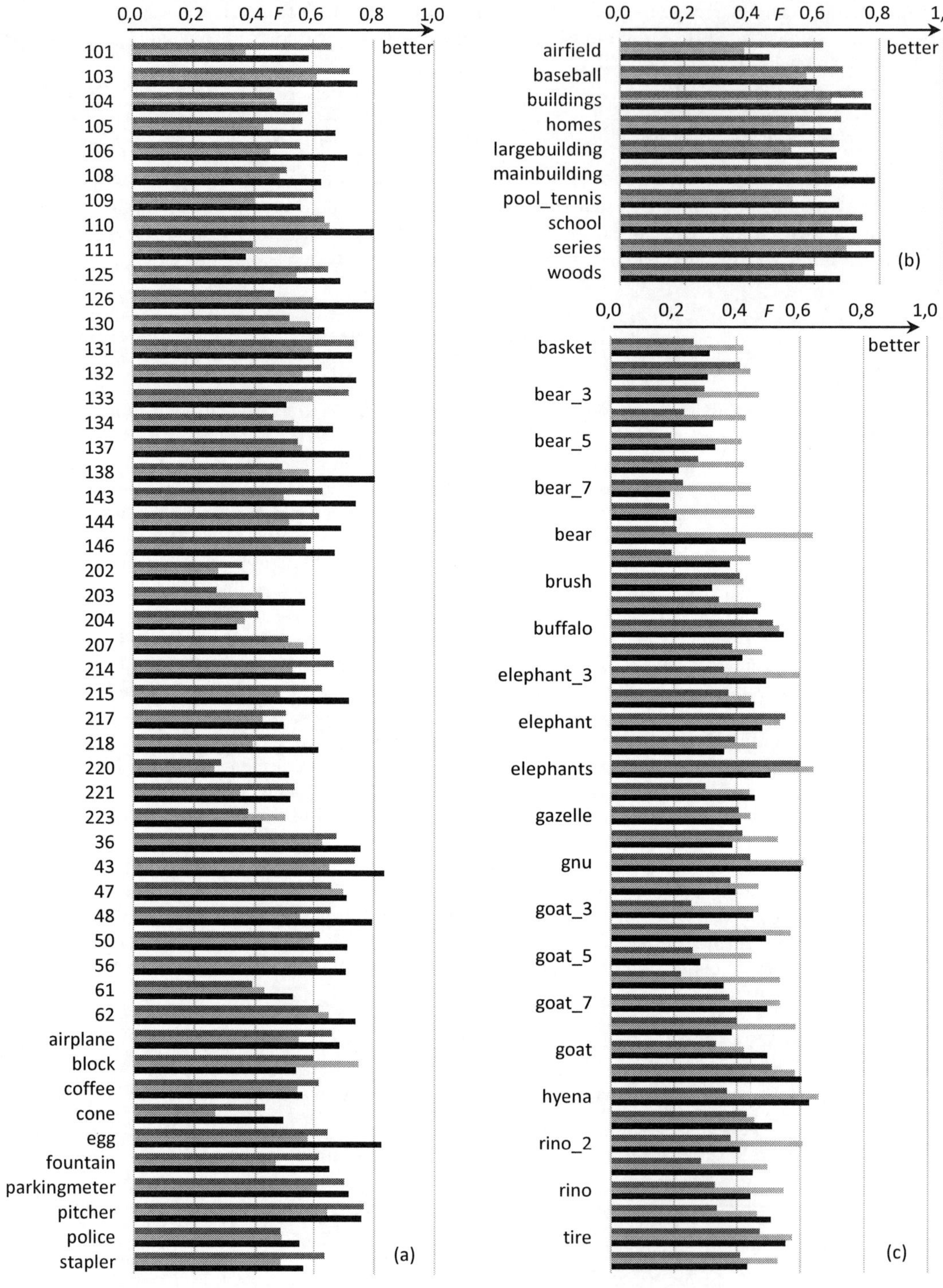

Figure 4. Edge detection results evaluated with F-measure on the data-sets (a) USFo, (b) USFa and (c) RuG

Algorithms were Canny (▩), BGTG (▩) and RD (■). Their average scores are shown in Table 2

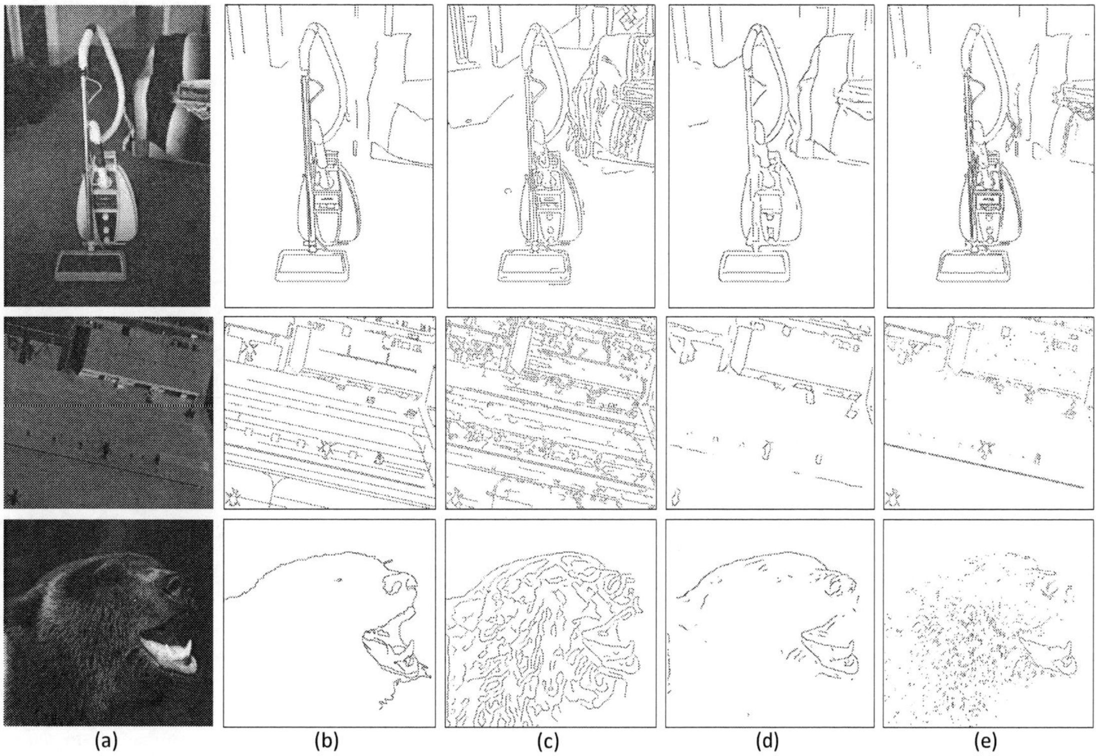

Figure 5. Edge detection results on the images: 'USFo-110' (481 × 711 pixels), 'USFa-airfield' (593 × 548 pixels) and 'RuG-bear_8' (512 × 512 pixels) from top to bottom. (a)The image and its edge maps of (b)the ground truth, (c)Canny, (d)BGTG, and (e)RD

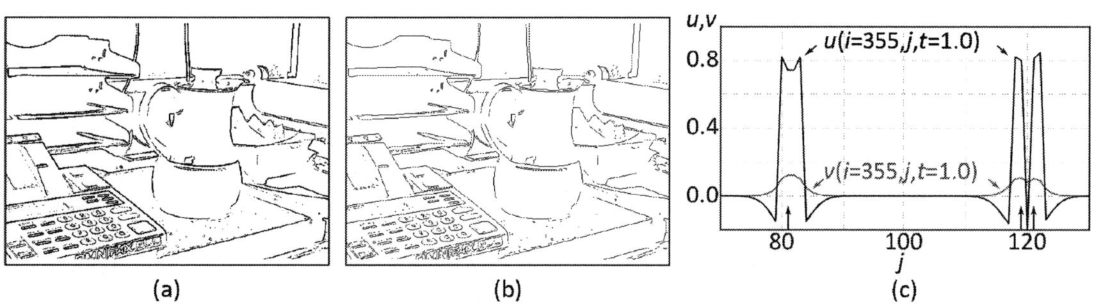

Figure 6. Demonstration of edge thinning on the image 'USFo-pitcher' (568 × 419 pixels). (a) Tentative edge map obtained by Eq. (6) at $t = 1.0$. (b) Result of the edge thinning. (c) Spatial distribution of $u_{i,j}$ and $v_{i,j}$ along the vertical line at $i = 355$ and $t = 1.0$; upward arrows show finally detected edge positions

4. CONCLUSION

The present paper proposed reaction-diffusion algorithm designed for image edge detection. The previous algorithm proposed by Nomura et al. (2016) takes image brightness as the initial condition of the algorithm; the algorithm proposed here takes its absolute gradient as the initial condition. In addition, edge thinning was also proposed and implemented in the post-processing stage of the proposed algorithm. By utilizing three image data-sets and two error measures, we evaluated quantitative performance of the proposed algorithm, in comparison with other two algorithms. The results show that the proposed algorithm has an advantage of detecting small and sharp edges on the artificial objects, and has a limitation in detecting contours on natural objects such as animals. Edge maps obtained by the reaction-diffusion algorithm were improved by the edge thinning.

ACKNOWLEDGEMENT

This research was partly supported by JSPS KAKENHI Grant Number JP17K00341.

REFERENCES

Aubert, G., and Kornprobst, P., 2006. *Mathematical Problems in Image Processing - Partial Differential Equations and the Calculus of Variations, Second Edition*. Springer-Verlag New York.

Bowyer, K. et al., 1999. Edge Detector Evaluation Using Empirical ROC Curves. *Proceedings of Computer Vision and Pattern Recognition.* Colorado, USA, Vol 1, pp 354-359.

Canny, J., 1986. A Computational Approach to Edge Detection. *In IEEE Trans. Patt. Anal. Mach. Intell.*, Vol. PAMI-8, No. 6, pp 679-698.

Comte, J. C. et al., 2001. Contour Detection Based on Nonlinear Discrete Diffusion in a Cellular Nonlinear Network. *In Int. J. Bif. Chaos.*, Vol. 11, No.1, pp 179-183.

FitzHugh, R., 1961. Impulses and Physiological States in Theoretical Models of Nerve Membrane. *In Biophysical Journal*, Vol. 1, pp 445-466.

Grigorescu, C. et al., 2003. Contour Detection Based on Non-classical Receptive Field Inhibition. *In IEEE Trans. Image Processing*, Vol. 12, No. 7, pp 729-739.

Koenderink, J. J., 1984. The Structure of Images. *In Biol. Cybern.*, Vol. 50, pp. 363-370.

Li, S. et al., 2015. Dynamical System Approach for Edge Detection Using Coupled FitzHugh–Nagumo Neurons. *In IEEE Trans. Image Processing*, Vol. 24, No.12, pp 5206-5219.

Lopez-Molina, C. et al., 2013. Quantitative Error Measures for Edge Detection. *In Patt. Recog.*, Vol. 46, pp 1125-1139.

Marr, D. and Hildreth, E., 1980. Theory of Edge Detection. *In Proc. R. Soc. Lond. B.*, Vol. 207, pp 187-217.

Martin, D. R. et al., 2004. Learning to Detect Natural Image Boundaries Using Local Brightness, Color, and Texture Cues. *In IEEE Trans. Patt. Anal. Mach. Intell.*, Vol. 26, No.1, pp 530-549

Morfu, S., 2009. On Some Applications of Diffusion Processes for Image Processing. *In Physics Letters A*, Vol. 373, pp 2438-2444.

Murray, J. D., 1989. *Mathematical Biology*. Springer-Verlag, Berlin.

Nagumo, J. et al., 1962. An Active Pulse Transmission Line Simulating Nerve Axon. *In Proceedings of the IRE*, Vol. 50, pp 2061-2070

Nomura, A. et al., 2003. Realizing Visual Functions with the Reaction-Diffusion Mechanism, *In J. Phys. Soc. Jpn.*, Vol. 72, No. 9, pp 2385-2395.

Nomura, A. et al., 2016. Preprocessing in a Reaction-Diffusion Algorithm Designed for Image Edge Detection. *Proc. IEEE Int. Symp. Signal Processing and Information Technology (ISSPIT).* Limassol, Cyprus, pp 166-171.

Perona, P. and Malik, J., 1990. Scale-Space and Edge Detection Using Anisotropic Diffusion. *In IEEE Trans. Patt. Anal. Mach. Intell.*, Vol. 12, No. 7, pp 629-639.

SONAR IMAGE DENOISING BASED ON WAVELET TRANSFORM USING NON-LOCAL MEANS FILTERING

Su In Lee[1], Wan-Jin Kim[2] and Kun Su Yoon[3]
[1]*Department of Informatics, Gyeongsang National University, 501, Jinju-daero, Jinju-si, Gyeongsangnam-do, Republic of Korea, 52828*
[2]*Agency for Defense Development, Jinhae PO Box #18, Jinhae-gu, Changwon-si, Gyeongsangnam-do, Republic of Korea, 51678*
[3]*Department of Aviation Control System, Aviation Campus of Korea Polytechnic, 46 Daehak-gil, Sacheon-si, Gyeongsangnam-do, Republic of Korea, 52549*

ABSTRACT

Comparing to optical images, sonar images experience more severe conditions such as degradation, light scattering, low contrast, and blurring. To guarantee the performance of the post processing such as object detection and classification, the need of a proper denoising method for sonar images has claimed. Conventional wavelet transform(WT) domain denoising method may be good candidates but they do not properly work for some cases which have ambiguity in edge and noise separation. Since image blurring after denoising is generally caused by the loss of edge information with low signal-to-noise ratio, the denoising performance may be improved by the introduction of a proper edge decision rule. In this paper, we propose a stationary WT denoising method with edge map and non-local means(NLM) filter for edge decision. Experimental results show that the proposed method has better performance than the three conventional methods(Visushrink, Sureshrink, and Bayesshrink) in terms of the edge preservation and the peak signal-to-noise ratio.

KEYWORDS

Image Denoising, Stationary Wavelet Transform, Non-local Means Filtering

1. INTRODUCTION

In the naval field, the operation of optical imaging devices is limited by the penetration depth and light intensity. As the alternative, imaging sonars using acoustic wave were introduced and they have been contributed to the marine exploration, and military operation. However, just same in optical images, the acquired sonar images suffer from noises. Many researchers had studied to repair or enhance images in various fields such as medical [Raju, V. et al. 2014], satellite [Kooshesh, M., & Akbarizadeh, G. 2015], and underwater [Cong, W., & Lu, J. 2016, Kumudham, R. et al. 2016, Padmavathi, G. et al. 2010].

Most of the past denoising methods are focused on the spatial domain processing and they generally improve image quality by manipulating pixel values. During the filtering, edges which have a similar characteristic with a noise is also removed, and it yields a performance degradation. For preserving edges, following transform domain filtering methods had been studied: Bayesian-based algorithm and dual tree complex wavelet transform [Isar, A. et al. 2005], roughness entropy fractal dimension fractal wavelet to the fractal matching process [Tin, H. W., et al. 2013], Haar wavelet transform and soft thresholding [Saurabh, A., et al. 2015], and soft thresholding based on wavelet transform [Donoho, D.L. 1995, Donoho, D.L. and Johnstone, I.M. 1995, Chang, S.G. et al 2000].

Conventional transform domain denoising methods showed the dramatically performance enhancement but their performance depends on the noise estimator and the image characteristic. If there exist many pixels including both of edge and noise, conventional methods have some difficulty to distinguish them. We inspired that edge information might be observed by extracting contour and proposed the adaptive noise estimator applying to noisy sonar images. The proposed method is consisted to two steps: edge map generation and adaptive filtering. For the first step, we applied the Canny edge detection algorithm to the all sub-band outputs of the à trous transform. In the second step, by referring the edge map and sub-band coefficients, non-local means(NLM) filter distinct the edge and noise. For performance evaluation, we adopted the peak signal-to-noise ratio(PSNR) which is widely used image quality assessment method and performed tests for several images.

2. BACKGROUND

In this chapter, we briefly describe transform domain filtering and denoising methods. The representative method of the former is the wavelet transform and it decomposes an image to multi-resolution sub-band.

Figure 1(a) shows the two level two-dimensional discrete wavelet transform(2D DWT). After the wavelet transform, the original image is divided four sub-band, and then the LL_1 sub-band decomposed into another four sub-band labeled as LL_2, LH_2, HL_2, and HH_2. Here, H and G denote the high-pass filter and the low-pass filter, respectively.

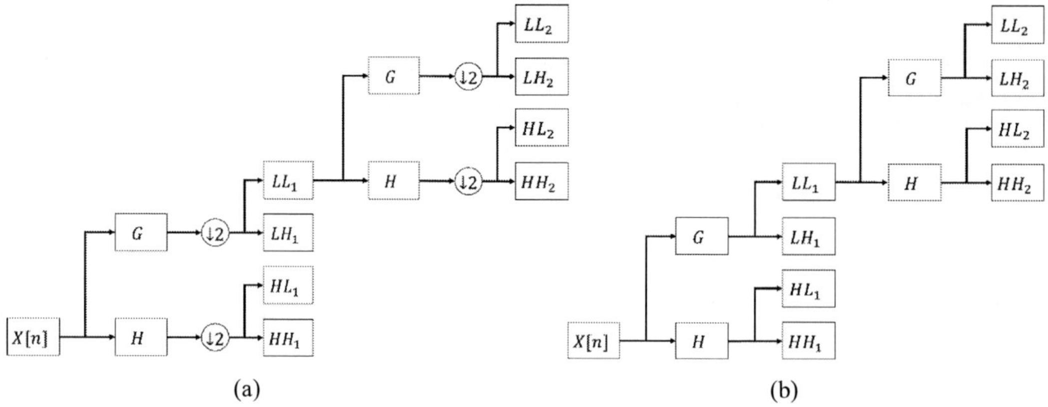

Figure 1. 2D Sub-band Decomposition: (a) DWT, (b) à trous Transform

As shown in figure 1(a), DWT is a non-redundant decomposition. The disadvantage of decimate transform is non-invariance in time-space, and the coefficients of a signal are not a time-shifted version of the original signal due to down-sampling [Fowler, J. E. 2005]. In decimated images, the edge information may disappear or distort. Hence, it is improper choice using the DWT for the edge map generation. The à trous transform, also known as the stationary wavelet transform(SWT), had proposed to overcome the disadvantage of the DWT [Fowler, J. E. 2005]. It has excellent performance in time-frequency decomposition and each decomposed output contains different frequency and direction information of the original image. Unlike the down-sampling DWT with one-fourth size of the original image, each sub-band is decomposed into the same size of the original image as shown in figure 1(b).

For the denoising, the most widely used methods are Visushrink, Sureshrink, and Bayesshrink. Visushrink adopts a threshold value corresponding to the standard deviation of the noise [Donoho, D. L., and Johnstone, J. M. 1992]. This method follows hard thresholding rules which is known as universal thresholds. Visushrink is a simple and efficient method but often yields excessively smoothed output due to the absence of consideration about minimizing the mean squared error. Sureshrink had proposed to overcome the defect of the Visushrink and is based on stein's unbiased estimate of risk [Donoho, D.L. and Johnstone, I.M. 1995]. It uses a combination of the universal threshold and unbiased estimate which follows soft thresholding rule. Sureshrink is possible to adaptively apply threshold to each sub-band and efficiently reduces noise. However, the performance depends on the similarity of the statistical characteristics between the original image and sub-band image. Comparing to Sureshrink which deals with non-parametric estimate, Bayesshrink had proposed to solve nearly optimal threshold by minimizing the Bayesian risk [Chang, S.G. et al 2000]. It shows good performance in terms of noise reduction but has limitation on edge preservation.

3. PROPOSED METHOD

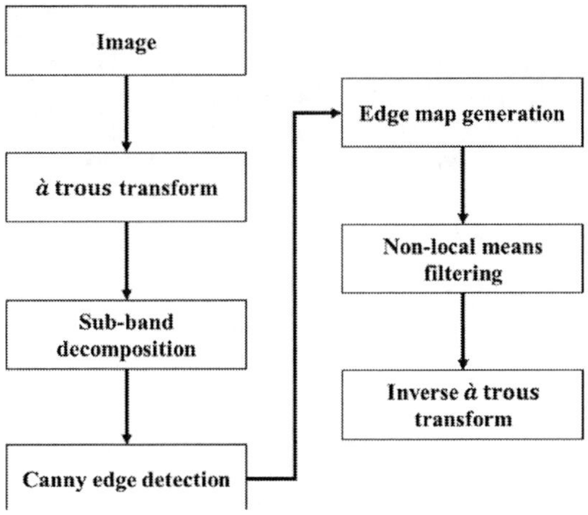

Figure 2. Procedure of the Proposed Method

As mentioned the previous chapter, Visushrink, Sureshrink, and Bayesshrink may cause not only blurring but also contour line or edge loss. Since our final goal is to guarantee the object detection and classification performance at sonar image, the critical point of denoising is to reduce noise while preserving edge information. To achieving this requirement, the proposed method(PM) grasps the edge orientation using the edge map and selectively removes noise using non-local means(NLM) filter. The procedure of the PM is illustrated on figure 2. In the PM, we used à trous transform [Fowler, J. E. 2005] which maintains image size for all sub-band and the sub-band decomposition is defined as

$$f(x,y) = c_J(x,y) + \sum_{j=1}^{J} w_j(x,y), \tag{1}$$

where f, c_J, and w_j are the original image, the low-pass, and the high-pass filtered image, respectively. c_J and w_j are reflecting detail of the original image. The à trous transform performs sub-band decomposition using B_3-spline filter [Starck, J. L. 2002] and it is defined as follow

$$f \rightarrow (P_0 f, \Delta_1 f, \ldots, \Delta_n f), \tag{2}$$

where P_0 is low-pass filter and $\Delta_1 \ldots \Delta_n$ are band-pass filters.

The next step is the Canny edge detection and it is well known as the reliable method for finding edges in image [Rong, W. 2014]. The convolution operation for image smoothing using 2D Gaussian function is performed, and then the intensity(magnitude) and direction of the edge(azimuth) are obtained by calculating the gradient of the 2x2 size region as follows

$$\begin{aligned} \|M(x,y)\| &= \sqrt{E_x[x,y]^2 + E_y[x,y]^2}, \\ \theta(x,y) &= arctan\left(\frac{E_y[x,y]}{E_x[x,y]}\right), \end{aligned} \tag{3}$$

where θ, E_x, E_y, and $\|M(x,y)\|$ represents the azimuth, the x and y direction gradient, and the magnitude, respectively. These magnitude and azimuth information compose the edge map. In the edge map, there exists not only edges but also artifacts. To reduce undesired artifacts, non-maximum suppression(NMS) is performed. The NMS compares the center coefficient with the neighboring coefficients corresponding to the azimuth θ and only choose the center coefficient larger than the neighboring coefficients as follows

$$NMS(x,y) = \begin{cases} |\Delta_s f(x,y)|, & if\ |\Delta_s f(x,y)| > |\Delta_s f(x',y')| \\ & and\ |\Delta_s f(x,y)| > |\Delta_s f(x'',y'')|. \\ 0, & otherwise \end{cases} \tag{4}$$

Here, $\Delta_s f$ is sub-band image and subscript s denotes decomposition level. $\Delta_s f(x,y)$ means center coefficient and $\Delta_s f(x',y')$ and $\Delta_s f(x'',y'')$ are neighboring coefficients.

(a) (b) (c) (d)

Figure 3. Edge Map for each Sub-band: (a) $L_1(\Delta_1 f)$, (b) $L_2(\Delta_2 f)$, (c) $L_3(\Delta_3 f)$, (d) $L_4(\Delta_4 f)$

The final stage of the Canny edge detection is to pick out potential and weak edges and it uses double threshold. The gradient magnitude values over the high-threshold are decided to the edge points, and the values under the low-threshold are considered as noise. The values between the high and low-threshold are classified to the weak edge. Edge map is generated by merging potential and weak edges and its result is presented in figure 3.

Conventional filters based on the transform domain performs denoising by referring to neighboring pixels. This approach sometimes works well but it causes the side effect such as edge loss and over smoothing. The NLM filter compares not only neighboring pixels but also all non-local regions with similarity to the current region, and thus it shows better performance than conventional filters. The NLM filter is defined as [Buades, A. 2005]

$$NL[v](i) = \sum_{j \in \Delta_s f} w(i,j)v(j), \tag{5}$$

where the weight $w(i,j)$ is

$$w(i,j) = \frac{1}{Z(i)} e^{-\frac{\|v(\mathcal{N}_i)-v(\mathcal{N}_j)\|_{2,a}^2}{h^2}}, \tag{6}$$

and normalizing constant $Z(i)$ is

$$Z(i) = \sum_j e^{-\frac{\|v(\mathcal{N}_i)-v(\mathcal{N}_j)\|_{2,a}^2}{h^2}}. \tag{7}$$

Here, i and j denote the pixel and v means the noisy image. And $v(\mathcal{N}_i)$ is the intensity gray level vector. The PM compares the generated edge map information and the NLM filter output for each sub-band as follows

$$NL[v][i] = \begin{cases} NL[v][i], & if\ NMS(x,y) = 0 \\ NMS(x,y), & otherwise \end{cases}. \tag{8}$$

For the case of $NMS(x,y) = 0$ corresponding to non-edge pixel, the NLM filtering is applied. The other cases, the value of $NMS(x,y)$ is applied to maintain the edge. Since noise reduction is only performed to the noisy pixel, it is possible to preserve more edge information compared to other filtering methods.

4. EXPERIMENTAL RESULT

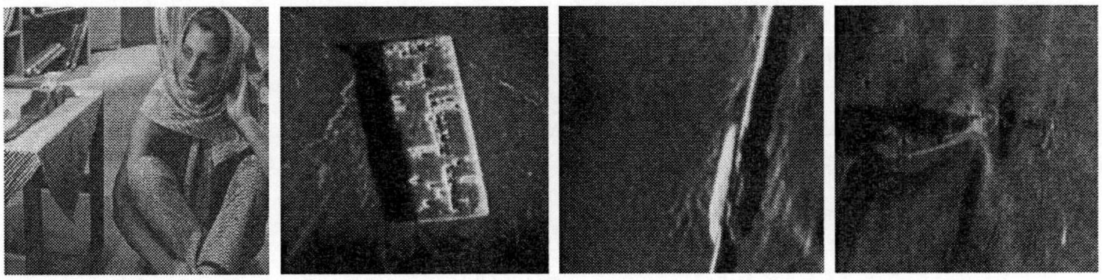

(a) (b) (c) (d)

Figure 4. Original Test Images: (a) Barbara, (b) Barge, (c) Pipeline, (d) Ship and Mooring

For the performance evaluation, Lena and Barbara images are generally used as the standard test image. However, unfortunately, there is no representative image for imaging sonar systems. To verify the performance of the PM, we chose four test images. One is the Barbara and the others is provided on the Kraken homepage [Kraken]. Test images are presented in figure 4 and detailed experimental conditions are described in Table 1.

Table 1. Experimental Conditions

Experimental condition	
Experiment environment	MATLAB
Image	Barbara, barge, pipeline, ship and mooring
Resolution	512 × 512
Noise levels	σ = 10, 20, 30, 40
Criterion	PSNR

For the experiment, we used the à trous transform with four levels sub-band decomposition and the Canny algorithm provided in the MATLAB.

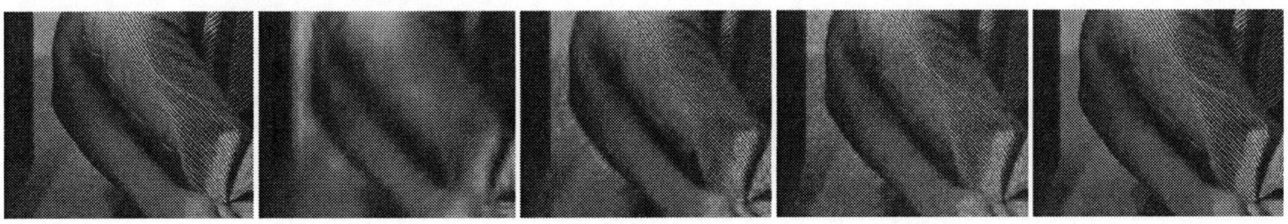

(a) (b) (c) (d) (e)

Figure 5. Experiment result images: (a) original, (b) Visushrink, (c) Sureshrink, (d) Bayesshrink, (e) PM

Figure 5 shows the experimental results of σ = 20. Comparing to the original image of figure 5(a), three conventional methods(Visushrink, Sureshrink, and Bayesshrink) produce blurred images as shown in figure 5(b)-(d). Since the conventional methods does not distinguish edge with noise and noise only pixel, numerous edges are collapsed after the denoising process. On the other hand, the PM shows similar output with the original by means of the adaptive sharpening. In terms of the output image quality, we can know that the PM works well for the general image. Table 2 presents the quantitative results for all noise levels(σ = 10, 20, 30, 40). The PM shows better performance than conventional method in most of cases and average performance improvement for three sonar images is about 2.68 dB, 2.07 dB, and 1.91 dB, respectively. These results means that the PM is effective for noisy sonar image.

Table 2. Comparison of the PSN

Noise level		($\sigma = 10$)	($\sigma = 20$)	($\sigma = 30$)	($\sigma = 40$)	Average
Barbara	Visushrink	24.4369	21.9983	21.0422	20.4606	21.9845
	Sureshrink	29.6980	26.9610	24.6044	23.6791	26.2356
	Bayesshrink	30.9164	27.5427	25.5002	24.7144	27.1684
	PM	**33.3226**	**30.2313**	**27.7059**	**25.9349**	**29.2986**
Noise level		($\sigma = 10$)	($\sigma = 20$)	($\sigma = 30$)	($\sigma = 40$)	Average
barge	Visushrink	24.2793	22.5045	21.606	21.0238	22.3534
	Sureshrink	29.2063	25.8815	24.2777	23.1772	25.6356
	Bayesshrink	30.5030	27.0374	25.4308	24.7495	26.9301
	PM	**30.5744**	**27.7110**	**26.7021**	**25.6292**	**27.6541**
Noise level		($\sigma = 10$)	($\sigma = 20$)	($\sigma = 30$)	($\sigma = 40$)	Average
pipeline	Visushrink	23.5738	22.032	21.5264	21.1745	22.0766
	Sureshrink	28.8808	25.2354	23.3822	22.4151	24.9783
	Bayesshrink	**29.8154**	**26.4617**	24.9191	24.1682	26.3411
	PM	29.4338	26.4405	**25.3352**	**24.9540**	**26.5408**
Noise level		($\sigma = 10$)	($\sigma = 20$)	($\sigma = 30$)	($\sigma = 40$)	Average
ship and mooring	Visushrink	23.0095	21.5742	21.0376	20.7043	21.5814
	Sureshrink	28.2116	24.2383	22.4444	21.3849	24.0698
	Bayesshrink	29.1053	25.8973	24.2400	22.8255	25.5170
	PM	**29.3456**	**25.9672**	**24.3622**	**22.8828**	**25.6394**

5. CONCLUSION

In this paper, we deal with the blurring issue of the conventional denoising methods. Since image blurring is directly linked to the collapse of the edge information, it is a critical problem in the object detection and classification. To achieve a contradictory objective, the noise reduction and the edge preservation, we proposed a new denoising method. The PM classifies edge with noise and noise only pixels by using edge map and effectively reduces noises using NLM filtering. In terms of qualitative and quantitative criterion, the proposed method shows better performance than the conventional methods (Visushrink, Sureshrink, Bayesshrink) for most of test cases.

The PM may be a good solution for denoising but there is still room for performance improvement. To enhance the performance, future works will focus on the more effective edge map generation by all level noise estimation and introduction of other transform such as the curvelet transform.

ACKNOWLEDGEMENT

This research was supported by the Agency for Defense Development, South Korea, under Grant (UD160014DD).

REFERENCES

Deepa, M. (2012). Wavelet and curvelet based thresholding techniques for image denoising. *International Journal of Advanced Research in Computer Science and Electronics Engineering (IJARCSEE)*, 1(10), pp-77.

Raju, V. V. K., & Kumar, M. P. (2014, April). Denoising of MRI and X-ray images using dual tree complex wavelet and curvelet transforms. *In Communications and Signal Processing (ICCSP)*, Melmaruvathur, India, (pp. 1844-1848).

Kooshesh, M., & Akbarizadeh, G. (2015, March). Despeckling algorithm for remote sensing synthetic aperture radar images using multi-scale curvelet transform. *In Artificial Intelligence and Signal Processing (AISP)*, Mashhad, Iran, (pp. 228-233).

Cong, W., & Lu, J. (2016, January). An improved three-dimensional block matching image de-noise algorithm and its application in a 3D imaging sonar. *In Ocean Acoustics (COA)*, Harbin, China, (pp. 1-4).

Kumudham, R., Swaminathan, A., & Rajendran, V. (2016, April). Comparison of the performance metrics of median filter and wavelet filter when applied on SONAR images for denoising. *In Computation of Power, Energy Information and Commuincation (ICCPEIC)*, Chennai, India, (pp. 288-290).

Padmavathi, G., Subashini, P., Kumar, M. M., & Thakur, S. K. (2010). Comparison of filters used for underwater image pre-processing. *International Journal of Computer Science and Network Security*, 10(1), 58-65.

Isar, A., Moga, S., & Isar, D. (2005, July). A new method for denoising sonar images. *In Signals, Circuits and Systems, ISSCS 2005*. Iasi, Romania, (Vol. 2, pp. 469-472).

Tin, H. W., Leu, S. W., Wen, C. C., & Chang, S. H. (2013, March). An efficient sidescan sonar image denoising method based on a new roughness entropy fractal dimension. *In Underwater Technology Symposium (UT), 2013 IEEE International*, Tokyo, Japan, (pp. 1-5).

Saurabh, A., Kumar, A., & Anitha, U. (2015, March). Performance analysis of various wavelet thresholding techniques for despeckiling of sonar images. *In Signal Processing, Communication and Networking (ICSCN)*, Chennai, India, (pp. 1-7).

Fowler, J. E. (2005). The redundant discrete wavelet transform and additive noise. *IEEE Signal Processing Letters*, 12(9), 629-632.

Donoho, D. L., & Johnstone, J. M. (1992). "Ideal spatial adaptation by wavelet shrinkage", *biometrika*, 81(3), 425-455.

Donoho, D.L. and Johnstone, I.M. (1995), "Adapting to Unknown Smoothness via Wavelet Shrinkage", *Journal of the American Statistical Association*, Vol. 90, No. 432, Dec 1995, pp. 1200-1224.

Chang, S.G., Yu B., and Vetterli, M. (2000), "Adaptive Wavelet Thresholding for Image Denoising and Compression", *IEEE Transaction on Image Processing*, Vol. 9, No. 9, 2000, pp. 1532-1546.

Starck, J. L., Candès, E. J., & Donoho, D. L. (2002). The curvelet transform for image denoising. *IEEE Transactions on image processing*, 11(6), 670-684.

Canny John, (1986) A Computational Approach to Edge Detection, *IEEE Transactions on Pattern Analysis and Machine Intelligence*, PAMI-8(6), pp. 679-698.

Rong, W., Li, Z., Zhang, W., & Sun, L. (2014, August). An improved CANNY edge detection algorithm. *In Mechatronics and Automation (ICMA)*, Tianjin, China, (pp. 577-582).

Buades, A., Coll, B., & Morel, J. M. 2005, June. A non-local algorithm for image denoising. *In Computer Vision and Pattern Recognition (CVPR)*, San Diego, USA, (Vol. 2, pp. 60-65).

Kraken, MINSAS and INSAS - Survey Imagery, http://krakenrobotics.com/gallery

ARPOSER: AUTOMATICALLY AUGMENTING MOBILE PICTURES WITH DIGITAL CHARACTERS IMITATING POSES

Gokcen Cimen[1], Christoph Maurhofer[1], Martin Guay[2] and Robert W. Sumner[2]
[1]*ETH Zurich, Switzerland*
[2]*Disney Research, Switzerland*

Figure 1. Examples of Poses Automatically Recovered and Augmented with a Digital Character Using our Method

ABSTRACT

We introduce *AR Poser*: a framework for posing *with, or as* a digital character. In this paper, we describe our first contribution to *AR Poser*: a technique for digital characters to recognize and automatically reproduce the same pose as a person in a picture (using only RGB information from a mobile device). 3D human pose estimation from RGB is an under-constrained and ambiguous problem that remains today an active field of study. Instead of addressing the general case of human pose estimation, we propose a solution that can be tailored to a specific scenario---such as entertainment poses for AR selfies. At the heart of our solution is a set of predefined poses (selfie poses) utilized to reduce ambiguities. In a nutshell, our method consists of two reliable steps: we first perform 2D pose estimation, and then perform a projection onto the 3D subspace to find the closest matching 3D pose. With our method, we are able to automatically create augmented reality selfies for a variety of different poses.

KEYWORDS

Augmented Reality, Pose Estimation, Intelligent Virtual Characters

1. INTRODUCTION

Digital augmentation of the real world opens new dimensions for ideation, communication and entertainment. For example, facial tracking combined with different mask overlays recently resulted in highly entertaining and popular mobile applications. In the future, we can imagine combining human shape estimation with digital character augmentation to unlock various entertaining selfie scenarios. Hence, we introduce *AR Poser*: a framework for posing with or as a digital character. In this paper, we describe our first contribution to *AR Poser*: a technique for digital characters to automatically reproduce the same pose as a person in a picture.

To automatically imitate the person's pose with a 3D digital character, we need to estimate the 3D pose of the person from a single monocular image (RGB). 3D human pose estimation from RGB is an under-constrained and ambiguous problem that remains an active field of study. Instead of addressing the general case of human pose estimation, we propose a solution that can be tailored to a specific scenario---such as poses AR selfies. At the heart of our solution is a set of predefined poses (selfie poses) utilized to reduce ambiguities associated with depth when estimating 3D poses. In a nutshell, our approach consists of breaking down the problem into two more reliable steps: first a 2D pose estimation, and then a projection onto our 3D subspace to find the closest matching 3D pose. With our method, we were able to automatically create augmented reality selfies for a variety of different poses.

2. RELATED WORK

There has been several entertaining applications of people augmentation in the recent years. Combining face tracking from RGB images with different 3D masks is a famous example popularized by the *Snapchat* app [Kazemi & Sullivan (2014)]. Recently, rapid progress has been made in estimating human poses and shapes from RGB images. To our knowledge, no works has yet fully automatically augmented people's bodies. For example, clothes has been added to images and video, but semi-automatically [Rogge et al. (2011), Rogge et al. (2014)]. There has been manual augmentation, where the application inserts a pre-defined character or object in the scene [Barakonyi and Schmalsteig (2006), Zünd et al. (2014), McIntosh et al. (2017)]. The seminal work of Barakonyi explores different interactions in AR with digital characters and objects [Barakonyi and Schmalsteig (2006)]. More recently, Zund et al. [Zünd et al. (2014)] evaluated different aspects of reality mixing techniques, and the McIntosh et al. [McIntosh et al. (2017)] created a magic bench where a character appeared on the bench on a display in front of the bench, and the character interacts with the person. Recently, the idea of tracking real world objects to interact with digital characters has been demonstrated using pre-defined marker-based tracking for rigid localization [Cimen et al. (2018)]. To our knowledge, there has not yet been a case of a person's pose automatically estimated and augmented with a digital character.

Estimating a 3D human pose skeleton from an image is a challenging problem due to the ambiguities associated to the depth projection, as well as the variations in human shapes. Using a depth camera, methods have been proposed where a large data-set of 3D skeleton poses and depth image pairs are created, to then train a model to map depth to 3D skeleton [Shotton et al. (2013), Buys et al. (2014), Zimmermann et al. (2018)], resulting in popular products such as *Kinect.*

Recently, researchers have experimented with a similar approach but using only a single monocular RGB image [Mehta et al. (2016), Tomè et al. (2017), Martinez et al. (2017), Mehta et al. (2017)]. At the heart of this approach is a human pose synthesis procedure that can creates a large data-set of human poses with various textures, from a which a model can be fitted. While it is showing promising results, it remains challenging to differentiate between different human shapes and cover a wide range of poses.

We are not the first to consider breaking down the problem into a first 2D pose estimation step, followed by a 3D re-construction step. A large set of human captured motion can be used to facilitate convergence to a natural 3D pose [Wang et al. (2014), Yasin et al. (2015), Chen & Ramanan (2016)]. Wang et al. [Wang et al. (2014)] represented 3D poses as a linear combination of a sparse set of bases learned from a large 3D pose dataset, and solve the 3D reconstruction as an optimization problem in the reduced space. Instead of online optimization, Yasin et al, [Yasin et al. (2015)] learned a direct mapping off line from 2D to 3D poses, and applied it to the task of 3D pose retrieval. Our approach does not rely on a large data set. A direct mapping blends between 2D skeletons as input and might yield 3D poses with artifacts. Hence a direct optimization method guarantees the 3D pose preserves its initial details. One additional problem with large set of poses is that while they may contain a variety of activities, they are complicated to gather and might not contain the entertainment poses desired for the application. Our approach is technically most similar to [Chen & Ramanan (2016)], but depends only on a small set of poses, geared towards the application.

3. 2D POSE ESTIMATION

We have recently seen rapid progress in 2D pose estimation from monocular images using deep learning "in the wild". There are now packaged solutions that offer robust solutions for multiple subjects and occluded parts. In this work, we use the pre-trained network *OpenPose* [Cao et al. (2017)], which was trained on the COCO [Lin et al. (2014)] and MPII [Andriluka et al. (2014)] datasets.

The pre-trained network takes as input the RGB image, and returns a list of joint positions y_i together with a confidence value c_i. For example, a partially visible body will result in a low confidence value for the joints outside the image. The neural network was trained over a large data-set of hand-annotated images---each with the skeleton of the people in the image.

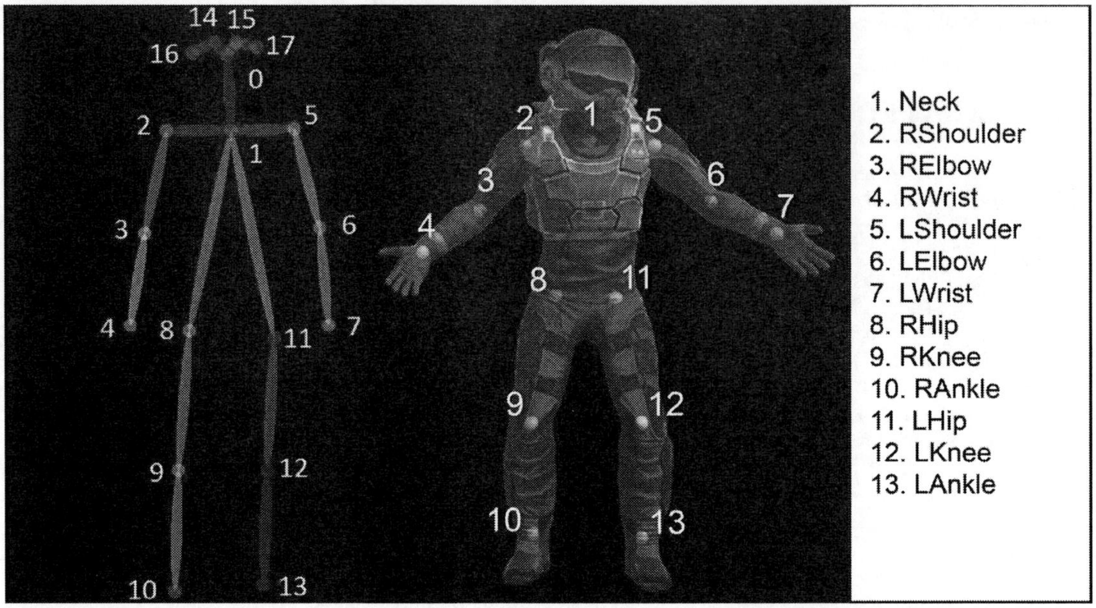

Figure 2. The 2D skeleton on the left is obtained from OpenPose. It has 18 joints. On the right is the 3D character that we used in our experiment. A common subset of joints need to be mapped for the 3D pose matching process

The 2D skeleton has a set of joint names that we associate to the 3D joints of our character, as shown in Figure 2. This map is defined manually in our case, but could be done automatically given corresponding T poses for example. With the 2D joint positions associated to 3D joints, we can proceed to the step of computing the best matching 3D pose.

4. 3D POSE PROJECTION

The way we project the 2D skeleton onto the 3D pose space is via local optimization. We assume a small set of 3D poses, in our case entertaining selfies, as shown in the results section. The 3D poses constrain the solution space to only plausible articulations of the characters body. Since possible selfie poses are symmetrical, we handle symmetries by mirroring the 3D poses in the dataset along y-axis.

For each pose in the database, we optimize for the rigid transformation that will bring the 3D pose, closest to the 2D projected skeleton, in terms for joint positions and bone direction similarity. The global transformation of a 3D pose is parameterized with 5 degrees of freedom, as we constrain the translation of the character along the y-axis, as shown in Figure 3.

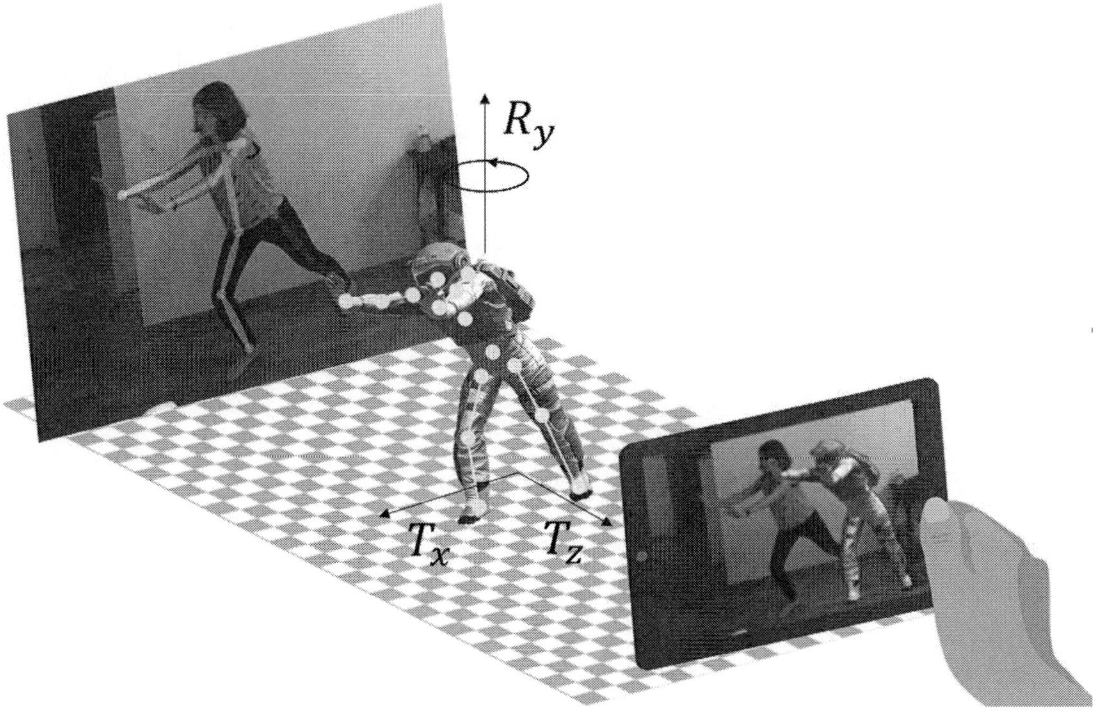

Figure 3. From 2D Pose Estimation to 3D Pose Subspace and Finding Optimal Character Pose

Formally, for each pose $X^k = \{x_i\}^k$ defined as a set of joint positions x_i, we optimize for a reduced rigid transformation M composed of a rotation around the y axis, R_y, and translations along the x and z axes T_x, T_z---resulting in $M = T_y\, T_x\, R_y$ and that minimizes the similarity cost between the 3D projected joint positions $P\, M\, x_i$ and the 2D joint positions y_i, where P is the view and projection transformation of the camera (see next section for how we estimate the mobile camera's parameters). Finally, we go through all the optimal transformations and poses pairs $< X^k, M >$, and pick the one that has the smallest cost value, resulting in the following optimization problem:

$$X^*, M^* = argmin_{\{<X^k,M>\}} \min_M \sum_i ||y_i - P\, M\, x_i\, ||^2$$

We solve the internal optimization for the transformation M using gradient-based optimization along numerical derivatives. This requires initializing the 3D pose front facing the camera as to ensure convergence towards a sensible solution.

We described how to match the 3D pose to the 2D skeleton, but this depends on 3D camera parameters for the projection. Next we describe how we estimate these for the mobile device given a known *a priori* marker in the scene.

5. AUGMENTATION AND MOBILE SETUP

To incorporate a 3D character into the real world picture using a mobile device, we need to estimate the camera parameters: a view and perspective matrix. The perspective matrix is given by the device, while we use marker-base technology (*Vuforia*) [Vuforia (2017)] to recognize and track the camera's transformations. Camera is located in space as Vuforia calculates its position based on marker detection. We print a real world marker that is about the size of a person, and process the texture for visual features. When the mobile device takes a picture, it contains the marker, which is then used to estimate the orientation and position of the camera.

The information about the scale of the AR character is lost during projection transformation. To address this, the 3D character pose used in the optimization (section 4), is initialized to roughly fit inside the bounding box of the marker. The optimization adjusts the character's depth translation to match the same size as the person's 2D skeleton. If the character is to be smaller, (e.g. a dwarf) we wait until the end of the optimization, to scale the final 3D pose back to its original size.

Finally, the neural network we use in section 3 (*OpenPose*) to estimate the 2D pose of a person is sizable and runs optimally on a graphics card. Deploying such a system on a mobile device represents a significant integration effort, and will suffer from a loss of performance due to the difference in hardware. Our solution is to place the 2D pose estimation "in the cloud", and send messages between the mobile device taking pictures, and the 2D pose estimation running on a server.

6. RESULTS AND DISCUSSION

We designed a creative concept around Space Exploration that resulted in 12 relevant poses. We started with a set of 10 poses, and invited people to experience the application. The subjects performed poses we did not have, which we then crafted and included in the dataset, removing the ones that were not relevant. After two such iterations, we 12 relevant poses shown below.

The pictures were taken from a mobile device, sent to a server for the 2D skeleton estimation (running *OpenPose*), and then the 3D pose matching was performed on the mobile device. The whole process took about 2 seconds.

7. LIMITATIONS

The sum of joint positions that we minimize is successful at matching the shape of the character, but does not always succeed at finding a perceptually similar size for the character. It can be seen in our results that sometimes the character is larger than others. We could fix this with a final pass that adjusts the size based on the shoulder and feet proportions, which seem to be visually important.

Naturally, poses not present in the database fail to be discovered. This is a limitation by design. Also, at the moment we only tackled and demonstrated pose similarity for body joints---excluding the face and the hands. In consequence, similar body poses that have different hand gestures will fail to be discriminated. We think this could be tackled with a 2 step matching where first the full body is matched, then the different hand poses are considered.

8. CONCLUSION

We proposed a practical approach to produce augmented reality selfies with digital characters. It relies on a set of predefined poses that are automatically selected and adjusted based on a 2D pose estimate of the character. While a few minor improvements are required to match people of different sizes, it unlocks possibilities to investigate new interactions not yet described in this paper. For example, we have the digital character be worn as a suit by the person in the picture---similar to augmenting clothes. We could estimate the shape of the person from a humanoid and utilize this 3D geometry estimation to support partial occlusions as well as casting approximate shadows from the subject to the character.

REFERENCES

[Andriluka et al. (2014)]Andriluka, M., Pishchulin, L., Gehler, P. & Schiele, B. (2014), 2d human pose estimation: New benchmark and state of the art analysis, *in* 'IEEE Conference on Computer Vision and Pattern Recognition (CVPR)'.

[Barakonyi and Schmalsteig (2006)] Barakonyi, I. & Schmalstieg, D. (2006), 2d Ubiquitous animated agentes for augmented reality., *in* 'Proceedings of the 5th IEEE and ACM International Symposium onMixed and Augmented Reality', IEEE Computer Society, ISMAR '06, pp. 145–154.

[Buys et al. (2014)] Buys, K., Cagniart, C., Baksheev, A., Laet, T. D., Schutter, J. D. & Pantofaru, C. (2014), 'An adaptable system for rgb-d based human body detection and pose estimation', *Journal of Visual Communication and Image Representation* 25(1), 39 – 52. Visual Understanding and Applications with RGB-D Cameras. http://www.sciencedirect.com/science/article/pii/S1047320313000515

[Cao et al. (2017)] Cao, Z., Simon, T., Wei, S.-E. & Sheikh, Y. (2017), Realtime multi-person 2d pose estimation using part affinity fields, *in* 'CVPR'.

[Chen & Ramanan (2016)] Chen, C. & Ramanan, D. (2016), '3d human pose estimation = 2d pose estimation + matching', *CoRR* abs/1612.06524. http://arxiv.org/abs/1612.06524

[Cimen et al. (2018)] Cimen, G., Yuan, Y., Sumner, R., Coros, S. & Guay, M. (2018), 'Interacting with intelligent characters in ar', *International SERIES on Information Systems and Management in Creative eMedia (CreMedia)* (2017/2).

[Kazemi & Sullivan (2014)] Kazemi, V. & Sullivan, J. (2014), One millisecond face alignment with an ensemble of regression trees, *in* 'Proceedings of the 2014 IEEE Conference on Computer Vision and Pattern Recognition', CVPR '14, IEEE Computer Society, Washington, DC, USA, pp. 1867–1874. https://doi.org/10.1109/CVPR.2014.241

[Lin et al. (2014)] Lin, T., Maire, M., Belongie, S. J., Bourdev, L. D., Girshick, R. B., Hays, J., Perona, P., Ramanan, D., Dollár, P. & Zitnick, C. L. (2014), 'Microsoft COCO: common objects in context', *CoRR* abs/1405.0312. http://arxiv.org/abs/1405.0312

[Martinez et al. (2017)] Martinez, J., Hossain, R., Romero, J. & Little, J. J. (2017), 'A simple yet effective baseline for 3d human pose estimation', *CoRR* abs/1705.03098. http://arxiv.org/abs/1705.03098

[McIntosh et al. (2017)] McIntosh, K., Mars, J., Krahe, J., McCann, J., Rivera, A., Marsico, J., Israr, A., Lawson, S. & Mahler, M. (2017), Magic bench: A multi-user, multi-sensory ar/mr platform, *in* 'ACM SIGGRAPH 2017 VR Village'.

[Mehta, Rhodin, Casas, Fua, Sotnychenko, Xu & Theobalt (2016)] Mehta, D., Rhodin, H., Casas, D., Fua, P., Sotnychenko, O., Xu, W. & Theobalt, C. (2017), Monocular 3d human pose estimation in the wild using improved cnn supervision, *in* '2017 Fifth International Conference on 3D Vision (3DV)'.

[Mehta, Sridhar, Sotnychenko, Rhodin, Shafiei, Seidel, Xu, Casas & Theobalt (2017)] Mehta, D., Sridhar, S., Sotnychenko, O., Rhodin, H., Shafiei, M., Seidel, H.-P., Xu, W., Casas, D. & Theobalt, C. (2017), 'Vnect: Real-time 3d human pose estimation with a single rgb camera', *ACM Trans. Graph.* 36(4), 44:1–44:14.

[Rogge et al. (2014)] Rogge, L., Klose, F., Stengel, M., Eisemann, M. & Magnor, M. (2014), 'Garment replacement in monocular video sequences', *ACM Trans. Graph.* 34(1), 6:1–6:10.

[Rogge et al. (2011)] Rogge, L., Neumann, T., Wacker, M. & Magnor, M. (2011), Monocular pose reconstruction for an augmented reality clothing system, *in* 'Proc. Vision, Modeling and Visualization (VMV)', Eurographics, pp. 339–346.

[Shotton et al. (2013)] Shotton, J., Fitzgibbon, A., Cook, M., Sharp, T., Finocchio, M., Moore, R., Kipman, A. & Blake, A. (2013), *Real-Time Human Pose Recognition in Parts from Single Depth Images*, Springer Berlin Heidelberg, Berlin, Heidelberg, pp. 119–135.

[Tomè et al. (2017)] Tomè, D., Russell, C. & Agapito, L. (2017), 'Lifting from the deep: Convolutional 3d pose estimation from a single image', *CoRR* abs/1701.00295. http://arxiv.org/abs/1701.00295

[Vuforia (2017)] Vuforia (2017), 'Qualcomm, http://www.qualcomm.com/vuforia'.

[Wang et al. (2014)] Wang, C., Wang, Y., Lin, Z., Yuille, A. L. & Gao, W. (2014), 'Robust estimation of 3d human poses from a single image', *CoRR* abs/1406.2282. http://arxiv.org/abs/1406.2282

[Yasin et al. (2015)] Yasin, H., Iqbal, U., Krüger, B., Weber, A. & Gall, J. (2015), '3d pose estimation from a single monocular image', *CoRR* abs/1509.06720. http://arxiv.org/abs/1509.06720

[Zimmermann et al. (2018)] Zimmermann, C., Welschehold, T., Dornhege, C., Burgard, W. & Brox, T. (2018), '3d human pose estimation in RGBD images for robotic task learning', *CoRR* abs/1803.02622. http://arxiv.org/abs/1803.02622

[Zünd et al. (2014)] Zünd, F., Lancelle, M., Ryffel, M., Sumner, R. W., Mitchell, K. & Gross, M. (2014), Influence of animated reality mixing techniques on user experience, *in* 'Proceedings of the Seventh International Conference on Motion in Games', MIG '14, ACM, pp. 125–132. http://doi.acm.org/10.1145/2668084.2668088

EVOLUTIONARY 3D SHAPE MODEL CREATION BY SHAPE BLENDING

Satoshi Yonemoto and Masaya Sugawa
Graduate School of Information Science, Kyushu Sangyo University, Japan

ABSTRACT

We propose a new method for creating evolutionary 3D shape models. Given several initial models and the mixing rate of them, our method creates novel and plausible 3D shapes. Our method is designed by evolutionary operations such as crossover and mutation. In this work, shape blending in crossover and in mutation is newly introduced. The created parts are stored in multiple family-tree structures, where each part of the initial models is the origin of the parts. Moreover, shape dis-similarity using shape histograms is used in fitness calculation. We demonstrate the effectiveness of our new evolutionary creation of 3D shapes.

KEYWORDS

Evolutionary Computation, 3D Shape Modelling, Shape Blending, Genetic Algorithm

1. INTRODUCTION

We propose an efficient way to create various 3D shape models from several models. Automatic 3D model creation is attracting, and starts to gain attention in many developers of 3D applications. In recent years, many procedural generation techniques are proposed (Sims, 1991; Smelik, 2009; Merrell, 2011; Guo, 2014; Yumer, 2015). A remarkable achievement of today's game development tools is the procedural generation of textures and materials. Previous approaches for procedural modelling either use stochastic models or generation rules which follow in shape genetics. Our method is one of such genetic approaches, and can evolve a population of individual models from several initial models.

Our method also enables a user to select a mixing rate with the user's own intention. Simultaneously, it can take shape diversity into account. In our previous work, we have verified our framework of evolutionary 3D shape model creation is effective (Yonemoto, 2017). Shape properties were treated as mixing at genetic code level, so that it was difficult to represent evolutionary shapes which were directly derived from the parents. Therefore, as the second step, we started efforts to introduce a shape blending algorithm in earnest.

In summary, we will introduce the following improvements:

- new shape blending algorithm in crossover and in mutation (part crossover and part mutation)
- re-definition of shape similarity measure using shape histograms
- management of multiple family trees during evolution process

Xu et al. (Xu, 2012) propose a 3D shape model mixing method by evolving original shape variations. According to this approach, evolutionary shapes are created by just mixing different shape models. The created models do not necessarily reflect a user's intention but, various interesting models can be created. This method is a kind of iterative mash-up model creation, rather than evolutionary creation. It is worthy of note that part crossover is used. Our work supports orthodox part crossover as an evolutionary process. As another method, a new shape synthesis method for mixing existing shapes is proposed by Kalogerakis et al. (Kalogerakis, 2012). Probabilistic model is designed to represent the structure class of shapes. Given 100 training models. This method can synthesis roughly 100 new shape models. It is interesting to note that the generation rules are automatically acquired from initial models. Alhashim, I., et al. (Alhashim, 2014) proposed a method for novel 3D model creation by topology-varying shape blending. This method enables creation of various intermediate shapes by shape blending. We introduce a similar shape blending scheme based on shape primitive adding and removing. Shape blending serves as gradual part evolution to generate new individuals.

2. EVOLUTIONARY 3D SHAPE MODEL CREATION

2.1 Our Framework

Figure 1 shows our framework of evolutionary 3D shape model creation. First, user prepares several initial models. The initial models are equivalent to shape seeds. User expects mixing the initial models and creating mash-up models. The mixing rate indicates the initial model's occupancy reflecting user's preference. To take shape diversity, initial set consists of the initial models and the other models which randomly selected from model database. The idea of our evolutionary process is based on evolutionary computation such as genetic algorithm. That is, our evolutionary process is executed according to the following procedures: selection, crossover and mutation. In crossover, first, part shuffling is executed among two individuals which are randomly selected (i.e., parents). Then, property crossover is executed. That is, their properties such as scale or bending may be exchanged by crossover at the genetic code level.

Figure 2 illustrates part shuffling and property crossover for a chair model, which has been already used in previous work. In part shuffling, using parent A and B, child C and D are created (then, A and B are replaced by C and D). In property crossover, their properties such as scale or bending may be exchanged (finally child C′ and D′ are generated). In this case, the parts of backrest are shuffled and then, their shapes are bended and the horizontal size is varied.

In crossover or in mutation, part evolution based on shape blending is also executed. The part evolution in crossover has several modes: part crossover, degeneration, change and reversion. The current mode is stochastically determined by roulette wheel selection. Part crossover is selected with the highest probability. In mutation, the part may be replaced with something new. This part replacement is occurred with a low probability (i.e., mutation rate). The part mutation is also supported. Shape primitive adding or removing may be executed. The generated models (i.e., the elite models) are picked up by user, and then they are displayed in a model gallery.

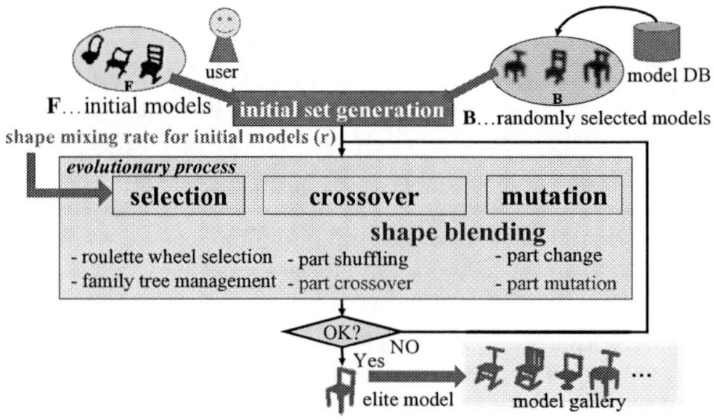

Figure 1. Evolutionary 3D Shape Model Creation

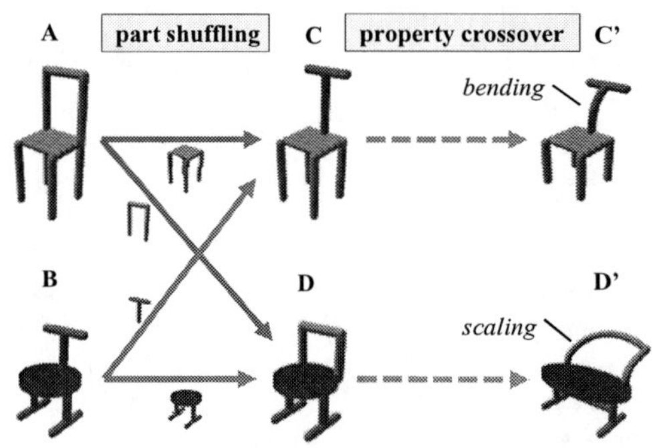

Figure 2. Part Shuffling and Property Crossover

2.2 3D Shape Model

2.2.1 Shape Primitive

In our work, 3D shape model consists of one or more parts. The parts configuration is defined as a structure graph (Zheng, 2013; Liu, 2015; Huang, 2016). Their parts are strongly connected. Each part is represented by grouping several shape primitives. Shape primitive is represented by deformable generalized cylinder. The shape primitive has several joint pins to connect with the other primitive. The part model is represented by grouping several shape primitives. This configuration is easily changed. Figure 3 illustrates an example of part model construction. The new primitive 4 and 5 (a cross decoration) are connected to the existing part model which has three primitives 1, 2 and 3.

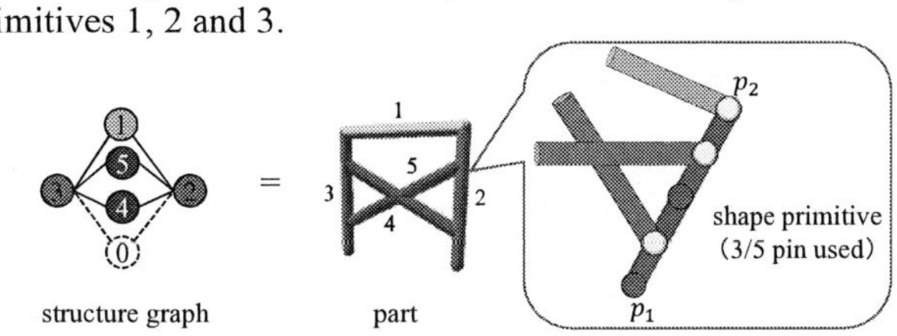

Figure 3. Part Model Construction

2.2.2 Shape Similarity

A histogram of direction distribution is used to grasp the shape properties. Each bin indicates the number of shape primitives which have the same direction and exist near $(v_1, \cdots, c_2)$. We call it shape histogram. Shape histogram is obtained for each part model. Figure 4 shows an example of 3D shape model and its two histograms. Their histograms have 8 bins respectively. Shape similarity is defined by determining the degree of dis-similarity between two histograms. As a similarity metrics for the histogram matching, we choose Bhattacharyya distance (Bhattacharrya, 1943). Scale similarity is also defined by using aspect ratio.

We verified the validity of our shape similarity. Figure 5 illustrates visualization of distance between parts with similar shapes. They are arranged concentrically to a most compact part (four-legs part). In the Figure, the dis-similarity corresponds to the radius of the circle, which is displayed by 0.1. The dis-similarity is greater in proportion to the increase in the number of shape primitives. It was found from the result that shape histogram served as a similarity measure.

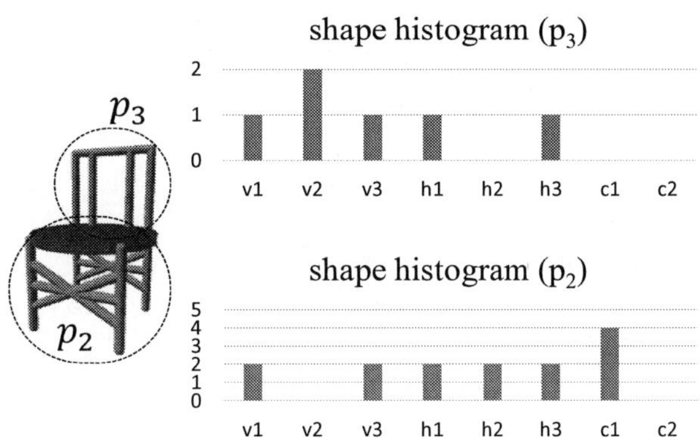

Figure 4. 3D Shape Model and its Shape Histograms

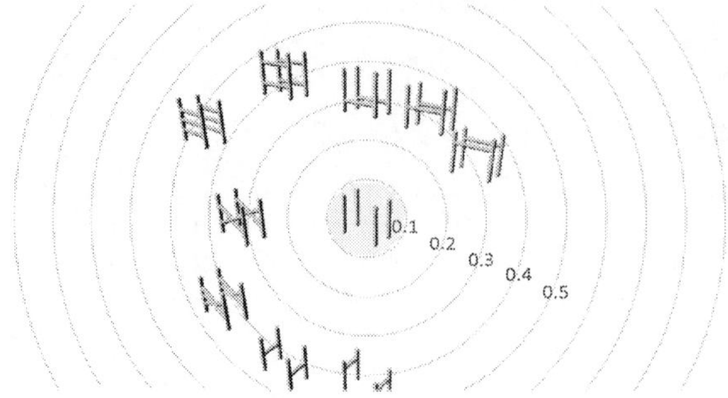

Figure 5. Visualization of Parts with Similar Shapes

3. SHAPE BLENDING

Shape blending serves as gradual part evolution to generate new individuals. Shape blending is used not only in crossover but in mutation.

3.1 Part Crossover

In part crossover, shape blending corresponds to direct copy operation from the other part. Shape blending in part crossover includes the following steps: First, find common structure of the shape primitives between parents. For example, the parallel shape primitives are valuable as such clues. Then, copy just the different primitives. They can be obtained by comparing their joint pins. As a natural result, a new part inherits the shape properties of parents. Figure 6(a) illustrates part crossover. An example of such common structure is highlighted in yellow. Child 2 inherits shape properties from parent 2. Two parallel shape primitives (in red) which correspond to the differences are directly copied from parent 1 to child 2.

Figure 7 illustrates the results of shape blending test for the backrest parts and for leg parts. As the first generations, two pairs of parents are used. The shape blending test was applied continuously three times, so the results were obtained from first generations to third generations.

3.2 Part Mutation

Figure 6 (b) illustrates part mutation. In part mutation, one or two shape primitives may be added or removed. The part mutation is executed for a randomly selected part with a low probability.

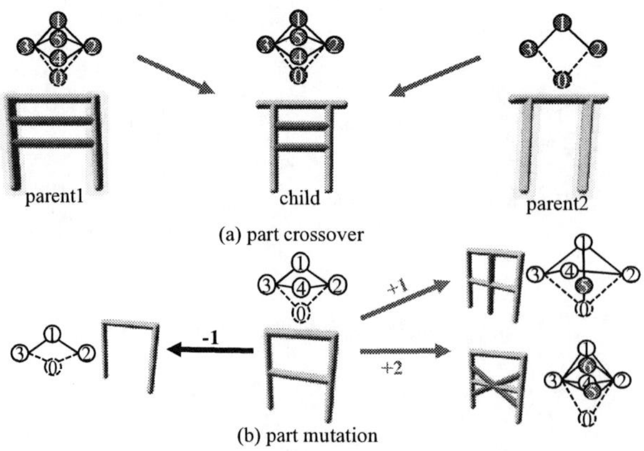

Figure 6. Shape Blending. (a) Part Crossover. (b) Part Mutation

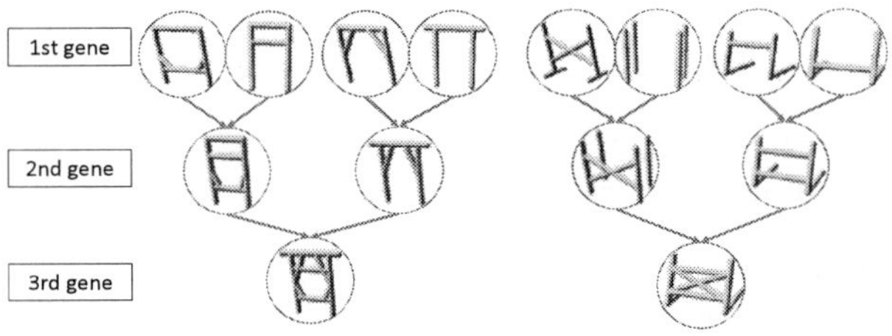

Figure 7. Results of Shape Blending Test

4. UPDATE OF FAMILY TREES

In our work, the created parts are stored in multiple family-tree structures. Each part of the initial models is the origin of the parts. First, the initial parts are registered as a root respectively.

4.1 Roulette Wheel Selection

The part evolution in crossover has several modes: part crossover (64%), degeneration (12%), change (12%) and reversion (12%). The current mode is stochastically determined by roulette wheel selection, which follows the fixed probabilities. Part crossover to add a new node is selected with the highest probability (about five times the other modes). That is, the probability of which the relative parts are reused is 36%. The current part is replaced by the relative part except for the part crossover mode.

4.2 Family Tree

Figure 8 illustrates how to update a family tree. The initial part (four legs) is registered as a root. In part crossover, a node (part) in the current family tree i and a node in the other family tree j (two L-legs registered as a root) may be selected as parents. Thus, a new node is added as a child. In part mutation which executes shape primitive adding and removing, a new node is also added to the corresponding family tree.

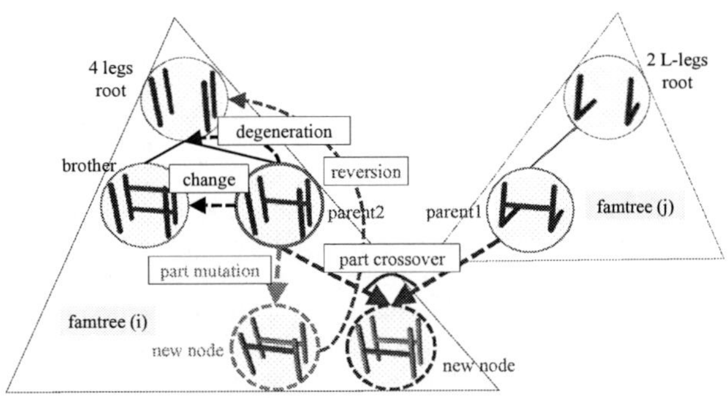

Figure 8. Update of Family Tree

4.3 Fitness

To keep the features inherent in the initial models, the mixing rate r is used as a parameter in the fitness function. Fitness value for individual j is given by the following equation 1:

$$f_j = Ke^{-\frac{\{e_j-(1-r)\}^2}{2\sigma^2}} \qquad (1)$$

where K and σ are coefficients. Error e_j is defined by the following equation 2:

$$e_j = \frac{1}{n}\sum_{k=1}^{n}\left\{(1-\alpha)\min_{i=\{1,\dots,M\}} d_s^k(i,j) + \alpha d_a^k(i^k,j)\right\} \quad (2)$$

where α is the blending strength of scale dis-similarity and it is set to 0.5, and M is the number of initial models. $d_s^k(i,j)$ and $d_a^k(i^k,j)$ means shape dis-similarity and scale dis-similarity between initial model i and individual j with part k, respectively. The index i^k means an initial model that takes the minimum value of shape dis-similarity with part k.

Figure 9 shows the effect of parameter r on the fitness function. As shown in Figure 9, when r is set to 1.0 and error e_j is about 0.0, the fitness value takes the maximum value 1.0. When r is set to 0.8 and error e_j is approximately 0.2, the fitness value approaches 1.0. Accordingly, the mixing rate that user defined can control shape diversity of the created models, based on shape and scale dis-similarity.

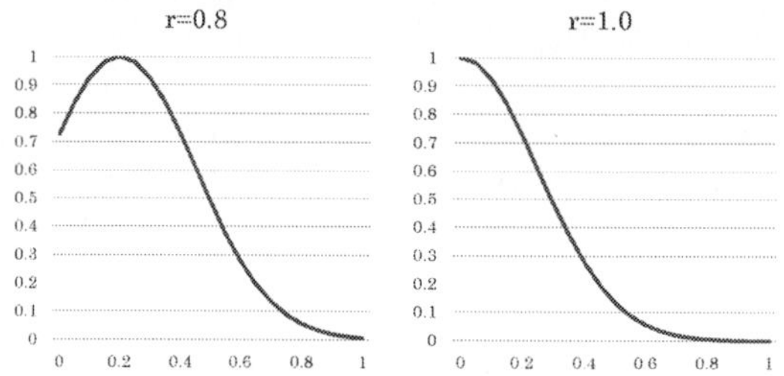

Figure 9. Effect of the Mixing Rate r

5. EXPERIMENTS

5.1 Evolutionary Creation Results

In our previous work, we have verified our framework of evolutionary 3D shape model creation was effective (Yonemoto, 2017). In this work, we introduced a new evolutionary creation method using shape blending and modified similarity measures. The occupancy of the initial models can be controlled by the mixing rate r. We tested for a chair model which consists of three parts as a typical object. Three initial models (I_1, I_2 *and* I_3) that user prepared in advance and an example of the descendant model A that evolved from them are shown in Figure 10. To take shape diversity, initial set consists of the initial models and the other models randomly selected from model database. In this experiment, the initial set consists of 18 individuals, where the initial models account for 50% of initial set. Thus, the remaining ones are randomly selected from unrelated models. Figure 11 shows all the individuals in 50th generations as the mixing rate r is set to 0.8. The elite model exists in the bottom-right corner (in red). Although in this case, most individuals just happened to have similar shape with the elite, we confirmed that their shapes take diversity. Figure 12 shows the other elite models with the fitness value. They were picked up by user under the same condition. When r is set to less than 1.0, various shapes which are not included in the initial models can be represented. Figure 13 shows the elite models which were acquired as the mixing rate r was set to 1.0. In this case, high-purity models which do not take diversity of shapes can be obtained.

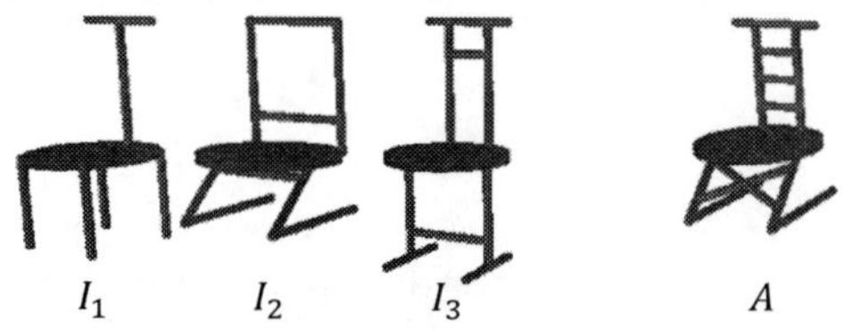

Figure 10. Initial Models and a Descendant Model A

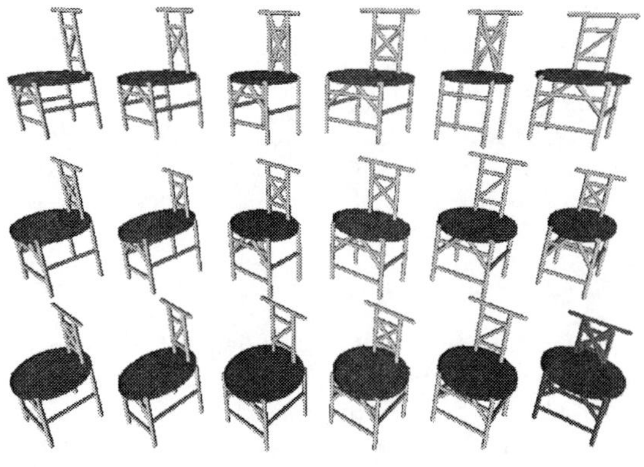

Figure 11. 50th Generations (80% Similar)

Figure 12. Acquired Elite Models (80% Similar)

Figure 13. Acquired Elite Models (100% Similar)

5.2 Verification of Fitness Function

In this work, we introduced a new dis-similarity measure for fitness calculation. Table 1 describes the shape dis-similarity and the scale dis-similarity between a test model A and each initial model I_1, I_2 and I_3. Their models are shown in Figure 10 respectively. In this case, scale parameters (i.e., d_a) are almost the same. In terms of p_2 shape (i.e., d_s^2), the model A is different from I_1 and I_3, but the model A is slightly similar to I_2. It is evident that I_2 is the root of A. In terms of p_3 shape (d_s^3), the model A is similar to I_3 for the same reason. From these results, it is found that the similarity measure is suitable to compare the descendants with the initial models. Table 2 describes the fitness values between individual A and the initial models, which are calculated under various fitness parameters (r, σ). The parameter σ means the distribution variance in the fitness function. When σ is small (e.g.,$\sigma = 0.1$), an influence of the amount of error e_j becomes great. On the other hand, when s is large (e.g., σ=1.0), the fitness values are slightly higher. Therefore, we often set the parameter σ from 0.25 to 0.5.

Table 1. Shape and Scale Dis-Similarity between a Test Model A and each Initial Model I_1, I_2 and I_3

	I_1		I_2		I_3	
	d_s	d_a	d_s	d_a	d_s	d_a
p_1	0.00	0.00	0.00	0.1	0.00	0.00
p_2	0.91	0.01	0.15	0.11	0.82	0.05
p_3	0.5	0.05	0.61	0.08	0.18	0.05

Table 2. Fitness Values under Different Parameter Setting

	$\sigma = 0.1$	$\sigma = 0.25$	$\sigma = 0.5$	$\sigma = 1.0$
r = 0.2	0.00	0.02	0.36	0.77
r = 0.8	0.49	0.89	0.97	0.99
r = 1.0	0.72	0.95	0.99	1.00

6. CONCLUSIONS

We presented an improved method for creating evolutionary 3D shape models, which reflects a user's preference and takes diversity of 3D shapes into account simultaneously. New shape blending algorithm which contains part crossover and part mutation upgraded the presentation capacity of the created shapes by directly mixing of shape properties of the parents. Using the mixing rate that user can control, plausible models can be created. In part crossover or in part mutation, multiple family trees which are introduced to take shape diversity are properly managed by roulette wheel selection. Consequently, shape evolutionary process proceeds gradually. Unlike mash-up methods which need complex management of heterogeneous shapes, our 3D model is represented in unified shape primitives, so evolutionary shapes can be completely managed in the family tree. New shape dis-similarity measure has also been incorporated into the fitness function. We demonstrated the effectiveness of shape dis-similarity using shape histograms. We demonstrated shape blending was just applicable for simple models like a chair or house, but our method is well-suited for complex structure design (Huang, 2016; Demir, 2016). Hence, in future work, we must examine its expansion for complex shape models with multiple parts. To represent more complex shapes, not only parallel shape primitives but also shape primitives arranged radially like objects that is leaf-shaped should be provided.

REFERENCES

Alhashim, I., et al. 2014. Topology-varying 3d shape creation via structural blending, *In ACM Transactions on Graphics*. vol.33, no.4.

Bhattacharrya, A. 1943. On a measure of divergence between two statistical populations define by their distributions. *Bull. Calcutta Math. Soc.* vol.35, pp.99-109.

Demir, I., et.al. 2016. Proceduralization for editing 3d architectural models, *in Proceedings of 3D Vision (3DV)*, pp.194-202.

Guo, X., et al. 2014. Creature grammar for creative modelling of 3D monsters. *Graphical Models*, vol.76, no.5, pp.376-389.

Huang, S., et al., 2016. Support substructures: support-induced part-level structural representation. In *IEEE transactions on visualization and computer graphics*. vol.22, no.8, pp. 2024-2036.

Kalogerakis, E., et al., 2012. A probabilistic model for component-based shape synthesis. In *ACM Transactions on Graphics*. vol.31, no.4, p.55.

Liu, H., et al., 2015. Replaceable Substructures for Efficient Part Based Modelling. In *Computer Graphics Forum*. vol.34, no. 2, pp.503-513.

Merrell, P., 2011. Model synthesis: a general procedural modeling algorithm. *IEEE transactions on visualization and computer graphics*. vol.17, no.6, pp.715-728.

Sims, K., 1991. Artificial evolution for computer graphics. In *Proceedings of SIGGRAPH*, pp.319-328.

Smelik, RM., et al., 2009. A survey of procedural methods for terrain modelling, In *Proceedings of the CASA Workshop on 3D Advanced Media In Gaming and Simulation*.

Xu, K. et al., 2012. Fit and diverse: set evolution for inspiring 3D shape galleries, In *ACM Transactions on Graphics*. vol.31, no.4.

Yonemoto,S, et.al., 2017. Evolutionary generation of 3D shape models, *In Proceedings of International Conferences Computer Graphics, Visualization, Computer Vision and Image Processing*, pp.47-54.

Yumer,M.E., et al. 2015 Procedural Modeling Using Autoencoder Networks. In *Proceedings of the 28th Annual ACM Symposium on User Interface Software & Technology*, pp.109-118.

Zheng, Y., et al., 2013. Smart variations: Functional substructures for part compatibility. In *Proceedings of Computer Graphics Forum*, pp.195-204.

COMPUTING THE SOLVENT EXCLUDED VOLUME BY GPU-BASED RAY CASTING

Martin Manak
University of West Bohemia, Department of Computer Science and Engineering
Univerzitni 8, 306 14, Pilsen, Czech Republic

ABSTRACT

The solvent excluded surface (SES) is a hypothetical boundary between atoms of a molecule and a solvent. The volume of space bounded by this non-linear surface is a useful quantity in computational biochemistry. Among the approaches for the computation of the volume, there is one which estimates the volume by a numerical integration. Several rays passing through the surface are generated and the parts inside the surface are summed up. The previous approach was designed primarily for CPU and tested on triangular surfaces. In this paper, the previous approach is adapted to GPU. This computational environment offers a high level of parallelism. Previous shaders, designed primarily for rendering SES by ray casting on GPU, were modified to compute volume contributions along a ray. The problem with losing precision in the computation of intermediate results is solved by transforming floating-point numbers to big integers. Thread-safety is ensured by using atomic operations. There were also problems with long computations on some systems. They are solved by using several synchronization objects (fence-sync). Thanks to these improvements it was possible to greatly increase the resolution and speed of the original solution.

KEYWORDS

Volume, Ray Casting, GPU, Solvent Excluded Surface

1. INTRODUCTION

The motivation for this work comes from the field of computational biochemistry. The study of molecular structures involves quantitative evaluation of properties related to their geometrical models. The Van der Waals model is a collection of partially-overlapping balls representing individual atoms. Proteins are surrounded by solvent molecules (water) and their atoms are tightly packed forming a stable shape with cavities and pockets specific for the protein and essential to its function.

A hypothetical boundary between a protein and a solvent is called the *solvent excluded surface* (SES). A spherical probe approximates a solvent molecule and SES is the topological boundary of the union of all probes of the given radius in such positions where the probe avoids collisions with the model. SES consists of convex and concave spherical patches and saddle-shaped toroidal patches as illustrated in Figure 1. SES volume is a quantity useful for the evaluation of cavities, energy-minimization, etc.

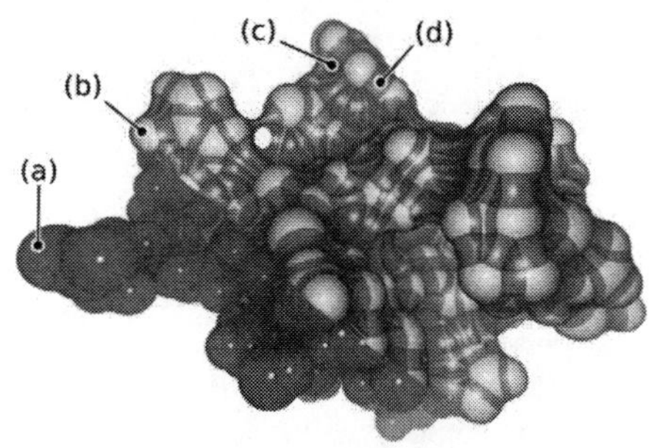

Figure 1. The model of insulin and SES elements: (a) atomic balls in the van der Waals model, (b) convex spherical patches, (c) concave spherical patches and (d) saddle-shaped toroidal patches

For some purposes such as fast visualization in high quality by ray casting on GPU, there is no need to compute the complete analytic description of all patches, because some problems can be solved directly on GPU. For volume computation, more effort is needed, but sometimes we can benefit from the approaches already used for visualization. Existing approaches use triangulation (Sanner et al. 1996), voxelization (Voss and Gerstein 2010), analytic computation (Connolly 1983; Quan and Stamm 2016), or numerical integration (Lindow et al. 2013; Phillips et al. 2010) to estimate SES volume.

This paper presents improvements to the numerical integration approach (Phillips et al. 2010), which allow to run the computation on GPU, achieve higher resolution and faster speed. Adapting existing shaders that were designed for SES visualization to perform numerical integration seemed much easier than implementing all the equations required by the analytic computation. The original shaders are available as supporting information to the article (Manak et al. 2017). Moving the computation to GPU introduced several challenges regarding computation in highly parallel environment and regarding precision of intermediate results. These problems are solved by transforming floating-point numbers to big integers and by atomic operations (OpenGL 4.2 – 4.6). There were also problems with long computations on some systems. They are solved by using several synchronization objects (fence-sync).

2. RELATED WORK

SES was initially introduced by Richards using the interpretation of a spherical probe that rolls over a molecule (Richards 1977). Connolly described the surface analytically and formulated the equations for computing the surface area (Connolly 1983).

A lot of work has been done regarding the computation and visualization of SES (Kozlikova et al. 2017). Traditional approaches had to prepare a triangular model (Ryu et al. 2009; Sanner et al. 1996) but this was computationally expensive. With the development of programmable GPUs, new methods emerged, which render SES patches directly from their analytical description by ray casting (Krone et al. 2009; Lindow et al. 2010; Manak et al. 2017). Few GPU-based methods can also triangulate SES (Decherchi and Rocchia 2013), implicit surfaces (Chen et al. 2015), or render complex convolution surfaces via ray-casting (Zhu et al. 2012).

If SES triangulation is available, the volume can be estimated by summing up the signed volumes of all tetrahedra formed by the triangles and the origin of the coordinate system. Many triangles are needed to achieve high quality. Nevertheless, this solution is quite widespread (Sanner et al. 1996).

If the space bounded by SES is filled with voxels, the volume can be estimated by counting the voxels and multiplying the result by the voxel-volume (Voss and Gerstein 2010). Disadvantages include the necessity to process all voxels that contribute to the volume, and resolution limits.

Volume can also be estimated by ray casting (Phillips et al. 2010). The idea is to generate rays parallel with the z-axis and measure the lengths of segments formed by intersections of rays and the space bounded by SES. The original method was designed primarily for CPUs and tested on triangulated surfaces.

Lindow et al. developed a method which can estimate the volume of SES cavities (Lindow et al. 2013). A cavity is filled with balls and ray casting is performed to measure the volume of their union. The computation was parallelized over rays and tested on GPU (OpenCL). The authors already had the implementation for rendering SES by ray casting on GPU, but they did not use it for volume computation.

The best option would be to compute the volume analytically (Quan and Stamm 2016), but this is quite difficult. A precise representation of patch boundaries is required for the evaluation of angles in vertices and for measuring the lengths and curvatures of edges. The Euler characteristic of patches must be computed. Holes in concave spherical patches must be filed. Also the volume of the union of balls must be computed.

3. BACKGROUND

The basic principle of computing the volume of a closed surface such as SES by ray casting is explained in this section (Phillips et al. 2010). The volume of an object is estimated as the sum of intersections of rays and the object. Ideally, rays should be boxes extruding infinitesimally small tiles of the xy-plane along the z-axis. Practically, lines are used instead of boxes and the result is multiplied by the tile-area.

More formally, the volume of a subset S of R^3 bounded by a closed surface can be expressed as $V(S) = \iiint \chi(x, y, z)\, dx\, dy\, dz$, where χ is the characteristic function of S giving one for each point of S and zero elsewhere. If we define a function $g(x, y) = \int \chi(x, y, z)\, dz$, we can rewrite $V(S) = \iint g(x, y)\, dx\, dy$.

The interpretation of g(x, y) is the sum of lengths of all line segments in the intersection of S and the line (a ray) parallel with the z-axis and passing through (x, y, 0). The function g can be evaluated when all intersection points of the ray and the boundary of S are known. Each intersection point is marked as an entry point if the ray enters the volume of S or as an exit point if the ray exits S in that point. The function g is then evaluated by subtracting each pair of exit and entry point z-coordinates (Phillips et al. 2010).

If N rays are generated in a rectangular area A in the xy-plane, the volume V(S) is estimated as $N/A \cdot \Sigma\, g(x_i, y_i)$, where (x_i, y_i) corresponds to the ray number i.

4. VOLUME COMPUTATION ON GPU

The proposed approach for the computation of SES volume on GPU is based on the shaders which have already been used for visualization (Manak et al. 2017). The analytic description of SES patches was computed by Aw-Voronoi 2.0-beta (https://sourceforge.net/projects/awvoronoi). This library computes SES elements from the Voronoi diagram of atoms (spheres, toruses and clip-planes) and detects cavities. Details regarding fast rendering of large numbers of SES patches by GPU instancing, computing the intersection of a ray and a torus, which leads to finding all roots of a quartic polynomial, clipping intersection points by planes and circular arcs stored in textures, will not be discussed here as they can be found elsewhere (Manak et al. 2017; Krone et al. 2009; Lindow et al. 2010). The shaders were adapted to perform volume computation in orthographic projection instead of visualization. The crucial points of this process are discussed here.

4.1 Resolution

Our ray casting relies on OpenGL rasterizer and the window size must be set up prior rendering. Resolution is specified in dots per angstrom (DPA). The window is a square with the side length computed as the maximal extent in the x- and y-axis of the bounding box multiplied by DPA and clamped to hardware limits (16384 on recent GPUs). Since we do not need rendering on screen, we can use the empty framebuffer with explicitly specified width and height (OpenGL 4.3).

4.2 Volume Contributions along a Ray

Ray casting provides intersection points of rays with SES patches. These points are computed directly in a fragment shader on GPU and the analytic description of each patch is available in the shader.

For volume computation, we also need to know whether the ray enters or leaves the space bounded by SES. This can be decided by the dot-product of the ray direction with the normal vector in the intersection point (exit points have this value positive, entry points negative).

Each ray can enter or leave SES many times, but we cannot afford to store all intersections for latter sorting and pairing. Instead, we can measure the absolute distance of the intersection point from the xy-plane and negate this value in entry points. The sum of all these values is the length of the ray in the space bounded by SES as illustrated in Figure 2. Theoretically, the summation order does not matter, which is good for parallel computation on GPU. Practically, the values are floating-point numbers with a limited precision and precision can be lost in intermediate operations. A solution is presented in the next section.

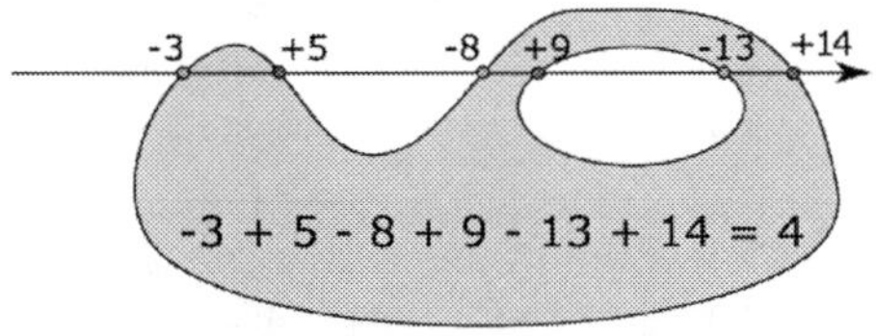

Figure 2. The absolute length of the ray is computed at each intersection point, negated when the ray enters the surface, and all these contributions are summed up

4.3 Computing the Sum of Volume Contributions Reliably on GPU

Volume contributions are computed in 32-bit floating-point numbers (floats). We need to sum them up reliably, but precision loss can lead to wrong results. Another problem is with thread-safety on GPU.

The problem of losing precision can be solved by transforming floats to big integers. According to the specification IEEE-754, a float can be written as $(-1)^{sign} \times 2^{exponent} \times significand$. The 32-bit format has `1` sign bit, `24` significand bits (including the implicit bit) and `8` exponent bits. According to IEEE-754, the maximal exponent is `127`, the minimal `-126`, the largest finite value is $2^{127} \times (2-2^{-23})$ and every finite value is an integral multiple of the smallest positive subnormal value $2^{-126} \times 2^{1-24} = 2^{-149}$. So, any finite float multiplied by 2^{149} is a whole number, which fits within $149 + 127 + 1 = 277$ bits.

The transformation of volume contributions from floats to big integers is done in the fragment shader. Binary representation (sign, exponent, significand) is obtained by the GLSL function `floatBitsToUint`, the big integer is constructed by bitwise operators and stored in a local array of nine unsigned integers. Negative numbers are represented in two's complement.

Now to the problem of thread safety. Ideally, the addition should be performed atomically. OpenGL 4.2 has a feature (`ARB_shader_image_load_store`) thanks to which shaders can load input and store output to images (texture-buffers). Atomic arithmetic is limited to 32-bit integers (`imageAtomicAdd`). OpenGL 4.3 provides a similar functionality (SSBO). OpenGL 4.6 enabled atomic arithmetic on atomic counters. Current GPUs usually have eight such counters.

So, we can allocate a buffer of few integers and use it in the fragment shader as the variable representing a big integer to which we will add volume contributions. A big integer is added to the variable (also a big integer) with the classic summation algorithm using a carry-flag and working on 32-bit integers as basic blocks. The trick here is that each block is added atomically and even if the whole operation is not atomic, it is thread-safe. The actual GLSL code be found in the appendix section of this paper.

4.4 Volume of Cavities

Full SES may contain cavities – partially overlapping regions of space, which can be occupied by the spherical probe but from which the probe cannot escape. When SES is rendered on screen, all overlapping parts must be removed. Only concave spherical patches may overlap this way. Clipping is performed in a fragment shader by testing the intersection point (ray vs sphere) against clip planes stored in a texture. If we want to compute the volumes of these regions by the proposed method, there are some problems to solve.

First, the boundary of each cavity must be a closed surface. This can be achieved by arranging the clip-planes in the texture before it is uploaded to GPU memory. Clip-planes of patches that belong to the cavity are stored before the clip-planes from other cavities. The shader that perform visualization will use all data, whereas the shader that performs the volume computation of cavities will use only a subset.

Next, each cavity must fit into the rendering window, ideally without wasting the resolution. We can compute the bounding box of each cavity as the bounding box of all spheres that were used to define the concave spherical patches of the cavity and compute translations that align cavities with the z-axis as it is depicted in Figure 3. These translations are then applied in the vertex shader.

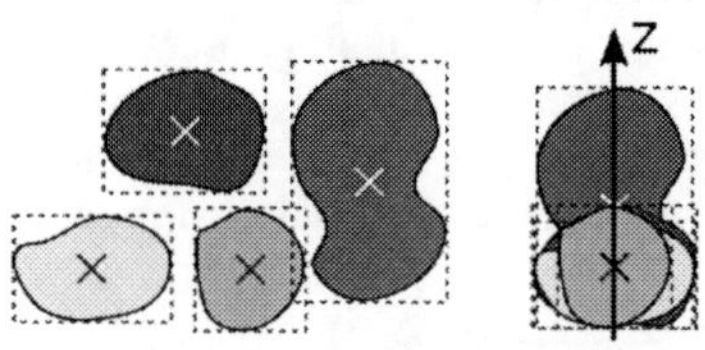

Figure 3. All cavities are aligned with the z-axis

It is generally faster to render all cavities at once. We need one counter per cavity to accumulate volume contributions and hence we must use atomic arithmetic on images or SSBO. Thread-contention issues can be mitigated by using more variables per cavity (accumulators for volume contributions) and choosing pseudo-randomly among them. It also helps to explicitly guard against adding zeros in the summation algorithm.

4.5 Waiting for GPU to Finish

We must wait for GPU to finish its work, otherwise we could get undefined results. After all drawing commands were called, a sync object is created and inserted into the command stream (`glFenceSync`). When the GPU finishes all commands, the sync will become signaled. A thread can flush all pending commands, block and wait for the signal with a timeout (`glClientWaitSync`).

Problems may arise with long runs when the resolution is very high and the surface too complex. Some drivers pretend the computation finished even if it did not. NVIDIA's proprietary drivers version 390.59 for Linux exhibit such behavior. After 11 seconds, the sync was incorrectly signaled that GPU completed all commands. Even calling `glFinish` did not help. AMD drivers were fine.

The solution is to set up a timeout, for example 5 seconds, and if the thread wakes up because the timeout expired, the old sync must be deleted and a new one created. The thread can then wait for the new sync (with a timeout) and this must be repeated until the computation really finishes.

Long runs are also problematic on Windows. There is a feature called Timeout Detection and Recovery (TDR). If GPU is occupied too long (2 seconds) or if a call to the GPU driver takes too much time (5 seconds), the system will intervene and show a dialog asking the user what to do next. To allow long runs, system registry keys `TdrDelay` and `TdrDdiDelay` must be explicitly created and set to higher values.

5. EXPERIMENTS AND RESULTS

Let us demonstrate the abilities and limits of the proposed method on few examples. We will start with trivial cases for which the analytic solution is known and then proceed to real data.

A simple yet informative test-case is a unit sphere ($V = 4\,\pi\,/\,3 \doteq 4.1887902$). Table 1 shows how many decimal digits we get for what resolution. For example, to achieve four digits (4.188), we need the resolution 65 DPA (dots per angstrom) corresponding to the rendering window 130×130, for seven digits 1621 DPA. Increasing the resolution even more would not help much, because volume contributions are computed in single-precision floats. Table 1 also compares the proposed method to MSMS (Sanner et al. 1996), which makes a triangulation and then computes the volume of the triangular mesh. To achieve four digits, MSMS needs a high density of 1423 vertices / A^2 (the default density is 1 for molecules with at least 1000 atoms).

The second test-case in Table 1 is SES of two atoms having their centers 2.0 A apart, van der Waals radii 1.2 A, and the probe radius 1.2 A. The SES has two spherical patches and one toroidal patch. According to (Quan and Stamm 2016), the volume is $V \doteq 14.75567\ A^3$. The proposed method computed six digits.

Table 1. The volume of a unit sphere and the SES volume on a pair of atoms, different quality settings

Unit sphere	Proposed method		MSMS	
V [A^3]	DPA	Window	Density	Triangles
4	2	4×4	11	248
4.1	7	14×14	23	556
4.18	39	78×78	215	5344
4.188	65	130×130	1423	35490
4.18879	316	632×632	–	–
4.188790	1621	3242×3242	–	–

2 atoms	Proposed method		MSMS	
V [A^3]	DPA	Window	Density	Triangles
14	1	5×5	5	276
14.7	5	23×23	64	4024
14.75	20	45×45	–	–
14.755	30	133×133	–	–
14.7556	201	885×885	–	–

We should mention here that these limits are just rough estimates obtained from experiments. Different drivers may compile shaders differently. Some precision bits can also get lost during the computation of transformation matrices, matrix multiplication in shaders, etc. These limits were obtained on NVIDIA GeForce GTX 780 running on NVIDIA's drivers for Linux, version 390.59.

The proposed method was also tested on real data. The molecule of insulin (Figure 1) was selected for demonstration purposes mostly because the SES on this model does not contain any cavity which could have been misinterpreted by MSMS. The data come from the first model in the PDB file 2HIU. The following Van der Waals radii were used: H 1.2, C 1.7, N 1.55, O 1.52, and S 1.8. The probe radius was set to the usual value of 1.4. The volume was computed for different resolutions by the proposed method and by MSMS. Fast convergence of the proposed method is apparent in Figure 4 and even if the results are not exactly the same, we can observe a consensus of about 99.9%.

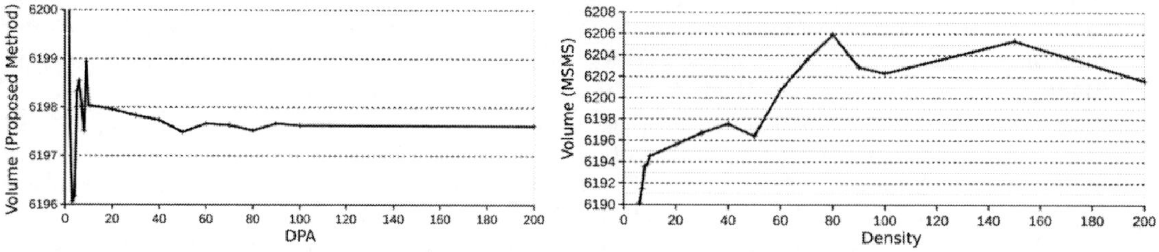

Figure 4. SES volume of insulin, different quality settings (PDB ID: 2HIU)

The proposed method was implemented as a plugin to CAVER Analyst (Jurcik et al. 2018). The new functionality is illustrated in Figure 5. The software detected 13 cavities in the model of a small enzyme and displayed a list with information about these cavities. The column "Volume (GPU)" displays the volume of each cavity as it was computed by the new method (resolution 100 DPA). The next columns "Volume" and "#Samples" display the volume computed by another method, which approximates each cavity by several filling balls and estimates the volume by the hit probability of random samples generated in the bounding box of the balls. This other method runs on CPU, requires many samples to deliver decent results and neglects toroidal patches. The proposed method that runs on GPU is generally faster and gives superior results.

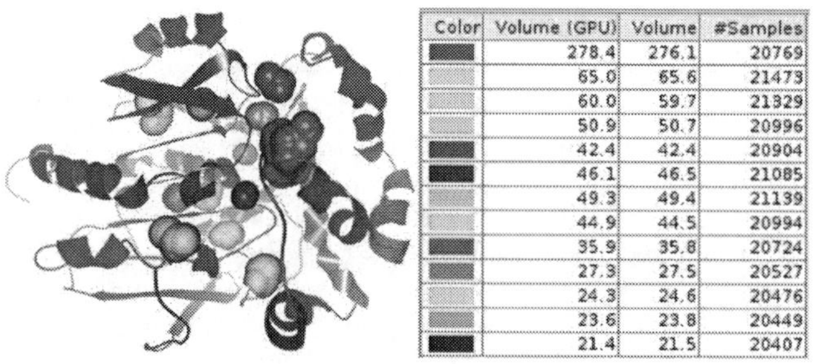

Color	Volume (GPU)	Volume	#Samples
	278.4	276.1	20769
	65.0	65.6	21473
	60.0	59.7	21329
	50.9	50.7	20996
	42.4	42.4	20904
	46.1	46.5	21085
	49.3	49.4	21139
	44.9	44.5	20994
	35.9	35.8	20724
	27.3	27.5	20527
	24.3	24.6	20476
	23.6	23.8	20449
	21.4	21.5	20407

Figure 5. Volume of SES cavities (probe radius 1.6A) in CAVER Analyst estimated by the proposed method using GPU ray casting and by another method using Monte Carlo sampling (PDB ID: 1CQW)

Performance results are listed in Table 2. SES was computed for the probe radius 1.4 A. The tests were performed on AMD Radeon RX 480 Graphics (POLARIS10) and time was measured from the moment when rendering started to the moment when the result was downloaded from GPU. Preprocessing (Voronoi diagram computation, cavities detection, computation of SES elements and upload to GPU) is not included but it usually takes a few seconds mainly because of Voronoi diagram computation. Table 2 also shows the number of intersection points produced by ray casting. Each of them contributed to the final volume. The numbers should be even but they are odd in some cases, because ray casting shaders suffer by negligible pixel artifacts. To avoid thread-contention issues, 32 accumulator variables were used in fragment shaders and a pseudo-random choice was made per fragment to choose the destination variable. It was about 25% faster than using one variable. The results in Table 2 were obtained with this optimization enabled.

Table 2. SES volume computation time for two molecular models (DPA - resolution in dots per angstrom, V - volume)

1A4U – 3926 atoms (medium size)				
DPA	Window	Intersections	V [A^3]	Time [ms]
1	62×62	10632	61542.2	3
4	248×248	169760	61571.9	3
10	620×620	1060913	61592.5	17
50	3098×3098	26489332	61592.1	83
100	6195×6195	105924522	61591.2	240
265	16384×16384	740891998	61590.4	1399

1AON – 58688 atoms (large)				
DPA	Window	Intersections	V [A^3]	Time [ms]
1	148×148	186292	868912.5	16
4	589×589	2953760	869336.3	18
10	1472×1472	18446945	869160.7	88
50	7357×7357	460809231	869154.5	1084
100	14714×14714	1843246275	869153.2	3936
111	16384×16384	2270912620	869117.1	4823

In the rest of this section, we will compare the performance with other approaches. The comparison is very rough, because different hardware configurations can have very different performance characteristics.

The original approach (Phillips et al. 2010) use smaller rendering windows. For 1A4U (the only test-case for which performance results are available), the maximal window was 200×200 and the computation took 270 ms on a single CPU core (Intel Core 2 Quad, 2.66 GHz). Our GPU method finished in less than 10 ms.

The MSMS program (Sanner at al. 1996) logs the amount of time spent in preparing SES triangulation and the number of triangular faces. Triangulation quality can be controlled by a density parameter, but this parameter is different from DPA. If we suppose each intersection point in our GPU method represents a tiny face, then we can guess the density parameter for which MSMS will produce a similar number of faces and compare against the triangulation time. For 1A4U and density 25.6, MSMS produced 1064270 faces (including cavities) in 1460 ms on a single CPU core (Intel Core i7-4930K, 3.4 GHz). This corresponds to 10 DPA and 17 ms in Table 2. For 1AON and density 3, MSMS produced 1818264 faces (excluding cavities) in 1940 ms. This corresponds to 10 DPA and 88 ms in Table 2.

6. CONCLUSION

The proposed method computes an estimate of the SES volume on GPU by ray casting, which has been used mainly for visualization so far. Bringing the computation to GPU made it possible to use larger rendering windows (16384×16384 instead of 200×200) with better performance. Fast computation was achieved by employing parallelism with atomic operations on GPU. A limitation is that numeric operations are performed in single-precision floating-point numbers. Experiments indicate the method can compute first four or five decimal digits of the result. The method also computes the volume of cavities in protein models. This is one of its most useful applications and the precision can be sufficient for this application area.

ACKNOWLEDGEMENT

This work was supported by the project 17-07690S of the Czech Science Foundation.

REFERENCES

Chen, J. et al, 2015. GPU-based polygonization and optimization for implicit surfaces. *The Visual Computer*, Vol. 31, No. 2, pp. 119-130.

Connolly, M. L., 1983. Analytical molecular surface calculation. *Journal of Applied Crystallography,* Vol. 16, No. 5, pp. 548-558.

Decherchi, S. and Rocchia, W., 2013. A general and robust ray-casting-based algorithm for triangulating surfaces at the nanoscale. *PLOS ONE*, Vol. 8, No. 4, pp. 1-15.

Jurcik, A. et al, 2018. CAVER Analyst 2.0: analysis and visualization of channels and tunnels in protein structures and molecular dynamics trajectories. *Bioinformatics,* pp. bty386.

Kozlikova, B. et al, 2017. Visualization of biomolecular structures: State of the art revisited. *Computer Graphics Forum*, Vol. 36, No. 8, pp. 178-204.

Krone, M. et al, 2009. Interactive visualization of molecular surface dynamics. *IEEE Transactions on Visualization and Computer Graphics*, Vol. 15, No. 6, pp. 1391-1398.

Lindow, N. et al, 2013. Exploring cavity dynamics in biomolecular systems. *BMC Bioinformatics*, Vol. 14, No. S-19, pp. S5.

Lindow, N. et al, 2010, Accelerated visualization of dynamic molecular surfaces. *Computer Graphics Forum*, Vol. 29, No. 3, pp. 943-952.

Manak, M. et al, 2017. Interactive analysis of Connolly surfaces for various probes. *Computer Graphics Forum*, Vol. 36, No. 6, pp. 160-172.

Phillips, M. et al, 2010. Measuring properties of molecular surfaces using ray casting. *2010 IEEE International Symposium on Parallel Distributed Processing, Workshops and Phd Forum (IPDPSW)*, Atlanta, Georgia, pp. 1-7.

Quan, C. and Stamm, B., 2016. Mathematical analysis and calculation of molecular surfaces. *Journal of Computational Physics*, Vol. 322, pp. 760-782.

Richards, F. M., 1977. Areas, volumes, packing, and protein structure. *Annual Review of Biophysics and Bioengineering*, Vol. 6, No. 1, pp. 151-176.

Ryu, J. et al, 2009. Triangulation of molecular surfaces. Computer-Aided Design, Vol. 41, No. 6, pp. 463-478.

Sanner, M. F. et al, 1996. Reduced surface: An efficient way to compute molecular surfaces. *Biopolymers*, Vol. 38, No. 3, pp. 305-320.

Voss, N. R. and Gerstein, M., 2010. 3V: cavity, channel and cleft volume calculator and extractor. *Nucleic acids research*, Vol. 38, No. Web Server issue, pp. W555-562.

Zhu, X. et al, 2012. Analytical solutions for sketch-based convolution surface modeling on the GPU. *The Visual Computer*, Vol. 28, No. 11, pp. 1115-1125.

APPENDIX

GLSL code – thread-safe accumulation of volume contributions with eight atomic counters `acb0`, ..., `acb7`.

```
layout(binding = 0, offset = 0) uniform atomic_uint acb0; ...
layout(binding = 0, offset = 28) uniform atomic_uint acb7;

void add(atomic_uint c, uint data, inout uint carry) {
 if (data + carry != 0u) {
  uint x = atomicCounterAddARB(c, data + carry);
  uint z = x + data + carry;
  carry = ((x & data) | ((x | data) & ~z)) >> 31;
 } else
  carry = data == 0 ? 0u : 1u;
}

uint[8] negate(uint[8] a) {
 uint carry = 1u;
 for (int i = 0; i < 8; ++i) {
  uint y = ~a[i] + carry;
  carry = carry & (y == 0 ? 1u : 0u);
  a[i] = y;
 }
 return a;
}

uint[8] floatToBigUInt(float f) {
 uint bits = floatBitsToUint(f);
 uint man = bits & 0x7FFFFFu;
 int ex = int(bits >> 23) & 0xFF;
 uint m = (ex == 0 ? 0u : (1u << 23)) | man;
 uint[8] a = uint[](0u,0u,0u,0u,0u,0u,0u,0u);
 for (int i = 0; i < 8; ++i) {
  a[i] = abs(ex) >= 32 ? 0u : (ex >= 0) ? (m << ex) : (m >> -ex);
  ex -= 32;
 }
 return a;
}

void accumulate(float f) {
 uint[8] a = floatToBigUInt(f); a = (f < 0.0) ? negate(a) : a;
 uint c = 0u;
 add(acb0, a[0], c); add(acb1, a[1], c); ... add(acb7, a[7], c);
}
```

Short Papers

PATIENT-MAINTAINED PROPOFOL SEDATION: THE ANAESTHETISTS' POINT OF VIEW

James Sprinks[1], Frank Worcester[1], Philip Breedon[1], David Hewson[2] and Nigel Bedforth[2]
[1]*Nottingham Trent University, Nottingham, UK, NG1 3FQ*
[2]*University of Nottingham, Nottingham, UK, NG7 2UH*

ABSTRACT

Many operations within the UK do not require general anaesthesia, and are instead carried out under sedation. A doctor normally provides this, and as the patient is not in control, they may be either under or over-sedated due to a misjudgement of patient anxiety. One solution would be to allow the patients to directly control their own sedation level. This paper presents an invention for innovation (i4i) project developing such a Patient Maintained Propofol Sedation Device (PMPSD). Due to the health risks associated with under and over-sedation, the anaesthetists' interface takes on an added importance to ensure they can oversee the process and intervene when needed. Through the project, a unique opportunity has arisen where anaesthetists have been involved throughout the interface design process, contributing to the development and testing of a prototype. We present this prototype, highlight its key features and how it differs from existing sedation pump interface systems. As the project continues, the interface will be used as part of a clinical trial at Nottingham University Hospitals NHS Trust involving 80 orthopaedic patients throughout the rest of 2018 and into 2019.

KEYWORDS

Participatory Design, Usability, Interface Design, Healthcare HCI

1. INTRODUCTION

In the UK, over 800,000 medical operations are performed annually with an anaesthetist present but without using general anaesthesia (Sury et al. 2014). During such procedures, a substantial number of patients report feeling anxious (Mitchell 2009), which in addition to being an intrinsically negative experience has also been consistently linked with deleterious surgical outcomes including post-operative pain (Munafò and Stevenson 2001). In order to reduce patient anxiety, a number of techniques have been found to have an effect, including visual distraction (Man et al. 2003), patient education (Jlala et al. 2010), music therapy (Bradt, Dileo, and Shim 2013), and pharmacological sedation (Mackenzie 1996).

Target Controlled Infusion (TCI) of Propofol, under the direction of an anaesthetist, is an often-preferred choice for intra-operative sedation due to the drug's pharmacokinetic profile; this is how the drug is absorbed, distributed, metabolised and excreted by the body (Schnider et al. 1998). However, judging the level of anxiety of the patient has proven difficult, and anaesthetists can be inaccurate judges of pre-operative patient anxiety (Badner et al. 1990). This can result in either over or under-sedation in comparison with the actual requirements of individual patients. One possible solution for overcoming this issue is to allow patients control over their depth of sedation.

Patient-maintained Propofol sedation has been previously tested in dental (Leitch et al. 2004), endoscopy (Stonell, Leslie, and Absalom 2006) and outpatient surgical (Yun et al. 2008) settings. Although this research has had favourable outcomes in terms of sedation concentration, patient recovery time and anxiety levels, to date there has not been a truly human-centred approach specifically considering the changing role of the anaesthetist in such a system. Previous work has acknowledged the inter-individual variability of patients' Propofol consumption (Irwin, Thompson, and Kenny 1997), but there has been little consideration of how such data is presented to the anaesthetist in order for them to ensure the procedure is safe and intervene when appropriate.

The interface design of an infusion pump can affect error rate, task completion times and the overall mental effort required of the supervising anaesthetist (Schnittker et al. 2016). Therefore, it is important that any such interface used as part of a patient-maintained system is designed so that the anaesthetist can safely and effectively monitor the process, as issues related to under and over-sedation are still a possible risk (Hewson et al. 2018).

This paper introduces an invention 4 innovation (i4i) project testing the suitability of a Patient Maintained Propofol Sedation Device (PMPSD) when used for lower limb orthopaedic surgery. In developing the system, a participatory design approach has been used, where anaesthetists have been fully involved in the process of creating the anaesthetist interface. In doing this, key HCI differences when considering a patient-maintained approach have been identified, and also improvements on some issues related to existing pump interfaces made.

2. PMPSD SYSTEM DESIGN

In order to investigate the suitability of patient maintained Propofol sedation for lower limb orthopaedic surgery, the following prototype system has been developed (see figure 1):

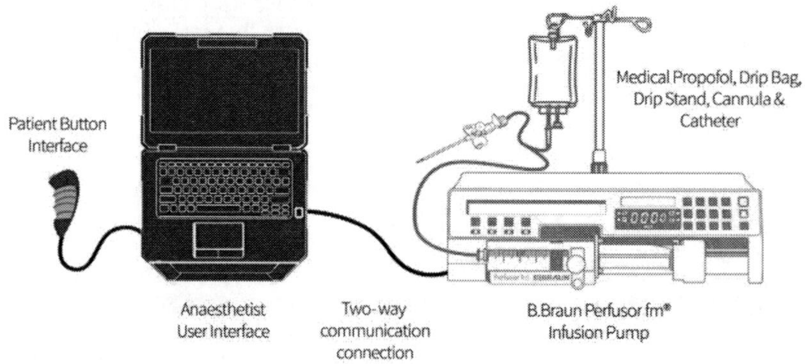

Figure 1. PMPSD Prototype System

The system consists of:

- Infusion pump (B.Braun Perfusor fm) and Drip setup. This is attached to the patient as per normal operating procedure.
- Anaesthetist User Interface. This is presented to the anaesthetist through a laptop that is both connected to the infusion pump (through a serial port connection), and to the patient button (through a USB port).
- Patient Button Interface: A trigger button that through pressing allows the patient an increase in sedation.

The principle component of the system is the anaesthetist interface, as it controls the pump's rate of infusion, monitors and responds to requests from the patient to increase sedation, and presents information regarding both to the supervising anaesthetist. It is also the pathway by which the anaesthetist can take back control of the sedation process, if the need arises for safety reasons.

3. USER AND INTERFACE REQUIREMENTS

Over a six-month design period, running from September 2017 to March 2018, monthly design review meetings were held to define the user and interface requirements, and evaluate the interface design iteratively as it was developed. Project members, software developers and anaesthetists who will be operating the system during the project, were in attendance. Through this process, the following initial requirements were derived, both in terms of functionality and features that ensure safe operation (see table 1):

Table 1. PMPSD User and Interface Requirements

Interface (System) Requirements	User Requirements
Baseline effect-site concentration of 0.5mcg.ml^{-1}: All patients start at a baseline level of sedation and do not drop below unless the system is deactivated	**Clear display of sedation metrics on screen:** Metrics like infusion rate, current sedation levels and total Propofol consumed clearly visible
Ceiling effect-site concentration of 2.0mcg.ml^{-1}: Patients' sedation level cannot go above ceiling unless anaesthetist feels it is appropriate	**Sedation pause:** Anaesthetist can pause sedation at any time (in order to replace syringe etc.)
Lock-out time of 2 minutes: After a request by the patient, further button presses will not cause an increase during lock-out time	**Anaesthetist override:** Anaesthetist can take over the system, disabling the patient button and controlling sedation level
Decrement of 0.1mcg.ml^{-1} every 15 minutes: If button not pressed by patient, sedation level slowly decreases over time	**Button Display:** Anaesthetist can see when/how often patient uses button to request increased sedation

4. ANAESTHETIST INTERFACE PROTOTYPE

Based on the previously mentioned requirements, and adhering to Nielsen's (Nielsen 1995) 10 heuristics for user interface design, the following anaesthetist interface prototype was developed for used with the PMPSD system (figure 2). The interface was developed using the C++ language and the Qt (www.qt.io) development environment:

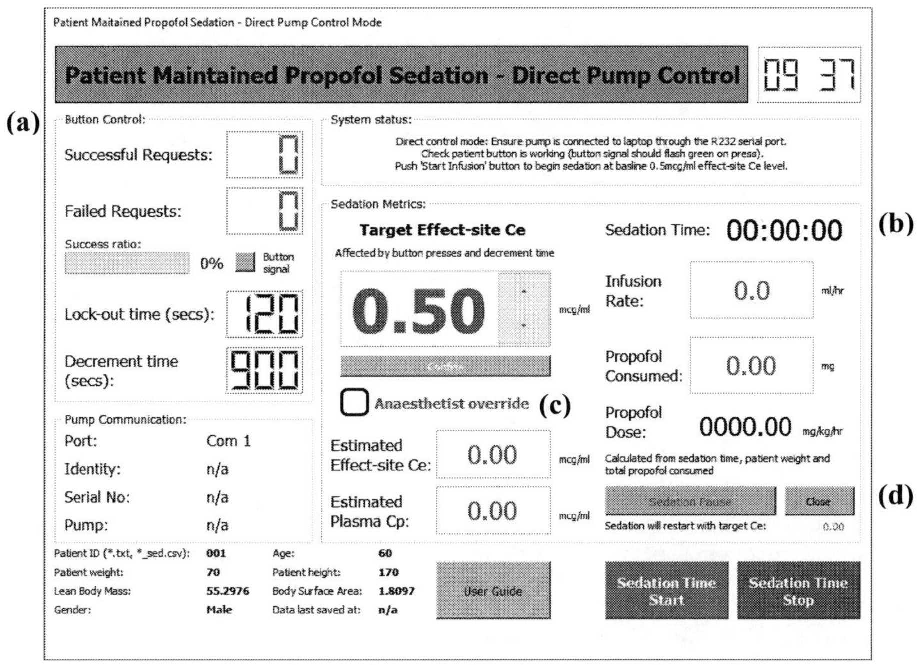

Figure 2. Prototype Anaesthetist Interface with the following displays: (a) – Button control display showing successful and failed patient requests for increased sedation; (b) – Sedation metrics display displaying sedation information; (c) – Anaesthetist override button allowing the anaesthetist to take system control; (d) – Sedation Pause button allowing the anaesthetist to pause sedation

4.1 Interface Prototype Evaluation

In order to evaluate the suitability of the prototype anaesthetist interface for use with patient maintained Propofol sedation, an evaluation workshop took place on a simulation version of the PMPSD system. On 16th February 2017 three anaesthetists from Nottingham University Hospitals NHS Trust took part in the workshop. They were asked to evaluate both the PMPSD interface prototype along with an existing infusion pump interface, considering their usability and to what degree they achieve Nielsen's design heuristics. As part of this process, they were asked to rate their agreement with statements regarding the interface design and its ease of use on a 9-point scale, with 9 meaning 'strongly agree' and 1 meaning 'strongly disagree'. Table 2 shows the scores given by the anaesthetists for each interface:

Table 2. Anaesthetists' Scores regarding Nielsen's Design Heuristics

Design Statement	Existing Pump Score	PMPSD Interface Prototype Score
The pump always keeps the user informed	7	8.5
The interface speaks the users' language	7	8.5
The interface supports 'undo' and 'redo'	5.5	7
The interface language is consistent	8	8.5
The interface is designed making it unlikely that problems occur	8	9
The interface minimises user memory load	7	8
Frequent actions are easy to access at speed	6	9
Dialogues only contain relevant information	7.5	7.5
Error messages are displayed in plain language	8	9
Documentation is easy to search, focused and list steps to carry out	4	8.5

Table 3 summarises some of the comments made during the workshop comparing the existing pump interface with the PMPSD interface prototype, adding context to the heuristic scores shown in table 2:

Table 3. Anaesthetists' Comments during the Evaluation Workshop

Existing Infusion Pump	PMPSD Interface Prototype
"The screen is way to small and crowded, you have to be directly in front of it to read it…"	*"Screen much clearer with button choices easy to read…"*
"Its not clear how to perform a syringe change, do you just pull the lever?"	*"The syringe change mode is easy to operate and clearly displayed on screen…"*
"It doesn't show all the sedation data at once, you have scroll through – not very helpful!"	*"All the sedation data is clear to read and on screen at the same time…"*

5. CONCLUSION

The involvement of the target user group (anaesthetists) throughout the design process of the PMPSD anaesthetist interface has resulted in a number of benefits to the process. These benefits are magnified by the fact that the software developers involved with the project do not have a medical or anaesthesia background, and so perhaps cannot identify so easily some of the more prevalent issues regarding patient maintained sedation.

At the beginning of the design process, the anaesthetists involved were able to clearly outline the initial system and user requirements that would need satisfying. Many of these requirements are unique to a patient maintained sedation system (anaesthetist override, button usage display etc.), and so would not have been easily derived through a review of existing infusion pump interfaces. Having this information early on in the process has made the development process more efficient, reducing the number of major changes required due to requirements being poorly understood or overlooked.

In addition to issues unique to a patient maintained system, more general problems regarding existing infusion pump interfaces were identified throughout the design process. Issues regarding the clearness of sedation data and its size and position on screen were pointed out as possible areas of improvement. Although there might exist a clear advantage due to the platform of the PMPSD being a laptop, allowing space for a greater amount of data to be displayed more clearly, the identification of such problems should still inform future designs of both patient and anaesthetist controlled infusion pump interfaces.

By taking a participatory design approach that involves anaesthetists throughout the process, it is hoped that the resulting PMPSD anaesthetist interface will be usable and therefore safe to operate in the upcoming clinical trials of the system throughout 2018 and 2019.

ACKNOWLEDGEMENT

This project was funded by the NIHR Invention for Innovation Programme (i4i), project no. II-LA-0716-20002. The views expressed are those of the authors and not necessarily those of the NHS, the NIHR or the Department of Health, UK. We are grateful to the anaesthetists of Nottingham University Hospitals NHS Trust that took part in and contributed to the design process.

REFERENCES

Badner, N. H. et al, 1990. Preoperative Anxiety: Detection and Contributing Factors. *Canadian Journal of Anaesthesia,* Vol. 37, No.4, p 444.

Bradt et al, 2013. Music Interventions for Preoperative Anxiety. In *Cochrane Database of Systematic Reviews*. John Wiley & Sons, Ltd.

Hewson, D. et al, 2018. Patient-Maintained Propofol Sedation for Orthopaedic Surgery: Patient Variability in System Use. *Contemporary Ergonomics and Human Factors 2018, Proceedings of the International Conference on Ergonomics & Human Factors.*

Irwin, M. G., Thompson, N., and Kenny, G. N. C., 1997. Patient-Maintained Propofol Sedation. *Anaesthesia,* Vol. 52, No. 6, pp 525–530.

Jlala, H. A. et al, 2010. Effect of Preoperative Multimedia Information on Perioperative Anxiety in Patients Undergoing Procedures under Regional Anaesthesia. *BJA: British Journal of Anaesthesia,* Vol. 104, No. 3, pp 369–374.

Leitch, J. A. et al, 2004. A Partially Blinded Randomised Controlled Trial of Patient-Maintained Propofol Sedation and Operator Controlled Midazolam Sedation in Third Molar Extractions. *Anaesthesia,* Vol. 59, No. 9, pp 853–860.

Mackenzie, N, 1996. Sedation during Regional Anaesthesia: Indications, Advantages and Methods. *European Journal of Anaesthesiology (EJA),* Vol. 13 (July), pp 2–7.

Man, A. K. Y. et al, 2003. The Effect of Intra-Operative Video on Patient Anxiety. *Anaesthesia,* Vol. 58, No. 1, pp 64–68.

Mitchell, M., 2009. Patient Anxiety and Conscious Surgery. *The Journal of Perioperative Practice; Harrogate,* Vol. 19, No. 6, pp 168–173.

Munafò, M. R., and Stevenson, J., 2001. Anxiety and Surgical Recovery: Reinterpreting the Literature. *Journal of Psychosomatic Research,* Vol. 51, No. 4, pp 589–596.

Nielsen, J., 1995. 10 Heuristics for User Interface Design: Article by Jakob Nielsen. Nielsen Norman Group. 1995. https://www.nngroup.com/articles/ten-usability-heuristics/.

Schnider, T. W. et al, 1998. The Influence of Method of Administration and Covariates on the Pharmacokinetics of Propofol in Adult Volunteers. *Anesthesiology: The Journal of the American Society of Anesthesiologists,* Vol. 88, No. 5, pp 1170–1182.

Schnittker, R. et al, 2016. Combining Situated Cognitive Engineering with a Novel Testing Method in a Case Study Comparing Two Infusion Pump Interfaces. *Applied Ergonomics,* Vol. 55 (July), pp 16–26.

Stonell, C. A., Leslie, K., and Absalom, A.R., 2006. Effect-Site Targeted Patient-Controlled Sedation with Propofol: Comparison with Anaesthetist Administration for Colonoscopy. *Anaesthesia,* Vol. 61, No. 3, pp 240–247.

Sury, M. R. J. et al, 2014. The State of UK Anaesthesia: A Survey of National Health Service Activity in 2013. *BJA: British Journal of Anaesthesia,* Vol. 113, No. 4, pp 575–584.

Yun, M. J. et al, 2008. Patient-Controlled Sedation vs. Anaesthetic Nurse-Controlled Sedation for Cataract Surgery in Elderly Patients. *International Journal of Clinical Practice,* Vol. 62, No. 5, pp 776–780.

PSYCHOTHERAPY CHATBOT DESIGN PROPOSAL: EMPIRICAL TESTS OF USER'S PSYCHOLOGICAL RESPONSES AND SELF-DISCLOSURE TO CHATBOTS WITH PERSONALITIES

Jieon Lee[1], Young June Sah[2] and Daeho Lee[1]
[1]*Sungkyunkwan University, South Korea*
[2]*Kangwon National University, South Korea*

ABSTRACT

The current research demonstrates empirical tests of user's affective responses and self-disclosure to text-based psychotherapy chatbots with personalities. Experiment 1 will identify how people would respond to chatbots that are either dominant or submissive. It will be conducted by a 2 (chatbot personality: dominant vs. submissive) X 2 (subject personality: dominant vs. submissive) between-subject experiment. Experiment 2 will provide evidence that intimate information disclosures influence how people behave in subsequent interactions with a chatbot. It will be conducted by a 2 (question-wording: reciprocal vs. non-reciprocal) X 2 (interview sequence: gradually vs. abrupt) between-subject experiment. I expect people will be more affected by chatbots with personalities, and will be more attracted to psychologically similar chatbots to themselves. In addition, when people are exposed to intimate information exchanges through the gradual conversation with chatbots, they will be more likely to disclose themselves to chatbots in turn.

KEYWORDS

Psychotherapy Chatbot, AI Therapy, Self-Disclosure, Mental Health, HCI

1. INTRODUCTION

Chatbots refer to computer software systems that can communicate with human users by employing natural languages. The chatbot technology first began in the 1960's to see how humans responded to a conversation with a chatbot (Shawar & Atwell, 2007). According to Gaggioli (2017), the earliest version of AI psychotherapy was derived from ELIZA. In 1966, Weizenbaum, MIT computer science professor, designed ELIZA to act as an artificial therapist by text-based conversation with a patient. What is intriguing about ELIZA is subjects were genuinely immersed themselves to their chatting with ELIZA as if interacting with a real person (Weizenbaum, 1966). Due to advances in natural language processing and deep learning algorithms, numerous researchers and startups are on the board attempting to create AI mental healthcare.

The two primary benefits of psychological AI are an affordable cost of mental health care and accessibility anytime anywhere when you are in need (Miner et al., 2017). Indeed, the cost of psychotherapy exceeded an approximate $187 in the United States in 2013 (Dieleman et al., 2016). What is worse is that over 75% of American college students who need clinical services do not receive a proper treatment (Hunt & Eisenberg, 2010) even though up to 74% of mental disorder diagnoses first occur in the early 20s (Kessler et al., 2007). In the light of these unpleasant conditions, that is why many experts are attempting to develop AI psychotherapy.

To my knowledge, therapist-client personality similarity and self-disclosure do not seem to be regarded in a chatbot design; however, personality similarity and self-disclosure play significant roles in human-to-human psychotherapy. In terms of Mendelsohn and Geller (1963)'s study, it indicated that the higher similarity of therapist-client personality was associated with longer and satisfying therapy. In addition, self-disclosure is useful therapeutic solution to help clients deal with their mental problems more effectively and productively (Goldfried et al., 2003). In line with these facets, the current research demonstrates empirical tests of people's psychological responses and self-disclosure to text-based chatbots with personalities.

2. BODY OF PAPER

2.1 Background on Human Reactions to Chatbots with Personalities - The Media Equation Paradigm

Simply put, the media equation refers to a state that people as users tend to respond to media such as TV and computer psychologically socially as if they are social actors (Reeves & Nass, 1996). The current research is based on this paradigm that individuals socially respond to computers without any doubt when computers possess human-like traits and social cues. The paradigm examines that humans tend to apply a social rule, "similarity-attraction or complementarity-attraction" to computers after they notice their personality (Isbister & Nass, 2000; Nass & Lee, 2001). Accordingly, I applied a personality aspect into a chatbot to see how users respond to the chatbot with personalities, and this association leads to two hypotheses:

H1: People will notice the personality of a chatbot when the chatbot represents a personality through its verbal and nonverbal cues.

H2: People will apply a social rule based on personality to a chatbot when the chatbot represents a personality through its verbal and nonverbal cues.

2.2 Similarity-attraction Theory

In the psychological literature, personality is a trait to see the differences between one another. The most prominent conceptualization of human personality is the Big Five personality dimensions (Digman, 1990). Out of Big Five Factors, extraversion (dominance vs. submissiveness) has been proved to indicate what a person is like and to predict their behavior the most (Williams, Munick, Saiz, & FormyDuval, 1995). Dominant people are more likely to be self-confident and decisive. They tend to direct others to act and make decisions for others, whereas submissive people are inclined to be self-doubt and passive. Correspondingly, they are likely to be easily followed and let others make decisions for them (Wiggins, 1979).

Along with these behavioral factors, the current study examines human's responses to chatbots with personalities: dominance and submissiveness. In the interpersonal interaction, the most pervasive aspect is the similarity-attraction theory, and this theory holds true that people tend to look for others with a similar personality to themselves and prefer to stay with similar people (Lee et al., 2006). In conclusion, given the rule, I propose a hypothesis of similarity-attraction theory:

H3: People will be more attracted to a chatbot that is similar to themselves depending on either dominance or submissiveness rather than a chatbot personality that is dissimilar to themselves.

2.3 Social Presence

According to Lee (2004), after his extensive review on presence, he defines the concept of presence as "feelings that people unnoticeably experience when they interact with the mediated or the artificial." Lee (2004) defined social presence as experiences that people interact with social actors mediated or artificially created by technology. I assume that social presence would be most likely to happen in human-to-chatbot interaction. Given the principle, I propose the following hypothesis:

H4: Social presence will mediate chatbot users' social responses to a chatbot.

2.4 Intimate Self-disclosure and Reciprocity

According to Altman and Taylor (1973), self-disclosure indicates personal information that a person reveals to another. Traditionally, people are more likely to like those who disclose personal information to us (Archer et al., 1980). In terms of self-disclosure, people generally like to disclose their thoughts and feelings to others, and by doing so, people have a feeling of closeness. Accordingly, self-disclosures involve greater the feeling of intimacy (Laurenceau et al., 1998).

However, it is necessary to consider degree or depth of self-disclosure according to an index of intimacy (Altman & Taylor, 1973). People feel uncomfortable with self-disclosure conveyed in the early stage of a relationship (Altman & Taylor, 1973). People would feel that's too much too soon. Altman and Taylor

(1973) found that people tend to disclose gradually, and exchanged information becomes more intimate over time. "Intimate self-disclosures" which refer to high-risk information that involves personal secrets and makes speakers feel vulnerable in a way (Kelly & Mckillop, 1996). The opposite of high-risk information is low-risk information that is rather light and shallow. In this regard, people tend to be reluctant to reveal their high-risk information to others (Kelly & Mckillop, 1996).

However, even if people are hesitant to disclose intimate information about themselves, they tend to engage in intimate self-disclosure even to strangers when they first receive intimate information from others (Cozby, 1973). This compelling phenomenon involves the principle of reciprocity. When people are first exposed to intimate self-disclosure from others, they feel as if they are required to disclose themselves in turn (Moon & Nass, 1996). Given the principles, I assume that people would feel the same way in relation to reciprocal interaction with chatbots; Accordingly, I propose the following hypotheses:

H5: People will tend to reveal greater amount of intimate information about themselves when they are interviewed by a chatbot that goes first for each interview question with its information.

H5a: People will be more attracted to a chatbot that goes first for each interview question with its information. Particularly, people in the reciprocal condition will tend to be more attracted to the chatbot than people in the non-reciprocal.

H6: People will tend to reveal more intimate information about themselves when they are interviewed by a chatbot that applies the socially proper sequence of self-disclosure. Particularly, people in the gradual condition will be more likely to engage in self-disclosure than people in the abrupt condition.

H6a: People will be more attracted to a chatbot that applies the socially proper sequence of self-disclosure. Particularly, people in the gradual condition will more likely be attracted to the chatbot than people in the abrupt condition.

2.5 Experiment 1

2.5.1 Method

A 2 (chatbot personality: dominant vs. submissive) by 2 (participant personality: dominant vs. submissive) between-subject experiment is being conducted. All subjects will be balanced for gender. A chatbot employed in this study is a text-based system on the mobile phone.

2.5.2 Participants

Participants will be 60 college students. Two weeks prior to the study, subjects are asked to complete the Bem Sex Role Inventory (BSRI; Bem, 1977) that indicates a degree of masculinity. Participants will be categorized as whether they are dominant or submissive based on their response to the BSRI results. Two weeks after finishing the BSRI subset, the same number of gender-balanced subjects from the dominant group and the submissive group will be asked to take part in the study.

2.5.3 Procedure

After completing the BSRI, dominant and submissive participants will be randomly paired with either the dominant or submissive chatbot in a 2 x 2 gender balanced and between-subjects design. When the subject arrives, they will be asked to counsel the given chatbot about whatever they have in mind by chatting on the smartphone. Meanwhile the chatbot will display their personalities (whether dominant vs. submissive) through verbal and nonverbal cues. Afterwards, the participant will be asked to complete a set of questionnaires to access the chatbots and their interaction.

2.5.4 Measures

On the pre-study, subjects will complete the BSRI to classify their personality into dominance and submissiveness. The dependent variables will be measured by a set of online questionnaires. In addition, the question items I will be employing are referred to the previous studies.

2.6 Experiment 2

2.6.1 Method

A 2 (question wording: NORECIP vs. RECIP) by 2 (interview sequence: GRAD, ABRUPT) between-subjects experiment is being conducted. All subjects will be balanced for gender. A chatbot employed in this study is a text-based system on the mobile phone.

2.6.2 Participants

Participants will be 60 college students.

2.6.3 Procedure

On arrival, the subject will be taken to the laboratory where it contains a smartphone that is activated the chatbot system. The experimenter will explain the chatbot would display the subject with a question, and the subject would respond to the question by typing on the screen on the phone. Once the participant completes a required response, they can move on to the next question by clicking on the "NEXT" button. When it comes to questions that will be given to participants, there will be two interview question parts. Part 1 consists of four questions regarding low intimate topics. Part 2 consists of 11 questions on high intimate topics. The low and high intimate questions were verified in previous studies (Davis & Sloan, 1974; Jourard, 1979; Jourard & Jaffe, 1970; Shaffer & Tomarelli, 1989). Subsequently, the participant finishes the given interviews with the chatbot; they will be asked to complete an online questionnaire.

2.6.4 Measures

According to Collins and Miller (1994), a degree of self-disclosure has been measured by two dimensions: depth and breath. "Depth" indicates the quality of the disclosed information and is measured by independent judges; conversely, "breadth" refers to the information quantity that is revealed and is measured by a word or time count.

Depth of Intimate Self-disclosure. I will measure the depth of intimate self-disclosure based on Moon's study (2000). Subjects will be told that definition of intimate self-disclosure and will be asked to rank the quality of the information that they receive during the interview with the chatbot on a five-point scale (1 = low intimacy; 5 = high intimacy).

Breadth of Intimate Self-disclosure. Breath of intimate self-disclosure will be measured by the length of the participant's comments during the interview with the chatbot. I will count words that the participants employed, and the total number of words in all responses will be scored (Collins & Millar, 1994).

3. CONCLUSION

3.1 Expected Results and Its Implication

With the technological development, psychological AI are arising over the world. The two primary benefits from psychological AI are an affordable cost of mental health care and accessibility anytime anywhere you want. Personality similarity and self-disclosure play important roles in human-to-human psychotherapy; nevertheless, to my humble knowledge, therapist-client personality similarity and self-disclosure do not seem to be regarded in a chatbot design.

Thus, in this study, I suggest a text-based psychotherapy chatbot design proposal through empirical two test of use's psychological responses and self-disclosure to chatbots with personalities. In the experiment 1, participants are expected to be affected by chatbots with characters whether it is dominant or submissive, and will be more attracted to psychologically similar chatbots in line with the theoretical background: the media equation, similarity-attraction theory, and social presence. In the experiment 2, I expect that when participants are exposed to intimate information through the gradual conversation with chatbots, they will be more likely to disclose themselves to chatbots in turn. As a result, the intimate information which can be quite significant source for psychotherapy to deal with patient's mental problems more effectively and productively.

REFERENCES

Altman, I., & Taylor, D. A. (1973). Social penetration: The development of interpersonal relationships. Holt, Rinehart & Winston.

Archer, R. L., & Burleson, J. A. (1980). The effects of timing of self-disclosure on attraction and reciprocity. *Journal of Personality and Social Psychology*, *38*(1), 120.

Bem, S. L. (1977). On the utility of alternative procedures for assessing psychological androgyny. *Journal of consulting and clinical psychology*, *45*(2), 196.

Collins, N. L., & Miller, L. C. (1994). Self-disclosure and liking: a meta-analytic review. Psychological bulletin, 116(3), 457.

Cozby, P. C. (1973). Self-disclosure: a literature review. Psychological bulletin, 79(2), 73.

Davis, J. D., & Sloan, M. L. (1974). The Basis of Interviewee Matching of Interviewer Self-disclosure. British Journal of Clinical Psychology, 13(4), 359-367.

Dieleman, J. et al (2016). US spending on personal health care and public health, 1996-2013. Jama, 316(24), 2627-2646.

Digman, J. M. (1990). Personality structure: Emergence of the five-factor model. Annual review of psychology, 41(1), 417-440.

Gaggioli, A. (2017). Artificial Intelligence: The Future of Cybertherapy?. Cyberpsychology, Behavior, and Social Networking, 20(6), 402-403.

Goldfried, M. R. et al (2003). Therapist self-disclosure in cognitive-behavior therapy. Journal of clinical psychology, 59(5), 555-568.

Hunt, J., & Eisenberg, D. (2010). Mental health problems and help-seeking behavior among college students. Journal of Adolescent Health, 46(1), 3-10.

Isbister, K., & Nass, C. (2000). Consistency of personality in interactive characters: verbal cues, non-verbal cues, and user characteristics. International journal of human-computer studies, 53(2), 251-267.

Jourard, S. M. (1971). Self-disclosure: An experimental analysis of the transparent self.

Jourard, S. M., & Jaffe, P. E. (1970). Influence of an interviewer's disclosure on the self-disclosing behavior of interviewees. Journal of Counseling Psychology, 17(3), 252.

Kelly, A. E., & McKillop, K. J. (1996). Consequences of revealing personal secrets. Psychological Bulletin, 120(3), 450.

Kessler, R. C. et al (2007). Age of onset of mental disorders: a review of recent literature. Current opinion in psychiatry, 20(4), 359.

Laurenceau, J. P. et al (1998). Intimacy as an interpersonal process: the importance of self-disclosure, partner disclosure, and perceived partner responsiveness in interpersonal exchanges. Journal of personality and social psychology, 74(5), 1238.

Lee, K. M. (2004). Presence, explicated. Communication theory, 14(1), 27-50.

Lee, K. M. et al (2006). Can robots manifest personality?: An empirical test of personality recognition, social responses, and social presence in human–robot interaction. Journal of communication, 56(4), 754-772.

Mendelsohn, G. A. (1966). Effects of client personality and client-counselor similarity on the duration of counseling: A replication and extension. Journal of Counseling Psychology, 13(2), 228.

Miner, A. S. et al (2017). Talking to Machines About Personal Mental Health Problems. Jama, 318(13), 1217-1218

Moon, Y. (2000). Intimate exchanges: Using computers to elicit self-disclosure from consumers. Journal of consumer research, 26(4), 323-339.

Moon, Y., & Nass, C. (1996). How "real" are computer personalities? Psychological responses to personality types in human-computer interaction. Communication research, 23(6), 651-674.

Nass, C., & Lee, K. M. (2000, April). Does computer-generated speech manifest personality? An experimental test of similarity-attraction. In Proceedings of the SIGCHI conference on Human Factors in Computing Systems (pp. 329-336). ACM.

Reeves, B., & Nass, C. (1996). The media equation: How people treat computers, television, and new media like real people and places. New York: Cambridge University Press.

Riggio, R. E., & Friedman, H. S. (1986). Impression formation: The role of expressive behavior. Journal of Personality and Social Psychology, 50(2), 421.

Shaffer, D. R., & Tomarelli, M. M. (1989). When public and private self-foci clash: Self-consciousness and self-disclosure reciprocity during the acquaintance process. Journal of Personality and Social Psychology, 56(5), 765.

Shawar, B. A., & Atwell, E. (2007). Chatbots: are they really useful?. In LDV Forum (Vol. 22, No. 1, pp. 29-49).

Weizenbaum, J. (1966). ELIZA—a computer program for the study of natural language communication between man and machine. Communications of the ACM, 9(1), 36-45.

Wiggins, J. S. (1979). A psychological taxonomy of trait-descriptive terms: The interpersonal domain. Journal of personality and social psychology, 37(3), 395.

UX DESIGN PRINCIPLES FOR MOBILE AUGMENTED REALITY APPLICATIONS

Anna Chakravorty[1] and Aidan Rowe[2]
[1]*Master of Design Candidate, Department of Art & Design, Faculty of Arts, University of Alberta*
[2]*Department of Art & Design, Faculty of Arts, University of Alberta*

ABSTRACT

Augmented Reality (AR), in which interactive virtual objects are seamlessly superimposed into real-world environments, is a growing area in mobile applications. With advancement in mobile devices capable of producing increasingly more persuasive compositions, the potential of Mobile Augmented Reality (MAR) has begun to be explored. To ensure the acceptance and success of future MAR systems and fill the gap in MAR research, it is vital to identify current UX guidelines that apply to MAR applications. This paper identifies existing UX design trends in MAR and surveys current MAR applications to discuss the potential areas of improvement.

KEYWORDS

Mobile Augmented Reality, Design Guidelines, User Experience, Survey

1. INTRODUCTION

As computer technology increases in power and decreases in size, and hardware-intensive applications are rapidly becoming feasible, mobile phones have become increasingly prevalent (Zugara, 2016). This evolution and the flexibility of mobile phones have created a perfect platform for Mobile Augmented Reality (MAR) (Zugara, 2016) applications, utilizing AR as a unique feature to produce an enhanced composite view of a user's surroundings by mixing real and digital information. While MAR applications has continued to gather intrigue and growth in development, a major concern is how user perceptions and experiences can be significantly limited by the design of the User Experience (UX). Since much of the previous work has been limited to AR technologies, research on MAR User Interface (UI) and UX design remains mostly unexplored. To overcome the limitations of MAR and to address the gap in MAR design research, this paper examines current MAR applications in different domains to determine the current user experience design patterns. Using previous research in AR as a starting point, this paper will first introduce the basic elements of user experience design. Then, a survey is conducted with the help of 5 volunteers using 10 noteworthy mobile apps in four distinct categories: education; business; entertainment; and social. Finally, the gathered data is used to discuss the effectiveness of current MAR application design and identify areas of improvement.

2. UX DESIGN PRINCIPLES FOR MAR APPLICATIONS

2.1 Environmental Design

Due to the intrinsic reality-based nature of AR in mobile applications, developers and designers must consider the context of the end user, which has three fundamental aspects: physical scenarios; spatial space; and accessibility (Webdesigner Depot, 2017).

2.1.1 Physical Scenario

A user's physical scenario indicates his/her usage when operating an AR application. UX designers must define user journeys and consider how the interface will react in each physical scenario. Rob Manson (Webdesigner Depot, 2017) from AR UX lists key examples of AR usage: Public, using the whole body to interact with the software; Personal, using a device in a public space; Intimate, sitting or standing with minor movement; and Private, using a wearable. It is vital to consider these physical scenarios (Webdesigner Depot, 2017) as it can place certain limitations on application functionality and design choices. Certain applications may require initial calibration or setup before the application can be run.

2.1.2 Spatial Space

Considering a user's spatial space involves examining the lighting, sound, and motion of a user's immediate surroundings (Unpingco, 2017). In all cases of augmented reality applications, moderate ambient light is required for the camera to detect real world elements. Harsh glare from the sun or extreme contrast between shadows and sunny areas indoors may interfere with the sensor's ability to detect real world elements, especially when using planer detection (Haller, Billinghurst, Thomas, 2018; Koelle, 2014). Similarly, ambient background noise is another concern if an application needs to generate adept volume to be heard or detect speech or other sound inputs (Koelle, 2014). Developers should accommodate for potential sound and light sources that would impact the system's fundamental abilities. Moreover, the environmental design should factor in the motion of the user. In MAR applications where the user is required to maneuver in the real environment, spatial awareness as well as safety needs to be addressed. Since much of the user's focus attends to the flat 2D screen of the MAR device, users may become unaware of their surrounding environment and potential elements of obstruction or hazard. There are a variety of precautionary alerts, and sensory feedback that can be implemented to ensure the safety of the user.

2.1.3 Accessibility (Unpingco, 2017; Koelle, 2014)

To strengthen the usability of MAR applications, flexible adjustments should be allowed for user preferences and ease of use. The following are some factors to be considered: user engagement time; one-hand control in app navigation; time restrictions to prevent unintentional operations; and effective audio cues for users who are unable to see and audio detection.

2.2 Interaction Design

An effective Interaction Design improves all aspects of user-system interaction, especially application navigation. Since most user interactions are spent on operating the application, the user interface should be easy to understand and use. A common technique to improve usability is to place the control buttons on frequently used and easy to reach areas of a device's touch display. Applying haptic feedback in MAR applications is another tool that can be used to provide helpful information and to reduce confusion (Haller, Billinghurst, Thomas, 2018). Another aspect that influences a user's mindset and experience is the design of user journey maps (Google, 2016). A successful journey map design should effectively organize the flow of information presented on the screen, ultimately assisting users to accomplish tasks as fast as possible. Efficient journey maps not only reduce the cognitive load on the user but also reduces learnability (Google, 2016). The UX design must also complement the application's purpose (UXmatters, 2018). For instance, the utilization of exciting AR filters and the design of the unique sharing platform in Snapchat enables users to improve their social interactions. For applications that require users to focus on the image produced by the camera, a reticle or raycast from the device may be useful (Unpingco, 2017). Moreover, designers and developers may also scale, or animate digital elements based on the orientation and position of the camera (Haller, Billinghurst, Thomas, 2018). Having virtual characters react with user movement or revealing more information about an object as a user approaches, are proximity cues (Unpingco, 2017) that encourages exploration and interaction via movement. The most exciting factor of MAR is the ability to capture and transmit a user's augmented view allowing for unique user communication opportunities. A user can draw, add or manipulate virtual elements in the realworld context captured from another user located elsewhere. While the technology in this area is still underdeveloped, some developers have already conceptualized this idea, in Holo for example (Haller, Billinghurst, Thomas, 2018). For effective user interactions, the terminology used should be consistent and understandable. Although there is currently no standardized terminology for MAR applications, a baseline of interoperability of terminology between MAR applications should be established (Koelle, 2014). While some terms used in traditional mobile application also apply in MAR applications, newer terms that are associated with the unique AR aspects may become confusing if a standard is not set. Development of a vocabulary along with different standard interaction gestures in MAR needs to be considered as a form of interaction design so that there is widespread adoption of these terms (Haller, Billinghurst, Thomas, 2018; Koelle, 2014).

2.3 Visual Cues

For users to experience the true potential of AR, it is essential for designers to apply visual cues to improve the presence of virtual objects and encourage users to explore their surroundings. There are multiple methods for enhancing an object's appearance: increasing an object's weight; utilizing depths maps; and choosing different material properties. Designers can also consider projecting virtual objects with specific choices of lighting techniques or casting shadows to improve overall object depth and presence. A common lighting model is simply placing a light source overhead at the 12 o'clock position, parallel to the device (Wilson, 2017). In addition, AR development platforms such as Google's ARCore allows devices to detect varying plane sizes or overlapping planes at different elevations (Unpingco, 2017) allowing for unique volumetric responsive designs and allowing creators to better react to the constraints of users' mobile play space. That said, designers must be aware of applying visual cues that force fixed paths on users or limits a user's view (Haller, Billinghurst, Thomas, 2018). While visual cues are essential in areas of projecting virtual imagery, visual cues also enhance UI elements and provides clues for better interaction. Similar to current mobile applications, UI elements such as icons, buttons, menus and text boxes must accommodate the application's purpose and function (Patricia, 2016). Developers should design UI elements to improve discoverability and user efficiency. To make buttons and other interactable elements more easily identifiable, hover states can be added to highlight objects of interest (Haller, Billinghurst, Thomas, 2018; Koelle, 2014). Similarly, UI elements that manipulate AR projected objects should give active visual cues in forms of realistic feedback. For instance, in a furniture shopping application, illusion of gravitational force can be emphasized when users drag and place a bookshelf (Koelle, 2014; Unpingco, 2017). Visual cues are also tools to differentiate the appearance of the UI from the user's surroundings. Principles such as the colour theory, typography and drop shadows, are just some of the rudimentary considerations for practical and usable UI design (Wilson, 2017; Patricia, 2016; Google, 2018).

3. DISCUSSION

To understand the UX of Mobile AR applications in the current landscape, I selected ten apps from different disciplines—retail, entertainment, productivity and social—to be evaluated in a survey. Next, five participants were chosen to understand varied perspectives; applicants came from networking, gaming, design, neuroscience and engineering backgrounds. For this exploration of UX design in existing MAR applications, the survey was made following the "The Questionnaire for User Interaction Satisfaction (QUIS)", a tool developed by the Human-Computer Interaction Lab (HCIL) at the University of Maryland (University of Maryland, 2018). The QUIS is a highly reliable measure, designed to assess users' subjective satisfaction across different human-computer interfaces. Figure 1 shows the evaluation of UX design for MAR application. The following are the findings from the analysis of the applications:

- 80% of the aps are easy to use and are quite flexible. Even though the apps have a good quality, they are either mostly satisfying or not stimulating enough. Potential improvements can be made in terms of social engagement, such as in the World Brush app, where users can create unique drawings that are anonymous but lacks tagging or sharing abilities.
- The information in 90% of the applications is readable but fails to structure and direct the flow of information presented. The game AR Runner, for example, offers different modes of play but lacks instruction on how to select different play modes or options. It is only after playing the application for a few times, that the user understands the flow.

- 10% of the MAR applications still face some issues with operation speed, especially if dependent on an internet connection. Applications, such as Google Translate, should offer offline assistance or operate with downloaded local files. Users mark 30% of the applications as requiring clearer input prompts. For instance, Graphmented, which creates charts and dashboards using AR, has buttons for control settings but they are not highlighted enough for participants.
- Users note that 80% of the applications feel that a tutorial or additional instruction is needed. This suggests a learning curve in many MAR applications. Inkhunter, where users try on virtual tattoos, shows user information once at the beginning and does not show any additional technical support when participants struggle with the task at hand. Inkhunter also increases the cognitive load and stress as it is harder to use the application with one hand.

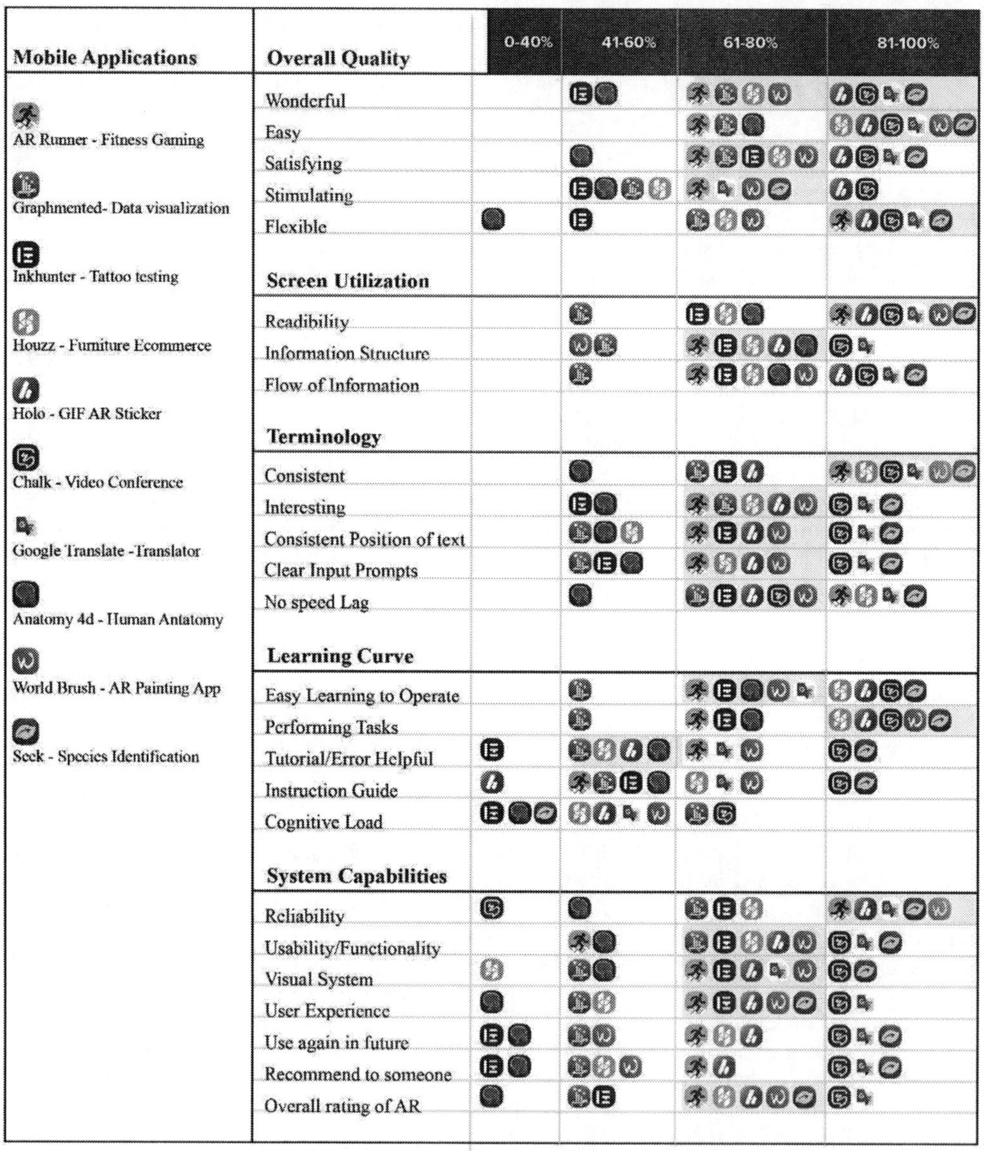

Figure 1. MAR Applications Survey Results Mapping

- Applications that focuses on functionality use case like Google Translate, Chalk and Seek were rated higher than other business or entertainment disciplines since they can increase efficiency.
- Most applications proved to be reliable, except Chalk, which requested access to contact details of the users arising some privacy concerns.
- Lastly, 70% of the users feel the visual system of applications needs further improvement and more active engagement. For example, user experience and interaction were hindered in Houzz, due to the absence of weight and depth in the virtual objects, and in Google Translate, where the interface is too conservative and rigid.

It is evident from the data gathered by the survey that there are several areas for improvements in MAR applications. The analysis shows more than 60% of users are willing to use these applications in the future and 50% would recommend them to others. The overall rating of the AR experience is above average for more than

60% of users. AR proves to be a stronger tool where the applications have functional usage. It seems current MAR applications still use traditional guidelines for mobile applications and thus suffer in certain areas involving AR. This brief discussion outlines the potential opportunities for AR applications and how these gaps can be addressed with ever-evolving AR technology.

4. CONCLUSION

Recent advances in mobile augmented reality is creating an exciting design space for new AR applications. While the UX community is still finding ways to participate in shaping this design probe into the experience of everyware, we still lack fundamental knowledge regarding how various design decisions will impact AR application effectiveness. This research analyzed existing user experience design guidelines and organized them into specific categories of environmental design, interaction design, and visual cues. Using the literature review of the UX design, ten MAR applications were evaluated to explore the challenges and opportunities in the current AR design scenario. While our experiment only assessed a subset of MAR applications, the survey framework was enough to examine the current trend in MAR industry and how these applications can be improved. Overall, the consensus demonstrates the need to enhance UX design for AR applications and the importance of considering design with these guidelines. The biggest misconception is we look MAR as a single user interface, and from that perspective, it doesn't add to what we already have. AR becomes strong when we look at situations where we have a high granularity of technology in the space where a standard desktop could lose control of these systems (Haller, Billinghurst, Thomas, 2018). We need to aim to improve the technology that is open and is owned and accessed by everyone.

REFERENCES

Google. Accessed March 20, 2018. Principles of Mobile App Design: Engage Users and Drive Conversions.

Koelle, Marion, Patrick Lindemann, Tobias Stockinger, and Matthias Kranz, May 2014.*Human computer Interaction with Augmented Reality*.

Michael Haller, Mark Billinghurst, Bruce Thomas, 2018. *Emerging Technologies of Augmented Reality: Interfaces and Design.* IGI Global. January 01, 0001.

Patricia Search, 2016. *Information Design Opportunities with augmented reality application*

University of Maryland. Accessed April 01, 2018. Questionnaire For User Interaction Satisfaction.

Unpingco, Alesha. December 13, 2017. Accessed March 20, 2018. Best Practices for Mobile AR Design. Google.

UXmatters. Accessed March 16, 2018. Inside Out: Interaction Design for Augmented Reality.

Webdesigner Depot. July 17, 2017. Accessed March 20, 2018. The Essential Guide to UX for AR.

Wilson, Tyler. November 13, 2017. Accessed March 16, 2018. The Principles of Good UX for Augmented Reality – UX Collective. [1] Skjoldbroder. August 11, 2017. Accessed March 16, 2018.Prototypr.

Zugara. May 02, 2016. Augmented Reality and Virtual Reality Accelerating Evolution Of User Interface Interaction.

USER INTERFACE DESIGN AND EVALUATION OF A MOBILE POLLEN TRACKING APPLICATION

Victor Jacobson, Cassandra Iglesias, and Patricia Morreale
School of Computer Science, Kean University, Union, NJ 07083, USA

ABSTRACT

The research presented here outlines the design and evalaution of a mobile application, which provides real-time reporting information on a variety of geographically specific naturally occurring pollens. Due to the complexity of pollen count data, a simplified data summary is presented in a graphical interface. The purpose of the mobile pollen tracking application is to make the data visually appealing and easy to understand. Early awareness of pollen counts allows people to practice preventative behaviors to avoid suffering from allergy symptoms. The mobile pollen app design is user-centered, and user feedback was incorporated throughout the design process. Four different types of pollen are reported simultaneously, computed from samples taken from a network of field pollen stations. Using visual identifiers, pollen types, persistence, and impact can be delivered on-demand to mobile users. Evaluation was conducted using the System Usability Scale (SUS) and the Usability Metric for User Experience LITE (UMUX-LITE). Users report positive experiences overall with the application, with support for several additional features. The application is currently available for use, and wider distribution is underway.

KEYWORDS

UI Design, Pollen Reporting, Mobile Application Design, Mobile Health, Behavior Modification

1. INTRODUCTION

Seasonal allergies affect millions of people annually and are one of the leading causes of chronic illness (CDC, 2018; ACAAI, 2018). While over-the-counter and prescription medicines can effectively counteract many of the uncomfortable or disabling symptoms experienced by allergy suffers, people must know when to take a medication or change their behaviors to avoid suffering. AccuPollen™ Allergy Tracker is a smartphone app which provides users with pollen counts measured at locations around the USA, providing information which may help people avoid misery. Pollen count data can be complex, so the mobile application presents a simplified summary of the data in a graphical interface. The purpose is to make the data visually appealing and easy to understand. Users can quickly see if pollens they are allergic to are present in the atmosphere and can use this information to proactively plan for the day.

An additional feature of AccuPollen™ is an allergy tracker. This feature is being implemented to allow users to track their allergy symptom severity and compare that to the pollen count. Users can also track their medication usage to help determine the effectiveness of their medicines. The allergy tracker will initially only track a few factors, with plans to grow. The interface will remain simple and polished but provide access to several layers of symptoms and medications. The app is free, featuring banner advertisements, and designed to encourage users to return to the app regularly for updated information.

2. PRIOR WORK

Prior research on pollen count applications had stressed the need for quality control in the eHealth service (Bastl et al., 2017). Pollen forecasts are known to be highly valuable for allergen avoidance, in part due to the historical nature of pollen data (Iglesia et al., 2015). The potential for improving the quality of life for individuals who suffer from allergies is high. Such services are recommended to be free and widely available. Predictive data analysis is also supported in the literature (Bocaj et al., 2017) and the important of including end-users in the design of any user-centered environment is well understood (Bruinessen et al., 2017; Preece, 2015).

Relevant work in atmospheric environmental impacts (Johnston et al., 2018) has been focused on asthma (Huckvale et al., 2015) and inhaled treatments (Jácome et al., 2017). The growth of mobile applications, and the accessibility of the app store for distribution (Gan et al., 2016) points towards the closer integration of users and health care providers for the management and monitoring of controllable chronic conditions.

The principle behind AccuPollen™ is to help patients see the pollen counts in their area. Support for this visualization is provided by human computer interaction (HCI) principles which support low cognitive load and feedback (Shneiderman, 2017). A *pollen count* is defined by the American Academy of Allergy Asthma and Immunology as "...measured by analyzing the number of mold spores or pollen grains in a cubic meter of air." This requires field pollen stations to identify the measurement of pollen. To analyze pollen count, a calculation is used to determine if the pollen count is low, moderate, or high, using a pre-determined scale. This type of calculation uses a *rotorod*, made up of silicon material left outside for 24 hours. The rotorod will test the air by examining the collection of pollen grains on the rods. Rotorod measurements are considered standard and reliable for pollen counts (Heffer, et al., 2005) AccuPollen™ reflects this measurement process, based on the limited amount of pollen reporting field stations per state.

3. USER INTERFACE DESIGN

AccuPollen™ is a free app which allows users to see real pollen counts around the U.S. Field pollen stations deployed throughout the USA measure pollen and upload pollen counts regularly to the AccuPollen™ database. AccuPollen™ automatically selects the closest pollen station based on the requesting user location. Users can also tap any station on the map to view its most recent pollen counts. The goal of the app for users to be able to easily see and understand accurate, correct pollen data and view pollen facts.

Figure 1. AccuPollen™ Welcome screen

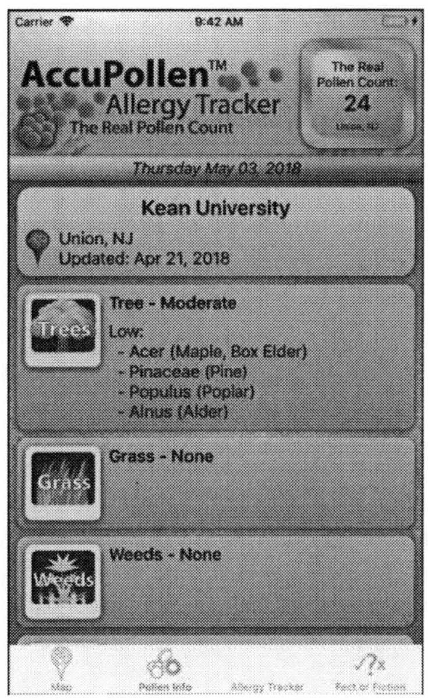

Figure 2. AccuPollen™ pollen information screen

The AccuPollen™ screen in Figure 1 illustrates the eastern coast of the USA. Location identifiers, looking like green pollen spores, show the pollen reporting stations in use. The buttons are located at the bottom of the screen, for ease of use. Four fixed pollen indicators, standard for pollen counting sites, are listed, providing information on trees, grass, weeds, and mold. The visual graphics presented were designed for the app, with the images made in Illustrator, using both color and visual indicators to reduce the cognitive load. The AccuPollen™ displayed is written in Swift, for the iPhone store; the Android version is in Java.

As the user navigates on the East Coast map, the landscape moves. The pollen thumb tacks give information on station location, and regularly update. A mix of active pollen reporting sites and inactive sites is present. The banner top is 25% of the screen, with the map occupying the remaining 75%, including pollen overlays, and advertising and navigation foot notes. A proprietary, privately held relational database is used to display the requested pollen information (Figure 2). The raw data of every pollen type is converted into a format for the app to use. Users are presented with geo-specific, visual single digit pollen numbers, and the exact calculations are done as part of the app. Pollen data is always ready for display.

4. USER INTERFACE EVALUATION

Evaluation of the user interface (UI) was done in two parts. Users were initially observed working with the AccuPollen™ app to understand their cognitive thinking while navigating the various features of the application. No prior details were given to the users on how to use the mobile application, besides background information of what the app was about. Upon observation, users investigated how to use the app by clicking on different features and navigating through trial and error. After the observation period concluded, the users were asked to complete a survey for the second part of the UI evaluation. The survey questions were based on the System Usability Scale (SUS) (Brook, 1996; Shneiderman, 2017) and modified in support of both the Usability Metric for User Experience (UMUX) (Finstad, 2010) and UMUX-LITE (Lewis, et.al. 2013). The survey consisted of seven statements, which were rated, and three short questions with free response text. For the first seven questions, users were asked to rate each statement on a Likert one to five scale, one being strongly disagree, and five being strongly agree. The statements included were:

- The App is easy to navigate (results in Figure 3),
- The App design is visually appealing,
- The individual pages are well designed (results in Figure 4),
- The App content is easy to understand,
- Overall the App was easy to use (results in Figure 5).
- The content of the App met my expectations, and
- Visiting the App was a positive experience.

The last three questions were short answer, which allowed the user to input their own feedback and thoughts. Those questions were:

- What do you like about the app?
- What do you wish was added?
- Did you encounter any problems using the app?

The human computer interaction (HCI) objectives of the testing were error identification and measurement of user efficiency and satisfaction.

Overall (n=8), users felt the app was easy to use, visually appealing, and the app met their expectations. The detailed "information of the various pollen stations" and "pollen per location" provided granular details which users had not seen before. The "pollen pointers on the map" were also appealing. Where users felt the mobile app scored lower was in the design of the individual pages. Users stated some text was cut off on certain pages, and pages appeared busy. Users also stated that they would like more information on pollen counts in different states, and the addition of a menu or instructions page on how to navigate the app.

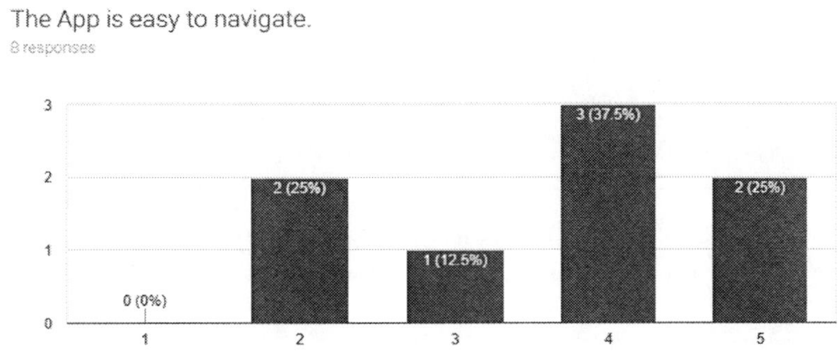

Figure 3. User assessment of AccuPollen™ navigation

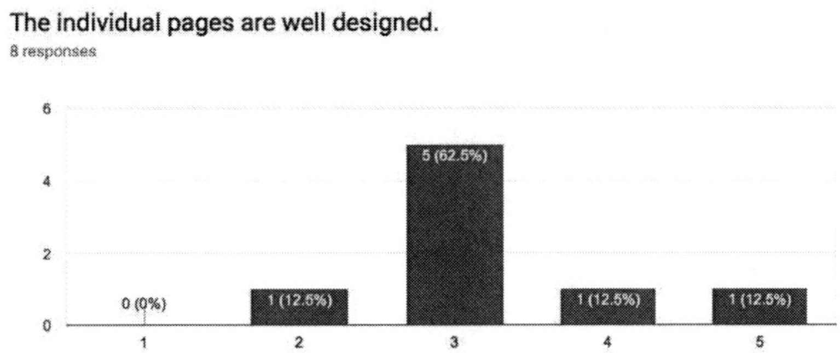

Figure 4. User assessment of AccuPollen™ mobile application pages

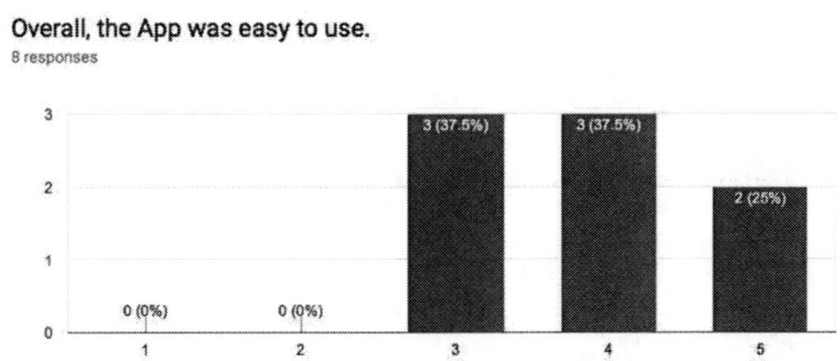

Figure 5. User assessment of AccuPollen™ usability

Currently, the app is freely available in the Apple store. An Android version is being developed, using the feedback received from the Apple product.

5. CONCLUSIONS AND FUTURE WORK

User adoption continues to increase, particularly as pollen season arrives. Future work includes updating the pollen thumb tacks with colors, to show how recently the site has been updated. If a pollen count has not updated recently, extrapolation is used by selecting a reading from a prior year, on the same or nearby date, and the data is presented to the user, in a historical context. Enhancements will include allergy tracking, additional information about where the pollen has come from, and specific thumbtacks which open for a discussion of the pollen site, with the map clear and visible, unless a specific pollen station is selected. Information about preventative behaviors can be added to the app, personalizing the experience for users, and encourage the use of the app in a pro-active manner to avoid or downgrade allergy symptoms.

An application such as this is expected to have additional environmental applications, such as wind speed for pilots or boaters, and other predictive situations where real-time atmospheric data analysis is required.

ACKNOWLEDGEMENTS

We would like to acknowledge support from STARx Technologies, LLC for the first author. We would also like to thank the users who participated in the initial evaluation and testing of AccuPollen™.

REFERENCES

American College of Allergy, Asthma, and Immunology (ACAAI). Online. https://acaai.org/news/facts-statistics/allergies Accessed June 25, 2018.

Bastl, K, et al., 2017. Evalation of Pollen Apps Forecasts: The Need for Quality Control in an eHealth Service, *In Journal of Medical Internet Research*, Vol. 19, Issue 5, pp. 1-8.

Bocaj, E., et al. 2017. M-Health Predictive Data Analysis of Daily Activities and Physiological Conditions. *In Proceedings of the International Conference on e-Health*, pp. 45-52.

Brook, J. 1996. SUS: A quick and dirty usability scale. *In Usability Evaluation in Industry*, Taylor and Francis Pub., UK.

Bruinessen, I., et al. 2017. Involving End-Users in the Development and Implementation of a Web-based, Physcial Activity Platform for Elderly. *In Proceedings of the International Conference on e-Health*, pp. 145-149.

Centers for Disease Control (CDC). 2018. Online. https://www.cdc.gov/nchs/fastats/allergies.htm June 25, 2018.

Finstad, K. 2010. The Usability Metric for User Experience. *In Interacting with Computers*, Vol. 22, No. 5, pp. 323-327.

Gan, S.K., et al. 2016. An overview of clinically and healthcare related apps in Google and Apple app stores: connecting patients, drugs, and clinicians. *In Scientific Phone Apps and Mobile Devices*, Vol. 2, pp. 1-9.

Heffer, M., et al. 2005. Comparison of the Rotorod to other air samplers for the determination of *Ambrosia artemisiifolia* pollen concentrations conducted in the Environmental Exposure Unit. *In Aerobiologia*, Vol 21, Issue 304, pp. 233-239.

Iglesia, D.H., et al. 2015. Pollen Allergies Prediction through Historical Data in Mobile Applications. *In International Journal of Artificial Intelligence*, Vol. 13, Issue 1, pp. 74-80/

Huckvale, K. et al. 2015. The evolution of mobile apps for asthma: an updated systematic assessment of content and tools, *In BioMed Central Medicine*, Vol. 13, pp. 1-15.

Jácome, C. et al. 2017. Inspirers: An App to Measure and Improve Adherence to Inhaled Treatment. *In Proceedings of the International Conference on e-Health*, pp. 135-139.

Johnston, F.H., et al. 2018. Using smartphone technology to reduce health impacts from atmospheric environmental hazards. *In Environmental Research Letters*, pp. 1-11.

Lewis, J., et.al. 2013. UMUX-LITE-When There's No Time for the SUS. *In Proceedings of the SIGCHI Conference on Human Factors in Computing Systems*, pp. 2099-2102.

Preece, J. et al. 2015. *Interaction Design: Beyond Human Computer Interaction*, 4th edition. Wiley, Sussex, UK.

Shneiderman, B, et al. 2017. *Designing the User Interface: Strategies for Effective Human-Computer Interaction*, 6th edition. Pearson Publishers, Hoboken, NJ, USA.

ELICITING REQUIREMENTS FOR DIGITAL SYSTEMS USING ACTIVITY AND TASK ANALYSIS

Alessandra Callado Bezerra de Mello and André Menezes Marques das Neves[1]
Universidade Federal de Pernambuco – UFPE, Brazil
[1]Dr

ABSTRACT

This research is focused on requirements capture based on understanding the activity system's context and on user-related task analysis as a resource for developing or adjusting digital systems. The study starts from a theoretical framework regarding Activity Theory (AT) and Usability Engineering in order to identify methods of data collection for generating information on requirements capture. It aims to compose and evaluate a method, through a case study, that considers both the activity system and the task analysis to understand the context of the problem to be solved. The proposition is a simplified approach, which might be an alternative to approximate user-oriented research application to agile dynamics.

KEYWORDS

User Requirements, HCI, Design Process, Activity Theory, Usability, Task Analysis

1. USER REQUIREMENTS CAPTURE

Both AT and Usability address requirements capture that can contribute to understanding the scenarios of human activities or problems to be solved. In both fields, the point of view of the actors involved in any particular activity is considered. In TA, the actors are the subject and the system's community members. In Usability, the actors are the users.

2. USABILITY

Comparing the structural activities required by Usability and Software Engineering, Leventhal & Barnes (2008) consider that there are many similarities between them and propose a variation of the Cascade model, integrating steps from the software development cycle to the user interface, considering usability principles and predicting iteration. According to the authors, in Software Engineering the problem consists in a system or process that requires a computerized solution, while in Usability the problem is focused in user context and its tasks. Among usability attributes, understanding the problem corresponds to the requirements capture stage. One needs to identify the variables that interfere with Usability in order to understand which user tasks require support in the interface to be developed. In this context, task analysis and specification is determinant to achieve satisfactory results. In the authors' definition, the analysis is described as the act of understanding and dismembering a problem, while Task Analysis is approached as the understanding of the user's tasks.

The analysis strategy presented by Leventhal and Barnes (2008) proposes combining three methods and aggregating elements of their approaches in software development: Scenario-Based Development (SBD), Unified Software Development Process and Hierarchical Task Analysis. The simplified task analysis method combines SBD and Use Case Analysis to represent high level tasks and it applies Task Analysis to identify and specify low level tasks' details. The technique enables the development of a document that can be used as a guide to the software design process. It aims to understand and present details about the user's problem (tasks) to be solved by the designer. It does not focus on describing the flow of activities, but rather the aspects to be considered.

3. ACTIVITY THEORY

In addition to the structure proposed by the cascade model and the identification of requirements proposed by Usability, the incorporation of the AT into the HCI design process signals the inclusion of the user context in social, cultural and psychological aspects. The historical socio-cultural AT model consists in a theoretical-conceptual framework to analyze human practices with interconnected individual and social levels (KUUTTI, 1996). The model considers the activity a basic unit represented by actions developed as people interact with their environment, which should never be considered separately when it comes to their social relations (LAZAROU, 2011). From the ideas of social and cultural mediation proposed by Vygotsky, Leont'ev (1978, 1981) developed the activity hierarchical model and proposed that the activity should be treated as a systemic and collective unit led to an object that is considered the activity's main motive and driving force (LAZAROU, 2011). This would be done through goal-oriented actions. Based on Vygotsky's views on the use of tools as process mediators, Leont'ev proposed that the activity's basic components would be the subject, the object and the mediation tools and categorized them in structuring levels, corresponding to the activity-action-operation triad. An expanded version of this model was proposed by Engeström (1987), that incorporates the social context, adding Social Rules, Community and Division of Labor, to the previously known components. The subject addresses the activity's individual and social nature. It is related to initiatives towards the satisfaction of the shared goal. The tools (artifacts) mediate the relationship between the activity's subjects and objects. They can be physical (material) or conceptual (symbolic). The community corresponds to the set of participants who share the same object and addresses the environment's social and cultural context. The rules comprehend explicit or implicit conventions and regulations that affect the means by which the activity is performed. The division of labor refers to social relations, responsibility allocation and variations of the subjects' work functions (MWANZA, 2001). In subsequent contributions, Frederick van Amstel (2010) presented the hexagonal module configuration, emphasizing that activity systems are not isolated entities, they interact with other systems, forming hives.

In a case study, Mwanza (2001) proposed a methodology to guide the AT-based data collection and interpretation process, so it can be applied during the requirements capture stage in order to identify the user's demands in a developing system. The operationalization process was divided in six stages: Modeling of the examined situation; Formulation of the situation's Activity System; Analysis of the situation's Activity System; Formulation of research questions; Conducting of detailed investigation; Interpretation of the findings.

4. EXPERIMENT APPLICATION

Both AT and Usability consider user-related demands and scenarios in their approaches. AT seeks to understand the activities by identifying their components as well as existing and potential conflicts between elements or between systems. Usability, however, seeks to understand the problem by observing the operation context and user needs. Would AT and Usability be two distinct options for collecting and analyzing user context and needs, or are they complementary?

Mwanza (2001) presents a systematization of what we propose calling Activity Analysis, by means of modeling the situation, formulating and analyzing the activity system and identifying its conflicts. Leventhal & Barnes (2008) propose the Task Analysis through use cases and scenarios. Apparently the two approaches are capable of capturing similar information about the user and their activity-task context. Based on this hypothesis, would it be correct to state that, by applying Mwanza's AT method, it would be possible to collect enough data to also develop the Task Analysis in a case study? The obtained results may indicate if the application of an AT method would be enough to capture requirements and subsidize the development or improvement of a system, or if it would be necessary to complement its application. The method will be applied in a case study where hopefully it will generate subsidies for formulating digital systems regarding the realtors' activity. The experiment will follow the following stages:

Stage 1 - Modeling of the examined situation: Questionnaire application in Focus Groups (FGs) with subjects of the activity. The FGs were chosen as a contribution to the method, aiming to collect data about the activity while observing the subjects in a collective context, in order to identify possible contradictions. In sessions recorded in a reserved environment, we gathered 3 groups of 6 to 8 realtors each. The questions were defined based on the Eight-Step-Model guidelines (Mwanza, 2001): 1. How would you describe the real estate (RE) activity?; 2. What is the purpose of the RE activity?; 3. Who are the people involved in the RE agent's activity?; 4. Which means or resources are used to carry out the activity?; 5. Which social norms, rules or regulations influence the development of this activity?; 6. What is the role of each actor involved in the activity and how are they organized?; 7. Where does this activity take place?; 8. What is the desired outcome when performing the RE agent activity?. In order to elucidate difficulties faced during the activity, a question was added: 9. If you could solve any aspect related to the real estate activity, what would it be?

Stage 2 - Formulation of the situation's Activity System From the data collected from the questions and FGs, it was possible to identify the components to formulate the subjects' Activity System. We proposed an adaptation to the procedure adopted by Mwanza, using Frederick van Amstel's (2010) Hexagonal Representation Diagram instead of Engeström's (1999) Second Generation Diagram, considering that the first represents more clearly the concept of contradictions between systems (hives).

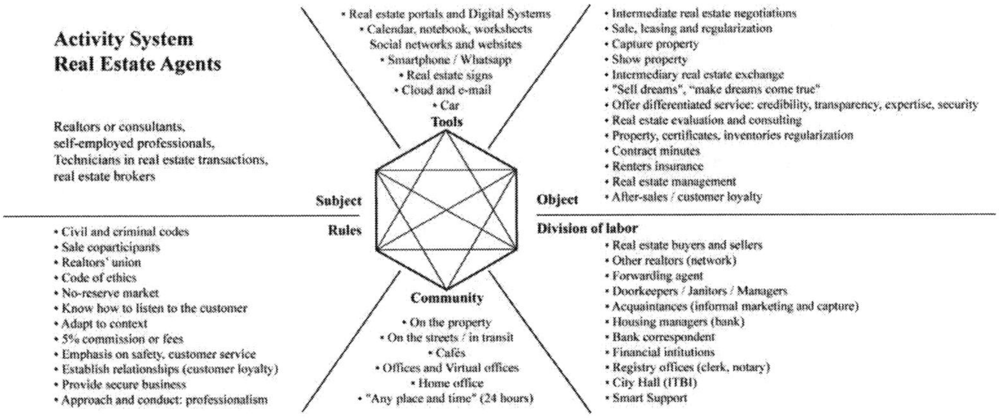

Figure 1. Freelance Realtors' Activity System, based on the Diagram from Frederick van Amstel (2010)

Stage 3 - Analysis of the situation's Activity System We sought to identify the possibility of grouping system components, in order to formulate structured and less repetitive questions. Based on the system analysis proposed by Mwanza, we used the Activity Notation structure to formulate the interview questions:

Table 1. Activity Notation

Actor		Mediator		Goal
Subject	how do they use →	Tool	to achieve →	Object
Subject	← how they affect	Rules	to achieve →	Object
Subject	← how they influence	Division of labor	to achieve →	Object
Community	← how they affect	Tool	to achieve →	Object
Community	← which ones they affect	Rules	to achieve →	Object
Community	← how they affect	Division of labor	to achieve →	Object

Stage 4 - Formulation of research questions: 1. How do realtors use systems to close real estate deals? 2. Which other tools do realtors use to complement the systems, and how? 3. In which ways the regulatory agencies affect realtors' work and the completion of their business? 4. Which aspects of a realtor's conduct can affect the success of their business and how? 5. Which aspects of the relationship with other realtors can influence the closing of deals? 6. Which aspects of the relationship with institutions and their agents can influence the closing of deals? 7. How does the use of Real Estate Systems and Portals affect the realtor's activity in the different contexts (socio-cultural environments) in which they operate, regarding the closing of deals? 8. How does the use of Whatsapp affect the realtor's activity in the different contexts in which they operate, regarding the closing of deals? 9. In which ways do the different work environments affect the realtor's activity and their goal of closing real estate deals?. We added a question about the activity's processes: 10. Could you describe in a step-by-step sequence how the real estate activity is carried out?

Stage 5 - Conducting of a detailed investigation: The formulated questions were applied in individual interviews with 10 real estate agents who use digital systems to manage their activities.

Stage 6 - Interpretation of findings (in progress): The contradictions identified during the interpretation of interviews were categorized in four levels, as per Table 2, and points out existing conflicts and problems that demand attention during the ideation phase.

Table 2. Classification levels

Contradiction	Description
Primary	Internal, within the elements of the Activity System
Secondary	Between the elements of the Activity System
Tertiary	Between the existing and potential forms of the Activity System
Quaternary	Between different Activity Systems

The following steps are not part of Mwanza's framework. They examine the documentation recommended by Leventhal's and Barnes's (2008) method regarding requirements capture in Usability. In these final stages, we will evaluate the need to complement the data collection procedure.

Stage 7 - Scenario Analysis: As the results of the Activity System (stage 2) is similar to the ones obtained through a Scenario Analysis, this stage is considered already achieved.

Stage 8 - Use Case Analysis: Developing a high-level diagram, the relationships between realtor and client are established on four main levels: identifying and meeting customer demands, forming partnerships with other realtors, obtaining real estate financing and issuing property documents. This is the base for next stage.

Stage 9 - Task Analysis (in progress): At this stage, we are developing the proposition of an alternative diagram that combines Task Analysis and Activity System results from the collected data.

5. CONCLUSION

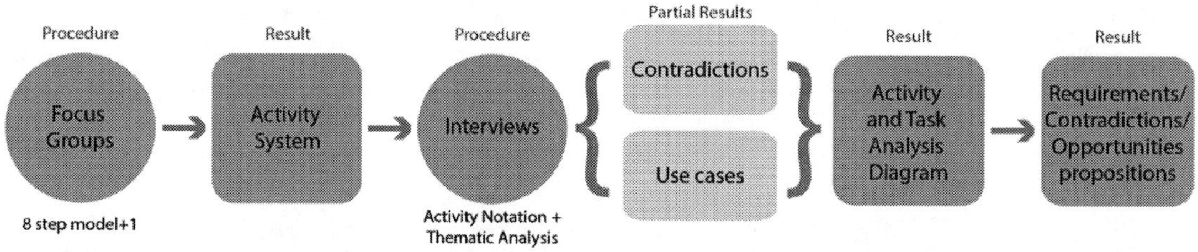

Figure 2. Structure of the Analysis of Activity-Task Analysis (AAT)

The study and proposition of a simplified method for requirements capture that integrates aspects of AT and Usability aims to contribute for structuring a systematic method as an alternative to stimulate user research applications even in contexts of low budget and restricted schedule. We can consider that the application of the method is helping us to understand and dismember the problem, identifying compositional elements, as well as their relationships and conflicts. When completed, will be possible to analyze the results obtained from the collected data and list their possible contributions and limitations. The analysis should consider if and how the results obtained in the application of this method might contribute to the digital interface developing process, as well as pointing out their shortcomings. The possibility of proposing a rearrangement of the method's stages and procedures and its structuring in diagram or canvas format will be evaluated as well as a proposition of an alternative diagram that combines Task Analysis and Activity System.

REFERENCES

Engeström, Y., 1987. *Learning by Expanding: An Activity Theoretical Approach to Developmental Research.* Orienta-Konsultit, Helsinki.

Kuutti, K., 1996. Activity Theory as a Potential Framework for Human-Computer Interaction Research. *In B. Nardi, Context and Consciousness: Activity Theory and HumanComputer Interaction*.MIT Press, Cambridge.

Lazarou, Demetris, 2011. Using Cultural-Historical Activity Theory to design and evaluate an educational game in science education. *Journal of Computer Assisted Learning*. Bristol, UK.

Leventhal, Laura; Barnes, Julie, 2008. *Usability Engineering: Process, Products and Examples*. Pearson Education, Inc., New Jersey.

Mwanza, D., 2001. Where Theory meets Practice: A Case for an Activity Theory based Methodology to guide Computer System Design. *In Michitaka Hirose (Ed), Proceedings of INTERACT'2001: Eighth IFIP TC 13 International Conference on Human-Computer Interaction*, Tokyo, Japan. IOS Press Oxford, UK.

Nardi, B., 1996. *Context and Consciousness: Activity Theory and Human-Computer Interaction.* Massachusetts Institute of Technology, Cambridge, USA.

Oliveira, Raquel Rodrigues Santos, 2014. *Information Design in Brazilian Education Social Networks: Analysis from Activity Theory.* Universidade Federal de Pernambuco (UFPE), Recife, Brazil.

THE EFFECT OF BACKGROUND INSTRUMENTAL MUSIC ON EMOTION AND PERFORMANCE

Brayan Rodríguez[1], Carlos Arce-Lopera[1], Ana María Arboleda[1], Javier Diaz-Cely[1], Julián Correa[2] and Pablo Montoya[2]
[1]*Universidad Icesi, Calle 18 No. 122-135 Pance, Cali, Colombia*
[2]*Musicar SAS, Avenida 2D No. 24N -75, Cali, Colombia*

ABSTRACT

Music affects the listener behavior and emotion, but this condition depends on variables of music design. In this regard, the present study aims to compare the emotional state, task load and performance under three different sound conditions determined by the tempo, articulation, mode, and metre of the songs. To achieve this end, we implemented a web-based tool in which the users' interaction was designed to be counter-intuitive and difficult. The tool collected several types of events during the interaction to measure the performance. The results revealed that the interaction was complicated and that required attention and effort to achieved a desired result. Besides, in general, the emotional state was not negatively affected by the condition. Nevertheless, outcomes illustrated important trends in task performance (i.e. final decisions, number of bad submissions, scroll direction changes, time spent, and time perceived) and task load (i.e. frustration) when comparing the three sound conditions. Thus, it is important to widen the experimental sample size to test for significance in the difference among different sound conditions.

KEYWORDS

Emotion, Music, User Performance

1. INTRODUCTION

The need to understand the effects of music on our behavior and cognitive processing has become increasingly important (Hallam *et al*, 2002). Music affects the listener behavior and emotion, but this condition depends on variables of music design. An increased tempo, for example, mostly has a positive impact in customers' emotions (arousal) (Michel *et al*, 2017) and consistently is related with faster behavior (Kämpfe *et al*, 2011); on the other hand, depending on the setting, volume has a special influence on the customer (Michel *et al*, 2017). Major and minor modes influence whether customers perceive the music as happy or sad (Peretz *et al*, 1998). Furthermore, genre (or subjective classification as calming or unpleasant) has an influence on cooperative behavior (Hallam *et al*, 2002) (Kniffin *et al.*, 2017) and school task performance (Hallam *et al.*, 2002) (Scott, 1970), reading tasks might be more disturbed by vocal than by instrumental music (Kämpfe *et al.*, 2011), and office workers with staccato music significantly decrease their cognitive performance in an isolated environment than workers with legato music (Schlittmeier and Hellbrück, 2009). Finally, the preferential dimension of the music influences the perception of time, for example, customers spend more time in a department store when they like the in-store music (Michel *et al.*, 2017); however, in the context of task performance, workers are able to differentiate between their personal music preferences and the sound conditions under which they preferred to perform a cognitive task (Schlittmeier and Hellbrück, 2009).

The influence on behavior and task performance of music is mediated through its effects on emotion: arousal and mood (Hallam *et al.*, 2002) (Michel *et al.*, 2017). Emotion is significantly associated with recall (Baumann *et al.*, 2015) and specifically arousal level increases task performance up to an optimal level beyond which over-arousal leads to a deterioration in performance (Hallam *et al.*, 2002). Moreover, for simple tasks, an increased level of arousal maintains the concentration and this yields a better task performance; but for complex tasks, the level of arousal may become too great and performance deteriorate (Hallam *et al.*, 2002).

Therefore, it remains unclear which attributes of music design can influence positively the task performance when the tasks are complex and require extensive use of cognitive processing. Particularly, sensory marketing solutions aim to improve office workers' task performance through instrumental music but the choice of the specific song is selected by music experts. Here, we aim at understanding the effect on emotional state and task performance of 27 instrumental background songs that are used in office settings. The songs differ in tempo, articulation, mode, and metre. The task performance was evaluated with a web-based tool simulating a complex and difficult attention-driven interaction.

2. METHODS

Twenty-seven instrumental songs were subjectively classified in terms of their tempo, articulation, mode, and metre by music experts. The resulting classes were motivating, mid, and relaxing. A difficult to interact web-based tool in which the user had to manipulate the mouse of a personal computer much more than usual and carefully read the instructions with a non-friendly and confusing graphic interface was used to test differences in emotional state when simultaneously hearing on of the three background instrumental music conditions.

2.1 Subjects

Twenty-four people voluntarily participated in the experiments: 10 females and 14 males. Age range was from 13 to 52 years old (27 on average) and 15 of them with little or no musical knowledge.

2.2 Materials

2.2.1 Music

The experimental conditions are given by three sets of background songs. The motivating condition mostly has songs in minor mode, staccato articulation, and with an average tempo of 119 bpm in the time signature 4/4. The mid condition is mostly in major mode, legato, and 91 bpm on average with the time signature 4/4. Lastly, the relaxing music is also mostly in major mode and legato, but the bpm is 48 on average with a time signature of 4/4, and in addition has some songs in the time signatures 6/8 and 3/4. Vocal characteristics of music can influence listeners' perceptions (Kämpfe *et al.*, 2011); thus, selected songs were only instrumental.

2.2.2 Interface

The sound conditions were accompanied by a tedious interface in which user will not intuitively find what she/he has to do with the tool. The input elements were modified in order to make it hard to express users' decisions. Besides, the website elements were positioned in a way that the user has to scroll down and up several times.

Subjects were requested to stay in an isolated room with computers in which the activity would be carried out. They are asked to use the same headphones every time to listen the background music in a fixed volume.

2.3 Procedure

Subjects were invited to participate in an experience where they are asked to be a travel agent who plans a vacation trip for a particular person with specific demands. The demands were carefully designed with different profiles and required the user to interact intensively with the interface. The purpose of the task was to have participants' involved within some decision making activities. However, this task takes place during annoying conditions: the web page where participants make their decisions is not intuitive or responsive (by design).

Participants faced the annoying interface in one of the three sound conditions. The instrumental songs were randomly chosen inside a certain condition and played back cyclically until the participant finished the task. Loudness was identical for each participant.

They received written instructions which state that the maximum available time to complete the vacation plan is 15 minutes and that maximum budget is COP $2.000.000. Besides, there were three profiles of the person or group of people for whom participants build the vacation plan. The profile was randomly chosen between three profiles: a 20 years old party youngster, a family with a kid and a baby, and a quiet student who is on vacation. To build a plan, participants must choose the vacation city, the hotel, number of days to stay, and budget for food. If the hotel amenities did not match with the priorities of the traveler, they have to keep trying until this is fulfilled or the 15 minutes are over.

The subject finished by clicking on the "submit decision" link. Next, the application appeared as if it were making some calculations, and the following message showed on the screen: "wait while we analyze all decisions." 30 seconds later, this message was followed by the last message "Thank you for waiting. Good-bye".

3. DATA COLLECTION

During the interaction, all interaction events including scroll changes, decision changes, final decision, time spent, number of bad submissions, and whether the time was over are collected. After the submission, an emotional state measurement is applied on the basis of determining the point in which a facial emotion changes in a carefully design video (Niedenthal *et al.*, 2001). This measurement is used to set the level of annoyance with the interface, namely a level greater than 30 out of 60 represents that the participant is feeling pleased. Moreover, the NASA Task Load Index (TLX) is applied to determine the perception of mental demand, physical demand, temporal demand, performance, effort, and frustration with the interface (Hart and Staveland, 1988). Next, time and music perception are also evaluated by asking the perception of minutes spent and if the background music was fast or slow.

Attitudes towards the experience are measured on a four-item seven-point semantic differential scale: very bad/ very good, unfavorable/favorable, not at all likable/ very likable, and unappealing/appealing. An overall satisfaction measurement in the same scale was added, asking if the participants were satisfied with their results. Attention to the music was evaluated on a seven point Likert scale, ranging from strongly disagree (1) to strongly agree (7), for the following four items: Paid much attention to the music in the interaction, followed the music more than the decisions, had the music in mind while taking decisions, and followed the music in the activity. Attitude and attention items were adapted from (Macinnis and Park, 1991). Moreover, likability of the music was assessed through three items (likable, pleasant, and good) on a Likert scale. Familiarity with the music was evaluated through three items (songs sound familiar, songs make me think about my past, and songs were personally relevant to me) in a Likert scale. The Likert scale ranges from totally disagree (1) to totally agree (7) (Macinnis and Park, 1991).

4. RESULTS AND DISCUSSION

The time spent interacting with the interface was 9 minutes and 52 seconds on average, with a minimum time of 3 minutes and 26 seconds and a maximum time of 15 minutes, the time limit. There was, on average, per participant, 59 scroll changes of direction, 5 errors (up to 21), and 14 decision changes until the correct plan was chosen or the time was up. These results show that the design of the web page indeed created a complicated interaction that required attention and effort to achieved a desired result.

The emotional state measurement gave us an average of 39 out of 60, indicating that users were inclined to feel pleased and the interface was not very annoying. The perception of the music was fast for the participants on motivating music condition and slow for the mid and relaxing condition. The time perception was from 1 to 18 minutes averaging 9 minutes and 30 seconds and the difference of each participant time perception with the actual time spent was 19 seconds on average. Regarding the NASA-TLX dimensions, the lowest scored was the physical demand with an average of 2 out of 10; the frustration was 4.1/10; the temporal demand, 4.5/10; the effort, 5/10; the mental demand, 5.2/10; and the performance, 5.6/10.

Furthermore, on average, attitudes towards the experience was 5.1/7, which means that attitudes were mostly positive. Attention to the music was 3.7/7, indicating that subjects did not significantly perceived the music. Music likability and familiarity was 5.1/7 and 3.9/7 respectively.

Three people (2 on mid music condition and 1 on relaxing music condition) couldn't finish the activity within the allotted time. Results also show that the participants under the motivating music condition took the best decisions, regarding to the budget for food and number of vacation days, when the traveler(s) profile was the party youngster or the family and, on the other hand, when the traveler was the quiet student, participants under relaxing music took the best decisions. According to music likability measurement, there was a significant difference in the scores under the motivating background music and the mid one ($t(8) = -2.57$, $p=0.045$) and, also, compared to subjects under the relaxing one ($t(8) = 3.82$, $p=0.003$); namely the relaxing and mid music was significantly more liked than the motivating music.

In the interaction, participants who listened to relaxing songs had more scroll direction changes but less bad submissions than ones who listened mid and motivating songs. The subjects under motivating music spent less time and perceived less time spent than the other ones. Nevertheless, the frustration measured by the NASA-TLX tool is on average higher under motivating music than under the other two sound conditions. Attention to the music was better scored by participants under relaxing music especially in the music in mind item. However, these differences are not statistically significant. Besides, in the NASA-TLX dimensions, music attention, nor time perception evaluation had significant differences among the three music conditions.

5. CONCLUSIONS AND FUTURE WORK

We designed and implemented a web-based tool in which the users had a difficult interaction when trying to register their decisions. This complex behavior was verified by measurements obtained from the interaction with the interface. Then, we were able to measure the influence of three different sound contexts on their task performance and load.

Most of the experiments in the literature measure the influence of background music on emotions specifically arousal and, by doing so, the effects on listener behavior or task performance. Whereas, this work in progress attempts to evaluate the emotion of the user when confronted with a complex task and using several measurement tools that can give insight on the complex relation between music and users emotion and performance.

Comparisons between the three music conditions did not reveal significant differences in the participants' emotional state but revealed better decisions regarding the traveler profile and some important trends on task performance and one dimension of task load.

In order to determine how to improve the task performance through the influence of background instrumental music, first we need to determine if the trends illustrated in the results can be significantly different by widening the sample size. Furthermore, in future work, the technology readiness should be taken into account because this could become decisive, for example, in the time spent in the activity.

ACKNOWLEDGEMENT

The authors acknowledge the support of INFIVALLE, of the Gobernación del Valle del Cauca, of PacifiTIC, of Musicar SAS and of Universidad Icesi for the logistics and financial support enabling the development of this research. Also, the authors acknowledge the collaboration of the i2T (grupo de investigación en Informática y Telecomunicaciones) research group members at Universidad Icesi.

REFERENCES

Baumann, C. *et al.*, 2015. Elsevier Limited. The role of brand exposure and experience on brand recall—Product durables vis-à-vis FMCG. *Journal of Retailing and Consumer Services*, Vol. 23, , pp. 21–31.

Hallam, S. *et al.*, 2002. The Effects of Background Music on Primary School Pupils' Task Performance. *Educational Studies*, Vol. 28, No. 2, pp. 111–122.

Hart, S. G. and Staveland, L. E., 1988. North-Holland. Development of NASA-TLX (Task Load Index): Results of Empirical and Theoretical Research. *Advances in Psychology*, Vol. 52, , pp. 139–183.

Kämpfe, J. *et al.*, 2011. SAGE PublicationsSage UK: London, England. The impact of background music on adult listeners: A meta-analysis. *Psychology of Music*, Vol. 39, No. 4, pp. 424–448.

Kniffin, K. M. *et al.*, 2017. The sound of cooperation: Musical influences on cooperative behavior. *Journal of Organizational Behavior*, Vol. 38, No. 3, pp. 372–390.

Macinnis, D. J. and Park, C. W., 1991. Oxford University Press. The Differential Role of Characteristics of Music on High- and Low- Involvement Consumers' Processing of Ads. *Journal of Consumer Research*, Vol. 18, No. 2, p. 161.

Michel, A. *et al.*, 2017. Pergamon. Thank you for the music – or not? The effects of in-store music in service settings. *Journal of Retailing and Consumer Services*, Vol. 36, , pp. 21–32.

Niedenthal, P. M. *et al.*, 2001. Taylor & Francis Group . When did her smile drop? Facial mimicry and the influences of emotional state on the detection of change in emotional expression. *Cognition & Emotion*, Vol. 15, No. 6, pp. 853–864.

Peretz, I. *et al.*, 1998. Music and emotion: perceptual determinants, immediacy, and isolation after brain damage. *Cognition*, Vol. 68, No. 2, pp. 111–41.

Schlittmeier, S. J. and Hellbrück, J., 2009. Wiley-Blackwell. Background music as noise abatement in open-plan offices: A laboratory study on performance effects and subjective preferences. *Applied Cognitive Psychology*, Vol. 23, No. 5, pp. 684–697.

Scott, T. J., 1970. Wiley/Blackwell (10.1111). The use of music to reduce hyperactivity in children. *American Journal of Orthopsychiatry*, Vol. 40, No. 4, pp. 677–680.

PREDICTORS OF GAZE AGENCY IN GAZE-CONTROLLED INTERFACES

Nadiya Slobodenyuk
Carleton University, Institute of Cognitive Science, 2201 Dunton Tower, 1125 Colonel by Drive, Ottawa, ON, K1S 5B6, Canada

ABSTRACT

Gaze-controlled interaction is gradually becoming a viable alternative to conventional input modalities beyond the realm of assistive technology. However, very little is known about what makes people experience control over gaze-contingent change in the interface and what makes gaze-controlled interaction feel natural. The sense of control over gaze-contingent interface change is referred to as gaze agency. The experiment presented in this paper explores 1) whether delay between the gaze action onset and display change (i.e. continuous dwell) predicts gaze agency, and 2) whether experience of gaze agency changes depending on whether participants consciously perceive the delay between the gaze action onset and display change or not. Results show that continuous dwell is a significant predictor of gaze agency and that participants experience greater agency when they are not conscious of the delay between the gaze action onset and its causal outcome as opposed to when they perceive the delay or have doubts whether there was a delay.

KEYWORDS

Gaze Agency, Gaze-Controlled Interfaces, Dwell

1. INTRODUCTION

Sense of agency is defined as a subjective experience of being in control of one's own actions that involves the feeling of the correspondence between intentions and actions and the attribution of the sensory outcomes of such intentionally generated actions to self. Gaze agency, also referred to as oculomotor agency, can be defined as an experience of control over gross eye movements and the attribution of change in the interface to one's own intentional gaze. It was previously suggested that considerations regarding the experience of agency in gaze-controlled interaction are paramount to cognitively grounded interface design (Slobodenyuk, 2016). Despite substantial efforts of making gaze interaction natural, little is known about gaze agency.

Research on sense of agency over hand movement shows that sense of agency is dependent upon a wide range of cues which include but are not limited to affective valence of the causal outcome (Wilke, Synofzik, & Lindner, 2012), beliefs about possible causality (e.g., Desantis, Roussel, & Waszak, 2011), and temporal and spatial mismatch between the predicted sensory outcome and the actual sensory outcome (e.g., Asai & Tanno, 2007). The temporal mismatch is experienced when the action outcome is perceived to occur before the onset of the action or later than predicted. However, the exact timing between the action and its causal outcome that leads to sense of agency is being debated. For example, Farrer et al. (2013) reported the full agency experience by their participants under the delays within the range [0, 334 ± 27 ms] and its decrease with longer delays, and loss of agency for delays beyond 707 ms. In Rohde, Scheller, and Ernst's (2014) study, the tolerance was to delays up to around 500 ms.

Temporal delay between the action and its causal outcome in the context of gaze-control interaction is a delay between the onset of gaze action and interface change. This delay is often referred to as continuous dwell and is widely used as a means of command initiation in gaze-controlled interfaces. A wide range of continuous dwell times has been used. For example, Bednarik, Gowases, and Tukiainen (2009) used a relatively long dwell time of 1000 ms. Jacob (1991) has used shorter dwell times of 100, 400, and 600 ms for various commands within one application. The present paper explores whether delay between the gaze action and its causal outcome (i.e. continuous dwell), in fact, predicts the gaze agency and whether conscious perception of such delay modulates gaze agency.

2. METHOD

2.1 Participants

Twenty-six undergraduate students (8 males and 18 females) from the American University of Beirut participated in the study for course credit. All participants had normal or corrected-to-normal vision and had no prior experience with eyetracking or gaze-contingent displays. None have self-reported color blindness.

2.2 Stimuli and Procedure

Participants were seated in front of a Tobii T120 eye tracker monitor (1280 x 1024 pixels). After the standard calibration procedure, they were given a simple demonstration of gaze-contingent display change. Participants saw a red circle following their gaze on the nine-point display and were told that focusing on specific points will switch the display to the next one. The demonstration of interface change due to focusing on the points on the display was necessary to make gaze-contingency salient to participants and to allow them to experience gaze agency.

The experiment was run in Tobii Studio 3.2.0. On each trial, participants saw a fixation cross followed by the stimulus display, and a feedback display with two questions (see Figure 1a). The stimulus display depicted a grid of 48 squares (105 x 105 pixels each). Two squares on each stimulus display were fully colored: one was red and the other one was green. The remaining squares were partially colored. The fully colored squares were the control zones of the display. The two control zones were located on the display as mirror reflections (see Figure 1b). Two types of displays were created with green control zone being more salient or red control zone being more salient. Salience was a function of adjacent partially colored squares being of the same color as the control zone. Participants were randomly assigned to complete either of the two versions. There were 20 possible locations of the salient control zone which, due to the mirror nature of the display, created 20 possible locations of the non-salient control zone in the same display.

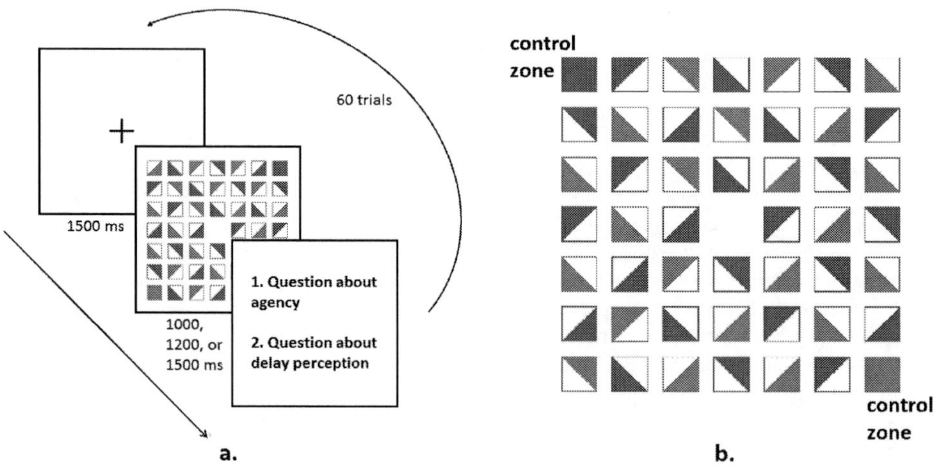

Figure 1. a. Sample stimulus. b. Experimental procedure

Participants were told that the fully colored squares are the control zones and that focusing on one of the control zones will switch the display to a feedback display. They were also told that on some trials the display would be switched to the next one by the computer and not because of their focusing on the control zone. In an actual experiment, participants never caused the display to switch as it was always switched automatically after a pre-set delay of 1000, 1200, or 1500 ms. On the feedback display that followed the stimulus display, participants saw a question prompting them to identify whether they switched the display, or the computer did (i.e. agency question) and another question prompting participants to identify whether there was a delay between their focusing on the control zone and the display change (i.e. delay question). Gaze agency question was answered using a six-point Likert scale, where the extremes were labeled "definitely me - 6" and "definitely not me - 1". Delay question was answered by choosing one of three options: "yes," "maybe," or "no."

3. RESULTS

3.1 Data Processing

Data from 4 participants was removed from the analysis: in one case, only 2% of the eye tracking data was available, in the second case, only 12% of the eye tracking data was available; two other cases were removed, as participants did not follow the instruction and did not focus on either of the control zones. Only cases where participants focused on one of the control zones and kept the focus in the control zone until the display switched were analyzed.

No differences in continuous dwell or gaze agency were found between a group of participants completing the version of the task where red control zone was salient and a group of participants completing the task where green control zone was salient were found. Therefore, data from both groups was analyzed together. The data was averaged across participants for each unique stimulus.

3.2 Delay and Gaze Agency

For the purpose of this analysis, gaze agency was reverse coded with higher gaze agency rating indicating greater agency loss. A simple linear regression was then carried out to determine whether delay between the gaze action onset and its causal outcome is a significant predictor of gaze agency. Average delay between the gaze action onset and its causal outcome statistically significantly predicted agency, $F(1, 58) = 45.865$, $p < .001$. Participant's agency loss increased with an increase in delay between the gaze action onset and its causal outcome. Average delay between the gaze action onset and its causal outcome accounted for 44.2% of the variation in gaze agency with adjusted R^2=43.2% which is indicative of the substantial effect size according to Cohen (1988).

3.3 Perception of Delay and Gaze Agency

A Kruskal-Wallis H test was carried out to determine if there were differences in agency scores between responses associated with cases where participants 1) perceived the delay between the gaze action onset (fixation on the control zone) and the causal outcome (display change), 2) did not perceive the delay, or 3) were unsure whether there was a delay or not. Median agency scores were statistically significantly different between groups, $H(2) = 91.244$, $p < .001$. Agency scores were the highest when participants did not perceive the delay (*Mdn* = 5.5), lower when they were unsure whether there was a delay (*Mdn* = 4.00) and lowest when participants perceived the delay (*Mdn* = 2.53). Pairwise comparisons using Dunn's (1964) procedure with a Bonferroni correction for multiple comparisons showed that there was a statistically significant difference between all three groups with $p < .001$.

4. CONCLUSION

The present paper explored 1) whether delay between the gaze action onset and display change (i.e. continuous dwell) predicts gaze agency, and 2) whether experience of gaze agency changes depending on whether participants consciously perceive the delay between the gaze action onset and display change or not. The results of the study show that delay between the onset of the gaze action and its causal outcome is a significant predictor of gaze agency. With an increase in delay participants experienced greater gaze agency loss. The analysis also showed that participants experienced significantly greater gaze agency when they did not perceive the delay in comparison to cases when they perceived the delay or had doubts whether there was a delay. These findings should be viewed as applied, as they suggest that the decision to use a continuous dwell of a specific duration for command initiation is directly related to whether participants will experience that they are in control of the display change or not. This initial investigation will be extended to outline the recommendations as to specific delays between the gaze action and its causal outcome that allow for the optimal experience of control in gaze-contingent displays.

REFERENCES

Asai, T., and Tanno, Y., 2007. The Relationship Between the Sense of Self-Agency and Schizotypal Personality Traits. *Journal of Motor Behavior*, Vol. 39, No. 3, pp 162–168.

Bednarik, R. et al., 2009. Gaze interaction enhances problem solving: Effects of dwell-time based, gaze-augmented, and mouse interaction on problem-solving strategies and user experience. *Journal of Eye Movement Research*, Vol. 3, pp 1–10.

Desantis, A. et al., 2011. On the influence of causal beliefs on the feeling of agency. *Consciousness and Cognition*, Vol. 20, pp 1211–1220.

Farrer, C. et al., 2013. The time windows of the sense of agency. *Consciousness and Cognition*, Vol. 22, No. 4, pp 1431-1441.

Jacob, R. J. K., 1991. The use of eye movements in human computer interaction techniques: What you look at is what you get. *ACM Transactions on Information Systems*, Vol. 9, No. 3, pp 152–169.

Rohde, M. et al., 2014. Effects can precede their cause in the sense of agency. *Neuropsychologia*, Vol. 65, pp 191-196.

Slobodenyuk, N., 2016. Towards cognitively grounded gaze-controlled interfaces. *Personal and Ubiquitous Computing*, Vol. 20, pp 1035–1047.

Wilke, C. et al., 2012. The valence of action outcomes modulates the perception of one's actions. *Consciousness and Cognition*, Vol. 21, pp 18–29.

TEXTURE REMAPPING AND MORPHING INTEGRATED WITH SPHERICAL MESH PARAMETERIZATION

Sabin Timalsena and Chao Peng
Department of Computer Science, University of Alabama in Huntsville, USA
301 Sparkman Drive, Huntsville, AL, USA 35899

ABSTRACT

The animation of character morphing is commonly used as a special effect in video games and movies. While existing mesh parameterization methods create smooth morphing effects for meshes, there is a lack of techniques to preserve the textures of meshes during mesh morphing. In this work, we present a novel method which morphs textures and is seamlessly integrated with the methods of spherical mesh parameterization, remeshing and mesh morphing.

KEYWORDS

Morphing, Texture Remapping, Mesh Parameterization

1. INTRODUCTION

Morphing is a mesh deformation technique that mimics an organic phenomenon in which an organism smoothly changes its shape over time. In computer graphics, morphing is used as a special effect in order to smoothly transform a virtual character from one form to another. Morphing is also used in games to allow players to customize the character by blending between several available 3D models.

The use of *blendshapes* (Lewis et al, 2014) is a popular deformation technique, in which a group of meshes are linearly combined. This has been extensively used in facial animations, where different expressions, each represented by a separate mesh, are blended together. However, blendshapes require the input meshes to be isomorphic (e.g., they must have a bijective vertex and triangle correspondence), and the vertices must be indexed consistently as well. For non-isomorphic meshes, Methods of planar parameterization (e.g., Kraevoy and Sheffer, 2004, Sorkine et al, 2002, and Aigerman et al, 2014) and spherical parameterization (e.g., Praun and Hoppe, 2003; Peng and Timalsena, 2016) have been proposed to transform meshes into parametric representations so that the features of the meshes can be lined up when the parameterizations are overlaid. In a planar parameterization, discontinuities may be introduced because the input mesh is cut and unfolded into flat pieces. Such discontinuities create limitations in morphing because interpolation of mesh properties cannot be done across the boundaries of the pieces. In contrast, cutting is not needed in a spherical parameterization. The recent work has demonstrated the success of mesh morphing with spherical parameterizations, where mesh features are warped and aligned in the spherical domain.

While existing parameterization methods create smooth transitions for meshes, textures are not well preserved during the animation of morphing. In this work, we add morphing effects for textures by extending the spherical parameterization method presented by Peng and Timalsena (2016). We present a texture remapping method which is seamlessly integrated with the methods of parameterization, remeshing and mesh morphing.

2. RELATED WORK

We discuss a few existing morphing methods that use mesh parameterizations. Alexa (2002) discussed various techniques and underlying problems of topology merging and morphing, focusing on relaxation based parameterization. Alexa (2002) also discussed possible alternative approaches for moving vertices during morphing compared to the traditional linear interpolation between target positions. Alexa's (2000) approach supported feature alignments, but it did not guarantee that features will be completely matched; features are moved on the spherical parameterization only to the extent that does not cause any triangle folds. Lee et al. (1999) supported mesh morphing with feature alignments; and the feature alignments in their case are done during the parameterization. The key idea is to parameterize both input meshes onto a common base domain, which is a very coarse mesh constructed to include the chosen feature points. After the parameterization, they constructed a metamesh by overlapping the parametric representations of the meshes and morph between them. Kraevoy and Sheffer (2004) adopted a similar parameterization method but used an adaptive method for remeshing, which results in a smaller number of vertices and triangles. Mocanu and Zaharia (2012) and Zhang (2011) presented the methods to support feature aligned mesh morphing. They used an adaptive subdivision method for remeshing and avoided having a large number of vertices and triangles after remeshing. Mocanu and Zaharia (2012) aligned features by deforming the parametric representations of the meshes according to a set of user-specified feature points, whereas Zhang (2011) introduced the notion of "feature regions" instead of feature points and focused on the alignment of small regions in the mesh instead of particular points.

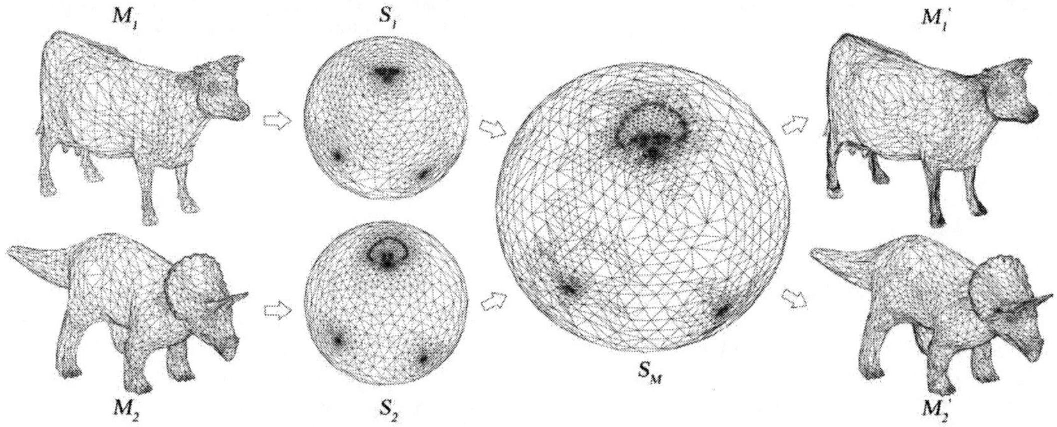

Figure 1. The example showing spherical parameterization and remeshing

Recently, Peng and Timalsena (2016) presented a spherical parameterization method to smoothly morph arbitrary genus-zero meshes. Given user-specified control points, the features of the meshes are aligned in the spherical domain to create surface correspondence. Then, a *supermesh* is generated after the process of subdivision. Here we briefly describe their spherical parameterization method. Figure 1 shows an example using Peng and Timalsena's (2016) method. Let's denote M_1 and M_2 as two input meshes. They are simplified to a tetrahedron by collapsing edges repeatedly in favor of removing high-curvature regions as early as possible. A tetrahedron is always a valid spherical embedding. Then, the vertices removed during edge-collapsing are inserted back iteratively into the spherical domain. A later removed vertex is inserted earlier and connects to the neighbor vertices of its 1-ring edge loop (local insertion). After the vertex insertion, spherical representations of M_1 and M_2 are obtained, which are denoted as S_1 and S_2, respectively. After that, a two-step feature alignment method is applied. The first step uses the least-squares rotation (Arun et al, 1987) to bring user-specified control points on S_1 and S_2 closer. The second step uses the radial basis function (RBF) (Mocanu and Zaharia, 2012) to deform and warp two spheres in order to exactly align the control points. Then, a supermesh denoted as S_M can be generated. To build S_M, the process starts with a triangulated octahedron embedded in a unit sphere. The vertices in S_1 and S_2 are overlaid on this unit sphere, and the triangles on the octahedron are progressively subdivided until only one vertex is inside a triangle. As a result, S_M is a semi-regular spherical mesh which can produce 3D shapes equivalent to M_1 and M_2. Here, M_1' is denoted as the equivalent shape of M_1 produced from S_M; and M_2' is the equivalent shape of M_2 produced from S_M. Finally, a morph is animated by linearly interpolating the positions of vertices between M_1' and M_2'.

3. TEXTURE MORPHING

Traditional texture mapping is a process of 3D to 2D parameterization, where each triangle in the mesh is assigned to use the color values from a patch on a 2D image. Texture mapping involves cutting the mesh along certain mesh edges, so texture seams are introduced to the mesh, and they still exist when the mesh is spherically parameterized. It is therefore not possible to directly assign texture coordinates or interpolated coordinates to the vertices of M_1' and M_2' unless we can make sure that there are no edges in S_M across texture seams of S_1 or S_2. In this work, we present a novel method which generates new texture charts without seams except at the boundaries of the 2D texture. This is done by assigning new texture coordinates to the vertices in S_M (which are carried over to M_1' and M_2') solely without regard to how the textures are originally mapped to the meshes. Section 3.1 explains the definitions of texture mapping and texture coordinates. Section 3.2 presents the details of our novel method for texture remapping and morphing.

3.1 Texture Mapping and Limitations on Interpolation

Associated to each triangle is a set of three pairs of texture coordinates (or UV coordinates), which specify where the three vertices of the triangle should be mapped to in the 2D texture chart. 3D artists generate such texture charts and may decide to create denser texture mappings in certain areas of the mesh compared to others (by making some patches proportionally larger than others). Figure 2 shows the texture charts for the cow and triceratops models. The bright lines on the cow and the triceratops indicate where the texture seams are. The resolution of the texture for the cow is 1024×1024 pixels, whereas the one for the triceratops is 512×512 pixels.

Figure 2. Textures for cow and triceratops meshes

It is possible that a vertex is on a texture seam, so it has to be split and mapped to multiple locations in the texture chart. The texture is not a continuous bijective map. Two adjacent triangles in the mesh may be mapped to two disparate locations in the texture chart. Also, there may be regions in the texture chart to which no triangle is mapped. We cannot interpolate texture coordinates across texture seams. We can only interpolate them within a patch, which associates to a group of connected triangles. Given a supermesh as described in Section 2, many edges of the supermesh created from the subdivision process cross the texture seams of M_1 and M_2, so the texture coordinates and texture layouts inherited from the original meshes of M_1 and M_2 cannot be directly used for M_1' and M_2'.

3.2 Remapping and Morphing

We generate new texture coordinates and correspondingly rearranged textures for M_1' and M_2'. We adopt an approach similar to Praun and Hoppe's (2003) approach to flatten the textures after applying them to S_1 and S_2.

We map the feature aligned S_1 and S_2 onto regular octahedrons embedded in a unit sphere. The octahedrons are then mapped to squares after unfolding them as shown in Figure 3. Note that the textures on S_1, S_2 and octahedrons are the original textures of M_1 and M_2, and they are associated with the original texture coordinates of M_1 and M_2. By doing this, we can effectively map the original input meshes M_1 and M_2 bijectively to squares, and use these square maps as new textures for M_1' and M_2', respectively. The square maps are then rasterized into pixels (we used the resolution of 1024×1024) to produce the actual color values for the new texture charts. Besides being bijective and seamless (except at octahedron's cutting borders), these new textures have the following properties:

1. Aligned features on S_1 and S_2 are preserved in square parameterizations after unfolding.
2. New texture coordinates of the vertices of M_1' and M_2' are determined solely by their parametric position on the sphere (e.g., vertex positions in S_M). This means the corresponding vertices of M_1' and M_2' can use an identical pair of new texture coordinates.

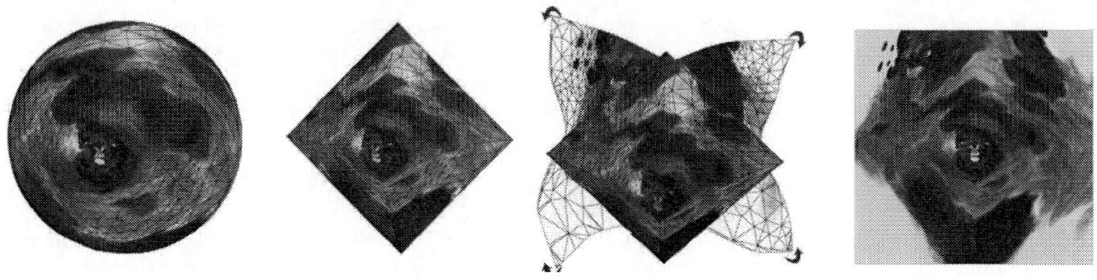

Figure 3. Texture remapping example for the cow

The same unfolding operation for S_1 and S_2 is also applied to the supermesh S_M, so that it is mapped to a square in the XY plane. As a result, the vertices of S_M can acquire 2D coordinates in the square. Those 2D coordinates are normalized to the range of [0,1] along both axes, and then become texture coordinates for the new textures. Note that M_1' and M_2' obtain the same texture coordinates because M_1' and M_2' are produced from the same supermesh S_M.

Let's see an example: assuming the octahedron is opened from the "back" vertex at *(0, 0, 1)*, prior to unfolding, the vertices that coincide with the x = 0 and y = 0 planes and fall behind the z = 0 plane must be split into two distinct vertices (they constitute the edges that map to the borders of the square). The back vertex from which the octahedron is opened is mapped to all four corners of the square. Also, prior to unfolding S_1 and S_2, they need to be cut along the x = 0, y = 0 and z = 0 planes to make sure there are edges to map onto the square's borders.

The texture coordinates calculated above are used to fetch color values from the new texture charts during the runtime. The color values are combined with alpha values for blending, so that the morphed texture fades between the two textures as the shape of the mesh is being morphed. Figure 4 shows the result of morphing which integrates with our texture morphing method.

Figure 4. Texture morphing example between cow and triceratops

4. CONCLUSION

In this work, we have presented a novel method to morph textures based on the technique of spherical parameterization. It is seamlessly integrated with the methods of spherical mesh parameterization, remeshing and mesh morphing. Our method blends the textures of the input meshes during mesh morphing, so it enhances the visual appearance of the morphing animation. The new texture maps are generated by rasterizing the original textures on unfolded octahedrons. Parts of the original textures might be squeezed to a small region in the new texture, which may lead to the issue of losing image quality. Thus, it is practically necessary to increase the resolution when rasterizing for new textures.

ACKNOWLEDGEMENT

This work was partially supported by the NSF grant, CNS1464323. We gratefully thank anonymous reviewers for their comments.

REFERENCES

Aigerman, N., Poranne, R. and Lipman, Y., 2014. Lifted Bijections for Low Distortion Surface Mappings. In *ACM Transactions on Graphics (TOG)*, Vol. 33, Issue 4, Article 69.

Alexa, M., 2002. Recent Advances in Mesh Morphing. *Computer Graphics Forum*, Vol. 21, Issue 2, pp.173–198.

Alexa, M., 2000. Merging Polyhedral Shapes with Scattered Features. *In The Visual Computer*, Vol. 16, Issue 1, pp. 26–37.

Arun, K. S., Huang, T. S. and Blostein, S. D., 1987. Least-Squares Fitting of Two 3D Point Sets. *IEEE Transactions on Pattern Analysis and Machine Intelligence*, Vol. 9, Issue, 5, pp. 698–700.

Kraevoy, V. and Sheffer, A., 2004. Cross-Parameterization and Compatible Remeshing of 3D Models. *In ACM Transactions on Graphics (TOG)*, Vol. 23, Issue 3, pp. 861–869.

Lee, W. F., Dobkin, D., Sweldens, W. and Schroder, P., 1999. Multiresolution Mesh Morphing. *In Proceedings of the 26th Annual Conference on Computer Graphics and Interactive Techniques (SIGGRAPH '99)*. Los Angeles, CA, USA, pp. 343–350.

Lewis, J. P., Anjyo, K., Rhee, T., Zhang, M., Pighin, F. and Deng, Z., 2014. Practice and Theory of Blendshape Facial Models. *In Eurographics (State of the Art Reports)*.

Mocanu, B. and Zaharia, T., 2012. A Complete Framework for 3D Mesh Morphing. *In Proceedings of the 11th ACM SIGGRAPH International Conference on Virtual-Reality Continuum and Its Applications in Industry (VRCAI '12)*., Singapore, Singapore, pp. 161–170.

Peng, C. and Timalsena, S., 2016. Fast Mapping and Morphing for Genus-Zero Meshes with Cross Spherical Parameterization. *In Computers & Graphics (C&G)*, Vol. 59, pp107-118.

Praun, E. and Hoppe, H., 2003. Spherical Parametrization and Remeshing. *In ACM Transactions on Graphics*, Vol. 22, Issue 3, pp. 340–349.

Sorkine, O., Cohen-Or, D., Goldenthal, R. and Lischinski, D., 2002. Bounded-Distortion Piecewise Mesh Parameterization. *In Proceedings of the IEEE Conference on Visualization (VIS'02)*. Washington, DC, USA, pp. 355–362.

Zhang, R., 2011. 3D Mesh Metamorphosis from Spherical Parameterization for Conceptual Design. *Iowa State University*, PhD thesis.

EVALUATING GAMES: A SECOND STAGE OF THE GAME DEVELOPMENT PROCESS

Ruth Torres Castillo and Carolyn Raynor
New Mexico State University, USA

ABSTRACT

Developing an educational game is a complex process with additional challenges to those found in other types of game development. In educational game development, a team is usually necessary to address the educational goals of the game, the content needed, and the applications of learning scientists and research in addition to multimedia design specialists. This paper shares a framework used for game review as a second stage of our research group's four-stage game development process. The process for review was used by an interdisciplinary educational game design team that evaluated existing games to inform the design and development of an early algebra game. The framework offers a structured means for assessing existing games and identifying how to incorporate missing elements of current games into our latest game design work.

KEYWORDS

Game design, Gamification, Educational Game Design, Game Design Models, Review Framework

1. INTRODUCTION

Game review is the second stage of our learning games lab's four-stage game design process. In terms of brief context, stage one of game design consists of a research study identifying the conceptual gaps in early algebra among U.S. students in grades 3-8. The results of this conceptual gap study informed the conceptual development of game-based mathematics learning materials. Once the team understands deeply the conceptual gaps students have in grades 3-8 mathematics through both an analysis of test data and many hours of observation in classrooms, the team moves on to Stage two. In this stage, research assistants from education, computer science, and the game lab complete a systematic game review identifying and understanding the strengths, weaknesses, and gaps in existing mathematics learning games. Stage three of game design is a ten-step digital design framework that utilizes the results of the stage one conceptual gap study and the second phase of game review to design innovative constructivist mathematics learning games and animations. Stage four of game design builds upon the results of the stage two game review and the extensive formative testing of games in Stage 3 to design appropriate supplemental materials and assessment tools to extend the learning initially experienced in the playing of the games. This paper focuses exclusively on stage two of the game design process. For details on the stage one conceptual gaps study, see Wiburg and Raynor (forthcoming).

Game review is often a way to assess games for use in a classroom, curate a list of educational games, or identify what games are available in a content area for a certain age group. These types of game reviews revolve around the identification of existing games for specific use, in this case for educational learning purposes. However, it is also valuable to review games as a means of identifying gaps in educational content and pedagogical usefulness in existing games. Moreover, when this type of review process is performed collaboratively as part of the design process, it engages the design team in a deeper level of pedagogical understanding about the content and design of existing games.

Interdisciplinary teams are important in designing effective learning games that incorporate learning objectives, content knowledge, and pedagogy. Effective educational game design teams constitute diverse backgrounds and disciplines (Chamberlin et al, 2012). Akin to being "well-read", it is important that all team members be "well-played". This analogy refers to game literacy, of having a diverse knowledge and experience of playing games (Davidson, 2009). Further, the collaborative design process unifies the team in articulating a shared vision for addressing game content, identifying valuable game mechanics, and deciding the best approaches for how a game should operate. Therefore, it is important to distinguish between types of game review; those that evaluate games for a given audience versus those that have the potential to inform future game design. Design teams that review games with a design lens a) look at overall game quality; b) identify content or pedagogical gaps; c) continually reframe problems; d) regularly question underlying assumptions; and e) establish a unique framework to guide game design.

Game review was used in the second stage of game design of our learning games lab. As part of the design process, the team reviewed learning games with the following shared elements: content (i.e., pre-algebra, algebra, patterns, ratios, properties, functions, expressions, equations); target audience (students in grades 4–7); and pedagogical approach (i.e., inquiry-based, problem solving, drill or practice).

2. BACKGROUND

The interdisciplinary game design team referred to in this study consists of a non-profit, educational game studio located in the Southwestern region of the United States specializing in developing early algebra learning games. The game design team is currently designing a new suite of games to enhance pre-algebra learning. The use of inquiry, especially inquiry-based learning (Edelson, 2001), constructivist principles, and knowledge building (Scardamalia and Bereiter, 2008) are at the core of the design team's principles. The affordances of games for learning is connected to what we know about how people learn (Bransford et al, 2000) and how teachers can stimulate that learning through inquiry-based practices (Gonzalez, 2013; Edelson, 2001). In terms of education, 'affordance' describes the relationship between the attributes of a digitally-enhanced learning environment and the particular learning needs and strengths of students (Kirschener, 2002). The affordances of technology can be used to assist different approaches to teaching and learning (Conole & Dyke 2004).

The guiding conceptual framework for the entire design team is based upon the collective years of teaching, research experience, and knowledge of the team. This conceptual framework encompasses a set of core beliefs: 1) All kids can succeed in mathematics if provided with the appropriate learning opportunities; 2) The power of technology and learning design can address the conceptual gaps we see; and 3) The power of research helps us to understand what kids do and do not know and why they do not know math concepts, as well as how well they are learning with the developing games.

The primary goal of the design team is to develop products using innovative design and pedagogical strategies to build in-depth knowledge of specific content. Keeping the principle that knowledge should be constructed by the learner rather than transmitted, the design team develops games in which mathematical concepts are learned as a natural means to playing and winning the game. A fundamental design scheme of the team is to design game-based learning materials resting on documented conceptual learning gaps in mathematical content and pedagogy, as well as to add supplementary problems that deepen the knowledge initially gained by playing the game.

2.1 Game Design and Review Models

The goal of successful game design is the facilitation of meaningful play, which is achieved by creating gameplay that enables discernible and integrated interaction by the player (Salen and Zimmerman, 2004). Critical to the design process is contributing new opportunities to learn content. Thus, educational game designers require an understanding of how to create games that enable interaction, provide ongoing feedback, grab and sustain attention, and have appropriate levels of challenge (Gee, 2003; Malone, 1981; Paras, 2005; Schell, 2014). Research in game development includes various models of educational game design, including: Learning Games Design Model (LGDM) (Chamberlin et al, 2012); Exploratory Learning Model (ELM) (De Freitas and Neumann, 2009); Four Dimensional Framework (4DF) (De Freitas and Oliver, 2006; Groff et al, 2015); E-Leadership and Soft Skills Educational Games Design model (ELESS) (De Freitas and Routledge, 2013); Affective Walkthrough Model (Dormann and Biddle, 2008); Relevance Embedding Translation Adaptation Immersion and Naturalization Model (RETAIN) (Gunter et al, 2008); Flow Experience Framework (Kiili et al, 2012); and Evidence-Centered Design (ECD) (Mislevy and Haertel, 2006).

Various game design models also include analytical game review in their design process. Such frameworks include MEEGA (Savi and Ulbricht, 2008), PLEX (Lucero et al, 2014), and GameFlow (Sweetser and Wyeth, 2005). For the MEEGA framework, the stated objectives of a software are compared to the experience of the learner and perceptions of learning (Petri et al, 2016). Moreover, the PLEX framework is designed to evaluate general games and categorizes playful experiences based on previous theoretical work on pleasure, game experiences, emotions, elements of play, and the motivations of why people gameplay. Further, the GameFlow model consists of eight elements (concentration, challenge, skills, controls, clear goals, feedback, immersion, and social interaction) which are used to review and understand how players achieve enjoyment in games. However, glaringly absent in each of these review models are the pedagogical motivations behind the game design. Thus, game development teams looking at pedagogy in games may need different approaches to support their design goals. For example, the review process for math games should identify both pedagogical and content gaps, as well as game quality. Further, while many of these game design models contain game review as part of their design process, many lack a specified protocol on how to conduct the game review. It is this gap that our second stage of game development, game review, aims to bridge.

2.2 Game Review Framework

Stage two of our game development, game review, begins once the learning goals and content area of the game under development have been identified (in stage one of game development). During stage two, game review, a five-member interdisciplinary team conducts a review process of 24 games. The team consists of mathematicians, math educators, educational researchers, learning scientists and game developers. Each team member identified a chosen criteria to review and narrowed the breadth of games down to a short list of top-rated games. Thereon, these top-rated games were evaluated jointly as a team. What follows is the five-step process involved in the stage two game review.

Step 1: Establish criteria. Building from the stage one conceptual gaps study, the team operationalizes the criteria to examine within each game to evaluate against the proposed game's learning goals. Criteria can be established based on the learning objectives, gameplay objectives, or goals of the game. The establishment of criteria is a milepost and serves to pinpoint content and pedagogical gaps that new game development should address.

Step 2: Identify existing games. The next step is to identify games and apps that introduce or teach equivalent content area of the proposed game (pre-algebra), utilize a similar learning pedagogy (constructivist, inquiry-based, knowledge-building), and/or have similar game mechanics as the proposed game.

Step 3: Play identified games/measure criteria. Each team member plays and rates the identified games according to the specified criteria with a rubric. Because the collection of games is likely large, this is a distributed task, with each team member delegated to play certain games. Ideally, multiple team members play each game; however, depending on the size of the corpus and team, this may not always be feasible.

Step 4: Refine game selection. The team refines the game selection, focusing on the games best fitting the identified criteria. The team then concentrates on the highest-rated games. At this stage, all team members play a subset of the top-rated games.

Step 5: Team review of top-rated games. Once the top-rated games have been played by each team member, the team engages in a group discussion. This provides the team opportunity to deeply discuss the features of selected games and how they relate to the proposed game under development.

3. RESULTS

While each of the steps in stage two of game design are important, steps one and five yielded particular new insights into the game development process. In step one, the design team had established areas for criteria in the content area of pre-algebra (based upon results of stage one of game development, see above). Criteria identified included games: a) teaching the same content as the proposed games (pre-algebra, algebra, patterns, properties, functions, expressions and equations), b) having the same pedagogical approach (inquiry-based learning reflecting a constructivist framework), and c) with mechanics lending themselves to learning (exploration versus simple practice). Incorporating the interdisciplinary team into the game review process provided the opportunity to integrate three core lenses (content, pedagogy, and game mechanics) into the second stage of game development. Derived from the team's guiding conceptual framework (see above), seven principles of game characteristics demonstrating a connection to math learning were identified. These seven principles were used as evaluation criteria and included: a) an inquiry-based approach to learning; b) embedded vocabulary; c) multiple representations of numbers and operations; d) easy entry to play, high ceiling to mastery; e) limited "instruction"; f) immediate and helpful feedback; and g) resources to expand learning from game to other learning environments.

4. DISCUSSION

The game review informed the team of the current state of existing algebra learning games. The review revealed differences between the evaluated games and the team's desired constructivist approach, particularly in areas related to math pedagogy. These differences correspond to the seven principles of game characteristics (refer to *a-g* above): 1) the game did not offer the player enough exposure to math vocabulary (*b*); 2) many games lacked multiple representations, using simple text representations of numbers and operations without a visualization (*c*); 3) games did not provide problems that could be solved in multiple ways, requiring players to accomplish tasks in exactly one specific way (*c*); 4) the game consisted of a typical drill and practice experience (*a*); 5) the game used typical pedagogical approaches, offering more of a quiz and reward structure (*a*); and 6) very few games gave clear feedback (*f*). In fact, only one of the 24 games introduced the player to concepts with an inquiry-based approach to learning.

The development team has been building and reviewing educational games for more than 20 years. However, this is the first time it has used a specific design process for the review of games. The implementation and proper documentation of the game review framework assisted in using a formal process for identifying and reviewing games and applying that review as a basis for discussion in the design process. The team found that when content experts, game designers, and educators were all involved in reviewing games, the resulting group discussion produced richer and diverse perspectives on a game's value.

Certain limitations were found by focusing this research article on stage two's game review process. Expressly, stage two is part of an interconnected four-stage game design process, and only one part of the game design process was examined in this review. Thus, the game design team did not have the opportunity to study what happens after stage two. Currently, the game design process has advanced, and the design team is in stage four of game design, developing supplemental materials to bridge gameplay to classroom instruction. Therefore, future research articles will focus on the unified four-stage process of game design.

5. CONCLUSION

Stage two's game review framework as an early exploration of algebra games yielded two primary benefits for the game design team. First, the curation of content and information was useful for the game development. The second benefit was a formalized process for reviewing games in terms of content, pedagogy, and game mechanics gaps. For game designers, it was beneficial to review the framework and see gaps among existing games. The process also helped new project members understand how games meet the design team's goals in diverse ways. Thereupon, the game review framework served as an effective second stage in the game development process for this multidisciplinary research team of game designers.

ACKNOWLEDGEMENT

This material is based upon work supported by the National Science Foundation under Grant #1503507. Any opinions, findings, and conclusions or recommendations expressed in this material are those of the author(s) and do not necessarily reflect the views of the National Science Foundation.

REFERENCES

Bransford, J.D. et al, 2000. *How People Learn* (Expanded ed.). National Academy, Washington, USA.

Chamberlin, B. et al, 2012. The learning games design model: Immersion, Collaboration, and Outcomes-Driven Development. *International Journal of Game-Based Learning (IJGBL)*, Vol. 2, No. 3,pp 87-110.

Conole, G. and Dyke, M, 2004. What are the Affordances of Information and Communication Technologies? *ALT-J,* Vol. 2, No. 2,pp. 113–124.

Davidson, D. (Ed.), 2009. *Well Played 1.0: Video Games, Value and Learning*. Lulu.com.

De Freitas, S. and Neumann, T., 2009. The Use of 'Exploratory Learning' for Supporting Immersive Learning in Virtual Environments. *Computers & Education*, Vol. 52, No. 2,pp 343-352.

De Freitas, S. and Oliver, M., 2006. How Can Exploratory Learning with Games and Simulations within the Curriculum be Most Effectively Evaluated?. *Computers & Education*, Vol. 46, No. 3,pp 249-264.

De Freitas, S. and Routledge, H., 2013. Designing Leadership and Soft skills in Educational Games: The E-Leadership and Soft Skills Educational Games Design Model (ELESS). *British Journal of Educational Technology*, Vol. 44, No. 6,pp 951-968.

Dormann, C. and Biddle, R., 2008. Understanding Game Design for Affective Learning. *Proceedings of the 2008 Conference on Future Play: Research, Play, Share*. ACM, pp. 41-48.

Edelson, D.C., 2001. Learning-for-Use: A Framework for the Design of Technology-Supported Inquiry Activities. *Journal of Research in Science Teaching*, Vol. 38, No. 3,pp 355-385.

Gee, J.P., 2003. What Video Games Have to Teach Us about Learning and Literacy. *Computers in Entertainment (CIE)*, Vol. 1, No. 1,pp 20.

Gonzalez, J.J., 2013. My Journey with Inquiry-Based Learning. *Journal on Excellence in College Teaching*, Vol. 24, No. 2.

Groff, J. et al, 2015. *Better Learning in Games: A Balanced Design Lens for a New Generation of Learning Games.* MIT Press, Cambridge, USA.

Gunter, G.A. et al, 2008. Taking Educational Games Seriously: Using the RETAIN Model to Design Endogenous Fantasy into Standalone Educational Games. *Educational Technology Research and Development*, Vol 56, No. 5-6,pp 511-537.

Kiili, K. et al, 2012. The Design Principles for Flow Experience in Educational Games. *Procedia Computer Science*, Vol. 15,pp 78-91.

Kirschner, P.A., 2002. Can We Support CSCL? Educational, Social and Technological Affordances for Learning. In P.A. Kirschner (Ed.), *Three Worlds of CSCL: Can We Support CSCL?* (pp. 7–47). Heerlen, The Netherlands, Open University of the Netherlands.

Lucero, A. et al, 2014. Playful or Gameful?: Creating Delightful User Experiences. *Interactions*, Vol. 21, No. 3,pp 34-39.

Malone, T.W., 1981. Toward a Theory of Intrinsically Motivating Instruction. *Cognitive Science*, Vol. 5, No. 4, pp 333-369.

Mislevy, R.J. and Haertel, G.D., 2006. Implications of Evidence-Centered Design for Educational Testing. *Educational Measurement: Issues and Practice*, Vol. 25, No. 4,pp 6-20.

Paras, B., 2005. Game, Motivation, and Effective Learning: An Integrated Model for Educational Game Design. Retrieved from https://pdfs.semanticscholar.org/3321/1b38d6fdf65f2c5a497d87512248a02e3ee9.pdf

Petri, G. et al, 2016. MEEGA+: An Evolution of a Model for the Evaluation of Educational Games. *INCoD/GQS*, Vol. 3.

Salen, K. and Zimmerman, E., 2004. *Rules of Play: Game Design Fundamentals.* MIT Press, Boston, USA.

Savi, R. and Ulbricht, V.R., 2008. Educational Games: Benefits and Challenges. *Revista Novas Tecnologias na Educação–Renote*, Vol. 6.

Scardamalia, M. and Bereiter, C., 2008. Pedagogical Biases in Educational Technologies. *Educational Technology,* pp 3-11.

Schell, J., 2014. *The Art of Game Design: A Book of Lenses.* AK Peters/CRC Press.

Sweetser, P. and Wyeth, P., 2005. GameFlow: A Model for Evaluating Player Enjoyment in Games. *Computers in Entertainment (CIE)*, Vol. 3, No. 3,pp 3.

Wiburg, K. and Raynor, C., forthcoming. Conceptual Gaps in Mathematics as a Research Base for a Successful Game-Based Mathematics Intervention. *EdMedia: World Conference on Educational Media and Technology.* Association for the Advancement of Computing in Education (AACE).

Zimmerman, J. et al, 2007. Research through Design as a Method for Interaction Design Research in HCI. *Proceedings of the SIGCHI Conference on Human Factors in Computing Systems*. ACM, pp. 493-502.

SURVEYING GAMES WITH A COMBINED MODEL OF IMMERSION AND FLOW

Ehm Kannegieser[1], Daniel Atorf[1] and Josua Meier[2]
[1]*Fraunhofer Institute of Optronics, System Technologies and Image Exploitation, Fraunhoferstraße. 1, 76131, Karlsruhe, Germany*
[2]*Karlsruhe Institute of Technology, Kaiserstraße. 12, 76131, Karlsruhe, Germany*

ABSTRACT

Detecting flow in games is key for successful adaptation processes. Until now, the method of choice to measure flow in games, is the usage of questionnaires. Because of the shortcomings of this method, the ultimate goal is, to establish an alternative measuring method through correlations of physiological sensor data. Beforehand the enhancement of the theoretical model of flow with the more fine-grained model of immersion is introduced. A unified flow/immersion model is proposed to allow a more detailed mapping of flow depth. In conclusion a way to evaluate the unified model is presented and a perspective towards preliminary test runs and future data recordings is given.

KEYWORDS

Flow, Immersion, Measurement

1. INTRODUCTION

Digital game based learning concepts should enable the player to fully immerse into a fictional world and story. All learning objectives should be integrated and not abstracted from real life, making the game feel like an entertainment title, but implicitly allowing to accomplish learning objectives with high learning motivation, resulting in better and sustainable learning outcome (Deci&Ryan, 1985; Krapp, 2009).

The ability to measure flow (Atorf et al., 2016), would provide a valuable input to adaptation processes, that try to improve the attractiveness of the game, regarding its potential of reaching a positive intrinsic motivational effect. Questionnaires, the standard method of flow evaluation until now (Nordin et al., 2014), only provide the means to answer whether a flow state is reached or not. A more fine-grained analysis of player experience would enable earlier adaptation and thus improving the quality of the game.

The method explained in this paper expands upon the flow model (Csikszentmihalyi, 1991), by adding Cairns' definition of immersion (Cairns et al., 2006). Cairns establishes immersion as a three-level construct, which is assumed as precondition for reaching the state of maximized intrinsic motivation (Figure 1). It is proposed that a clear relationship between both immersion and flow can be established and linked into one unified model, thus improving the ability to detect flow and its precursors.

If the thesis of the combined model is correct, the incorporated immersion questionnaires will tend towards total immersion during identified phases of flow.

2. CONSIDERING A COMBINED MODEL OF FLOW AND IMMERSION

Cairns' three levels of immersion are elicited by the immersion questionnaire, published by Cheng (Cheng, 2015). While flow is considered the psychology of optimal experience, immersion is known as the psychology of sub-optimal experience (Cairns et al., 2006). As such, these concepts appear to be linked by definition. However, the exact nature of this link is still unclear. Georgiou et al. define flow as part of the most extreme state of immersion, which puts it into the total immersion category of Cairns' model (Georgiou, 2017).

Existing methods used to elicit flow, focus on questionnaires. These questionnaires are based on the definition of immersion employed in these studies. Csikszentmihalyi described flow as the optimal experience of an action (Csikszentmihalyi, 1991), as a state of extreme focus on an activity. Flow is achieved, when the individual becomes engrossed in the activity to a point, where their surroundings no longer appear relevant. Csikszentmihalyi considers this the optimal experience, the optimal way to enjoy an action. He links this with the idea of an autotelic personality, a personality that performs actions for the enjoyment derived by the action itself, instead of external gains. This is special because it means that enjoyment can even be derived from work and other taxing activities. It is achieved when a balance between challenge and skill of the subject is struck.

The problem when defining immersion is, that immersion is used to refer to two different things known as spatial immersion and emotional immersion. The definition of spatial immersion is synonymous with the definition of presence. As such, it refers to the psychological sense of perceiving a virtual reality as real while being physically located in another (Zhang, 2017). The model proposed in this paper concerns itself with emotional and engagement-based immersion. This type of immersion deals with the intensity of user engagement with a task. Cairns defines engagement-based immersion in their series of papers (Cairns et al., 2006) (Jenett, 2008) as a three-level construct.

The first level is called engagement. It is automatically achieved when the subject interacts with a task. As such, its entrance barrier is "time". The second level, engrossment, is achieved when the subject becomes emotionally involved in the activity. It is synonymous with the feeling of the controls becoming invisible. The highest stage of immersion is referred to as "total immersion". In this state, the subject is completely cut off from reality and experiences both spatial real world dissociation as well as a loss of a sense of time.

Based on this definition, Cairns developed a questionnaire to measure immersion. They define five main factors: Cognitive involvement, real world dissociation, challenge, emotional involvement and control. Many of these factors overlap with flow. The main difference between flow and immersion is that immersion may be a sub-optimal experience. Cheng improved upon Cairns' model of immersion by adding dimensions to the three layers (Cheng, 2015). Engagement is broken into Attraction, Time Investment and Usability.

Engrossment, the second level of Cairns' immersion levels can be broken down into emotional attachment of the user to the task and decreased perceptions of time and spatial surroundings. The final level of Cairns' immersion model, "total immersion", has two components: The first refers to the loss of spatial awareness, and is identified by Cheng as "presence", the feeling of physically being present in a virtual reality. The second term is given by Cheng as "empathy", the state in which the player relates to their avatar on an emotional level and shares the character's emotions.

Georgiou et al. notice that term and define it as synonymous with "flow" (Georgiou, 2017). This fits well with Cairns' definition of immersion as the "psychology sub-optimal experience" (Cairns et al., 2006), while flow is referred to by Csikszentmihalyi as the "psychology of optimal experience" (Csikszentmihalyi, 1991). This would make "flow" the highest state in Cairns' multi-level immersion model.

At the base of the proposed model, Cairns' multi-level immersion model is employed. Additionally, Cheng's model is used to extend the multi-level immersion model. Csikszentmihalyi's flow model of optimal experience comes into play as part of the highest level of Cairns' immersion model, "total immersion": it depicts an increase in flow among the diagonal through eight sub states. Given this diagonal increase, the lower levels of immersion, engagement and engrossment resemble the lower to medium flow levels in the bottom left to center area of the model, while total immersion resembles the highest flow level in the upper right corner (Figure 2).

Looking at the components of flow and immersion, a large overlap can be seen. Challenge and control are a part of both flow and immersion. Real world dissociation is also found as part of both immersion and flow, both as temporal dissociation and spatial dissociation (when interacting with virtual environments). The flow state's concentration aspect is synonymous with the most extreme version of immersion' cognitive involvement.

Contrary to immersion, flow does not identify emotional involvement. Arousal is defined as the strength of emotional experience. Strength of emotional experience can be mapped directly to challenge. Mapping valence to skill is more difficult. Such a mapping would require identifying an emotional component to skill. Such an approach would be to introduce the concept of dominance, an emotional dimension related to a person's sense of feeling control (Mäntylä, 2016). Measuring such an emotional dimension, would prove to an interesting field of research by itself and therefore it is not evaluated here.

Flow is also strengthened by direct feedback from the interaction, which is not required in order to become immersed in an activity. This can be explained with flow being an extreme version of immersion. As thus, our model proposal can be summed up as a unification of flow and immersion, which treats flow as the most extreme state of immersion (Figure 2).

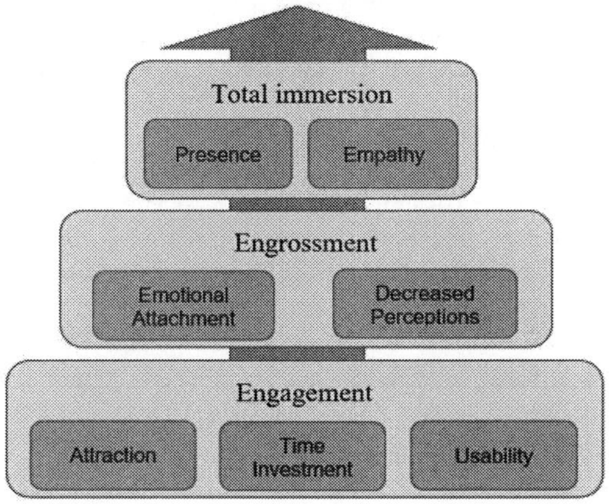

Figure 1. Cairns' 3-level Immersion Model

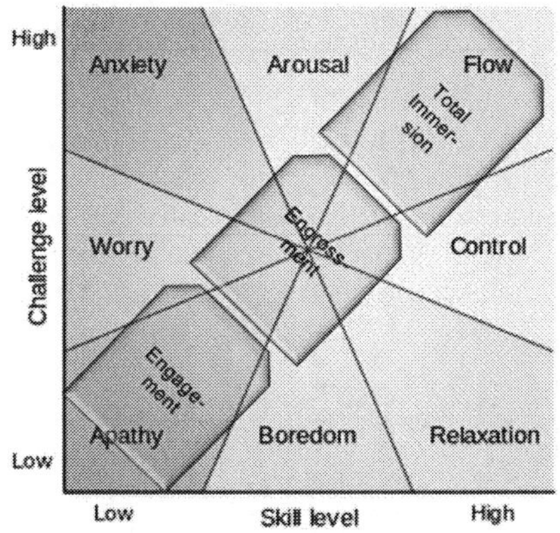

Figure 2. Combined 8-channel Flow/Immersion

3. CONCEPT OF MEASURING FLOW AND IMMERSION

In the procedure of evaluating our proposal, 40 randomly selected people go through a gaming phase and an assessment phase. Test runs showed, that 30 minutes were enough time to reach a relatively high state of immersion; accordingly, the gaming phase was set to 30 minutes of game play. The game can be selected freely; this choice was made in order to make it easier for test subjects to reach high states of immersion. During the gaming phase, game play and player footage are recorded. During the following assessment phase, the player watches the previously recorded gaming session and answers flow and immersion questionnaires periodically. These questionnaires elicit the player's flow state at the specified time in the video recording.

The questionnaires are shown multiple times, in a three level hierarchical fashion, throughout the footage evaluation in differing time intervals. The first level of questionnaires is measuring which level of immersion the player is currently in. It is based on Cheng's immersion questionnaire (Cheng, 2015), which adds multiple dimensions to Cairns' definition of immersion (Cairns et al., 2006) and presented every three minutes.

The second level of questionnaires measures flow, based on the Flow Short Scale questionnaire (Rheinberg, 2003) and is presented every six minutes. The final level of questionnaires is presented at the end of the game footage playback. It is based on the Game Experience questionnaire (IJsselsteijn et al., 2013) and entails a complete elicitation of flow, immersion and related experiences. The questionnaires were rewritten into past tense for consistency, additionally; some points were rewritten for clarity. As it was unclear to participants, they were also altered to reflect which span of time they referred to.

This way, the theory that flow is an extreme version of immersion can be tested by comparing phases of immersion, identified in the first and third level (Immersion/Game experience questionnaire) to corresponding phases of flow, identified in the second and third level (Flow Short Scale/Game experience questionnaire).

4. CONCLUSION AND PERSPECTIVE

The work in progress presented, proposes a unified model of flow and immersion. The model will be verified by data elicited by flow and immersion questionnaires in the context of serious games. If the model is proven, a qualitative evaluation and steps towards an adaption process are enabled.

The procedure is composed of a gaming phase and an assessment phase, the former to record player and gameplay footage, the later to identify phases of flow and immersion. It is an attempt to find proof, that flow and immersion are linked in the multi-level immersion model by Cheng (Cheng, 2015). It will be performed at Fraunhofer IOSB in the near future, as soon as preliminary tests are completed.

Furthermore, the approach will enable experiments towards establishing a method for measuring player flow/immersion levels automatically through physiological measurements. These experiments will be about, whether physiological parameters correlate during identified phases of flow or immersion, allowing a less intrusive, less biased and more automated analysis of player experience, during the activity under test.

REFERENCES

Atorf, D., L. Hensler, and E. Kannegieser (2016). "Towards a concept on measuring the flow state during gameplay of serious games". In: European Conference on Games Based Learning (ECGBL). ECGBL 2016. Paisley, Scotland, pp. 955–959. isbn: 978-1-911218-09-8. url: http://publica.fraunhofer.de/documents/N-438328.html.

Bach, Dominik R., Karl J. Friston, and Raymond J. Dolan (2010). "Analytic measures for quantification of arousal from spontaneous skin conductance fluctuations". In: International Journal of Psychophysiology, pp. 52–57. doi: 10.1145/1920778.1920801. url: http://doi.acm.org/10.1016/j.ijpsycho.2010.01.011.

Cheng, M.-T., H.-C. She, and L.A. Annetta (June 2015). "Game Immersion Experience: Its Hierarchical Structure and Impact on Game-based Science Learning". In: J. Comp. Assist. Learn. 31.3, pp. 232–253. issn: 0266-4909. doi: 10.1111/jcal.12066. url: http: //dx.doi.org/10.1111/jcal.12066.

Csikszentmihalyi, Mihaly (Mar. 1991). Flow: The Psychology of Optimal Experience. New York, NY: Harper Perennial. isbn: 0060920432. url: http://www.amazon.com/gp/product/0060920432/ref=si3_rdr_bb_product/104-4616565-4570345.

Georgiou, Yiannis and Eleni A. Kyza (Feb. 2017). "The Development and Validation of the ARI Questionnaire". In: Int. J. Hum.-Comput. Stud. 98.C, pp. 24–37. issn: 1071-5819. doi: 10.1016/j.ijhcs.2016.09.014. url: https://doi.org/10.1016/j.ijhcs.2016.09.014.

Rheinberg, F., R. Vollmeyer, and S. Engeser (2003). "Die Erfassung des Flow-Erlebens". In: Diagnostik von Motivation und Selbstkonzept. Göttingen: Hogrefe, pp. 261–279.

Zhang, C., A. Perkis, and S. Arndt (May 2017). "Spatial immersion versus emotional immersion, which is more immersive?" In: 2017 Ninth International Conference on Quality

of Multimedia Experience (QoMEX), pp. 1–6. doi: 10.1109/QoMEX.2017.7965655

Cairns, P., Cox, A., Berthouze, N., Jennett, C., & Dhoparee, S. (2006). Quantifying the experience of immersion in games. In: Cognitive Science of Games and Gameplay workshop at Cognitive Science, 2006.

Nordin, A., Denisova, A. and Cairns, P. (2014). Too many questionnaires: measuring player experience whilst playing digital games. Seventh York Doctoral Symposium on Computer Science & Electronics, pp.69-75.

Allen, Christopher (2014, July 22). "The Proficiency Ladder". Life With Alacrity. Retrieved July 22, 2014, from http:// www.LifeWithAlacrity.com

IJsselsteijn, W. A., de Kort, Y. A. W., & Poels, K. (2013). The Game Experience Questionnaire. Eindhoven: Technische Universiteit Eindhoven.

Mäntylä, Mika et al. (2016). "Mining Valence, Arousal, and Dominance - Possibilities for Detecting Burnout and Productivity?" In: CoRR abs/1603.04287. arXiv: 1603.04287. url: http://arxiv.org/abs/1603.04287.

INVESTIGATION OF GAME PREFERENCE IN THE UNIVERSITY STUDENT

Noppon Choosri[1, 2], Noppon Wongta[1], Patison Palee[1], Waritsara Jitmun[1] and Napatsayod Swangtrakul[2]
[1]*College of Arts, Media, and Technology, Chiang Mai University, Thailand*
[2]*Center of Data Analytics and Knowledge Synthesis for Healthcare, Chiang Mai University, Thailand*
239 Huaykaew Rd., Suthep, Muang,Chiang Mai, Thailand 50200

ABSTRACT

Understanding gaming preference of users can increase the chance of success in game production. Under the concern in developing effective education game for undergraduate students, this study investigates the game preference of Thai university students in the different field of studies to benefit the ongoing education game projects. The important findings from the survey showed the difference in preference in some game genres between male and female which are Action, Action adventure, Role-playing and Strategy game. There is no significant impact of the field of studies to game preference. It has also been identified that the students who have physical activities in their leisure times tend to like to play the strategy games. Further, the study primarily examines the reason for preferences from some of the famous games. The most identified satisfactory criteria of game selections are whether the game is fun and the graphic of the game are attractive.

KEYWORDS

Survey, Game preference, Thai students, Gender Difference, Physical Activity, Sedentary Activity, Education Game

1. INTRODUCTION

The market research has revealed the rapid growth of the market value of the online game in Thailand from 3,700 Million baht to 4,190 Million baht between 2008 and 2011. A similar trend is seen in mobile and tablet game market in which the value is increased from 224 Million Baht (2008) to 2,012 Million Baht (2011) (Software Industry Promotion Agency 2011). The National statistical office of Thailand stated that in 2008, 2011, and 2014 Thai adolescence age 13-24 increasingly spent their free time playing computer games more than other activities; the statistical ratio is 5.8%, 12.3%, 21.0% respectively (National statistical office Thailand 2011, Thailand 2014). In fact, Thai teenager surprisingly spends the longest time in Asian countries playing games (60.7 minutes each day), whereas the other countries such as Singapore, Hong Kong, Korea and China are 59.4, 56, 46 and 43.2 minutes respectively (National statistical office Thailand 2012).

Recently, the genre of serious game which is a game designed for the primary purpose of enhancing the performance of operations has emerged. One of the serious game applications is an education game. The Game -based learning approach is applied to support learning outcomes successfully in several domains of higher education such as civil engineering (Ebner and Holzinger 2007), software engineering (Cagiltay 2007), medical education entrepreneurial skills in management students (Williams 2015), Learning art history (Froschauer, Zweng et al. 2012). To develop an educational game successfully, it requires a game developer to understand players preference so that the 'fun factor' can do its job effectively in developing knowledge and skills. Related research involved a correlation between players preference and their demographic background are typically focused on the gender difference on game interest. It has been agreed that males spent more time playing computer games than females (Chou and Tsai 2007, Greenberg, Sherry et al. 2010, Homer, Hayward et al. 2012). This paper has the primary purpose of exploring the game preference between male and female of Thai undergraduate. This is the new research population for the research in this area. Importantly, the research is also aimed to explore the novel demographic parameters that possibly significant to game preference. We suspected that students who are studying in the different field of study might have the interest in game genre differently. Another research question is to investigate the preference of game genre is affected by the characteristic of lifestyle pattern, i.e. physical and sedentary lifestyle.

The remainder of this paper is organised as follows. Game genre classification is discussed in Section 2. The method and results, as well as, the hypotheses of the research are to be discussed in Section 3 and finally Section 4 is discussion and conclusion.

2. GAME GENRE CLASSIFICATION

Several game researches refer to the game classification, but currentl there are many of them exists as sampled in Table 1. One of the possible reasons is because no global classification fits all research purposes. Different classification usually means the different number of genres and categories. Also, different methodologies were applied to define classification. For example, the study of Lucas and Sherry (2004) examined gender differences in gameplay, 14 genres were used in that research which was defined by consulting multiple sources of literature. Gros (2007) discussed the approaches of using games in formal education to make digital society, 7 genres were mentioned based on author perspective. Zammitto (2010) explored the correlation between the gamers personality and their gaming preferences, 7 genres taken from the modification of Rollings and Adams (2003) were included in the survey. Phan, Keebler et al. (2016) explored a solution to measure video game satisfaction, 12 genres of the game were included in the survey based on consulting various popular gaming websites.

Table 1. Current game genres

Authors	No. of genres	Game genres
Lucas and Sherry (2004)	14	Action/Adventure, Arcade, Card/Dice, Classic board, Fantasy, Fighter, Racing/Speed, Role playing, Shooter, Simulation, Sports, Strategy, Puzzle, and Quiz/Trivia
Gros (2007)	7	Action, Adventure, Fighting, Role-playing, Simulations, Sports, and Strategy
Zammitto (2010)	7	Action, Adventure, Simulation, Sports Strategy, Puzzle, and Role Playing
Phan et al. (2016)	12	Action, Action, Adventure, Driving/Racing, Fighting, Music/Dance, Puzzle/Card/Board, Role-playing, Simulation, Sports, Strategy, Trivia/Game show, and Other

This research decides to follow the study of (Phan et al., 2016) because the classification is practical-oriented and the explicit examples of the popular games belong to each category are given as shown in Table 2.

Table 2. Example of games by genres (Phan et al., 2016)

Main Genre	Example
Action	Destiny, New Super Mario Bros. Wii, Dynasty Warriors6
Action adventure	Minecraft, Grand Theft Auto, The Last of Us
Driving/racing	Mario Kart Wii, Forza Horizon 2, Gran Turismo
Fighting	Super Smash Bros. for Wii U, Skullgirls, Mortal Kombat
Music/Dance	Guitar Hero, Taiko Drum Master, Just Dance 2015
Puzzle/card/board	Candy Crush Saga, Words With Friends, Tetris
Role-playing	World of Warcraft, Dark Souls, Pokemon X
Simulation	The Sim3, Space Engineers, Tropico5
Sports	NBA 2K15, FIFA 15, SSX
Strategy	DotA 2, Sid Meier's Civilization V, League of Legends
Trivia/game show	Trivia Crack, QuizUp, You Don't Know Jack
Other	Wii Fit Mario Party, Clicker Heroes

3. METHODS AND RESULTS

The cross-sectional survey was conducted at the large university of northern Thai from October to December 2017. Participants were about the similar ages between 20-24 years of age. The participants are from four diverse fields of study, including medicine, software engineering, animation, and management. Possession of game devices from participants was surveyed; the choices were indicating game devices were provided and multiple selections are allowed. 78 participant response the survey. General information about the participants is summarized in Table 3.

Table 3. Sample information

Variable	Frequency	%
Gender		
Male	44	56.40
Female	34	43.60
Field of study		
Med	19	24.40
Ani	21	26.90
SE	16	20.50
MMIT	22	28.20
Posession of game devices		
PC	71	88.75
Console	27	33.75
Smartphone	52	65.00
Other	2	2.50

The online self-administered questionnaire was distributed to the participant. The survey questions explored the respondents' preferences in 2 stages. First, the study examined the correlation between the demographic background of samples and their game interest. Second, the study explored further the primary reasons underpinning the preference of particular game.

The following hypotheses related to demographical data of participant were tested. In general, the participants were asked to rate their preference for each game genre on a five-point Likert-type scale:

Hypothesis 1 (H1): Video game genre preferences will differ between males and females

The survey from the sample in Table 4 indicates that the preferences of four types of games are statically different between males and females ($p<0.05$) which are the Action, Action adventure, Role-playing and Strategy game. All of the four-game genres show the same pattern of difference that male noticeably has a stronger interest in the games than females.

Table 4. Game Genre Preferences by Gender

Game	Male		Female		P-Value
	Mean	SD	Mean	SD	
Action	3.95	1.077	3.32	1.036	0.009
Action Adventure	4.25	1.014	3.21	1.200	< 0.001
Racing	3.14	1.231	3.29	1.268	0.001
Fighting	3.36	1.222	3.12	1.149	0.580
Music	3.02	1.532	3.12	1.225	0.322
Puzzle	3.07	1.437	3.62	1.181	0.881
Role-playing	4.16	1.098	3.59	1.131	0.082
Simulation	3.66	1.200	4.06	1.071	0.013
Sport	2.80	1.733	2.26	1.136	0.127
Strategy	4.34	1.055	2.82	1.314	0.313

*statistical significant p-value < 0.05

Hypothesis 2 (H2): game genre interest will differ by field of study.

The result from Figure 1 showed that when separate the concern of participant by the field of study, there is no difference in game genre preference among them. So, the average scores indicating game preference in each genre from the whole participant are computed. Figure 1 depicts the top five most preferred game which are Roleplaying (M=4.16, SD=1.098), Simulation (M=3.66, SD=1.200), Action Adventure (M=4.25, SD=1.014), Action (M=3.95, SD=1.077), and Strategy (M=4.34, SD=1.055).

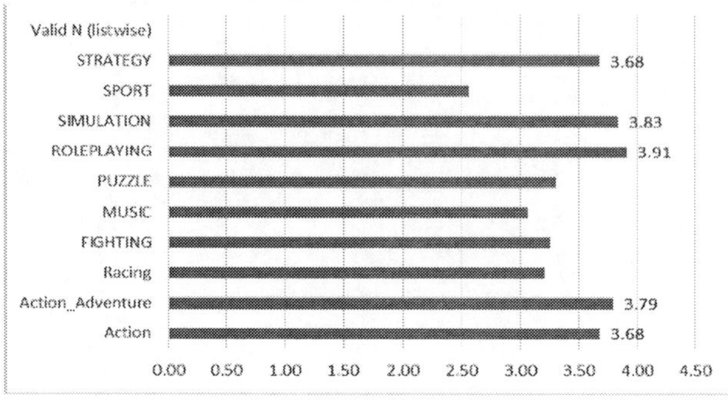

Figure 1. The most preferred game genre

Hypothesis 3 (H3): game genre interest will differ by the type of free time activities.

It was suspected that a free time hobby besides playing computer games is related to game preference. The hobby of this research is focused on two kinds of categories which are sedentary activities such as reading, watching television, chatting with friends and physical activities such as doing sports, exercising and trekking. The only game that shows statistical differences between the participant who like sedentary and physical e hobby is a Strategy game. The game is more preferable for participants who like physical hobby as shows in Table 5.

Table 5. Game Genre Preferences by Hobby Characteristics

Game	Hobby=Easy (N=63)		Hobby=active(N=15)		P-Value
	Mean	SD	Mean	SD	
Action	3.65	1.073	3.81	1.223	0.485
Action Adventure	3.69	1.262	4.19	0.911	0.191
Racing	3.23	1.273	3.13	1.147	0.756
Fighting	3.24	1.155	3.31	1.352	0.849
Music	3.10	1.434	2.94	1.289	0.613
Puzzle	3.32	1.352	3.25	1.390	0.833
Role-playing	3.79	1.189	4.38	0.806	0.077
Simulation	3.79	1.118	4.00	1.317	0.307
Sport	2.39	1.453	3.25	1.612	0.061
Strategy	3.50	1.400	4.38	1.147	0.013

*statistical significant p-value < 0.05

The second phase of the survey in the research is involved investigation the reasons why ones feel enjoy particular game were examined. A game representing each game genre is used as the sample to ask participants if they like the games. The questions to explore gratification are selectively adopted from (Phan et al., 2016), the reasons include: R1= I think it is easy to learn how to play the game, R2= I enjoy the fantasy or story provided by the game, R3= I tend to spend more time playing the game than I have planned, R4= I think the game is fun, R5= I feel the game allows me to be imaginative, R6=I enjoy the music in the game., R7= I feel successful when I overcome the obstacles in the game, R8= I like to play this game with other players, R9= I enjoy the game's graphics.

The research selects one game from each genre to primarily investigate enjoyments factors. The selection of game is mainly considering from popularity suggested in the selection is demonstrated in Table 6.

Table 6. The Selection of Game Representing each Genre

Main Genre	Example
Action	Mario Bros
Action adventure	Grand Theft Auto (GTA)
Driving/racing	Need for Speed
Fighting	Street Fighter
Music/Dance	Dance Dance Revolution
Puzzle/card/board	Tetris
Role-playing	Final Fantasy
Simulation	The Sims
Sports	Pro Evolution Soccer
Strategy	Star Craft

The top five reasons that best describe preferences of the most preferred game from samples were extracted as demonstrated as follows:

Final Fantasy→R9,R2,R3,R5
The Sims→ R5,R3,R2,R4,R9
GTA→R2,R4,R5,R9,R3
Mario Bros→R4,R1,R7,R6,R9
Star Craft→R4,R3,R5,R7,R9

The results showed the common reasons for preferences in all game genres are "I think the game is fun" and "I enjoy the game graphic". Another significant observation is that the only satisfactory reasons of playing the Mario Bros, which is a categorized as an action game, are "I think it is easy to learn how to play the game" and "I enjoy the music in the game".

4. DISCUSSION AND CONCLUSION

The research examines game genre preferences of the undergraduate from the large university in the north of Thailand. The finding from this research is to be used to support the ongoing project involved the development of the serious educational games for the sample population. The participants were recruited from four study programs which are medicine, software engineering, animation, and management. The results confirm previous evidence of Greenberg, Sherry et al. (2010) and Homer, Hayward et al. (2012) that male has a stronger interest in physical oriented games such as sport games and car racing games, action as shown by the predominant of the preference in Action and Action Adventure. One observation to be made from the findings is that male possibly prefer more sophisticated game as they showed more interest in the Role-playing and Strategy games.

The comprehensive review from Kuss and Griffiths (2012) indicated that the personal trait contributes a diversity in gaming behaviour. To this point, we suspected that students in the different area of studies might have the unique personal trait which might be seen from their game genre preference, this study, however, found no implication between these two variables. So, education game designers are not necessary to take this demographic background into account.

The results from the investigation of the lifestyle pattern and game preference are in contrast with previous evidence. Thorne, Smith et al. (2014) found that the 'sports and racing' group was significantly more active overall than the 'strategy' group associated with physical activities, whereas the result from this study showed that the strategy game is the only game type that associated with the physical activity preference.

Although the research contributes some useful findings for practical purpose, the improvement should be made to the method of study to produce stronger academic contribution. The sample size of the survey should be larger, and the diversity of study areas should be more varieties to enhance the accuracy of the survey. The latter part of the research where the study has initially investigated the reasons to be 'Like' the games. This research surveys the opinion of the participant by using one popular game representing each game genre. So, the result reflects only the attitude on that game not on the game genre that the game belongs to. Future research with more proper research design is required to draw conclusion related to this question.

REFERENCES

Cagiltay, N. E. (2007). "Teaching software engineering by means of computer-game development: Challenges and opportunities." British Journal of Educational Technology 38(3): 405-415.

Chou, C. and M.-J. Tsai (2007). "Gender differences in Taiwan high school students' computer game playing." Computers in Human Behavior 23(1): 812-824.

Ebner, M. and A. Holzinger (2007). "Successful implementation of user-centered game based learning in higher education: An example from civil engineering." Computers & Education 49(3): 873-890.

Froschauer, J., J. Zweng, W. Merkl, M. Arends, D. Goldfarb and M. Weingartner (2012). ARTournament: A Mobile Casual Game to Explore Art HistoryVortrag ISBN: 978-0-7695-4702-2; S. 80-84. 12th IEEE International Conference on Advanced Learning Technologies, Rome, Italy.

Greenberg, B. S., J. Sherry, K. Lachlan, K. Lucas and A. Holmstrom (2010). "Orientations to video games among gender and age groups." Simulation & Gaming 41(2): 238-259.

Gros, B. (2007). "Digital games in education: The design of games-based learning environments." Journal of research on technology in education 40(1): 23-38.

Homer, B. D., E. O. Hayward, J. Frye and J. L. Plass (2012). "Gender and player characteristics in video game play of preadolescents." Computers in Human Behavior 28(5): 1782-1789.

Kuss, D. J. and M. D. Griffiths (2012). "Internet gaming addiction: A systematic review of empirical research." International Journal of Mental Health and Addiction 10(2): 278-296.

Lucas, K. and J. L. Sherry (2004). "Sex differences in video game play: A communication-based explanation." Communication research 31(5): 499-523.

National statistical office Thailand (2011). The 2011 survey on conditions of society and culture. Ministry of information and communication technology. Bangkok, National statistical office Thailand: 57.

National statistical office Thailand. (2012). "Adolescent: Internet: game online " Retrieved 10 April, 2018, from http://service.nso.go.th/nso/nsopublish/citizen/news/news_internet_teen.jsp.

Phan, M. H., J. R. Keebler and B. S. Chaparro (2016). "The Development and Validation of the Game User Experience Satisfaction Scale (GUESS)." Hum Factors 58(8): 1217-1247.

Rollings, A. and E. Adams (2003). Andrew Rollings and Ernest Adams on game design, New Riders.

Software Industry Promotion Agency (2011). Digital Content Market Values.

Thailand, N. s. o. (2014). The 2014 survey on conditions of society and culture

Bangkok, National statistical office Thailand.

Thorne, H. T., J. J. Smith, P. J. Morgan, M. J. Babic and D. R. Lubans (2014). "Video game genre preference, physical activity and screen-time in adolescent boys from low-income communities." Journal of adolescence 37(8): 1345-1352.

Williams, D. (2015). "The Impact of SimVenture on the Development of Entrepreneurial Skills in Management Students." Industry and Higher Education 29(5): 379-395.

Zammitto, V. L. (2010). Gamers' personality and their gaming preferences, Communication, Art & Technology: School of Interactive Arts and Technology.

GAME DESIGN TOOLS FOR MAXIMUM EFFECTIVENESS

Pedro Henrique Roscoe Lage de Oliveira[1], Carlos Alberto Silva de Miranda[1]
and Joao Victor Boechat Gomide[2]
[1]*Minas Gerais State University, Avenida Antônio Carlos, 7545 – Belo Horizonte, MG – Brazil – 31.270-010*
[2]*FUMEC University, Rua Cobre, 200 – Belo Horizonte, MG – Brazil – 31.310-190*

ABSTRACT

This paper demonstrates alternatives to replace items of the game design document (GDD) during the development of digital games. The creation and development of a game, in general, is carried out using a GDD, containing all the indications, information and the script of the game, for the team to follow throughout the development process. There is no exact formula for producing a GDD. Various templates are proposed and misunderstood information at different levels of responsibility may create irreparable problems after deployment to production. This paper proposes the analog prototyping as an efficient alternative to GDD, in association with benchmarking and agile development.

KEYWORDS

Game Design, Analog Prototyping, Benchmarking, Agile Development, Game Design Document

1. INTRODUCTION

This paper analyses a set of methods used as efficient alternatives to GDD topics to increase the team efficiency and communication. The game design goals and topics are commented on (CRAWFORD: 1982, 49-50): "A game must have clearly defined goal. This goal must be expressed in terms of the effects that it will have on player. It is not enough to declare that a game will be enjoyable, fun, exciting or good; the goal must establish the fantasies that the game will support and the types of emotions it will engender in its audience. (…) Once you have settled on your goal, you must select a topic. The topic is the means of expressing the goal (…)"

The game designer can be defined as the professional who determines the gameplay basic guidelines of the product and the development methods that will be used to produce the final product by the development team. (ROUSE: 2001, 18) states that "at its most elementary level, game design consists of inventing and documenting the elements of a game."

Jesse Schell shows that the game designer must cultivate many skills, ranging from knowledge in technical writing to mathematics (Schell, 2008: 2-4). The designer will use every skill he has to communicate the ideas and to reach the conclusion of the project with minimum expenses and maximum result.

The first phase of a game development starts before programming, art, marketing or any other subject related to game development. The game designer is responsible for planning the product development strategies, goals and topics, before even involving other professionals. (CRAWFORD. 2016, pg. 51) says that "during this phase it is critical that you commit little to paper and above all, write no code! (…) You will generate during this phase a great variety of specific implementation ideas for your game. They will not all fit together neatly (…). Indulge yourself in creating implementation ideas, but be prepared to winnow the ruthlessly during design."

To Ernest Adams, "a game is designed by creating a concept and identifying an audience in the concept stage, fleshing out the details and turning abstract ideas into concrete plans in the elaboration stage, and adjusting the fine points in the tuning stage (…)." (ADAMS: 2009, 62). Rouse points that "in many ways, developing a game is all about understanding your limitations and then turning those limitations into advantages." (ROUSE: 2001, 47-54)

The construction of a digital game depends on the teamwork of a diverse crew with a wide range of technical skills. One of the most delicate parts of development is the efficient and cost-effective use of each member´s effort. The team must seek a scenario where the professionals work with functional independence and their performances are not limited by product scope, harmonizing each personal set of skills in order to create a coherent product. As observes Rouse, the development team must be organized to divide the product in parts and build the game incrementally. "Instead of working a little bit on all the different components of the game, you should try to complete one system before moving on to the next. Work on the most basic and essential systems first, and then build the systems that depend on that system. This allows you to implement a system, test it out, see if it "feels" right, and only then move on to the next system." (ROUSE: 2001, 254)

The development of game design tools boost the team effectiveness, since the game designer will be able to perform typical gameplay design tasks independently. (ROUSE: 2001, 378) notes that "in order to create superior content, the design team will need to be equipped with well-designed, robust game creation tools. Therefore, one can conclude that designing a good game is about designing good game creation tools".

In this paper, analog prototyping, benchmarking and agile development processes are presented as processes for the game designer, which can replace some GDD topics in many productions. Those resources are poorly approached in the literature, never analyzed together, and rarely used by development teams.

2. GAME DESIGN DOCUMENT

During the development, the design process follows phases of the product creation, starting with the overall planning, designation of responsibilities and set of the tools that will be developed and/or used by the team. The final stage is dedicated to polishing, which involve a large number of iterations with individuals inside and outside the development group.

Writing a GDD is considered a relevant part of the process. It is assumed, in general, that the lack of a GDD guiding the project culminates in failure. There is no perfect formula for a GDD production, along with huge controversies on how to build it. As Adams notes, "As part of their job, game designers produce a series of documents to tell others about their game design. Exactly what documents they produce and what the documents are for vary from designer to designer and project to project (ADAMS: 2009, 54)

The document has the function of recording decisions and agreements that have been made orally or making explicit the ideas that have been ventilated and approved by the developers. Although there is no standard for composing a GDD, there are proposed structures and recommendations. Those who support the use of GDD as the backbone of game development understand that this document should include several sessions. However, as noted by Rouse, "different companies may have different standards for what documentation pieces they create in order to assist and guide a game´s development." (ROUSE. 2001, 302)

The documents that usually are part of the GDD are listed in Adams (ADAMS: 2009, 56-58): High Concept Document, which defines the central concept of the game; Game Treatment Document: the most detailed game description document, considered an extended version of the High Concept Document; Character Design, World Design, Narrative Design and Level Design Documents: those are specifically directed to specific parts of the game; Game Script document: according to Adams, this document cover the stories and mechanics that shape the game core.

Some practical issues brought by writing all these documents within the game creation process are justifying the time and effort needed to write them, along with the effectiveness of these documents while producing the game. It is well known that many game developing professionals only read these documents superficially. Others prefer a more informal and intuitive approach, as seen in many productions. The game designer has to be a good communicator to make the others understand the GDD and must track the work of the other professionals, as points (Schell: 2008, 3). Richard Rouse (2001: 292) points out that "the necessity of game development documentation is a side effect of the increasing size of game development teams. In the early days of game development, when a development team consisted of one multi-talented individual, documenting the functionality of the game was less important. If that one person was able to establish and implement a vision for the project's gameplay, it did not especially matter if she wrote it down or not."

3. ANALOG PROTOTYPING

Prototyping is an important process for creating a product. The quickness, inexpensiveness and clarity are characteristics of the prototyping process which can be divided into two categories, high fidelity and low fidelity, according to the proximity they have from the final material. Jesse Schell (2008: 86-87) understands that "every prototype must be created to answer a question and sometimes more than one. (...) Your goal is to loop as usefully and as frequently as possible. So if you can manage it, why not just get the software out of the way? If you are clever, you can prototype your fancy videogame idea as a simple board game, or what we sometimes call a paper prototype. (...) This lets you spot problems sooner."

,On the subject Kay et al (2003, 6) states that the prototype points out e serves to communicate information and show tangible ideas to the development team, internal management and external clients. Testing and refining the interactions of a game in the prototyping phase means that all other individuals involved in the development are less likely to rebuild parts of the product due to problems identified in later phases.

Digital and analog games have outstanding differences, notably the interactions with physical pieces on the first ones and the graphical interface interactions in the second. In addition, there are differences in how they deal with the mechanics and complexity. Digital games have the game system as a final referee for rules. In the other hand, if a rule is contradictory in an analog game, players may discuss and decide what is the best way to apply it. The analog game system is adaptable, while the digital game system is rigid. Moreover, the complexity in digital games can be hidden in the feedback system, which allows the game to remove certain tasks from the player, operations, for example, can be made instantly by the computer.

However, it is possible to state that a set of systems present in a board game can represent a significant fraction of the systems presented by digital games. As an example, *he Dark Souls* board game captures the fundamentals of the *Dark Souls* digital game, absorbing its mechanics and translating them into a turn-based combat system..

Analog prototyping can be used as a key resource in development since it is a quick tool to validate the iteration possibilities of a digital product. Also, the developer must consider that the financial and human expenses implicated in the making of an analog prototype are objectively lower than that of a digital prototype. This method gives the designer superior implementation effectiveness; mechanics can be created and tested without the need to translate them with code, placeholders or art implementation. Furthermore, understanding a game using an analog prototype is easier than reading a GDD, making the game experience perception more fluid to the team since they will actually play the game, being able to perform all critical balancing and mechanics modification before the digital development begins.

(SNYDER: 2003, 12) describes the advantages of paper prototyping for interface prototyping, which she says are good to provide feedback early in the development process, encouraging creativity, promoting rapid iterative development, facilitating communication with the team and customers, enabling a multidisciplinary team to work together since it does not require any technical skills.

4. BENCHMARKING

Benchmarking techniques can be utilized in the game design process aiming to analyze and applying the best principles in the game development. Benchmarking, according to Elmuti and Kathawala (1997: 229) "is the process of identifying the highest standards of excellence for products, services, or processes, and then making the improvements necessary to reach those standards, commonly called ′best practices′. The justification lies partly in the question: ′Why re-invent the wheel if I can learn from someone who has already done it?' "

Through benchmarking, the game designer can set each goal and topic of his game based on examples of solutions he found in other games, facilitating the set-up of the project and guiding the work of team members. Watson (2007: 3) remembers that "benchmarking is a process of comparing in order to learn how to improve. Motivation for a benchmarking study is the desire to improve and become more competitive."

Elmuti and Kathawala (1997: 229) states that "the process of benchmarking is more than just a means of gathering data on how well a company performs against others (...). It is also a method of identifying new ideas and new ways of improving processes and, therefore, being better able to meet the expectations of customers." The benchmarking used in the early phases of development intent to support the team organization. Watson (2007: 8) points out that "(...) benchmarking will provide productivity improvement by concentrating on specific activities that will improve the effectiveness, efficiency, or economy of routine business operations."

By looking outside, the game designer can identify best practices, qualities and flaws within other games in the same genre typically have, along with ways to fix it. With the use of benchmarking, the game designer can light better ways to reach a high-quality ultimate product. As an example of benchmarking use, there is the game Forsaken Dungeons, created by Jet Dragon Studios. The game used as a main reference for its creation the universe of Battlechasers. Dofus was the benchmark for scenarios, while base gameplay was benchmarked by the boardgame Gloomhaven. The Level Design Document was replaced by a Level Editor, while the Game Script document was replaced by the analog prototype.

5. AGILE DEVELOPMENT IN GAME DEVELOPMENT

Analog prototyping and benchmarking are put together in their maximum effectiveness when used inside agile development processes, as opposed to traditional cascade development. The fundamental problem of the cascade development is that game creation is a constant process of learning and iteration. Agile development techniques increase the speed of the development by establishing a workflow capable of allowing the materialization of the project instead of exhaustive documentation, as observed by Clinton Keith (2010: 13): "We are uncovering better ways of developing software by doing it and helping others do it. Through this work we have come to value: 1. Individuals and interactions over processes and tools; 2. Working software over comprehensive documentation; 3. Customer collaboration over contract negotiation; 4. Responding to change over following a plan."

The creation of a game using agile development is divided into pre-defined time intervals called sprints. Each sprint's objective is to fullfil a specific functionality required by the customer, referred as "user story". Each sprint is only completed after development and testing of the corresponding user story features. The next sprint will be planned by prioritizing which features are the most important, and so on, until all the development goals are met. This mindset saves time and removes obstacles that will invariably arise during development.

Analog prototyping and benchmarking work as guides, to define the initial sprints and the first short-term goals, in the agile development process. If the entire team had the opportunity to iterate with the analog product and the benchmark games, the definition of the project scope will be clearer to the developers and much re-work will be avoided as the iterations have been already made, ensuring the effectiveness of the game mechanics and the fun of the product-player interactions.

The most commonly methodology used to apply agile development methods and practices is called Scrum. It names three main roles: Product Owner, Scrum Master and Development Team. The Product Owner (usually the game designer) has the final say in the game concepts, while the Scrum Master enables the interaction between all involved parts, removing any obstacles arisen during the development, and the Development Team carries on the technical development of the product.

The game development success comes from the effectiveness of the methodologies applied to detect problems and find solutions during the game creation process. To achieve team-efficiency, the communication between the members is of paramount importance to allow features of the product to be effectively delivered. Furthermore, it isimportant to integrate potential consumers in the iteration process to ensure the optimal user experience. To achieve these objectives, the use of analog prototyping, benchmarking and agile development techniques can result in the improvement of the team communication and workflow, as well as aiding on solving emergent problems that will during the project evolution.

6. CONCLUSION

This article demonstrates that there are alternative processes to the game design document to create and develop a game. Analog prototyping, associated with benchmarking, can replace parts of the GDD or the entire document, and those methods can be integrated in agile development processes for maximum efficiency. The capability to detect problems and create high-quality communication between the game designer and the rest of the development team and customers makes analog prototyping, benchmarking and agile techniques powerful techniques for creating and iterating with the features of the game.

The game design document, despite being the most used instrument in game development, presents limitations associated with lack of synergy between the records put on paper and the development stages of a game. There is no single way to work with game design. The alternatives presented in this paper, although much less used in the mainstream production, have great results when applied. Those methods give as outcome an improvement in the use of human and financial resources, as well as easy and timely identification of flaws during the project, enabling their solution.

ACKNOWLEDGEMENT

The authors are grateful to CNPq and FAPEMIG for the financial support to this work.

REFERENCES

Adams, E. 2009. *Fundamentals of Game Design.* 2nd Ed. New Riders. California

Buxton, Bill. 2007. *Sketching User Experiences – Getting the Design right and the Right Design.* Morgan Kaufmann, California.

Chua C. K, Leong, K.F., Lim, C.S.. 2003.*Rapid Prototyping.* 2nd Ed. World Scientific. New Jersey.

Crawford, C. 1982. *The Art of Computer Game Design.* Vancouver.

Elmuti, D.; Kathawala, Y. 1997. *An Overview of Benchmarking Process: a tool for continuous improvement and competitive advantage.* Lumpkin College of Business And Applied Sciences, Illinois.

Keith,Clinton.2010. *Agile Game Development with Scrum.*Addison-Wesley. Boston

Rouse, R. 2001.*Game Design – Theory & Practice.* Wordware Publishing, Texas

Schell, J. *The Art of Game Design – A Book of Lenses.* 2008. Morgan Kaufmann, California

Snyder, C. 2003.*Paper Prototyping – The Fast and Easy Way to Design and Refine User Interfaces.* Morgan Kaufmann. San Francisco

Stapenhurst, T. 2009.*The Benchmarking Book – A How-To-Guide to best practice for managers and practitioners.* Butterworth-Heinemann. Oxford.

Watson, G. H. 2007*Strategic Benchmarking Reloaded with Six Sigma – Improve Your Company's Performance Using Global Best Practice.* John Wiley & Sons. New Jersey.

MECHANICAL PERFORMANCE ASSESSMENT SYSTEM FOR ENDOTRACHEAL TUBE INTRODUCERS USING MOTION DETECTION AND OBJECT TRACKING

Francesco Luke Siena[1], Philip Breedon[1], James Armstrong[2], Paul Watts[1], Kristofor Inkpin[2] and Andrew Norris[2]

[1]*Nottingham Trent University, 50 Shakespeare Street, Nottingham, NG1 4FQ, UK*

[2]*Nottingham University Hospitals NHS Trust, Derby Road, Nottingham, NG7 2UH UK*

ABSTRACT

Failure to secure the airway with an endotracheal tube in a timely manner on induction of anaesthesia can lead to serious complications, including death. Equipment design and selection can often contribute to procedure success or failure, although current equipment does not always provide optimum solutions. Most anaesthetists consider endotracheal tube introducers (bougies) essential equipment; however, there are many different types available, with little relative performance data to inform choice. To date, no performance assessment system exists that is capable of assessing the shape retention properties of bougies. This paper discusses the design development process of the Shape Retention Testing System (SRTS) that utilises motion detection, object tracking and image processing to assess the relative performance of bougie introducers.

KEYWORDS

Airway Management, Bougie, Difficult Airway, Image Processing, Motion Detection, Object Tracking

1. INTRODUCTION

Endotracheal intubation is fundamental to safe anaesthetic practice and the procedure continues to challenge experienced of anaesthetists. Serious consequences, including death and disability can occur (Cook et al, 2011). A UK national survey of major complications suggests improvements can be made in practice, design and choice of equipment (Cook et al, 2016). A bougie (also known as a bougie introducer) is one of the most common intubation aids used. Bougies are long, flexible, relatively narrow rods that have some intrinsic "shape memory". They are used when the view is limited, making direct placement of the endotracheal tube (ET tube) itself difficult. Bougies are manually manipulated to match the curve of the patient's airway and act as a physical guide over which the ET tube can be placed and the bougie removed.

If a bougie fails to retain its shape during use, it must be removed and reshaped. Limiting the number of reshaping processes required is vital for this time-critical procedure, therefore understanding the mechanical properties of bougies is desirable when designing new equipment and selecting it for use in practice. The Difficult Airway Society (2018) provides a comprehensive list of bougie introducers used in UK; however, these vary in diameter, length, tip design and material construction. Mushambi et al (2016) identified the re-usable Eschmann Tracheal Tube Introducer "Gum Elastic Bougie" (GEB) as the gold standard device.

Currently there is no standard testing equipment to accurately assess bougie performance, especially the shape retention properties. Siena et al, (2017) first proposed the construction of suitable testing equipment, including an analysis system for the assessment of the shape retention properties utilising vision based tracking.

Single use tracheal tube bougies/introducers are becoming more common due to their significantly lower price point compared to the GEB and the elimination of concerns over cleaning, disinfection and sterilisation. Mushambi et al (2016) suggests urgent further evaluation of the single use devices is required before they replace the GEB entirely. Specific device selection is often based on operator personal preference, availability of equipment within the NHS supply chain and hospital-designated suppliers.

Any new or existing device should conform to the UK's Difficult Airway Society's ADEPT principles (Pandit et al, 2011); however, many devices have not undergone any formal evaluation. An accurate, reliable testing system could inform device selection and usage decisions. Previous studies of the relative performance of bougie introducers suffer from several limitations including unreliability, inaccurate measurement, poor standardisation of applied pressures, calibration, accuracy of data acquisition equipment, repeatability of positional tracking and application of forces within desired angles and orientations. An objective, reliable system capable of assessing mechanical and physical properties of endotracheal tube introducers could overcome these limitations. We considered that the use of motion capture technologies to provide a repeatable and accurate method of measuring bougie motion and shape retention capabilities would be a reliable cost effective approach.

2. TESTING SYSTEM (SRTS)

The Shape Retention Testing System (SRTS) is a concept recently presented by the authors (Siena et al, 2017) as a method of analysing the shape retention characteristics of bougie introducers. This system utilises motion detection and object tracking in combination with image processing techniques for data acquisition and analysis. Annamaneni et al (2003), Hodzovic et al (2004a; 2004b) Jackson et al (2009), Janakiraman et al (2009) have previously completed studies to assess the uses, properties and risks associated with bougie-assisted intubation within simulated difficult intubations and considered factors such as the effect of tip pressures, placement considerations and comparative assessment between multiple use and single use bougies. However, many of these studies do not use standardised or even suitable testing techniques with the required accuracy to provide precise results. Using a motion detection and object tracking based system, in combination with image processing, the SRTS has been designed to overcome the above-mentioned issues.

2.1 Hardware: SRTS Construction

The SRTS utilises an Intel® RealSense™ SR300 camera to identify motion detection and object tracking. The SR300 is one of the smallest 3D depth and 2D camera modules currently available on the market utilising a short range, coded light 3D imaging system. The SR300 utilises depth sensing with a 1080p RGB camera, enabling users to complete tasks such as dynamic background segmentation, object tracking, facial recognition, gesture recognition, hand and finger tracking and augmented reality tasks (Intel® RealSense™, 2016). Figure 1 presents a 3D schematic diagram of the SRTS setup with key technical features highlighted:

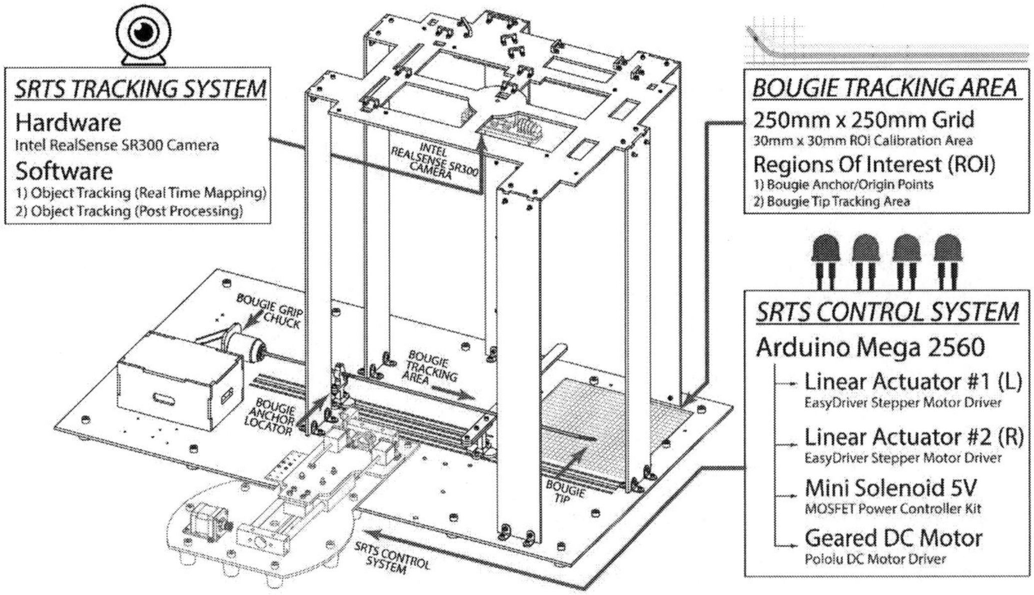

Figure 1. Shape Retention Testing System (SRTS) Setup

2.2 System Control

The SRTS has been designed to function in three key stages. First, the STRS control system uses the linear actuator pushers to manipulate the shape of the bougie at one or more points to generate a curve similar to that of a patient's airway. Secondly, once in position, the SRTS tracking system, utilising object tracking (real time mapping), is activated and begins tracking, the linear actuator pusher system (LAPS) then retracts and the bougies shape retention is tracked; simultaneously a video recording of the movements is taken.

Finally, once the video recording is completed, the post processing data analysis software is utilised to analyse device performance. There are multiple components to the SRTS that overcome many of the limitations discussed. The LED lighting system creates a standardised lighting environment when used in combination with the blackout hood that encompasses the testing systems support frame; this ensures ambient room lighting is minimised. The mechanical chuck grips the bougie and works in combination with the bend location anchor that can be adjusted based on the bougie being assessed. The linear actuator pusher system (LAPS) is controlled by an Arduino Mega 2560 and utilises several motor drivers and power control modules. Control parameters have been programmed within the code to ensure commands can be altered based on the required input parameters, but also an automatic reset command is utilised to ensure the system has a calibrated home position.

The SRTS has been designed with the capability to alter testing parameters, creating a repeatable testing system adaptable for variable equipment assessment. The camera system provides accurate camera/video tracking with a fixed frame rate and appropriate field of view (FOV) to track the bougies bend angles, tip movements, speed of movement and shape retention within pre-defined regions of interest (ROI) (Figure 2). Accurate camera tracking data, captured in combination with interchangeable angle measurement grids, allows the assessment of data over clinically relevant ranges both pre and post processing.

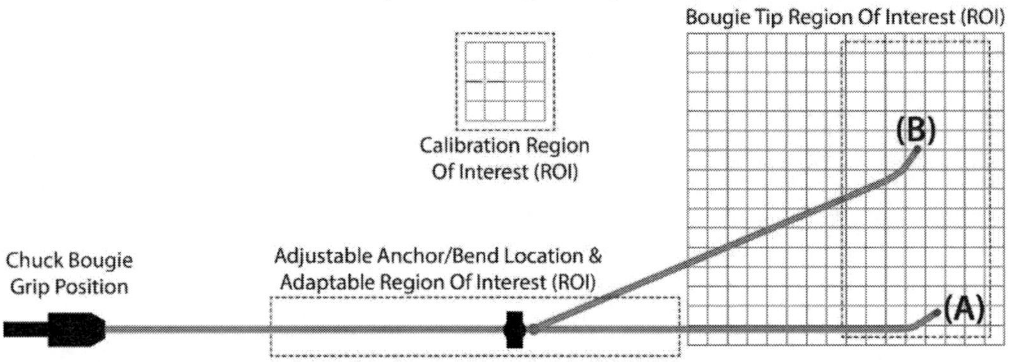

Figure 2. Bougie Tracking Regions of Interest (ROI)

2.3 Software: Motion Detection, Object Tracking and Image Processing

The SRTS uses two software packages to assess the shape retention properties of bougie introducers. The Real Time Mapping Software (RTMS), which has been adapted from an open source object tracking C# program that utilises a live camera video feed to assess the colour and size of objects (Gupta, 2013). This program is used for motion detection and object colour tracking to plot/map the bougie tip movements. The RTMS identifies coloured objects and tracks their positional movement. The X and Y co-ordinate data is captured and plotted onto a position-tracking map as the object is moved providing a mapped image.

The Object Tracking Post Processing Software (OTPPS) analyses a recorded video of the bougie introducer movements to determine the starting angle (degrees), change in angle (degrees), the distance moved (mm) and the speed of movement recorded in millimetres per second (mm/s). The OTPPS tracks over a set number of frames tracking the anchor/origin location and the tip of the bougie, both of which are defined by coloured markers. Data points are then monitored and captured during bougie manipulation (Figure 2b) as the bougie attempts to return to its original shape (Figure 2a). The OTPPS software requires a number of input parameters in order to function correctly. Initially, it is imperative to identify the key colours within the image that we wish to identify as our targets; each target also has a Region of Interest (ROI) defined (Figure 2). The ROI instructs the software the location to search for the given target colour. This not only reduces the area that the system will need to search, thereby speeding up the process, but will also reduce the chance of any object outside of our search area being identified by the camera and being incorrectly tracked by the system. The OTPPS software breaks down the video into individual video frames, extracting the pixel data from each frame, isolating the pixels of our given target colour and creating a digitised array representation of the image that the computer can now search (Figure 3). Pixels are extracted from the source image and are converted into a digitised map Figure 3 (Left). Figure 3 (Right) shows a 4x4 extract of an image, showing the converted digitised version with target colours turned into numerical values.

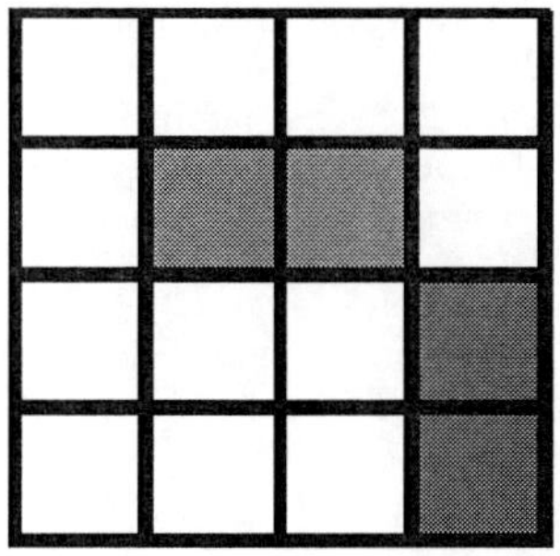

0	0	0	0
0	1	1	0
0	0	0	2
0	0	0	2

Figure 3. Original image in pixels. (Left) Digitised map of the pixel image (Right)

Once the system has this array of data, it now isolates the centre of the required object and use this point as the coordinates for any measurements collected. Two targets were required to be tracked to calculate the required angle and speed of the bougie tip movement. The first target is located at the base of the bougie where it will be shaped; this is a fixed anchor point which will not move during testing. The second is the tip of the bougie (Figure 2(a)); this is the part of the bougie that will move and will be tracked (Figure 2(b)).

As the video runs at a fixed frame per second (FPS) rate, it is therefore possible to calculate an exact timestamp for each frame and set of coordinates. Using this data, it is possible to calculate the movement of the target points between two specified timestamps. By calculating the angle between the anchor and the bougie tip for each of the two frames and subtracting the first angle from the second, the amount of rotation that has occurred within the specified timeframe is calculated. An important part of the measurement calculation is to define the scale of the camera image, to convert the pixel coordinates into measurements of distance (mm). To do this, a grid system is utilised with a fixed sized grid width of 10mm. An ROI is setup for this grid and requests the camera to find the location of the grid. Once the camera system locates the first line in the grid, it scans to the right-hand edge of the line and then scans across to the start of the next line. The distance between the two points gives the number of pixels per 10mm, which is then divided by 10 to give pixels per 1mm. This can now be used when converting from pixels into mm's. To calculate the distance moved, the bougie tip start frame is subtracted from the bougie tip end frame; this defines the distance in pixels between the two points. By dividing this new value by the number of pixels per mm it is possible to discover the number of millimetres moved by the bougie tip between the start frame and the end frame.

The analysis of video frames is a processor intensive task. As a result, this image-processing task was optimised within the program to allow the processing of video frames in parallel, thereby utilising all of the cores available on the computer/workstation. The main thread of the program controls the file access to the video file and extracts frames as and when they are needed. Once extracted, the image from the frame is passed into a parallel thread, which then proceeds to process the image and extract the required coordinates and data.

Once complete, the thread returns the result to the main thread, which then collates the data into a single data set and writes the output video frame into the output video file. Using this framework, the program is capable of running any number of threads, this is easily modified within the program code to increase or decrease the threads as needed. During testing, the program was set to use eight threads to best utilise all the available cores on our test computer/workstation.

3. CONCLUSION

Utilising object detection and tracking in combination with image processing has ensured that the development of the Shape Retention Testing System (SRTS) has been possible. Developing the SRTS has demonstrated that an accurate, repeatable and reliable testing system can be manufactured to provide anaesthetists and the medical device industry with a testing system capable of providing data to inform device selection and usage decisions. The data collected by the developed SRTS will be utilised to provide evidence for device selection and purchase decisions. In addition, the data collected can also be used to provide evidence to professional societies and academics to inform their guidelines for best practice; this in turn could place the device manufacturers under pressure to conform to a strict device performance criteria. Using object detection and tracking, the SRTS has demonstrated its capability to standardise and monitor many elements not previously considered in studies conducted and published within academic case studies and equipment assessment literature. The SRTS can also be adapted for paediatric equipment assessment in the future. The SRTS will now be used to assess the performance of the extensive bougie introducer range available for purchase within the UK.

ACKNOWLEDGEMENTS

Mr F.L. Siena is a funded PhD student at Nottingham Trent University by a Vice Chancellors PhD Bursary. A Nottingham University Hospitals Charity and NUH Department of Research and Development Pump Priming grant is being used for product development and the manufacture of a Steerable Bougie. The authors would like to acknowledge Mr Frank Worcester's (NTU) contribution to the images produced for this paper.

REFERENCES

Annamaneni, R. et al, 2003. A comparison of simulated difficult intubation with multiple-use and single-use bougies in a manikin. Anaesthesia, 58(1), pp.45-49.Behringer, E.C. and Kristensen, M.S., 2011. Evidence for benefit vs novelty in new intubation equipment. *Anaesthesia*, 66(s2), pp.57-64.

Cook, T.M. et al, 2011. Major complications of airway management in the UK: results of the Fourth National Audit Project of the Royal College of Anaesthetists and the Difficult Airway Society. Part 1: anaesthesia. *British journal of anaesthesia*, 106(5), pp.617-631.

Cook, T.M. et al, 2016. A national survey of the impact of NAP4 on airway management practice in United Kingdom hospitals: closing the safety gap in anaesthesia, intensive care and the emergency department. BJA: *British Journal of Anaesthesia*, 117(2), pp.182-190.

Difficult Airway Society. (2018). Tracheal Tube introducers/exchangers/guides. [Online] Available at: https://www.das.uk.com/content/tracheal-tube-introducersexchangersguides [Accessed 22 Feb. 2018].

Gupta, K. (2013). Detect and Track Objects in Live Webcam Video Based on Color and Size Using C# - CodeProject. [Online] Codeproject.com. Available at: https://www.codeproject.com/Articles/139628/Detect-and-Track-Objects-in-Live-Webcam-Video-Base [Accessed 10 Mar. 2018].

Hodzovic, I. et al, 2004. Evaluation of Frova, single- use intubation introducer, in a manikin. Comparison with Eschmann multiple- use introducer and Portex single- use introducer. *Anaesthesia*, 59(8), pp.811-816.

Hodzovic, I. et al, 2004. Bougie- assisted difficult airway management in a manikin–the effect of position held on placement and force exerted by the tip. *Anaesthesia*, 59(1), pp.38-43.

Intel® RealSense™. (2016). Intel® RealSense™ Camera SR300. [Online] Available at: https://software.intel.com/sites/default/files/managed/0c/ec/realsense-sr300-product-datasheet-rev-1-0.pdf [Accessed 21 Feb. 2018].

Jackson, G.N.B. et al, 2009. Forces required to remove bougies from tracheal tubes. *Anaesthesia*, 64(3), pp.320-322.

Janakiraman, C., Hodzovic, I., Reddy, S., Desai, N., Wilkes, A.R. and Latto, I.P., 2009. Evaluation of tracheal tube introducers in simulated difficult intubation. *Anaesthesia*, 64(3), pp.309-314.

Mushambi, M.C. et al, 2016. A national survey of tracheal tube introducers and associated complications. *Anaesthesia*, 71(7), pp.853-854.

Pandit, J.J. et al, 2011. The Difficult Airway Society 'ADEPT' guidance on selecting airway devices: the basis of a strategy for equipment evaluation. *Anaesthesia*, 66(8), pp.726-737.

Siena, F. et al, 2017. Performance analysis for difficult airway equipment: Standardising for success. *Journal of Health Design*, 2(4), pp.39-41.

SP-LOOP: A LOOP CLOSURE DETECTION METHOD FOR RGB-D SLAM USING SEMANTIC AND POSITION INFORMATION

Xueshi Li[1], Fei Qiao[1], Qi Wei[1], Yi Yang[1], Xinjun Liu[2], Huazhong Yang[1]
[1]*Dept. of Electronic Engineering,*
[2]*Dept. of Mechanical Engineering*
Tsinghua University, Beijing, China

ABSTRACT

Loop closure detection is an important part in a simultaneous localization and mapping (SLAM) system. This paper presents a loop closure detection method for semantic RGB-D SLAM, which makes use of both semantic and position information. Compared with widely used feature-based loop closure detection method, proposed method increases the recall rate of loop closing by 20.3% in texture-less environment.

KEYWORDS

SLAM, Loop Closure Detection, Semantic Segmentation, RGB-D

1. INTRODUCTION

Simultaneous localization and mapping (SLAM) is the problem of constructing a map of surroundings while estimating the camera's pose within it. SLAM is a fundamental problem in robotics. It is widely implemented in various applications which requires the information of surrounding environment and camera pose, such as autonomous driving, unmanned aerial vehicle, augmented reality etc.

With the development of computer vision and deep learning in recent years, many semantic SLAM systems began to emerge. The addition of semantic information can make SLAM systems have a higher level understanding of the surroundings, which enables SLAM systems to complete complex tasks.

Loop closure detection is an important part in a SLAM system, which aims to detect once arrived place and helps SLAM to build a global consistency map by providing extra constraints. The most widely used loop closure detection methods in SLAM systems are based on the bag-of-words (BoW)(Nistér & Stewénius, 2006) model, which makes use of hand-crafted features, such as SIFT, SURF and ORB etc. However, feature-based loop closure detection may fail in conditions such as illumination changing, viewpoint changing and texture-less environment.

In this paper, we propose a loop closure detection method for semantic RGB-D SLAM, using both semantic and position information, named as SP-Loop. A semantic segmentation algorithm, FCIS(Li, Qi, Dai, Ji, & Wei, 2016), is used to extract semantic information from images. The similarity score between two images depends on the similarity of relative positions of detected objects in each image. The main contributions of this work are:

1. A novel method loop closure detection for semantic RGB-D SLAM;
2. Evaluating the similarity of two images at the level of object instead of features;
3. A better performance than feature-based method in texture-less environment.

2. METHOD OF SP-LOOP

The proposed method has three stages to detect loop closures. First, images are preprocessed and the database of image sequence is set up. Second, we calculate the similarity score of images. And finally, temporal consistency is checked. These three steps are detailed as below:

2.1 Set Up Database

Images captured by cameras need semantic segmenting before detecting loops. In this paper, semantic segmentation is handled by FCIS. The output of FCIS gives the masks of detected objects as well as their categories. The centroids of objects are calculated in the camera coordinate system, according to depth information and camera intrinsic parameters. These centroids are used to represent the positions of objects.

Each frame also keeps an index of categories, recording the amount of objects detected in each category. When an image is queried in the database, the index can help to list the candidates of possible loop closing frames in the database quickly.

2.2 Calculate Similarity Score

The score represents the similarity of objects' positional relationship, which is calculated by lengths and angles of corresponding vectors pointing from one object to another in two images. Calculating similarity score including 4 steps as follows:

1. Check the number of objects in each category. Only two images that have exactly the same number of objects in each category may be considered as a loop.

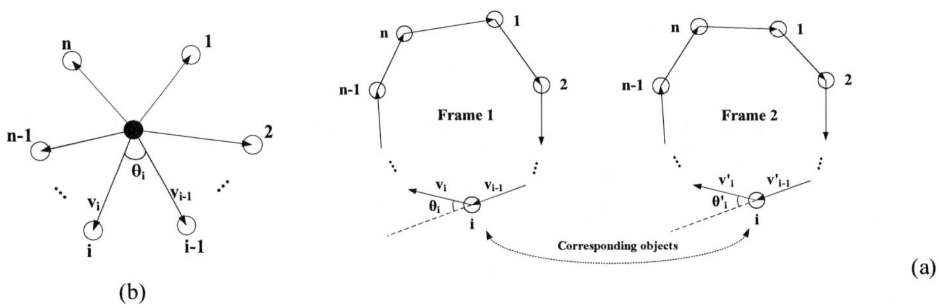

Figure 1. Each Circle Represents the Position of Object Centroids. (a) Shows the Relative Postion of One Object (Black Circle in the Middle) to the Other Objects; (b) Shows the Corresponence of Arranged Objects In Two Images

2. Arrange objects in order. Correspondences of objects are determined in this step.

a) If there is at most one object in each category, the correspondences are simply determined by comparing the categories of objects.

b) If there is at least one category that contains more than one object, the correspondences of the objects in this category are determined by comparing their relative position to objects in other categories. Objects in two images with the most similar position to other objects are treated as corresponding objects. The similarity is calculated using the lengths and angles of relative position vectors, as defined in Figure 1(a). Calculation is the same as step 3 and 4 detailed below.

As the correspondences are determined, arrange the objects in a predefined order according to their categories as shown in Figure 1(b).

3. Calculate vectors between centroids of adjacent objects and angles between adjacent vectors. As shown in Figure 1(b), vector v_i points from the i-th object to the (i+1)-th object, angle θ_i represents the angle between vector v_{i-1} and v_i.

4. Calculate similarity score according to corresponding vectors. By comparing the relative errors of lengths of vectors and the relative errors of angles between vectors, the similarity of relative position of objects are determined. The definition of average relative length error and average relative angle error is shown as (1) and (2).

$$E_{\text{length}} = \frac{2}{n}\sum_{i}\frac{|\|v_i\| - \|v'_i\||}{\|v_i\| + \|v'_i\|} \quad (1)$$

$$E_{\text{angle}} = \frac{2}{n}\sum_{i}\frac{|\theta_i - \theta'_i|}{\theta_i + \theta'_i} \quad (2)$$

The similarity score of two images is defined as

$$Score = (1 - E_{\text{length}})\,(1 - E_{\text{angle}}). \quad (3)$$

2.3 Check Temporal Consistency

A high similarity score usually represents a place once reached. However, since error may occur in any steps during the calculation, the similarity score may go wrong too. For example, instance segmentation may wrongly detect or categorize an object.

To avoid this, we check the images for temporal consistency. If the queried image is similar to images in a period of time, and so do the images near the queried image, it is then considered as a closed loop. Then take the image pair with the maximum similarity score as the loop.

3. EXPERIMENT

Results of experiments in case of normal and texture-less environment are shown in this section. Proposed method and DBoW2(Galvez-Lopez & Tardos, 2012) are compared. Images in datasets are taken using Kinect2 depth camera with resolution of 960×540. The dictionary of DBoW2 has 6 levels and each level has 10 branches, which is generated using ORB features. It is trained using images captured from the same scenes as datasets used in experiments. Semantic segmentation of SP-Loop is handled by FCIS, as mentioned earlier. The FCIS model is trained on MSCOCO(Lin et al., 2014) dataset.

The comparison of precision-recall curves between SP-Loop and DBoW2 is shown in Figure 2. On dataset of normal environment, DBoW2 performs slightly better than SP-Loop. While on dataset of texture-less environment, since feature detection easily fails in texture-less environments, DBoW2 has a decreased performance in this case too. Results show that the recall rate of SP-Loop can reach a maximum of 76.6% when precision rate is 100%, while DBoW2 reaches a maximum of 56.3%, which is 20.3% lower than that of SP-Loop.

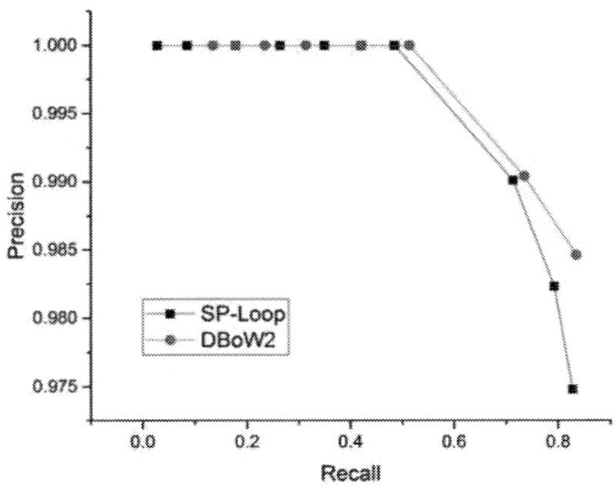

(a)

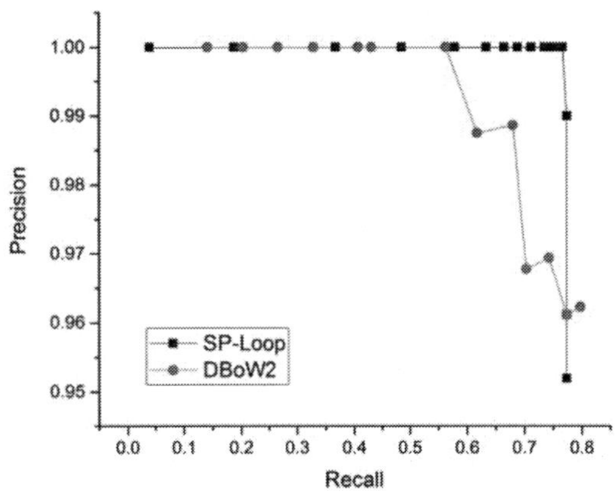

(b)

Figure 2. Precision-Recall Rate On Dataset of (a) Normal Environment (b) Texture-Less Environment

4. CONCLUSION

This paper presents the SP-Loop algorithm, a loop closure detection method for RGB-D SLAM making use of both semantic and position information. SP-Loop provides a feature-free method for loop closing in semantic SLAM system. The similarity of two images is determined by the similarity of relative position of the objects in the images. Experiments show that proposed semantic method can reach a recall rate 20.3% higher than DBoW2, classic feature-based method, in the case of texture-less environment.

Future work is going to realize a map-to-map method rather than the image-to-image one. Since semantic segmentation algorithm is not accurate enough, a single image often has errors. A local map is built making use of recent images and is able to correct the errors by voting scheme. Map-to-map method is able to obtain a better recall rate. Map-to-map method is also able to solve the problem when there are too few objects in an image to calculate similarity score.

Another consideration is to change the semantic segmentation algorithm from FCIS to another method making use of RGB-D image in order to obtain more accurate and robust segmentation results.

REFERENCES

Nister, D., & Stewenius, H. (2006). Scalable recognition with a vocabulary tree. In *Computer vision and pattern recognition, 2006 IEEE computer society conference on* (Vol. 2, pp. 2161-2168). Ieee.

Filliat, D. (2007, April). A visual bag of words method for interactive qualitative localization and mapping. In *Robotics and Automation, 2007 IEEE International Conference on* (pp. 3921-3926). IEEE.

Gálvez-López, D., & Tardos, J. D. (2012). Bags of binary words for fast place recognition in image sequences. *IEEE Transactions on Robotics*, *28*(5), 1188-1197.

Mur-Artal, R., Montiel, J. M. M., & Tardos, J. D. (2015). ORB-SLAM: a versatile and accurate monocular SLAM system. *IEEE Transactions on Robotics*, *31*(5), 1147-1163.

Cummins, M., & Newman, P. (2011). Appearance-only SLAM at large scale with FAB-MAP 2.0. *The International Journal of Robotics Research*, *30*(9), 1100-1123.

Salas-Moreno, R. F., Newcombe, R. A., Strasdat, H., Kelly, P. H., & Davison, A. J. (2013, June). *Slam++: Simultaneous localisation and mapping at the level of objects.* In Computer Vision and Pattern Recognition (CVPR), 2013 IEEE Conference on (pp. 1352-1359). IEEE.

Li, Y., Qi, H., Dai, J., Ji, X., & Wei, Y. (2017, July). Fully convolutional instance-aware semantic segmentation. In *IEEE Conf. on Computer Vision and Pattern Recognition (CVPR)*(pp. 2359-2367).

Lin, T. Y., Maire, M., Belongie, S., Hays, J., Perona, P., Ramanan, D., ... & Zitnick, C. L. (2014, September). Microsoft coco: Common objects in context. In *European conference on computer vision* (pp. 740-755). Springer, Cham.

Williams, B., Cummins, M., Neira, J., Newman, P., Reid, I., & Tardós, J. (2009). A comparison of loop closing techniques in monocular SLAM. *Robotics and Autonomous Systems*, *57*(12), 1188-1197.

Lowry, S., Sünderhauf, N., Newman, P., Leonard, J. J., Cox, D., Corke, P., & Milford, M. J. (2016). Visual place recognition: A survey. *IEEE Transactions on Robotics*, *32*(1), 1-19.

ADAPTIVE SCREEN SAMPLING ALGORITHM ACCELERATION FOR VOLUME RENDERING

Sergey Belyaev[1], Vladislav Shubnikov[2] and Nikita Motornyi[1]
[1]*Peter The Great St.Petersburg Politechnic University, St.Petersburg, Russia*
[2]*Epam Systems, St.Petersburg, Russia*

ABSTRACT

Adaptive screen sampling that allows to yield an image by calculating a volume integral for just a part of pixels is one of volume rendering acceleration methods. This method is efficient if source data is highly coherent. The efficiency of the method decreases rapidly as source data coherence decreases. We propose a modification of the above-mentioned method that makes it less dependent on source data coherence. The modified method is a two-pass one. On the first pass, performed for only a part of pixels, volume integral values for the set of intervals where the transfer function value is not zero are calculated and saved to the G-buffer. On the second pass, these volume integral values are used for fast calculation of the remaining pixels' colors. This method allows to increase the speed of the standard adaptive screen sampling method by 1,6 times on the average, depending on the source data.

KEYWORDS

Volumetric Rendering, Performance Acceleration, Adaptive Sampling

1. INTRODUCTION

Direct volume render, whereby volume integral values are calculated for each pixel of the image, is the principal scientific (e.g. medical) data visualization method. This method allows to efficiently research data volumes by setting various transfer functions, but it is computationally expensive. Its run time is proportional to the number of pixels in the visualization window, so the method's optimization for high-resolution displays and/or low performance devices (e.g. mobile devices, laptops and PCs with low performance video boards, and VR devices that require minimal FPS 60 with two-camera rendering) is an important objective. Adaptive screen sampling is one of the optimization methods for direct volume render. For the first time this method was proposed in (Levoy, 1990), whereby the image space was broken down into same-sized blocks and volume integrals were calculated for the corners of these blocks. If integral values for these corners have relatively small difference, the colors of the pixels inside the blocks were calculated by bilinear interpolation. Otherwise, a block was recursively split into four parts. (Kratz, 2011) proposed a variation of Levoy's approach for GPU-based rendering. They have replaced the comparison of integral values for corner points of the blocks with a more sophisticated technique based on finite elements methods (FEM) to achieve explicit error control. In their implementation, ray casting was performed on GPU, and hierarchical data structures block support (quadtree) was performed on CPU. Methods to remove artifacts arising from the fact that the volume integral is not calculated for all pixels are discussed in (Kim, 2016). Recursive splitting in the GPU implementation leads to multi-pass algorithms that prove inefficient because of certain GPU architecture aspects. Therefore, a two-pass algorithm was used in (Lesar, 2015). For this algorithm, the colors of all pixels inside the block were calculated either by bilinear interpolation or by volume integral calculation. A two-pass algorithm was also used in (Bruder, 2016) for ray tracing implementation on mobile devices.

In practice, most source data (medical as well) show relatively high spatial coherence, so after the first iteration, the number of pixels that must be additionally sampled during the subsequent iteration is approx. 5-40% of the final image pixel count. Implemented on GPU, adaptive screen sampling yields an almost double speed-up if additional sampling is required for less than 10% of pixels. If this proportion increases, adaptive screen sampling efficiency decreases considerably. The reason is that on GPU, pixels are processed group by group, and a processing time for a group is the same as the longest time required to process its constituent pixels.

The method we propose is a two-pass one. On the first pass, performed for selected pixels, volume integral values for the set of intervals where the transfer function value is not zero are calculated and saved to the G-buffer (for example Kaufman, 2005). On the second pass, these volume integral values are used for fast calculation of the remaining pixels' colors. Thus, the method speeds up the processing of pixels whose colors cannot be calculated by linear interpolation of the adjacent pixels calculated on the first pass.

Section 2 describes what we perceive as our main contributions, i.e. a method to accelerate volume rendering by preliminary calculation of volume integral values for a part of pixels. Section 3 describes the results of our research. Section 4 sums up our work.

2. ALGORITHM

The algorithm we propose employs a two-pass adaptive screen sampling method. In accordance with the method, a pixel set is broken down into n*n sized blocks, and one pixel for each block is processed during the first pass. However, apart from calculating the color of pixel C, the L_i intervals where the transfer function value is not zero and volume integral I_i values on such intervals are also determined during the ray casting process. The calculated values are saved to the G-buffer. On the figure 1, the processed pixels (for n=2) are denoted as A.

I_i is a four-component vector that contains color C_i (three components vector) and transparency a_i (scalar). L_i is a 2-components vector, contained distances from ray start point to start and end of the i-th interval. The other pixels are processed during the second pass. Figure 2a depicts the algorithm of the second pass (in a two-dimension case for the sake of simplicity). We assume that the transfer function values are not zero only in the area painted grey. The boundary values for intervals L_i^1 and L_i^2 and volume integral values for these intervals I^1_i, I^2_i are calculated and stored in the G-buffer. The pixel under processing is on ray *r*.

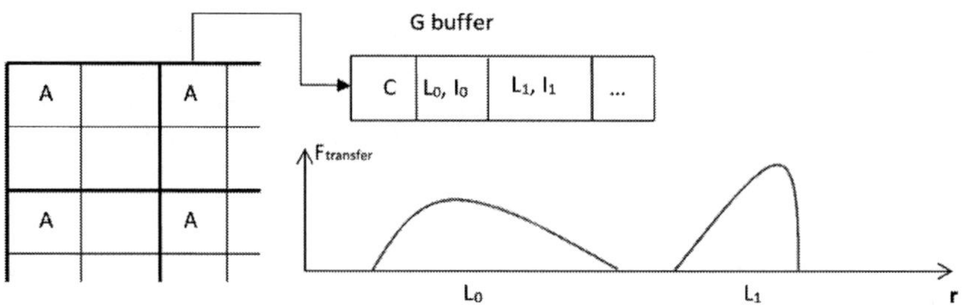

Figure 1. The G-buffer contains the color of pixel C, the intervals L_i on the ray **r**, where the transfer function value is not zero, and volume integral I_i values on these intervals

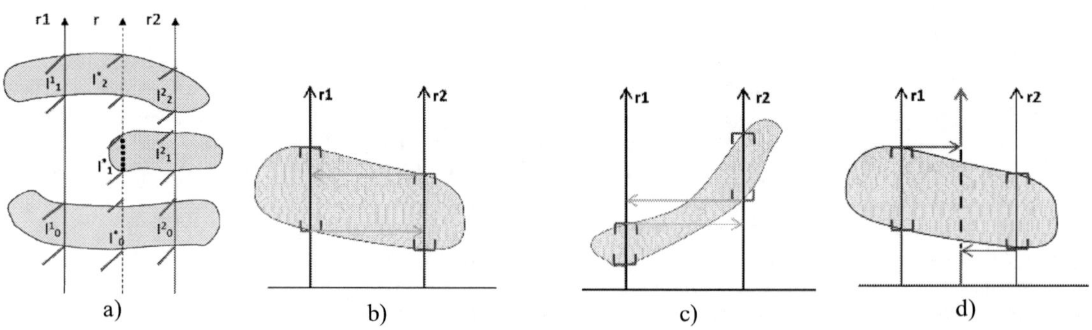

Figure 2. Volume Integral Calculation

Let $|I^1_0|$, $|I^2_0|$ and $|I^1_1|$, $|I^2_2|$ have pairwise proximate values. Then I^*_0 и I^*_2 can be calculated by bilinear interpolation. Thus, calculating I^*_1 is sufficient to calculate the volume integral on ray ***r***. The problem of integration along the whole ray is reduced to the problem of integration on a part of this ray. Algorithm uses similarity of such intervals. Intervals are considered similar if their projections onto the ray under processing are intersecting. Figure 2 depicts similar (b) and dissimilar (c) intervals, respectively. For similar intervals, their volume integral values are checked for proximity. If the difference matches to the following condition:

$$|I_i - I_j| < \delta \quad (1)$$

a bilinear interpolation of volume integral values on the four investigated intervals is performed. Otherwise, a volume integral value is calculated on the ray under processing from the minimal boundary for all intervals up to the maximum one, as shown on the figure 2d. If the intervals are not similar, the algorithm proceeds straight to volume integral value calculation. The integration interval is determined just as in the above-mentioned case. Interval selection and processing are performed in accordance to the following algorithm:

1. Let Index[k] (k=1...4) be the indices of the current intervals on neighboring rays to be processed
2. If (for all k intervals are similar) {
3. Process intervals;
4. for (k=1;k<5;k++) Index[k]++;
5. }
6. else {
7. Let j be such that Index[j] is the index of the interval most proximate to the ray's start point.
8. Process interval with index Index[j];
9. Index[j] ++
10. }

For example, for the two-dimension case shown on Figure 3, the algorithm's operation will yield the following sequence of intervals: (1,4); (2); (5); (3,6).

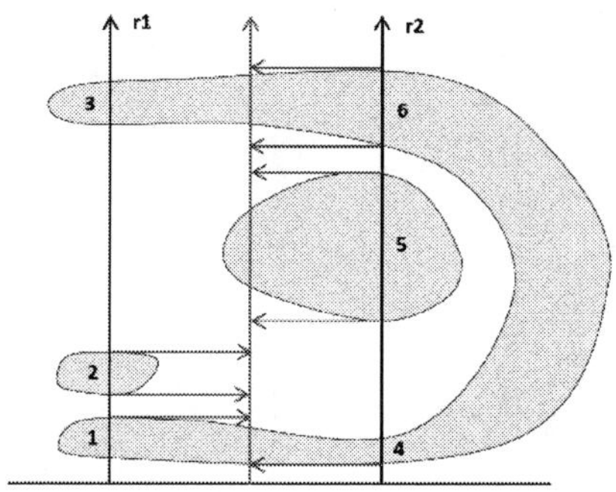

Figure 3. Interval Processing Sequence

3. RESULTS

All tests were performed on a 3.4GHz Intel Core i7-2600 CPU with 4.0GB of main memory with NVidia GForce GTX 780 Ti graphics hardware with 3072MB of texture memory and implemented GPU-based algorithm на Unity, using OpenGl ES 3.1. 6 CT data sets were used as source data. Refer to Table 1 for their parameters and screenshots.

Table 2 contains the data on the achieved performance (FPS) during the visualization of these data sets. Volume integral values calculation used the standard method (Kruger, 2003), with an invariable step equal to (1/2048) of voxel size. A rectangular parallelepiped was used as a delimiting volume. The visualization window resolution was 1200x900 pixels. The n value (block size) was set at 3.

Table 2 is laid out as follows. The cells in the table's first column contain data set numbers (according to the Table 1). The columns A, B, and C contain FPS values obtained under the following conditions:

A. No optimization

B. Two-pass adaptive screen sampling

C. Two-pass adaptive screen sampling, optimization using the stencil buffer and integration interval splitting into 8 parts.

The following two columns contain visualization acceleration values achieved using the standard two-pass adaptive screen sampling algorithm and the algorithm we propose, respectively. The penultimate column contains acceleration values that can be ascribed only to the use of the proposed algorithm. The last column contains the ratio K (the proportion of the number of pixels whose colors could not be calculated by linear interpolation and the total pixel count). The K ratio describes the extent of source data non-coherence for the selected transfer function.

Table 1. Source Data

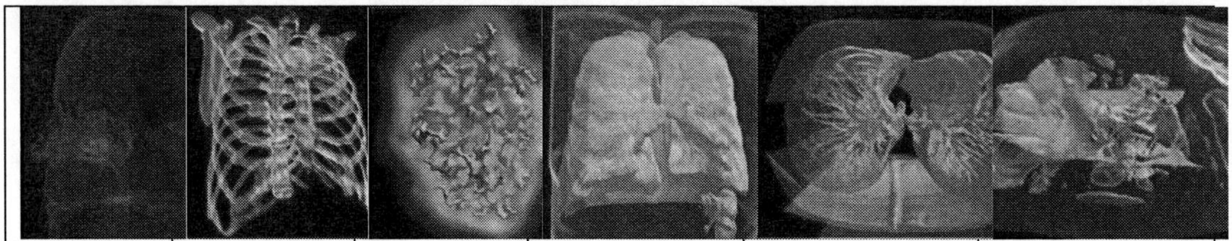

Head 256x256x256	Lungs 256x256x256	Molecule field 128x181x168	Lungs 512x512x136	Lungs 512x512x136	Pelvis 512x512x150

Table 2. Comparison with the Basic Method

Data set Number	FPS			B/A ratio	C/A ratio	C/B ratio	K ratio
	A	B	C				
1	32	72	118	1,19	2,25	3,69	1,64
2	48	92	116	0,96	1,92	2,42	1,26
3	34	68	112	1,00	2,00	3,29	1,65
4	40	66	74	0,95	1,65	1,85	1,12
5	18	32	50	1,11	1,78	2,78	1,56
6	20	42	74	1,10	2,10	3,70	1,76

The table 2 shows that a standard two-pass adaptive screen sampling increases FPS by a factor of 1.95 on the average, while the FPS increase for the method we propose is by a factor of 2.95. Thus, the method we propose speeds up the basic adaptive screen sampling method by a factor of 1.6 on the average. Acceleration values lower than this average are attested in the cases, when the early ray termination condition is satisfied for a significant number of rays (bones in source data sets 2 and 4). In opposite cases, the acceleration is higher than the average, inversely proportionally to source data coherence for the selected transfer function.

As source data coherence decreases, the number of pixels to be processed on the algorithm's second pass increases. This is what happens when parameter δ value in (1), determining the applicability of bilinear interpolation, is decreased. At the first approximation, the relationship between the method's efficiency and source data coherence can be evaluated by applying the method at various δ values. Figure 4a depicts in blue the pixels that were processed on the second pass of Data Set 4 visualization with δ values at 0.2, 0.1, and 0.05, respectively. For these values, the non-coherence ratio K values are 0.05, 0.15, and 0.32, respectively.

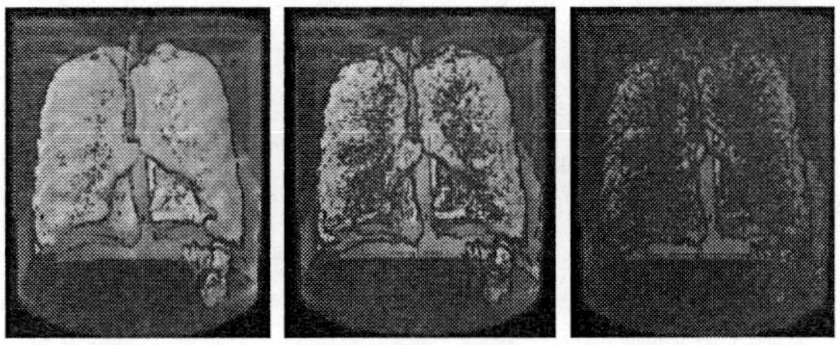

a

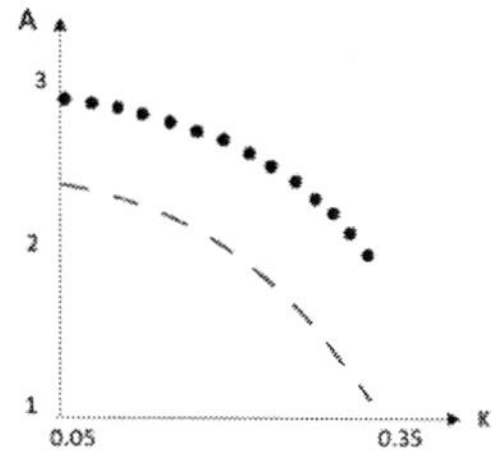

b

Figure 4. a) The pixels processed at the second pass of data set 4 visualization for δ = 0.2; 0.1; 0.05. b) The relationship between volume rendering acceleration (A) and data incoherence K ratio, for the basic method (dashed) and the proposed method (dotted)

These data were used to plot the curves depicting the relationship between acceleration an incoherence K values (see Figure 4b) for the basic method and the proposed method, respectively.

4. CONCLUSION

In this article, we propose a modification of the adaptive screen sampling method that allows to speed it up by a factor of 1.6 on the average. The efficiency of the modified method depends on the source data coherence to a lesser extent, albeit it does decrease as data coherence decreases. Described algorithm can be used for visualization of the medical volumetric data with large spatial coherency.

REFERENCES

Bruder V., Frey S., Ertl T., 2016. Real-time performance prediction and tuning for interactive volume raycasting. *Proceedings of SIGGRAPH ASIA 2016 Symposium on Visualization.*

Kaufman A., Mueller K., 2005. Overview of Volume Rendering. *Chapter of Visualization Handbook (2005).*

Kim, Y., et al. 2016. Adaptive undersampling for efficient mobile ray tracing. The Visual Computer (*Proceedings of Computer Graphics International 2016*), 1–11.

Kratz, A., et al., 2011. Adaptive screen-space sampling for volume ray-casting. *Tech.report Konrad-Zuse-Zentrum fur Informationstechnik Berlin* (2011).

Kruger J., Westermann R., 2003. Acceleration techniques for GPU-based volume rendering. *In Proceedings of IEEE Visualization 2003* (2003), pp. 287–292.

Lesar Z., 2015. Real-time ray casting of volumetric data. *Proceedings of EUROCON 2015 - International Conference on Computer as a Tool* (EUROCON), IEEE. DOI: 10.1109/EUROCON.2015.7313802

Levoy M., 1990, Volume rendering by adaptive refinement. *In Visual Computing*. 6, 1 (1990), 2–7.

MORAN'S Z BASED ADAPTIVE IMAGE FILTER

Tzong-Jer Chen
School of Information Engineering, Baise University, Baise, Guangxi, 533000 China

ABSTRACT

A medical image filtering algorithm based on spatial autocorrelation is proposed. The Moran's Z calculation is used to adapt the average filter. The noisy PET image is reconstructed using MLEM iteration with a low-pass filter applied in image quality improvement post-reconstruction. In practice, a Gaussian filter is often performed for post-filtering. Although this low-pass filter removes the noise in reconstructed PET images, it is associated with significant quantitative information loss. Two phantoms, Huffman and Utah, are used in this work to simulate a Siemens PET scanner using the GATE algorithm. The sinogram was reconstructed using the OSEM algorithm on Matlab. The image noise level with different numbers of iteration were then calculated and filtered using an average filter with or without Moran's Z adaptation. Image qualities were estimated using PSNR calculation. The PSNR of images using the proposed scheme are higher than those using the non-adaptive average filter. The algorithm visual processing is good but more forward research is required.

KEYWORDS

Image De-Noise, Moran Statistics, Adaptive Filter, PET

1. INTRODUCTION

Radiography is a widely used technology in medical applications. In the diagnostic medicine field, digital image applications have led to their rapid expansion. Digital images may be contaminated by a variety of noise sources during acquisition, processing, transmission and reconstruction. Image filtering or enhancements are required for medical image visual quality improvement [Ruikar J.D. et al, 2013].

In the nuclear medicine field, the positron emission tomography (PET) was used to generate activity distribution images to extract a patient's physiological information. The activity distribution projections obtained first by the detector rings around the patient. Images are then created using reconstruction algorithms. The filtered back-projection (FBP) algorithm is the most common image reconstruction method. However, due to the limited number of projection sets, the FBP algorithm introduces streak artifacts into the reconstructed images [Huesman R.H., 1977].

For better image quality the maximum-likelihood expectation–maximization (MLEM) [Shepp L.A., Vardi Y., 1982] and ordered subsets expectation–maximization (OSEM) [Hudson M. and Larkin R.S., 1994] algorithms for iterative image reconstruction were recently developed. These algorithms are iterative methods for computing maximum-likelihood.

In iteration process low frequency image components appear first and then gradually the detailed parts are developed as the iterations progress. The reconstructed image quality gradually improves in the beginning iterations. However, after a certain point in the number of iterations the image quality becomes noisier [Snyder D.L. and Miller M.T., 1985]. At higher iteration numbers, images produced by the MLEM algorithm become noisier even though the likelihood still increases. To yield a quality image, one can stop the algorithm before this deterioration phase develops or after a fixed number of iterations [Bissantz et al, 2006]. In practice, the MLEM iteration is stopped prematurely and a post-reconstruction low-pass filter is then applied [Hamill J. and Bruckbauer T., 2002]. Post-filtering can be easily optimized for specific tasks. In clinical practice, a Gaussian filter (GF) is often performed for post-filtering. Although GF improved quality in reconstructed PET images but it was associated with a significant loss of quantitative information.

The adaptive un-sharp masking and nonlinear module was recently proposed [Fu S.J. et al., 2007]. These algorithms enhance images while effectively decreasing the noise. The development of adaptive, nonlinear modules for image enhancement may be a good approach. Chen et al. and Shiao et al. proved Moran's Z to be a good index for determining image smoothness or sharpness [Chen T.J. et al, 2006, Shiao Y.H. et al, 2007]. These statistics also showed that it had ability to distinguish between image noise and edges [Chen T.J. et al, 2016]. Both Chen et al. and Hung et al. recently proposed adaptive filters using Moran statistics [Chen T.J. et al, 2016, 2017, Hung C.C. and Chang E.S., 2017]. They found that, the average [Chen T.J. et al, 2017] and median filter [Hung C.C. and Chang E.S., 2017] could be used successfully in noise filtering with adaptive Moran statistics.

A post-filtering method using Moran statistics as an adapting priori on PET image filtering was presented. This statistical method was applied to determine if an image area belongs in the edge, noise or smooth areas. Following that, the average filters without or with Moran's Z calculations were then applied to this noisy image. The results showed that this filter worked better than the non-adaptive filter.

2. METHODS AND MATERIALS

2.1 Phantom and Simulation

Two phantoms, Huffman and Utah, were used in this research. The GATE (GEANT4 application for tomographic emission V3.1 x64) algorithm was used to simulate the ECAT 951/31 (CTI, Knoxville, TN) PET scanner. The scanner has a radius of 300mm with 256 parallel detector tubes per angle and a total of 192 angles. The PET sinogram was produced when the simulation reached 900 Mega counts and without any post correction. PET images were then obtained using the OSEM reconstruction algorithm in a division of four subsets. Two 128×128 Hoffman and Utah phantoms, as shown in Figure 1, 2 were used for simulations, respectively. Iterations up to one hundred were made for each phantom.

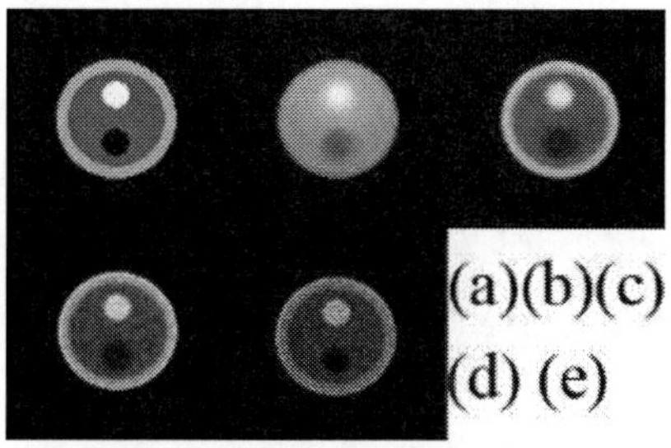

Figure 1. Utah phantom with various iterations, (a)Utah phantom, (b) one iteration,(c)22 iterations, (d)36 iterations, (e)100 iterations

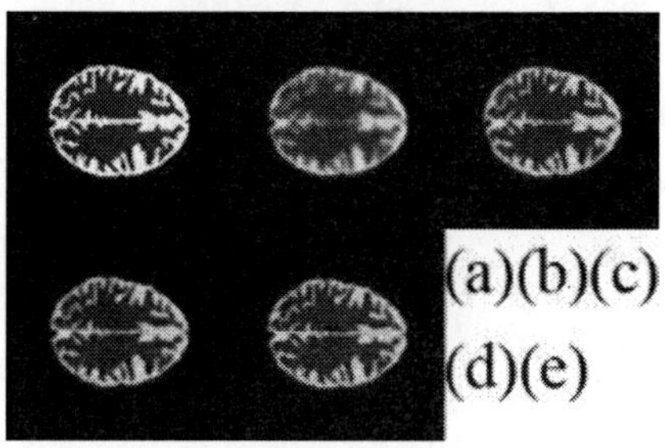

Figure 2. Hoffman phantom with various iterations, (a) Hoffman phantom, (b) 5 iterations, (c) 22 iterations, (d) 48 iterations,(e) 97 iterations

2.2 The Moran's Z

The Moran statistics are used to evaluate the randomness of mapped data by measuring the spatial autocorrelation [Cliff A.D .and Ord J.K., 1981]. The Moran parameter measurement R in a window (a window is part of an image) was calculated as:

$$R = \frac{N \sum_{j=1}^{mxn} \sum_{i=1}^{mxn} \delta_{ij} (x_i - \bar{x})(x_j - \bar{x})}{S_0 \sum_{i=1}^{rxc} (x_i - \bar{x})^2} \quad (1)$$

Where x_i is the gray level for pixel i, $\bar{x}$ is the mean gray level of the window, $S_0 = 2(2mn - m - n)$, m and n are the number of rows and columns in the window, N is the total number of pixels in the window, and $\delta_{ij} = 1$ if pixel i and j are adjacent and 0 otherwise. The numerator and denominator are measures of the covariance and variance among the pixels, respectively. When the size of N is large enough, the variable M approximately follows a normal distribution with the mean and variance given by

$$a = -1/(N-1) \quad (2)$$

and

$$\sigma^2 = \frac{N[(N^2 - 3N + 3)S_1 - NS_2 + 3S_0^2] - K[N(N-1)S_1 - 2NS_2 + 6S_0^2]}{(N-1)(N-2)(N-3)S_0^2} - a^2 \quad (3)$$

where $K = N\sum(x_i - \bar{x})^4 / [\sum(x_i - \bar{x})^2]^2$, $S_1 = 2S_0$, and $S_2 = 8(8mn - 7m - 7n + 4)$. The standardized normal statistic,

$$Z = \frac{R - a}{\sigma} \quad (4)$$

, will show randomness in the image data. It can be used to determine noise, blurring and edge in an image. The 5×5 window was used for Moran's Z calculation, in this report.

2.3 Image Noise Calculation

Olsen [Olsen S.I., 1993] proposed a method to calculate the noise levels in images. He found that using standard deviation (STD) to estimate Gaussian or uniform additive noise in a residual image was most reliable. A residual image can be obtained by subtracting the pre-filtered image from the original, in which the filtered image is produced using an average or median filter. The 3×3 and 5×5 windows were used for the average filter and STD calculation, respectively.

2.4 Image Quality Evaluation

The peak signal to noise ratio (PSNR) is an index of the fidelity between the original and the manipulated image or signal [Chen T.J. et al., 2017]. PSNR has generally been widely used to estimate the quality of reconstruction for lossy image compression algorithms [Lin L.H. and Chen T.J., 2018]. PSNR is an approximation of human vision evaluations of reconstruction quality. The higher the PSNR the better fidelity between images.

$$PSNR(dB) = 10 \log_{10} \left[\frac{(2^n - 1)^2}{\frac{1}{N} \sum_i [P_A(i) - P_B(i)]^2} \right] \quad (5)$$

, where n is the depth of the bits in a pixel and N is the total number of pixels. The pixel values are denoted as $\boldsymbol{P_A}$, original, and $\boldsymbol{P_B}$, manipulated image, respectively.

3. RESULTS

3.1 Noise Levels

The PET image noise levels were estimated using average STD calculation on residual images. The residual image was produced by subtracting the filtered image from the original. Figure 3 shows the average STD vs. number of iterations for two phantoms. The noise levels in PET images are ascending with the iteration numbers increasing for both phantoms. This result is consistent with the previous reports [Snyder D.L. and Miller M.T., 1985].

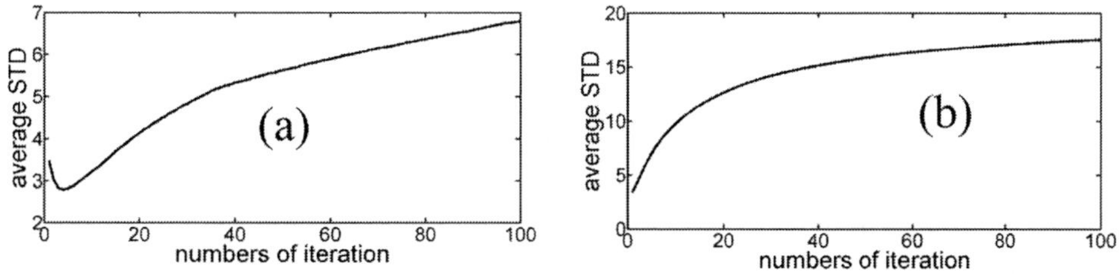

Figure 3. The Average STD of Various Iterations of (a) Utah Phantom, and (b) Hoffman Phantom

3.2 Image Quality

The PSNR results, image quality, corresponding to increasing numbers of iterations for the Utah and Hoffman phantoms are shown in Figures 4 and 5, respectively. The PSNR becomes steady after some iteration points. However, the filtering caused PSNR degradation in the images. The image noise was reduced after low-pass filtering but the quality decreased, as in Figure 4 (a) and Figure 5 (a). Image areas can be categorized as structural areas and noise [Chen T.J. et al, 2016]. The Z value on an image can be used to distinguish between the noise and structure. Both Figure 4 (b) and Figure 5 (b) show that the PSNR of filtered phantoms using the Moran adaptive filter is better than the traditional average filter, shown in Figure 4 (a) and Figure 5 (a). The Z value is set at 3.4 based on previous study [Chen T.J. et al, 2016, 2017]. The area was treated as a noise area if the Z value is lower than the setting point.

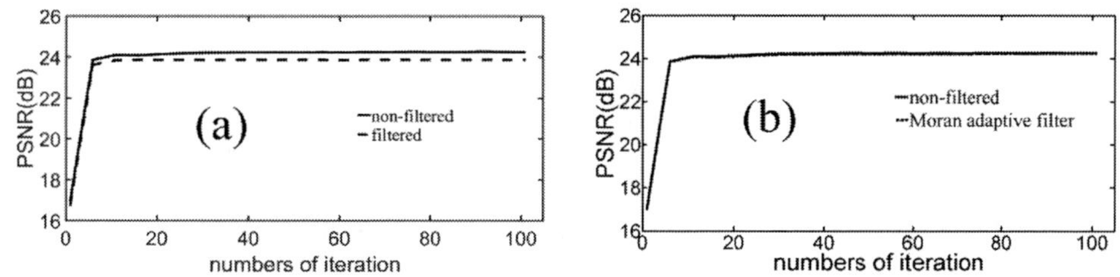

Figure 4. The PSNR of the Utah phantom for various iterations. (a) non-filtered, filtered (b) Moran adaptive filter

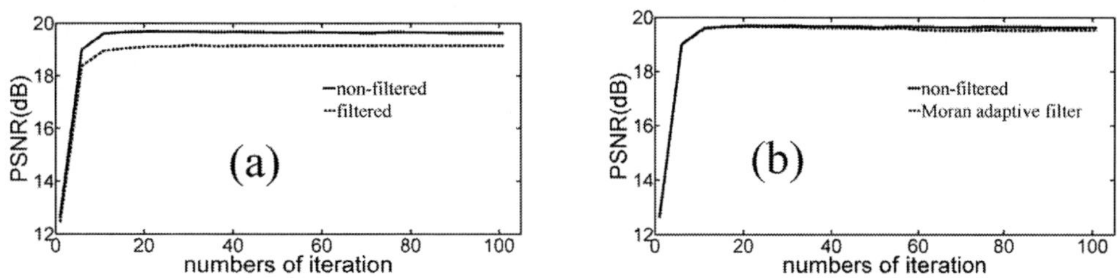

Figure 5. The PSNR of Hoffman phantom for various iterations. (a) non-filtered, filtered (b) Moran adaptive filter

4. CONCLUSIONS

The Moran's Z calculation was successfully used as an adaptive average filter cintroller. Two phantoms, Huffman and Utah, were used to prove the effectiveness of this method. The proposed scheme promotes image PSNR better than the non-adaptive average filter. The Z value is set at 3.4 based on a previous study. Areas were treated as a noise if the calculation Z value is lower than the setting point, or treated as a structure area if higher than the setting point. For effectiveness testing, we varied the Moran's Z and set at 1.5. Figure 6 shows PSNR for the Utah phantom for non-filtered and Moran adaptive filter. The PSNR for the Moran adaptive filter is slightly higher than that of the non-filtered line. The algorithm visual processing is good but more forward research is required.

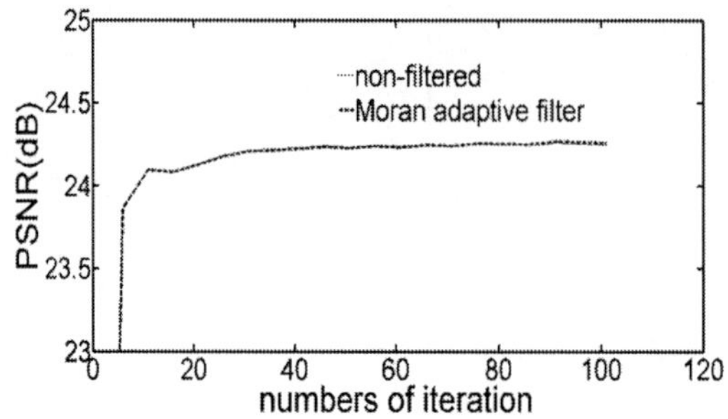

Figure 6. The PSNR (part) of Utah phantom for non-filtered and Moran adaptive filter, Moran's Z was set at 1.5

REFERENCES

Bissantz N., Mair B.A, Munk A., 2006. Amulti-scale stopping criterion for MLEM reconstruction in PET. *In: IEEE medical imaging conference proceedings*. San Diego, CA, USA, pp. 3376-3379.

Chen T.J. et al, 2017. A novel edge-preserving filter for medical image enhancement. *CGVCVIP 2017*, Lisbon, Portugal, pp. 279-284.

Chen T.J. et al, 2017. Compressed Medical Image Quality Determination Using the Kolmogorov Smirnov Test. *Current Medical Imaging Reviews*, 13(2), pp.204-209.

Chen T.J.et al, 2016. A pilot study on a new image enhancement method using spatial statistics. *Joint International Information Technology, Mechanical and Electronic Engineering Conference (JIMEC 2016)*, XiAn, China, pp.33-38.

Chen T.J.et al., 2006. A blurring index for medical images. *J Digital Imaging*, 19, pp.118-125.

Cliff A.D. and Ord J.K., 1981. *Spatial process: models and applications*. Pion, London, UK.

Fu S.J. et al., 2007. A feature dependent fuzzy bidirectional flow for adaptive image sharpening. *Neurocomputing*, 70, pp. 883-895.

Hamill J. and Bruckbauer T., 2002. Iterative reconstruction methods for high-throughput PET tomographs. *Phys Med Biol.*, 47, pp.2627–36.

Hudson M. and Larkin R.S., 1994. Accelerated image reconstruction using ordered subsets of projection data. *IEEE Trans Med Img.*, 13, pp.601–609.

Huesman R.H., 1977. The effects of a finite number of projection angles and finite lateral sampling of projections on the propagation of statistical errors in transverse section reconstruction. *Phys Med Biol.*, 22(3), pp511–521.

Hung C.C. and Chang E.S., 2017. Moran's I for impulse noise detection and removal in color images. *J. Electron. Imaging*, 26(2), pp. 309-318.

Lin L.H. and Chen T.J., 2018. Mutual Information Correlation with Human Vision in Medical Image Compression. *Current Medical Imaging Reviews*, 14(1), pp.64-70.

Olsen S.I., 1993. Estimation of noise in images: an evaluation. *CVGIP* , 55, pp. 319-323.

Ruikar J.D.et al, 2013. Review of image enhancement techniques. *International Conference on Information Technology in Signal and Image Processing-ITSIP.* Mumbai, India, pp.18-19.

Shepp L.A. and Vardi Y., 1982. Maximum likelihood reconstruction for emission tomography. *IEEE Trans Med Img.*, MI-1(2), pp.113–121.

Shiao Y.H. et al, 2007. Quality of Compressed Medical Images. *J of Digital Imaging*, 20, pp.149-159.

Snyder D. L. and Miller M. T., 1985. The use of sieves to stabilize images produced with the EM algorithm for emission tomography. *IEEE Trans. Nucl. Sci.* , NS-32, pp.3864-3872.

PROBABILISTIC AND BOTTLENECK TANDEM FEATURES FOR EMOTION RECOGNITION FROM VIDEOS

Salma Kasraoui[1], Zied Lachiri[1] and Kurosh Madani[2]
[1]*University of Tunis el Manar, LR-SITI Laboratory*
National Engineering School of Tunis, BP.37 Le Bélvedère, 1002, Tunis, Tunisia
[2] *Université Paris-Est, University Paris-Est Créteil, LISSI EA-3956 Laboratory,*
Senart-FB Institute of Technology, 36-37 rue Charpak, 77127, Lieusaint, France

ABSTRACT

This paper proposes a tandem based approach for handcrafted features optimization in facial expression recognition (FER) in the wild. The approach trains an artificial neural network (ANN) to generate new trainable features: probabilistic features and bottleneck features. The former are generated from the class probabilities estimates and the latter are obtained from the activations of a narrow hidden layer in the ANN. In this work, we train a multi-layer perceptron (MLP) on Local Binary Patterns on Three Orthogonal Planes (LBP-TOP) features to extract the so-called probabilistic and bottleneck features. Support Vector Machines (SVM) are used to predict one of the seven emotion categories (anger, disgust, fear, happiness, sadness, surprise and neutral) from the Acted Facial Expression in the Wild (AFEW) database. Noteworthy improvements are shown in the classification accuracy.

KEYWORDS

FER, LBP-TOP, Tandem Features, MLP, SVM

1. INTRODUCTION

Human emotional states understanding has been for a decades the main focus of diverse research communities namely psychology, neuroscience and cognitive science (Poria et al, 2016). To characterize emotions, several definitions were formulated despite the simplicity of the term. In affective computing, scientists use Sherere's definition who considers emotions as an 'episode of interrelated, synchronized changes in five components in response to an event of major significance to the organism' (Scherer, 2005). Automated emotion analysis aims to develop an autonomous human-like cognitive machine with the ability to analyze, interpret and reproduce human emotions based on the biological human cognitive system. The task involves facial expressions, head movement, vocal channel, physiological signals and body gestures as cues from which relevant informations are extracted and processed to make a decision about the emotional state. Facial expressions based automatic emotion recognition systems are the most investigated because of the major contribution of the face in interpersonal communication (Mehrabian, 1968).

Data, descriptors and machine learning classifier or regressor are the base components of any FER system. Existing databases are collected either under acted and posed scenario or under scenario with spontaneous interactions. In the former, subjects, *usually actors,* are asked to reproduce certain emotions. Emotions are portrayed in a fully controlled settings i.e. bad illumination conditions and head motions are restrained. In the latter, data is collected in real-life conditions from movies, TV-shows, interview. The subject's behavior is natural, spontaneous and free ("in the wild"). To represent the collected data (still images or videos), achievements in FER task make use of hand-crafted descriptors such as facial landmarks, relationships between face salient components, Local Binary Patterns (LBP) (Chao et al, 2015), Histogram of Oriented Gradients (HOG) (Carcagnì et al, 2015), Gabor Wavelets (Zhang B., 2016) (Ruiz-Garcia et al, 2016), and Optical Flow (Niese et al, 2012) followed by standard classifiers like SVM, Adaboost and neural network. Recent trends employ deep networks to perform end-to-end emotion classification (Shin, 2016).

The aforementioned approaches performed steadily and efficiently on acted databases (Chao et al, 2015) (Carcagnì et al, 2015) (Zhang B., 2016) (Ruiz-Garcia et al, 2016) (Niese et al, 2012) (Shin, 2016) (Ghimire D. and Lee J., 2013). However, under spontaneous context, traditional methodologies are not robust enough to recognize natural emotions accurately. Spontaneous FER still needs further investigations either in the feature-level or in the model-level. In this paper, we investigate a new approach in the field of FER based on tandem features extracted from a neural network. Tandem systems have contributed to a noticeable improvement in automatic speech recognition (ASR). The architecture incorporates an ANN discriminatively trained to engender probabilistic features (Hermansky et al, 2000) or bottleneck features (Grzl et al, 2007). Probabilistic features use the posterior probabilities of the ANN class estimation. However, bottleneck features are generated from the activations of a narrow hidden layer in the middle. Motivated by the potential proven by this features extraction method in ASR task, we aim to evaluate the behavior of tandem features in FER in the wild task.

In our experimental setup, we train the two sets of tandem features on standard LBP-TOP features. Our experiments are tested on the AFEW database. Our results show gratifying improvement in the classification accuracy by the use of tandem features rather than LBP-TOP features only. The remaining of the paper is structured as follows: section 2 describes the proposed methodology. Section 3 presents the dataset, the features sets and the obtained results. Finally section 4 concludes the paper.

2. FRAMEWORK DESCRIPTION

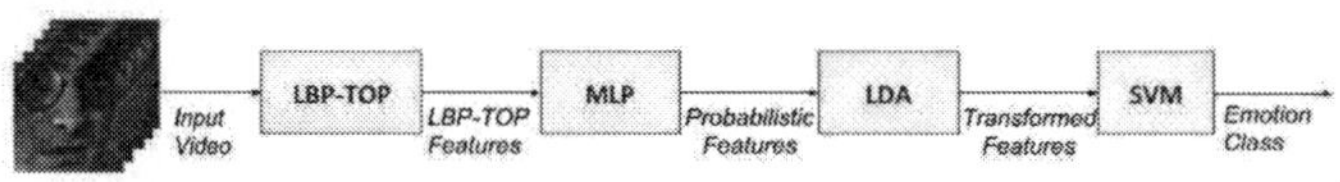

Figure 1. Block Diagram of the Probabilistic Tandem Framework

The proposed frameworks are implemented individually. Figure 1 depicts the overall architecture of the probabilistic features based framework. The training procedure is as follows: Given a video sequence, LBP-TOP features are extracted and stored in a feature vector that we denote $X = \lfloor x_1 .. x_n \rfloor$ where n is the features vector dimensionality. A fully connected MLP is then trained by backpropagation on X to estimate the desired classes denoted $y = [0, ..., 6]$. The probability of each class is derived from the output of the last layer by the softmax function formulated in the equation 1:

$$P\langle y = i|X\rangle = \frac{\exp(x_i)}{\sum_{i=0}^{n} x_i} \quad (1)$$

These probabilities form the probabilistic features set. Support Vector Machines (SVM) are then employed for emotion classification after features decorrelation by Local Discriminant Analysis (LDA).

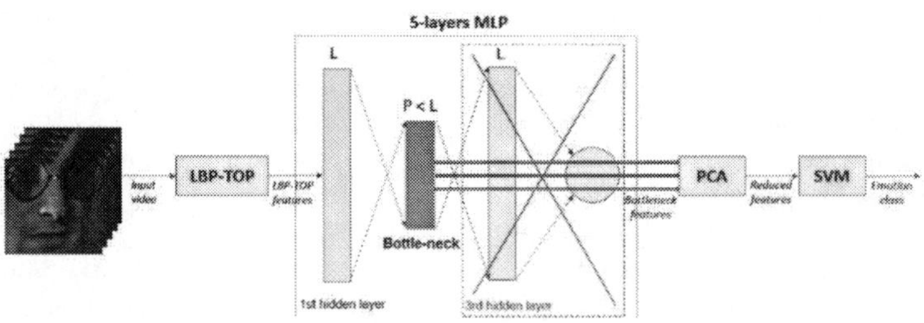

Figure 2. Block Diagram of the Bottleneck Tandem Framework

Figure 2 illustrates the overall architecture of the bottleneck features based framework. The difference compared to the first framework is that in this case the network includes three hidden layers with narrow-size hidden layer in the middle. The bottleneck features are extracted from the activation of that hidden layer. Principal Component Analysis (PCA) is then applied to reduce the dimensionality of the resulted features vector. Details about the neural network representation and learning can be found here (Rumelhart et al, 1986).

3. EXPERIMENTS AND RESULTS

We conduct our experiments on the Acted Facial Expression in the Wild (AFEW) database (Dhall et al, 2011). AFEW was proposed for the purpose of emotion recognition in the wild challenge (EmotiW) since 2012 and year by year several changes are added in order to provide a more natural data with a large amount. The dataset is composed of audio video sequences obtained from films and reality TV shows. The data is labelled using a semi-automatic annotator (Dhall et al, 2012). Annotation labels are the basic six emotions (anger, disgust, fear, happiness, sadness and surprise) with the neutral emotion. We use the latest version of the AFEW dataset which differs from the oldest ones by the adding of a test set with TV shows videos. The data is split into three sets: a training set, a validation set and a test set (see Table 1).

Table 1. AFEW Emotion Class Samples Repartition on the Train and the Validation Sets

Emotion	Train	Validation
Anger	133	60
Disgust	74	39
Fear	80	45
Happiness	147	61
Neutral	138	60
Sadness	80	61
Surprise	71	45
Total	**723**	**371**

3.1 Features Sets

LBP-TOP is used as the appearance descriptor to represent the video data. The choice is made based of its ability of extracting local informations and its illumination changes invariance (Zhao G. and Pietikainen M, 2007). The extraction procedure is the same as (Dhall et al, 2016). LBP-TOP is computed on a 128x128 frames after the face detection and alignment. Each frame is split into 4X4 non-overlapping blocs. For each bloc, LBPTOP histograms are extracted and concatenated into one histogram representing the feature vector of the given video sequence.

For probabilistic features extraction, we train a MLP with one to three hidden layers, with hidden units varying from one hundred to one thousand. The hidden layers size is the same. LDA is applied then to decorrelate the probabilistic feature vector variables. In some cases the dimensionality is reduced. To extract bottleneck features, we train 5-layers MLP. The first and the third hidden layers are of the same size (1000). The bottleneck layer has a narrow size in the range of [25, 30, 35, 40, 45, 50, 75, 100]. The resulted feature vector is processed by PCA to reduce the dimensionality. We also employ LDA for comparison.

For the two features sets, the net is trained with the softmax function for the output layer, with LBFGS solver for weights optimization and the log-loss function. We also varied the non-linear activations. We evaluated the logistic sigmoid function $a^{[i]}(z) = \frac{1}{1+\exp(-z)}$, the hyperbolic *tan* function $a^{[i]}(z) = \tan(z)$ and the identity function $a^{[i]}(z) = z$ in addition to the ReLU function $a^{[i]}(z) = \max(0, z)$.

3.2 Emotion Classification

SVM stands for the state-of-the-art discriminative machine learning algorithm which has been widely and efficiently used in both classification and regression tasks (Cortes C. and Vapnik V., 1995). To pick up the optimal hyper-parameters we performed 5-fold cross validation on the kernel, penalty and gamma parameters: kernel ϵ [linear, polynomial, RBF, sigmoid], C ϵ $[10^{-4} \ldots 10^{0} \ldots 10^{3}]$, gamma ϵ $[10^{-4} \ldots 10^{0}]$. The best parameters were obtained for C = 100, gamma = 1 and the RBF kernel. As we do not have the test set annotations, we evaluated our models on the validation set. The final result is got after performing 10-fold cross validation and retrieving the mean accuracy. For SVM implementation, we used the liblinear library in sklearn (Pedregosa et al., 2011).

3.3 Results and Classification Discussion

The experiments are evaluated on the validation set of the AFEW database. It turns out that applying PCA to reduce the dimensionality is system impairing. The employment of LDA, however, led to improvement of the overall accuracy. The best score is achieved with tanh as activation function and a narrow hidden layer of 100 units. This result outperforms the results got in (Dhall et al, 2016) on the validation set.

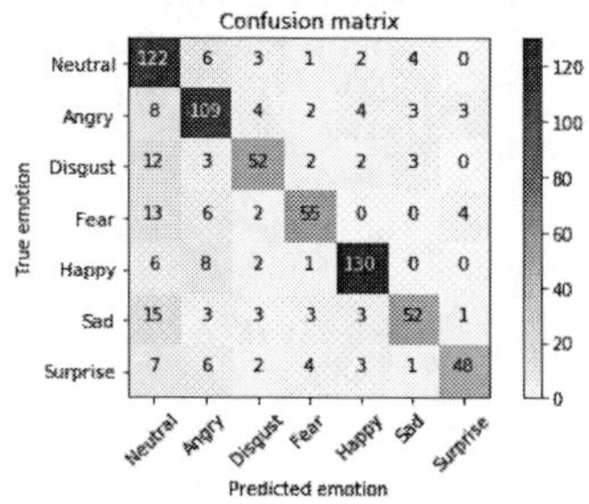

Figure 3. Confusion matrix of LBP-TOP features classification on the train set

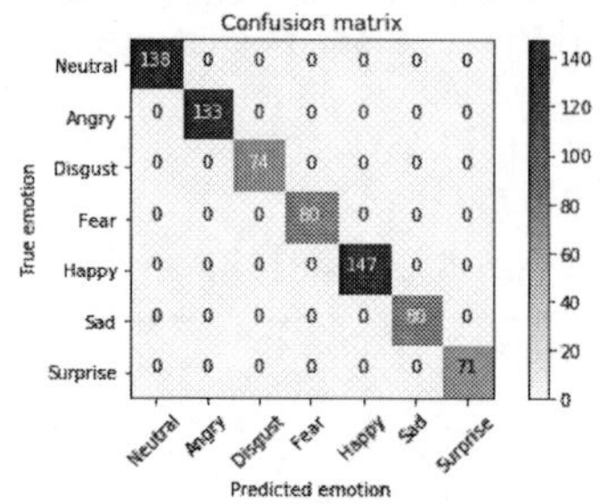

Figure 4. Confusion matrix of probabilistic features classification on the train set

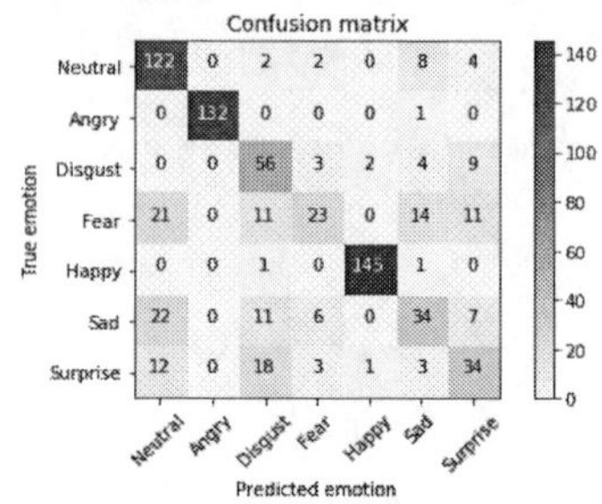

Figure 5. Confusion matrix of bottleneck features classification on the train set

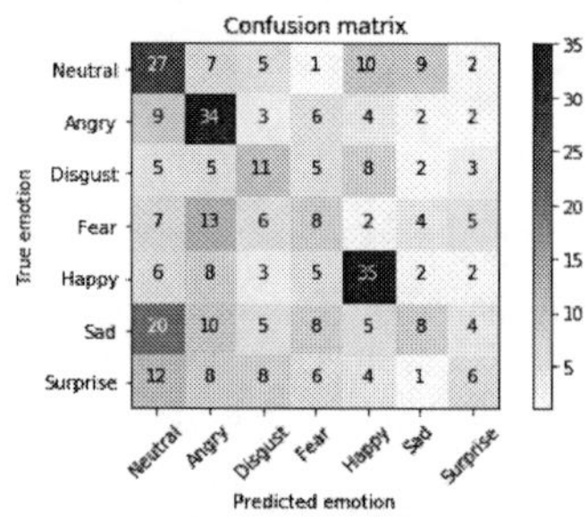

Figure 6. Confusion matrix of LBP-TOP features classification on the validation set

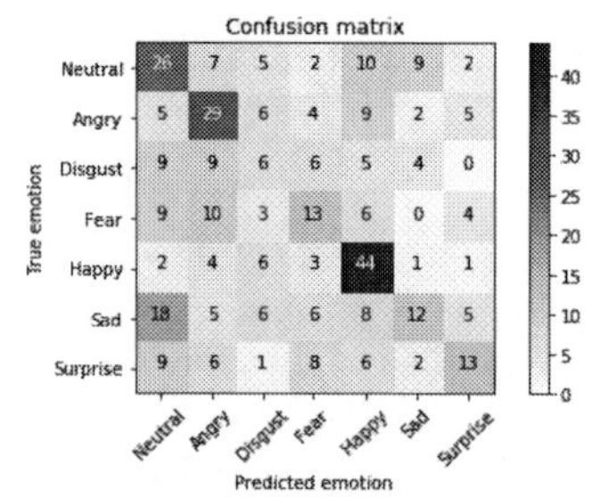

Figure 7. Confusion matrix of probabilistic features classification on the validation set

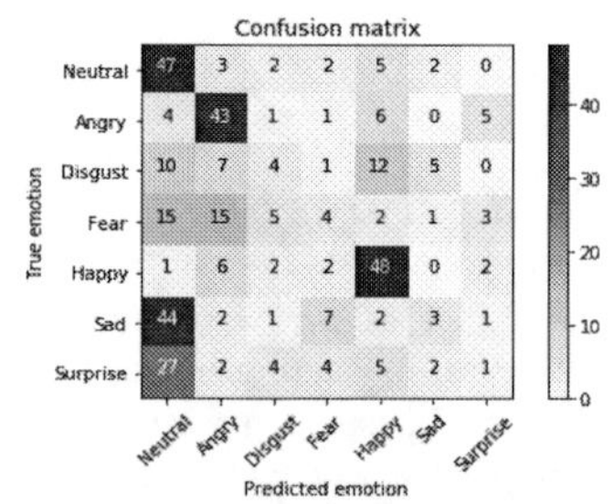

Figure 8. Confusion matrix of bottleneck features classification on the validation set

Confusion matrices of the proposed models on the validation set are illustrated in Figure 3, Figure 4, Figure 5, Figure 6, Figure 7 and Figure 8 respectively. One can remark that neutral, angry and happy expressions are well recognized. It can also be seen that bottleneck features perform better classification accuracy (77.04 %, 71.66 % and 78.68 % respectively). However, bottleneck features fail for recognizing fear, sad and surprise expressions. We can observe from those figures that fear expression is confused with neutral and angry expressions. Sad and surprise expressions are extremely confused with the neutral expression.

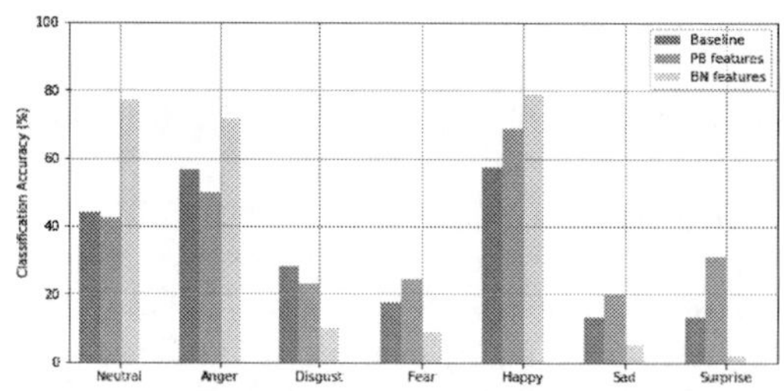

Figure 9. Comparison of the Baseline, Probabilistic (PB) and Bottleneck (BN) Models Performance on Each Class

We compare the baseline, the probabilistic and bottleneck based systems in Figure 9. One can remark that probabilistic and bottleneck features play a complementary role. Probabilistic features augment fear, happiness and surprise expressions with an improvement of 6 %, 11 %, 6 % and 17 % respectively. However, bottleneck features augment neutral, anger and happiness expressions by an increase of 32 %, 15 % and 21 % respectively which completes the probabilistic features gaps.

The confusion matrices show that disgust, fear and surprise are mainly confused with neutral, anger and happy expression which are the majority classes. It turns out also that the identity function has shown to be effective in this work and it outperforms ReLU and tanh activation functions.

4. CONCLUSION

In this paper, we proposed a tandem features based approach in order to classify the six basic emotions completed by neutral attitude. The samples (of images) corresponding to the above-mentioned emotional categories are provided by realistic videos from the AFEW database. Tandem features may offer an advantage in improving classification accuracy for some of the considered classes: improvement achieved is significant in the case of neutral, angry and happy expressions with bottleneck features. However, fear, sad and surprise expressions recognition is still poor despite the improvement offered by probabilistic features.

REFERENCES

Carcagnì et al. (2015). Facial expression recognition and histogram of oriented gradients : a comprehensive study. *SpringerPlus*, 1-25.

Chao et al. (2015). Facial expression recognition based on improved local binary pattern and class-regularized locality preserving projection. *Journal of signal processing*, vol 117, 552-561.

Cortes C. and Vapnik V. (1995). Support-vector networks. *Machine Learning*, Volume 20, Issue 3, pp 273–297.

Dhall et al. (2011a). *Acted Facial Expressions in the Wild Database.* Technical Report.

Dhall et al. (2012). Collecting Large, Richly Annotated Facial-Expression Databases from Movies. *IEEE MultiMedia*, Volume: 19, Issue: 3, 34 - 41.

Dhall et al. (2016). Emotiw 2016: Video and group-level emotion recognition challenges. *Proceedings of the 18th ACM International Conference on Multimodal Interaction. ACM*, (pp. 427-432). Tokyo, Japan.

Ghimire D. and Lee J., G. (2013). Geometric Feature Based Facial Expression Recognition in Image Sequences Using Multi-Class AdaBoost and Support Vector Machines. *Journal of sensors*, vol.13, pp. 7714-7734.

Grzl et al. (2007). Probabilistic and bottle-neck features for LVCSR of meetings . *IEEE International Conference on Acoustics, Speech and Signal Processing - ICASSP '07*, (pp. 757-760). Hononulu, Hawaii, USA.

Hermansky et al. (2000). Tandem connectionist feature extraction for conventional HMM systems. *IEEE International Conference on Acoustics, Speech, and Signal Processing. Proceedings (Cat. No.00CH37100)*, (pp. 1635–1638). Istanbul, Turkey.

Loconsole C., M. C. (2014). Real-time emotion recognition novel method for geometrical facial features extraction. *International Conference on Computer Vision Theory and Applications (VISAPP).* Lisbon , Portugal.

Mehrabian, A. (1968). Communication without words. *Psychology Today*, vol. 2, no. 4, 53-56.

Niese et al. (2012). Facial expression recognition based on geometric and optical flow features . *IET Computer Vision*, vol. 6, no. 2, pp. 79-89.

Pedregosa et al. (2011). Scikit-learn: Machine Learning in Python. *JMLR 12*, 2825-2830.

Poria et al. (2016). Fusing audio, visual and textual clues for sentiment analysis from multimodal content. *Neurocomputing*, 50_59.

Ruiz-Garcia et al. (2016). Emotion recognition using facial expression images for a robotic companion. *Engineering Applications of Neural Networks*, vol 629, pp 79-93.

Rumelhart et al. (1986). Learning Internal Representations by Error Propagation. *Parallel distributed processing: explorations in the microstructure of cognition*, vol. 1, 318-362.

Scherer, K. R. (2005). What are emotions? And how can they be measured? *Social Science Information*, 695–729.

Shin, M. K.-S. (2016). Baseline CNN structure analysis for facial expression recognition. *25th IEEE International Symposium on Robot and Human Interactive Communication (RO-MAN)*, (pp. 724-729). New York, NY, USA.

Zhang B., L. G. (2016). Facial expression recognition using LBP and LPQ based on Gabor wavelet transform. *2nd IEEE International Conference on Computer and Communications (ICCC)*, (pp. 365–369). Chengdu, China.

Zhao G. and Pietikainen M. (2007). Dynamic Texture Recognition Using Local Binary Patterns with an Application to Facial Expressions. *IEEE Transactions on Pattern Analysis and Machine Intelligence*, Volume: 29, Issue: 6, 915 - 928.

ARTIFACT REMOVAL AND LESION SEGMENTATION FOR MELANOMA DETECTION IN SKIN LESION IMAGES

Julie Ann Salido, Conrado Ruiz Jr. and Nelson Marcos
College of Computer Studies, De La Salle University, Manila, Philippines

ABSTRACT

Melanoma is a severe form of skin cancer characterized by the rapid multiplication of pigment-producing cells. There are new techniques for automated analysis of skin lesions for classification of melanoma using images from digital cameras and smart phones. A problem on analysis of these images are interesting because of the existence of artifacts and noise such as hair, veins, water residue, illuminations and light reflections. An important step in the diagnosis of melanoma is the removal of artifacts and reduction of noise that can inhibit the examination to accurately segment the skin lesion from the surrounding skin area. In this paper, a new method for extraction of skin lesion is implemented based on image enhancement and morphological operators. The experimental results show that artifact removal and lesion segmentation in skin lesion images can perform a true detection rate of 95.37% for melanoma skin lesion segmentation.

KEYWORDS

Artifacts Removal, Lesion Segmentation, Melanoma

1. INTRODUCTION

Melanoma is a severe form of skin cancer characterized by the uncontrolled growth of pigment-producing cells. According to the American Cancer Society, there is an estimated 87,110 cases of melanoma, with about 52,172 in males and 34,940 in females. It is estimated that 9,320 people will die from melanoma in 2018 (Siegel et al., 2018). Melanoma is treatable when detected early, but advanced melanoma can spread to other internal organs, which can result to death. Dermoscopy is used as a non-invasive method (Johr, 2002) that allows an in vivo evaluation of colors and microstructures of the skin specifically the epidermis, dermo epidermal junction, and papillary dermis. Dermoscopy allows examination of the skin and its patterns.

There are several studies that implement traditional telemedicine across the world especially in the developing countries, but the efforts have been characterized with challenges such as the high-cost of sustaining telemedicine solutions and insufficient access to medical expertise when needed. In recent years, there have been high expectations for techniques such as dermoscopy in aiding diagnosis. However, evaluation of pigmented skin lesions is not only expensive to other communities but also complex and highly subjective, thus motivating researches in diagnosis automation. The advances of smart-phones and ordinary cameras led to implementation of other applications for skin disease classification. The most challenging tasks are border detection or lesion segmentation especially on skin images from ordinary cameras. Due to the presence of artifacts and noise such as veins, hairs, illuminations, and light reflections, it is difficult to do border detection and image segmentation of lesion on skin images.

In this study, a simple method to detect and segment lesion from skin images using image analysis on ordinary skin images is employed. The lesion segmentation technique is tested on DermIS (Diepgen & Eysenbach, 1998) and DermQuest (Galderma, 2014) datasets. Some examples are shown in Figure 1.

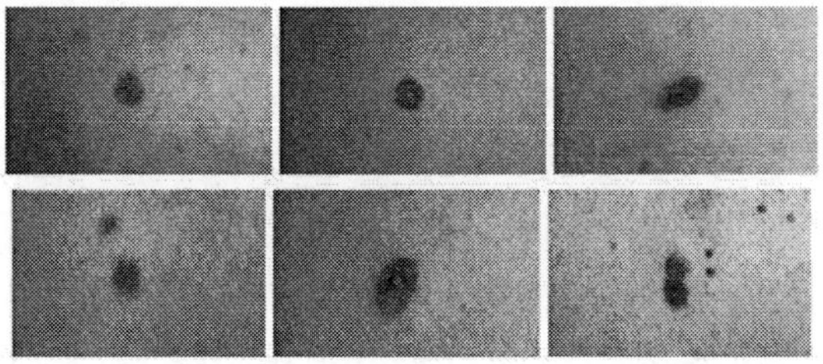

Figure 1. Sample Melanoma (Row 1) and Non-Melanoma (Row 2) Images from DermIS and DermQuest

2. BACKGROUND

In pre-processing, color space transformation is an important step in skin images. The skin image colors are in RGB (red, green, blue) values, either directly (in an RGB image) or indirectly (in an indexed image, where the colormap is stored in RGB format). In this case, the CIE L*a*b* color space was used.

In regular skin images, artifacts and noise include blood vessels, skin lines and illuminations, light reflections and the presence of hairs (see Figure 2). The direct way to remove these artifacts is to even and smoothen the image using general purpose filters. Noise in skin images such as luminosity, reflections, and others lead to different specifications of color spaces. The presence of noise and artifacts in skin images could lead to erroneous lesion segmentation of images. Image reconstruction, scene completion or area restoration might be necessary. The task of restoring a missing part of an image using information from the known part, in this case the skin image minus the hair can be done using image inpainting technique. To repair removed artifacts information from skin images, a harmonic inpainting method (Chan & Shen, 2001) is used for each color space. Figure 3 shows an example of hair removal.

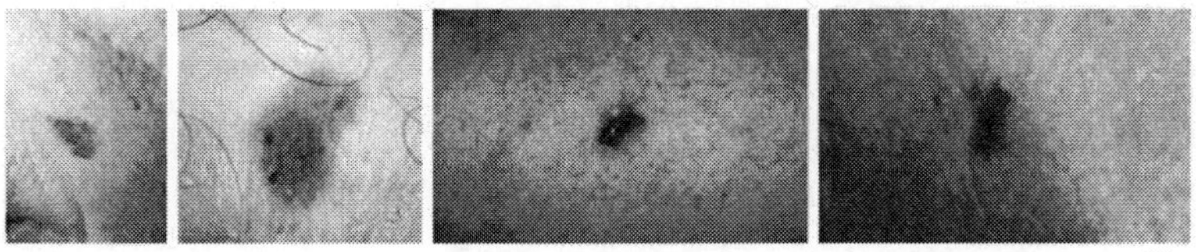

Figure 2. Sample Melanoma & Non-Melanoma Images from DermIS & DermQuest with Artifacts & Noise

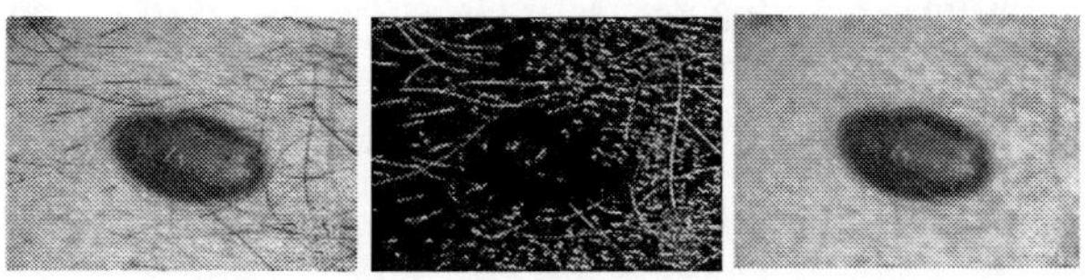

Figure 3. Example of Hair Removal

Creating a mask for artifacts and filtering of identified noise will be done followed by image multiplication. This step will create a new dermoscopy image minus the artifacts and identified noise. Inpainting on the new skin image will be performed for area restoration. Lesion segmentation will be performed in the new skin image using morphological operators. This will enable the system to detect borders and diameter of the lesion, and perform testing for symmetry on the lesion.

The existence of artifacts and noise are a predominant problem in skin images. In this case, if a skin lesion has artifacts and noise, the skin lesions segmentation, pattern analysis, and classification tasks will be affected. Thus, an automatic artifact and noise reduction which preserves the lesion features, while keeping the computational cost low for real-time implementation, is a must. The different means to accomplish image segmentation are using thresholding methods, color-based segmentation (Otsu, 1979), edge detection (Canny, 1987), and texture methods (Sonka et al., 2014).

The most recent correction algorithms for skin lesion images can only be applied to dermoscopy images, which already have some filtering due to the dermatoscope. Other studies have improved lesion segmentation by using color calibration (Haeghen et al., 2000) and normalization for classification or contrast enhancement (Celebi et al., 2009) combined with illumination correction.

3. METHODOLOGY

The dataset used for lesion segmentation are from DermIS (Blum et al., 2004) and DermQuest (Galderma, 2014). The skin images are of irregular sizes, and taken with different lightings and camera. Skin images are subdivided into melanoma and non-melanoma from both databases with ground truth (GT). Examples of skin images with GT are shown in Figure 4. Melanoma skin images total to 116, with 42 from DermIS and 74 from DermQuest, and 82 non-melanoma images of which 24 are from DermIS and 58 from DermQuest. These images have varying illuminations and light reflections. Some have veins and hair that overlaps with the lesion, and others parts of the body can be seen.

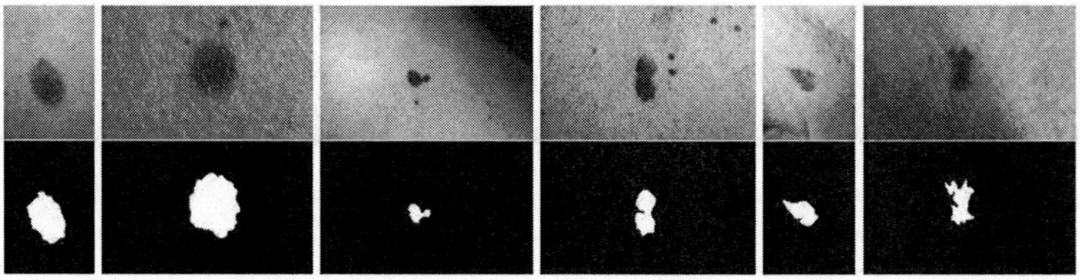

Figure 4. Sample Images from DermIS and DermQuest with their Ground Truth

The existence of hair is a predominant problem in some skin images. In this case, if a skin lesion is covered with hair, the skin lesion's segmentation tasks will be affected. An automatic hair removal method which preserves the lesion features using the technique in the study of (Salido & Ruiz Jr, 2017) is used. A CIE L*a*b* color space is identified to process the first layer for brightness and illumination. Grayscale and binary image is used as a different color space in some part of the new approach. Skin images are converted to CIE L*a*b* to determine the maximum luminosity of the skin images. Image adjustment is then performed that maps the intensity values in grayscale image original skin image to new values in the updated skin image. A denoising technique using Gaussian filter is used for image filtering of shadows and unnecessary textures in skin image. Histogram matching is performed to a defined image to denoise skin image before edge detection is performed (see Figure 5).

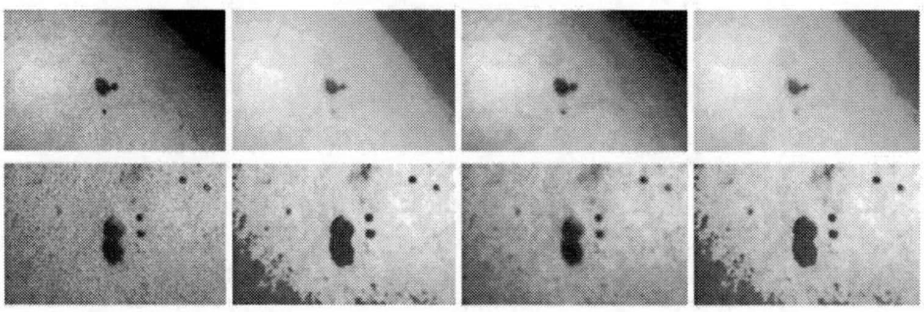

Figure 5. Sample Images During Preprocessing; 1st Column are Original Images, 2nd Column Luminosity Layer, 3rd Column is the Output in the Gaussian Filter, 4th Column is the Histogram Match Skin Image

Edge detection is done to divide a skin images into multiple parts for lesion segmentation. This is done using Canny method with a threshold of 0.3 for all histogram match images. Some image processing techniques applied on the images include dilate, fill, erode, and getting the perimeter for the edge outline. All connected components are then indexed, and the maximum connected components is determined from the list of index elements. The mask for the maximum connected components of the skin image is created and added to the original image.

4. RESULTS AND DISCUSSION

There are available GT binary masks, as a reference image with the same size as the original image. The GT in the dataset is used to evaluate the performance of the new approach. The artifact removal and lesion segmentation approach was implemented in Matlab 9.2.

A quantitative evaluation is performed on segmentation using statistical metrics. The border detection outcomes were compared with the reference images. As mentioned in Section 2.1, one of the factors that complicate the detection of borders in skin images is the insufficient detection of contrast between the lesion and the skin. Based on the new approach, the contrast between the lesion and the background skin is increased. This study takes two inputs: an RGB skin image X with n three-component pixels and its GT.

For the pre-processing results, some are shown in Figure 5. The first column shows the original skin image, the second column shows the luminosity layer, then the corrected skin image using Gaussian filter, and the last column is the output of image matching. The results of the new method for lesion segmentation are shown in Figure 6. The first column shows the original skin image, next is the corrected or enhanced skin image denoising and image matching, next is the identified lesion border, next column shows the skin image with the lesion border detected, and the last column shows the area of the identified skin lesion. For the lesion segmentation analysis, the work of (Celebi et al., 2015) is used. These are the mean border error (MBE), true detection rate (TDR), and the false positive rate (FDR).

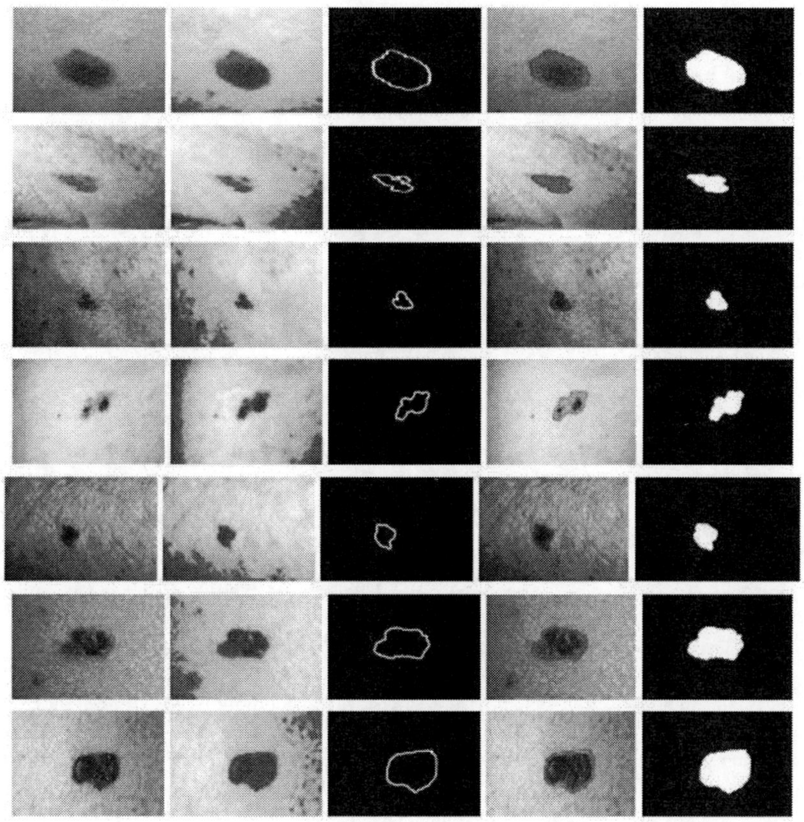

Figure 6. Examples of Results for the New Method on Lesion Segmentation

The results of the three metrics to measure the skin lesion segmented are acceptable, with as much as 96.77% TDR and as low as 3.23% FDR. Table 1 shows the performance of the new approach in the skin images based on the dataset from discussed in Section 3.1. The lesion segmentation difficulty is on detection the difference between the skin of different type, color, or texture. The problem is that the lesion area is sometimes diffused on the skin and is not well separated in the skin. This is because the lesion has two types of segmented regions overlapping each other, and only the innermost regions are segmented.

Table 1. Performance Results in three Metrics

Metric	Non-melanoma	Melanoma
TDR (%)	96.77	95.37
FDR (%)	3.23	4.63
MBE	72.43	81.50

5. CONCLUSION

This study has presented a simple algorithm for lesion segmentation for melanoma detection in skin lesion images. In artifact removal and noise reduction, morphological operators and inpainting techniques were used. This approach was shown to be as effective as other methods in detecting, removing, and correcting skin images for lesion segmentation. For lesion segmentation, morphological operators, image enhancement, and matching technique were used. This is an important pre-processing step in the identification and classification of melanomas. With a true detection rate of 96.77% for non-melanoma and 95.37% for melanoma lesion segmentation, it can be concluded to have achieved a very satisfactory skin lesion region recognition. In the future, more image segmentation methods for detecting lesion border on skin images may be explored. Possible enhancement on a model for classifying skins may also be useful, especially looking into the problem of varying skin color for different ethnicities.

REFERENCES

Blum, A., Luedtke, H., Ellwanger, U., Schwabe, R., Rassner, G., and Garbe, C. 2004. Digital image analysis for diagnosis of cutaneous melanoma. development of a highly e ective computer algorithm based on analysis of 837 melanocytic lesions. *British Journal of Dermatology*, 151 , 1029-1038.

Canny, J. 1987. A computational approach to edge detection. *In Readings in Computer Vision* (pp. 184-203). Elsevier.

Celebi, M. E., Iyatomi, H., and Schaefer, G. 2009. Contrast enhancement in dermoscopy images by maximizing a histogram bimodality measure. *In Image Processing (ICIP), 2009 16th IEEE International Conference* on (pp. 2601-2604). IEEE.

Celebi, M. E., Mendonca, T., and Marques, J. S. 2015. *Dermoscopy image analysis volume 10.* CRC Press.

Chan, T. F., and Shen, J. 2001. Nontexture inpainting by curvature-driven difusions. *Journal of Visual Communication and Image Representation*, 12 , 436-449.

Diepgen, T. L., and Eysenbach, G. 1998. Digital images in dermatology and the dermatology online atlas on the world wide web. *The Journal of dermatology*, 25 , 782-787.

Galderma, S. 2014. *Dermquest image library.*

Haeghen, Y. V., Naeyaert, J. M. A. D., Lemahieu, I., and Philips, W. 2000. An imaging system with calibrated color image acquisition for use in dermatology. *IEEE transactions on medical imaging*, 19 , 722-730.

Johr, R. H. 2002. Dermoscopy: alternative melanocytic algorithmsthe abcd rule of dermatoscopy, menzies scoring method, and 7-point checklist. *Clinics in dermatology*, 20 , 240-247.

Otsu, N. 1979. A threshold selection method from gray-level histograms. *IEEE transactions on systems, man, and cybernetics*, 9 , 62-66.

Salido, J. A. A., and Ruiz Jr, C. 2017. Using morphological operators and inpainting for hair removal in dermoscopic images. *In Proceedings of the Computer Graphics International Conference* (p. 2). ACM.

Siegel, R. L., Miller, K. D., and Jemal, A. 2018. Cancer statistics, 2018. *CA: a cancer journal for clinicians*, 68 , 7-30.

Sonka, M., Hlavac, V., and Boyle, R. 2014. Image processing, analysis, and machine vision. *Cengage Learning.*

EFFICIENT COMMAND BUFFER RECORDING FOR ACCELERATED RENDERING OF LARGE 3D SCENES

Viacheslav I. Gonakhchyan
Ivannikov Institute for System Programming of the RAS, 109004, Moscow, Alexander Solzhenitsyn st., 25, Russia

ABSTRACT

Interactive rendering of 3D scenes with a big number of objects is computationally intensive. It is hard to determine an efficient way of rendering command recording and submission. Command buffers can be recorded each frame, but that incurs a performance penalty. Command buffers can be created as a pre-processing step and then included in the primary command buffer during rendering, but that requires additional memory for holding multiple buffers. Command buffers can be created for a node in a decomposition hierarchy, but we need to determine the proper number of levels and fit them into the limited amount of memory. We propose a rendering algorithm, which is based on the space decomposition hierarchy with the determined height. It performs frustum culling and occlusion culling during the CPU idle time to improve the rendering performance. We show that the proposed algorithm efficiently handles scenes with a big number of objects and high depth complexity.

KEYWORDS

3D Rendering, Command Buffers, Vulkan

1. INTRODUCTION

Interactive rendering of large 3D scenes can be limited by different stages: CPU-GPU communication, vertex transformation, pixel shading. In this paper, we focus on improving the first one for a number of reasons. Modeling applications in architecture deal with a large number of dynamic objects, where each object can be selected, moved, deleted. In recent years GPUs gained more video memory to store geometry, more performance when processing vertices and pixels, but in many cases that power cannot be fully utilized because of the slow rendering command submission. In this paper, we analyze command recording and submission performance and propose a rendering algorithm that aims to reduce CPU-GPU communication bottleneck.

The rendering algorithm proposed in the paper is founded on three research areas: graphics APIs, occlusion culling methods, rendering performance. Let's consider each of them in more detail.

Drivers based on OpenGL versions up to 1.4 submitted graphics commands to GPU in immediate mode. All graphics commands and vertex data were sent to GPU each frame. OpenGL 1.5 introduced vertex buffer objects that allowed storing vertex data in video memory (Khronos Group, 2003). That helped to alleviate bandwidth problems for communication between CPU and GPU. But the problem of command buffer composition and state validation still remained. Also, OpenGL standard had no capabilities for well-defined control of memory allocation and command buffer submission. In 2015 NVIDIA introduced extension NV_command_list that addressed the problem of command buffer submission. It raised the efficiency of CAD scene rendering with millions of small objects (Lorach, 2014). In 2016 new graphics API Vulkan appeared. Vulkan further reduced the overhead by removing state validation from a driver. It introduced a conceptual model for multithreaded memory management and command submission. Vulkan objects VkCommandPool, VkCommandBuffer allow for granular control of memory allocation and command submission.

Let's consider the previous work dealing with command buffers in Vulkan. Blackbert noticed that in Vulkan there is a clear separation between generating rendering commands and executing them but analyzed only one way of command buffer usage — when multiple threads record their own command buffers, containing rendering commands for a specific set of objects (Blackbert, 2016). Shiraef measured drawcall overhead for an increasing number of rendered objects using Vulkan and OpenGL and showed that Vulkan performed better in terms of the CPU and GPU utilization. Although command buffer composition was done in a loop for each object, command buffer granularity was not considered (Shiraef, 2016).

Hierarchical occlusion culling methods can significantly reduce the number of visible objects and decrease the number of commands being sent to GPU. Let's consider important papers investigating hierarchical occlusion culling. Bittner et al. investigated occlusion queries for visibility determination of nodes of space decomposition hierarchies (Bittner et al., 2004). Rendering performance is decreased because of CPU stalls and GPU starvation. Authors proposed approaches to solve the performance problems: rasterize previously visible objects at the beginning of a frame, send visibility queries for leaf nodes of a hierarchy, check visibility results in the next frame. Guthe et al. observed that in many cases visibility queries make performance worse than frustum culling, proposed a probability criterion to minimize the number of queries, a performance model which helps to avoid queries when rasterization is cheaper (Guthe et al., 2006). Mattausch et al. suggested further ways of minimizing the number of queries like sending one query for a group (Mattausch et al., 2008). It groups visibility queries when objects are invisible for several frames, which results in rendering performance improvement.

Let's consider the previous work on rendering time estimation. Funkhouser et al. described an adaptive algorithm to maintain uniform frame rate. Each frame an appropriate level of detail was chosen for objects to achieve the target frame rate (Funkhouser et al., 1993). Wimmer et al. Proposed a graphics hardware model for rendering time estimation where objects are sent to GPU via command buffer (FIFO) each frame. More importantly for our paper, they analyzed idle time and described the problems that break CPU-GPU parallelism: GPU starvation when CPU is not supplying rendering commands fast enough, CPU stalls when GPU cannot perform rendering in time and CPU waits for it to finish. Graphics hardware should strive for maximum parallelism and avoid backend starvation (Wimmer et al., 2003).

Although there is a lot of technical information about command buffer usage, we have not found papers with analysis of command buffer performance when using space decomposition hierarchies. The goal of the paper is to investigate CPU utilization and frame rendering time depending on the approach to command buffer composition and to propose the algorithm based on space decomposition that maximizes rendering performance of large 3D scenes. We assume that all of the scene's geometry and rendering commands can fit into memory.

2. COMMAND BUFFER RECORDING PERFORMANCE

There are two approaches to command buffer recording in Vulkan: inlining, referencing secondary buffers. Inlining of rendering commands must be performed each frame, which requires more computation on CPU. Referencing of secondary command buffers is faster because they are pre-recorded, but they require separate areas of mapped memory (see fig. 1). So, having too many secondary buffers is not memory efficient because of unused space in pages of memory.

Let's consider the benchmark to show the difference in memory consumption and CPU utilization when using the described approaches to command buffer recording. The rendering algorithm performs the following steps: wait for swapchain image to become available (CPU idle time), record the primary buffer, submit the primary buffer to the graphics queue. These three stages determine the frame rendering time. Let's consider the first stage in more detail. In case of triple buffering, we have three swapchain images. Idle time is the time CPU waits for GPU to complete the submitted work and show the framebuffer image on display. Zero idle time means that GPU is faster than CPU, resulting in CPU bottleneck that we want to avoid. Non-zero idle time means that we have free CPU time to do other tasks.

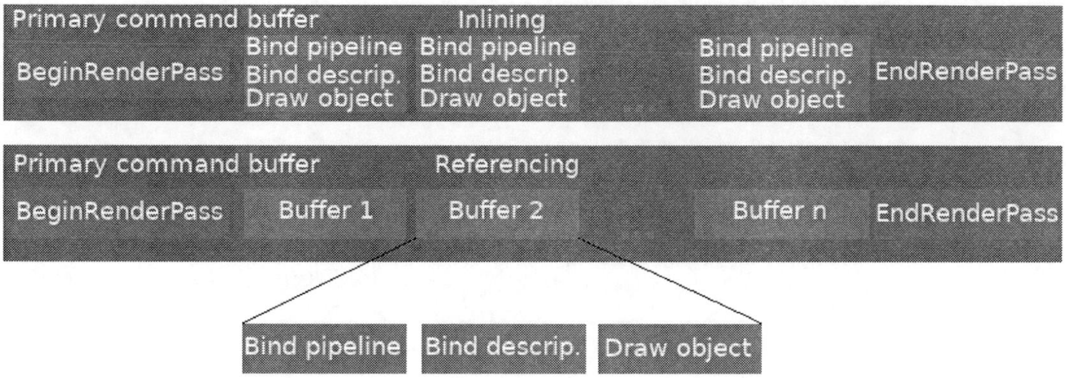

Figure 1. Inlining and referencing approaches to command buffer recording in Vulkan. When inlining (see the top rectangle), rendering commands are included in the contents of the primary command buffer. When referencing (see the bottom rectangle), rendering commands are stored in separate regions of memory and referenced from the primary command buffer

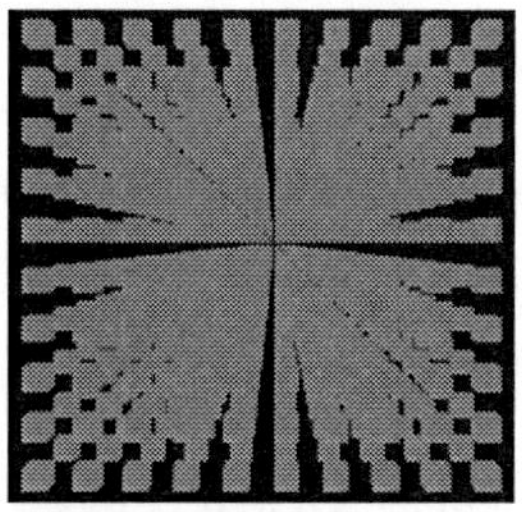

Figure 2. Test Scene with Cubes

We load the specified number of cubes arranged in a three-dimensional grid (see figure 2). We perform primary command recording and rendering. The results are measured for increasing number of cubes typical for CAD scenes. System configuration: AMD FX-8320 3.3GHZ, NVIDIA GeForce GTX 1070 8GB.

The tests are performed for three different types of primary command buffer recording: inlining all rendering commands in the primary command buffer (table 1), using one secondary command buffer per object (table 2), using one secondary command buffer per 1000 objects (table 3). When inlining, most of the CPU time is spent on the command recording, while GPU is waiting for work. When using one secondary command buffer per object, most of the CPU time is spent on the command submission, and memory consumption is much higher. Increasing the number of objects per secondary command buffer solves the problem — we no longer have CPU bottleneck (idle time can be spent on other tasks), memory consumption is reduced. Note that memory consumption is even lower than when recording with inlining. This happens because inlining requires three command buffers to exist at any given moment, because up to three frames can be pending execution. So, assigning multiple objects to a secondary command buffer gives the most efficient performance.

Table 1. Rendering Performance when using Inlining

Number of cubes	Idle time, ms	Buffer recording time, ms	Buffer submission time, ms	Memory consumption, MB
10000	0	1.8	0.03	183
50000	0	9.6	0.05	239
100000	0	19.6	0.06	310
300000	0	55.5	0.07	641

Table 2. Rendering performance when using one secondary command buffer per object

Number of cubes	Idle time, ms	Buffer recording time, ms	Buffer submission time, ms	Memory consumption, MB
10000	0	0.15	1.4	324
50000	0	0.9	7.0	1008
100000	0	1.9	14.5	1868
300000	0	5.8	43.0	5313

Table 3. Rendering Performance when using one Secondary Command Buffer per 1000 Objects

Number of cubes	Idle time, ms	Buffer recording time, ms	Buffer submission time, ms	Memory consumption, MB
10000	0.7	0.02	0.08	160
50000	3.6	0.02	0.10	189
100000	7.3	0.03	0.12	228
300000	22.5	0.03	0.18	400

Note that high memory consumption is due to command buffers, not geometry or textures. GPU has a limited amount of memory, and we need to determine the maximum number of command buffers that can be pre-allocated. It can be estimated by creating 10000 command buffers, which render one cube with different matrices, and measuring virtual memory consumption increase. For our system configuration command buffer size is 16KB, and 8GB of VRAM can hold approximately 500000 command buffers. However, other configurations with integrated graphics may allow for only 60000 command buffers (1GB of memory). The maximum number of command buffers is used in the proposed algorithm below.

3. PROPOSED ALGORITHM

When rendering a 3D scene with a lot of objects, inefficient performance is caused by GPU starvation, which is, in turn, caused by CPU bottleneck. We can avoid CPU bottleneck by minimizing the command buffer recording time on CPU, minimizing the number of commands being sent each frame. To reduce the recording time, we can use pre-allocated secondary command buffers. To reduce the number of commands, we can use a hierarchy, pre-record rendering commands for a node and cull invisible nodes. There are two popular algorithms to cull invisible objects: frustum culling, occlusion culling based on occlusion queries (Bittner et al., 2004). Both algorithms have associated costs, so we have to make sure that we do not exceed the time budget.

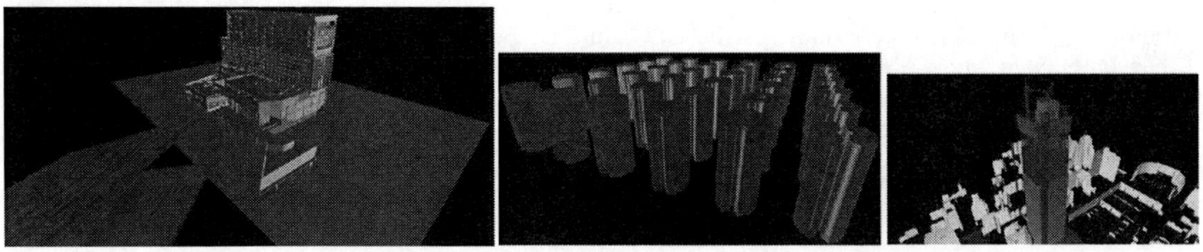

Figure 3. Scene 1 (on the left) with 10.8 million triangles, 71961 objects. Scene 2 (in the middle) with 10.2 million triangles, 154025 objects. Scene 3 (on the right) with 11.5 million triangles, 109991 objects

We already established that pre-recording command buffers achieves 2-3 times faster rendering than recording commands each frame. Let's consider further ways of improving performance by using a hierarchy. For simplicity, we use the single-reference octree to hold objects. Single-reference octree is more efficient than multiple-reference octree because every rendering command is recorded only once. Secondary command buffers are pre-recorded for octree nodes and included in the primary command buffer (referencing). Let's consider rendering performance of scene 1 depicted on fig. 3, when all objects fall into view. Results show that this approach is efficient, and we have free CPU time to perform other tasks (table 4). Note that for lower octree height the idle time is slightly higher, but lower height also results in less efficient culling. The proposed algorithm takes advantage of the idle CPU time to perform frustum culling and occlusion culling.

Table 4. Rendering performance of scene 1 when commands are pre-recorded for each octree node

Octree height	Number of nodes	Idle time, ms	Buffer recording time, ms	Buffer submission time, ms	Memory consumption, MB
3	129	7.8	0.02	0.09	637
4	449	7.5	0.03	0.12	644
5	1953	6.7	0.05	0.33	700
6	9017	5.8	0.12	0.97	1129

During the pre-processing the proposed algorithm performs the following steps:

1. Set $H = \lfloor \log_8 B \rfloor$, where B is the maximum number of command buffers that can be pre-allocated;
2. Create the octree with H levels, add objects of the passed scene;
3. Render the scene using the command buffer referencing and measure the idle time;
4. If the idle time is zero, then set H=H-1 and repeat from step 2.

This process determines the octree height H for efficient rendering. Setting the initial value of H based on B is important to avoid the problem with some drivers that exit when all available video memory is used up. It is unlikely to get H less than 3, because at that point CPU has very little work to do. Although gathered performance statistics do not show the zero idle time, it is possible when the number of octree nodes is high.

During the rendering the proposed algorithm performs the following steps each frame:

1. Wait for the rendering completion of a pending primary command buffer;
2. Get the results of occlusion queries and compose the array of visible nodes;
3. Perform frustum culling of the visible nodes;
4. Record secondary command buffers of the visible nodes to the primary command buffer;
5. Record occlusion queries for the octree nodes inside frustum to the primary command buffer;
6. Submit the primary command buffer to the graphics queue for rendering.

The rendering algorithm has essential steps (1,4,6) and optional steps (2,3,5). Essential steps must be completed regardless of the time budget (the idle time plus the time spent on frustum culling and occlusion culling). Optional steps should be performed without exceeding the time budget. Assuming that temporal coherence of visibility holds, we can expect the rendering load to be approximately the same from frame to frame. This allows us to use the idle time of the next frame in the current frame to perform the optional steps. In case of the zero idle time (GPU starvation), the next frame should reduce the time budget by a constant time (e.g. 3 milliseconds).

Let's consider the occlusion culling in more detail (steps 2 and 5). Occlusion queries are recorded for three frames. Temporal coherence allows us to use the visibility results from the previous frame in the current frame. Query results are checked after the rendering of the corresponding frame has finished (frame k waits for completion of frame k-3). Occlusion query commands are inlined in the secondary command buffer (step 5), which is executed after the rendering of objects in the visible nodes. Octree can contain tens of thousands of nodes. Skipping occlusion queries for some of them gives conservative visibility results.

We measured how the proposed algorithm performs in practice in comparison to frustum culling (table 5). Overall, frame rendering time improved for scenes 1 and 2, because these architectural scenes have high depth complexity, and visibility queries significantly reduced the number of visible nodes.

Table 5. Frame Rendering Time of Scenes 1, 2, 3

Scene	Frustum culling with command inlining, ms	Frustum culling with command buffer referencing, ms	Proposed algorithm, ms
1	25.5	7.5	4.6
2	32.2	14.0	10.0
3	26.6	10.8	8.0

4. CONCLUSION

We analyzed the command buffer recording performance. Analysis showed that pre-recording command buffers is more efficient for rendering of large 3d scenes than recording commands for each object each frame. We proposed the rendering algorithm that pre-records command buffers for nodes of the single-reference octree and takes advantage of the idle CPU time to do the frustum culling and occlusion culling. Results showed that using the idle CPU time to perform culling improves the rendering performance of large 3D scenes with high depth complexity.

REFERENCES

Bittner, J. et al., 2004. Coherent hierarchical culling: Hardware occlusion queries made useful. *In Computer Graphics Forum*, Vol. 23, No.3, pp. 615-624.

Blackert, A., 2016. Evaluation of multi-threading in Vulkan.

Funkhouser T. A., Sequin C. H., 1993. Adaptive display algorithm for interactive frame rates during visualization of complex virtual environments. *In Proceedings of SIGGRAPH 93,* Vol. 27, No. 2, pp. 247–254.

Guthe, M. et al., 2006. Near Optimal Hierarchical Culling: Performance Driven Use of Hardware Occlusion Queries. *In Eurographics Symposium on Rendering.* pp. 207–214.

Khronos Group, 2003. History of OpenGL. [ONLINE] Available at: https://www.khronos.org/opengl/wiki/History_of_OpenGL#OpenGL_1.5_.282003.29. [Accessed 07 April 2018].

Lorach, T., 2014. Approaching Zero Driver Overhead. *Nvidia Professional Visualization Group (SIGGRAPH 2014).*

Mattausch, O. et al, 2008. CHC++: Coherent Hierarchical Culling Revisited. *EUROGRAPHICS*, Vol. 27, No. 3

Shiraef, J. A., 2016. An exploratory study of high performance graphics application programming interfaces.

Wimmer M., Wonka P., 2003. Rendering time estimation for real-time rendering. *In Proceedings of Eurographics Workshop on Rendering*, pp. 118–129.

A MOBILE APPLICATION BASED ON AUGMENTED AND VIRTUAL REALITY FOR DYNAMIC TRAINING AND TESTING OF THE ROAD-RULE SKILLS

Tatiana N. Tomchinskaya, Nikolay Yr. Dudakov and Aleksander D. Filinskikh
Alekseev State Technical University of Nizhny Novgorod, Russia

ABSTRACT

An application for real-time visualization of augmented and virtual reality is considered, which enables the consideration of traffic accidents on a mobile platform with the Android operating system. The application developed by authors on the basis of Unity 3D is able to visualize various types of road accidents and link them to a terrain, different conditions of urban environment, and map of the accident statistics. The system has a bank of video for the accident 3D-scenes. This application may be used for training and examine road rules.

KEYWORDS

Augmented Reality, Virtual Reality, Road Traffic Accidents, Dynamic Tests, Virtual Driving School

1. INTRODUCTION

The problem of accidents associated with road transport has become particularly acute in the last decade due to the mismatch of the road transport infrastructure with the needs of the society for safe road traffic, inadequate efficiency of the road safety system and extremely low discipline of road users.

According to statistics, annually more than 1 million people over the world die and about 50 million people are injured. In the Russian Federation only, there are more than 150 thousand road accidents per year. At the same time, more than three quarters of all road accidents are related to violations of the Russian Federation Road Traffic Regulations by drivers of vehicles and a high percentage of participants in road accidents are drivers with experience up to three years.

The solution of emerging problems is not limited to the development of the urban road network. Various intelligent transport systems are offered. For example, Hanshin Expressway Company Limited considers the risk of an accident as one of the important concepts of its safe driving assistance and traffic management for the next generation. The company offers to use information about the risks of accidents for comfortable and safe driving (T. Kodama, D. Yabukami, T. Daito, Y. Ozawa, 2015). An interesting study proposing an architecture for interactive motion-based motion modeling Environment. The proposed architecture combines several types of modeling, including: motion-based modeling of driving, simulation of pedestrians, modeling of motorcycles and bicycles and traffic modeling (Paz, A.; Veeramisti, N.; Khaddar, R.; de la Fuente-Mella, H., and Modorcea L., 2015)..

Typically, the main function of these systems is the analysis of accidents; however, they do not support the possibility of realistic visualization of a particular accident in a living environment.

One of the "last trends" in the construction of transport systems is the technology of displaying objects in 3D format with the help of augmented reality on the windshield of the car. Applications of augmented reality are mainly intended for navigation, which helps drivers better navigate the road (https://newsroom.konicaminolta.eu). Such an application can be more useful for experienced drivers. partially covers the windshield and the novice driver who does not know how to "scan" the environment quickly enough cannot cope with the additional flow of information. So, during the research it was revealed that for the novice drivers and cadets of driving schools the most acute problem is the problem of correctly recognizing the road situation on the road, in which there can be almost no time for making a decision. It is necessary to act as quickly as possible and, at the same time, take into account all aspects of the current situation, such as the signal of a traffic light, marking, signs, the position of cars and their speed. In addition, when you get into an extreme situation, the student may become confused, which can lead to even more deplorable results.

The solution to this problem can be the proposed application for a mobile platform intended, primarily for novice drivers and cadets driving schools.

Two ways of ensuring road safety are considered.

1. Preview an unfamiliar path section using the augmented reality. Pointing the camera smartphone on a map of the city, for example, on Yandex map, the driver can see a realistic model of a specific section of the road infrastructure on the smartphone screen with all signs and markings.

2. By immersing in virtual reality, a driver can see in a stereo mode a living situation of an accident that occurred on a particular section of a realistically modeled part of a particular city. View this situation from different points of view, like the victim, the culprit or the casual witness and understand all the reasons for this incident. And also for the cadets of driving schools, a system of dynamic tests is offered, performed on really existing sites with increased statistics of road accidents in specific cities.

2. MOBILE APPLICATION

The most dangerous parts of the road network are considered. Since the application is aimed at obtaining traffic information, the following risk factors are studied as the contextual information (Hardy Pundt, 2017): speed, lateral interval, priority, distance; weather conditions: ice conditions, black ice, snow-covered road, snowfall, rain, fog; road surface. Each factor may be described by corresponding coefficient as below:

Ki = OP/N, where OP is the number of traffic accidents with this factor at a given location; N - average for all similar events in the city. All factors are modeling parameters.

The most dangerous sections of the city roads, corresponding to each factor Ki, are identified, and dangerous road situations are modeled on these sections. Recorded video showing: 1) erroneous behavior of the driver and 2) how to properly act in a similar situation. A video bank has been prepared, which stores videos demonstrating traffic rules. Figure 1 shows the dangerous areas with a factor - speeding.

2.1 Augmented Reality Unit

To implement the application on the Android platform, the integrated development environment of Unity 3D is used. For the traffic-accident areas the proper scenes were developed, the ones simulate the typical accidents connected with this place. Models of scene's participants are pre-created in the Autodesk Maya and 3DsMax tool environment as the low-polygon objects having trajectories parameterized relatively to the road, roadside objects and other traffic participants. These scenes are then embedded in the Unity3D environment (Figure 1).

Figure 1. Images of low-polygonal three-dimensional scenes (bottom), which are examples of Object for recognizing via the Vuforia Object Scanner one of the city square from the positions marked by tags on the map (top)

The augmented reality functionality was realized using Vuforia SDK (www.vuforia.com), the worlds widely used as AR platform for Unity 3D. Blocks of our application are united via the C# programming language. The augmented reality realized in the application via the Vuforia Object Scanner. Vuforia plug-in launches a mechanism for searching for tags, created in advance for the city map, and reproduces as the augmented reality a tooltip about the degree of danger or the correspondent accident 3D scenes for this part of the road.

The scenes for the most dangerous areas can be also integrated onto the map via special labels for learning such places. The Vuforia plug-in recognizes the image of one of the label on the map received from the smartphone's camera, based on information about the position of the label (marker) in space.

Figure 2. Loading a Scene on a Smartphone by a Map Label

Figure 3. Control Buttons for Navigation and Orientation in the Space

For 3D reconstruction of the scene the calculation of the reference points with simultaneous tracking is performed, thereby the objects of three-dimensional scene will be correctly oriented in the space. The application projects the corresponding model onto the label, and the scene of the accident case is loaded on the screen. The scene is also played in the third person view mode (Figure 2).

2.2 Virtual Reality Unit

Block VR (virtual reality) is designed to view the model in virtual reality mode without using a label. From the list of suggested scenes, the user selects the model of interest. The screen of the smartphone or tablet is loaded with a scene, with the ability to view it from different angles and from different road users with full or partial immersion.

For a full immersion, a virtual reality helmet is required. A virtual camera layers added to the scene. The choice is made in favor of the product Fibrum SDK, because it has all the necessary settings, and it does not overload the system with additional plug-ins. Using the Fibrum SDK object, two cameras are installed, for each eye, respectively, the distance between the cameras, the distortion of the image and the required cylindrical distortion. To view the virtual reality with full immersion requires a screen with a diagonal of 4 to 6 inches, as it is necessary to have in the phone sensors accelerometer and gyro. This is required to monitor the position of the smartphone in space and as a consequence - the location of the virtual camera in the "in-game" space.

To manage the view mode the standard internal plug-in Unity 3D - Characters Controller is used. When you download a scene on a smartphone in the virtual reality mode, you can view the situation from various road participants, whether the culprit, the victim or the free movement of the scene. When the user is in the free travel mode, he can look around, explore the terrain and the road infrastructure surrounding it, or navigate around the stage using the standard control joystick (Figure 3). Buttons for selecting the view mode are at the top of the screen. Back button - to exit the scene, to the main menu.

In the virtual reality scene view mode using the virtual reality glasses (Figure 4), the user does not have the ability to move freely around the scene. To switch to viewing a scene from another participant in traffic, the user must "look" at the button until the load bar appears. After loading it, within a few seconds, the program will redirect the user to the selected menu item. To select a view of scene from another participant of the road, the user needs to "look" at the corresponding button on the screen. For a more complete immersion, objects inside the scene cast a shadow from static and dynamic light sources.

Figure 4. Two Cameras for Stereo Imaging

For this, a three-dimensional object cylinder is added to the parent prefect of Rigid Body FPS Controller. He casts a shadow from the character, but in order for the polygons of the object to fall into the camera, he is excluded from the renderer. To make the body have its volume and could collide with other objects, a standard Mesh Collider script is added, which makes all faces of the character physical and does not allow it to pass through the walls. The same plugin should be installed on objects through which the user is forbidden to pass.

2.3 Dynamic Testing Unit

During the studding in driving schools trainees are offered static illustrations in a book with tests that give the student time to think, against the dynamic situation on the road, in which time is very short for making a decision. The system of dynamic tests, performed on really existing sites with increased statistics of road accidents, considered on the example of a particular city, is proposed. During the implementation of the project, the most dangerous parts of the road-transport interchange of a particular city are taken as a basis.

As a result of the investigation of these areas and road accidents, a number of test tasks were compiled with situations in which accidents most often occur, as well as a number of complex road sections with which drivers have problems. On each site, several variants of tasks are considered, based on the real location of traffic signs, marking and possible obstacles (for example, other cars that violate the rules, so the driver may not notice the traffic sign).

Figure 5. Example of the Usual Test Strategy

Figure 6. Example of the Dynamic Test System

In the opposite to standard test (Figure 5), during the passage of the dynamic test, the view from the driver's seat is displayed on the monitor screen just before the learner (Figure 6). The test person can turn his head around, as it does in real life.

The procedure of passing the test is as follows. When the user's machine approaches the testing stage, for example, the intersection, the candidate is offered a choice of several answer options that may contain one or another action.

If the tested person chooses the correct answer, then the score is recorded, and the machine continues to move to a predetermined position. If an incorrect answer is selected, the score is not recorded, which will be informed to the tested person. In some cases, if an incorrect choice can lead to an accident, the scene of the accident is reproduced.

In total there are 20 tasks during testing, according to the results of which the final score is announced and tips are given on the incorrectly passed stages, if any. The level of complexity of the task and the number of earned points is determined based on the complexity of road segment via the integral factor Ki (like the level of difficulty in a game) and determines the level of the driver's qualification.

At each stage, from 1 to 5 possible outcomes are realized, where each outcome is a next task that is randomly loaded into the system, depending on the choice made earlier.

This decision was made because some tested persons can memorize the position of the answer to the question, while not fully understanding why the chosen option is correct. It is also possible to rearrange the variants of answers in some places to further complicate the task.

You can make no more than two errors in one block. After the wrong answer, the program adds five random questions, in which the cadet, for successful surrender, has no right to make a mistake.

There are three options for loading tests: in mono visualization mode, in stereo-visualization mode and in full immersion mode using a virtual reality helmet or its light version, VR glasses.

3. CONCLUSION

The application of virtual and augmented reality technologies during driver training in real emergency areas of the city is investigated. To build scenarios for the creation of accident-dangerous cases, statistics and situational descriptions of accidents were used. The mode of dynamic training and testing in the mode of virtual and augmented reality with various degrees of immersion is offered.

The technology for implementing an application for a mobile platform that can implement scenarios for training and testing on crashes-dangerous situations in several modes of using virtual and augmented reality is proposed. The implementation is performed in the Unity 3D integrated development environment.

It is intended to use the application in practical classes in driving schools. As is known in driving schools there is no possibility to pass all difficult sites of roads and to disassemble all non-standard situations with the cadet. In view of the fact that new spatial methods of experience can be created by connecting physical and Virtual spaces in different ways (Gallastegui, S., 2016), and there is a sufficient amount of literature that contributes and proves that the effective use of 3D virtual worlds improves learning experience and improves learning outcomes (Georgios Dafullas, Noha Saleb and Martin Lumes, 2017). Therefore, it can be assumed that the use of this application will significantly improve the level of training of cadets driving schools, will acquaint them with the complex situations that arise in specific places of the road infrastructure, and teach them dynamic tests in the virtual reality mode.

The application is only a pilot project and works on smartphones with mid-price segment processors. Testing was carried out in three driving schools of the city. The greatest interest in using the application showed students – 98% and drivers with driving experience up to three years – 93%.

The technology of virtual and augmented reality can also be applied when new complex traffic junctions are put into operation. For example, in Nizhny Novgorod, when the metro bridge was put into operation, many drivers did not use it due to difficult, in their opinion, entrances the bridge both from one side of the river and on the other. Timely information of drivers via virtual reality will avoid many dangerous situations and, accordingly, will contribute to improving road safety.

REFERENCES

Dafoulas, G., Saleeb, N., Loomes M., 2017. What learners want from educational spaces? A framework for assessing impact of architectural decisions in virtual worlds. IADIS International Journal on Computer Science and Information Systems Vol. 14, No. 2, pp. 72-90.

Gallastegui, S., 2016. Between immersion and emersion: orientating digital games towards virtual and physical spaces. IADIS International Journal on Computer Science and Information Systems Vol. 11, No. 1, pp. 49-62.

Kodama, T., Yabukami, D., Daito, T., Ozawa, Y., 2015. Informing drivers on accident risks: a case of Hanshin Expressway's web-based tool "Safety Drive / Smart Choice". //22nd ITS World Congress, Bordeaux, 2015, 11 pages.

Paz, A.; Veeramisti, N.; Khaddar, R.; de la Fuente-Mella, H., and Modorcea L. 2015. Traffic and Driving Simulator Based on Architecture of Interactive Motion. // The Scientific World Journal, Article ID 340576, 9 pages.

Pundt, H., 2017. Integration of context-information to support spatial decision systems. IADIS International Journal on Computer Science and Information Systems. Vol.12, No. 2, pp. 50-64.

Reflection Papers

DEVELOPMENT OF SUPPORT TOOL TO IMPROVE INDIRECTLY CONSCIOUSNESS OF ENERGY SAVING

Takumi Shida, Hiroshi Sugimura, Moe Hamamoto and Masao Isshiki
Graduate School of Engineering, Kanagawa Institute of Technology
1030 Shimo-ogino Atsugi Kanagawa 243-0292 Japan

ABSTRACT

This paper proposes a human interface in the home energy management system, HEMS for short. The aim of the interface is improving the persistence and frequency of the user's power consumption behavior for economy in electric power consumption at home. The principal idea of our proposal is that control/status functions on network-connected home appliances are each displayed as an icon, which is called "annotation", on the visualization screen of power consumption. A period of time of operation that exceeds the pre-specified threshold about power consumption is shown at a specialized area on the screen. A view at the screen allows users to visually grasp a home appliance having effective power saving. According to the result of the questionnaire, the interface that we developed was evaluated.

KEYWORDS

HEMS, Visualize Power Consumption, Annotation, Energy Saving

1. INTRODUCTION

With the spread of network-connected home appliances, the Home Energy Management System (HEMS) is attracting attention. HEMS supports the power-saving behavior of a user by the visualization of power consumption and remote/concentrated controlling of home appliances. HEMS demonstrates a power saving effect from the study by Kato et al. (2011). Visualization of power consumption by being displayed in a graph view on the screen motivates the user to behave in a power-saving manner. However, visualization function of HEMS has a problem in terms of not being used for a long time from the study by Yagita et al. (2014). The existing visualization that is mostly limited to visualization of power consumption for the entire home is likely to provide insufficient information for users who lack electric knowledge. There have been several recent studies to resolve this problem. Komatsu et al. (2014) proposed a system of proposing the generic advice on energy-saving based on power consumption and peak hours. This system itself selects the advice of high energy-saving effect for the user through a list of advice. However, since this advice is not optimized for the use conditions of each user, energy-saving may be a burden to the user. Morimoto et al. (2016) and Kato (2013) propose an energy-saving method by automatic control of home appliances. However, this method does not include external factors such as seasonal variation, weather and the time of day. On the one hand, power-saving behavior may become a burden for the user. After all, by considering a burden for the user, it is important that the tool is needed to improve farther consciousness of power-saving for the user. The tool should show power consumption and information of home appliance to the user, and assist the user with understanding various methods of energy-saving of home appliances. This improvement allows users to make a plan for power-saving with their own lifestyle and to tackle reasonably power-saving. We propose the tool that adds an annotation to visualize information about home appliances in visualization. An annotation consists of operated time when using home appliances and information about home appliances having high power consumption. A view at the screen allows users to visually grasp a home appliance having effective power saving. In this paper, the tool to raise consciousness of power-saving for the user is developed, and at the same time, the tool is evaluated by the result of a questionnaire.

2. SUMMARY OF THE SYSTEM

Figure 1 shows the overall image of the tool. An annotation is indicated by using icons. The visualization screen is divided into top and bottom areas, and the information of the icons changes depending on the area. In figure 1 (A), icons in the upper area indicate appliances that are using instantaneous current more than the pre-specified threshold, e.g. over 4 amperes (400 wattages). This icon visualizes the operation time by its horizontal size with respect to the axis. In figure 1 (B), icons in the bottom area are indicated when the corresponding home appliances are in operation. In figure 1 (C), the screen visually shows the consumption current by using data of the day and previous day. the upper limit of the rated maximum current of the switchboard is also shown. The indication of the rated maximum current in the visualization screen allows the user to recognize the reference level of the current consumption.

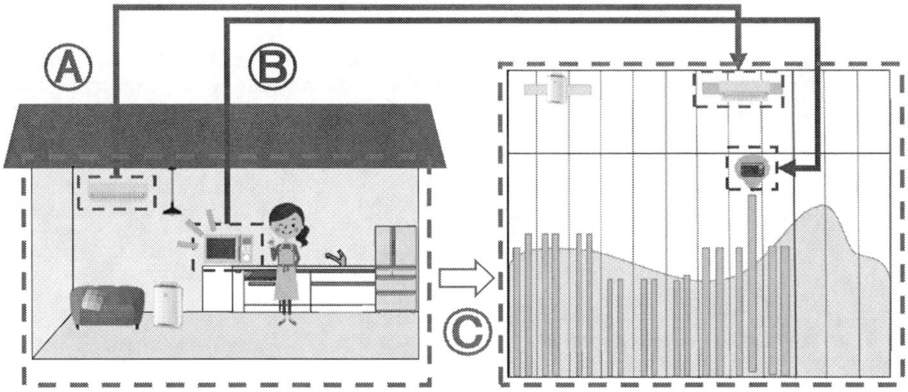

Figure 1. The overall image of the tool

(1) The acquisition of current consumption

Current consumption is obtained with the data from the switchboard. The whole current consumption is obtained with the data from the main circuit breaker, and current consumption of each home appliances is obtained with the data from the circuit breaker.

(2) The acquisition of home appliances of operating state.

The tool obtains information on the control/status of home appliances from ECHONET Lite communication. For example, it acquires the ON-OFF state of the air conditioner, cooling/heating mode, and air volume.

(3) The annotation of display.

Figure 2 shows the example of the shape change of the icons. The annotation uses icons to indicate the operating state of home appliances by illustrations, shapes, and colors. Each icon has a unique color assigned to each home appliance to enable immediate recognition of the home appliance. There are two kinds of round and square icons. A round icon indicates the ON-OFF state of the home appliance. A gray icon means that the corresponding appliance is in the OFF state. Icons in other colors represent active home appliances. A rectangular icon shows the control/status change of the home appliance. The illustration shows the content of operation or setting of the home appliance.

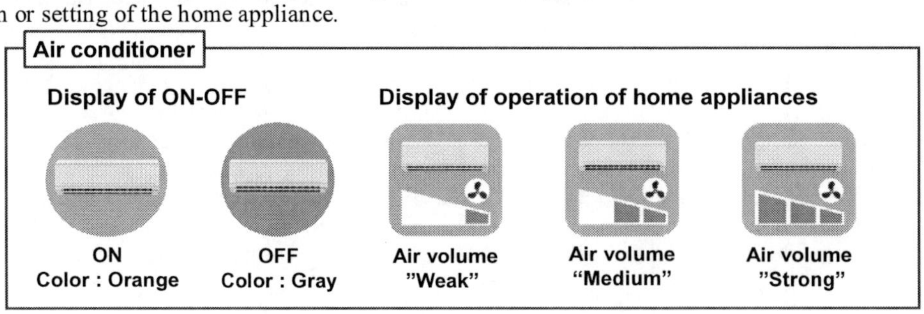

Figure 2. The example of shape change of icons.

2.1 Implementation

Figure 3 shows an entire system configuration. The switchboard uses a network-connected switchboard. Current consumption can be obtained from the sensor built in the switchboard. The data is acquired by using ECHONET Lite communication. ECHONET Lite is a standardized (ISO/IEC 14543-4-3), OSI-based network communications protocol for home automation, and an Open Specs. The server acquires the control/status of each home appliance by using ECHONET Lite communication. The data is stored in the database (DB) in the server. The interface is implemented by the Web application (Ruby on Rails), and it is displayed on Web browsers using HTML 5.

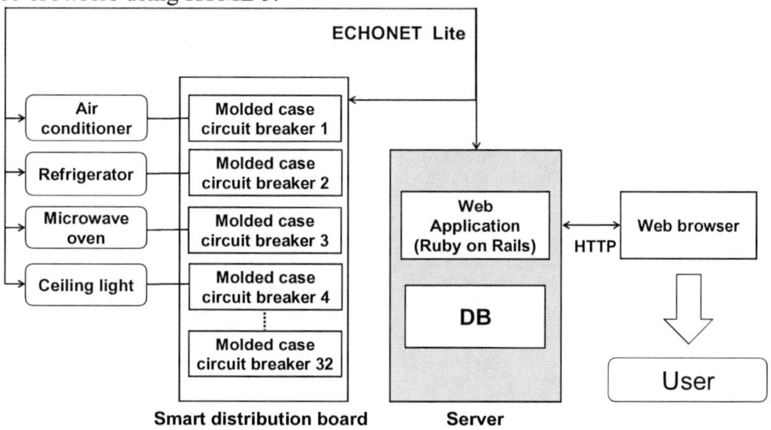

Figure 3. An entire system configuration.

Figure 4 shows an example of the display screen. The consumption current of the day is indicated by orange bars, while that of the previous day is shown by a blue line chart. A vertical blue line is drawn at the current time to help the user locate the latest consumption current at a glance among a lot of data displayed on the graph. The red broken line indicates the rated maximum current of the switchboard. An annotation shows current consumption with high current consumption at the top of the graph and shows information of control/status of home appliances at the bottom of the graph. As many annotation icons may overlap each other on the display, the tool possesses the function of switching the display/non-display of each annotation at the bottom of the visualization screen.

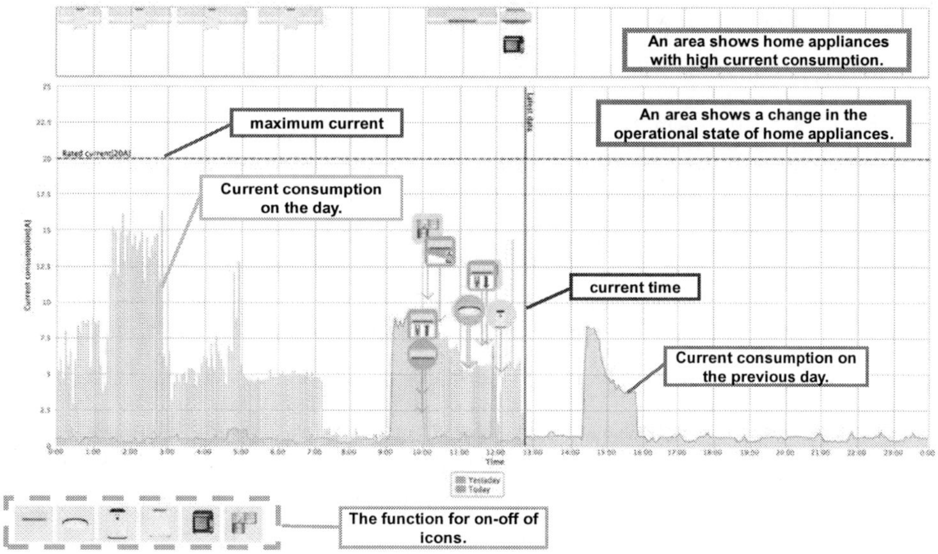

Figure 4. A screen of the tool.

3. EVALUATION OF THE SYSTEM

We have carried out a questionnaire to evaluate the effectiveness of the tool. We conducted questionnaires for a total of 11 people of 9 men in their twenties and 2 women in their forties.

Figure 5 shows the results of the change in consciousness of energy-saving due to the tool. From this result, it is possible to expect that the tool can improve the consciousness of energy-saving. The tool obtained a particularly favorable result from "people with the consciousness of energy-saving". This result suggests that users with high consciousness of energy-saving find the annotation and visualization to be useful for locating home appliances that need more actions than their usual energy-saving practice. Many people with no consciousness of energy-saving answered "energy-saving is slight possible". This result suggests that the tool must provide more information to motivate people with no consciousness of energy-saving to take energy-saving actions.

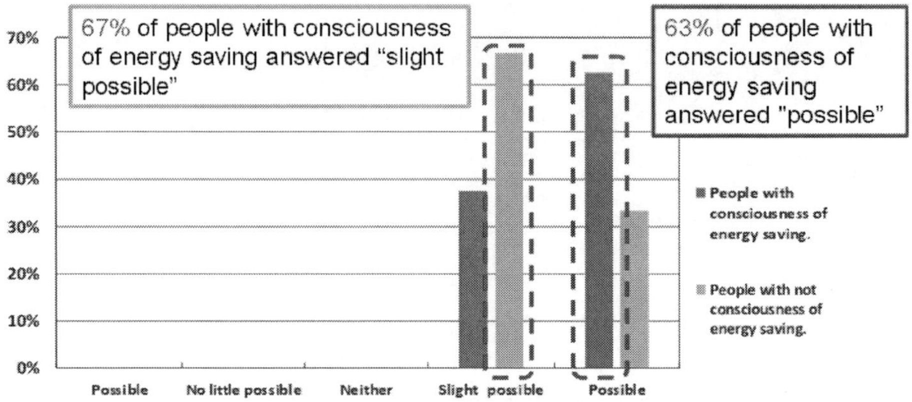

Figure 5. The results on the change in consciousness of energy saving by the tool.

4. CONCLUSIONS

In this paper, we developed the tool to support energy-saving behaviors of the user and evaluated its usefulness by the questionnaire. As the tool adds an annotation to visualization, it is easy for users to understand which home appliance is highly energy-saving. The questionnaire showed that the tool obtains an especially favorable evaluation from people with the consciousness of energy-saving. In future studies, we will improve the tool to more clearly support energy-saving of the user by adding various information of home appliances and showing more methods of energy-saving. We will also verify whether a continuous energy-saving effect can be obtained by the tool.

REFERENCES

Kato, R. 2011. Issues of the penetration of Home Energy Management System-Summarizing issues by the investigation of past demonstration projects, *Central Research Institute of Electric Power Industry Research Report Y 12011,* Japanese.

Kato, T. Yuasa, K and Matsuyama, T. 2013. Energy On Demand, *Information Processing Society of Japan*, Vol.54, No.3, pp.1185-1198.

Komatsu, H. Nishio, K. Mukai, T. and Shinohara, Shinohara, 2014, Automatic Generating System for Reports on Energy Conservation Tips Based on Electricity Demand Data, *IEEJ Transactions on Electronics, Information and Systems*, Vol.134, No.9, pp.1394-1405.

Morimoto, N. 2016 Energy-on-Demand System Based on Combinatorial Optimization of Appliance Power Consumptions, *Journal of Information Processing*, Vol.25, No.1.

Yagita, Y. Iwafune, Y. and Hata, Y. 2014. HEMS Browsing Behaviors and the Communication Effects, *Journal of Japan Society of Energy and Resources*, Vol. 35, No.4, pp50-58, Japanese.

KISS (KEEP IT SIMPLE, STUPID) FOR TRUST!

Mehak Sharma and Muktha Hiremath
SAP Labs India Pvt. Ltd., India

ABSTRACT

Data is the new oil of the world and like any precious resource, it must be regulated for the benefit of people. The General Data Privacy Regulation (GDPR) directive is the first step in this direction. The embarkation to achieving conformity to the GDPR is to understand the needs of the user or the data subject. This paper focuses on the user research conducted with the data subjects, on their awareness and knowledge about data protection and GDPR. It highlights the insights from the interviews with the data subjects, and also provides, high level recommendations for designing, keeping data protection in mind, with the data subjects' needs at the center of it. The insights and the recommendations indicate that user experience and design play a critical role in designing for trust and transparency.

KEYWORDS

User Experience Design, Data Privacy, Security, Transparency, Design in Tech

1. INTRODUCTION

In today's extensive digital landscape, organizations are gathering immense quantities of data about users' activities, online as well as offline. Users have access to intelligent products that gather and transfer detailed personal information. Users' data is a fast-growing source of competitive advantage and therefore for organizations, gaining users' trust is crucial. However, the available flood of data presents vast opportunities for abuse and loss of user's trust.

Facebook has been in the news for the Cambridge Analytica data scandal for the same reason. Such divulgement about organizations make users lose goodwill and trust, ultimately resulting in lesser business for organizations. With the advent of the General Data Protection Regulation as the primary law across the European Union, it is mandatory for organizations to protect citizens' personal data or face a penalty up to €20 million, or 4% annual global turnover. As more and more organizations are reviewing their policies, it's becoming increasingly clear that the user experiences will play a central role in shaping trust in minds of the users.

2. GENERAL DATA PROTECTION REGULATION (GDPR)

The GDPR directive expands the rights of citizens and residents (data subjects) and how much control they exert over their personal data. The GDPR directive lists data subject's rights in detail. GDPR affects all organizations in Europe as well as organizations on other continents.

2.1 User Research

The responsibility of complying with GDPR guidelines now lies with organizations. Central to the process of complying with GDPR, is to understand the data subject, how they grasp GDPR and how is an organization viewed as worthy of their trust? Our organization and its products also have to comply with GDPR, hence this was a trigger for holding detailed user research sessions with the data subjects. Although there are plenty of resources that offer generalized GDPR related Ux best practice, there is a lack of a 360-degree feedback which elaborates data privacy from a data subjects' view point.

To address the topic of trust and understanding of GDPR, we adopted the user interview methodology for user research to interview data subjects followed by a cognitive walkthrough based on an early prototype of the product to gain pertinent insights. Feedback from these sessions gathered via cluster analysis were incorporated into the product that was implemented and released. The user research was conducted with 8 European citizens in Germany with a moderator and notetaker. The study group was diverse in profession (Real-estate, Airport technician, Sales representative, Public administrator, Pre-school teacher, Pedagogue, Student, Cultural sector), education, age (mean age: 30 years, youngest: 24 years and oldest: 67 years) and gender.

2.2 Research Findings

The research findings are grouped into 3 parts, general awareness about the GDPR from the data subjects point of view, their ideas about what trust consists of and their ideas about the GDPR rights.

General awareness about GDPR: 75% data subjects currently don't have sufficient knowledge about GDPR. But when explained, they indicated that they would access their data after GDPR is rolled out - they believed they would get data faster, in a more trustworthy manner. Data protection is understood as a mandatory requirement, and as a basic right. According to them, only the organizations that they authorize to receive their data, should do so. Organizations are seen as having a greater obligation with the new regulations. Even the government agencies should strictly comply to GDPR.

Insight: Organizations should endeavor to transparently educate the data subject about their rights - it needs to be an integral part of every organization.

Data protection and trust: 62.5 % of data subjects expressed skepticism in trusting organizations with their data.13% trusts the government to keep the data confidential. In their words, trust is promoted via a serious presentation of the organization, a clear path to access their data, and a quick response to queries. Data subjects are aware that their data is saved by various customers in many different locations. In this context, 50% data subjects explicitly mentioned need for a central system to access their data. They also believed that a central system could be subject to data breach and hacking.

Insight: A clean look of the organization's website promotes trust. Data subjects want to have an easy access to personal information. Need for a central system to access data, but there are also concerns about who gets to collect data. A trustee or central administration can arrange this.

GDPR Rights:

Right to erasure: When data subjects were asked if they had requested for data deletion for an application/website they used, 38% data subjects indicated to requesting deletion of data. Topics of deletion included information like email account, personal identifiers related to physical attributes, job application entries. Expectation is that data should be wiped clean when data subjects want it to be deleted. 25% data subjects cited examples such as job applications, whereby the data is stored in the organization database.

Insight: When data subjects request for deletion, they expect data is completely deleted, and usually they are not aware about retention policies. Deletion process and retention policies needs to be clearly defined and made transparent to the data subject.

Right to rectification: Data subjects indicated that they have requested changes in data on instances such as moving a house, change in address, change in bank information for applications/website they use.

Right to access: Right to access encompasses the following points:

Recipients of personal data : 38% of the data subjects want to keep track of organizations and third parties – where are the organizations getting their data from and to which third parties the data is transferred. According to the data subject, data transfer should only be done with their explicit consent.

Requesting information: 50% of the data subjects have not tried requesting for personal information. 38% have tried to request information out of curiosity. The Information request was initiated online/website, email, by phone and personally. The expectation is, the data report is sent via a registered mail in a protected email format and a secure transmission process.

Revoke consent: 50% stated that it is clear that once they accept a business's general terms and conditions, the transfer of their data will occur, failing which the service will be unavailable or not fully available. 37% data subjects expressed explicitly incidents when they received newsletters or requests after a purchase or a restaurant visit. It wasn't clear to them at that instance, it was only clear to them later that had given their consent.

Insight: Data subjects require ability to revoke consent for individual instances of data transfer. Companies need to be transparent and indicate instances when and how they are utilizing data subjects consent.

3. DESIGN RECOMMENDATIONS

In summary, the remarks and observations of our end users elicited several design recommendations (more specifically based on our observation and understanding of the users). The design recommendations are grouped into 3 parts, creating awareness and trustworthiness about organizations, having a human touch and facilitating GDPR rights.

Creating awareness and trustworthiness about the organization: Post GDPR, the obligation is on organizations to provide the data subject information about the motives, beliefs of the organization and data retention policies – as this is the first step of trust creation. When accepting terms and conditions of organizations, a full disclosure of all the information that will be utilized by the organization, should be provided to the data subject in a human readable format. The interface should not use dark patterns, for example, highlighting particular information that might mislead the data subject to take a wrong decision.

Trusting a human touch: Interface navigation should be simple, minimum and intuitive. Terminologies should be understandable (locally sensitive). The interface should explicitly indicate a private 'profile' of the data subject. For communication with the organization, the data subjects need telephone numbers along with email addresses, as this creates trustworthiness in the mind of the data subject. There should be a possibility to create a personal, individual request to the organization. The product should guide the user so that the experience is not frustrating.

Facilitating GDPR rights:

Simplifying information and personal data access: Data subjects have the right to view their personal information and obtain knowledge about the recipients of their personal data. Access to personal data should be easy to reach by the data subject at the system level. The data subjects expect to be able to view their information such as: Personal details (name, telephone number, addresses), their card details, social security number, insurance history and a record of all their previously deleted data. When a data subject requests a download of the personal data report – request processing needs to be quick and the system should inform the data subject about their request status. Access into the secure system should not be complicated. The report should be human readable and intuitively structured within one document.

Table 1. Chart illustrating the categories of data the data subject wants to view

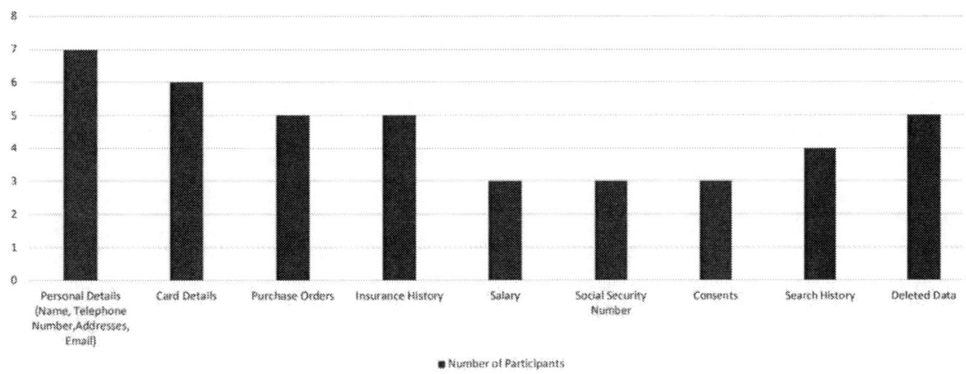

Streamlining data erasure and data rectification: Data subjects expect an immediate and full deletion of their data. Expectation is that the data subjects should be able to delete the data themselves. In some cases, immediate deletion might not be possible – as the organization may be utilizing the data presently, and an immediate deletion would mean that the organization may lose its capability to serve the data subject. Therefore, when a deletion request is made, the status and time taken for deletion should be made clear to the data subject. In a case where complete deletion isn't possible, for example, the need to adhere to legal compliance (a bank keeping data for 7 years) the data subject should be informed about such an instance. Therefore, there is a need of a section within the system, which makes it transparent to the data subject the time taken to process a deletion request and information on associated retention policies. Capabilities to raise a request, revoke a deletion request if needed, edit/rectify request should be provided by the system, where the data subjects can raise the fore mentioned actions themselves, or by the help of a customer care executive.

Demystifying right to object: It is established from user research that data subjects want clarity when giving out their consent to receive further communication from organizations. The duty of organizations is to clearly notify when the data subject is giving permission to receive extra communications and services.

The interface should not mislead the data subject.

4. CONCLUSION

Designing for trustworthy systems is not complex. However, it requires addressing the basic needs of a common citizen – transparency of all data, appropriate and easy to understand communication (without miring in legalese) and the very human aspect of trustworthiness. As mentioned in the paper, there are several small ways in which a company can project its trustworthiness, via its interfaces and experiences. Keep it Simple, Stupid, (KISS)[10]the well-known design principle, is quite applicable as a guiding design principle for GDPR.

ACKNOWLEDGEMENT

This research was supported by SAP. The authors thank colleagues and internal stakeholders from SAP who provided expertise that greatly assisted the research. We thank Alexandra Matz (user researcher) for assistance with user research sessions and collating the data. We thank the "anonymous" user research participants for their insights.

REFERENCES

Alan Calder, 2016. *EU GDPR: A Pocket Guide*. IT Governance Publishing. (eBook)

Patrick O'Kane (author), Kristy Grant-Hart (foreword), 2017. *Fix It Fast Apply GDPR to your company in 10 simple steps.* Brentham House Publishing Company, Covent Garden

Steve Portigal, 2013. *Interviewing Users*. Rosenfeld Media Brooklyn, New York.

Welderufael B. Tesfay, Peter Hofmann, Toru Nakamura, Shinsaku Kiyomoto, Jetzabel Serna, 2018. *Privacy Guide: Towards an Implementation of the EU GDPR on Internet Privacy Policy Evaluation.* Proceeding

IWSPA '18 Proceedings of the Fourth ACM International Workshop on Security and Privacy Analytics

https://en.wikipedia.org/wiki/Facebook%E2%80%93Cambridge_Analytica_data_scandal

https://en.wikipedia.org/wiki/Dark_pattern

https://experience.sap.com/skillup/debugging-design-cognitive-walkthrough-with-build/

https://en.wikipedia.org/wiki/KISS_principle

https://hbr.org/2014/11/with-big-data-comes-big-responsibility

A REVIEW OF THE ROLE OF EXPLANATIONS FOR USER ACCEPTANCE IN BLACK BOX SYSTEMS

Norman G. Vinson, Heather Molyneaux and Jean-Francois Lapointe
National Research Council Canada
Ottawa, Ontario, Canada

ABSTRACT

The opacity of black box AI systems' decision-making has led to calls to modify these systems so they can provide explanations for their decisions. In this article we discuss what these explanations should address and what their nature should be in order to meet the concerns that have been raised and to prove satisfactory to users.

KEYWORDS

Explanation, AI, User Acceptance, Automated Decision Systems, Black Box

1. INTRODUCTION

Artificial Intelligence (AI) systems are increasingly moving out of the lab into the world. As they do, the decisions these systems make will affect people's lives. AI systems can potentially make decisions about medical treatments or diagnoses, hiring and promotion, loans and the interest rates borrowers pay. Concerns have been raised about how these systems make their decisions (Guidotti et al., 2018; Wachter et al., in press). For example, in 2016 Amazon restricted some visible minority neighborhoods from participating in a free same day delivery service even though nearby areas were eligible. This lead to public outcry over alleged racial bias. Soon thereafter, Amazon extended the service to the neighborhoods in question (Ingold & Soper, 2016). Such concerns have led to calls for AI systems to explain their decisions. The question we deal with in this article is what must explanations address to be acceptable to users of AI systems and to the people who are subject to those decisions.

However, before we delve into the issue of acceptable explanations, we will provide some context by discussing the black box characteristic of many AI systems. This will lead into a discussion of the concerns that have been raised about AI decision-making. We will then discuss the issue of user acceptance of explanations.

2. BLACK BOXES

Very generally, a so-called black box system is one in which only inputs into the system and its outputs are observable (Bunge, 1963). In the context of AI, this term is also applied to systems whose input-output relationships are so complex that they cannot be understood by examining the code. Indeed, many AI systems use machine learning in which the code itself does not describe the input-output relationships but instead allows the system to build a model that encodes those relationships. This model then allows outputs to be predicted from inputs (Mohammed et al., 2017). Consequently, in such systems, examining the code cannot tell us why any particular input generates its corresponding output. Moreover, the resulting model is sometimes so complex that examining it does not provide such an understanding either.

To make matters worse, many AI decision-making systems are proprietary so that the models cannot be inspected and, in some cases, the inputs are not disclosed to protect trade secrets, privacy of the users or to ensure users do not manipulate the decision-making (Wachter et al., in press). It is for these reasons that AI decision-making systems are considered black boxes.

3. AI DECISION-MAKING CONCERNS

The black-box nature of AI systems has raised concerns that could limit adoption. The primary concern is one of fairness, in that AI decisions could be based in whole or in part on an input that should not have any influence on the decision (Zemel et al., 2013). Many jurisdictions have laws and regulations to prevent such discrimination, but it can occur with AI systems due to their black box nature (Guidotti et al., 2018).

Obviously, AI decision-making systems should refrain from using inputs that are considered discriminatory, such as race and gender. However, discrimination can creep into an AI system via the training corpus for machine learning systems (Kiritchenko & Mohammad, 2018). If the training corpus is assembled with real world cases that involve discrimination, the system will incorporate that discrimination into its predictive models. For example, if loan officers discriminated against loan applicants with foreign-looking names, an AI system model built with that data would do the same. Even if the discriminatory features are not directly input into the system, discrimination can still occur on the basis of proxy features (like location of residence) that correlate highly with the discriminatory feature (like race) (Zemel et al., 2013) This happened in the Amazon free delivery case mentioned above (Ingold & Soper, 2016).

Wachter proposed that the explanation should be in the form of a counterfactual that expresses the most similar possible world that provides the opposite decision (Wachter et al., in press). For example, a system may deny someone a loan. The corresponding counterfactual statement takes the form *<the opposite decision> would have occurred if <some condition that was not actually met had been met>*. For example, *you would have been approved for a loan if your income were 10% higher.* To limit complexity, the conditional statement should describe the closest possible world to the real world.

However, simply providing a counterfactual for each case is not sufficient to allay concerns over discrimination. Following our example, the system could discriminate on the basis of gender by requiring higher income levels for women than men. A man with a certain income could be told he would have received the loan if his income were 10% higher, but a woman with the *same* income could be told that she would need an income *15% higher* to obtain that loan. Neither that man nor that woman would know the system is discriminatory. Analyses must be conducted over *several* decisions to detect discrimination.

Contestability of a decision is also a concern (Wachter et al., in press). Decisions organizations make in regard to individuals can often be appealed. An appeal requires an understanding of *which* inputs led to the decision as well as an understanding of *how* these inputs led to the decision.

It is also important that the system be competent; that it performs well. An AI loan officer could be unbiased but if it sets low interest rates for high risk loans, the lender will lose money. To support user adoption, there would have to be evidence that the AI system has an acceptable level of performance.

Issues of fairness, contestability and competence require that explanations:

- Identify the inputs that lead to each decision,
- Show that identifiable groups of people are not intentionally or accidentally disadvantaged,
- Provide a rationale for why the identified inputs are related to the decisions,
- Provide evidence of sufficient performance.

4. USER ACCEPTANCE

Where fairness, contestability, or competence is involved, we can argue that explanations are important. However, explanations may also be important for user satisfaction and acceptance in general (Peters, 2011).

Research on recommender system explanations can shed some light on the features of explanations that support user acceptance. Recommender systems are AI-systems that make recommendations about products or services (a book, an e-learning course) to a user, based on that user' personal characteristics or preferences. These characteristics or preferences are typically collected in a personal profile (Lapointe et al., 2017). The profile is then matched in various ways with items that are potentially of interest to the user. Interestingly, many recommender systems are not black boxes, and as a result can provide explanations for their recommendations. Researchers have studied the characteristics of recommendations that make them more acceptable to users.

Zanker (2012) found that explanations about spa recommendations increased users' perception of the system's usefulness, which increases user acceptance (Davis, 1989). The explanations revealed how the recommended items matched the users' profile. For example, one explanation could be that a recommended spa was "family friendly" for users with families. Note that it would be useful to a user to know that this was a reason for the recommendation even if the user did not intend to go to the spa with her family.

However, users have a greater preference for more complex explanations that reveal the trade-offs of various recommendations. For example, a spa may be family friendly but it may be farther away than the others. The trade-off here is family friendliness versus distance. A trade-off formulation adds other factors to a single factor explanation and supports choice-making (Pu & Chen, 2007). Indeed, users seem to prefer complex explanations over single factor explanations (Muhammad et al., 2016), especially when the issue is important to them (Pu & Chen, 2007).

Perhaps not surprisingly, people's desire for complexity is limited. Kizilcec (2016) found that people preferred more complex explanations when the results did not meet their expectations, but simpler ones when the results were expected. The added complexity involved describing the decision-making procedure. This explained why the users' expectations were violated, thus increasing user perception of fairness. However, there was a point at which additional information became confusing. For black box systems, it would be impossible (by definition) to provide a sufficiently simple and understandable explanation of the decision-making process.

Much of the research on explanations is couched in the construct of trust. Trust in electronic or computer systems is a complex construct that involves a variety of components. Some of these components, like fairness, can be addressed by explanations (Kizilcec, 2016). However, many of these components are not directly related to the characteristics of explanations provided by the system. For example, the system's reputation influences the users' trust in the system (Grabner-Krauter & Kaluscha, 2003), but reputation is not a characteristic of an explanation.

5. CONCLUSION

Many AI systems behave as black boxes, raising concerns of fairness and competence. As a result, some authors are calling for AI systems to be required to provide explanations for their decisions (Wachter, et al. in press). From a technical perspective, this poses a problem. Black box systems are not black boxes simply because their explanation feature is turned off. They are black boxes because the code does not specify which inputs lead to specific decisions and the decision-making models are typically too complex to provide sufficiently simple explanations.

Research on recommender systems that are not black boxes, and therefore can provide explanations, have revealed features of explanations that influence user acceptance. Interestingly, these features also address some of the concerns about AI decision-making raised in the literature:

- The explanation should refer to the personal characteristics of the person about whom the decision is made.
- The explanation should provide the inputs that influenced the decision (including tradeoffs).
- The explanation should describe the procedure by which inputs led to the decision, though this may not be possible for black boxes.

Since the preference for complexity seems to depend on context (Pu & Chen 2007, Kizilcec 2016), it may be preferable for people to have the opportunity to adjust how much complexity is provided by the explanation.

In addition, organizations that serve the public interest, regulators, and organizations that use AI systems themselves should want to ensure that the systems can demonstrate:

- That identifiable groups of people are not intentionally or accidentally disadvantaged.
- An acceptable level of performance.

These demonstrations require an analysis over the whole body of a system's decisions, as opposed to explanations for individual decisions. As a group, these explanations features' are far beyond what many proprietary AI decision-making systems currently provide (Wachter et al., in press). Moreover, while the concerns over AI decision-making currently focus on undesired biases, users prefer even more transparency. What exactly these preferences are, what types of explanations would be satisfactory, and how they may differ across contexts and user types remains a topic for investigation. Explanations of AI decisions is certain to be a fruitful topic for future AI and HCI research.

REFERENCES

Bunge, M., 1963. A General Black Box Theory. *Philosophy of Science*, Vol. 30, No. 4, pp. 346-358.

Davis, F. D., 1989. Perceived usefulness, perceived ease of use, and user acceptance of information technology. *MIS Quarterly*, Vol. 13, No., pp. 319–340.

Guidoitti, R. et al., 2018. A Survey of methods for explaining black box models. *arXiv preprint arXiv*:1802.01933

Grabner-Krauter, S., Kaluscha, E., 2003. Empirical Research in On-line Trust: A Review and Critical Assessment. *International Journal of Human-Computer Studies*, Vol. 58, pp. 793-812.

Ingold, D., & Soper, S., 2016. Amazon Doesn't Consider the Race of its Customers. Should it? *Bloomberg*. https://www.bloomberg.com/graphics/2016-amazon-same-day/

Kiritchenko, S., & Mohammad, S.M., 2018. Examining Gender and Race Bias in Two Hundred Sentiment Analysis Systems. In Proceedings of the *7th Joint Conference on Lexical and Computational Semantics (*SEM)*. New Orleans, LA, USA.

Kizilcec, R.F., 2016. How Much Information? Effects of Transparency on Trust in an Algorithmic Interface. Proceedings of the *CHI 2016 Conference ojn Human Factors in Computing Systems*, San Jose, CA, USA, pp. 2390-2395.

Lapointe, J.-F. et al. 2017. A Review of Personal Profile Features in Personalized Learning Systems. In: Andre T. (ed.) *Advances in Human Factors in Training, Education, and Learning Sciences (AHFE 2017); Advances in Intelligent Systems and Computing*, Vol. 596, pp. 46-55, Springer.

Mohammed, M. et al., 2017. *Machine Learning: Algorithms and Applications*. CRC Press, New York, USA.

Muhammad, K. et al., 2016. A Live-User Study of Opinionated Explanations for Recommender Systems. *In proceedings of IUI'16, 21st International Conference on Intelligent User Interfaces*, Sonoma, CA, USA pp. 256-260.

Peters, W., 2011. Explanation and trust: what to tell the user in security and AI? *Ethics and Information Technology*, Vol. 13, Issue 1, pp. 53-64.

Pu, P., & Chen, L., 2007. Trust-Inspiring Explanation Interfaces for Recommender Systems. *Knowledge-Based Systems,* Vol. 20, Issue 6, pp. 542-556.

Wachter, S. et al., in press. Counterfactual explanations without opening the black box: Automated decisions and the GDPR, *Harvard Journal of Law & Technology*.

Zanker, M. 2012. The Influence of Knowledgeable Explanations on Users' Perception of a Recommender System. Proceedings of the sixth *ACM Conference on Recommender Systems RecSys'12*, Dublin Ireland, pp. 269-272.

Zemel, R. et al., 2013. Learning Fair Representations. In Proceedings of the *30th International Conference on Machine Learning (ICML 2013)*, Atlanta, Georgia, USA. *Journal of Machine Learning Research, Workshops and Conference Proceedings (JMLR: W&CP)*, Vol. 28, No. 3, pp. 325-333.

PASSWORD MEMORIZATION MADE EASY -- AN AUGMENTED-REALITY APPROACH

Chuan-Kai Yang, Hsuan Chin and Yuan-Cheng Lai
National Taiwan University of Science and Technology, Taipei, Taiwan

ABSTRACT

Using password to protect privacy is quite common nowadays, especially for web services. However, to avoid a password from being potentially cracked, every user is usually advised to regularly change the password from time to time. Moreover, different web services may impose different password setting constraints, thus leading to different passwords. As a result, it has become more and more challenging for people, let alone the elder ones, to memorize all the passwords. To address this, we propose to design an augmented-reality approach that can display the desired password for the corresponding web service. Furthermore, to keep others from taking a peek at the passwords, a face detection mechanism is also implemented to alert the undesired existence of the third-party.

KEYWORDS

Augmented Reality, Face Recognition, Password Protection

1. INTRODUCTION

As data security or privacy becomes more and more important, especially for web services such as online shopping/banking, password is often used for its convenience. However, due to the existence of various password cracking tools, most web services would suggest each user to constantly change his/her password. Furthermore, pertaining to different security levels/concerns, different web services may enforce different password setting constraints, such as the existence of lower and upper cases, and/or both alphabets and numbers, thus leading to the scenario that different passwords are used for different web services. As a consequence, it has become more and more difficult for people, and especially the elders, to keep track of all the related passwords for the use of different web services. To solve this issue, in this paper, we propose to make use of the technique of marker-less augmented reality to display the desired password when the corresponding web service login screen is matched or detected. Furthermore, as there is still the risk of exposing the password to undesired third-party during the password displaying phase, we equip our system also with the capability of face detection to prevent others from stealing the secret password. However, there still remains one challenge: detecting the undesired face involves the front-camera (of a cell phone), while displaying the desired password as an overlaid image requires the use of the back-camera. In spite of the support from few mobile phones to use both the front and back cameras simultaneously, we hope our developed APP can fulfill all functionalities while still being able to run on most current mobile phones. We address this by adopting a multi-thread approach so that as if both cameras can be simultaneously used for their dedicated purposes.

The rest of the paper is organized as follows. Section 2 reviews related studies related to this work. Section 3 describes our system in more detail. Section 4 presents the results produced by our system. Section 5 concludes this work and hints for some potential future directions.

2. RELATED WORK

There are mainly three types of studies that are related to this work: augmented reality, called AR hereafter for short, face detection, and concurrent usage of both the front and back cameras. The first type of study is on augmented reality. As the name suggests, unlike its close counterpart of "virtual reality", which usually couples with a head-mounted display to allow a user to feel virtually immersed in reality, AR is to overlay some visual information on top of the original display devices to augment the reality. Louis Rosenberg (Roenberg 1993) developed one the first AR systems, and Hirokazu Kato created AR ToolKit, the first open-source AR library (http://artoolkit.org), while there are also other commonly used AR SDK like Vuforia (https://www.vuforia.com/). In terms of classification, AR can be divided into two categories: marker-based and. markerless. The first category corresponds to the case where a marker is represented by some particular pattern, normally a black-and-white pattern is used, while in the second category nearly any image can be used as a marker, and thus it is called markerless. For example, Xiao and Lifeng (Xiao and Lifeng 2014) proposed to display 3D models using AR on a mobile phone, while Kulpy and Bekaroo. (Kulpy and Bekaroo 2017) showed how to present associated nutritional information for detected fruits and Wang et al. (Wang et al. 2017) demonstrated how to track multiple targets in a mobile navigation system.

The second type of studies is on face detection/recognition, and there are many existing researches in this regard. Recently, Ye and Zhu (Ye and Zhu 2017) improved video face recognition accuracy by fusing multiple features. Ren et al. (Ren et al. 2017) proposed to make use of face detection for detecting suspicious people from staying in a place for too long in a real-time manner. Wati and Abadianto (Wati and Abadianto 2017) applied face detection and recognition for smart-home security applications.

The third type of studies is regarding the concurrent activation of both the front and back cameras. There exist few mobile phones, such as Samsung Galaxy S4, that can activate both the front camera and back camera, while a software approach should be applied for most other mobile phones if we want to use both the front camera and back camera simultaneously. Since we are writing a Java-based APP on the Android system, we could apply a multi-thread approach to simultaneously activate both the front and back cameras. In terms of multi-thread Java programming, Gong et al. (Gong et al. 2007) has demonstrated how it can be achieved. In general, this multi-thread technique has many applications, such as on Sorting, as shown in (Qian and Xu 2011), or on smart energy management, as shown in (Chen et al. 2012). Once we can access both the front and back cameras simultaneously, no matter it is done through hardware or multi-threaded implementation, many applications can be realized, such as the system designed by Jain et al. (Jain et al. 2014)..

3. PASSWORD REMINDER VIA AUGMENTED REALITY

The design of our system can be divided into three parts, which will be illustrated in the following three sub-sessions, and the system flow is shown in Figure 1.

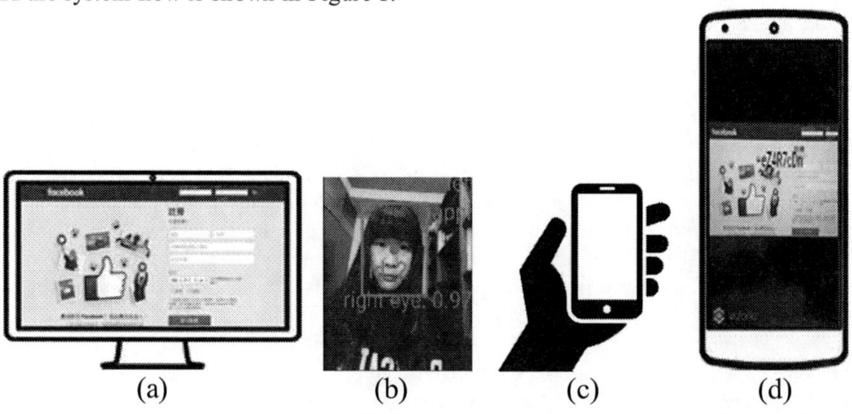

Figure 1. The system flow of this work. (a) The website (of login) containing the password that a user wants to memorize. (b) The front camera needs to check if there's any undesired face. (c) The user needs to hold the mobile phone on top of the website login screen. (d) Once the website matches with the one stored in our database, the desired password gets displayed through an AR mode

3.1 Augmented Reality Engine

The augmented reality engine we used is Vuforia (https://www.vuforia.com/), which is a widely used platform for AR development, and can be used in mobile phones, tablets and eyewear. Developers of Vuforia can implement many advanced computer-vision related functionalities in Android or iOS in order to create realistic and interactive AR experience. In this work, we make use of Vuforia SDK for developing our desired functionality, that is, treating the image of the website (of login) as the marker, called *image target* in Vuforia, so that later on at the run time, a user can hold his/her mobile phone on top of the website that he/she forgets about the password, and the desired password can be displayed. Note that there are two things worth mentioning. First, the original functionality is to display a 3D model once the image target is matched, and this display class can be changed to a *textPlane* class, which is used to show the desired password. Second, the displayed password is in fact in the form of an image, and can be made *transparent* so that it will not occlude the original website's content too much.

3.2 Face Detection

As mentioned previously face detection is needed in our system as we would like to prevent others from taking a peek at the password when it is displayed on the screen of the mobile phone. Currently we make use of *Google Face API*, as the goal is to build a prototype, but not to reinvent the wheel. Note that a detected face, as shown in Figure 2, its corresponding information of size, orientation and some landmarks (facial features) will be displayed once it is identified.

3.3 Turning on both the Front and Back Cameras

As the mobile phone used in our experiment is not equipped with the functionality of concurrently opening the back and front cameras, we adopt the technique similar to Gong et al. (Gong et al. 2007) by running multi-threads in Java to support two display windows corresponding to two cameras: the front camera is used to detect the users in front of the mobile phone, i.e., to detect all the faces that are close enough to the screen of a mobile phone, so that any person, except the desired user, who wants to take a peek at the shown password, can be identified and an alert can be signaled if more than one faces are detected.

4. RESULTS

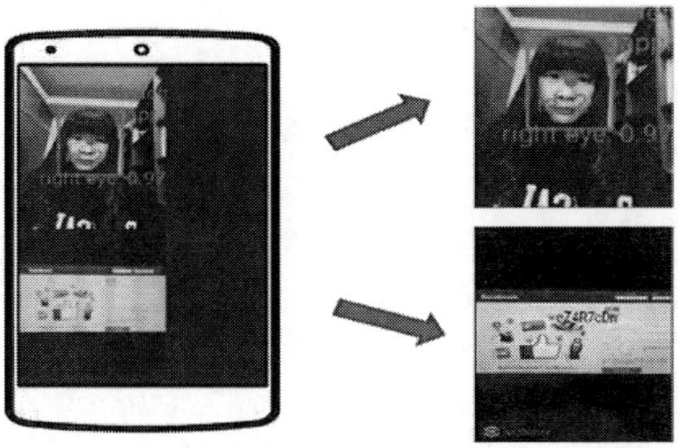

(a) (b)

Figure 2. Example results.. (a) The upper window contains the information of a detected face, while the lower window shows the login screen of a website. (b) The upper window stays the same, while the lower window demonstrates how the desired password (,in black) is shown on top of the matched website image.

Figure 2 shows some testing example where our APP can simultaneously opens two windows for both the front camera and the back camera. The front camera is responsible for detecting the faces of the users in front of a mobile phone, as shown in the top image in Figure 2(a) with some associated face information, while the back camera should be placed on top of the website login screen, as shown in the bottom image in Figure 2(a), which has been captured and stored as a marker or image target at the preprocessing time to match against the video frames in the AR mode at the run time. Once the website image target can be identified, the desired password is retrieved and displayed on top of website login screen, as shown in Figure 2(b).

5. CONCLUSION AND FUTURE WORK

We have successfully implemented a prototype for retrieving and displaying the associated password for logging into a website by adopting an AR approach, i.e., the login screen of a website can be recorded and used as a marker in an AR engine at the preprocessing time so that it can be matched against at the run time to display the desired password should it be forgotten. To provide more safety, both the front camera and back camera are used to detect the faces of users to avoid the password from leaking to undesired persons.

A potentially better solution is to incorporate face recognition in our system so that only the authorized user can get to trigger the AR functionality for retrieving the password. However, Google Face API currently does not support this feature and we need to turn to other engines/APIs to carry out this functionality. Another possibility is just to request the user to enter a PIN number that is consistently used for a mobile phone to enhance the security if the mobile phone is lost or used by an unauthorized user.

ACKNOWLEDGEMENT

This work was supported in part by the Ministry of Science and Technology of Taiwan under the grants MOST 104-2221-E-011-083-MY2, MOST 105-2218-E-011-005, MOST 105-2218-E-001-001, MOST 106-3114-E-011-003, and MOST 106-2221-E-011-148-MY3.

REFERENCES

Rosenberg, 1993. Virtual fixtures as tools to enhance operator performance in telepresence environments. SPIE Manipulator Technology.

Xiao and Lifeng, 2014. Implementation of mobile augmented reality based on Vuforia and Rawajali. *2014 IEEE 5th International Conference on Software Engineering and Service Science*, Beijing, China, pp 912-915.

Kulpy and Bekaroo, 2017. Fruitify: Nutritionally Augmenting Fruits through Markerless-Based Augmented Reality. *2017 4th IEEE International Conference on Soft Computing and Machine Intelligence*, Republic of Mauritius, pp. 149-153.

Wang et al., 2017. A Markerless Augmented Reality Mobile Navigation System with Multiple Display Function. *2017 IEEE International Conference on Applied System Innovation*, Sapporo, Japan, pp. 408-411.

Ren et al., 2017. A Real-Time Suspicious Stay Detection System based on Face Detection and Tracking in Monitor Videos. *2017 10th International Symposium on Computational Inteligence and Design*, Hangzhou, China, pp. 264-267.

Wati and Abadianto, 2017. Design of Face Detection and Recognition System for Smart Home Security Application. *2017 2nd International Conferences on Information Technology, Information Systems and Electrical Engineering*, Yogyakarta, Indonesia, pp. 342-347.

Ye and Zhu, 2017. The Video Face Recognition Method and System Based on The Fusion on Multiple Features. *2017 10th International Congress on Image and Signal Processing, BioMedical Engineering and Informatics*, Shanghai, China.

Gong et al., 2007. On Testing Multi-threaded Java Programs. *Eighth ACIS International Conference on Software Engineering, Artificial Intelligence, Networking, and Parallel/Distributed Computing*, Qingdao, China, pp. 702-706.

Qian and Xu, 2011. Optimization and implementation of sorting algorithm based on multi-core and multi-thread. *2011 IEEE 3rd International Conference on Communication Software and Networks*, Xi'an, China, pp. 29-32.

Chen et al., 2012. Smar Energy Management of Multi-threaded Java Applications on Multi-core Processors. *13th ACIS International Conference on Software Engineering, Artificial Intelligence, Networking, and Parallel/Distributed Computing,* Kyoto, Japan, pp. 260-265.

Jain et al., 2014. Imaging Techniques for Secure Photograph using Dual Camera. *2014 Recent Advances in Engineering and Computational Sciences*, Chandigarh, India, pp. 1-6.

Posters

AUTOMATIC TABLE TENNIS SCORING SYSTEM BASED ON SMART WEARABLE DEVICES

Sangwoo Noh, Yejoon Lee, Youmin Kim, Jinwoo Cho, and Ahyoung Choi[1]
Department of Software, Gachon University, Seongnam, 13120 Republic of Korea

ABSTRACT

Recently people's interests in health care are increasing, and many wearable device manufacturers have released various kind of fitness trackers for exercises and activities. However, most of them are focused on personal activities not on group activities. In this paper, we propose a system that automatically scores a table tennis game by using smartwatches and smartphones. The system analyses sensor data from the smartwatches, detects sound of a ball and calculates scores based on table tennis scoring algorithm. To evaluate the system, we collected 521 swing data and 50 ball sound data from 5 people, and the accuracy was 97.8%(510/521) and 82%(41/50), respectively. We expect that this system can be applied in a wide range of group activities with a low expense.

KEYWORDS

Table Tennis, Activity Recognition, Wearable Device, FFT

1. INTRODUCTION

As the interest in healthcare, many manufacturers have produced various kind of wearable devices, such as Samsung Gear Fit Pro2, Apple Watch3, Garmin Vivoactive, etc. However, the abandonment rate of smartwatch and fitness tracker is 29 and 30 percent, respectively [Susan Moore, 2016]. The users mostly said those products are not useful enough. In addition, those trackers are mostly focused on personal activities and don't support group activities. Eric O.Boyer and his team proposed low-cost motion sensing of table tennis players [Eric Boyer, 2013]. They attached sensors on the racket and used Gaussian low pass filter to analyze data in real time. However, they had to tag manually in the graph to classify types of swings. This is not an appropriate way to classify swing types in real time. Other researchers used Kinect to detect a user's swing action [Geon Heo, 2015, Liming Zhang et al., 2016]. They read 3D information of a user's action and converted the information into spherical coordinates. Then, through LDA coordinates reduction and k-means clustering, they extracted feature points of the action and classified the swings into 2 types by using the HMM. The study showed 80.2% of accuracy. However, that study was hard to be applied in the real game because all players had to stand in front of Kinect. To enhance usefulness of wearable device and reduce the cost for exercise, we propose a system, Automatic Table Tennis Scoring System(ATTSS).

2. PROPOSED METHOD

The proposed ATTSS consists of three steps: swing recognition based on smartwatches, ball sound detection based on smartphones, and scoring algorithm based on table tennis rules. First, for swing detection, we collect accelerometer and gravity sensor signal from the smartwatch and develop a pattern recognition algorithm to detect whether a user performs a swing or not. From the preliminary study, we find out that x and y represent an event of swing action. To see the integrated force of accelerometer, Signal Vector Magnitude (SVM) was applied on x and y value. The reason z value was not included is that z value not only represented little difference but also affected accuracy of swing detection algorithm. After SVM, we used

[1] Corresponding author, email: aychoi@gachon.ac.kr

thresholding 150 and made all value below the threshold to zero. We also used peak detection algorithm to extract only one peak from a cluster of peaks in the graph: other peaks in a certain window size (e.g. 10) were ignored before a next swing. In addition, to differentiate a swing with other actions, gravity sensor z value was used. Figure 1 below is a result of 19 swings. The left in Figure 1 shows that raw x, y and z value of accelerometer: red is y, purple is x and green is z. The right in Figure 1 shows that the result of swing recognition algorithm. Secondly, system detects sound of ball dropping on the table based on sound signal with the microphone of a smartphone device. The microphone in the smartphone was used to collect sound data to determine whether a ball was dropped on the table. The original sound signal collected is time domain data in 22,050Hz. To see the range of frequency of a ball sound, Fast Fourier Transform algorithm was applied and converted time domain into frequency domain with a total block size 512. Amplitude from block No. 180 ~ block No.270 (7,751Hz ~ 11,627Hz) became higher than other sound frequency. We determined if a ball was dropped on the table by using this algorithm: check whether amplitude from block No.180 ~ block No.270 exceeds a specific threshold (e.g. |13|), and check whether amplitude between 80 and 180 exceeds a specific threshold (e.g. |3|).

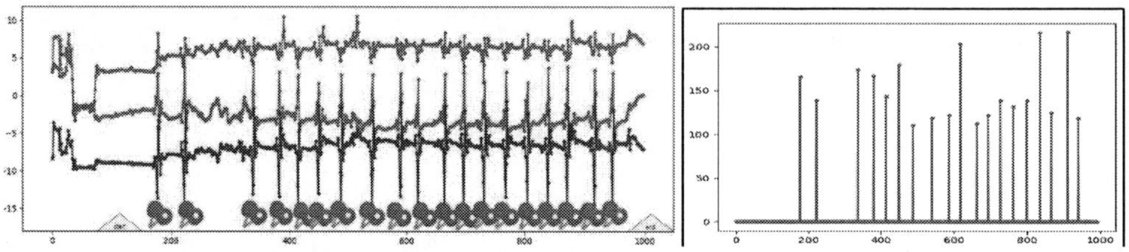

Figure 1. Raw accelerometer(left) and result of swing recognition algorithm (right)

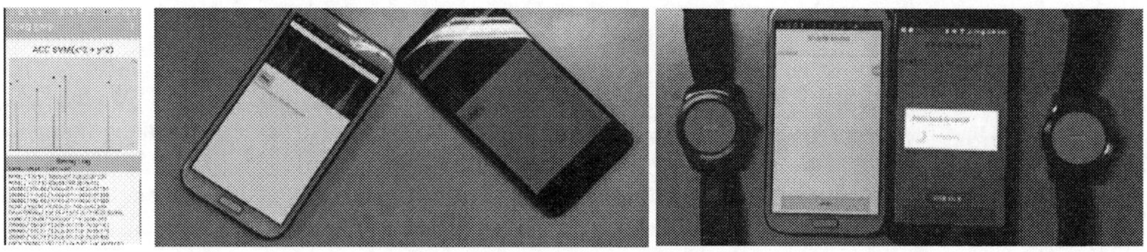

Figure 2. Implementation: Swing recognition (left), sound detection (middle) and implementation result (right)

Finally, a referee smartphone device collects all the analyzed data from each player, and determines a winner or a loser based on table tennis scoring algorithm. The winner could be determined by checking an event occurring while playing game. The event is swing event and ball-dropping event. In a general case, there are a sequence of events: Player A swings the ball → Ball drops on Player B table → Player B swings the ball → Ball drops on Player A table → Player A swings the ball → and so on. Based on a sequence of events, each player has an array of expected events. Each player compares 'now-event' with 'expecting-event'. If it is equal, they keep playing, otherwise, each player checks whose event it was in the previous event. If it was A, B is winner and vice versa. To see if the algorithm works, we watched the video clip of a real game, Ryu (South Korea) vs Wang Liqin (China), on YouTube and recorded the sequence of events for an input data. The scoring algorithm produced a correct output,11:6, for the input data. Figure 2 above is implementation of each function. Left is an app for swing recognition, middle is an app that detects ball sound, and right is a smartwatch app ready for a game and two smartphones matching other players. To evaluate the system, we collected 521 swing data from 5 people, and the accuracy was 97.8%(510/521). For sound detection test, the accuracy was 82%(41/50). In a further study, we are going to enable the system to be and go through usability evaluation.

ACKNOWLEDGEMENT

This research was supported by the MSIT (Ministry of Science and ICT), Korea, under the National Program for Excellence in Software supervised by the IITP (Institute for Information & Communications Technology Promotion) (2015-0-00932) and was supported by Basic Science Research Program through the National Research Foundation of Korea (NRF) funded by the Ministry of Education (NRF-2016R1D1A1B03935104).

REFERENCES

Susan Moore, 2016. "User Survey Analysis: Wearables Need to Be More Useful", Gartner, Sydney Australia.

Eric Boyer et al., 2013, Low-cost motion sensing of table tennis players for real time feedback, *International Journal of Table Tennis Sciences,* Paris, France, pp.1-4.

Geon Heo et al. 2015. Analysis of Table Tennis Swing using Action Recognition. *Journal of Institute of Control*, Vo1.21, No. 1, pp40-45.

Liming Zhang et al., 2016, Kinect based 3D video generation, *In proceedings of IADIS*, Madeira, Portugal, pp.278-282.

AUTOMATIZATION OF ALGORITHMS FOR VISUAL QUALITY CONTROL OF COATINGS AND CONTOURS ON THE PRODUCTS FOR MEDICAL PURPOSES

Olga E. Baklanova, Elena V. Ryzhkova and Madina M. Iskakova

D. Serikbayev East Kazakhstan State Technical University, Kazakhstan

ABSTRACT

The study aims to development of production technologies of titanium and its coatings of domestic production of medical products. In this study were considered Sobel operator and Gabor filter, which are of greatest interest for the development and improvement of quality control systems. The analysis of the image gives an assessment of quality of production, reveals existence of defects that allows to correct the processing line of production, and also to reveal malfunction of the equipment. Using of new algorithms for visual quality control of geometric parameters and coating texture, allows processing of medical products with minute and high performance.

KEYWORDS

Texture, Biocompatible Coating, Gabor Filter, Sobel Operator, Digitalization, Machine Vision, Image Recognition, Image Processing Methods, Quality Control, Medical Products, Implants

1. INTRODUCTION

The development of health care program of Republic of Kazakhstan "Densaulik"*(денсаулық(kazakh) - health)* is aimed at improving the social well-being of the population of the Republic in the interests of vulnerable groups, such as victims of environmental problems associated with testing at the Semipalatinsk nuclear test site and the activities of industrial enterprises, as well as for groups suffering from cancer, bone tuberculosis, elderly people in need of quality and affordable prosthetics (Nazarbayev N., 2010). The study aims to development of production technologies of titanium and its coatings of domestic production (JSC (open joint-stock company) "Ust-Kamenogorsk Titanium and Magnesium plant") of medical products.

Research object: medical titanium alloys of production of JSC UK TMP and biocompatible powders of hydroxyapatite. Relevance of the study: improving the social welfare of citizens of the Republic of Kazakhstan. Research methods: modern analytical methods of structure research (transmission and scanning electron microscopy with energy dispersive analysis, x-ray phase analysis), complex thermal analysis, tests of operational properties, computer simulation of technological processes and tests of physical and chemical properties of experimental samples of medical products. Area of research: applied materials research and development of new algorithms of automation and control, obtaining medical materials and products. Field of application: metallurgy, materials science, automation and control, medical materials and products. The results can be used to product medical products: biocompatible coatings, implants and medical instruments.

2. VERIFICATION ALGORITHMS MATCHING OF THE PRODUCT'S SHAPE AND OF BIOCOMPATIBLE COATING'S TEXTURE

In this study were considered Sobel operator and Gabor filter, which are of greatest interest for the development and improvement of quality control systems.

The implant is checked in two stages:

1st stage: control of the contours of the implant (Sobel operator);

2nd stage: control of biocompatible coating (Gabor filter).

2.1 Sobel Operator. Mathematical Apparatus of Sobel Operator

The Sobel operator is the discrete differential operator calculating approximate value of a gradient of brightness of the image. Application of the Sobel operator in each point of the image is a vector of a gradient of brightness in this point, or its norm. In the field of image processing it is often used in algorithms for detachment boundaries. The Sobel operator is based on the convolution of images by small separable integer filters in vertical and horizontal directions, so it is relatively easy to compute. The operator calculates the gradient of the brightness of the image at each point. The result is how "sharply" or "smoothly" the brightness of the image changes at each point, and hence the probability of finding a point on the face, and also the orientation of the boundary. In practice, the calculation of the magnitude of the change in brightness (the probability of belonging to the edge) is more reliable and easier to interpret than the calculation of the direction.

Mathematically, the gradient of a function of two variables for each image point (which is the brightness function) is a two-dimensional vector, the components of which are the derivatives of the image brightness along the horizontal and vertical lines. At each point of the image, the gradient vector is oriented to the direction of the greatest increase in brightness, and its length corresponds to the magnitude of the brightness change. This means, that the result of the Sobel operator at the point lying in the region of constant brightness is the zero vector, and at the point of the region of different brightness lying on the boundary, a vector crosses the boundary in the direction of increasing brightness (Parker, James R., 1997).

The operator uses 3x3 kernels with which the original image is folded to calculate the approximate values of the derivatives horizontally and vertically. Let the "A" be the original image, and *Gx* and *Gy* be two images on which each point contains approximate derivatives with respect to x and y. They are calculated as follows:

$$Gy = \begin{bmatrix} -1 & -2 & -1 \\ 0 & 0 & 0 \\ +1 & +2 & +1 \end{bmatrix} * A \text{ and } Gx = \begin{bmatrix} -1 & -2 & -1 \\ 0 & 0 & 0 \\ +1 & +2 & +1 \end{bmatrix} * A$$

Where *(*)* denotes a 2-dimensional convolution operation.

The coordinate x here increases "to the right", and y - "down". At each point of the image, the approximate value of the gradient value can be calculated by using the approximate values of the derivatives obtained: $G = \sqrt{G_x^2 + G_y^2}$ (element-by-element).

Using this information, we can also calculate the direction of the gradient: $\theta = \arctan\frac{G_y}{G_x}$. Where, the angle θ is equal to zero for the vertical boundary, which has the dark side to the left (Mark S., 2008).

2.2 Gabor Filter. Mathematical Apparatus of Gabor Filter

The algorithm based on Gabor's filters is very useful in identifying the direction of the texture. This is the main advantage of the algorithm. In digital image processing, this filter is applied to detect edges of objects. RGB and HSL color models are suitable to use this algorithm. It should be noted that this algorithm is not as popular as, for example, graph theory algorithms. Therefore, the algorithm based on Gabor filters is of the greatest interest for its development and further implementation.

The algorithm using Gabor's filters is based on the work with two matrices: image matrix and filter matrix. The original image can be represented as a matrix I, the image matrix filled with pixel values. These values are placed in each cell of the matrix. The filter matrix and image matrix are superimposed on each other (Kozlova I.V., 2012).

The fundamental formula used in the implementation of the algorithm is:

$$g(x, y, \delta, \theta, \varphi, \sigma, \gamma) = e^{(-\frac{x'^2 + y^2 y'^2}{2\sigma^2})} * \cos\,(2\pi\frac{x'}{\delta} + \varphi)$$

Where: $x' = x\cos\theta + y\sin$; $y' = -x\sin\theta + y\cos\theta$; δ – wavelength of the cosine factor; θ – determines the orientation of the normal of the parallel bands of the Gabor function in degrees; φ – determines the phase shift in degrees; γ – compression ratio.

3. OUTCOME

The presented figures illustrate the results of the application of the Sobel operator (figure 1) and Gabor filter (figure 2).

Figure 1. Control of the Contours of the Implant

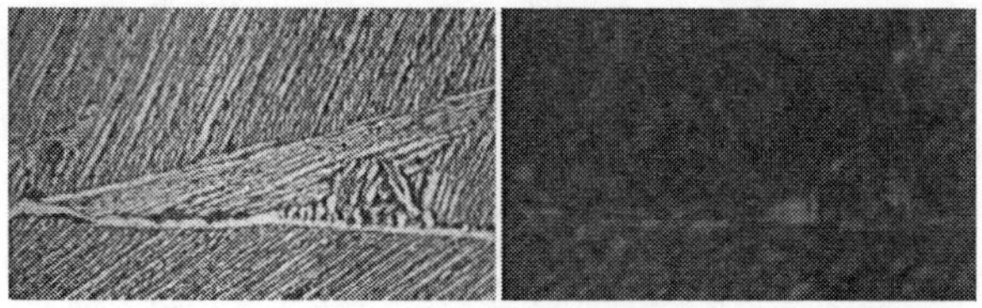

Figure 2. Control of Biocompatible Coating

Conducted research on digital images of the medical implant (checking coating and contour) give the opportunity to assess product quality and identify defects.

4. CONCLUSION

The analysis of the image gives an assessment of quality of production, reveals existence of defects that allows to correct the processing line of production, and also to reveal malfunction of the equipment. Using of new algorithms for visual quality control of geometric parameters and coating texture, allows processing of medical products with minute and high performance. Possible further expansion of the possibilities of checking the quality of the implant in the form of automation of quality control products.

ACKNOWLEDGMENT

The study was conducted with the financial support of the science Committee of the Ministry of Education of the Republic of Kazakhstan within the program-target funding for scientific and technical program: "Target scientific and technical program of D.Serikbayev East Kazakhstan state technical University, focused on the development of new types of products for production at leading industrial enterprises of East Kazakhstan region" for 2017-2019, under the subprogramme 0006/PCF "Production of titanium products for further use in medicine".

REFERENCES

Kozlova I.V., 2012. Image textural segmentation Algorithm based on Gabor filter // Scientific study, 2012, №10 pp. 442-444.

Mark S., 2008. Nixon and Alberto S. Aguado. Feature Extraction and Image Processing, Academic Press, 2008, p. 88.

Nazarbayev N., 2010. Health care program of Republic of Kazakhstan "Densaulik"(денсаулық (kazakh) - health [open source] https://www.enbek.gov.kz/ru/node/332663

Parker, James R., 1997. Algorithms for Image Processing and Computer Vision. New York: John Wiley & Sons, Inc., 1997.

VOXEL REPRESENTATION OF LOCAL GEOMETRY

Alexey Tolok[1], Natalya Tolok[2] and Mikhail Loktev[1]
[1]*Moscow State Technological University "Stankin", Russia*
[2]*V. A. Trapeznikov Institute of Control Sciences of Russian Academy of Sciences, Russia*

ABSTRACT

The method of functional-voxel modeling (FVM) to build a voxel-geometric model is considered. The FVM method is based on the linear approximation of the area describing the geometric object by an algebraic function. In the process of approximation, the normalized coefficients are determined with the arguments of the obtained linear function at each point of the area. These coefficients are local geometric characteristics and are displayed using the corresponding color in the voxel space.

KEYWORDS

Local Geometry, Voxel, Functional-Voxel Modeling, Algebraic Function

1. INTRODUCTION

Voxel modeling in the existing context allows us to explore the area of an explicitly defined algebraic function (for example, the construction of quadrics with perturbation functions [Vyatkin and Dolgovesov, 2004]), but often such a model reduces to a receptor model for visualization. It should be borne in mind that the algebraic function on a given area takes three main states: the positive values domain (it is customary to refer to the area of a geometric object), the negative values domain (accordingly, the area outside the object) and the area of zero values (the geometric object border). Such approach allows to save the important geometrical position information of a normal in a space point.

2. FUNCTIONAL-VOXEL GEOMETRIC MODEL

Constructing the functional voxel model (FV-model) is based on the principles of linear approximation of the function space to calculate its local geometric characteristics (Tolok, 2016). Unlike existing approaches to linear approximation, local geometrical characteristics of this model are represented by the components of a normal of the space increased dimension based on the **statement:** *In the space* E^{m+1} *a hyperplane of the kind* $n_1x_1+\cdots+n_mx_m=p$ *is presented as* $n_1x_1+\cdots+n_{m+1}x_{m+1}=0$. Linear approximation defines a flat neighborhood at the point of the 3D space by components of the normal $\vec{n}(n_1,n_2,n_3,n_4)$ for the normal equation $n_1x_1+n_2x_2+n_3x_3+n_4x_4=0$. Consider an example of a functional-voxel representation for the function:

$$x_3^f(x_1,x_2)=5(x_2 sin\pi x_1+x_1^2 cos\pi x_2).$$

Definition. A graphic image, commensurate with an algebraic function and displaying its local geometrical characteristic, is called a graphic image model of a prototype, or a graphic M-image.

Imagine an approximate model $x_3'=g(n_1,\ldots,n_4,x_1,x_2)$ of the function $x_3^f=f(x_1,x_2)$ (figure 1) as a normal vector field, expressed by four scalar fields $\vec{n}=(n_1,n_2,n_3,n_4)$ according to the conditions of the statement. Install some scalar fields conformity n_1,n_2,n_3,n_4, defined by the period $[-1;1]$ with their voxel representation C_1, C_2, C_3, C_4. These values are set in accordance with the gradation of the monochrome palette $p \in P = [0; 255]$ (figure 1): $C_i = \frac{P(1+n_i)}{2}$.

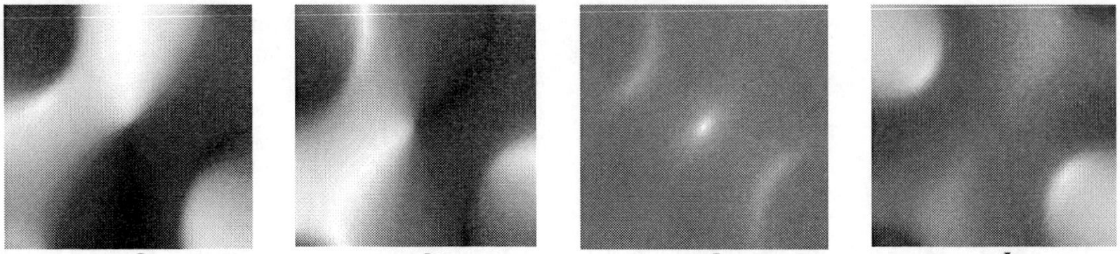

C_1^f C_2^f C_3^f C_4^f

Figure 1. Basic M-images for the Function $f(x_1, x_2)$ for $P = [0; 255]$

At this stage for computer operation with the function, it is enough to use its basic M-images (FV-model) for implementation of different computation.

3. FUNCTIONAL-VOXEL ARITHMETIC

This work (Tolok, 2016) provides basic arithmetic operations over algebraic features for the computer presented by FV-model. To demonstrate the basic principle of such operations, consider the sum of two functions with the same scope of definition, which can be written as a function $(g + f)(x) = g(x) + f(x)$. Hereby each of these functions must be specified explicitly: $x_i^f = f(x_1, \dots, x_{i-1}, x_{i+1}, \dots, x_m)$, $x_i^g = g(x_1, \dots, x_{i-1}, x_{i+1}, \dots, x_m)$ then we write the value of the sum as $x_i^{Add} = x_i^f + x_i^g$.

As example, consider two functions heterogeneous according to their structure for summing up. As the first function we use the above-mentioned x_3^f, and the second function will be presented by the exponential law:

$$x_3^g = (x_1 - 1)e^{-(x_1^2 + (x_2+1)^2)} + 10(0.2x_1 - x_1^3 - x_2^5)e^{-(x_1^2 + x_2^2)} + e^{-\frac{x_1^2 + x_2^2}{3}}.$$

Figure 2 shows the voxel representation of the function $x_3^g = g(x_1, x_2)$.

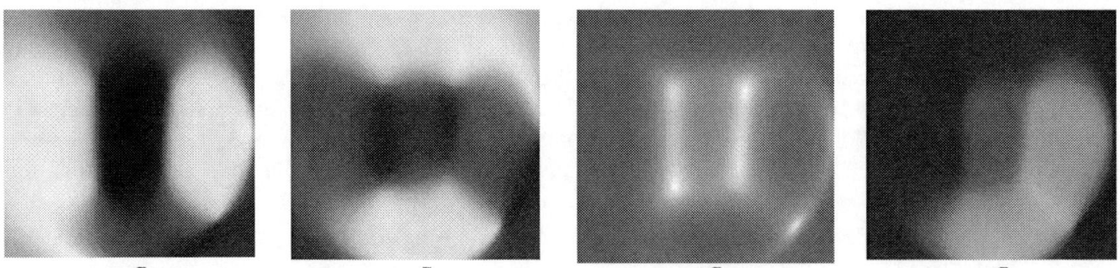

C_1^g C_2^g C_3^g C_4^g

Figure 2. Example of Voxel M-Image Function $x_3^g = g(x_1, x_2)$

It's notable that by voxel M-image of the component n_i is expressed $n_i = (C_i - P/2)/P$, and the function of any complexity and dimension (m) turns into linear image:

$$x'_i = \frac{n_{m+1}}{n_i} - \sum_{j=1}^{j=i-1} x_j \frac{n_j}{n_i} - \sum_{j=i+1}^{j=m} x_j \frac{n_j}{n_i}.$$

In this case, we have the sum of two expressions of functions (*f*) and (*g*):

$$x_3^{Add} = \left(-\frac{n_1^f}{n_3^f}x_1 - \frac{n_2^f}{n_3^f}x_2 + \frac{n_4^f}{n_3^f}\right) + \left(-\frac{n_1^g}{n_3^g}x_1 - \frac{n_2^g}{n_3^g}x_2 + \frac{n_4^g}{n_3^g}\right)$$

Having regrouped the equation and having expressed coefficients, we obtain:

$a_1^{Add} = n_1^f n_3^g + n_1^g n_3^f$, $a_2^{Add} = n_2^f n_3^g + n_2^g n_3^f$, $a_4^{Add} = n_4^f n_3^g + n_4^g n_3^f$, $a_3^{Add} = n_3^f n_3^g$.

Figure 3 shows the M-images of the function (f + g). In [2], the main arithmetical operations using M-images are given.

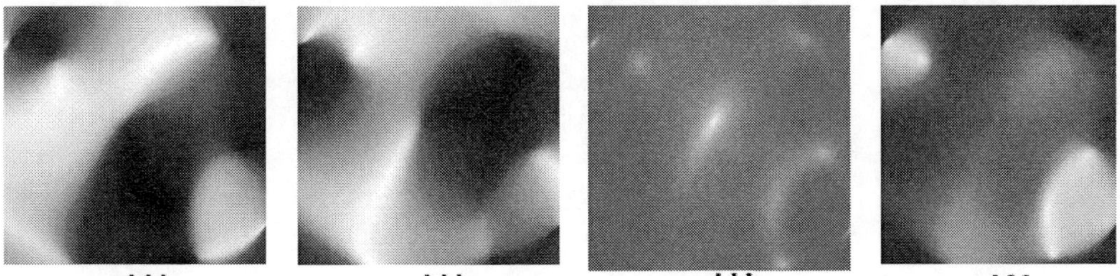

C_1^{Add} C_2^{Add} C_3^{Add} C_4^{Add}

Figure 3. Voxel Representing the Domain of the Sum of Functions (f) and (g)

4. GEOMETRIC TRANSFORMATIONS OF FV MODEL SPACE

Expanding record $X \cdot N^T = p$ into a normal equation of such kind as $n_1x_1 + \dots + n_{m+1}x_{m+1} + n_{m+2} = p$. Consider the shift in the example of the plane of the general position along the axes on $(\Delta x, \Delta y, \Delta z)$ given by equation $n_1x + n_2y + n_3z = p$. With such a shift, the equation gets the following form: $n_1(x - \Delta x) + n_2(y - \Delta y) + n_3(z - \Delta z) - p = 0$. Opening the parentheses and regrouping components leads to the expression

$$n_1x + n_2y + n_3z - (p + n_1\Delta x + n_2\Delta y + n_3\Delta z) = 0,$$

$$[n'_1 \quad n'_2 \quad n'_3 \quad p'] = [n_1 \quad n_2 \quad n_3 \quad p] \cdot T^T,$$

$$T^T = \begin{bmatrix} 1 & 0 & 0 & -\Delta x \\ 0 & 1 & 0 & -\Delta y \\ 0 & 0 & 1 & -\Delta z \\ 0 & 0 & 0 & 1 \end{bmatrix}.$$

The FV-model of function $x_3^C = 1 - x_1^2 - x_2^2$ is shown in the figure 4.

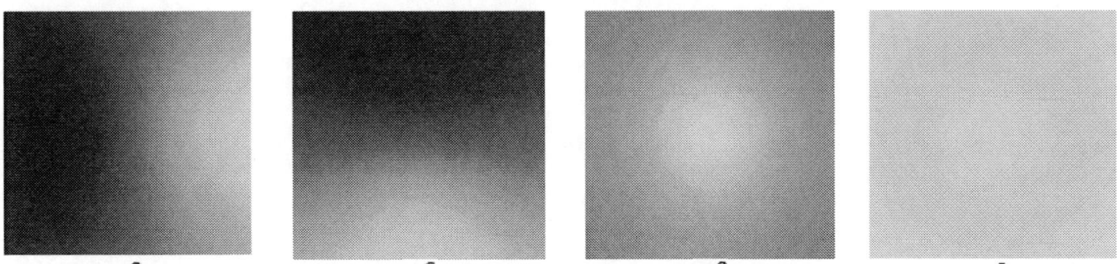

C_1^C C_2^C C_3^C C_4^C

Figure 4. FV-Model of the Area of the Unit Circle Function

Despite the lack of visibility of the expected paraboloid surface, the FV-model provides the computer with all the necessary geometric characteristics for the image of the object. In a figure 5 characteristic change of M-images in case of shift operation on 10 units along an x-axis is watched. By analogy statements about applicability of matrixes of turn and scaling for conversions of local characteristics are proved.

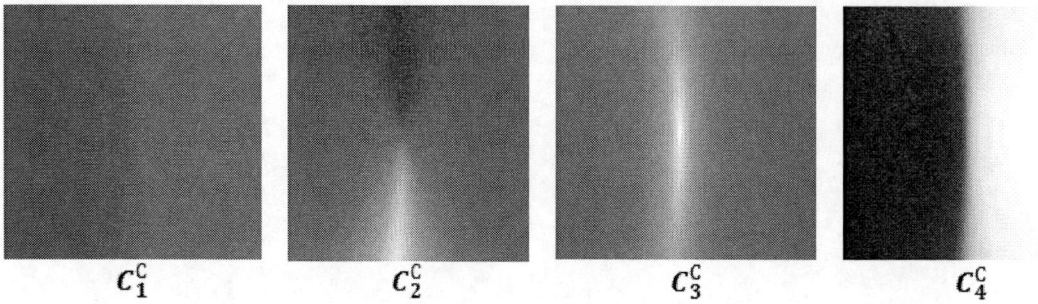

Figure 5. FV-model is shifted along the x-axis by 10 units along the unit circle

5. CONCLUSION

The main advantage of the FVM method and its perspective is a significant increase in the level of computer model geometrization, which allows us to simplify calculating such conditional mathematical constructions, as differentiating and integrating the function. All the demonstrated computational constructions of the method are based on using local geometric characteristics of the increased functional space and focused on applying to complex multidimensional functions.

REFERENCES

Vyatkin S. I., Dolgovesov B. S. Perturbation Function in Geometric Modeling / / International Conference Graphicon 2004, Moscow, Russia, http://www.graphicon.ru/

Tolok A.V. Functional-voxel method in computer modeling / edited by academician S. N. Vassilyev. - M.:FIZMATLIT, 2016. - 112 p. - ISBN 978-5-9221-1680-0.

DENOISING APPROACH FOR HIGH-RESOLUTION COMPUTED TOMOGRAPHY DATA

Jakub Šalplachta, Tomáš Zikmund and Jozef Kaiser
CEITEC - Central European Institute of Technology, Brno University of Technology
Purkyňova 656/123, 612 00, Brno, Czech Republic

ABSTRACT

Noise presence in CT (computed tomography) data distorts acquired information and negatively affects data interpretation, therefore denoising has become important pre-processing step of CT data analysis. Until today many efforts have been done regarding noise reduction in field of low-dose (medical) CT but no complex denoising methodology and noise properties knowledge exist for submicron computed tomography. This poster presents preliminary results of ongoing research regarding noise reduction in submicron CT data. New algorithms for noise properties estimation and noise reduction were proposed and their functionality tested on data from laboratory based system (Rigaku nano3DX machine) equipped with CCD detector.

KEYWORDS

CT, High-Resolution Data, Noise Variance Estimation, Noise Reduction

1. INTRODUCTION

X-ray computed tomography (CT) noise reduction approaches can be divided into: projection domain, reconstruction domain and tomogram domain [Kim, J.H. et al., 2016]. In presented research only projection domain denoising is considered. As projection data are regarded data after flat-field correction where detector photoresponce non-uniformities are corrected. Resulting data contain noise that is related to acquisition process and can be modelled as a compound of photon shot noise (related to quantum nature of light modelled by Poisson distribution representing photon-counting statistics) and read noise (related to additive electronic noise followed by Gaussian distribution) [Ding, Q. et al., 2006]. Another not negligible component is the random valued impulse noise with probable cause by detection of cosmic ray during the acquisition process. Noise reduction can lead to certain loss of edge and structural information, which is inevitable by use of traditional denoising methods. Therefore, sophisticated methods in terms of noise reduction effectivity and structural information preservation are only considered in this work. However, exact noise properties knowledge is essential for optimal noise reduction. Data acquired by Rigaku nano3DX machine equipped with CCD detector (achieved spatial resolution in micron and submicron space) were used for noise properties characterization and denoising approach development. All selected and developed algorithms were evaluated in terms of noise reduction effectivity and preservation of spatial resolution and computational and time consumption.

2. DENOISING APPROACH FOR HIGH-RESOLUTION CT DATA

2.1 Noise Properties Study

In presented research, bright images (i.e. flat-field corrected projection data without sample) were used to evaluate noise properties. Series of bright images were acquired for several settings of acquisitions parameters, for each combination 100 frames were acquired. Noise extraction for each acquisition settings was realized by subtraction of mean bright frame from all acquired bright frames. Consequently, noise properties were determined and noise model was established. For exact noise variance estimation in projection data new algorithm was proposed. This algorithm is based on Immearkear method [Immerkaer, J., 1996] and inspired by its modification published by Tai [Shen-Chuan Tai and Shih-Ming Yang, 2008]. The resulting noise model is different from well-known noise model at medical data.

2.2 Denoising Methodology

Acquired noise knowledge was subsequently incorporated into proposed denoising approach consisting of two subsequent steps: impulse noise reduction and a compound of Read+Shot noise reduction. Various methods were tested as possible solutions to each step, such as: Non-Local means ([Buades, A. et al., 2005], [Coupe, P. et al., 2008]), Total variations based noise removal ([Rudin, L.I. et al., 1992], [Getreuer, P., 2012]), Block Matching algorithm [Chen, Q. and Wu, D., 2010] and switching median filters for impulse noise reduction ([Garnett, R. et al., 2005], [Dong, Y. et al., 2007], [Fei Duan, L.I. et al.,]). For evaluation of the noise reduction functionality several quality parameters, such as Signal to Noise Ratio (SNR) or Structural Similarity index (SSIM), were used.

2.2.1 Proposed Impulse Noise Reduction Algorithm

Median filter has been widely accepted as solution for impulse noise reduction with high computational efficiency. However, using this algorithm all image pixels are affected leading to blur and certain loss of information by removal of desirable details (see Figure 1). To overcome these drawbacks new impulse noise reduction algorithm was proposed. This algorithm can be seen as switching median filter having the first step noise pixels detection and followed by noise pixels correction in second step. Detection of affected pixels is based on a local image statistic called ROAD ("Rank-Ordered Absolute Differences") published by Garnett [Garnett, R. et al., 2005]. To improve identification of random-valued impulse noise affected pixels we proposed to calculate ROAD values for input image and also median filtered image and subtract results from each other and then apply logarithmic function to the subtraction result. This leads to suppression of negative structural effect and to amplification of differences between affected pixels with small dissimilarity and non-affected pixels in their neighborhood. As noise-affected pixels are subsequently identified those pixels which achieved statistically significant high dissimilarity values. For correction of detected noise pixels standard median filter is used in order to achieve good computational effectivity. Result of proposed impulse noise reduction algorithm is shown in Figure 1, where it can be seen that this algorithm is able to preserve structural information and causes no blur unlike standard median filter.

Figure 1. Comparison of impulse noise reduction results acquired by median filter (left image) and proposed algorithm (right image) - Rigaku nano3DX projection data of bamboo stick

3. CONCLUSION

Results of presented research will make available for users of submicron computed tomography a methodology for complex projection domain noise reduction. To achieve high denoising effectivity, noise properties of high-resolution projection data were studied and their knowledge incorporated into proposed noise reduction approach. Noise model of submicron CT projection data was established. This model was revealed to differ from known medical noise model. The noise reduction effectivity and structural information preservation were tested on several selected methods. New algorithms for exact noise variance estimation and random-valued impulse noise reduction were also developed. Testing of all selected methods and algorithms was conducted on data with submicron resolution acquired by Rigaku nano3DX machine equipped with CCD detector.

ACKNOWLEDGEMENT

This research was carried out under the project CEITEC 2020 (LQ1601) with financial support from the Ministry of Education, Youth and Sports of the Czech Republic under the National Sustainability Programme II and CEITEC Nano Research Infrastructure (MEYS CR, 2016–2019).

REFERENCES

Buades, A. et al., 2005. A Non-Local Algorithm for Image Denoising. *2005 IEEE Computer Society Conference on Computer Vision and Pattern Recognition (CVPR'05)*, pp.60-65.

Coupe, P. et al., 2008. An Optimized Blockwise Nonlocal Means Denoising Filter for 3-D Magnetic Resonance Images. *IEEE Transactions on Medical Imaging*, 27(4), pp.425-441.

Chen, Q. and Wu, D., 2010. Image denoising by bounded block matching and 3D filtering. Signal Processing, 90(9), pp.2778-2783.

Ding, Q. et al., 2006. Modeling mixed Poisson-Gaussian noise in statistical image reconstruction for X-ray CT. *Proc. 4th Intl. Mtg. on image formation in X-ray CT*, pp.399-402.

Dong, Y. et al., 2007. A Detection Statistic for Random-Valued Impulse Noise. *IEEE Transactions on Image Processing*, 16(4), pp.1112-1120.

Fei Duan, L.I. et al., 2010. A Highly Effective Impulse Noise Detection Algorithm for Switching Median Filters. *IEEE Signal Processing Letters*, 17(7), pp.647-650.

Garnett, R. et al., 2005. A universal noise removal algorithm with an impulse detector. *IEEE Transactions on Image Processing*, 14(11), pp.1747-1754.

Getreuer, P., 2012. Rudin-Osher-Fatemi Total Variation Denoising using Split Bregman. *Image Processing On Line*, 2, pp.74-95.

Immerkaer, J., 1996. Fast Noise Variance Estimation. *Computer Vision and Image Understanding*, Vol. 64, No. 2, pp. 300-302.

Kim, J.H. et al., 2016. Denoising of polychromatic CT images based on their own noise properties. *Medical Physics*, 43(5), pp.2251-2260.

Rudin, L.I. et al., 1992. Nonlinear total variation based noise removal algorithms. *Physica D: Nonlinear Phenomena*, 60(1-4), pp.259-268.

Shen-Chuan Tai and Shih-Ming Yang, 2008. A fast method for image noise estimation using Laplacian operator and adaptive edge detection. *In 2008 3rd International Symposium on Communications, Control and Signal Processing.* IEEE, pp. 1077-1081.

AUTHOR INDEX